A History of Malawi
1859–1966

Other related James Currey titles

Obasanjo, Nigeria & the World
JOHN ILIFFE

Bulawayo Burning: The Social History of a Southern African City
1893–1960
TERENCE RANGER

A Victorian Gentleman & Ethiopian Nationalist
PETER P. GARRETSON

Thomas Pringle: South African Pioneer, Poet & Abolitionist
RANDOLPH VIGNE

The Freetown Bond: A Life under Two Flags
ELDRED DUROSIMI JONES

Slaves of Fortune: Sudanese Soldiers & the River War
1896–1898
RONALD M. LAMOTHE

Germany's Genocide of the Herero:
Kaiser Wilhelm II, His General, His Settlers, His Soldiers
JEREMY SARKIN

Ethiopia: the Last Two Frontiers
JOHN MARKAKIS

A History of Malawi
1859–1966

JOHN McCRACKEN

Honorary Senior Research Fellow
Stirling University

 JAMES CURREY

James Currey
is an imprint of Boydell & Brewer Ltd
PO Box 9
Woodbridge, Suffolk IP12 3DF (GB)
www.jamescurrey.com

and of

Boydell & Brewer Inc.
668 Mt Hope Avenue
Rochester, NY 14620-2731 (US)
www.boydellandbrewer.com

British Library Cataloguing in Publication Data
A catalogue record is available on request from the British Library

ISBN 978-1-84701-064-3 James Currey (Paperback)

The publisher has no responsibility for the continued existence or accuracy of URLs for
external or third-party internet websites referred to in this book, and does not guarantee that
any content on such websites is, or will remain, accurate or appropriate.

Papers used by Boydell & Brewer are natural, recycled products
made from wood grown in sustainable forests

Typeset in 10.5/11.5 Monotype Ehrhardt
by Avocet Typeset, Chilton, Aylesbury, Bucks
Printed and bound in Great Britain by
CPI Group (UK) Ltd, Croydon CR0 4YY

For Juliet

Contents

Contents

List of Maps, Photographs & Tables

Maps

Photographs

Tables

Acknowledgements

In the years since I first conceived the idea of this book I have received support from more individuals and institutions than I can name. Among the many scholars from whose work I have benefited I must single out George Shepperson, Elias Mandala, Andrew Ross, Jack Thompson, Robin Palmer, Terence Ranger, William Beinart, Malyn Newitt, Matthew Schoffeleers, Landeg White, Leroy Vail, Owen Kalinga, Joey Power, Colin Baker and my former colleagues (and in some cases, students) in the History Department at Chancellor College: Kings Phiri, Megan Vaughan,Wiseman Chirwa and Wapulumuka Mulwafu. Joseph Mfuni, J. Kazembe, J.A. Juma, C.C. Kamcholoti, Mary Mpanje and Mercy Thawe carried out interviews on my behalf. Student presentations made at History seminars at Chancellor College have been a regular source of information. Many of my ideas have been honed through discussions at Stirling University with final year students taking my special subject: 'The Colonial Experience in Malawi'. I have also benefited from my contacts with a new generation of historians of Malawi including H.A. Badenoch,Tim Lovering, Agnes Rennick, Markku Hokkanen and Zoe Groves. On my visits to Malawi, I have enjoyed the generous hospitality of Cornell and Sandy Dudley and of Sean and Barbara Morrow. Sean Morrow subsequently made it possible for me to see the personal files of Malawi students at Fort Hare.

My thanks are also due to the custodians of the Malawi National Archives, from whose helpfulness in often trying conditions I have benefited for nearly 50 years, the National Archives at Kew (formerly the Public Record Office), the National Library of Scotland, Edinburgh University Library, Rhodes House Library, Oxford and the Zimbabwe National Archives. My researches in Malawi have been financed in part through the British Academy Small Grants Fund and the Carnegie Trust for the Universities of Scotland.

Passages in the book have appeared in *The Journal of African History*, 39, 2, 1998, in *African Affairs*, 97, 387, 1998 and in *The Journal of Southern African Studies*, 28, 1, 2001. I am grateful to the publishers for allowing me to reproduce them. I would also like to thank HarperCollins for granting permission to publish an amended version of the map of Blantyre that appears in *Atlas for Malawi* (Collins-Longman, Limbe, 1969).

All efforts have been made to trace the copyright holders, where this is appropriate, for the photographs. I am grateful to the Trustees of the National Library of Scotland for permission to publish 'Girls' Tea Party' and to the family of Peter Mackay for allowing me to use the photographs of 'The Prison Graduates' and of 'Dr. Banda after being sworn in as Prime Minister' which appeared in his book, *We Have Tomorrow: Stirrings in Africa, 1959–1967* (Michael Russell,

Norwich, 2008). Dr Jack Thompson kindly supplied the print I have used of the ordination of Livingstonia's first Malawian ministers.

There are three special debts which I must acknowledge. The first is to my former colleague in Dar es Salaam, John Iliffe, whose *Modern History of Tanganyika* presents a daunting challenge to scholars seeking to write the history of an African country while also setting the standard for what can be achieved. The second is to Kings Phiri who, for more than three decades, has provided me with advice, assistance and friendship in my engagement with Malawi and its past. The final debt is to my wife Juliet, who has read and edited every word, assisted me in my researches and encouraged me to get the work finished. In love and thanks I dedicate this book to her.

Abbreviations

ADMARC	Agricultural Development Marketing Corporation
ALC	African Lakes Company
BCAG	*British Central African Gazette*
BCGA	British Cotton Growing Association
B&EAC	Blantyre and East Africa Company
BSAC	British South Africa Company
CAT	*Central African Times*
CCAP	Church of Central Africa Presbyterian
CDC	Colonial Development Corporation
CDWF	Colonial Development and Welfare
CSHFMR	*Church of Scotland Home and Foreign Missionary Record*
DRC	Dutch Reformed Church
FMC	Farmers Marketing Board
ICU	Industrial and Commercial Workers Union of South Africa
ITC	Imperial Tobacco Company
JAH	*Journal of African History*
JSAS	*Journal of Southern African Studies*
KAR	King's African Rifles
LWBCA	*Life and Work in British Central Africa*
MCP	Malawi Congress Party
NTB	Native Tobacco Board
RNLB	Rhodesia Native Labour Bureau
SOMJ	*Society of Malawi Journal*
TZR	Trans-Zambesia Railway
UMCA	Universities' Mission to Central Africa
WNLA	Witwatersrand Native Labour Association

Note on Terminology

Place names have been spelt in many different ways in Malawi in the past century. I have employed names that were current in the colonial period (hence Port Herald rather than Nsanje and Cholo rather than Thyolo). I have also standardised spellings except where quoting from a contemporary source or providing a contemporary reference. The term 'Malawi' is used for the geographical region covered by the modern nation state and 'Nyasaland' for the British protectorate. 'Malawian' and 'Nyasa' are both used in describing the territory's inhabitants. Chiefly names can create particular problems. In reference to the northern Ngoni paramount chief, I use the spelling 'Mbelwa' in preference both to 'Mombera', the term most commonly employed in the early colonial period and also 'M'mbelwa', a term that has gained in popularity since the 1950s. For almost all of the colonial period, the currency used in Malawi was British sterling. Twelve pence equalled one shilling and 20 shillings one pound.

Glossary

Askari	African soldier (Boma askari: African policeman)
Beni	costumed dance parodying military activities
Boma	government office
Capitao	foreman, overseer
Chibaro	contract labour; slave labour
Chibuku	African beer
Chifwamba	belief that individuals consume corpses to achieve magical power
Chikoti	whip
Chikunda	armed slaves; later, warrior hunters; Sena immigrants
Chiperoni	dry season rains
Dambo	wetland; alluvial floodplain
Dimba	agricultural system involving cultivation on floodplain
Ganyu	worker hired by the day
GuleWamkulu	Great Dance of the secret Nyau society
Hijab	Muslim woman's veil or headscarf
Kachasu	locally distilled spirit
Kwacha	dawn (national symbol)
Lobola	bride price
Madrassa	Quranic school

Malimidwe	agricultural conservation rules
Malingga	stockaded village
Malipenga	military-style dance
Mankhwala	medicine: herbal or magical
Matutu	cultivation mounds
Mbumba	matrilineage group
Mchapi	witchcraft eradication/medicine
Misere	contour ridges
Mphala	dryland, rain-fed agricultural system
Mthandizi	Rhodesian Native Labour Supply Commission
Muzungo	Afro-Portuguese
Mzungu	European
Mwalimu	Muslim teacher
Mwavi	poison ordeal
Nkhoswe	senior maternal uncle or brother
Njala	seasonal hunger; famine
Nomi	youth labour association
Nyau	secret Chewa/Mang'anja cult involving masked dancers
Prazos	estates
Ruga–ruga	Swahili henchmen
Tengatenga	porterage
Thangata	system imposing labour as exchange for rent
Ulendo	journey, tour by district officer
Vyanusi	sprit possession cult in the North
Visoso	millet cultivation method, involving felling and burning
Zunde	large cotton fields

Map 1 Malawi Region, late 19th century

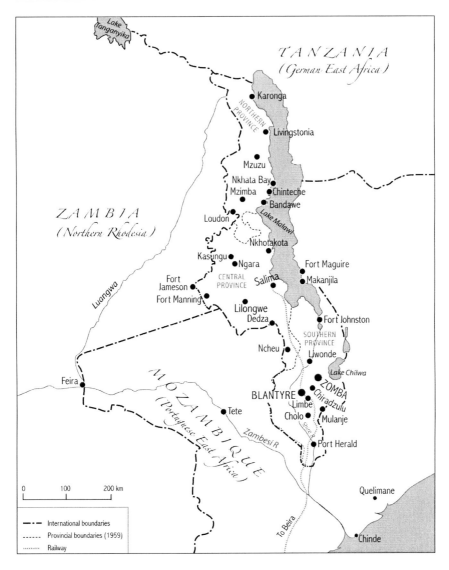

Map 2 Malawi, mid-twentieth century

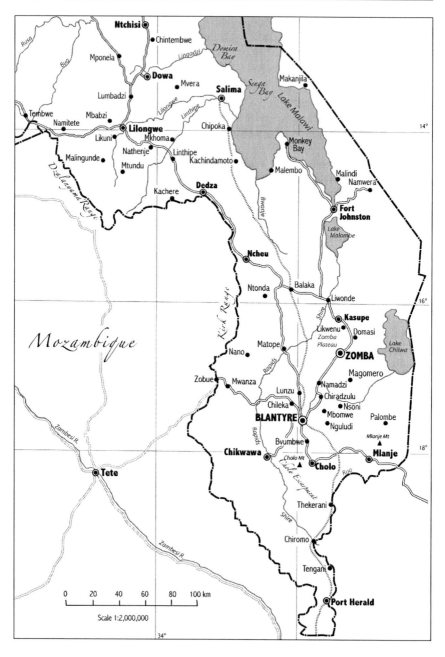

Map 3 Southern Malawi

Introduction

There can be no better introduction to the character of colonial rule in Malawi than the view from the lip of Zomba plateau looking down on the old colonial capital. In the distance, nearly 50 miles away, rears Mulanje Mountain, a rocky massif divided from its neighbour Mchesa by the Fort Lister Gap, a pass used by slave traders in the late nineteenth century. Further to the south, on the road to Blantyre, looms the jutting eminence of Chiradzulu and, closer to Zomba, the small hill known as Magomero, once the site of the headquarters of A.L. Bruce's Magomero estate, the epicentre of the 1915 Chilembwe Rising. To the north lies Lake Chilwa, a shallow, saline expanse of water, 800 square miles in extent when water levels are high but, on occasions, shrinking to a cluster of pools. Beneath the mountain, the town of Zomba is so overhung with trees as to be only partly visible. Despite the rash of new buildings that have extended its boundaries in all directions, the physical contours of the colonial capital are easy to detect. To the right, on the road to Blantyre, stands the neat army barracks, originally constructed in 1895 with, alongside it, the King's African Rifles Memorial from the First World War and the notorious Zomba prison. Directly below, obscured by trees, is Government House (now one of the Malawi President's numerous State Houses), constructed in stages between 1898 and 1905 and the residence of successive Governors. Lower down the slope is the Gymkhana Club, formerly the social hub of the European community, separated from the commercial zone on the lower side of the road to Blantyre by a golf course and by a cricket field on which the KAR band once played to celebrate the British monarch's birthday. Climbing up the lower slopes of the mountain stand the former homes of colonial officials, high-ceilinged, single storied houses, fronted by wide verandas, all with their own extensive gardens. In a demonstration of colonial hierarchy, the highest houses, those coolest and with the best views to Mulanje, were reserved for the most senior officials. To the left, near to the plunging gorge of the Mulunguzi River, are the twin towers of the Old Residency (now an hotel), built in 1886, five years before the Protectorate was declared by the disgraced Scottish missionary, John Buchanan, on instructions from the British Consul A.J. Hawes. Below are the Botanical Gardens, originally laid out from 1889 by Harry Johnston, the first Consul-General. Near at hand is the two-storied Secretariat, built in 1897, burnt down in 1919 and not re-built until 1950, the nerve-centre of the colonial administration.

Together, Zomba's older buildings provide a remarkable insight into the nature of colonialism. The army barracks and adjacent prison point to the importance of coercion in sustaining colonial rule though the openness of Government House (the brick wall surrounding it was not built until 1966) suggests that, for much of the colonial period, personal security was not regarded as a problem. The apparently innocuous golf course bordering the main road was a key element in physically enforcing racial segregation. European officials and their families lived on the mountain slope above the golf course, where there had once been several villages; Indian traders and African clerks were directed to locations below the road, close to the market. In a further refinement, junior officers could find themselves relegated almost to the roadside, although never across it. With each promotion came the opportunity to climb higher on the mountain. The modest size of the secretariat and adjacent government buildings demonstrates how limited were the number of officials that the colonial government employed. The lack of architectural ostentation in those buildings suggests that there were few resources available, as well as little appetite among Malawi's colonial rulers for the grand imperial statements in stone made by the Germans in Dar es Salaam and by the British in Pretoria and Delhi. Seen from Zomba Mountain, colonialism in Malawi thus appears as a superficial phenomenon, one that lasted little more than 70 years and influenced only marginally the agricultural practices and social structures of Malawi's people. Yet this would be a misleading conclusion. For, as will be demonstrated, the interactions of local people both with colonial officials, settlers and missionaries in Malawi, as well as with social and economic forces beyond its boundaries had profound if complex consequences that remain of great importance today.

This book is a general history of Malawi, focusing mainly on the colonial period but seeking to place that period in the context of the pre-colonial past. Its notional starting date, 1859, the year of David Livingstone's first visit to the region, has been chosen as marking the initial informal involvement of Britain in the area. The closing date, 1966, marks both the formal withdrawal of Britain with the departure of the Governor General Sir Glyn Jones and the consolidation of the Banda regime with the establishment of the republic of Malawi. Many Malawians in much of the intervening period had only limited awareness of the British involvement; other external actors, ranging from Southern African mineowners to Italian entrepreneurs and French Catholic missionaries also played their part. Nevertheless, it is the contention of this study that in the century under review British people, starting with Scottish Presbyterian missionaries and including soldiers, speculators, colonial officials and politicians, played a crucial role in shaping the territory. Such an assertion might lead to the charge that what is intended here is a twenty-first century Malawian version of 'East Africa and its Invaders', top-down history written from the perspective of the colonisers.[1] This, however, is not the case. If one central theme is how Britain as a state and the British as people shaped Malawi, an even more important theme is how Malawian people have shaped their own history, often in overt defiance of the colonial order but sometimes too through communal activities unrelated to the colonial presence. There is much here on armed resistance to the colonial occupation, on religious-inspired revolt, on the rise and fall of a fragile labour movement and on the growth of popular nationalism. But room is also given to the creation of dance societies, the eruption of witchcraft eradication movements and the emergence of football as a popular national sport. In particular, the book seeks to reconstruct the life stories of a variety of Malawians, some of them well-

[1] Reginald Coupland, *East Africa and its Invaders* (Oxford, 1938).

2

known, some of them not, in ways that throw light on specific themes.

Over the past 40 years, popular perceptions of the history of Malawi under colonial rule have been dominated by two contending approaches. The first, developed from the late 1960s and expressed most clearly in the work of Bridglal Pachai, concentrates on nation-building, an activity seen as having its roots in the distant past and reaching a climax with the attainment of political independence in 1964.[2] Colonial rule is depicted as important: positively for its role in dissolving tribal divisions and creating the infrastructure for national unity; negatively for the impetus it gave to the emergence of a united nationalist movement which ultimately challenged British authority and created the basis for the new nation state. The alternative view, most persuasively argued by Leroy Vail in a series of distinguished contributions published in the 1970s and early 1980s, presents the history of Malawi as being, above all, about 'the making of an imperial slum.'[3] This process of impoverishment and underdevelopment began, Vail argued, in the mid-nineteenth century but accelerated with the establishment of colonial rule. Of fundamental importance was the satellisation of Malawi as a labour reserve for the mines and farms of Southern Africa, a process which resulted principally from the policies pursued by imperial and colonial governments in London and Zomba.

It is the contention of this book that, despite their genuine merits, neither of these approaches provides a satisfactory analysis of Malawi's colonial history. 'Nation-building' historians are correct to identify the emergence of a powerful Malawian nationalist movement as a significant theme in the history of the territory (no less than four chapters in this book are devoted to the subject). Indeed, there is a strong case for arguing that without the eruption of popular nationalism in Malawi in the late 1950s the Federation of Rhodesia and Nyasaland would not have been dissolved. Nevertheless, to focus too narrowly on nation-building is to ignore a whole range of political initiatives and social developments not directly connected with the emergence and triumph of the Malawi Congress Party. As Vail and White have demonstrated, evolving patterns of ethnic and regional identity were no less important than the creation of national identity in the shaping of modern Malawi.[4] Social change divided communities rather than contributing to a wider unity. Territorial frontiers provided peasants with zones of opportunity as well as boundaries demarcating national allegiance. Even at the level of political action, it would be wrong to assume that popular protest was necessarily related to nationalist objectives. Workers more frequently went on strike for economic reasons than to advance the cause of national liberation. In some cases at least, peasants involved in popular protests turned for support to traditional religious institutions with the ultimate aim of restricting the

---

[2] Bridglal Pachai, *Malawi: the History of a Nation* (Longman, London, 1973).

[3] H.L. Vail, 'The Making of an Imperial Slum: Nyasaland and its Railways, 1895–1935', *JAH*, 16, 1, 1975, pp. 89–112; Leroy Vail, 'Railway Development and Colonial Underdevelopment: the Nyasaland Case' in Robin Palmer and Neil Parsons (eds), *The Roots of Rural Poverty in Central and Southern Africa* (Heinemann, London, 1977), pp. 364–395; Vail, 'The State and the Creation of Colonial Malawi's Agricultural Economy' in Robert I. Rotberg (ed.), *Imperialism, Colonialism and Hunger: East and Central Africa* (Lexington Books, Lexington, 1983), pp. 89–112; Vail, 'The Political Economy of East-Central Africa' in David Birmingham and Phyllis Martin (eds), *History of Central Africa* Volume Two (Longman, London, 1983), pp. 200–250.

[4] Leroy Vail and Landeg White, 'Tribalism in the Political History of Malawi' in Leroy Vail (ed.), *The Creation of Tribalism in Southern Africa* (James Currey, London, 1989), pp.151–92.

advances of the state rather than taking control at the centre.

If the 'nation-building' approach is inadequate, however, so too is the once fashionable 'underdevelopment' alternative: the belief that international capitalism and the establishment of global markets impoverished third world countries. This is not to dispute that exceptional material poverty existed in colonial Malawi, often exacerbated by inappropriate government policies. Colonial planners paid only intermittent attention to the interests of Malawi's African inhabitants, being frequently more concerned with fostering the settler section of the economy and of mining interests further south. Nevertheless, exponents of underdevelopment tend to oversimplify the impact of capitalism in Malawi by stressing only its negative features and ignoring its more positive qualities. Peasants and migrants are seen simply as victims rather than as tenacious individuals carving out opportunities for themselves with varying degrees of success. The portrait of colonial Malawi as a labour reserve for Southern Africa, while accurate for some northern parts of the country, was by no means true of the whole. By the 1940s several competing colonial economies had emerged, with the labour exporting districts of the north being balanced by the settler estate section of the Shire Highlands and by areas where peasant production dominated, notably in the Central Region. In certain respects, indeed, the economic history of colonial Malawi ran contrary to wider Central African trends. Whereas, in the interwar years, white farmers in Southern Rhodesia established their dominance over African producers partially as a result of the intervention of the settler government, in parts of Malawi peasant producers became actively involved in commercial agriculture at a time when the settler sector was in decline. Cash-crop producers in Malawi battled against a host of problems including high transport costs, irregular international prices, an often exploitative marketing system and damage from drought and pests. Yet their story is as much one of achievement and survival as it is of the enduring struggle against poverty.

Back in the 1960s it was almost an article of faith that newly independent African states should be equipped with their national histories but that belief has declined in recent decades, along with faith in the transformative power of national governments and politicians. In some respects, therefore, the unit of study employed in this book is a controversial one. As defined by its arbitrarily established boundaries, the territory known successively as the British Central Africa Protectorate, Nyasaland and Malawi, was an artificial construct, one that brought together a variety of peoples equipped with different languages and cultures upon whom it imposed itself only intermittently during the colonial period. To a great extent, its economy was explicable only as part of the wider regional economy. Most of the ideas and assumptions that influenced its rulers originated in centres far from Zomba. For many of its inhabitants, external events, notably the First World War and the 1930s Depression, had a greater impact than developments originating locally. In this book the terms 'Malawi' and 'Malawians' are employed as useful labels but it is important to stress that virtually no-one used these terms prior to the foundation of the Malawi Congress Party in 1959 (Dr Banda is a partial exception). 'Nyasaland' and 'Nyasa' have a longer heritage, although up to at least the First World War the label 'Nyasa' was largely employed of local people by outsiders rather than by local people to describe themselves.

4

If the concept of Nyasaland/Colonial Malawi has its problematic features, there are, however, good reasons why it should be employed as the unit of study. For all their apparent fragility, the colonial boundaries have stood the test of time in defining the limits of the post-colonial state. Colonial administrative policies enacted in the Protectorate differed in a number of respects from those introduced in Northern and, especially, Southern Rhodesia. The financial resources available in the three territories varied widely. Discrepancies in access to education and to economic opportunity within Nyasaland created rivalries between communities and regions. Above all, by 1938, Malawian labour migrants in Southern Africa had become acutely aware of perceived differences in racial policies between what they saw as their homeland, Nyasaland, and settler-dominated Southern Rhodesia. In the early 1950s, Malawian activists, many of whom had spent extensive periods abroad, were often drawn towards a regional approach to politics but in practice, with very few exceptions, they eventually became committed to the liberation of the single territory, Nyasaland. Despite valiant attempts to link the new nation to the pre-colonial 'Maravi Empire', the idea of modern Malawi is of relatively recent origin. However, there can be no doubting its reality today.

Two further features are integral to this study. The first is the influence of Christian missions, a central issue in the history of many African countries but one of particular importance in Malawi as a consequence of the exceptional weakness of the colonial state and the remarkable responsiveness to the pioneer missions of many societies in the area. One aspect of this influence was the extent to which the provision of education and health care remained in the hands of missions for much of the colonial period. Of equal importance was the emergence of vigorous, new Christian communities, shaped in a variety of ways by their missionary contacts yet displaying distinctive, African-based forms and beliefs.

The second feature is one that has been stressed by John Iliffe both in his magisterial *Modern History of Tanganyika* (in many respects, the model for this book) and also in his study, *Africans: the History of a Continent*.[5] This is the ongoing struggle, beginning long before colonialism and continuing long afterwards, between peasants and their enemies in the natural world, a struggle complicated by the process of demographic change. At one level, this involved the continuing attempts of rural communities, assisted and sometimes obstructed by colonial experts, to counter the ravages of wild animals and intrusive pests: tsetse fly, rinderpest, red bollworm and others. At another level, it involved the impact of environmental change: soil erosion, the rise and fall of water levels, drought and flooding. As Iliffe has noted, changes in the world of nature have frequently interacted with human interventions: among them the spread of long-distance trade, warfare and the growth of cash-crop farming. In addition, since the Second World War, the struggle has intensified as a consequence of the rapid growth of population in a territory which historically has supported some of the densest concentrations of population in rural Africa. Central to this book is the story of how Malawians responded to the intrusion of imperialism and colonialism in a variety of forms and the role they played in the

5 John Iliffe, *A Modern History of Tanganyika* (Cambridge, Cambridge University Press, 1979); John Iliffe, *Africans: the History of a Continent* (Cambridge, Cambridge University Press, 1995).

5

dissolution of the colonial state. However, as Mandala has emphasised, 'ecological change was almost as important as capitalism in the social transformation of the region.'[6] Behind the struggle for political liberation lay population growth, land shortage and increased pressure on natural resources.[7]

---

[6] Elias C. Mandala, 'Capitalism, Ecology and Society: the Lower Tchiri (Shire) Valley of Malawi, 1860–1969', Ph.D. dissertation, University of Minnesota, 1983, p. 261.

[7] The most recent study on the topic is Wapulumuka O. Mulwafu, *Conservation Song: A History of Peasant-State Relations and the Environment in Malawi, 1860–2000* (White Horse Press, Cambridge, 2011).

1
The Land & the People

Introduction

For the peoples living in what is now the modern state of Malawi, the forty years prior to the establishment of colonial rule in 1891 was a period of exceptionally violent and rapid change. During those decades, groups of refugees from Southern Africa, collectively known as Ngoni, stormed northwards and again south, seizing people, cattle and agricultural resources and eventually creating three major and two minor conquest states in the region. Yao-speaking peoples from the east of Lake Malawi, wielding guns and trading in slaves, conquered much of the Upper Shire Valley and Shire Highlands; in the Lower Shire Valley, other groups of invaders, Kololo and Portuguese-speaking adventurers, carved out further petty kingdoms. These political upheavals interacted with the dramatic expansion of the slave and ivory trades; this in turn resulted in important shifts in the distribution of population. Many cultivators abandoned the dispersed settlements on fertile ground within easy reach of water where they had previously lived to take refuge instead in stockaded villages, often perched in inaccessible mountainous or island locations. In a number of communities, the concentration of military power led to the increasing subordination of vulnerable groups in society – notably women. Where drought coincided with violent disorder, as most notably in the Shire Highlands and Valley in 1862–63, famine of calamitous proportions resulted, sparing neither young nor old, man nor woman. It is necessary to be wary of the more dramatic versions of the 'disaster school' of central African history. The descriptions of Mang'anja villages in the Shire Highlands in 1859 given by David Livingstone and John Kirk are of near idyllic settlements, well watered and surrounded by shady trees, in which men passed their time quietly smoking cannabis or tobacco and drinking beer when they were not involved in a rich array of agricultural and non-agricultural tasks.[1] Nevertheless, the point must be made that the impact of the colonial state was felt in a region already undergoing many types of change

---

[1]   David and Charles Livingstone, *Narrative of an Expedition to the Zambesi and its Tributaries* (London, 1865), p. 109; R. Foskett (ed.), *The Zambesi Journal and Letters of Dr John Kirk*, 2 vols, (Edinburgh, 1965), pp. 236–42

and was inevitably influenced by previous developments.

This chapter offers a description of rural economies and societies before and during the period of disruption as well as an account of the processes of change which provide the background to the emergence of the colonial state.[2] At the broadest level, the history of the Malawi region in the nineteenth century is similar to that of Eastern Africa as a whole in involving the expansion of long distance trade and an intensification of the relationships of agricultural societies with the larger international economy. However, it is the contention of this chapter that there are at least four features that distinguish the pre-colonial Malawian experience with significant consequences for the region's subsequent history. First, levels of population density, particularly near rivers and the Lake, were markedly higher than among any of Malawi's neighbours, as they have remained up to the present day, thus creating the potential for intense disputes over land. Secondly, this land was largely inhabited by matrilineal peoples, members of a cultural belt that extended through Zambia into Mozambique, with forms of social organisation different from those of the patrilineal peoples to the north and south and resulting in somewhat different relations between men and women. Third, while the impact of an expanded slave trade came relatively late to the Malawi region, it struck it with exceptional force and had a variety of important consequences. The significance of the fourth feature will be explored more fully in chapters two and three. The central geographical feature of the Malawi area is the Lake Malawi – Shire River drainage system which extends south to the great Zambesi river and from there to the Indian Ocean. For people with boats, and particularly with steamboats, this waterway was attractive as a means of communication. But this was to ignore the drainage system's most conspicuous characteristic: that over lengthy periods water levels fluctuated dramatically with major consequences for navigation on the Shire.

The natural environment

Malawi is a narrow country, 530 miles long and never more than 100 miles wide. Its boundaries are artificial, the product of colonial treaties. Yet to a certain extent they give shape to a rough physical unity for the whole area is part of the southern extension of the Rift Valley which stretches down Lake Malawi (355 miles long) to the Shire Valley, with high plateaux rising on either side.

The variety of terrain enclosed in Malawi's modern borders has influenced the history of people in the area over many centuries.[3] Stretching from north to south five main mountain ranges – the Nyika and Viphya plateaux and the Dedza, Zomba and Mulanje mountains – rise abruptly from rolling highlands to altitudes of between 6 and 8,000 feet, producing heavy precipitations of rain.

[2] For the problems involved in this undertaking see Megan Anne Vaughan, 'Social and Economic change in Southern Malawi: A Study of Rural Communities in the Shire Highlands and Upper Shire Valley from the Mid-Nineteenth century to 1915', Ph.D. dissertation, University of London, 1981, pp. 11–12.

[3] J.G. Pike and G.T. Rimmington, *Malawi: a Geographical Study* (London, 1965); Swanzie Agnew, 'Environment and history: the Malawian setting' in Bridglal Pachai (ed.), *The Early History of Malawi* (London, 1972), pp. 28–48; F. Dixey, 'The Distribution of Population in Nyasaland', *Geographical Review*, 18, 1928, pp. 274–90.

Cold and windswept, these mountain ranges have rarely attracted human settlement. However, on the Nyika plateau iron smelting was conducted by Phoka smiths until the 1930s and, on Zomba mountain, refugees established villages during the disruptive wars of the late nineteenth century.

More important in the human history of Malawi are a series of upland plateaux, including the Mzimba plain in the north, the Lilongwe or Central Province plateau in the centre and the Shire Highlands in the south, all important centres of population in colonial times and beyond. These upland plateaux range in height from 2,500 to 4,000 feet and compose some three quarters of Malawi's land surface. Soils are variable ranging from the leached sandy soils of the Kasungu district, covered in the 1890s with extensive Brachystegia woodlands, to the much more fertile, better drained ferruginous soils of the Lilongwe plain, marked by the presence of Combretum (Acacia) woodlands. To the north of this central plateau region stretches the Mzimba highlands and the Rukuru plain, an area of light sandy soils, innumerable ant hills and scattered stunted trees; in the south-east, in the Shire Highlands, open canopy Brachystegia woodland remained the dominant vegetation type. Except in times of extensive warfare, people tended to settle within easy walking distance of streams or rivers or else by *dambos*, shallow, marshy depressions which retained moisture into the dry season and hence could be used to graze cattle or else for the cultivation of supplementary crops.

Steep escarpments divide these plateau areas from the very different environment of the Lake Malawi-Shire littoral in the trough of the Rift Valley. Less than 200 metres above sea level for much of its length, this valley is considerably hotter and, in the southern sections more arid than the hills rising adjacent to it. Yet by the late nineteenth century it was providing refuge to a substantial although unevenly distributed population, attracted to the area by the availability of year-round water supplies and by the existence of rich alluvial flood plains permitting the cultivation of a variety of crops independent of rainfall, notably at the Karonga plain at the north-west of the lake and in the Lower Shire Valley. Also important was the presence of abundant supplies of fish – most particularly at the southern end of Lake Malawi where the shallow waters and gently sloping beaches made for better fishing than did the steep, rocky shores and deeper waters further north.

It is partly because of the favourable conditions available in this environmental zone that, ever since records have been kept, population density in the Malawi region has always been considerably greater than in any of her East and Central African neighbours: three times that of Tanganyika and Mozambique, four times that of Zimbabwe and over eight times that of Zambia whose overall population today remains smaller than Malawi's[4]. Over the last century Malawi has had the reputation of being a peculiarly impoverished territory, well known for its export of labour. Yet, as Webster has suggested, for much of its pre-colonial history, the region appears to have functioned as a place of refuge at times of drought for people from less well endowed areas.[5]

[4] Figures calculated from Lord Hailey, *An African Survey* (London, 1938) pp. 108; CIA World Factbook, November 2004, www.cia.gov. See also B R Kuczynski, *Demographic Survey of the British Empire* (London, 1949).
[5] J.B. Webster, 'Drought, Migration and Chronology in the Lake Malawi Littoral', *Transafrican Journal of History*, 9, 1 and 2, 1980, pp. 70–90.

Access to permanent water supplies was one factor which attracted immigrants into the Malawi region; another was the comparative reliability of rainfall in the area. Like other parts of southern tropical Africa, Malawi's rainfall is largely influenced by the weather system known as the Inter-Tropical Convergence Zone. This passes southward to its southern limit over Zimbabwe in December and January and then retreats northwards in February and March, the whole period being known as the rainy season. In much of Malawi, however, in contrast to more arid territories further south, the South-East Trades, blowing across the Indian Ocean, bring further rain in April, which, in the north, continues sporadically into May. Malawi also benefits from its proximity to the East African coast which means that, even in the dry season, incursions of light rain and drizzle known as *chiperoni* occur over high ground facing south-east. Malawi in consequence enjoys a mean annual rainfall of 45 inches – a figure higher than that of any of her immediate neighbours – with only five per cent of the country in receipt of less than 30 inches of rain, the figure generally considered to be the minimum required for successful dry land farming.

As in much of the rest of Eastern and Southern Africa, however, rainfall can never be taken for granted. Dramatic fluctuations exist within limited areas, with, for example, Mulanje and Cholo districts enjoying average rainfalls of between 65 and 80 inches a year compared with the meagre 33 inches received on average in the immediately adjacent Lower Shire Valley. Moreover, good rains in one year can easily be followed in all but the most favoured districts by drought in the next. Such is the diversity of Malawi's natural resources that no single territory wide drought or famine has yet been recorded (the famine of 2002, the worst in modern times, came close to being territorial-wide).[6] In the Lower Shire Valley, however, drought or semi-drought conditions occurred every six years or so on average and similar conditions prevailed in the Kasitu Valley, north of the Mzimba plain, where hardly a year passed in the 1880s without members of the Livingstonia mission being accused by their Ngoni neighbours of having held up the rain. Fear of drought and famine was thus central to Malawian ideologies.[7] 'When there is no rain at the proper season there ensues much distress. Famine is dreaded above all other evils', wrote an early missionary based in the Shire Highlands in the late 1870s.[8] The central function of all of the major territorial cults in the region was the calling of rain and the prevention of drought; when the rains failed in northern Ngoniland in 1885–86, Scottish missionaries were enlisted to provide additional assistance.[9]

Seasonal fluctuations in rainfall have interacted with more gradual ecological changes. For many centuries, long term variations in the level of Lake Malawi, the Shire River and Lake Chilwa have profoundly influenced economic activities on their shores. All are subject to annual variations of water level of about four feet between the dry and wet season. But they also have been subject to

---

[6] John Iliffe, 'The Poor in the Modern History of Malawi', Centre of African Studies, *Malawi: An Alternative Pattern of Development* (Edinburgh, 1984), p. 251. See also J.J. Stegman, 'Nyasaland Droughts', *Nyasaland Journal*, 4. 1,1951.

[7] J. M. Schoffeleers and A. A. Roscoe, *Land of Fire: Oral Literature from Malawi* (Likuni Press, Lilongwe, 1985), p. 10.

[8] Duff Macdonald, *Africana or the Heart of Heathen Africa* (London, 1882, 2 vols, reprinted 1969), vol. 1, p 88. See also Iliffe, 'Poor in the Modern History of Malawi', p. 251,

[9] John McCracken, *Politics and Christianity in Malawi* (Cambridge, 1977), pp. 91–92.

substantial changes in the mean annual water level over lengthy periods.[10] Starting around the time of Livingstone's last visit to Lake Malawi in 1866, the level of the lake and river gradually fell to reach the lowest known levels in 1915 by which time the colonial vision of using the waterway as a major highway into Central Africa had been dashed. Lake levels then rose, covering reefs and inundating fertile rice fields on the south-east arm of the lake. Initially, the rise in the level of the lake had no effect on the Upper Shire River, where water levels fell so low by 1924 that Lake Malombe dried up almost entirely with food gardens being planted on its bed.[11] But in the decade after 1927 the level of the river rose rapidly, permanently engulfing extensive stretches of rich floodland in the Lower Shire valley.[12] Meanwhile, the water level of Lake Chilwa fluctuated in an even more dramatic manner. A shallow, saline expanse of water, Lake Chilwa extended almost to the northern foot of Mulanje Mountain in 1859, at the time of Livingstone's first visit, only to shrink to almost nothing in 1910. Further low levels were reported in 1914–6, 1920–2 and in 1934, resulting on each occasion in heavy mortality among fish stocks, with the survivors taking refuge in surrounding swamps to re-emerge a couple of years later when the lake returned to its normal size.[13]

Production & exchange

Famine, drought, rain and fire constitute the four great motifs in the oral literature of Malawian societies.[14] They come together in one of the most powerful creation stories among the Chewa and Mang'anja peoples, the Kaphirintiwa myth, which starts with the earth, waterless and lifeless. One day, rain falls in a great shower, bringing down a man and woman from the sky with a hoe, a winnowing basket and a mortar. Chiuta (God) also comes down, accompanied by all the animals. Plants and trees grow in the watered earth; there is food in abundance. God, man and animals live together in peace. But eventually the man rubs two sticks together and invents fire. This sets the grass ablaze and the animals run away, filled with rage against him. Chiuta is too old to escape by climbing a tree. But he is rescued by a spider which puts down a thread and lifts him to safety. So God, now driven from earth, announces that man must die and join him in heaven.[15]

The story's significance can be read at a number of levels. Firstly, it comments on the introduction of agriculture and the dichotomy between field and forest, a central theme in Central African history from the beginning of the Iron Age

---

[10] J.G. Pike, 'The hydrology of Lake Malawi', *Society of Malawi Journal*, 22, 2 (1968); Pike and Rimmington, *Malawi*, pp. 114–18; Robert Crossley, 'Ancient Flood Levels on Lake Malawi', *Malawi Review*, 1, 1 (1982), pp. 11–14.

[11] South Nyasa District Report for 1931, MNA NSF 4/1/3.

[12] John McCracken, 'Fishing and the Colonial Economy: the Case of Malawi', *Journal of African History*, 28 (1987), p. 418.

[13] N. Lancaster, 'The Changes in the Lake Level', in Margaret Kalk, A.J. McLachlan, C. Howard-Williams (eds), *Lake Chilwa: Studies of Change in a Tropical Ecosystem* (The Hague, 1979).

[14] Schoffeleers and Roscoe, *Land of Fire*, p. 10.

[15] This account is drawn from Schoffeleers and Roscoe, *Land of Fire*, pp. 19–20 and from the slightly different version provided by Matthew Schoffeleers, *River of Blood: The Genesis of a Martyr Cult in Southern Malawi* (Madison, 1992), pp. 32–33.

around 200 AD right on into the nineteenth century when peasant farmers were still struggling to cut back and domesticate the bush. Second, it notes the reciprocal relationship between the world of animals and that of the village as expressed most vividly in the ancient *Nyau* cult of the Mang'anja and Chewa peoples where male dancers in masks representing spirits and wild animals [*zilombo*] took part in mourning rites and initiation ceremonies.[16] Animals were dangerous, threatening crops and cultivators alike. But they were also a source of food, hunted by groups of men. It was through hunting as much as through warfare that the ideal masculine attributes of bravery, virility and fierceness could be most fully expressed.[17] Third, it points to the significance of fire as a source of civilisation and authority but also of conflict associated with the arrival in the Malawi region of Phiri immigrants from Katanga. And finally it also touches on the ritual importance of Kaphirintiwa, a 'little flat-topped hill' to the west of the south end of Lake Malawi, believed to be the site of the first of a network of territorial shrines spreading down from central Malawi into the Lower Shire valley and including the Mbona shrine at Khulubvi. It was to the mediums and officials of these shrines that peasant farmers turned for advice and support when confronted by the ever-present threats of blights and pests, floods and drought.[18]

Religious functionaries might provide inspiration and explanation at times of natural disaster brought about by drought or flood. Only skilful cultivators could ameliorate its consequences.[19] The nature of that skill, so John Iliffe has noted, was very different from the skill of the modern large-scale farmer. 'He seeks to control the environment and produce a few specialised crops. The [Malawian] cultivator sought to adapt to the environment and produce as many crops as possible.'[20] In the Lower Shire Valley, successful cultivators were admired for their ability to choose 'the right plots for particular crops', judging 'not only by the nature of the soil itself but by the grass which may be growing on it'. As one informant explained:

> 'Mphumbu' soil will produce a good crop of bullrush millet, 'Ncecha', a light sandy soil, is the best type for groundnuts. 'Ndrongo', a black soil, is ideal for cotton. 'Nsangalabwe', while not suited to most crops, is very favourable for 'Maere' (finger millet, used in brewing the best beer). Of the grasses, 'Nsengere' and 'Nsonthe' show a suitable soil for maize.[21]

---

[16] The literature on *Nyau* is extensive. I have particularly benefited from the analyses by Schoffeleers, *River of Blood*, pp. 34–41 and by Laurel Birch de Aguiler, *Inscribing the Mask: Interpretation of Nyau Masks and Ritual Performance among the Chewa of Central Malawi* (Fribourg, Switzerland, 1996).

[17] For an extended discussion of this theme see Brian Morris, *The Power of Animals: An Ethnography* (Oxford, 1998), especially pp. 69–74.

[18] J.M. Schoffeleers, 'Introduction' in Schoffeleers (ed.), *Guardians of the Land* (Gwelo, 1979) pp. 2–5.

[19] The discussion that follows is based largely on the following sources: Kings M. Phiri, 'Production and Exchange in Pre-Colonial Malawi', in *Malawi: An Alternative Pattern of Development*, pp. 3–32; Phiri, 'Pre-Colonial Economic Change in Central Malawi: the Development and Expansion of Trade Systems 1750–1875', *Malawi Journal of Social Science*, 5, (1976); Edward A. Alpers, *Ivory and Slaves in East Central Africa* (London, 1975), pp. 1–38; Vaughan, 'Social and Economic Change', pp. 35–81; Elias C. Mandala, *Work and Control in a Peasant Economy* (Madison, WI, 1990); P. T. Terry, 'African Agriculture in Nyasaland', *Nyasaland Journal*, 14, 2 (1961) pp. 27–35.

[20] Iliffe, *Modern History*, p. 14.

[21] A.W.R. Duly, 'The Lower Shire District: Notes on Land Tenure and Individual Rights', *Nyasaland Journal*, 1, 1948, pp. 1–44.

By the second half of the nineteenth century, Mang'anja farmers in the Shire Highlands were growing 'sorghum, beans, millet, pumpkins, cucumbers, cassava and various kinds of Eleusine [finger millet]'.[22] They were also growing maize, the most important of the so-called American crops, high yielding but vulnerable to drought, which had been introduced from the east coast, perhaps in the eighteenth century, and by the 1880s had become 'the chief article of cultivation' in the area.[23] On the *mphala* drylands of the Lower Shire River sorghum and finger millet remained staple crops, often intercropped with pumpkins, groundnuts, cucumbers and peas. But on the *dambo* floodplains adjacent to the river, maize (*chimanga*) was cultivated in greater quantities along with a remarkable variety of lesser crops: beans, sugar-cane, rice and many types of vegetables. Finger millet supplemented by sorghum was the main staple of the Nyanja people of the Upper Shire valley. But around the south end of Lake Malawi maize was once more king, supplemented by sorghum, pumpkins, groundnuts and rice. Further north on the west coast, millet and the easily harvested cassava were convenient crops for peoples harassed by Ngoni raiders; while on the heavily watered Karonga floodplain bananas provided 'a great source of nourishment' for the Ngonde people, supporting denser populations than long-fallow agriculture and requiring less labour than other crops. Maize and finger millet were the main crops grown by Ngoni and Tumbuka cultivators on the Mzimba and South Rukuru plains. Further south, however, it was not until the 1880s and 1890s, according to Kings Phiri, that maize was introduced alongside sorghum and millet as a staple crop among the Chewa.[24]

The variety of crops grown reflected diversity in the type of agricultural systems employed. All over Malawi, as in East-Central Africa more generally, agricultural production was household based, using human labour exclusively rather than the labour of animals, and employing a limited range of agricultural implements: axes, digging sticks and hoes, the latter usually made of iron although, in some parts of central Malawi, of wood. Almost everywhere types of swidden (slash and burn) shifting agriculture were practised, although, as Vaughan has shown, there appears to have been a tendency in the Shire Highlands for the 'woodland' or forest-fallow system, involving the planting of seeds directly into the ashes following the felling and burning of trees, to be replaced by the more labour-intensive 'grassland' or bush-fallow system in which hoes were extensively employed.[25] Under this system, cultivators planted seeds on earth-covered mounds of ash and vegetation (*matuto*). In the neighbouring Shire valley, most crops were planted on flat ground. Among the Ngonde on the Karonga plain it was customary to plant on long ridges composed of grass and weeds covered by earth.[26] Wherever conditions allowed, rain fed, dry land farming was supplemented by the cultivation of maize and other crops in *dambos*. The result, so Livingstone's Makololo porters informed him, was 'that "here the maize had no season" – meaning that the whole year was proper for its growth and ripening'. In times of drought such gardens were particularly appreciated;

22 John Buchanan, *The Shire Highlands* (Edinburgh, 1885), p. 122.
23 Ibid.
24 Phiri, 'Production and Exchange', p. 9.
25 Vaughan, 'Social and Economic Change', pp. 49–51.
26 Terry, 'African Agriculture', p. 32.

there are many accounts of people seeking refuge on the banks of the Shire after their upland crops had failed.

In contrast to the importance placed on agriculture, animal husbandry was largely neglected. No purely pastoralist peoples lived in the Malawi regions; among the indigenous population cattle were kept in extensive numbers only by the Ngonde, who housed them in long sheds kept scrupulously clean. According to Owen Kalinga slightly more than half the population possessed cattle in 1900 with the largest herds being owned by members of the Ngonde political elite who distributed some of them among clients on a temporary basis.[27] Cattle were also of importance in the economy and society of the two major Ngoni kingdoms. 'Each village along the road seemed to have its herds of cattle, some twenty or thirty, others about one hundred in number', Robert Laws remarked of northern Ngoniland in 1878.[28] However, with the exception of Mwase Kasungu and his brother, Chipawila, who owned a 'magnificent' herd of 'perhaps four hundred head' in the late 1880s, only limited numbers of cattle were herded by Chewa farmers on the tsetse-free Lilongwe plain and hardly any in the Shire Valley or Highlands where pockets of tsetse acted as a deterrent.[29] In these districts, chickens, goats and fat-tailed sheep made a more substantial contribution to the food supply and the last two were also used as a form of currency, being exchanged for foodstuffs, iron or salt.

Hunting for meat or skins has been ignored by most historians. But, as Morris has noted, hunting was important in many Malawian communities not just, or even primarily, for the food it provided but also as a social activity associated with the assertion of a particular form of masculinity.[30] In the 1860s, game appears to have been in short supply in the Shire Highlands.[31] But in the Shire Valley, all the way from the Zambesi River to Lake Malawi, there were large herds of hippopotami and elephants along with antelopes of many description: kudu, reedbuck, hartebeest and impala.[32] No hunting guilds of the type that flourished among the Bisa in the Luangwa Valley appear to have existed either here or elsewhere in the Malawi region.[33] But there were a number of professional hunters, hung with charms, using flint muskets and accompanied by hunting dogs, who went in search of larger game.[34] And there were also groups of specialist hippopotami hunters who made a precarious living out of harpooning hippos from canoes, then exchanging the flesh for maize and selling the teeth to Portuguese traders.[35] Traps to catch game were many and varied, ranging from pitfalls used to trap elephants to smaller traps for antelopes and

[27] Owen J. M. Kalinga, 'Towards a Better Understanding of Socio-Economic Change in 18th and 19th century Ungonde', *Cahiers d'Etudes Africaines*, 93, 24–1, 1984, p. 94.
[28] Laws to Convenor, Livingstonia Committee, February 1879, *Free Church of Scotland Monthly Record*, 2 June 1879, p. 136.
[29] Carl Wiese, *Expedition in East-Central Africa, 1888–1891 A Report,* edited by Harry W. Langworthy, (University of Oklahoma Press, Norman, 1983), p. 253.
[30] Morris, *Power of Animals*, pp. 72–74.
[31] R.H. Rowley, *The Story of the Universities Mission to Central Africa* (London, 1866), pp. 172–733.
[32] Livingstone, *Zambesi Journal*; Foskett, *Zambesi Journal*; Alice Werner, *The Natives of British Central Africa* (London, 1906), pp. 185–92.
[33] Morris, *Power of Animals*, pp. 65–66.
[34] For a vivid description see Henry Faulkner, *Elephant Haunts* (London, 1868), pp. 173–79.
[35] E.D. Young, *The Search for Livingstone* (London, 1868), pp. 239–43; Mandala, *Work and Control*), p. 88.

lesser game, down to and including field mice.[36] At times, these were employed in conjunction with communal hunts in which groups of men and boys, led by chiefs or headmen and armed with arrows, knobkerries and spears, drove animals into nets or pitfalls. Meat was always much prized; but the excitement with which its appearance was greeted suggests that it was only infrequently eaten.

If meat was in short supply in the Malawi region in the mid nineteenth century, fish, fresh and dried, was available in relative abundance. The richest fishing grounds (among the best in Eastern Africa) were Lake Chilwa and the southern end of Lake Malawi. But *chambo, utaka, usipa* and *mpasa* were also caught in considerable quantities in the Shire River and throughout Lake Malawi, notably in the vicinity of Likoma and Chizumulu islands.[37] Fishing techniques were influenced by the character of the local environment. At the north end of the lake and around the islands, where the shores are rocky and steep, fishermen made use of two types of net: the *chilimira*, an open water seine net worked from two canoes, and the *matchela*, a gill net, usually left in the water overnight. At the southern of the Lake, however, the existence of gently sloping beaches made possible the use of *makoka*, large meshed seine nets varying in length from 50 to 400 yards, which were manoeuvred into place by fishermen in a single canoe and then pulled to the beach by ropes. Fish weirs and basket traps were employed on the Shire River and its tributaries. Dugout canoes provided the essential means of transport. They were usually hollowed out of the much-prized *chonya* tree (Breonadia microcephala) or else from *masangu* which was less durable, being a softer wood, but quicker and easier to work. Nets were constructed of local fibres (*bwazi* or *chopa*) and were much admired for their strength and lightness by early European observers.[38]

Fishing played a particularly important role in the economy of the Lakeside Tonga, on the western shore of Lake Malawi, and of the Nyanja people living at the south end of Lake Malawi, near Lake Chilwa and in the vicinity of the Shire River.[39] In contrast to agriculture, which involved men and women in relatively equal numbers, fishing was a gender-specific activity, monopolised almost entirely by men who made use of kinship ties in order to mobilise labour. Among the Nyanja, communal tasks such as setting nets, hauling them to shore and constructing canoes were normally performed by male members of an *mbumba* or matrilineage group, although fish trapping was often undertaken individually. Most fish caught were consumed within the fishermen's *mbumba*, but there was a regular trade to the more agriculturally productive highland regions adjacent to Lake Malawi involving the exchange of dried fish for maize and beans; by the 1860s fish traders from Lake Chilwa were also active in the Shire Highlands.

Dried fish was only one among a variety of commodities – including earthenware pots, tobacco, and foodstuffs – that were widely traded between ecologically diverse districts by the 1860s. Even more important were cotton cloth, ironware and salt, the three main staples of the regional economy.

---

[36] Werner, *Natives*, pp. 189–90.
[37] John McCracken, 'Fishing and the Colonial Economy: the Case of Malawi', *Journal of African History*, 28 (1987), pp. 413–29.
[38] William Percival Johnson, *Nyasa the Great Water* (Oxford 1922), p. 59.
[39] Vaughan, 'Social and Economic Change', pp. 40–60.

There is evidence that, in the Shire Valley at least, cotton production played a significant role going back at least to the seventeenth century. Two main types of cotton were grown, the indigenous *Tonje Kadja* and the imported *Tonje Manga*, and it was noted that although the former yielded less cotton and was inferior in quality to Tonje Manga, 'many people prefer it to foreign cotton' because it made stronger cloth.[40] As a variety of European pioneers observed, spinning and weaving were 'painfully slow' processes, largely dominated by men and resulting in the manufacture of what was a relatively expensive item beyond the means of all but the more affluent customers.[41] Most people living in the Shire Highlands, which were too cold for the successful production of cotton, continued, therefore, to clothe themselves in bark cloth but, when the opportunities arose, they also participated in a vigorous trade in regional commodities as the missionary, Rowley explained: 'The people in the highlands were rich in iron, those in the valley were poor; so when a highlandman wanted cotton to make himself a cloth, he sent down hoes, and such like things, to the valley, and obtained cotton in exchange.'[42]

Cotton cloth was also produced in more limited quantities by Chewa craftsmen in the Mchinji-Kasungu district of the Central region and by Mambwe immigrants from the Lake Malawi-Tanganyika corridor who settled under Ngoni protection in the Rukuru valley from the mid-nineteenth century. In a number of areas, however, cotton cloth was neither produced nor sold. Ngonde cultivators and herdsmen were highly successful in maintaining a balanced and variegated economy, yet the wearing of clothes other than brass girdles and bead aprons was virtually unknown among the Ngonde as late as the 1880s. In the Maseko Ngoni kingdom of Chikusi in 1878, men wore skins or bunches of feathers, with rings of hide on their legs and arms; most women were clothed in pieces of bark cloth although a few instead wore locally produced cotton cloth, described by one observer as being 'rough, strong, and durable'.[43]

If cloth was a luxury, albeit one much in demand, ironware and salt were essentials for the maintenance of the household economy. Outcrops of ironstone were irregularly dispersed: common in the Shire Highlands where Kirk noted that 'Every village has its forge and in the forest are the smelting furnaces'; much rarer in the Shire valley where little iron ore was to be found.[44] On much of the south-west shore of Lake Malawi iron hoes and spears were in short supply and, according to Kirk, 'the people do not appear to know how to work iron.'[45] Inland, in the upland district known as Chimaliro, Livingstone observed 'at every third or fourth village...a clay, fire-hardened furnace, for smelting iron. ... As we passed along, men sometimes ran from the fields they were working in, and offered for sale new hoes, axes and spears of their own workmanship.'[46] Further north, on the eastern edge of the Nyika plateau, Phoka smiths were renowned for the quality of their iron hoes, although some abandoned their smelting furnaces

[40] Livingstone, *Zambesi*, p. 111.
[41] Foskett, *Zambesi Journal,* Vol.1, pp. 240–41.
[42] Rowley, *Story,* pp. 230–31.
[43] Robert Laws, 'Journey along the Western Side of Lake Nyasa in 1878', *Proceedings of the Royal Geographical Society*, 1878, p. 308.
[44] Foskett, *Zambesi Journal,* Vol. I, p. 237.
[45] Foskett, vol. 2, p. 375.
[46] Livingstone, *Narrative*, p. 536.

in the 1850s as a consequence of the Ngoni invasion.[47]

Because of the skill required in the smelting of iron, it tended to be a specialist activity, conducted in the bush in secret and often involving the use of religious rituals. Men appear to have largely monopolised production, although east of the Luangwa Valley in the 1820s, Chewa women miners and smelters were employed by a Portuguese entrepreneur.[48] In the Shire Valley headmen and chiefs were mainly responsible for smelting the ore they obtained from the Highlands. But in the Highlands themselves, so Rowley noted, 'all may be blacksmiths', although he added that 'but few excel in ironwork'. Mang'anja smiths were claimed to be more skilled than Yao ones 'and the Manganja of the hills better than those of the valley'. Many of the articles produced – knives, spearheads, arrowheads and axes – were 'of such excellent workmanship', so Rowley believed, 'that they might have come from the hands of some of our own workmen'.[49] In the Shire Valley wooden hoes continued to be used alongside iron hoes which only well-to-do families could afford. Wherever they were traded, iron hoes served as items of exchange as well as instruments of agricultural production. Even the heavy Phoka hoe was frequently used for the payment of bridewealth.

Iron-working, like hunting, was overwhelmingly the preserve of men. Salt production, by contrast, was largely dominated by women. As Kjekshus has noted, salt was a vital element throughout East Central Africa for all people existing on a predominantly vegetarian diet.[50] Small quantities could be acquired relatively widely by burning reeds or grasses and then evaporating the ash but high quality sites were in short supply. The best and most famous were on the shores of Lake Chilwa where salt-making took place between May and November on land flooded during the rainy season. Production was in the hands of women of post-childbearing age, perhaps because to indulge in sexual intercourse while making salt was believed to undermine the operation. Salt-bearing soil was washed in baskets or earthenware pots with the residue being distributed through a woman's matrilineage or else traded throughout the Shire Highlands.[51] Women were also mainly responsible for the distillation of salt from the saline soils to be found at the confluence of the Shire and Mwanza rivers.[52] They also played a leading part in distilling salt from the salt springs (*vikulo*) located in a number of streams in the vicinity of Kasungu. Salt, indeed, was the basis for a lively trade extending through much of central Malawi into eastern Zambia and involving the exchange of salt for iron hoes, goats and various types of cloth.[53] Almost wherever salt was produced, political rulers appropriated a carefully assessed proportion of the product as a form of tribute. In the Kasungu area,

[47] Augustine W.C. Msiska, 'A note on iron working and early trade among the Phoka of Rumphi, Malawi', *SOMJ*, 34,1 1981, pp. 36–44; Hangson B.K. Msiska, 'Established on Iron, Undermined by Ivory: the Mwaphoka, c. 1380–1810', unpublished paper, Department of History, University of Malawi, 1979.

[48] A.C.P. Gamitto, *King Kazembe and the Marave, Cheva, Bisa, Bemba, Lunda, and Other Peoples of Southern Africa* trs.. Ian Cunnison, (Lisbon, 1960), pp.54–5.

[49] Rowley, *Story*, p. 245.

[50] Helge Kjekshus, *Ecology Control and Economic Development in East African History* (Heinemann, London, 1977), p.92.

[51] Rowley, *Story*

[52] Mandala, *Work and Control*, p. 44; Livingstone, *Zambesi Journal*, p. 101.

[53] Phiri, 'Production and Exchange', pp. 15–16.

chiefs Kawoma and Mwase derived substantial revenues from their control of the industry. The same was true at the south end of Lake Malawi where the Yao chief Mponda benefited from the presence of salt-pans adjacent to his main village. In 1866 Livingstone witnessed three to four hundred people making salt on this plain.[54] Seventeen years later, it was noted that 'the people in [Mponda's] village are well supplied with cloth …as people come from all quarters to buy salt, of which there is the material for making plenty.'[55]

Trade brought Malawians into contact with a wider international economy. Southern Malawi has a long history of involvement in international trade, going back at least to the late sixteenth century, by which time the Portuguese had occupied the ancient port of Sofala (the site of modern Beira) and seized control of the Swahili trading settlements in the Zambesi Valley at Sena and Tete. Over the next 150 years, the Portuguese focused their attention very largely on the gold trade of the Zimbabwean plateau, south of the Zambesi. However, they also made contact with the Maravi peoples of the Shire region from whom they obtained ivory, *machila* cloth, ironware, salt and food in exchange for Indian-produced cloth, beads and brassware.[56] At this period, Maravi traders regularly travelled to Mozambique Island to sell their ivory. However, by the early eighteenth century Yao ivory traders from east of Lake Malawi had come to dominate long distance ivory trade to the coast, thus rendering this route obsolete and relegating Mang'anja and Chewa communities to the role of primary producers.[57] Whereas, by the mid-nineteenth century, Yao men had come to regard the experience of trade and travel as essential ingredients of Yao male identity, the Mang'anja of the Shire Valley, so Livingstone believed, were 'much more fond of the home pursuits of spinning, weaving, smelting iron and cultivating the soil than [they were of] foreign travel'.[58]

Nevertheless, the Malawi region remained an important centre for international trade, partly as a result of the intervention of new groups of entrepreneurial middlemen. In southern Malawi, it was the expulsion of the Portuguese from the Zimbabwean plateau in the 1690s that provided the initial impetus. By this time, a variety of frontiersmen and adventurers, making use of armed slaves, *chikunda*, had carved out estates for themselves in the Zambesi Valley which the Portuguese Crown came to recognise as *prazos*. Portuguese-speaking and nominally Catholic, these *muzungos* frequently contracted marriages with African women and increasingly adopted African styles of dress, government and warfare.[59] Following the Portuguese defeat south of the Zambesi, some *muzungos* turned north to the lower Shire valley and the grasslands to the west where they and their *chikunda* hunted and traded for ivory. Some groups of *chikunda* broke away from their masters; others found themselves in direct competition with Yao traders who from the mid-eighteenth century had begun to sell ivory from the Malawi region to Swahili traders at Kilwa. They again both competed and

54 Horace Waller (ed.), *The Last Journals of David Livingstone* (London, 1874), Vol. I, p. 106.
55 Diary of Frederick Morrison, entry for 2 March 1883, Edinburgh University Library [EUL].
56 Malyn Newitt, *A History of Mozambique* (London, 1995), pp.77–8; Kings Phiri, 'Northern Zambezia from 1500 to 1800', *SOMJ*, 32, 1, 1979, p. 15. See also M.D. Newitt, *Portuguese Settlement on the Zambesi* (London, 1973).
57 Alpers, *Ivory and Slaves*, p. 58, 76–85; Newitt, *History*, p. 178, 184.
58 Livingstone, *Narrative*, p. 522 quoted in Alpers, *Ivory and Slaves*, pp. 17–23.
59 Newitt, *History*, pp. 217–42.

collaborated with Bisa traders from beyond the Luangwa Valley, who were active in western Malawi and along the banks of the Upper Shire from at least the 1830s. The Bisa, in their turn were in contact with Balowka (possibly Yao) traders from east of Lake Malawi who entered the elephant-rich Nkhamanga area in northern Malawi in the 1770s and 1780s and began hunting and trading for ivory and skins.[60]

By this time slaves from west of Lake Malawi were also reaching such coastal ports as Kilwa, although up to 1800 the flow does not appear to have been large. After 1805, however demand for slaves expanded sharply on the East African coast leading to the more systematic exploitation of the lands west of Lake Malawi. In the 1820s and 1830s some 8,000 to 10,000 slaves annually were exported from this region, so Kings Phiri has calculated, although it is important to stress that many of these were drawn from eastern Zambia and western Mozambique rather than from within the modern boundaries of Malawi.[61] Although the slave trade to Quelimane expanded sharply in the 1820s and 30s, most slaves were drawn from the *prazos* of the Zambesi valley, at this period, leaving the Shire Highlands and Valley relatively undisturbed.[62] Many, however, came from central Malawi where a large number of war captives were available as a consequence of fighting between the various small autonomous chiefdoms that had emerged following the disintegration of the Maravi state system in the eighteenth century.

Political & social organisation

European travellers and missionaries entering the Malawi region in the second half of the nineteenth century believed that people were grouped into tribes, distinguished from each other not only by language, culture and political system but also by physical appearance. Mang'anja men had tattoos composed of raised lines; Yao (Ajawa) of small isolated spots.[63] Later investigation has revealed a more complex and fluid picture, although one that involves a reinterpretation of the concept of ethnic identity rather than its abandonment. In the early 1830s, as the Portuguese explorer Antonio Gamitto recognised, apparently separate tribes in Central and Southern Malawi shared a common cultural and linguistic heritage. Diverse peoples, including the Mang'anja, Nyanja and Makua in southern Malawi and the Chewa and Chipeta in the centre, were 'totally independent of each other, and each is known by its own name. Nevertheless it is beyond dispute that all are of the same Marave race, having the same habits, customs, language etc'.[64] Tribal names often defined a people living in a specific environment: 'Nyanja', the people of the lake; 'Chipeta', the people of the grasslands. For many people, clan rather than tribe was the most important unit of group identity: Yao migration into southern Malawi from the eighteenth century

[60] H.L. Vail, 'Suggestions towards a reinterpreted Tumbuka history', in Pachai, *Early History*, pp. 154–55.
[61] Phiri, 'Pre-Colonial Economic Change ', p.25.
[62] Leroy Vail and Landeg White, *Capitalism and Colonialism in Mozambique* (London, 1980), pp. 22–7.
[63] Foskett, *Zambesi Journal*, September 4 1859, p. 243; Livingstone, *Narrative*, p. 376–77. See also Macdonald, *Africana*, p. 16; Rowley, *Story*, pp. 239–40.
[64] Gamitto, *King Kazembe*, p. 64.

was greatly facilitated by the manner in which common clan membership was used as a 'vehicle of assimilation across tribal boundaries', linking Yao immigrants with their Nyanja hosts.[65] At a political level, conflicts between chieftaincies frequently took place within an ethnic group, whether Maravi or Yao. At a cultural level, tribes were dynamic organisms, not static institutions, regularly incorporating people of diverse background and, at times, redefining their social boundaries. Many of the Yao who spread east to the southern shores of Lake Malawi were the proud descendants of Nyanja and Lomwe people who had become assimilated into Yao society. By the same token, the term *Chikunda*, initially applied to armed slaves employed on Portuguese estates (*prazos*) in the Zambesi valley, came to be used first of bands of independent warrior hunters and then as an ethnic designation for the thousands of immigrants from the Zambesi region (later still to be known as Sena) who moved in the late nineteenth century into the Shire Valley.[66] Ethnic categories were thus subject to fluidity and change, although this does not imply that they have no explanatory value. Indeed, from the mid-nineteenth century tribal identities in the Malawi region tended to become more distinct at precisely the time that cultural intermingling intensified.

By the early 1860s, when the first party of explorers and missionaries entered the region, a political situation of considerable complexity had been created through the interaction of indigenous and immigrant peoples. Most of those living in central Malawi and south of the lake shared a common language, Chinyanja or Chichewa – spoken with considerable regional variations – and a common culture and clan organisation. Pre-colonial historians disagree about many of the most fundamental features concerning the early history of these people.[67] But it is generally accepted that their origins lie in an intermingling between the earliest inhabitants, the Kafula or Batwa, and immigrants from the Katanga region of modern-day Congo, sometimes identified with the Banda clan, who moved south during the early second millennium. In many traditions, the Banda are portrayed as having a special affinity with the land along with the power of making rain. They were followed, perhaps as early as the fourteenth century, although conceivably as late as the sixteenth, by Phiri clansman (also known as Maravi) who tacitly accepted Banda claims to ownership of the land while asserting their rights to chiefly power over a previously stateless population.[68] Much of the detail of their subsequent political history remains problematic, but there is no dispute that by the seventeenth century three main

---

[65]   Vaughan, 'Social and Economic Change', pp. 61–3.
[66]   Schoffeleers, *River of Blood*, p. 22; Allen Isaacman, 'Ex-Slaves, Transfrontiersmen and the Slave Trade: The Chikunda of the Zambesi Valley, 1850–1900' in Paul E. Lovejoy (ed.), *Africans in Bondage: Studies in Slavery and the Slave Trade* (Madison, Wisconsin, 1986), pp. 273–391; H.H. Johnston, *British Central Africa* (London, 1898), p. 391.
[67]   For the central debate on the timing and nature of the Maravi incursions see: M.D.D. Newitt, 'The Early History of the Marave', *Journal of African History*, 23 (1982), pp. 145–62; Matthew Schoffeleers, 'The Zimba and the Lundu State in the late Sixteenth and Seventeenth Centuries', *JAH*, 28 (1987), pp. 337–55; Alpers, *Ivory and Slaves*, pp. 46–58. Newitt's revised argument can be found in Newitt, *History*, pp. 71–8.
[68]   Schoffeleers, *River of Blood*, pp. 22–32; Phiri, 'Northern Zambezia', pp. 1–22; Phiri, 'Chewa History in Central Malawi and the Use of Oral Tradition', (PhD dissertation, University of Wisconsin, 1975); H.W. Langworthy, 'Chewa or Malawi political organisation in the precolonial era' in Pachai, *Early History*, pp. 104–22.

Maravi kingdoms were in existence: that of Kalonga (usually regarded as the founder state) at the southwest end of the Lake; of his kinsman Undi between the Luangwa and the Zambesi rivers; and of his fellow kinsman, Lundu, initially based in the Lower Shire Valley although briefly extending his authority eastwards as far as the Indian Ocean. On several occasions early in the early seventeenth century bands of Maravi mercenaries, renowned for their ferocity, took part alongside the Portuguese in wars of expansion against Karanga rulers on the Zimbabwean plateau.

By the end of the century, however, the Maravi states were in disarray. Lacking effective centralising institutions, they suffered from the increasing devolution of political power to subordinate chiefs like Mankhokwe who emerged as the dominant figure in the Lower Shire Valley, taking the title *Lundu* to himself. Yao traders squeezed them out of the major trade routes to the coast. Afro-Portuguese and *Chikunda* adventurers in search of gold penetrated into Maravi territory north of the Zambezi where they established independent mining camps *(bares)* and intervened repeatedly in local politics. By the early 1800s, the Lundu kingdom was reduced to a section of the Lower Shire Valley and the king was politically impotent. As for Undi, his authority was already well on the wane when the Portuguese official, Gamitto, travelled through his kingdom in 1831 and the decline accelerated during the next three decades. In the grasslands west of Lake Malawi Mwase Kasungu's powerful kingdom arose in an area previously dominated by Kalonga but elsewhere village groupings re-emerged as the most important political units. Rowley's comments on the Shire Highlands in the early 1860s indicate both the extent to which traditions of hierarchy survived along with the degree to which they had been undermined in practice:

> Each little community had its head man, its chief, and too often its separate interest; and although the subordinate chiefs were nominally under a superior … and these superior individuals nominally subject to the Rundo, to whom tribute was paid from all the chiefs, yet this arrangement produced but little good. Central authority existed but in name, unity of action was not the result of it, and patriotism did not exist.[69]

The very name Maravi (often associated with flames) receded into a state of obscurity that was to last for nearly a century.[70] Instead, people of similar culture were identified by regional place names: Nyanja for the people round the south end of the lake and Mang'anja for those in the Lower Shire valley and Highlands; Chewa (a term used by Gamitto in 1830s) for those living west and south-west of the lake; Chipeta, the people of the high grass, a term used for descendants of the earliest pre-Phiri immigrants, now scattered through the Dedza, Dowa and Ntcheu districts of the Central Region.[71]

A somewhat different pattern existed among the Maravi's northern neighbours: the Tumbuka and related peoples to the west of the lake, the Tonga on the lake shore itself and the Ngonde on the plain to the north-west. Despite their sense of ethnic identity, the Tonga and Tumbuka are both mixed peoples with

---

[69] Rowley, *Story*, pp. 264–5.
[70] Schoffeleers, 'The meaning and use of the name *Malawi* in oral traditions and precolonial documents' in Pachai (ed.), *Early History*, pp. 91–103.
[71] Schoffeleers, *River of Blood*, pp. 25–32.

variegated cultures. The Tonga are an amalgam of at least four different groups, some of Chewa origin, some from the north, while the Tumbuka likewise have been influenced both by the matrilineal Chewa to the south and by patrilineal peoples from western Tanzania. Both originally lacked large-scale centralised authorities, although among the Tumbuka, certain chieftaincies, notably that of Luhanga, controlled more than a single clan. By the mid-eighteenth century, however, the demand for soft, easily carved African ivory in India was leading to a rise in prices firstly in the market towns of Mozambique but increasingly, as time passed by, in the expanding port of Kilwa. Soon traders from the east of Lake Malawi, dressed 'as Arabs', although drawn in particular from Unyamwezi, were making their way to Nkhamanga, the home of the northern Tumbuka, in search of ivory and to a lesser extent, of slaves. Known collectively as Balowoka, 'those who have crossed over the water', they established a loose confederation of states running from the lakeside port of Chilumba west to the elephant-rich Luangwa valley. By the 1820s, however, the authority of this Chikulamayembe dynasty was already on the wane. Lacking effective military or bureaucratic institutions, it was unable to respond effectively to changes in the pattern of trade in the Luangwa valley which diverted the region's ivory away from the trade routes to the east. New traders entered the Henga valley, purchasing slaves and undermining the Balowoka's commercial monopoly. 'When the Ngoni arrived on the scene in the mid-nineteenth century', writes Vail, 'they found a politically disorganised, militarily weak, and socially fissiparous society that proved easy to defeat.'[72]

Some historians have suggested that the Ngonde were also influenced by ivory traders who reached them from the east side of the lake but, in an authoritative study, Owen Kalinga has demonstrated that no such trading contacts existed prior to the late nineteenth century. The Ngonde were related not to other groups in Malawi but to a variety of peoples in western Tanzania with whom they shared a distinctive form of centralised monarchy. In the seventeenth century the Kyungu had been a sacred religious figure, living like the Lwembe of the culturally similar Nyakyusa north-east of the Songwe River in strict religious seclusion. But for reasons possibly connected with the favourable environment of the Karonga plain and the dense settled population attracted to it, the Kyungus from the third quarter of the eighteenth century entered more actively into secular politics while succeeding in limiting the powers of their previously dominant councillors (*makambala*). They also gradually extended the boundaries of the Ngonde state and established reasonably effective control over outlying villages.[73]

It is probable that for most Malawians in the mid–nineteenth century political authority at the level of the chieftaincy was of less importance than the social organisation of villages and households. Mang'anja cultivators in the Shire Highlands and Valley in the early 1860s retained some sense of allegiance to

[72] Leroy Vail, 'The Making of the "Dead North": A Study of Ngoni Rule in Northern Malawi, c. 1855–1907' in J.B. Peires (ed.), *Before and After Shaka: Papers in Nguni History* (Grahamstown, 1981); Vail, 'Suggestions', pp. 150–60; T. Cullen Young, *Notes on the History of the Tumbuka-Kamanga Peoples in the Northern Province of Nyasaland* (London, 1932), pp. 31–47, 82–4; J. van Velsen, 'Notes on the History of the Lakeside Tonga of Nyasaland', *African Studies*, 18, 3, 1959, pp. 108–13.

[73] Godfrey Wilson, *The Constitution of the Ngonde*, Rhodes-Livingstone Papers No. 3, 1969; Owen J.M. Kalinga, *A History of the Ngonde Kingdom of Malawi* (Mouton, Berlin, 1985).

Mankhokwe or even to his rival, the descendant of the original Lundu. But this rarely involved the provision of tribute to the paramount and was most effectively demonstrated in religious terms. Veneration for Mbona, the martyred spirit closely associated with the Lundu paramounts, continued to be widely expressed in the early 1860s and beyond. Mankhokwe, however, lacked military resources and was unable to provide assistance to other Mang'anja chiefs when they were attacked.[74]

By contrast, villages and households continued as viable social units. In common with other peoples of Maravi descent, the Mang'anja were matrilocal and matrilineal: a man normally moved into his wife's home village when he married; succession followed from uncle to maternal nephew rather than from father to son.[75] The consequence was that within a village the core was provided by one or several matrilineal groups (*mbumba*) made up of married sisters, their daughters and unmarried sons. With the exception of headmen, married men in the village were incomers. Bridewealth (the transfer of objects, often cattle, from the bridegroom's family to the family of the bride) was not employed. Instead, the prospective bridegroom performed arduous agricultural services (*chikamwini*) for his mother-in-law, who treated him as an *mkamwini* or workhorse. The upbringing of children and the settlement of disputes both remained responsibilities for members of the *mbumba*, and specifically of the *Nkhoswe*, a senior brother or maternal uncle to whom the group of sisters were presumed to turn for advice.

In this situation, the Mang'anja household, consisting of a wife and her husband, the wife's children and her elderly relatives, functioned effectively as an agricultural unit but less so as a social one. Women and men worked together in the fields, with women probably playing the larger part. However, women ate with their female relatives in separate groups from men and combined together with other women on specific tasks such as beer brewing and the pounding of maize. Husbands did not control the reproductive activities of their wives: children of the union belonged to the wife and her matrikin rather than to her husband. Equally, ownership of land went to the wife; if she and her husband divorced, the land remained with her.

It was, therefore, only in northern Malawi among such patrilineal, cattle-keeping peoples as the Ngonde and, to a lesser degree, the Tumbuka, that marriage could be interpreted as an unambiguously exploitative institution, cementing the dominance of senior men over their wives and other subordinates. Elsewhere, the relations between men and women were much more complex: Mang'anja women performed rituals of humility and respect to men, such as kneeling when they met; yet, in times of peace, they achieved a considerable degree of control over their domestic lives through their ownership both of land and of the produce of their labours.[76] It was women, not men, who had control of grain bins – although it should be added that, as in many other societies, it was

---

[74] Mandala, *Work and Control*, pp. 16–18.
[75] The discussion that follows is drawn predominantly from the following sources: Megan Vaughan, *The Story of an African Famine* (Cambridge, 1987), pp. 54–56; Vaughan, 'Social and Economic Change', pp. 40–42; Mandala, *Work and Control*, pp. 21–25; Landeg White, *Magomero* (Cambridge, 1987), pp.33–34; K.G.M Phiri, 'Some Changes in the Matrilineal Family System among the Chewa of Malawi since the Nineteenth Century', *JAH*, 24, 1983, pp. 257–274.
[76] Macdonald, *Africana*, p. 35. See also Morris, *Power of Animals*, pp. 56–57.

also women not men who took responsibility for child rearing and for such labour-intensive activities as gathering firewood and carrying water as well as cooking and pounding grain.[77] Although there were some women headmen and chiefs, political office-holders were very largely men. However, women played a major role in rain-calling ceremonies and as the 'spirit' wives of Mbona, where they took the lead in organising the shrine.[78] Hunting and warfare, however, remained a monopoly of men, a feature that would grow in significance in the 1860s as the violence associated with slave raiding intensified.

Less ambiguous forms of inequality involved the dominance exercised by elders over youths and of free men over slaves. It was through their control of marriage that elders could most easily exploit the labour of their juniors. Generational tension has been described as probably the most important form of social conflict in pre-colonial East Africa, although, as Iliffe notes, 'exploitation was masked by every man's expectation of becoming an elder.'[79] Among the Ngonde, this tension was institutionalised by the creation of age villages or else of communal dormitories in which young men of a similar age would sleep. Only when they married were these young men recognised as full adults, capable of inheriting cattle from their fathers. Yet marriage was dependent on the payment as bridewealth of several cows which by definition would belong to the father or his fellow senior kinsmen rather than to the son. Consequently young men were often forced to labour in their fathers' fields for several years before being given sufficient cattle to allow them to secure a wife.[80] Those young men whose families did not have sufficient cattle might instead render agricultural services to their prospective wife's parents as a substitute for the payment of bridewealth.[81]

Mang'anja youths were also subject to the dominance of their elders. Expressly excluded from participation in the communal rituals integral to the proper ordering of society, they were also denied access to certain economic activities – notably iron working and salt distillation. Marriage, once more, came to dramatise their subordinate position. Obliged to provide labour services for their prospective mothers-in-law, they were frequently employed on the hardest tasks – opening new fields and maintaining them for a full season – before being permitted to marry.[82] Unlike domestic slaves, however, they could look forward to making the full transition to adulthood.

There can be no doubt that the proportion of Malawians who were domestic slaves increased substantially with the expansion of the slave trade but, even earlier, domestic slavery existed. Unfree labour came in three main categories: children offered as pawns, sometimes in settlement of disputes; women, who either voluntarily enslaved themselves, often at times of famine, or else became victims of the legal process; and war captives of either sex, obtained through kidnapping or military raids.[83] In most parts of Africa, slaves were largely

---

[77] Rowley, *Story*, p. 246.
[78] Mandala, *Work and Control*, pp. 23–25.
[79] Iliffe, *Modern History*, p. 17.
[80] Godfrey Wilson, 'The Nyakyusa of South-Western Tanganyika', in Elizabeth Colson and Max Gluckman (eds), *Seven Tribes of British Central Africa* (Manchester, 1951), pp. 259–60.
[81] Kalinga, 'Socio-Economic Change', p. 93.
[82] Mandala, *Work and Control*, pp. 29–32.
[83] White, *Magomero*, pp. 33–34.

obtained through warfare and similar violence.[84] But in the Malawi regions prior to the Ngoni eruption chiefs and headmen more commonly acquired domestic slaves (*akapolo*) through the manipulation of the legal system.[85] Women slaves were valued both for their productive and reproductive capacities. By taking 'slave wives' Chewa and Mang'anja headmen and chiefs could bypass matrilineal kinship obligations, increase the number of dependants directly under their control and hence expand the labour resources available to them. Free women also were alert to the need to acquire extra labour for their households – an especially pressing consideration in a society where high rates of child mortality prevailed. At Magomero, the mission station founded in the Shire Highlands in 1860, married women frequently seized young girls who had been given refuge by the missionaries. Because slave women and children born into free families were normally assimilated into lineages over time it is frequently suggested that their lot was of a different order to that of plantation or chattel slaves. Nevertheless, it would be wrong to underestimate the extent to which *akapolo* were exploited. Traditions collected by Kings Phiri in the Central region suggest that Chewa slaves 'were generally ill-treated unless they came from local lineages. They were forced to do onerous work with blunt instruments such as worn-out hoes, eat their food from the floor like dogs, and drink their beer from broken or dirty gourds.'[86] Elias Mandala records a similar tradition from the Lower Shire Valley: 'Whenever there was a hard job to be done, they always gave it to a kapolo. He or she would work the whole day without rest; and no one really cared because a kapolo was not a real human being.'[87] Like the youths whom they resembled, domestic slaves were not permitted to participate in iron working or in salt production. Although they worked in the fields alongside freemen, they did not control the product of their labour.

Trade & conquest

From the middle of the nineteenth century the peoples of Malawi were exposed to two new disruptive external influences. The first was the extension and enlargement of the trade in slaves and ivory. As we have seen, long-distance commerce between the Lake Malawi area and the east African coast was already well underway by the late eighteenth century. From the early decades of the nineteenth century, however, a number of developments took place contributing to a dramatic expansion in the scale of trade from the 1840s onwards. Prices paid for East African ivory began to rise sharply from the mid-1820s as a consequence of the growth in the market in Western Europe and America for luxury items made of that material. The cost of trade goods imported into East Africa, particularly mass produced *merikani* cloth, fell steadily as a result of the improvements in production techniques. On the Mozambique coast there was an increased demand for slaves, initially fuelled by plantation owners in Brazil and Cuba and continued from the French Indian ocean island of Reunion. As requests from

---

[84] Paul E. Lovejoy, *Transformations in Slavery* (Cambridge, 1983), p. 4.
[85] Mandala, *Work and Control*, p. 33.
[86] Phiri, 'Pre-Colonial Economic Change', pp. 24–5.
[87] Mandala, *Work and Control*, p. 35.

these quarters declined from the early 1850s the pattern of trade shifted northwards to the coastal port of Kilwa, which was strategically placed to meet the new demand for slaves on the clove plantations of Zanzibar and Pemba and, somewhat later, on the grain-producing plantations of Mombasa and Malindi. Not until the 1870s, after the Sultan of Zanzibar had been finally pressurised by the British to sign treaties banning slave trading by sea or on land, did the trade begin to decline although it was at least another decade before the number of slaves taken from the Malawi region fell off appreciably.

Estimates of numbers involved must be treated with considerable caution but it would appear that they roughly doubled between the 1820s and 1860 when Consul Rigby claimed that '19,000 slaves were brought to Zanzibar from the coast of Africa' of whom 'fifteen thousand were from the neighbourhood of the great lake of Nyassa'.[88] Later in the mid-1860s, the number of slaves annually exported from Kilwa, most of them from the interior, was reported to be in excess of 22,000. By this time, so many slaves were being taken from the lake region that, in the vicinity of Zanzibar, 'Wanyasa' had become the name commonly applied to people of slave origin.[89] Decades later the term was still being used on the coast as an expression of common identity and pride, linking ex-slaves to their mythical country of origin. Some even succeeded in making their way back to Nyasaland early in the twentieth century, although none of these is recorded as having made contact with relatives.[90]

The expansion in demand for slaves resulted in fundamental changes in the organisation of long distance trade. Up to the 1830s, Arabs and Swahili on the East Coast of Africa had been content to provide markets for caravans from the interior which were largely controlled by African peoples such as the Bisa, the Nyamwezi and the Yao. From this period, however, the growing profitability of the trade led to the first full-scale Swahili penetration of the interior. The actual numbers involved were small but the Swahili had the advantage over their African competitors of access to capital lent by Indian financiers at Zanzibar and to the most modern firearms available with which they equipped mercenary allies. They were not at first generally concerned with extending their territorial powers, although in the 1840s a trader from Zanzibar, Salim bin Abdallah, settled at Nkhotakota on the west shore of Lake Malawi, where he established a thriving commercial staging post and agricultural settlement. Instead they concentrated in the Malawi regions on dominating the northern trade routes to Nkhotakota and Deep Bay [Chilumba] while sharing the southern routes with Yao traders with whom they had extensive commercial dealings.[91]

Their expansion, however, was not without political consequences. By 1863 Salim bin Abdallah had seized control of the whole Nkhotakota district from neighbouring Chewa chiefs and was regularly sending dhows filled with slaves and ivory to the entrepot at Losewa, described by James Stewart as 'the port or

[88] C.P. Rigby, Report on the Zanzibar Dominions, 1 July 1860 in Mrs Charles E B Russell, *General Rigby, Zanzibar and the Slave Trade* (London, 1935), p. 333.
[89] Frederick Cooper, *Plantation Slavery on the East Coast of Africa* (New Haven and London, 1977), p. 120.
[90] Cooper, pp. 240–41, 265–66.
[91] Marcia Wright and Peter Lary, 'Swahili Settlements in Northern Zambia and Malawi', *African Historical Studies*, 4, 3, 1971; H.W. Langworthy, 'Swahili Influence on the Area between Lake Malawi and the Luangwa River', *African Historical Studies*, 4, 1971.

landing-place from the western side of the lake for all slave caravans converging towards Kota-Kota and...also the point of departure for newly formed and rearranged caravans leaving the eastern shore of Nyassa for Kilwa'.[92] Following his death in the mid-1870s, his successors consolidated their position by sending groups of ivory hunters to Kasungu and beyond into the Luangawa Valley and by hiring their fleet of between four and six dhows to other traders who wished to transport goods across the lake. They also made use of slave labour to grow a variety of crops – rice, cassava, onions, vegetable marrows, mangoes and paw paws – for sale to passing caravans. Diplomatic alliances were established with a number of local rulers such as Mwase at Kasungu and Kalumo at Ntchisi who were supplied with guns as a consequence of their involvement in long distance trade. By 1879, a separate group of Swahili had moved south from Ujiji on Lake Tanganyika and taken up residence among the Senga people in the upper Luanga Valley where large herds of elephants were still to be found.[93] Two or three years later a group of these Swahili, headed by the wealthy trader, Mlozi, were introduced to the rulers of Ungonde by a commercial ally, the African elephant hunter, Kalumwenzo Sichinga.[94] They quickly established stockaded settlements in the area which they used as bases for the transport of slaves and ivory from the Chitipa highlands and the Luangwa valley to Chilumba and from there by dhow across the lake to Manda.

Further south, Yao traders benefited from commercial contacts with the Swahili which went back at least to the seventeenth century. Over the next hundred years they came to dominate trading networks extending from their homeland in northern Mozambique east to the coast and west through the Shire Highlands to the Luangwa valley while at the same time absorbing members of other ethnic groups – Nyanja, Lomwe and Makua – into a multi-ethnic, clan-based community linked only by the use of a common trading language, ChiYao, and a common set of economic interests.[95] Up to the late eighteenth century Yao traders do not appear to have made their homes in the Malawi region. From the 1790s, however, small groups of refugees, coming in search of food at a time of famine, began settling in the Mangochi Hills to the south west of Lake Malawi. A few years later they were uprooted from this district and forced to move further south by better-armed members of the Mbebwe clan, led by Mkata and Kawinga; they in turn clashed with later immigrants arriving in the 1830s and 1840s led by Msamala and Malemia.

At first, Mang'anja and Yao lived together in comparative harmony. But in the early 1860s disputes arose, explained by Livingstone as a consequence of the inability of the Mang'anja to provide food supplies to meet the considerable body of traders. 'When the provisions became scarce, the guests began to steal from the fields, quarrels arose in consequence', and violent warfare broke out.[96] Unlike

---

[92] George Shepperson, 'The Jumbe of Kota Kota and some aspects of the history of Islam in British Central Africa' in I.M. Lewis (ed.), *Islam in Tropical Africa* (London, 1966), p. 196; James Stewart, 'The Second Circumnavigation of Lake Nyasa', *Proceedings of the Royal Geographical Society*, vol. 1, 1877, p. 292.

[93] John W. Moir, 'Mambera's to the Basenga Country – Notes', 29 December 1879, NLS 7904.

[94] Kalinga, 'Ngonde Kingdom', pp. 121–26.

[95] Vaughan, *Story*, p.56; Vaughan, 'Social and Economic Change', pp. 60–63; J. B. Webster, 'From Yao Hill to Mount Mulanje', History Seminar paper, Chancellor College, University of Malawi, 1977.

[96] Livingstone, *Narrative*, p. 171. See also Vaughan, 'Social and Economic Change', pp. 143–44.

the Mang'anja, the Yao appear to have had no tradition of large-scale centralised political organisation, but through their involvement in the international economy prominent military and commercial leaders had emerged who owed their power to the acquisition of slaves and the distribution of imported cloth. Possession of guns and ammunition may also have contributed to their military superiority although the few flintlocks they held in the 1860s are likely to have been more important for their psychological effect than as effective military instruments.[97] At all events, Yao chiefs were generally successful in the fighting and within a few years had either eliminated their Mang'anja and Nyanja rivals in the Shire Highlands, the Upper Shire Valley and round the south end of Lake Malawi or else had reduced them to the status of village headmen in Yao-controlled states. Yao traders had also penetrated into the heartland of the old Maravi empire west of Lake Malawi, killing Kalonga Sosola, the last ruler of that title, and establishing a number of rival states, including those of Pemba at the mouth of the Linthipe river, of Tambala inland and of Bibi Kaluundu, on the shores of Lake Malawi, a few miles north of Pemba's settlement.

Culturally and in some respects politically, the Yao resembled the Maravi peoples. Like them they were members of Central Africa's matrilineal belt, tracing inheritance through the female line from uncle to nephew and normally practising uxorilocal marriage. Many shared common clan names with the people among whom they settled, thus providing justification for the view that they were kinsfolk, perhaps returning to their places of origin. Their contacts with the east coast, however, as pioneers of the Arab trading frontier, introduced a new factor into economic and cultural relationships. By the 1870s, coastal influence was apparent among the Yao in the square houses they built, some of them 'with substantial carved doors such as one sees in Zanzibar';[98] in the richly embroidered clothing worn by members of the political elite; and in the fact that at least one chief, Makanjira, on the south eastern shore, had already been converted to Islam. The most important Yao settlements near the lake, Mponda's and Makanjira's, were substantial towns, with populations variously estimated at between 4,000 and 6,000 inhabitants. Dhows were built at Makanjira's, as at Nkhotakota, to carry caravans across the lake. Coastal delicacies – mangoes, paw paws and coconuts – were grown 'with the object' so Abdallah wrote, 'of making the Lake-shore resemble the Coast'.[99]

As Livingstone noted in 1866, Yao men, including Chief Mponda, periodically participated directly in agriculture.[100] Nevertheless, it is clear that in contrast to the Mang'anja, they tended to place the greatest priority on trade, leaving work in the fields largely, although not exclusively to women. Songs sung at the departure of caravans frequently castigated those men who remained at home 'thinking too much about food'.[101] Yao society in consequence tended to be at once more stratified than Mang'anja society and also perhaps more heavily

---

[97] E.A. Alpers, 'The Yao in Malawi: the importance of local research in Pachai', *Early History*, pp. 171–3.

[98] Consul Goodrich to Foreign Office, 19 March 1885, TNA FO 84 1702.

[99] Morrison diary entry for 8 March 1885, EUL; Robert Laws, *Women's Work at Livingstonia* (Paisley, 1886), p. 4; Yohanna B. Abdallah, *The Yaos* (Zomba, 1919), pp. 43–4. See also Edward A. Alpers, 'Trade, State and Society among the Yao in the nineteenth century', *JAH*, 10, 3 1969.

[100] Waller, *Last Journals*, vol. 1, p. 108.

[101] Vaughan, 'Social and Economic Change', p. 67.

reliant on its involvement in a wider economy. Vaughan postulates that 'the absence of male labour for clearing new land had led to the cultivation of increasingly infertile soils in the eighteenth century and that this contributed to the famine which propelled the first Yao immigrants into southern Malawi.'[102] By a similar token, chieftaincies formed were based on the prowess of their leaders in the closely allied occupations of trade and war and in their hold over supplies of ammunition and guns. Trading expeditions were usually organised by chiefs but frequently sons or nephews were deputed to lead them in their place. Such men could rapidly expand their own personal retinues armed with guns and hence increase the military resources available to them.

Yao expansion interacted with the penetration into the Shire Valley and Highlands of Afro-Portuguese and *Chikunda* slavers. By the 1840s, demand for slaves was drawing powerful Afro-Portuguese families north of the Zambesi into the area once dominated by the Maravi states. The pioneer family, the Caetano Pereiras, established themselves as the dominant force between the Luangwa and the Shire by 1840, but within a matter of years their authority had been overshadowed by that of the Vas dos Anjos family, led by Paul Marianno Vas dos Anjos II. Known widely by his African title, Matakenya, 'the causer of trembling', Paul Marianno constructed a formidable *aringa* (fortress) at Shamo at the southern extremity of the Shire River from 1853. Using this *aringa* as his base, he bought slaves from Mang'anja elders before turning to raiding as a primary occupation. This alarmed the Portuguese authorities who sent troops to capture his *aringa* in 1858. By the early 1860s, however, Paul Marianno was back on the Shire, where he launched his *Chikunda* in a series of raids up the river and into the Shire highlands, looting and raiding villages. In 1863, he destroyed the Mbona shrine at Khulubvi and killed one of the leading Mang'anja chiefs, Tengani. By the time of his death later that year, he had drawn together Mang'anja and Sena refugees into a new state, Massingere, which stretched from the Ruo to the Zambesi.[103] These people constituted the first wave in the mass immigration into the Shire Valley of predominantly patrilineal *Chikunda* or Sena refugees, bringing with them a variety of new cultural and linguistic influences, including associations of adolescents, known as *nomi* societies.[104]

The impact of the slave trade was immensely complicated by the simultaneous intrusion into the Malawi region of invaders from the south. In the 1820s the rise and expansion of the Zulu kingdom in Natal was accompanied by the migration out of the area of a number of groups of Nguni-speaking people.[105] Two of these, described both as Maviti and Ngoni, entered Malawi in the 1840s having incorporated a variety of conquered peoples on the way. One, led by Zwangendaba, crossed the Zambesi near Zumbo in 1835, halted for four years in Nsenga country, and then continued their northwards advance up the Malawi-

---

[102] Ibid., p. 69.

[103] Newitt, *History*, pp280, 286, 304–5, 312–3; Newitt, *Portuguese Settlement*, pp. 278–80; Vail and White, *Capitalism and Colonialism*, pp. 30–1; 37; Mandala, *Work and Control*, pp. 67–72.

[104] Vail and White, *Capitalism and Colonialism*, pp. 71–72,170.

[105] The classic account, still useful on the movement of Nguni-speaking people, is J. D. Omer-Cooper, *The Zulu Aftermath* (London, 1966). However, its analysis of the causes of the process of fragmentation and aggregation of chiefdoms in south-western Africa has now been superseded. See Norman Etherington, *The Great Treks: The Transformation of Southern Africa, 1815–1854* (Harlow, 2001) and Carolyn Hamilton (ed.), *The Mfecane Aftermath* (Johannesburg, 1995).

Luangwa watershed as far as Ufipa on the east side of Lake Tanganyika where Zwangendaba died about 1848. The other, led by Mputa ('The Smiter') Maseko, spent a brief period in the Ntcheu area to the southwest of Lake Malawi before making their way up the eastern side into the Songea district which they reached in the early 1840s.

The return of these Ngoni groups into the Malawi regions began in the mid-1850s and led to the establishment of four main kingdoms either within or abutting on the borders of the modern state. Following Zwangendaba's death, a succession dispute occurred resulting in the creation of several factions, all but one of them headed by sons of Zwangendaba. The most powerful of these, that of Mbelwa, moved southwards in the mid-1850s up the Henga valley into the rolling highlands beyond, reducing most of the Tumbuka to subjection and destroying the last vestiges of the Chikulamayembe state. This group finally settled in the tsetse-free Kasitu Valley where Mbelwa was joined by three other brothers, Mtwalo and Mabilabo, who had accompanied him in the march south, and Mpherembe, whose faction joined up with that of Mbelwa's in the early 1870s after several years spent fighting against Bemba chiefs. The Northern Ngoni kingdom thus differed from that of most breakaway Nguni states in that it contained a number of distinct segments, each with its own semi-independent ruler, who nevertheless recognised the ultimate sovereignty of the paramount.

The creation of the Northern Ngoni kingdom marked only one among a number of political developments. Over the next few years Chiwere Ndlovu, an experienced war-lord, raided south into the hinterland of Nkhota Kota, finally establishing a new kingdom deep in Chewa country at Mvera. Meanwhile, Mpezeni, a brother of Mbelwa, led his followers first to Bemba country and then, about 1871, into the area straddling the modern boundary between Zambia and Malawi at Chipata. At almost exactly this time, the prolonged journeying – as much the evasive wandering of refugees as the triumphant march of conquerors – of the Maseko Ngoni was coming to an end. Driven from Songea by a rival group of Ngoni, that of Zulu Gama, they retreated southwards into the Shire Highlands in the early 1860s and then moved again, perhaps under pressure from Yao gunmen, to Domwe Mountain in modern Mozambique from where they could dominate the grasslands stretching north towards Mount Dedza and Ntcheu.[106]

Despite their varied experiences, the Ngoni kingdoms shared a number of organisational features in common. All were 'snowball' states, dependent for their expansion during their period of wandering on the forcible incorporation of a steady stream of male and female captives from the communities among whom they moved. Their basic economic unit remained the household, usually incorporated into a larger village, but in addition young men around the age of fifteen were recruited into age regiments extending across the whole society which were intermittently employed in seizing captives from the Ngoni's neighbours and in carrying off cattle and grain. All made use of Zulu-type military technology – the short stabbing spear and heavy oxide shield – and they also placed a high premium on the accumulation of cattle, the most valuable source of capital available within Ngoni society. Unlike the Yao, they involved them-

---

[106] T. Jack Thompson, *Christianity in Northern Malawi* (Leiden, 1995), p. 1–15; J. A. Barnes, *Politics in a Changing Society* (Oxford, 1954), pp. 7–23; Newitt, *History*, 257–64.

selves only to a limited extent in the East Coast trade but (popular assumptions to the contrary) they were by no means inexperienced in agriculture, even though it was usually the women who played the largest part. Ngoni kingdoms tended to be hierarchical in nature. Power and privilege was concentrated very largely on members of aristocratic clans originating from South Africa; but outstanding warriors, whatever their backgrounds, could rise to positions of military leadership. Ng'onomo, the senior general in the northern Ngoni paramountcy by the 1870s, was the son of a captive from Delagoa Bay. Chiwere Ndhlovu, eventually the leader of an independent state, was an Nsenga by birth and himself a former captive.

Patterns of violence

The mounting cycle of violence that enveloped central Africa from the 1860s brought in its wake profound changes, political, social and economic, that set the scene for the establishment of colonialism in Malawi. The starting point relates to the changing character of the slave trade. Up to the late 1850s most of the slaves sold to traders by members of the Mang'anja political elite were marginal, sometimes kinless figures on the periphery of society: friendless orphans, criminals and unfortunates accused of witchcraft.[107] As violence escalated, however, these social restraints collapsed. War captives remained an important category of slaves but they were now accompanied by ordinary villagers, seized in raids by armed gangs of Yao or *Chikunda* gunmen, who were no longer prepared to purchase what they could obtain through force of arms. Members of different Yao clans routinely preyed on each other. Individual acts of kidnapping regularly took place. It was more than ever the assumption, in the words of the Jumbe of Nkhotakota, that 'slaves were not like … free people, they were like dogs or cattle, just fit to be done with as he or their masters pleased.'[108]

The journal kept in the late 1870s by members of the Livingstonia mission at Cape Maclear close to the slave route running round the south end of Lake Malawi provides numerous examples of the insecurity that prevailed. One man, Chawisa, a blacksmith by trade, who had sought refuge at the station, had escaped from a slave gang at Nkhotakota, only to be enslaved by a second master, then sold to a third, before ending up making a living by 'mending native guns at the Mission village'.[109] A woman, Nambewe, had been sold and resold several times before running away from her master and taking up with a man, Chikondwi, who fled with her to the station when his owner threatened to sell him. Some husbands sent their slave wives to work at the station for cloth as an alternative to selling them to the coast. Others arrived by altogether more circuitous routes. One woman, Msumata, was kidnapped from her village by an Ngoni raiding party in 1877. They sold her to Swahili traders who abandoned her at Nkopi when she fell ill. She was then enslaved by a local villager and finally moved in 1878 to the refuge of the station. The complexity of motivation among those joining the mission is well revealed in the case of a young man, Saiti, a

---

107 Livingstone, *Narrative*, p. 125.
108 Quoted in Morrison diary entry for 7 December 1882.
109 Cape Maclear Journal, entry for 9 October 1877, National Library of Scotland [NLS], Ms. 7909.

slave of the local village headman, Mtalika, who 'ran away', the Journal records, 'because having been here on a former occasion working, his master was dissatisfied at his not having given him part of his pay. Further, he has made a large garden and is afraid that on this account he will be poisoned. He also heard that his chief intended to sell him, and also he had a love disappointment.'[110]

What emerges from these stories and from the numerous others available is a systematic pattern of behaviour involving three developments of particular importance.[111] First of these, as White accurately notes, was the establishment of new political linkages in which 'the relationship that came to matter was not that based on kin or "tribe" but that between patron and client, the protector and the protected.'[112] Whoever possessed guns in significant numbers and could offer security was likely to attract dependents to them. In the 1860s and 70s the example set by Paul Marianno and his *chikunda* henchmen was copied not only by a variety of Yao chiefs but also by the Kololo porters brought by Livingstone from Barotseland to the Lower Shire, who successfully created chieftaincies for themselves out of the prevailing conditions of uncertainty.

This is linked to a second development: that with very few exceptions (for example that of the Yao chief Bibi Kulundu) it was men who emerged as patrons and women who became their clients. European observers of Mang'anja society in 1861 were impressed at the extent to which women were able to compete on relatively equal terms with men.[113] However, the upsurge of violence put women particularly at risk, in part because it was men who controlled the means of destruction in society – fighting and hunting with guns and spears. Moreover, the growth of *ukapolo* domestic slavery affected women disproportionately. Yao chiefs in the 1880s employed male slaves 'in farming, building, making baskets, sewing garments, and such masculine pursuits', so a Scottish missionary commented. But they prized women more and were prepared to pay higher prices for them: partly because of their value 'in hoeing the farm, and all such female duties'; more particularly because of their reproductive powers – the fact that they could be utilised as slave wives.[114]

The third development, the growth of domestic slavery, was thus frequently related to the exploitation of women. Historians have at times been chary of using the term 'slavery' as a description of unfree status in African societies. Although it is true that the social distance between slave and master on an American plantation was much greater than that between master and 'slave wife' in a Yao territorial chieftaincy, aspects of the relationship remain the same. Slaves had this in common that they were legal and often real outsiders, removed from their kinship group and hence denied the rights and privileges of the society in which they lived.[115] This was perhaps of particular importance in the case of matrilineal societies like the Yao. In such societies, as Cooper notes, 'children

---

[110] Cape Maclear Journal, 16 February 1878, NLS Ms. 7909.

[111] For an excellent study of the life stories of slaves from the Nyasa-Tanganyika corridor see Marcia Wright, *Strategies of Slaves and Women* (London, 1993).

[112] White, *Magomero*, p. 49.

[113] Rowley, *Story*, p. 208.

[114] Macdonald, *Africana*, pp. 147.

[115] Lovejoy, *Transformations*, pp. 1–6.; Cooper, *Plantation Slavery*, pp. 2–6; Igor Kopytoff and Suzanne Miers, 'African "Slavery" as an Institution of Marginality' in Miers and Kopytoff, *Slavery in Africa* (Madison, Wisconsin, 1977), pp. 3–78.

normally were considered part of their mother's kinship group and the father, no matter how wealthy he became, had trouble converting wealth into strengthening his own kinship group.' Slave mothers, on the other hand, had no kinship group and their children went to swell the ranks of their father's dependents.[116] Chief Mponda was described in 1876 as having 90 wives;[117] the most powerful of the Kololo chiefs, who built up kingdoms for themselves in the Lower Shire valley, had at least 40. What is most striking is that by the 1870s it was not only members of the political elite, as among the Sena in the Zambesi valley, who were on the lookout for *akapolo*.[118] Unattached women became the prey of men; free married women took to kidnapping defenceless girls.

Special problems of interpretation exist in the case of the Ngoni states, the overwhelming majority of whose members were drawn from families initially incorporated by force into the society. What appears true, however, is that while families incorporated south of the Zambesi or 'on the march' were accepted fully as members of the Ngoni communities, those incorporated through raid or conquest in the Malawi regions were in a much more indeterminate category, liable both to be sold as slaves or to be to put to work by members of the aristocracy.[119] In the major Ngoni kingdoms in consequence, the gap between chiefs and commoners was impressively large. Controlling by far the largest herds of cattle in the state, and the greatest number of dependents, the rulers of both the northern and southern kingdoms were able to lavish privileges on their wives and immediate families of a different order to those available to members of most other political elites. Looking back to pre-colonial times in the 1930s, members of the Ngoni aristocracy were unanimous in remembering that the *amakosikazi* (royal women) never worked, even consigning responsibility for their children to their domestic slaves (*micetho*) and girl companions (*izidanani*). Instead they devoted their time to leisure activities – dressing their hair in elaborate styles, dancing and drinking beer. Special clothing was reserved for their use – kilts made of soft dressed leather; they alone were permitted to wear leopard and lion claw ornaments set among layers of beads.[120]

The reverse side of this picture of luxury can be found in the densely packed stockaded villages, extending into Lake Malawi established by Tonga and other refugees fleeing from Ngoni raids. The extent of this shift in settlement patterns should not be overestimated. Euphorbia hedges surrounding Mang'anja villages existed prior to the intensification of the slave trade, although their number and size increased during the time of troubles.[121] Nevertheless, there can be little doubt that, as violence increased, dramatic changes took place. In the Lower Shire Valley the dual agricultural system based on the *dimba* floodland and *mphala* dryland zones was disrupted as people took refuge in the small islands of the Shire River and within the surrounding marshes. In the Shire Highlands people abandoned the fertile but open plain stretching from Zomba to Soche, turning instead to mountain sanctuaries or to more easily protected settlements

---

[116] Cooper, *Plantation Slavery*, p. 17.
[117] Livingstonia Mission Journal, 20 January 1876, NLS Ms. 7908.
[118] Barbara Isaacman and Allen Isaacman, 'Slavery and Social Stratification among the Sena of Mozambique' in Miers and Kopytoff, *Slavery in Africa*, pp. 107–18.
[119] Margaret Read, *The Ngoni of Nyasaland* (London, 1956), pp.4–10.
[120] Read, *Ngoni of Nyasaland*, pp. 81–5; Vail, 'Making of the Dead North', pp. 243–44.
[121] Mandala, *Work and Control*, pp. 20–21.

on Chisi Island on Lake Chilwa.[122] Similarly, in northern Malawi, the establishment by the Ngoni of large concentrated villages, housing both people and cattle, was accompanied by the mass flight of local villagers and the creation of a bush–covered belt of depopulated territory fifty miles wide in some sections.[123] The Henga valley, formerly a centre of Tumbuka population, 'was made a wilderness...the favourite resort of game and beasts of prey'.[124] Stockaded villages in the Kasungu district were clustered in clearings a few miles in radius beyond which the bush stretched as far as the horizon.[125] Cultivation of cassava, a root crop largely proof against Ngoni raids, gave the Tonga an element of food security. Other people, however, were less fortunate.

The severe famine of 1861–63 which devastated the Shire Highlands and Valley was at once both consequence and cause of the disruption of agricultural communities. As so often in Africa it was the combination of violence with drought that converted a period of temporary food shortages into a famine that kills.[126] The rains failed in the Shire Highlands in January 1861 at a time when food supplies had already been diminished as a result of Yao and Ngoni raids. Thousands of people fled to the Shire Valley hoping to obtain crops from *dimba* gardens on the floodland only to finds that cultivation had virtually ceased in the face of further raids from Matakenya (Paul Marianno). When the short rains failed in November 1862 the results were catastrophic. At first it was children and the vulnerable who suffered most severely but by January able-bodied adults too were starving. 'Wild-looking, famished men, with cords tied tightly round their waists to lessen the pains of hunger, roamed about grubbing up roots, until, unable to go on any longer, they sank down and died.'[127] Men with guns and access to canoes, like Livingstone's Kololo, were able to able to avoid the worst affects by seizing gardens or by obtaining provisions from the Lower Zambesi. But for the great majority this was not an option. Coming up the Shire in January 1863, John Kirk was met by a steady flow of bodies floating down the river: 'These have died of hunger. The few we meet are skin and bone, some evidently about to follow their comrades.'[128] In scenes reminiscent of those that greeted observers during the great Ethiopian famine of the early 1980s, missionaries attempted to distribute grain to the famished survivors:

> Men who had carried heavy burdens with ease up the hills tottered towards us attenuated beyond recognition; others too weak to stand dragged themselves along on their hands and knees; women in the prime of life crawled to the doors of their huts, and could get no further; and the little children were in such a horrible condition from long famishing, that the sight of them was more than one could bear.[129]

---

[122] Vaughan, 'Social and Economic Change'; White, *Magomero*, pp. 79–81.
[123] T. J. Thompson, 'The Origins, Migration and Settlement of the Northern Ngoni', *SOMJ*, 34, 1, 1982, pp. 19–20; Vail, 'Making of the Dead North', pp.240–41.
[124] *Aurora*, 1897.
[125] *Aurora*, 1900.
[126] Detailed contemporary accounts appear in Livingstone, *Narrative*, Foskett, *Zambesi Journal*, and especially Rowley, *Story*, pp. 430–51. The best modern analyses can be found in Iliffe, 'Poor in the Modern History of Malawi', pp. 251–52 and Mandala, *Work and Control*, pp. 73–80.
[127] Rowley, *Story*, p. 447.
[128] Foskett, *Zambesi Journal*, p. 500.
[129] Rowley, *Story*, p. 450.

One well informed first-hand witness believed that, by February 1863, 90 per cent of the Mang'anja population had died from famine or warfare. Although the casualties were great this is almost certainly an exaggerated figure.[130] Nevertheless, the traumatic effects of the famine should not be ignored. Not only did it greatly accelerate the tendency for women and the vulnerable to put themselves under armed protectors, it also temporarily disrupted the agricultural and commercial economy of the Shire Valley, bringing 'an oppressive stillness' to an area 'where formerly crowds of eager sellers appeared with the various products of their industry'.[131] Furthermore, in combination with the impact of raiding, it resulted in the abandonment of villages in extensive parts of the Middle and the Upper Shire and the Shire Highlands, leading to an expansion of the wild animal population and the reforestation of land previously cleared for human habitation.[132] When British colonisation got underway from the mid 1870s, therefore, it was to happen in an area changed in significant respects from those that existed only fifteen years before.

In later years, missionary propagandists were to claim of the Malawi region of the 1860s: 'Almost everywhere there were indications of a large population having existed shortly before; but now all was desolation through the withering curse of slavery.'[133] The reality was somewhat different. Widespread disruption undoubtedly existed as is demonstrated by the numerous abandoned iron forges and burnt villages witnessed by observers in the 1870s and 80s. But this must be balanced against the remarkable ingenuity and tenacity demonstrated by villagers in the face of exceptional adversity. By 1875, cotton was once more being grown in the Lower Shire Valley, although probably not on the scale that had existed earlier.[134] People at the south end of Lake Malawi, who had taken refuge in the neighbouring hills, were now 'making stealthy runs to their gardens' in order to grow their crops.[135] Tonga villagers preserved their stocks of grain from Ngoni raiders by storing it in bins on an island 100 yards from the shore.[136] With the retreat of cultivators into places of safety far from fertile land, agricultural productivity in some areas is likely to have declined. But there is no evidence of a long-term fall in population levels. Indeed, from the time of Harry Johnston's first census in 1895, which estimated the population of the territory at 845,000 (only just less than the population of Zimbabwe in 1921), population densities in the Malawi area were always higher than in neighbouring Eastern African territories.[137]

What this may imply is that the period of maximum violence in the 1860s was followed by a further period of lesser devastation during which the new intruders consolidated their authority. The case of the Ngoni kingdoms has attracted particular controversy.[138] Tumbuka historians claimed that 'the Ngoni have come

[130] Rowley, *Story*, p. 384.
[131] Livingstone, *Narrative*, p. 450.
[132] Vaughan, *Famine*, p. 58.
[133] James W. Jack, *Daybreak in Livingstonia* (Edinburgh, 1901), p. 18.
[134] Livingstonia Mission Journal, 4 September 1875, NLS Ms.7908.
[135] Ibid., 10 April 1876.
[136] Stewart, 'Second Navigation of Lake Nyassa', 1877, pp. 298–99.
[137] G. Coleman, 'African Population of Malawi: An Analysis of the Censuses between 1901 and 1966', *SOMJ*, 27, 1, 1974; Robin Palmer, *Land and Racial Domination in Zimbabwe* (London, 1977), p. 12.
[138] For a useful discussion of the controversy see Thompson, *Christianity*, pp. 15–29.

and spoiled this land';[139] Ngoni intellectuals responded that Ngoni rule brought justice to a frightened and divided people:

> Before the Ngoni came to this country the villages were small and isolated from each other. There was constant pouncing on people to catch them as slaves.... When the Ngoni came they had one law for all the people and they had courts to hear cases where this law was enforced. There was freedom to travel in the land where the Ngoni ruled, because they had peace within their boundaries.[140]

Tonga villagers in the West Nyasa district struggled to maintain their independence against raids from Mbelwa's Ngoni in the 1870s. Other groups deliberately put themselves under Ngoni rule or else paid a regular tribute in order to avoid attack.

Equally controversial has been the question of the Ngoni's economic impact. As Thompson notes, an initial phase of raiding for grain was followed by the establishment of mixed pastoral-agricultural economies involving the cultivation of maize and millet conducted largely by women and serfs.[141] It is Vail's contention, however, following the analysis of the pioneer Livingstonia missionaries, that this system, unlike the Tumbuka long-fallow system that preceded it, was ecologically disastrous. The land was put under pressure by the overgrazing of cattle and the creation of centralised villages. However, the key problem was the introduction by the Ngoni of the *visoso* system of cultivating millet for the production of beer, which involved the large-scale cutting down and burning of trees and hence a decline in the water table.[142] Vail's conclusion that by the mid-1880s the land had been spoiled and the Ngoni economy was in ruins almost certainly exaggerates the extent of the crisis.[143] Nevertheless, it is the case that in the 1890s many of the Northern Ngoni abandoned their homes in the Kasitu valley in order to open new gardens further south near Mzimba.

Closer to the lake, the growth of the major Swahili and Yao commercial centres also had ambivalent consequences. As caravans required provisioning, settlements like Mponda's, Makanjira's and Nkhotakota were drawn into the commercial production of food crops long before British rule was established. Visitors to Nkhotakota, in the early 1880s were made uncomfortably aware of the prevailing culture of violence, as demonstrated in the rotting heads of Ngoni attackers decorating the stockade surrounding the town. But they were also impressed by the remarkable range of crops being sold including maize and rice, the basic staples, along with onions, paw paws, vegetable marrows, coconuts and mangoes.[144] At Makanjira's main village, 'gardens stretch for some miles round the town and are well stocked with rice, maize, mapira, pumpkins etc.' The people possessed '[an] abundance of cattle, goats and fowls'.[145] At Nkhotakota,

---

[139] Saulos Nyirenda, 'History of the Tumbuka-Henga People', *Bantu Studies*, 5 (1931), p. 4.
[140] Ishmael Mwale quoted in Read, *Ngoni of Nyasaland*, pp. 88–89.
[141] Thompson, *Christianity*, pp. 22–4.
[142] Vail, 'Making of the "Dead North"', pp. 238–43.
[143] For further discussion see John McCracken, 'Conservation and Resistance in Colonial Malawi: the "Dead North" Revisited', in William Beinart and JoAnn McGregor (eds), *Social History and African Environments* (Oxford, 2003), pp. 157–63.
[144] Morrison Diaries, 7 May 1882, 18 September, 8 December 1885, EUL; Goodrich to FO, 19 February 1885, TNA FO 84/1702.
[145] Goodrich to FO, 19 March 1885, TNA FO 84/1702.

the 'sale of grain to caravans' was regarded as one of the Jumbe's main sources of revenue along with the sale of ivory and slaves and the hire of dhows for ferrying goods across the lake.[146]

Equally important was the emergence in these densely crowded towns of a cosmopolitan culture, drawing at once on Chewa and Yao traditions and on those of the Swahili coast. Leading merchant princes like the second Jumbe, Mwinyi-Mguzo, and his Yao counterpart, Makanjira, now dressed resplendently in Arab fashion, although Chief Mponda confined himself to 'a red handkerchief tied round his head in half turban form [and] round his loins…some strong blue cloth'.[147] Makanjira, like many of the inhabitants of Nkhotakota, spoke Swahili 'well and fluently'.[148] The Jumbe carried out an extensive written correspondence with the Sultan of Zanzibar and with other dignitaries on the coast.[149] Makanjira employed a *mwalimu* who taught reading and the Koran on an open veranda in front of the mosque, so an Anglican missionary noted in the late 1870s.[150] There was also a school and small mosque at Nkhotakota, although the latter appears to have been reserved for the Arab population.[151] Both Makanjira and the Jumbe were committed to Islam, and the Jumbe, at least, observed Ramadan scrupulously. However, among his followers in Nkhotakota, its end was celebrated with the loud *ngoma* drumming often associated with Chewa rites of passage and with the consumption of a great deal of beer.[152]

It is tempting to speculate on what would have happened in the Malawi region had the European scramble for Africa not taken place when it did. Linkages with the East Coast would surely have been strengthened. The Swahili language might well have become a common *lingua franca*. Islam would have spread as the major world religion. Arab political authority, linked loosely to the Sultanate of Zanzibar, would have grown. In the south of the country, Afro-Portuguese *muzungos* might have extended their power up the Shire Valley until they reached the lake. At the same time, it is more than likely that the process already under way by which intruding invaders were assimilated into the society of the people they had conquered would have continued unabated. Through intermarriage and child-rearing, the fundamental institutions of the Tumbuka, Chewa and Mang'anja would probably have been preserved. Swahili and *muzungos* alike would have become increasingly Chewaised. All this, however, is simply speculation. On 29 December 1858 David Livingstone entered the Shire from the Zambesi in his small steamer, the *Ma-Robert*. By the time he finally left the region in January 1864 the seeds of British colonisation had been sown. It would take another 25 years, however, before they finally germinated.

---

[146] *British Central Africa Gazette*, 20 August 1894.
[147] Morrison Diary, entries for 3 Aug., 18 September 1885, EUL; J. F. Elton, *The Lakes and Mountains of Eastern and Central Africa* (London, 1879), p. 288.
[148] Elton, *Lakes and Mountains*, p. 288.
[149] Goodrich to FO, 7 Oct 1885, TNA FO 84/1702.
[150] W. P. Johnson, 'Seven Years Travels in the Region East of Lake Nyasa', in W. J. Campbell (ed.), *Travellers Records of Portuguese Nyasaland* (London, no date), p. 60.
[151] Goodrich to FO, 19 Feb 1885, TNA FO 84/1702.
[152] Elton, *Lakes and Mountains*, pp. 297–8, 300. See also Shepperson, 'Jumbe of Kota Kota', pp. 193–207.

2

Commerce, Christianity
& Colonial Conquest

Missionary imperialism:
Livingstone & his legacy

During debates in Nyasaland's legislative council in the run up to independence the nationalist politician, Henry Masauko Chipembere, used to delight his supporters and scandalise his opponents by describing David Livingstone as a 'tourist'. In certain respects, Chipembere's comment was sound. Livingstone, despite his vehement claims to the contrary, was not the first European to 'discover' Lakes Malawi and Chilwa; nor did he travel over previously unknown territory: almost wherever he went, he was guided by local Africans who escorted him along well used tracks, employed in both regional and international trade.[1] Yet if Livingstone's claims as a pioneer explorer are open to challenge, his importance for the history of Malawi cannot be denied. It was through his initiative that Britain's involvement with the Malawi regions began. Moreover, much that we know today concerning the Shire Valley and Highlands in the 1850s and 60s derives from the observations that he and his companions made, although it was not until the publication of several of their journals a century later that the full value of their work was revealed.[2]

Livingstone's strategy for the development of Africa dates from the return of the missionary-explorer to Britain in December 1856, following the completion of his epic trans-continental journey to Luanda on the west coast and from there to Quelimane on the east. His central message, the need to introduce Christianity and civilisation through commerce, had a long pedigree going back to the beginning of the British missionary movement in the 1780s.[3] But it was Living-

---

[1] See Timothy Holmes, *Journey to Livingstone* (Edinburgh, 1993), pp. 187–99; Oliver Ransford, *Livingstone's Lake* (London, 1966), pp. 45–57.

[2] See J.P.R. Wallis (ed.), *The Zambezi Expedition of David Livingstone, 1858–1863* (2 vols, London, 1956); J.P.R. Wallis (ed.), *The Zambesi Journal of James Stewart, 1861–1863* (London, 1952); Foskett, *Zambesi*; Norman R. Bennett and Marguerite Ylvisaker, *The Central African Journal of Lovell J. Procter, 1860–1864* (African Studies Center, Boston University, 1971). A more recent publication is Gary W. Clendennen, *David Livingstone's Shire Journal 1861–64* (Scottish Cultural Press, Aberdeen, 1992).

[3] Brian Stanley, *The Bible and the Flag* (Leicester, 1990), pp. 70–73.

stone's achievement, based on his status as a national hero, to imbue the slogan with new-found authority. The speeches he delivered in Britain in the latter part of 1857 reinforced the message contained in his best-selling *Missionary Travels*, published in November of that year. The opening of the African continent to free trade and its incorporation into the world economy was a necessary precondition for the spread of Christianity: 'The promotion of commerce ought to be specially attended to as this, more speedily than anything else, demolishes the sense of isolation which heathenism engenders, and makes the tribes feel them mutually dependent on, and mutually beneficial to, each other.' This would involve 'the preparation of the raw materials of European manufactures in Africa, for by that means we may not only put a stop to the slave-trade, but introduce the negro family into the body corporate of nations, no one member of which can suffer without the others suffering with it.'[4] All this, Livingstone maintained, could be achieved through the employment of steamboats on the Zambesi, pushing past the decaying Portuguese settlements in the low-lying coastal region and opening up markets and sources of raw material in the healthy Batoka plateau in modern Zambia. This, he hoped, would be the future site of a small British colony, though one, he emphasised, that would have more in common with the monasteries of medieval Europe than it would with modern South Africa.[5]

In March 1858 the government-financed Zambesi Expedition left Britain, taking with it the steam launch *Ma-Robert,* designed to transport the party into the Central African interior. By December the discovery that the Cabora Bassa rapids presented an insuperable barrier to navigation had brought the Zambesi project to a halt. Instead, in January 1859 Livingstone turned his attention to the Shire River which was said to flow from a large lake to the north. This time, the presence of cataracts 100 miles upstream did not divert him from his purpose. In April he and John Kirk, a young Scottish doctor and botanist, travelled to Lake Chilwa and the Shire Highlands which they both regarded as a suitable site for a Christian mission and cotton-growing colony. Four months later they came back to the region with a larger party and on 17 September reached the south-end of Lake Nyasa (as they named it). In September 1861 Livingstone returned to the lake once more with a small boat which he sailed two thirds of the way up the western shore to Nkhata Bay. By then, however, he had been joined in the region by a further small group of Britons, members of the Universities Mission to Central Africa [UMCA], an Anglican society, founded in response to Livingstone's lectures in Oxford and Cambridge in 1857. Led by the newly consecrated Bishop Charles Mackenzie, shotgun in one hand, bishop's crozier in the other, the missionaries made their way up the escarpment in July 1861 to a village, Magomero, which Livingstone had suggested as a site. In the final stages of their journey they were accompanied by 98 refugees, freed from slave gangs on Livingstone's instructions.[6] In 1862 they were joined on the Shire by the moody, young Free Church of Scotland probationary minister, James Stewart, who had come out alone on a

[4] David Livingstone, *Missionary Travels and Researches in South Africa* (London, 1857), p. 28.
[5] Holmes, *Journey*, pp. 146–7.
[6] There are excellent accounts of the ill-fated UMCA expedition in White, *Magomero*, pp. 3–70 and in Owen Chadwick, *Mackenzie's Grave* (London, 1959).

tour of reconnaissance with the aim of establishing a Presbyterian mission in the area.[7]

The failure of the Zambesi Expedition is one of the most extensively researched topics in missionary history. In North America at this very time, cities such as Chicago were being transformed as a consequence of the combined impact of railways and steamboats, linked to the exploitation of lake and river routes. It was always doubtful, however, whether the leaking *Ma-Robert* or her successor, the *Lady Nyassa*, could have had remotely similar results. In the 1860s the Shire River had gained close to the highest level it would reach prior to the late 1930s. But as a navigable highway it had many faults, starting with the 30 miles of cataracts dividing the Upper Shire from the Lower and including numerous shifting mud banks; these enlarged during the dry season when the river became virtually unusable by steamers. For all her iconic qualities as a symbol of Victorian technological achievement, the *Ma-Robert*, with her insatiable demand for firewood, served Livingstone much less well than a fleet of canoes would have done.

Other problems were equally pressing. Although Livingstone's robust constitution protected him from the worst impact of tropical diseases, several of his companions, including his wife and Bishop Mackenzie, died of malaria and dysentery. Portuguese officials, concerned by what they saw as a European rival's intervention in their sphere of influence, grew increasingly hostile; African rulers became alarmed. Livingstone, as Landeg White has commented, 'was a reliable and often acute observer of people, plants, animals and geographical structures. But as an interpreter of local structures of power he was reliable only in the sense that he was usually wrong.'[8] By associating himself with the adventurer, Chibisa and thus alienating the paramount Mankhokwe he stored up problems for the expedition on his pioneering ascent of the Shire. Later, by encouraging the UMCA missionaries to intervene militarily against Yao traders he further added to their difficulties.[9] Even the most expert diplomat, however, would have found himself hard pressed to withstand the combination of accelerating violence associated with the Yao expansion into the Shire Highlands and the prolonged drought and acute famine that enveloped the Shire region in 1861–62. In July 1863 Livingstone received the government order of recall. At almost the same time Mackenzie's successor, Bishop Tozer, determined to withdraw the Universities Mission. Livingstone made one further lengthy journey along the western shore of Lake Malawi in October 1863. In February 1864, however, he departed on the *Lady Nyassa*, bringing the first phase of British intervention in the Malawi region to an end. A year earlier the London *Times* had assessed the results of the Expedition: 'We were promised cotton, sugar and indigo … and of course we got none. We were promised trade; and there is no trade…We were promised converts and not one has been made. In a word, the thousands subscribed by the Universities and contributed by the Government has been productive only of the most fatal results.'[10] James Stewart, who had arrived at the

---

7   For Stewart's expedition see Sheila Brock, 'James Stewart and David Livingstone' in B. Pachai, *Livingstone: Man of Africa* (Longman, London, 1973), pp. 86–110.
8   White, *Magomero*, p. 23.
9   For a detailed discussion see Schoffeleers, 'Livingstone and the Mang'anja Chiefs' in Pachai, *Livingstone*, pp. 111–29.
10   Quoted in Tim Jeal, *Livingstone* (London, 1973), p. 269.

very time that the famine was beginning take its toll, expressed his disillusionment with Livingstone even more sharply: 'His accursed lies have caused much toil, trouble, anxiety and loss of life, as well as money and reputation and I have been led a dance over half the world to accomplish nothing.'[11]

The legacy of the Zambesi Expedition can be explored at a number of levels. In the Malawi region the most immediate effect resulted from the impact of the 15 men conventionally described as Makololo who joined Livingstone in the Lower Shire Valley in 1859. Most of them were subject peoples from the Kololo-dominated Lozi state whom he had recruited along with nearly 100 other porters in the mid-1850s during his trans-continental expedition. In 1856 these men were left by Livingstone at Tete where they hunted elephants and cultivated land under the guardianship of the Governor, Sikard. Livingstone made an attempt in 1859 to take them all back to Barotseland. But several preferred to remain where they were rather than to risk their lives in the now disintegrating Lozi state. Livingstone, therefore, employed them on his various forays up the Shire and paid them in guns and cloth. In November 1861 the Kololo settled under Chibisa at Chikwawa just south of the cataracts and in the next few years increased their strength by hunting for elephants and attracting numerous dependents. By 1862 they had driven out most of the original inhabitants and were employing their retainers to open up new gardens and grow food.[12]

The departure of their patron in January 1864 served only to increase the Kololo's political ambitions. Assisted by the further supply of guns and ammunition which Livingstone had left with them they took the offensive against local Mang'anja chiefs, defeating Mankhokwe in 1867 and killing the Lundu paramount. By 1870 they had established six independent chieftaincies in the Lower Shire valley, the largest being those of Chipatula in the south and Kasisi (often known as Ramakukan) in the north, each about 500 square miles in extent. Much of their political organisation was similar in form to that utilised by the *muzungos* and their *chikunda* followers in the Zambesi valley. But they continued to value their connections with 'the English' and particularly with their patron, Livingstone. Makololo chiefs enthusiastically welcomed Edward Young, the leader of the Livingstone Search Expedition, when he made his way up the Shire in 1867.[13] Eight years later, they responded equally enthusiastically to the appearance of the pioneer Livingstonia Mission party by bringing firewood and provisions for sale and sending hundreds of their dependents to carry loads on the long hike round the cataracts. This did not prevent the Kololo subsequently becoming deeply embroiled in fierce disputes with Scottish traders. Nevertheless, they remained in general strong opponents of Portuguese and *muzungo* expansion in the Shire valley, even if their support for the British was much more equivocal than contemporary imperial narratives suggest.[14]

Equally important in understanding the legacy of the expedition was its impact on those caught up in the withdrawal. Although several members left deeply disillusioned, Livingstone himself remained committed to the idea of

[11] Wallis, *Zambesi Journal of James Stewart*, entry for 17 September 1862, p. 125.
[12] Much of my discussion of the Makololo draws on the excellent account by Elias Mandala, 'The Kololo Interlude in Southern Malawi, 1861–95', M.A. thesis, University of Malawi, 1977.
[13] E.D. Young, *The Search After Livingstone* (London, 1868), pp. 103–6.
[14] Mandala, 'Kololo Interlude', pp. 121–41.

establishing a small colony of British immigrants in the Shire Highlands. Some of his admirers went a good deal further.[15] Horace Waller, the UMCA's passionate young lay superintendent, provides the most striking example. Convinced by his experiences in the Shire region of the evils of the slave trade, Waller spent much of the rest of his life as an influential and bellicose spokesman for the anti-slavery movement which he came increasingly to equate with the extension of British imperial interests in Africa.[16] His commitment to the Malawi region remained particularly strong. Time and again in the 1870s and 1880s he and his circle of like-minded correspondents made use of Livingstone's legacy in demanding that Britain's title-deeds to 'Nyassa-Land' (a term coined by Waller) should be recognised; that the moral investment made by missionaries, traders and others should result in the establishment of British suzerainty in the area in which they had worked and died.[17]

Also affected by the withdrawal of the mission were the 44 survivors of the group of captives released from a slave gang by Livingstone in 1861. Most accompanied Waller to Cape Town. But two 13-year old boys, Chuma and Wekotani, were taken by Livingstone across the Indian Ocean to Bombay where they were enrolled in a Free Church of Scotland school. The subsequent experiences of these displaced people demonstrate the significance of the intermediary role played by Malawians in the pioneering phase of British expansion. One man, Chinsoro, proved 'invaluable' on Young's 1867 expedition but was summarily shot by the homicidal ex-army officer, Henry Faulkner, on a hunting expedition the following year.[18] Four others joined the pioneer Livingstonia party at Cape Town in 1875; one of these, Tom Boquito, acted as the interpreter on the expedition to find a suitable site for the Blantyre mission in 1876.[19] Chuma, arguably the first Malawian international celebrity, accompanied Livingstone throughout his final expedition to Africa between 1866 and 1873, and was later immortalised in imperial circles, along with his colleague Susi, as the 'faithful follower' responsible for bringing the explorer's embalmed body 1,500 miles to the coast. As a result of the intervention of Waller, the editor of Livingstone's Last *Journals*, he and Susi then travelled to Britain where Waller drew heavily on their first-hand description of Livingstone's final days in his seminal account of the explorer's death.[20]

Historians concerned with Livingstone's role as a missionary imperialist have tended to concentrate on his proposals, first made in 1859, for the settlement of small communities of industrious and God-fearing English or Scottish immigrants in the Shire Highlands. These proposals were largely ignored by government. But by 1864 they did give credence to the paternalistic vision of Britons 'taking a leading part in managing the land…extending the varieties of production of the soil…and in trade and in all public matters': a vision that was later to

[15] W.G. Blaikie, *The Personal Life of David Livingstone* (London, 1889), p. 332.
[16] A full account is provided in Dorothy O' Helly, *Livingstone's Legacy: Horace Waller and Victorian Mythmaking* (Athens OH 1987).
[17] Horace Waller, *'The Title-Deeds to Nyasa-Land* (London, 1887). See also Helly, *Livingstone's Legacy*, pp. 262–74; 323–27.
[18] White, *Magomero*, pp. 69–70.
[19] For Boquito see John McCracken, '"Marginal Men": the Colonial Experience in Malawi', *JSAS*, 15, 4, 1989, pp. 538–44.
[20] Helly, pp. 107–23.

be utilised by humanitarian imperialists like Waller in justifying their calls for the introduction of British rule.[21]

More important, however, than these fanciful schemes – firmly rejected in the 1860s both by government ministers and by Livingstone's supporters – was the systematic accumulation of western knowledge concerning the Malawi region that the Zambesi Expedition inspired. Livingstone's companions included both 'a practical mining geologist from the School of Mines [Richard Thornton] to tell us of the mineral resources of the country' and 'an economic botanist [John Kirk] to give a full report of the vegetable productions – fibrous, gummy and medicinal substances together with the dye stuffs – everything which may be useful in commerce.'[22] Although Thornton was dismissed before he had time to carry out research in the area, Kirk put together an extensive collection of arte-facts and botanical specimens which he sent to the Royal Botanical Gardens at Kew; and Livingstone also collected artefacts, although on a smaller scale.[23] His greatest contribution, however, was the systematic notes, accompanied by detailed sketch maps, which became the basis for his path-breaking study, *Narrative of an Expedition to the Zambesi*, published in 1865. Prior to 1859 British knowledge of the Malawi region was virtually nil as the only European descriptions, notably Gamitto's *King Kazembe*, remained untranslated.[24] Now, through his *Narrative* as well as through his frequent letters, Livingstone provided his fellow-countrymen with a reading of the Malawian landscape and of the people who inhabited it that has survived virtually unchallenged through the colonial period and beyond.[25] Iconic images conjured up by Livingstone – of Mang'anja 'men, women and children hard at work, with the baby lying close by beneath a shady bush'; of the beauty and fertility of the Shire Highlands and the devastation inflicted by the slave trade – entered the Victorian imagination. In addition, Livingstone's 'appropriating gaze', like that of other nineteenth-century explorers, extended to the practice of 'naming space', giving the names of influential friends and acquaintances to prominent natural features: the 'Murchison' cataracts on the Shire River and 'Cape Maclear' at the south end of Lake Nyasa.[26]

Add to this the symbolism of sacrifice and ownership invested in the graves (carefully tended by subsequent visitors) of Mary Livingstone at Shupunga and

---

[21] Blaikie, *Personal Life*, p. 332. The most comprehensive discussion of Livingstone's colonisation schemes can be found in Helly, *Livingstone's Legacy*, pp. 240–48. See also Jeal, pp. 185–88; Holmes, *Journey*, pp. 145–47.

[22] Livingston to Adam Sedgwick, 6 February 1858 in Timothy Holmes, *David Livingstone: Letters and Documents 1841–1872* (London, 1990), pp. 49–50.

[23] Jeanne Cannizzo, 'Doctor Livingstone Collects' in National Portrait Gallery, *David Livingstone and the Victorian Encounter with Africa* (London, 1996), pp. 139–65.

[24] Ian Cunnison, editor of the 1960 translation, notes in the Preface that a rough English version of part of the section on the customs of the Lunda was included in F.T. Valdez, *Six Years of A Traveller's Life in Western Africa* (London, 1860). Subsequently, Livingstone's exploits inspired the Council of the Royal Geographical Society to commission Richard Burton to translate a further collection of Portuguese travellers' narratives, mainly in North East Zambia, under the title *The Lands of Cazembe* (London, 1873).

[25] Felix Driver, 'David Livingstone and the Culture of Exploration in Mid-Victorian Britain' in *David Livingstone and the Victorian Encounter*, p. 122.

[26] Sir Roderick Murchison, President of the Royal Geographical Society and Sir Thomas Maclear, Astronomer Royal at Cape Town, were close friends, patrons and regular correspondents of Livingstone.

of Bishop Mackenzie at the confluence of the Shire and the Ruo and the significance of the Expedition's legacy in shaping British and, more specifically, Scottish humanitarian attitudes becomes clear. In government circles, by the
mid-1860s, Lord Palmerston's belief that Livingstone 'must not be allowed to
tempt us to form colonies only to be reached by forcing steamers up cataracts'[27]
had solidified into the conviction that little or nothing was to be gained from
providing administrative or financial support to missionary parties seeking to
operate in the area. Among Scottish churchmen, however, the response was
different. James Stewart's critical report on his pioneering expedition brought
the proposal for an industrial mission to a temporary halt but it did not extin-
guish it entirely. In 1867 Stewart, now Principal of the influential Lovedale Institution in South Africa raised the possibility of a further expedition to the
Zambesi area where he would recruit fifteen or twenty young men who would be
sent for education at Lovedale.[28] Dr Alexander Duff, the Convener of the Free
Church of Scotland Foreign Missions Committee, refused to let him go but did
not abandon the idea outright. Instead, over the next few years two separate
developments took place: the first, the improvement of communications between
Europe and the Indian Ocean, marked by the opening of the Suez Canal in 1869;
the second, the popular resurgence of interest in Livingstone which reached its
peak following his lonely death at Ilala south of Lake Tanganyika and the return
of his body to Britain. The opening in 1872 of a monthly steamer service between
Aden and Durban via Zanzibar by the British Steam Navigation Company, a
Scottish firm owned by William Mackinnon, was a particularly significant development. As Duff later explained: 'Owing to the establishment of a monthly line
of steamers along the Eastern Coast, thereby rendering its principle ports easily
accessible, the attention of the [Foreign Missions] Committee had … been
anxiously turned to the discovery of some suitable locality in that direction.'[29]

At first, it was to Somaliland that the Free Church looked. But this scheme
was discarded following Livingstone's funeral in Westminster Abbey when
Stewart, on a brief visit to his homeland, once more revived his proposal for an
industrial mission named 'Livingstonia' at the south end of Lake Malawi. Placed
'on a carefully selected and commanding spot in Central Africa' this station,
Stewart promised, would 'grow into a town, and afterwards into a city and
become a great centre of commerce, civilisation and Christianity.'[30] The Church
of Scotland was equally enthusiastic. Within days of Stewart's speech, its
General Assembly authorised the establishment of a mission 'among the natives
of that part of Africa which had been hallowed by the last labours of Dr Livingstone.'[31] Its name, 'Blantyre', would commemorate the town in which the
explorer had been born and bred.

The decision of the two great national churches of Scotland to act in this way
can be seen as the last and perhaps the most important aspect of Livingstone's
legacy. For all his evident Scottishness, Livingstone operated within a largely

[27] Jeal, p. 222.
[28] Brock, 'James Stewart and David Livingstone', pp. 105–06.
[29] Alexander Duff, *The Proposed Mission to Lake Nyassa* (Edinburgh, 1875), p. 8.
[30] Quoted in Jack, *Daybreak*, p. 26. See also John McCracken, 'Livingstone and the Aftermath: the
Origins and Development of the Livingstonia Mission', in Pachai, *Livingstone*, pp. 220–22.
[31] Quoted in Andrew C. Ross, 'Livingstone and the Aftermath: the Origins and Development of the
Blantyre Mission' in Pachai, *Livingstone*, p. 191.

British (he would have said 'English') context: first as a Congregationalist working for the London-based, interdenominational London Missionary Society; and then through his association with the Foreign Office and the Royal Geographical Society. His most famous appeal for missionaries to work in Central Africa had been made to Anglicans in the Senate House, Cambridge rather than to Presbyterians at the universities of Edinburgh or Glasgow. Even his funeral was a great British imperial ceremony, held at the very heart of empire in Westminster Abbey. Yet if Livingstone was clearly a British national hero he was also a proud Scot, convinced of the benefits that 'twenty or thirty good Christian Scotch families and their ministers and elders' would bring to the Shire Highlands and scathing in his comments on Bishop Tozer's withdrawal.[32] The disasters suffered by the UMCA made it inadvisable to proceed with Stewart's scheme, he agreed: 'though had the Scotch perseverance and energy been introduced, it is highly probable that they would have reacted, most bene-ficially, on the zeal of our English brethren, and desertion would never have been heard of.'[33]

The Scottish missions now had the opportunity to succeed where the Angli-cans had failed and appropriate Livingstone's legacy to themselves. Central problems of recruitment and of financial support remained. As Ross has noted, neither Livingstone's death nor the revival movement led by Moody and Sankey in 1874 were successful in persuading more than a tiny trickle of candidates to offer themselves as missionaries for Blantyre.[34] The first ordained minister did not come forward until 1878, leaving the initial party woefully lacking in lead-ership. Nevertheless, it is from this time that a central feature in the history of Britain's relationship with the Malawi region emerges: the involvement of Scot-tish missions, supported by significant industrial and commercial elements, linked to powerful national churches, and consciously drawing both on Living-stone's developmental strategies and on his growing reputation as a Presbyterian saint.

Financed by a small group of predominantly Glasgow-based industrialists, leading figures in the economic revolution that made nineteenth century Scot-land 'the workshop of the world', the pioneer Livingstonia party brought with them a prefabricated steamer, the *Ilala*, named after the place of Livingstone's death. On 12 October 1876 they sailed into Lake Malawi. A week later, they settled at Cape Maclear. Almost exactly a year on they were joined by a group of reinforcements led by Dr Stewart and including four African missionaries from Lovedale, at least one of whom, William Koyi, was to play an important part in Livingstonia's subsequent history.[35] At the same time, October 1875, the Blan-tyre mission was established in the Shire Highlands on a ridge stretching south-ward from Mount Ndirande. Back in Scotland, relations between the Church of Scotland and the breakaway Free Church, created in the great Disruption of 1843, were often fraught. But in Malawi from the first the two missions tended to cooperate with each other. Indeed, in December 1876 Stewart and Robert

[32] Blaikie, p. 261.
[33] Livingstone, *Narrative*, p. 414.
[34] A. C. Ross, 'Scottish Missionary Concern 1874–1914: a Golden Era?' *Scottish Historical Review*, 60 (1972), pp. 52–72.
[35] For the story of these men see T. Jack Thompson, *Touching the Heart: Xhosa Missionaries to Malawi, 1876–1888* (Pretoria, 2000).

Laws, the two senior missionaries at Livingstonia, responded to a desperate appeal for help from the demoralised agents at Blantyre by agreeing to temporarily assist in the running of the station. It was under the civil engineer, James Stewart, Dr Stewart's cousin that the Christian colony of Blantyre began to take shape.[36]

Christian colonies

There are examples elsewhere in Eastern and Southern Africa – in Buganda, Barotseland and among the northern and southern Tswana – of Protestant missionaries taking on the role of spiritual and diplomatic advisers to independent African rulers who would then establish the parameters within which Christianity could develop. In southern Malawi, however, the situation was very different. By the mid-1870s, Yao chiefs including Kapeni on Mount Soche and Malemia on Mount Zomba had established a tenuous control over local Mang'anja villagers. However they were themselves harassed by rival Yao chiefs such as Kawinga at Chikala and Matapwiri at Nsanje as well as by Chikusi's Ngoni who carried out raids from their base near Dedza Mountain. In these conditions of political insecurity it was always likely that the missionaries, with their plentiful supplies of guns and cloth, would be propelled into an independent political role. This was particularly true of Blantyre, whose organisers saw it from the first as a mission colony exercising civil as well as spiritual authority.

In the event, both missions evolved as tiny Christian states, each directly responsible by 1880 for several hundred dependants living in villages adjacent to the central station and composed of a mixture of refugees, escaped slaves and local people exchanging the protection of one local patron for another. As the number of refugees grew, relations between the missions and neighbouring authorities – chiefs and headmen, who had lost followers – intensified, resulting in an increase in the number of robberies and raids around the settlements. This in turn led to a shift from the paternalistic control which characterised relationships at Cape Maclear in the early years to the increasing use of arbitrary violence. At Cape Maclear a small prison, probably the first in Malawi, was built in 1878 to house both male and female offenders.[37] Stocks (long discarded in Britain) were constructed and used to punish errant dependents. Several cases of flogging took place, both there and particularly at the out-station at Bandawe (established in 1878) where lay missionaries imposed a savage code of discipline on their workers involving the flogging of up to 31 men at a time.[38]

At Blantyre conditions were even worse. Taking advantage of a leadership vacuum in the early years, a handful of youthful Scottish artisans rapidly built

---

[36] Andrew C. Ross, *Blantyre Mission and the Making of Modern Malawi* (Kachere Series, Zomba 1996), pp. 39–47; McCracken, *Politics and Christianity* pp. 34–8.

[37] Cape Maclear Journal, 21 September 1878, NLS Ms. 7909; Lucy Bean and Elizabeth van Heyningen (eds), *The Letters of Jane Elizabeth Waterston 1866–1905* (Cape Town, 1983), p. 164. According to Dr Waterston, 'the *utterly dark cell* which they have for a prison here is the punishment at home for unruly prisoners and not for ordinary prisoners...and yet they had put a woman into it here who had a child at the breast, of course taking the child away.'

[38] McCracken, *Politics and Christianity*, pp. 62–3.

up their potential wealth and individual status by gaining title to thousands of acres of land in dubious deals with local chiefs.[39] When faced by crimes committed near their station, they reacted with a brutality completely at odds with Yao and Mang'anja systems of justice, although not dissimilar from those imposed by Makololo chiefs who had been influenced by what they had seen of Portuguese *prazos*.[40] Corporal punishment involving the infliction of up to 200 lashes from a triple-thonged buffalo hide whip was routinely employed, even in cases where evidence of wrongdoing appears to have been entirely lacking. One man was flogged to death. Another was wounded in almost every part of his body by a firing squad before being finally put out of his misery by a compassionate Malawian spectator.[41] It was not until the dismissal in 1881 of three of the agents involved and the re-founding of the mission under the visionary David Clement Scott that the worst abuses in the system were eradicated. Scott continued to exercise 'a right of arbitration and rough jurisdiction' over neighbouring villages, according to Frederick Lugard, later to become famous as the architect of 'indirect rule'.[42] But he did so not by violence but by making use of *milandu* – meetings in which he came together with headmen and elders to settle disputes brought before them.[43] By 1890, a year before colonial rule was established, Blantyre had become an 'an oasis of civilisation' containing 'well-stocked kitchen-gardens, carpenters' shops, brick-making and laundry establishments'. It also had an exemplary boarding school, Lugard reported, in which the 'spotless clothes of the children, the neatness and order and discipline enforced were like nothing I have ever seen in Africa'.[44] The mission had also become a major employer of labour with some 2,000 people a year working on Scott's great new church between 1888 and 1891 in addition to the core of skilled and semi-skilled workers employed permanently on the station.[45]

Meanwhile, at Livingstonia an even more comprehensive reappraisal took place. Robert Laws, who took over from Stewart as head of the mission in December 1877, reached the conclusion in 1880 that the exercise of magisterial powers was hindering his role as a minister of the Gospel.[46] The next year, after lengthy discussion, the missionaries abandoned Cape Maclear, perceiving it to be an unhealthy site lacking in fertile land and sailed half way up the west coast of the lake to Bandawe where residents were informed that 'here it was not intended that Civil Jurisdiction should be exercised by the English Missionaries and that they must decide where they would like to settle.'[47] Over the next decade, Livingstonia missionaries were frequently called upon to play an influential political role in their dealings with Tonga and Ngoni chiefs at Bandawe, Njuyu and Ekwendeni. But their central concern was with extending their evangelistic and educational influence through the creation of a network of village schools rather than seeking to impose a system of secular justice.

[39] Macdonald, *Africana*, Vol. 2, pp. 82–3.
[40] Macdonald, *Africana*, Vol. 1, pp. 201–2.
[41] Alexander Chirnside, *The Blantyre Missionaries – Discreditable Disclosures* (London, 1880).
[42] Captain F.D. Lugard, 'A Glimpse of Lake Nyassa', *Blackwood's Magazine*, January 1890, p. 20.
[43] Ross, *Blantyre Mission*, pp. 70–1.
[44] Lugard, *The Rise of Our East African Empire* (Edinburgh, 1893), Vol. I, p. 72.
[45] *LWBCA*, Dec 1889, June 1891.
[46] Laws to Smith, 3 Feb 1880. Quoted in Livingstonia sub-committee minutes, entry for 2 June 1880, NLS Ms. 7912.
[47] Bandawe Journal entry for 18 April 1881, NLS Ms. 7911.

Developments among the lakeside Tonga were particularly striking. By the late 1870s these people lived under the rule of a dozen or more fiercely competing chiefs, pressed together in four or five large stockaded villages (*malingga*) created to provide defence against raids from their Ngoni neighbours to the west. In 1877 they succeeded in defeating an Ngoni *impi* at Chinteche but this did not prevent the recurrence of raids in later years. Consequently Tonga chiefs welcomed the mission both as a diplomatic ally and, over time, as a source of spiritual strength. 'The Atonga attribute their deliverance from the Angoni to some powerful medicinal charm exercised by the white man', noted a Livingstonia missionary in November 1884, explaining the large numbers that had taken to attending the Sunday service.[48] It was only in 1889 that the first Tonga converts were baptised but by that time there were more than a dozen schools, spread through the district, with over 1,300 pupils regularly attending.[49] Some young Tonga men were already working as porters and storemen in the infant colonial economy of the Shire Highlands; others had been employed as mercenaries in a British-led military expedition against Arab traders at the north end of the lake.[50]

Livingstonia's readiness to reduce its political role was in part related to the creation of the Livingstonia Central Africa Company – later known as the African Lakes Company – in 1878. The impulse behind the formation of the company came from the offer by the two brothers, John and Fred Moir, to introduce 'legitimate trade' as a means of eradicating the slave trade.[51] James Stevenson, a wealthy Scottish chemical manufacturer who was the convenor of the Livingstonia committee, took up the challenge, joined by the Govan shipbuilder John Stephen and by a small group of fellow entrepreneurs who were all supporters of the Livingstonia Mission. Nominal capital of £20,000 was raised and in September the Moirs arrived at Quelimane along with three artisans from Govan, a large quantity of trade goods and a small, flat-bottomed steamer named after Livingstone's *Lady Nyassa*.[52]

The subsequent experiences of the ALC demonstrate the formidable difficulties involved in seeking to provide an alternative to the east coast trade in slaves. In the Zambesi Valley extending as far as the Lower Shire, the late 1870s and 1880s witnessed what has been described as an 'agricultural revolution' – the expansion in the production by African growers of oilseeds, copra and groundnuts which were purchased by Indian traders and sold on to international companies.[53] In the Malawi region, however, conditions were different. Because of its close links with the missions, the Company was obliged to take responsibility for transporting goods from the Zambesi to Lake Tanganyika as well as trading over the whole area but it was starved of working capital and hence suffered from serious shortages of manpower and transport. Carrying capacity on its steamers was extremely limited; cancellations and delays abounded. The Moirs accordingly down-played plans for the development of cash crops in the Shire Highlands and instead concentrated on the export of ivory. In the early years, many

[48] Bandawe Journal entry for 23 Nov 1884 in *Free Church of Scotland Monthly Record,* June 1885.
[49] W. P. Livingstone, *Laws of Livingstonia* (London, 1921), p. 246.
[50] McCracken, *Politics and Christianity*, pp. 75–83.
[51] Livingstonia Sub Committee minutes, 6 Nov 1877, NLS. Ms. 7912.
[52] H.W. Macmillan, 'The Origins and Development of the African Lakes Company, 1878–1908' (PhD dissertation, University of Edinburgh 1970), pp. 98–113.

of the elephants killed for their ivory were shot by the Moirs themselves and by other ALC employees supported by teams of Malawian hunters. The Company also made strenuous efforts to purchase ivory from Mponda, Makanjira, the Jumbe of Nkhotakota and other Yao and Swahili traders on the lake, but the prices they offered were frequently rejected as these traders could make greater profits by selling their ivory at the coastal ports. Commercial arrangements were modified in the three years from 1883 when the ALC agent, Monteith Fotheringham, struck up an extensive trade in ivory at Karonga with Mlozi and other Swahili entrepreneurs. However, the trade in slaves was not thereby affected and Yao long distance trading patterns continued as before.[54] In the mid-1880s, Fred Morrison, the ALC engineer on the *Ilala*, witnessed frequent caravans passing through Mponda's head village and the number of Swahili visitors to the entrepot appears to have increased.[55] The chief was 'entirely in the hands of the coast men who surround him', Consul Hawes noted in June 1886, 'and every care is taken on their part to prevent the trade slipping out of their hands'.[56] Many of the major Yao trading chiefs had little or no dealings with the Lakes Company at all.

It was in the Lower Shire Valley that the impact of the ALC was most markedly felt. By the late 1870s, Makololo chiefs had obtained a virtual monopoly over the killing of elephants and the sale of ivory between the cataracts and the confluence of the rivers Shire and Ruo. But further south they were challenged by a group of *chikunda* followers of Matakenya under the leadership of his son, Paul Mariano III, who maintained a tenuous hold over the area known as Massingere. In consequence the Makololo were unable to use the Shire-Zambesi waterway to transport their ivory to the coast and initially welcomed the ALC as a convenient trading partner. By the mid-1880s, however, the relationship had deteriorated. Not only was the Company unwilling to trade in spirits, guns and gunpowder, it had also supplied guns and ammunition to its own specially recruited contingent of African ivory hunters (including the Blantyre headman, Kumtaja). Several of the hunters had flouted the claim of local chiefs to the 'ground tusk' of each elephant shot in their district. One option open to the Makololo was to bypass the services of the ALC by opening relations with the growing number of European private traders operating on the river. One such was the notorious George Fenwick, a man with a penchant for violence displayed both during his service as a joiner with the Blantyre mission and as a hunter with the ALC. However, in January 1884 Fenwick killed Chipatula and was himself killed in revenge over a disputed cargo of ivory and oil seeds which he had taken to the coast. A general crisis then erupted during which the ALC's store at Matope was ransacked and the *Lady Nyassa* sunk. Only after John Moir agreed to pay Kasisi a regular subsidy to keep the river open did transport services resume.[57]

By this time, however, the Shire region had begun to attract the attention of a growing number of European speculators. A key figure was John Buchanan, a

[53] Vail and White, *Capitalism and Colonialism*, pp. 64–9.
[54] Macmillan, 'African Lakes Company', pp. 211–17.
[55] Morrison, Diary entry for 2 March 1883, EUL.
[56] Hawes to FO, 3 June 1886, TNA FO 84/1751.
[57] Hugh Macmillan, 'The African Lakes Company and the Makololo, 1878–84' in R.J. Macdonald (ed.), *From Nyasaland to Malawi* (Nairobi, 1975), pp. 65–85.

young gardener from rural Perthshire. Following his dismissal from the Blantyre mission in 1881, he had set up as an innovative farmer and land agent on the estate he had acquired near the Mulunguzi River in the shadow of Zomba Mountain. During the 1880s Buchanan claimed title to some 170,000 acres of land for himself and his two brothers. He also acted as intermediary in further large-scale land transactions, acquiring large estates for a variety of absentee landlords, among them Horace Waller, the missionary propagandist, By 1888, he had been joined by further adventurers, including the two elephant hunting brothers, George and Henry Pettitt, and by Eugene Sharrer, a fellow land speculator and trader. They, in turn, went out of their way to recruit African hunters who could negotiate with local rulers as well as significantly increase the total amount of ivory shot. With their knowledge of English, mission residents at Blantyre were prime targets for the European newcomers. Commenting on the situation in January 1889, David Clement Scott compared the excitement of ivory hunting for his teachers with 'the gold digging fever to Europeans'. 'It is perhaps the place here to say that very many of the best workers have been spoilt by indiscriminate loans of guns and powder for elephant hunting.'[58] Among those men was Donald Malota, described in 1886 as one of the best two teachers at the mission and recruited by George Pettitt in 1888.[59] In the same year, Kumtaja, a man of 'unusual enterprise and cunning', as a colonial official later noted, added to his success as an elephant hunter by acquiring a considerable extent of land from Kapeni in the Michuru Valley.[60] He also exploited his contacts with Ngoni headmen settled in the Upper Shire Valley by setting up business as a labour recruiter, providing John Buchanan and the ALC with a supply of 'Ngoni' (many probably Chewa) carriers and agricultural workers, some of whom were employed in clearing land prior to the planting of coffee.[61] Thus, more than three years before the establishment of British colonial rule in the Shire Highlands, virtually all the ingredients of the colonial economy were already in place.

The colonial occupation: treaties & flags

There was never much doubt from the mid-1880s that the Malawi region would come under European colonial rule but the questions remained as to which European power would dominate and what form occupation would take. In the 1870s the Scottish missions had frequently requested the appointment of a British consul in the area as a means of reinforcing the anti-slave trade campaign, only to be informed that the government 'can hold no hope of the appointment of an accredited British agent'.[62] Livingstone's legacy and the work of the missions might have influenced attitudes in humanitarian circles in Britain, but successive governments saw no financial or strategic value in intervening directly, particularly as access to the Zambesi and Shire continued to be controlled by

---

[58] *LWBCA*, Jan 1889.
[59] Malota's life story is recounted in McCracken, 'Marginal Men', pp. 545–50.
[60] Note by F. Moggridge, MNA Blantyre District Book, Vol. 1, 1907; *LWBCA*, September 1888.
[61] *LWBCA*, June, September 1888, April 1889; John Buchanan, 'Coffee: Its Position and Prospects', *CAT,* Oct 1895.
[62] Quoted in the minutes of Livingstonia Sub Committee, 30 June 1880, NLS Ms. 7912.

the Portuguese. In 1883, in the aftermath of the Blantyre scandals, the government relented to the extent of appointing a Consul, Captain Foot, to 'the territories of the African kings and chiefs in the districts adjacent to Lake Nyasa' but, as Lord Salisbury was later to note, his power was strictly confined. 'To please the missionaries we send a representative of the government; to spare the taxpayers, we make him understand that he will in no case be supported by an armed force. The only weapon left to him is bluster.'[63] Foot played a useful diplomatic role in brokering an agreement between Kasisi and John Moir following the murder of Chipatula. But neither he nor his successor, A. G. Hawes, was in possession of any real administrative or judicial authority.[64]

The change in attitude can be dated from the Berlin Conference of October 1884, perceived by some historians as the starting point of the partition of Africa. In previous years Portugal had negotiated a draft treaty with Britain that would have guaranteed free navigation on the Zambesi and fixed the confluence of the Ruo and Shire rivers (the southern limit of Makololo authority) as the northern limit of Portuguese power. Neither the Scottish missions nor Bishop Mackenzie's gravesite would fall under Portuguese jurisdiction. With the convening of the Berlin Conference, however, the treaty fell and a new, more aggressive period of colonial expansion began, premised on the principle that effective occupation of territory by European powers rather than informal predominance would be the criterion for international recognition. The day after the conference ended, in February 1885, the German Chancellor Bismarck declared a protectorate on the Tanzanian mainland, thus striking a fatal blow to Zanzibar's informal empire in the area. In the same year, the Portuguese Foreign Ministry produced its famous rose-coloured map, showing a broad band of territory claimed by Portugal, stretching across the continent from Angola to Mozambique and including the greater part of modern Malawi. A few weeks later, Serpa Pinto and his lieutenant Augusto Cardoso embarked on an expedition from Ibo on the East African coast, aimed at making treaties with the leading Yao chiefs on Lake Malawi. Meanwhile, the African Lakes Company in a sudden burst of energy obtained treaties of friendship from the Makololo chiefs as well as from Tonga and Ngonde chiefs on the north-west side of the lake.

This sudden spurt of treaty-making intensified political rivalries. The ALC's aim in making treaties was to obtain a charter from the British Government giving it the legal right to establish political control over the Shire-Nyasa route. This scheme was shelved in 1886 following bitter protests from the Blantyre missionaries, who were convinced that the Moir brothers would be incapable of shouldering the responsibility effectively. The following year, however, hostilities broke out between the Company and Swahili traders at the north end of the Lake, fuelled in part by the growth of mutual suspicions. In the early 1880s, Mlozi, Kopakopa, Msalemu and Salim bin Najim established a number of stockaded settlements in Ungonde from where they carried out an active trade in ivory with the ALC depot at Karonga. Because of the unreliable performance of the company's steamers, long delays often occurred in the arrival of European trade goods with the result that Swahili merchants and their followers from the

[63] Salisbury, Minute, 15 May 1888, FO 84/1922 quoted in R. Robinson and J. Gallagher, *Africa and the Victorians* (Macmillan, London, 1961), p. 24.
[64] A.J. Hanna, *The Beginnings of Nyasaland and Northern Rhodesia* (Oxford, 1956), pp. 74–5.

Luangwa valley and Lake Tanganyika were forced to delay their departure for months at a time.[65] As in the Shire Highlands thirty years earlier, the demands of traders for food supplies put great strains on the indigenous agricultural community. Quarrels between the Swahili and their Ngonde hosts culminated in July 1887 with the killing of an Ngonde headman.

It was at this point that international political rivalries impinged on what in other circumstances might have been an entirely local dispute.[66] Threatened by the well-armed Swahili and their formidable *ruga-ruga* allies, several Ngonde chiefs responded by demanding that Monteith Fotheringham, the Lakes Company agent at Karonga, should honour the treaties they had made with the ALC only two years earlier and take military action against the Swahili. At the same time, Mlozi (alarmed perhaps by the collapse of the Sultan of Zanzibar's informal empire) signalled his determination to assert his authority by taking the title 'Sultan of Konde'. Fotheringham initially attempted to bring the warring parties together. But when the Swahili accelerated their advance and on 1 November sacked the village of Kyungu, the Ngonde paramount, he reacted with alarm. When the Ngonde fled to the station, Fotheringham gave sanctuary, building a brick wall around his house and store. By the end of November, the Swahili-Ngonde war had become a Swahili-European one, exalted in the eyes of the whites involved into an anti-slavery crusade. Company agents recruited a substantial contingent of Mambwe spearmen from the Nyasa-Tanganyika corridor. The Swahili, in their turn, made use of Henga mercenaries, who had entered Ngonde country as refugees from the Ngoni about 1881. After a lapse in the fighting between December 1887 to April 1888, hostilities were renewed but with inconsequential results. Even the arrival of the Indian army officer, Frederick Lugard, accompanied by a small band of white South African mercenaries, failed to break the stalemate. In June 1888 and then again in January and March 1889 Lugard mounted attacks on the Swahili stockades, only to be rebuffed each time.

Had the ALC been successful in asserting its military dominance at the north end of the lake it is at least possible that its political claims would have been accepted in London and Lisbon. In the event, its striking failure encouraged others to become involved. By 1888 the Company's attempts to ship large quantities of arms into the interior had seriously alarmed the Portuguese authorities on the Lower Zambesi, who renewed their efforts to control the trade route. But they also encouraged a new generation of Portuguese imperialists to attempt to establish effective occupation in the area.[67] In July 1888, Antonio Maria Cardoso, a former governor of Quelimane, received secret instructions from the Portuguese government to make treaties with Yao chiefs at the south east end of Lake Malawi and in the eastern portion of the Shire Highlands. At almost the same time, the experienced explorer and convinced imperialist, Serpa Pinto, set out on a diplomatic mission to France to persuade Cardinal Lavigerie to establish a White Fathers mission near Lake Malawi. The dual danger represented by Scottish Presbyterian missionaries and Scottish traders was to be challenged by the twin

---

[65] L. Monteith Fotheringham, *Adventures in Nyassaland* (London, 1891), pp. 34–41.
[66] For the origins of the war see H. W. Macmillan, 'Notes on the Origins of the Arab War' in Pachai, *Early History*, pp. 263–76; Wright and Lary, 'Swahili Settlements', pp. 561–70.
[67] Newitt, *Mozambique*, pp. 344–45.

forces of Portuguese diplomacy and the influence of the Roman Catholic Church. In November, Cardoso set out on his expedition with a large force of *chikunda* mercenaries. Six months later, the five White Fathers chosen to open the Nyasa mission were waved off by Lavigerie in a ceremony that closed with the playing of the Portuguese national anthem. Although the Fathers were all French, it had been agreed that Portuguese would be the medium of instruction in their schools and that their station would be considered to be Portuguese property.[68] Accompanied by the Portuguese agent, Teixira de Sousa, they reached Mponda's head village on the Shire River crossing just south of Lake Malawi on 28 December 1889 and were immediately invited to stay. In the same month, a Portuguese military column under Serpa Pinto's command moved up the Shire to Chiromo, repulsing an attack from the Kololo on the way. By this time at least 25 chiefs or headmen, most from the Shire Highlands and the south-east arm of the lake, had accepted flags and made treaties with the Portuguese.[69]

It is an indication of Lord Salisbury's lack of enthusiasm for the extension of British formal rule to the Nyasa area that he rejected missionary calls for imperial protection throughout 1888 in the face of a well-planned campaign mounted by the two national churches in Scotland. 'It is not our duty to do it', he told the House of Lords. 'We should be risking tremendous sacrifices for a very doubtful gain.'[70] Speaking to a powerful Scottish delegation in April he made clear that while he was prepared to insist on the free navigation of the Zambesi he would 'on no account ...send an armed expedition to the Nyasa region' and 'on no account ...annex Nyasaland or declare it British territory'.[71] If the Lakes Company and the missionaries wished to expel the Arabs they would have to do so themselves.

The news (received in London in December) of Cardoso's expedition, with its aim of asserting Portuguese claims over the Shire region, was a more troublesome issue because Salisbury had already promised the missionaries that while the British government would not annex Nyasaland it would not allow the Portuguese to do so either.[72] One possible answer lay in the draft agreement reached in Lisbon in March 1889 between the newly appointed consul for Mozambique, Harry Johnston, and the Portuguese Foreign Minister, Barros Gomes. In a daring move, going well beyond what the Foreign Office was planning, Johnston persuaded the Portuguese to drop their claims to Mashonaland and northern Zambesia, including the western shore of Lake Malawi, while obtaining the Shire Highlands and Valley in their place. Livingstonia's stations would be freed from the Portuguese threat; Blantyre's stations would not.[73]

Although some Free Church officials privately welcomed this deal, most Scottish churchmen were opposed. In April and May 10,500 ministers and elders signed a memorial calling on Salisbury to reject the proposal: this time he was more forthcoming.[74] It was accepted on all sides that the African Lakes Company

[68] Ian Linden, *Catholics, Peasants and Chewa Resistance* (London, 1974), pp. 15–16.
[69] Hanna, p. 130.
[70] Salisbury quoted in R.E. Robinson and J. Gallagher, *Africa and the Victorians,* London, 1961 p. 224.
[71] Dr Lindsay quoted in Livingstonia Sub Committee minutes, 26 July 1888, NLS Ms. 7912.
[72] *Ibid.*
[73] Roland Oliver, *Sir Harry Johnston and the Scramble for Africa* ((London, 1959), pp. 146–50.
[74] For alternative views on this episode see Oliver, *Harry Johnston,* pp. 150–51; Ake Holmberg, *African Tribes and European Agencies,* (Goteborg, 1966) p. 262.

was too weak and disorganised to assume responsibility for governing Nyasa-land but a larger, more powerful company might serve the purpose. Cecil Rhodes, the millionaire mining speculator, was anxious to persuade the govern-ment to grant him powers of administration over mineral-rich Mashonaland and this provided him with the perfect opportunity. In return for a Royal Charter for his newly-created British South Africa Company, Rhodes signalled his readi-ness to extend the Company's operations into Northern Zambesia, to take over the ALC, and to pay an annual sum of £9,000 a year for the administration of Nyasaland. In July 1889 Consul Johnston took a gunboat into the Zambesi through the recently discovered Chinde mouth, bringing with him the sum of £2,000 donated by Rhodes to make treaties with chiefs. On the Shire he met Serpa Pinto with a force of about 300 camped a short distance below the Ruo. He then moved on to Blantyre where the manse dining room at the mission had become 'a factory with half-a-dozen sewing machines, for the manufacture of Union Jacks – made of calico, red, white and blue – for presentation to chiefs in the district'.[75] Before his departure for the north, he held discussions with John Buchanan, the Acting Consul. It was Buchanan who, in a prearranged move, sent a letter of protest, dated 19 August, to Serpa Pinto from the British residents of Blantyre in which he announced that 'the Makololo country and the Shire Hills, commencing at the Ruo river, has been placed under the protection of Her Majesty the Queen.'[76]

Even at this stage, there is no indication that Salisbury was committed to the establishment of a British protectorate. Johnston's instructions were to make treaties to forestall the Portuguese, not to proclaim British rule. Buchanan's proclamation, made without prior reference to the Foreign Office, was aimed at halting Serpa Pinto's advance rather than making that rule a reality.[77] Events, however, now took their own momentum. Following the death of Kasisi in May 1888, Mlauri had emerged as the most important of the Kololo chiefs. An inde-pendent-minded pragmatist, his central concern at a time of unprecedented European pressure was to play off the Portuguese and British against each other and to retain his independence.[78] Thus, in the second half of 1888 he had held several meetings with Portuguese officials at his head village, Mbebwe, but had also had courteous discussions with John Moir of the ALC. As the European presence became more intrusive, Mlauri's hostility grew. In June 1889 some of his followers fired on the Company's steamer, the *Lady Nyassa*. Two months later, he refused to give free access up the Shire to the Pinto expedition and was subsequently involved in minor skirmishes with its members over several weeks. As he explained to Harry Johnston, with whom he had an acrimonious meeting in August, Mlauri had become 'convinced … that all white men were equally bad'.[79] In consequence, he was one of the few chiefs to refuse to sign any treaty with the Company; an action explained by Buchanan, perhaps more accurately than he intended, as arising from Mlauri's 'superstitious fear of the British flag'.[80]

[75] Alexander Hetherwick, *The Romance of Blantyre* (Dunfermline, nd), p. 69.
[76] Quoted in Hanna, pp. 144–45.
[77] My analysis follows Holmberg, pp. 265–68 at this point.
[78] The best account of Mlauri's actions can be found in Mandala, 'Kololo Interlude', pp. 140–50.
[79] Johnston, *British Central Africa*, pp. 84–5.
[80] Quoted in Mandala, 'Kololo Interlude', p. 146.

In October, matters came to a head. Confronted by an increase in violent incidents between his villagers and the Portuguese expeditionary force, Mlauri accepted arms and ammunition from Moir in exchange for a British flag which he flew in full view of the Portuguese camp at Mpatsa. His 'superstitious fear' was demonstrated to be well founded. Up to now, Serpa Pinto had acted with extreme caution in refraining from moving north of the Ruo in force. But the sight of the Union Jack flying from Mlauri's flagpole was more than Portuguese honour could bear. In a rapid turn of events, Portuguese soldiers crossed the Shire and uprooted the flag only to be attacked at Mpatsa by Mlauri's followers. The Portuguese struck back, killing over 70 of Mlauri's men. Reinforced by two armed launches, they then thrust northwards up the Shire, occupying Chiromo early in November. Serpa Pinto, who was seriously ill, departed for the coast but the expedition continued northwards under Lieutenant João Coutinho as far as Katunga, the port closest to Blantyre, which it reached on 2 January 1890, by which time much of the Lower Shire was in Portuguese hands. Some Kololo chiefs took refuge with the British in Blantyre. But Mlauri, true to his independent nature, made Thyolo Mountain his hiding place.[81]

In a matter of days, these events on the Lower Shire became the subject of newspaper headlines in Britain and Portugal. On reaching the coast, Serpa Pinto had cabled Lisbon to announce a great victory: 'The Kololo people, decimated in the fighting, are completely submissive. The route to Nyasa is secure for the commerce of all nations.'[82] Portuguese editors rejoiced; the mood in London and Edinburgh was more sombre. Nearly a quarter of a century of anti-Portuguese humanitarian rhetoric duly took its effect. Correspondents claimed that the Portuguese had insulted the British flag; that Livingstone's faithful servants had been massacred because they had attempted to hold the country for Britain. Old suspicions of the Portuguese as slave dealers surfaced; as did rooted Protestant prejudices against the Roman Catholic Church.[83]

Salisbury, of all British politicians, was the one most impervious to waves of popular emotion. But even he was affected by the news. For all the scepticism he had displayed concerning the economic or strategic value of the Malawi region to Britain, the Prime Minister had been persuaded by 1889 that there were good reasons for protecting Scottish missionary and commercial interests in the area, particularly if a large part of the cost were to be met by Rhodes rather than the British taxpayer. The providential discovery of the Chinde channel, sufficiently deep to allow ocean-going ships to sail into the Zambesi without touching Portuguese territory, reduced the concern that Portugal could impose prohibitive tariffs. Getting the Scottish churchmen off his back would be an added bonus. Nevertheless, the ferocity of Salisbury's response comes as a surprise. On 23 December the British cabinet agreed on plans to send a naval force to occupy Mozambique Island if the Portuguese refused to stay south of the Ruo. Three days later Salisbury ordered the Channel and Mediterranean naval squadrons to Gibraltar to put pressure on Lisbon. On 8 January 1890 he formally

[81] Mandala, 'Kololo Interlude', p. 148.
[82] Quoted in E. Axelson, 'Portugal's attitude to Nyasaland during the period of the partition of Africa' in Pachai, *Early History*, p. 259.
[83] *The Times*, 'Portuguese Aggression in Africa', 14 Dec 1889; 'Portuguese Invasion of British Nyasaland', 16 Dec 1889; letter from Horace Waller, 20 Dec 1889.

demanded that Portuguese forces on the Shire withdraw. On 11 January he presented the Portuguese Government with an ultimatum. Faced by the greatest naval power of its day, the Portuguese government reluctantly acceded. In Portugal, press and public united in condemnation of Britain and the government was forced to resign. Newitt may be overstating the case when he describes Salisbury's actions 'as one of the major blunders in British policy in the nineteenth century'. But he is right to note that this was one of only two occasions during the partition of Africa (the other was the confrontation in 1898 between Britain and France over Fashoda) when there was a real possibility of European powers coming to blows.[84]

The sequel in the Malawi region can be briefly related. On 8 February the Portuguese commander at Katunga received an order to withdraw below the Ruo and quickly obeyed. On 12 March the last Portuguese troops evacuated Chiromo. Mlauri, however, did not return to power: in one of the first acts of the new government-in-waiting, Buchanan descended to the valley and evicted him from office. Although Mlauri lived on until 1913, widely respected by the people around him, he was never reinstated as chief.[85] Elsewhere, vestiges of Portuguese influence took longer to disappear. The White Fathers, with their Portuguese agent at Mponda's village at the south end of Lake Malawi, heard of Serpa Pinto's withdrawal only in May 1890. The agent left two months later, the day after Mponda had raised the British flag at his village, but the missionaries stayed on until June 1891 when they left to found a mission in Bembaland. Mponda flew the Portuguese flag alongside the British as late as November 1890.[86]

Meanwhile, the diplomatic niceties were concluded in Europe. On 20 August 1890 Britain and Portugal signed a convention defining the boundaries of their territories. Portugal, as a result of the successful treaty-making expedition carried out by Augusto Cardoso in 1885, secured territory extending westwards as far as Mulanje Mountain, but almost the whole area in which the Scottish missions had worked, extending from the Lower Shire valley through the Highlands to the Lake, came into the British sphere. The one British mission that lost out was the UMCA, which had relocated to Zanzibar in 1864. In 1882, the saintly William Percival Johnson began his remarkable forty-six year period of service evangelising on the eastern lake shore. The greater part of the territory he covered was allocated to Portugal.[87] In September the Portuguese parliament refused to ratify the treaty, but after further strong-arm pressure from Britain, a final agreement was reached on 11 June 1891. The main modification was the extension of British territory in the south beyond the Shire's confluence with the Ruo to Nsanje, an area once under Mariano's control but now dominated by a small group of Mang'anja chiefs, the most important of whom was Tengani. The other modification was the granting to Britain of a 99-year lease over a piece of land at the Chinde mouth to be used for the transhipment of goods to and from British territory.[88] In time, Chinde was to develop as a strange little British possession, stuck on a sandbank between the Zambesi and the India Ocean, with

[84] Newitt, *Mozambique*, p. 347.
[85] Mandala, 'Kololo Interlude', pp. 149–50.
[86] Linden, *Catholics*, pp. 27–31.
[87] Charles M. Good Jr., *The Steamer Parish* (University of Chicago Press, Chicago, 2004) pp. 74–81.
[88] Hanna, pp. 171–72.

its own famous bar and hotel, Murray's, and its jumble of Indian stores and warehouses.[89]

One issue that remained to be determined concerned the identity of the government in waiting. Rhodes's original intention had been to absorb the ALC into his British South Africa Company as a first step towards establishing territorial dominance north of the Zambesi. Negotiations with the Lakes Company stalled, however, and Rhodes, now preoccupied with the construction of a colony in Mashonaland, agreed, as an interim measure, to provide the ALC with an annual sum of £9,000 from 1 January 1890 to protect the mission stations and keep open the route to Lake Tanganyika. By this time concession hunters, anxious to obtain land and mineral rights, had begun to move into the area, and the ALC took the lead in making a series of largely fraudulent claims on behalf of the Chartered Company, amounting in the Northern region to some 2.75 million acres. For several months, debate continued over the proposal that the BSAC should take over the administration of the 'Nyasaland Districts'. But David Clement Scott and Alexander Hetherwick of the Blantyre Mission were firmly opposed to 'the relegation of all interests, missionary, trader, settler and especially native interests, to the sole judgement of a large monopolizing Commercial concern', and it was their view that eventually won out.[90] In February 1891 Lord Salisbury approved a compromise scheme whereby British-claimed territory north of the Zambesi would be divided in two. Everything west of the western watershed of the Lake would come under Company rule; everything east, including all the mission stations, would be part of a Protectorate, administered directly by the Foreign Office. Harry Johnston would take on the dual role of Administrator of the Company's sphere as well as Commissioner and Consul-General of Nyasaland. The Company would pay him £10,000 for the purposes of general administration. He would control both the British Government's and the Company's armed forces, employing them wherever he wished.[91] On 10 September Johnston arrived at Zomba, a convenient 40 miles from the disputatious Scots at Blantyre. There he took over the impressive two-storied Residency, built by John Buchanan for Consul Hawes, as the headquarters of his embryo state. In a typically flamboyant gesture, he misleadingly named it 'British Central Africa', with the Nyasaland portion being 'the British Central Africa Protectorate'. It was not until 1907 that 'Nyasaland' became the official name of the territory.

Conquest & resistance

The years between 1891 and 1895 were dominated by the bruising military campaign dedicated to transforming the paper partition into the reality of formal rule. John Moir, in a valedictory paper written shortly before his retirement as Manager of the ALC, argued that colonial rule would best be achieved 'by disturbing the existing state of affairs as little as possible'. He warned against

[89] For a lively account of Chinde in 1894 see R C F Maugham, *Africa as I Have Known It* (John Murray, London 1929), pp. 24–35.
[90] *LWBCA*, August 1890.
[91] Hanna, pp. 181–82.

the dangers of 'anything approaching the *Military Occupation* lately attempted by the German East African Co.' and instead recommended that Yao and Swahili potentates should be weaned from their involvement in the slave trade by subsidising the price paid for their ivory.[92] Johnston, however, had very different intentions. Of distinctly unmilitary appearance and background – he was only five foot three inches tall, spoke in a high-pitched voice and had been educated at an art college – Johnston was a gifted artist, naturalist and linguist but not a natural soldier.[93] Nevertheless, when he arrived at Chiromo in July 1891, accompanied by 70 Indian troops under the command of Captain Cecil Maguire, 10 Swahili irregulars and a seven-pounder gun, he was already convinced of the necessity of using force in order to establish territorial hegemony.[94] One of his very first actions, taken weeks before he moved to Zomba, was to dispatch a military expedition to Mulanje where the Yao chief, Chikhumbu, had incurred the displeasure of a couple of planters by demanding an additional payment for the land that he had sold them. As the Blantyre missionaries complained, this was a disagreement that 'could without much difficulty have been settled by Mlandu.'[95] Johnston, however, took the opportunity to use force instead.

Chikhumbu's defeat served as prelude to the extension of British rule over the Shire Highlands and Upper Shire Valley. Johnston had noted as early as December 1890 that 'Our Policy in Nyasaland in our present state of weakness must be "Divide and Rule"'; to that end he went out of his way to confirm the subsidy of £200 a year paid by the Lakes Company to the Jumbe of Nkhotakota as a means of detaching him from the north end Arabs.[96] His central concern, however, was to isolate and defeat Makanjira, the most important of the Yao chiefs on the eastern lakeshore. With that in mind, Johnston advanced up the Shire in October with the ostensible aim of settling a dispute between the Yao chiefs Makandanji and Mponda. He then attacked Makandanji's town before going on to Mponda's which was shelled by the seven-pounder and burnt. Only then did Mponda agree to submit. Next, he set off on board the ALC steamer, *Domira*, to Makanjira's main town, a settlement of some 6,000 people, containing 'the largest and best houses we have met with in this part of Africa'. The town was bombarded from the boat using incendiary shells which set it alight in several places. Then the Indian troops landed and started to pillage in earnest. All the houses for over a mile were burnt as were three of Makanjira's six dhows that were used for transporting slaves, food and ivory across the lake. Johnston then returned to the other side of the lake and forced Kazembe, a relative of Makanjira's, to sign a treaty of allegiance to the British. Finally, he returned to his base at Zomba from where a further attack was made on the Yao chief, Kawinga.[97]

[92] John Moir to Directors of the British South Africa Company, 9 Oct 1889, photostat, private Shepperson Collection. Hermann von Wissman had launched first stage of his campaign to overcome coastal resistance and establish German control over Tanganyika in April 1889.

[93] The standard, somewhat uncritical biography of Johnston is Oliver, *Sir Harry Johnston and the Scramble for Africa*. See also Robin H. Palmer, 'Johnston and Jameson: a comparative study in the imposition of colonial rule' in Pachai, *Early History*, pp. 293–322.

[94] See Eric Stokes, 'Malawi Political Systems and the Introduction of Colonial Rule, 1891–1896' in E. Stokes and R. Brown, *The Zambesian Past* (Manchester, 1966), pp. 355–539.

[95] *LWBCA*, August 1891 quoted in Andrew Ross, 'The African – A Child or a Man' in Stokes and Brown, *Zambesian Past*, p. 342.

[96] Johnston's memo on Makanjira, 29 Dec 1890, TNA FO 84/2052; Stokes 'Malawi Political Systems', pp. 360–61.

Johnston's early successes were followed by a stiff reversal. Faced by the sudden appearance of the Indian troops, armed with machine guns and modern rifles as well as a seven-pounder that could strike with devastation from any distance up to half a mile, many chiefs reluctantly submitted to the British; others attempted to engage them as allies in their struggle with local rivals. Makanjira, however, was made of sterner stuff. In December 1891 Maguire led a further expedition against him aimed at destroying his two remaining dhows. This time Makanjira was prepared. When Maguire and the Indian troops landed off the *Domira* they ran into an ambush laid by the chief and were forced to retreat to the beach. Maguire and three sepoys were killed, as were a military surgeon and ship's engineer who came ashore the following day. Eventually, the *Domira*, which had been stuck on a sandbank for three days, had to sail away leaving Makanjira in command of the field. With his prestige boosted as a result of this victory, Makanjira then crossed over the lake, drove Kazembe from power as a punishment for allying himself to the British, and installed Kulundu, the woman ruler, in his place. Thereafter, he gave support to a Yao ally, Chiwaura, in his revolt against Jumbe at Nkhotakota.[98] Meanwhile, in an unrelated incident in February 1892, the Yao chief, Zarafi, in the hills southeast of the lake, repulsed a force sent against him by J. G. King, the Collector at the newly established station of Fort Johnston. Nine soldiers fighting for the British were killed; King was shot through both lungs. In the panic that followed, the Administration's only piece of artillery, the seven-pounder gun was abandoned along with quantities of rifles and ammunition. Several of the Indian soldiers ran away and did not return to their base until a fortnight later.[99]

For Johnston, this was 'the nadir of our fortunes'.[100] Yet it was also the point at which the inherent strengths of the new administration became apparent. Much has been made of the 'slender financial and military backing' available to Johnston but this does not take account of the reserves upon which he could call.[101] The British South Africa Company was initially reluctant to provide additional assistance but in 1893 Cecil Rhodes came to Johnston's aid with a special grant of £10,000 to be used in subjugating Makanjira. The Indian contingent was expanded with the recruitment of 200 Jat Sikhs, conventionally regarded as the best troops in the Indian army; Makua mercenaries from Mozambique were added to the force; and three gunboats were supplied by the Admiralty, two for service on the Lake and one on the Upper Shire. Fresh British officers (nine in all by 1895) arrived, attracted by the prospects of rapid promotion that service with Johnston provided. In addition, starting in February 1892, increasingly large contingents of local troops were recruited. In the early stages, most of these were occasional levies supplied by chiefs such as Mponda and the Ngoni warlord, Chifisi, who were seeking short-term alliances with the British. Such men were uncertain allies, restricted largely to carrying loads, and frequently deserting. However, they were supplemented from February 1893 by bands of Tonga mercenaries, employed as carriers and agricultural workers in the Shire

[97] H.H. Johnston, 'Report on Measures taken to suppress the Slave Trade in British Central Africa, July–Dec 1891', *Papers relative to the suppression of the Slave-Raiding in Nyasaland, 1892*, Cmd. 6899.
[98] Johnston to Salisbury, 26–7 Dec 1891, *Ibid*, 1892; W P Johnson, *African Reminiscences*, p. 205.
[99] Johnston to Salisbury, 25 Feb 1892, *Papers relative to the suppression of Slave-Raiding …1892.*
[100] Johnston, *British Central Africa*, p. 107.
[101] Stokes, 'Malawi Political Systems', p. 358.

Highlands by Buchanan Brothers and the ALC. These forces proved more reliable. By 1895, some 200 Tonga regulars were serving in the army, led by their courageous though brutal commander, Sergeant Bandawe. By this time, they had been joined by the first contingent of Yao regulars, men who in some cases had once fought against the British and had now come over to their side.[102]

With reinforcements in place, Johnston went onto the offensive again. Once more, his principle target was Makanjira and, once more, the campaign proved less successful than he had hoped. Early in November 1893, the expedition left Fort Johnston for Nkhotakota where the ageing Jumbe faced a serious challenge from Chiwaura and his Yao supporters. After a heavy bombardment, Chiwaura's village was taken by force and the chief killed. The expedition then crossed the lake where, on 19 November, Makanjira's large new town, rebuilt a mile from the old, was subjected to continuous bombardment from the gunships. The Sikhs then landed, destroyed the town, burnt Makanjira's last dhow and ranged up and down the coast for a distance of 36 miles, seizing loot, destroying grain supplies and burning almost every village that they found. Over the next few weeks, the imposing Fort Maguire was erected close to the spot where Makanjira's main town had once stood; it was garrisoned by a contingent of Sikhs and irregulars reinforced by two powerful guns. In an attempt to break Makanjira's power once and for all his rival, the female chief Kumbasani, was persuaded to take up residence, along with her people, near the fort.[103]

It was at this point that Makanjira's tenacity revealed itself. Elsewhere in southern Malawi, Yao chiefs fought bravely in their initial encounters with the British but, when defeated, tended to submit. What made Makanjira different is by no means clear although it seems likely that the chief's sense of personal honour was reinforced by a deep commitment to Islam shared by a number of his supporters but not, at this period, by other Yao rulers. During the course of the sacking of his town, his men had fought with courage before being overwhelmed by the accuracy of the firepower brought against them. Nevertheless, although they were forced to withdraw to the hills, they remained disinclined to submit. During the second half of December, they carried out skirmishing operations against the Sikhs and on 6 January they struck. In a sudden move that wrong-footed the Administration forces some 2,000 men attacked the fort and settlement, seizing possession of Kumbasani's town. She was captured and beheaded and it was only after two hours' hard fighting that the attackers were driven off.[104] Some of Makanjira's headmen now submitted but the chief remained as obdurate as ever. With all his dhows now destroyed, he could no longer continue the struggle from the lake. Instead, he withdrew to the hills, close to the Portuguese border, from where he carried out a series of guerrilla raids on villages close to Fort Maguire (and not far from where Masauko Chipembere, seventy years later, was to conduct his doomed campaign against Dr Banda).[105] His popularity appears to have remained undiminished. When Major Edwards launched a further expedition against him in November 1895,

[102] John McCracken, 'Authority and Legitimacy in Malawi: policing and politics in a colonial state' in David Anderson and David Killingray (eds), *Policing and Decolonisation* (Manchester, Manchester University Press, 1992), pp. 161–62.
[103] Hanna, pp. 197–98; *BCAG* Jan 1894.
[104] *BCGA* Feb 1894.
[105] Edward Alston diary, entries for 3 and 30 Oct, 1895, MNA.

he found Makanjira to be the undisputed ruler of a large valley, thickly populated with villages, containing, it was claimed, some 8,000 houses, many of them 'built in the coast style'.[106] Forewarned of the advance, Makanjira and his followers withdrew in a classic guerrilla manoeuvre, leaving his main town deserted when the British arrived.[107] Subsequently, he continued to carry out occasional raids by exploiting the colonial boundary which allowed him to cross into Portuguese territory whenever the pressure grew too great. At the time of his death in 1915 he was still independent, still breathing defiance at the British.[108]

With Makanjira expelled from the lake, the way was open for the Administration to establish its dominance over the last remaining independent Yao chiefs. Ever since 1891, Harry Johnston had combined his campaign against the slave trade with the imposition of hut tax, first in the Shire Highlands and subsequently in the Shire Valley. Chiefs were instructed to bring in taxes at a rate of six shillings – later three shillings – a hut, paid initially either in foodstuffs or else in labour for the government. If they resisted, their villages and grain stores were burnt.[109] In 1895 this strategy was extended in a series of brief military expeditions against Kawinga, Matapawiri, Zarafi and Mponda. Kawinga initiated the process in February, not long after Makanjira had launched his attack on Fort Maguire, by sweeping down from his mountain stronghold at Chikala in a raid on Malemia's villages situated in the shadow of Zomba Mountain near the Blantyre mission outpost, Domasi. In a rapid sequence of events, he was repulsed there by a mixed contingent of Sikhs and Tonga irregulars under their leader, Bandawe, and then driven from his capital at Chikala.[110] Kawinga's defeat was followed by the subjugation of Matapwiri. A Muslim Yao, commanding an important trade route to the coast from his base east of Mulanje, Matapwiri had obtained a considerable supply of guns and ammunition from the Portuguese in exchange for ivory, but he was unable to make effective use of them during the whirlwind campaign launched against him in September 1895.[111] During an operation conducted with great brutality by the Sikh and Tonga troops, men, women and children were indiscriminately bayoneted and extensive looting took place. Among the items recovered – an indication of the multicultural character of this trading frontier – were 'a sacramental cup, a gaudy crucifix …plenty of drums, a few Arabic books …a good many Zanzibari boxes containing some rupees …a tin of quinine, bottle of eau de cologne, snider cartridges'.[112]

A month later came the attack on Zarafi near Mangoche Mountain. The largest expedition mounted by the British up to this time involved 240 newly trained Tonga and Yao soldiers as well as 68 Sikhs. The activities of snipers, shooting from behind rocks, slowed the advance but could not prevent the capture of Zarafi's town on 27 October.[113] The seven-pounder gun, captured

[106] Alston diary, entry for 18 Nov 1895.
[107] Alston diary, entry for 17 Nov 1895.
[108] Johnston to Salisbury, 6 Jan 1896, *Correspondence respecting Operations against Slave Traders in British Central Africa, 1896*, Cmd. 7925; 'Tribal History', Fort Johnston District Book, Vol 1, Part II.
[109] H.H. Johnston to Hetherwick, 3 December 1892, MNA Blantyre Mission Papers; Wordsworth Poole to his mother, 11 September 1895, MNA PO 1/1.
[110] W. Henry Rankine, *A Hero of the Dark Continent* (Edinburgh, 1897), pp. 283–96.
[111] Hanna, pp. 62, 199.
[112] Wordsworth Poole to his mother, 9 October 1895, MNA PO 1/1.
[113] Wordsworth Poole to his mother, 5 November 1895.

more than three years earlier, was retaken, but – having previously sent off his ivory, cattle and most of his women – Zarafi escaped, to reappear in 1896 on the Portuguese side of the border. In a striking indication of continuing divisions in Yao society, Kawinga supplied the British with guides to lead them to Zarafi's stronghold.[114]

Mponda's fall was a further blow to Yao political dominance at the lake. Mponda I, the associate both of Livingstone and of the Livingstonia missionaries at Cape Maclear, had flourished thanks to his involvement in the slave and ivory trades. However, following his death in 1885 disputes broke out between the new Mponda, Nkwate, the son of a slave wife, and a number of other candidates for the succession. For several years Mponda II demonstrated a sure touch in playing off internal rivals against each other, just as he did in switching alliances between the rival Ngoni chiefs, Gomani and Kachindamoto, and between the British and Portuguese.[115] Johnston's government provided a greater challenge, however, particularly following the location of the colonial *boma*, Fort Johnston, on the Shire river crossing south of the lake and close to Mponda's main town. After his traumatic defeat in October 1891, Mponda shrewdly nurtured his alliance with the British, sending men and food supplies to Fort Johnston in January 1892 at a time when several Yao chiefs were threatening to take up arms against them.[116] But the grant of a subsidy of £100 was insufficient to prevent him turning to slave trading once more, no doubt as a means of bolstering his economic and political power. He therefore withdrew westward from the immediate vicinity of Fort Johnston to the Mayuni hills, only to discover that this was the signal for the former chief's senior sister, her young son and several of Mponda's headmen to take up residence near the fort and seek the assistance of the British. Accordingly, in November 1895, Johnston ordered Mponda to surrender and when he did, deposed him from the chieftainship.[117] The young boy chief was officially recognised as the rightful heir but with drastically reduced prestige and power.

The subjugation of the Yao chiefs marked the beginning of the final stage of colonial conquest. Ever since 1889, when he and Mlozi had agreed to a truce, Johnston had deliberately avoided confrontation with Mlozi and the 'north-end Arabs' and they in turn had not sought to interfere with the activities of the ALC at Karonga. With his reinforcements in place, however, Johnston was in a position to strike. On 24 November an armada of ships, including the German steamer, *Hermann von Wissmann*, sailed from Fort Johnston with the largest force employed during the period of colonial conquest; it consisted of over 400 Sikh and African riflemen, nine British officers (three of them mercenaries 'up for the shooting'), two Nordenfeld machine guns and six powerful pieces of artillery.[118] No warning of the unilateral ending of the treaty was given to the Arabs. Instead, at dawn on 2 December, Kopakopa's and Msalema's stockades were successfully assaulted and the much larger stockaded town of Mlozi was

[114] Johnston to Salisbury, 13 Nov 1895; 6 Jan 1896, *Corr …respecting Operations against Slave Traders…, 1896.*
[115] See introduction by Ian Linden to 'Mponda Mission Diary, 1889–1891: Daily Life in a Machinga Village', *International Journal of African Historical Studies*, 7, 2 (1974), pp. 274–82.
[116] Johnston to Salisbury, 16 Feb 1892, *Papers relative to suppression of Slave-raiding…., 1892.*
[117] Johnston to Salisbury, 13 Nov 1895, *Corr…respecting operations against Slave Traders…,1896.*
[118] Edwards to Johnston, 1 Jan 1896, *Ibid.*

surrounded. Over the next two days, Mlozi's town, about half a mile in extent and containing around 3,000 people, was subjected to a steady bombardment from seven-pounder and nine-pounder guns firing shrapnel and incendiary shells. However, the walls of the double-fenced stockade remained unbreached and the defenders continued to resist. Not till Mlozi had been severely wounded by a shell fired at his stone house did a large group of fighting men burst out of the town with the intention of surrendering, only to be massacred almost to a man.[119] Even then, the British still faced stiff opposition in their final assault on the stockade. Mlozi, who had taken refuge in an underground room, was captured by Sergeant Bandawe, given a cursory trial and hanged the next day. 'He died like a man and I admired him immensely', one of the British officers noted in his diary.[120] Some of the defenders, including Kopakopa, managed to escape but two to three hundred died outside the town and many more in it.[121] In a belated act of mercy, the single doctor on the expedition made a futile attempt to treat the wounded, many of whom were suffering from 'horrible wounds' that required the amputation of legs or arms. 'They were nearly all women who had been struck by shell or shrapnel, the lack of males being accounted for by the fact that the men were probably all polished off.'[122]

With Mlozi dead, attention switched to the hills west of the lake where a colonial presence hardly existed. Johnston's most likely target was the northern Ngoni kingdom which had gone through a period of instability following the death of the paramount, Mbelwa, in August 1891. Several raiding expeditions into adjacent territory had taken place in 1892 and 1893, leading the missionary, Kerr Cross, at Karonga to claim: 'It is to crush and render impossible atrocities of this character that the domain of British civilisation must be extended to Central Africa.'[123] For Johnston, however, other considerations carried greater weight. Unlike the north-end Arabs, the northern Ngoni did not threaten trade routes that the British wished to monopolise; unlike the Maseko Ngoni at Domwe they placed no obstacles to the European recruitment of labour. The Livingstonia Mission's influential position in the kingdom was a further factor disposing Johnston to caution: first because he was reluctant to disrupt the work of the mission stations[124] and second because on more than one occasion missionaries in the area acted as intermediaries between the administration and Ngoni chiefs, settling disputes that otherwise might have resulted in war. The northern Ngoni, accordingly, escaped colonial conquest in the 1890s and accepted British rule only in September 1904. Even then, the terms agreed fell far short of the 'treaty or your life' demands more characteristic of Johnston's

[119] Harry Johnston provides detailed but highly unreliable accounts of this expedition in *British Central Africa*, pp. 135–43 and in *The Story of My Life* (Indianapolis, 1923) pp. 299–304. These should be supplemented by the first-hand accounts of Edward Alston (Alston Diaries 2–5 December 1895) and Wordsworth Poole (letter to his mother 23 Dec 1895, MNA PO 1/1) and also by David Stuart-Mogg, *Mlozi of Central Africa* (Central Africana Limited, Blantyre, 2010).

[120] Alston diary entry for 5 Dec 1895, MNA. In an act of barbarism by no means untypical of the times, the big game hunter, Gordon Cumming, acquired Mlozi's head as a trophy. See Alston's diary entry for 20 Jan 1896.

[121] Johnston, *British Central Africa*, p. 141.

[122] Wordsworth Poole to his mother, 23 Dec 1895.

[123] *Central Africa*, April 1893, pp. 50–1.

[124] *Report …on the Trade and General Condition of the British Central African Protectorate*, 1895–6, Cmd. 8254, p. 13.

approach. Taxation would be introduced only in 1906, 15 years after it had been imposed in the Shire Highlands; six chiefs, headed by the new paramount, Chimtunga, were to receive subsidies; no Yao or Tonga police would be employed in the district. The Ngoni kingdom would be preserved as a nation rather than destroyed.[125]

The other major centralised states on the hills and upland plateau west of the lake were treated very differently. No sooner had the Arabs been defeated than Edwards, the British commander, despatched Lieutenant Edward Alston with a contingent of Sikh and African troops to join the recently appointed administrator at Nkhotakota, A. J. Swann, in an attack on the Chewa chief, Mwase Kasungu. Mwase, so Swann alleged, had given sanctuary to an ally of Makanjira, Saidi Mwazungu. More important, he 'had prevented the industrious inhabitants of the country ... from going to work in the coffee plantations round Blantyre'.[126] Joined by a force of some 4,000 irregulars from Nkhotakota commanded by Chief Mbaruku, they assaulted Mwase's town in a blinding rainstorm on 31 December and came away with 300 head of cattle and 546 lbs of ivory.[127] In Britain, the event was trumpeted as a great victory and both Queen Victoria and the Princess of Wales, the future Queen Alexandra (Alston was her godson), sent their congratulations. Wordsworth Poole, who had spoken to some of the Tonga soldiers involved, commented that hardly a shot had been fired.[128] In a follow up attack, Chief Tambala successfully evaded Alston's expeditionary force only to be defeated in October alongside the Chewa chief, Odete, when Captain Manning stormed the latter's stronghold on Chirenje Mountain.[129]

A few days later the last major military expedition in the Protectorate took place. Throughout much of the 1870s and 80s, the Maseko Ngoni kingdom in the Dedza highlands had been the largest and probably the most powerful political force in southern Malawi: capable, as demonstrated in the dramatic raid inflicted on the Shire Highlands in 1884, of terrorising Yao, Mang'anja and European alike. It was only through the payment of a substantial bribe in cattle that David Clement Scott ensured that the Blantyre mission would go unmolested.[130] In subsequent years, the protracted civil war between the chief, Chikusi, and his main rival, Chifisi – carried on from 1891 by their successors Gomani and Kachindamoto – seriously weakened the kingdom as, to an even greater extent, did the accumulation of firearms in Yao hands. During the mid-1880s, Mponda paid a regular tribute in cloth and salt to Chikusi but in 1891 Chikusi's warriors were rebuffed with contemptuous ease by a well-aimed volley when they attacked Mponda's stockade.[131]

Gomani, like Chikusi before him, initially went out of his way to sustain a

[125] For further details see McCracken, *Politics and Christianity*, pp. 110–13.
[126] Report by A.J. Swann enclosed in Johnston to Salisbury, 24 Jan 1896, *Corr ...respecting Slave-Trade*, 1896.
[127] Alston diaries, entries for 26 Dec 1895–2 Jan 1896.
[128] Alston diaries, entries for 5 April and 7 June 1896; Wordsworth Poole to his mother, 9 July 1896.
[129] Sharpe to Sir Clement Hill, 28 Oct 1896, PRO FO 2/108; *BCAG*, November 1896.
[130] Hetherwick, *Romance of Blantyre*, pp. 50–52; Elmslie, 12 Dec 1884, *Free Church of Scotland Monthly Record*, April 1885; William Harkess to Laws, 28 March 1885, NLS Acc. 9220.
[131] Morrison Diary, entry for 5 May 1885, EUL; Consul Hawes to Foreign Office, 7 July 1886, TNA FO 84/1751; Linden, 'Maseko Ngoni', p. 241.

friendly dialogue with missionaries and officials, but by 1893 relations had begun to sour. Not only had Gomani, in making an alliance with his old enemy Mponda, become involved in the trade in slaves, he had also grown concerned at the seasonal drain of labour from his kingdom to the Shire Highlands and its impact on his supply of warriors.[132] Seriously alarmed by news of the deposition of Mponda in November 1895, Gomani reacted by forbidding his subjects to pay taxes to the British and by harassing mission stations below the escarpment.[133] At a time when the most lurid rumours concerning the outbreak of the Matabele and Mashona risings were circulating in Zomba, this was more than the acting commissioner, Alfred Sharpe could take. Two columns of troops were despatched up the escarpment and attacked on 23 October 1896. The Ngoni responded by inaccurately firing muzzle-loaders rather than charging in formation and were quickly dispersed. Gomani, little more than a youth, 'about 18, over 6 feet and ... very fine looking', was captured on 27 October and shot.[134] 'The rest of the days up there was occupied in going out on patrols and burning villages and collaring cows and prisoners', the doctor on the expedition relates. 'Altogether we got about 200 cows. My share will come to about 20 cows which represents about £50.'[135] With the Ngoni economy disrupted, the flow of labour to the plantations increased. By March 1897, a year after Johnston left the Protectorate, some 5,000 people from the kingdom were said to be working in the Blantyre area.[136]

The aftermath of invasion:
collectors & chiefs

By the late 1890s the colonial conquest was virtually complete and the British Central Africa Protectorate had begun to take administrative shape. A chain of fortified government posts (*bomas*), typically manned by a collector or his assistant and supported by a small contingent of Sikh and Malawian soldiers, extended from Port Herald (Nsanje) and Chiromo to Fort Johnston (Mangoche), which moved to its present site in 1897, and on to Deep Bay and Karonga in the north.[137] Military encampments such as Fort Maguire, on the site of Makanjira's first town, Fort Mangoche, near to Zarafi's former stronghold, and Fort Lister, on the slave route past Mulanje, were all positioned with the aim of breaking up overland trade routes to the east coast utilised by slavers, thus making room for steamer-borne traffic under British control going south. Rough tracks had been constructed from the river ports, Chikwawa and Matope to Blantyre and over the 40-mile stretch from Blantyre to Zomba. Surveyors, first appointed in 1895, had demarcated colonial boundaries as well as the bound-

[132] Stokes, 'Malawi Political Systems' p. 368–69.
[133] *Half Yearly Livingstonia Report, July–Dec, 189*, report by T.C.B. Vlok; *BCAG*, 15 Nov 1895.
[134] Capt Stewart to Sharpe, 5 Nov 1896, FO 2/108; Wordsworth Pole to his father, 4 Nov 1896, MNA PO 1/1.
[135] *Ibid.*
[136] *Report...on the Trade and General Conditions of the British Central Africa Protectorate, April 1896 to March 1897*, Cmd. 3729.
[137] C.A. Baker, *Johnston's Administration 1891–1897* (Department of Antiquities Paper No. 9, Zomba, 1971), pp. 74–87.

aries of the huge areas of land acquired by settlers under certificates of claim approved by Harry Johnston. On the ground, the appearance of the Malawi region did not change markedly between the late 1880s and the 1890s. But in the imagination of the colonisers, a fundamental shift had taken place, given visible expression in the elaborate maps produced for Johnston's parliamentary reports of 1894 and 1896. 'Nyasaland' (British Central Africa) was for the first time given tangible identity. In a remarkable foretaste of the future, the Shire Highlands were divided up in a few curved lines between the state and a handful of named European companies and individuals.[138]

The influence of the surveyor was reinforced by the coercive power of the soldier. Johnston, a confirmed evolutionist, was committed to the maintenance of European military superiority. One aspect of his policy was the restriction of African ownership of firearms through the introduction of a gun tax and the prohibition of the import of gunpowder (officially proclaimed in late 1894, though not effective for several more years).[139] Another more controversial aspect was the creation of a locally recruited military force, initially to supplement, subsequently to replace the Sikhs, who finally withdrew in 1912. It was based at the military camp at Zomba, opened in June 1895, and drew predominantly on Tonga and Yao recruits attracted by the pay of four rupees a month and the prospect of ample booty. Designated the Central African Rifles in 1896, this body performed so effectively that in a highly unusual development a second battalion, 1,000 strong, was raised in January 1899 under the command of the War Office for employment in defence of the Royal Navy's coaling station in Mauritius.[140] Three years later, in 1902, both battalions were incorporated into the King's African Rifles, the regional army for Britain's East African possessions. Thereafter, Malawian soldiers were employed in three main roles: internal defence: a decreasing concern in the years after Mlozi's defeat; colonial wars beyond Malawi's boundaries: notably in Ghana, Somaliland and the Gambia; and as a source of paramilitary policemen, the *boma* askari, who were posted to administrative centres from 1895.[141] In the years leading up to the First World War, the latter's most important duties, according to a district resident, consisted of 'the checking of hut taxes and the obtaining of labour and the carrying of orders from the Resident to the chiefs and information from the chiefs to the Resident'.[142]

For Malawians in general the impact of the colonial conquest was severe. With the exception of the attack on Mlozi, numbers killed in battle appear to have been relatively small. But to this must be added the disruption caused by the widespread burning of villages, looting of cattle and the destruction of grain bins. 'I saw the ruins and the half-burned maize lying scattered over the ground – and a sore sight it was, when one thought of the famine of last season', wrote

---

[138] *Report by Commissioner Johnston of the First Three Years Administration, 1894,* Cmd. 7504*; Report by Commissioner … Johnston on the Trade and General Condition of the British Central Africa Protectorate, 1895–96,* Cmd. 8254.

[139] Hanna, p. 218.

[140] Timothy Lovering, 'Authority and Identity: Malawian Soldiers in Britain's Colonial Army, 1991–1964', PhD dissertation, University of Stirling, 2002, p. 26.

[141] McCracken, 'Authority and Legitimacy', pp 162–63; McCracken, 'Coercion and Control in Nyasaland: Aspects of the History of a Colonial Police Force', *JAH* 27, 1, 1986, p. 128.

[142] Resident Fort Johnston to Chief Secretary Zomba, 16 Mar 1921, MNA S1/850/20.

Alexander Hetherwick, commenting on the destruction of Chief Mitioche's village in 1893.[143] There was no large-scale famine of the type that had devastated the Shire Valley and Highlands in the early 1860s. However, severe food shortages occurred in several places, including the area around Makanjira's former town, although the worst effects were avoided in 1895 through the distribution of rice and maize purchased by government officials and UMCA missionaries.[144] Certain incidents, notably the killing of Chief Gomani, entered folk memory and were eagerly recalled 80 years later.[145] Overall, however, what was most striking about African responses to invasion was the variety of reactions it provoked. Where people felt that some room for compromise existed, the creation of short-term alliances with the British became possible. Ngonde headmen, threatened with extinction by Swahili traders, actively supported Johnston in his assault on Mlozi. So too did Tonga chiefs, who sent mercenaries to fight beside the Administration's forces. The latter, in particular, came through the period of military occupation largely unscathed. Where, however, the economic interests of the British clashed with those of African chieftaincies, conflict was often the result. Johnston's rooted determination to impose his rule by force ensured that there was little chance that even the most diplomatically astute of Yao chiefs could have avoided being sucked into the war. But given that their authority rested on the use and sale of slaves and of ivory, the probability of confrontation was always going to be high. As will be discussed in the next chapter, Yao economies were peculiarly badly hit by the forced construction of the colonial economy. In the final analysis, however, European intentions were of much greater importance in assessing responses to conquest than the character of African societies. Despite the militarised nature of the Ngoni kingdoms, Mbelwa, Gomani and Mpezeni in North-Eastern Rhodesia were all ready to negotiate with the British and to make concessions in order to retain their major interests unharmed. But whereas the northern Ngoni were sufficiently remote from the seats of European economic and administrative power to avoid confrontation, Gomani's attempt to prevent his subjects taking employment with settlers in the Shire Highlands resulted in a full-scale attack, the confiscation of cattle and the opening of the kingdom to labour recruiters who behaved with all the brutality of slave traders

Yet if colonial violence was similar in some respects to the violence of the slave trade, albeit with more accurate rifles and more destructive cannon, its effects were strikingly different. Slave raiding had pushed whole communities onto mountain slopes and into stockaded villages. The suppression of raiding, unevenly spread over a number of years, had directly opposite results. The start of the process in the Shire Highlands was described by Hetherwick on his return to Domasi in December 1892.

> After a year's absence one is struck by the extensive migration of the native population which has taken place. The mass of the native population has moved off the hill down to the plain below. The low hill below Domasi basin where successive Malemias have had their principal village is now deserted. Only a few huts occupy the surrounding slopes of

---

[143] Quoted in Ross, 'Blantyre Mission and the Administration', p.344.
[144] *The Life and Letters of Arthur Fraser Sim* (London, 1896), p. 181.
[145] Vaughan, 'Social and Economic Change', p. 109.

Malosa and Zomba, on which the greater part of the native population once lived … Fear of Angoni and Makwangwara, as well as mistrust of each other, kept the people on the hills which became a refuge for men as well as for conies. Now the stream of native population is flowing down to the plains again where good soil affords hope of good crops.[146]

Four years later the same process was at work in the Dedza area. By 1900 it had spread to northern Malawi. In the Nkhata Bay area, Tonga villagers abandoned the use of stockades; elsewhere dispersed Tumbuka groups moved away from places of sanctuary. In the Henga valley, so a Livingstonia missionary noted, 'a rapid increase of redistribution of the population proceeded. The Poka left the perches which they had dug out for themselves on the Nyika Plateau to build on the flats, forming along with the Henga, who were making back to their old home in the Rukuru plain, a long straggle of villages parallel to the path going to Ekwendeni …. The visible population more than doubled.'[147]

Back in southern Malawi the shift in settlement patterns intensified as the risk from warfare declined. By 1904 many villages located on Mulanje Mountain had been abandoned and new ones built on the plains below.[148] New villages had been established in the Chiradzulu area and across the plain east from Blantyre. Wherever they went, the returnees found themselves confronted by European planters claiming legal title to land which the former's ancestors had cultivated.

For Malawian political elites, the consequences of invasion were traumatic. Several rulers were killed, committed suicide or were forced into exile during the series of wars conducted by Johnston and Sharpe. None, not even the Jumbe of Nkhotakota, succeeded in coming to the type of political accommodation with the British achieved by the Kabaka of Buganda and by Lewanika in Barotseland. For a short period, Jumbe III (Mwene Kusutu) established a working relationship with Johnston, as a result of which he received a subsidy and continued to rule his territories virtually unchecked in exchange for keeping his political distance from the north-end Arabs and occasionally supplying the British forces with food and mercenaries. But, by the time of his death in 1894, opposition from rival forces in his state was threatening to make this policy untenable. A few months later, the British resident recently sent to Nkhotakota ousted the new Jumbe and took over responsibility for ruling the state as chairman of a council of headmen.[149]

Colonial occupation, however, did not involve fundamental changes in the nature of African societies. Although rulers were often displaced during the conquest period, the social and political systems over which they had presided survived in almost every case, the exception being that of the 'north-end' Arabs, almost all of whom were killed or left the country. No systematic attempt was made to displace 'alien' Yao, Ngoni or Makololo chiefs by chiefs of Chewa or Mang'anja origin. No campaign was launched against the continuation of domestic slavery. Johnston's propaganda involved listing the number of slaves that had been freed. But as Wordsworth Poole noted, this was often, literally, a paper exercise in which women, 'whom we call slaves' are given 'papers of manu-

---

[146] *LWBCA* Dec 1892.
[147] Livingstonia Education Diary, Report for 1904, Livingstonia Papers, MNA. See also McCracken, *Politics and Christianity*, pp. 115–16.
[148] White, *Magomero*, pp. 85–6.
[149] Stokes, 'Malawi Political Systems', pp. 362–4.

mission which papers are found afterwards thrown away in heaps, for obviously a paper saying that "so and so has been freed by me this day – signed so and so" is really not much use to a free woman.'[150] At Nkhotakota, in the mid-1890s, the first collector made some attempt to prevent slaves being used in carrying ivory to the east coast, but with very indifferent results. 'Hundreds, almost thousands, have passed before Mr Nicoll, and have, without exception declared that they were not slaves; and yet I have no doubt that they were slaves all the time', as an Anglican missionary observed.[151] He also noted that

> The Administration, while forbidding buying and capturing people, recognises a kind of feudal system… This is not liberty as we know it, but without a large force of soldiers and much expenditure no other way of governing the people is possible …To do away with this feudal system would be to revolutionise the country, and might lead to serious outbreaks.[152]

Domestic slavery thus continued virtually unchecked into the early years of the twentieth century in large parts of what became the Central Region.[153] It was not until much later, with the spread of Christianity and the growing influence of local courts, that former slaves began to assert their independence and, even then, the slur of slave status remained.

Three features define the character of the early British administration: the hybrid nature of the colonial state, the heterogeneous character of colonial officials and the priority given to the collection of revenue. As a political entity, the British Central Africa Protectorate was a hybrid, legally subordinate to the will of the imperial government but in practice functioning as a semi-autonomous body, with much important decision-making being left to the Commissioner, Harry Johnston and, from 1897 to 1910, to his successor, the big-game-hunting lawyer, Alfred Sharpe. In an early attempt to legitimise colonial rule through an emphasis on the monarch as the personification of imperial authority, Johnston and his successor went out of their way to present themselves to chiefs as the local representatives of Queen Victoria and of her successor, Edward VII.[154] In practice, responsibility in London was vested up to 1904 in the Foreign Office, a prestigious institution but one with little first-hand experience of Africa. However, as the territory up to 1912 was the recipient of significant annual imperial grants in aid, it was also subjected to the scrutiny of the British Treasury which was anxious to ensure that colonies and protectorates would become financially self-sufficient in the quickest possible time. For Johnston and his successors, therefore, local autonomy was something of an illusion in that the relative independence of the 'man-on-the-spot' was tightly restricted by the financial restraints under which he worked. By the same token, it was not until after the First World War that the Colonial Office became an initiator rather than a super-

---

[150] Wordsworth Poole to his mother, 16 April 1896, MNA PO 1/1.

[151] *Life and Letters of Sim*, p. 202.

[152] *Ibid*, 1 January 1895, p. 171.

[153] *Report on the Trade and General Condition of the British Central Africa Protectorate for 1903–04*, Cmd. 2242.

[154] Queen Victoria's status in relation to the Protectorate became a subject of controversy in the 1950s when opponents of the Federation argued that the government would be breaking its treaty obligations, made in agreements between chiefs and the Queen's representatives, if sovereign power in Nyasaland was transferred to another state.

visor of policy and, even then, governors in Nyasaland remained capable of pursuing certain lines of action of which their superiors in London disapproved.[155] Policy-making in the new Protectorate thus became subject to pressures from a variety of interests, colonial, imperial and financial, all with their own agendas.

One area in which Johnston retained autonomy was in his selection of colonial officials. By the 1890s the Indian Civil Service had become renowned as an elite body, entry to which was achieved through competitive examination followed by further study at Oxford or Cambridge. However, neither the Foreign nor the Colonial Office operated an equivalent system, with the result that Johnston was obliged to make his own appointments prior to 1895 when he handed over the task to the Foreign Office. It was not until 1897 that the first attempt was made to create a regular local civil service with different grades and a separate system of promotion; and only in 1904, when the Colonial Office took over responsibility for the Protectorate, was this system regularised with the introduction of compulsory language and legal examinations.[156]

In the intervening period, colonial administrative responsibilities in Malawi were assumed by a small, almost entirely untrained group of European frontiersmen, recruited because they were available. They included former big-game hunters, ex-soldiers, ex-missionaries and former employees of the ALC. Johnston declared himself opposed to the employment of white South Africans whom he considered to be without 'any concept of justice where natives were concerned'.[157] Otherwise, he was happy to accept almost anyone he could get: a few, men with university degrees; others virtually uneducated. Several of these emulated the Portuguese *muzungos* in displays of casual violence involving the flogging, punching and even sexually molesting of Africans without apparent detriment to their subsequent careers.[158] When two fellow Europeans, a naval captain and doctor, visited the assistant collector, John Yule, at his remote station at Songwe in 1895, he led them in a prolonged drinking session before sending the *boma* askaris to a neighbouring village to procure women against the protests of their husbands. When a missionary complained, the leader of the askaris was flogged and sentenced to three months' hard labour. Yule, 'a very energetic man as well as tidy and artistic', escaped with a reprimand and was later promoted.[159] His experience can be contrasted with that of John L. Nicoll, one of the most perceptive and liberal-minded among the pioneer officials, who was dismissed from the Blantyre mission, where he had worked as a teacher in 1883, because his wife, by then deceased, had conceived their child two months before they were married.[160] An apprentice joiner, Nicoll, found work with the ALC before

155 For the wider context see Bruce Berman, *Control and Crisis in Colonial Kenya* (James Currey, London, 1990), pp. 1–9 and Andrew Roberts, 'The Imperial Mind' in A. Roberts (ed.), *Cambridge History of Africa, Volume 7, 1905–1940* (Cambridge, Cambridge University Press, 1986), pp. 26–40.
156 L H Gann, *The Birth of a Plural Society* (Manchester, 1958), p. 104; Robert Boeder, *Alfred Sharpe of Nyasaland* (Blantyre, Society of Malawi, 1981), p. 102.
157 Johnston to Salisbury, 31 May 1897, TNA FO 2/128 quoted in Gann, *Birth of a Plural Society*, p. 104.
158 Boeder, *Alfred Sharpe*, pp. 59–63.
159 Kerr Cross to Dr Smith, 4 Oct 1895 with enclosure Richard Crawshay to James B. Yule, 4 April 1895, NLS Ms. 7878; Col Edwards to Johnston, 31 March 1897, Johnston Papers, JO 1/1/1, Zimbabwe National Archives.
160 Morrison diaries, entry for 9 Dec 1883; Report of the Foreign Missions Committee, *Church of Scotland Assembly Papers*, p. 197.

being recruited by Johnston in 1891. At the end of that year, he was one of the half dozen district officers (the apt official title was Collector of Revenue) appointed to the new administration. Their number increased to 27 in 1897 and to 38 in 1905: twelve Collectors and 26 Assistant Collectors.

District administration took varying forms in different parts of the territory but the collection of revenue remained a major priority throughout. In many colonies in East and Central Africa, several years elapsed between colonial occupation and the initial demand for hut tax with its direct challenge to chiefly power. In Tanganyika, hut tax was not imposed until 1898, thirteen years after the German protectorate had been declared; in North-Eastern Rhodesia it was 1900 and in North-Western Rhodesia 1904. In Malawi, however, as we have seen, the initial demands were made in the Shire Highlands in 1891 within weeks of Johnston's arrival, with the result that in this area local compromises with African rulers were almost entirely rejected and direct force was employed instead. Land alienation and the rapid emergence of functioning settler estates added to the marginalisation of chiefly authorities on alienated land so that by the mid-1890s estate-owners in Mulanje, Blantyre and Zomba districts had become *de facto* rulers, judging cases among their tenants, inflicting punishments and collecting hut tax direct. Collectors were largely confined to receiving hut tax from the estate owners, assisting in the acquisition of labour and dealing with such cases as were passed to them. Both Johnston and Sharpe introduced measures intended to regulate relations between European employers and their African labour force but, in practice, these were largely ignored.[161] By the same token, when official recognition was given to chiefs in the 1912 District Administration (Native) Ordinance the decision was taken to exclude Zomba, Blantyre and Mulanje districts from its provisions.[162]

Elsewhere in the Protectorate, two different patterns emerged. In certain financially or strategically important transport centres including Chiromo, Nkhotakota and Fort Johnston, the Collector from an early period was provided with relatively substantial military and administrative resources and in consequence was able to play an active, varied role. At Nkhotakota, Nicoll and his successor, A J Swann, supervised the collection of customs duties from Swahili traders, presided over many civil and criminal cases and chaired meetings with local chiefs following the eviction of Jumbe.

Over much of the territory, however, fewer resources were available to collectors and hence greater reliance was placed on African intermediaries: *boma* askaris, messengers, local chiefs and headmen. The role of local government staff has been largely ignored by historians of colonial administration but they played a part of considerable significance at the cutting edge of imperial authority, collecting taxes, seizing hostages, forcing labour and even, on occasions, 'beating up people and robbing the men who had gathered to pay their tax'.[163] Most policemen were former soldiers such as Chiwadai, a Yao from Makanjira's area, who served for six years, winning two medals, with the KAR before being appointed as a policeman to Port Herald in 1907. In the 1920s he was station

[161] See 'Native Labour Regulations', *Report on the Trade and General Condition of the British Central African Protectorate for 1903–4*, Cmd. 2242.

[162] S.S. Murray, *A Handbook of Nyasaland* (Zomba, 1922).

[163] Lewis Mataka Bandawe, *Memoirs of a Malawian* (Blantyre, Malawi, 1971), p. 71.

sergeant at Lilongwe where, between 1910 and 1913, 21 out of 22 policemen employed had previously served in the army.[164]

Of even greater importance were the capitaos, later clerks, who acted as interpreters for the collectors, thus providing the main communications link between the new administration and local communities. Occasionally, as with Sergeant Jacobi at Mzimba, 'a good man in dealing with delicate cases with Angoni chiefs', the collector made use of senior policemen.[165] More frequently, mission-trained civilians were employed, among them Hezekiah Mwanza, an Ngoni from Ekwendeni, who joined the administration at Mzimba as capitao and interpreter in 1906 and was still working in the same district as senior clerk more than two decades later.[166] Such men have sometimes been described as 'collaborators' but to do so is to ignore the extent to which their independent interpretation of events shaped the views of successive British collectors and residents.

Chiefs and headmen constituted the final segment in the triangular equation. Sharpe, like Johnston before him, was initially unwilling to incorporate African rulers within the new system of colonial autocracy and tended to fall back on coercion whenever any challenge to his authority was made. As late as 1902, he reacted to protests from Tonga chiefs, supported by Livingstonia missionaries, against the introduction of a new six shilling hut tax by sending a contingent of KAR troops to the Chinteche area, where they humiliated the chiefs by forcing them to send men to work unpaid for the *boma*.[167] The agreement he reached in September 1904 with Mbelwa and his fellow Northern Ngoni chiefs thus appeared to mark an important step in the transition from the politics of conquest to those of consent. Mbelwa and five other chiefs were promised annual stipends for agreeing to assist the Resident (the new term for Collector) with his work. Disputes continued, particularly over the vexed question of raiding for cattle, but this did not prevent chiefs from being incorporated in a Native Court, alongside the Resident, H. C. McDonald, or in the formation in 1907 of a council of Ngoni chiefs, the forerunner of the Mbelwa African Administrative Council, established in 1931.[168]

With the Ngoni precedent established, the question remained as to whether it could form a model for local administration elsewhere. The issue was raised shortly after Sharpe's retirement in 1910 and became the subject of vigorous discussion in the Nyasaland Legislative Council. Officials, led by the Acting Governor, Hector Duff, pressed for the introduction of officially recognised Headmen to act as communicators between village communities and European administrators. Settlers successfully opposed the measures, ostensibly because of the consequences they might have on African life; in reality because they saw them as a threat to their control of labour.[169] In 1912, however, similar measures were reintroduced in the District Administration (Native) Ordinance and this

---

[164] Lilongwe District Book, police character record, 1918–23.
[165] Mzimba (Mombera) District Book, police character record, 1907–10.
[166] *Ibid*, 1918–23.
[167] Sharpe to TNA FO, 19 May 1902, FO 2/606; Sharpe to FO, 14 Oct 1902, FO 2/607; Daly to Macalpine, 8 Oct 1902, NLS Ms. 7864; Boeder, *Alfred Sharpe*, p. 75.
[168] Boeder, *Alfred Sharpe*, pp. 99–100.
[169] Timothy Kiel Barnekov, 'An Inquiry into the Development of Native Administration in Nyasaland, 1888–1937' (Maxwell Graduate School of Citizenship and Public Affairs, Syracuse University, Occasional Paper No. 48, 1976), p. 46.

time they were approved. In an enabling measure that by 1913 had been put into operation in only nine out of 19 districts or sub-districts, provision was made for the appointment by the Governor of Principal Headmen, chosen predominantly but by no means exclusively from the most prominent chiefs: on Likoma the first Principal Headman was the Anglican missionary, Archdeacon Glossop, who served in that role for many years.[170] Under the terms of the Ordinance, the Principal Headmen had no judicial powers; no officially-recognised courts; and no tax-collecting or tax-raising functions, other than those delegated to them by the residents. However, the elasticity of the system meant that in some areas Principal Headmen and village headmen under them were still able to exert considerable authority. In the Chikwawa district, six of the seven leading Makololo chiefs (the exception was Mlauri) were appointed as principal headmen. In exchange for their cooperation, the local Resident tacitly accepted their continuing hegemony in a number of areas. 'Indirect rule' as a set of beliefs would not be introduced to Nyasaland until 1933. But in the intervening period, as Mandala has noted, chiefs and headmen continued to shoulder a wide range of traditional duties, including settling disputes and allocating land, undisturbed by British officials.[171]

At Government House, however, the importance of coercion continued to be trumpeted. In his hand-over notes, written in 1913 for the new Governor, Sir George Smith, Major Pearce, the Acting Governor, welcomed the appointment of principal headmen as subordinate members of the colonial administration but expressed his concern at the powers that had accumulated in the hands of the Ngoni chiefs:

> The Mombera District is to my mind a standing example of the undesirability of propagating the tribal system and perpetuating the rule by chief. I do not think that any progress can be expected from such a system and such people will always prove a potential danger to a country. The people instead of looking to the Resident as their head look to the hereditary chiefs.

Pearce's recommendation, eagerly seized on by Smith in 1915, was that 'if trouble ever does arise in the Mombera District it will be met not by interviews or arbitration but by a short sharp lesson at the hands of our military forces.' Nothing, he claimed, would better benefit the Northern Ngoni 'than to shoot a few down, burn their villages, deport their so called chiefs and confiscate their cattle.'[172] Thus, two years before the deportation of the Ngoni paramount, Chimtunga, his fate had been effectively sealed. Colonial authorities in Nyasaland now accepted an administrative role for local chiefs. But on the brink of the First World War they were still committed to an ideology of domination that left little space for African political initiatives.

---

[170] *Nyasaland Protectorate Report for 1912–13;* S.S. Murray, *A Handbook of Nyasaland* (Zomba, 1922).
[171] Mandala, *Work and Control*, pp. 101–07.
[172] Major Pearce's Confidential Notes on Nyasaland, MNA GOA 5/3/1.

3
The Making of the Colonial Economy 1891–1915

Introduction

No period in the colonial history of Malawi is more important than the two decades following the declaration of a British Protectorate. During these years the British not only established their territorial hegemony through force, they also brought about a fundamental reshaping of the country's economy along lines that are still familiar today. Long distance trade in gathered items such as ivory declined and was gradually replaced by trade in agricultural staples: principally coffee, cotton and tobacco. In the Shire Highlands much land was alienated to a small group of settlers. But the plantation economy they created had to compete for labour from the early years of the twentieth century with a peasant sector based principally on the Upper and Lower Shire Valley and with a labour exporting zone, located principally but not exclusively in the north. At different times the colonial state gave precedence to different sectors of the economy. Overall, however, its impact was notably uneven in the sense that while some local communities were massively affected by its interventions, others survived the first stage of colonial penetration largely unscathed. In all cases, however, the general tendency was for non-agricultural economic activities to diminish and, particularly in the southern third of the country, for the production of food to become increasingly commercialised.

Capitalist penetration was also connected with the emergence of new forms of poverty, both relative and absolute. Hard statistical evidence is impossible to obtain but whatever the very real economic deprivation that existed in the Malawi region, particularly at the time of maximum disruption from the slave trade, there is no reason to believe that natural resources and living standards were inferior in the late 1880s to those in much of East-Central Africa although in certain places, for example, the high-rainfall area around the Lakes Victoria and Tanganyika, regular agricultural surpluses were, and remain, easier to achieve. By 1913, however, the gap as measured in domestic exports between Nyasaland and most of its neighbours had become apparent and in the inter-war period it notably widened, in part as a result of the exploitation of mineral resources in Northern Rhodesia, Southern Rhodesia and Tanganyika but also as a consequence of the greater productivity achieved by African and European farmers alike in Uganda and Kenya. A central theme of colonial Malawi's economic century history concerns the growth, intermittent and irregular it was, of the export economy. However, this took place more slowly than in the region as a whole, with inevitable consequences both for government revenues and for family incomes. Undoubtedly in the 1930s there were what Mandala has described as 'deserts of famine' in southern Tanganyika, in eastern Northern Rhodesia and in northern Mozambique at least as, and probably more, severe than any that existed in Nyasaland. Overall, however, it is clear that Nyasaland by this time had a lower wage economy, less capital investment and less foreign trade than almost any of its neighbours.

Settlers & the state

Harry Johnston was a natural optimist, convinced that 'Nyasaland ought to become another Brazil for the wealth of tropical produce it is fitted to yield under cultivation.' Yet from the beginning, he and his successors were confronted by a number of constraints that were to have a long-lasting impact on economic performance. Firstly, political geography was not in his favour. As a result of their vigorous campaign, the Scottish churches had saved Nyasaland from Portuguese rule but the result was a curiously elongated, landlocked territory, never more than 100 miles wide and over 500 miles long, which was separated from the coastal ports, through which all exports and imports had to flow, by lengthy stretches of Portuguese or German controlled territory.

Had Livingstone's legacy, the Zambesi-Shire highway, functioned as the explorer had hoped, as a smoothly functioning artery for international trade, the problem of Nyasaland's geographical isolation might have been overcome. But even in the 1880s, its shortcomings had been cruelly revealed and as water levels fell they became even more evident. By the 1890s, Katunga (Chikwawa) had been virtually abandoned as a port. By 1903 its successor, Chiromo, was also coming under threat, with the result that steamers from Chinde had to unload their cargoes onto barges at the Portuguese station of Villa Bocage some 40 miles below the colonial border, to be transported north.[1] By the end of the dry season much of the river was transformed into a combination of shallow pools and sand-banks; although transport by steamer improved, the rough road built from Katunga to Blantyre disintegrated during the rains, resulting in serious traffic congestion.[2] Tsetse fly and the steep gradient of the Katunga road from the valley to the highlands precluded the use of oxen. Instead, transport work became the preserve of a shifting population of head porters (*tengatenga* carriers), many of whom suffered severely on the demanding trek up the escarpment from the steamy valley floor to the chill of the Shire Highlands. Nyasaland thus became saddled with a notoriously inefficient transport system, yet one in which freight charges were among the highest in southern-central Africa.

---

[1] *Report on Trade and Conditions in the BCA Protectorate, 1902–03*, Cmd. 1772 and *1903–04*, Cmd. 2242.

[2] Elias Mandala, 'Feeding and Fleecing the Natives: How the Nyasaland Transport System distorted a New Food Market, 1890s-1920s', *JSAS*, 32, 3, 2006, pp. 508–09.

The third constraint, interconnected directly with the others, involved the limited input of the metropolitan government. All over Africa, wherever it had administrative responsibility, the British Foreign Office in the 1890s saw its central function as ensuring that colonies should not become long-term financial burdens to the metropolis and this was also true of Nyasaland, which had been occupied largely as a result of missionary pressure and was not regarded in London as being of any great economic or strategic importance. Contrary to some views, this did not mean that financial support was not forthcoming. Ministers were anxious to ensure that the new protectorate did not fail. The Treasury was persuaded to sanction imperial grants in aid totalling £54,352 for the years 1891–96, thus facilitating the military conquest of the region. In this period, 72 per cent of Nyasaland's revenues came from external sources. More significantly, grants in aid averaging nearly £30,000 a year (£294,000 in total) continued to be paid under Colonial Office rule from 1904 to 1912, a time when such grants were being phased out in most parts of British Africa.[3] However, with Treasury money went Treasury scrutiny which resulted in persistent demands for economy and a virtual boycott on large-scale investment. In other parts of Africa before the First World War, colonial governments were able to raise funds in Europe to build railways or improve harbour facilities, but in Nyasaland this was not possible. Plans for a railway from Blantyre to Quelimane on the Indian Ocean coast or, if that proved too expensive, from Blantyre to Chiromo on the Lower Shire River, were mooted from the early 1890s only to fall foul of the Foreign Office and the Treasury. Neither was prepared to invest in schemes that involved constructing a track through a foreign territory. Until Nyasaland became capable of supporting itself from locally-raised revenues, there was no question of raising external funds on guarantees provided by Britain.[4]

It was against this background of financial stringency that Harry Johnston grappled with the central problem of how best to develop an export-based cash economy that would provide the wherewithal for taxes and make his administration self supporting. In Southern Rhodesia the British South Africa Company looked to encourage large-scale white settlement, but Johnston rejected this approach for Nyasaland on health grounds, arguing that it was only on high plateaux like the Nyika that European families would be able to live in safety, free from the scourge of malaria.[5] At a time when the annual European death rate in the territory averaged more than eight per cent, no 'low class' settlers lacking in capital would be welcomed. More pragmatically, there was little chance of large-scale European immigration into a territory lacking exploitable minerals. Although gold had been mined at Missale in northern Zambesia up to the 1830s, none was discovered in payable quantities further east.[6]

The main alternative was the West African solution: an export economy based on peasant production. However, Johnston was equally emphatic in ruling this out. Shifting cultivation, he asserted, was a 'heedless system, ruinous to the future interests of the country'. If peasant agriculture was to flourish, it would only be through the importation of Indian cultivators: 'who might serve to instruct the

3   Vaughan, 'Social and Economic Change', pp. 109–112, 326.
4   Vail, 'Railway Development', pp. 366–69.
5   *Johnston, First Three Years.*
6   Newitt, *Mozambique,* pp. 208–10, 305; Johnston, *British Central Africa,* pp. 49–51.

natives as to higher modes of agriculture than their present thriftless procedure'.[7]
Not until 1895 did lack of funds persuade him to abandon this scheme.

It was against this background that Harry Johnston turned his attention to the small community of European adventurers now living in the Shire Highlands. Most of these were primarily engaged in 1891 as traders, transporters and ivory hunters. John Buchanan had introduced coffee growing on a small scale on his Mulungusi estate at Zomba, and ten years later, several other Europeans turned to coffee, attracted by the dramatic boom in world prices dating from the late 1880s.[8] Exports in 1891 constituted a negligible 10 tons, worth perhaps £1,000. By this time, however, 'coffee [was] being planted in all directions', most notably by Eugene Sharrer, whose estates 'had more land under cultivation than anyone else' according to the Scottish missionary paper, *Life and Work*.[9] For Johnston, this development seemed the answer to his problem. 'It would almost seem as though the welfare of this Protectorate will be first founded on its coffee plantations', he wrote. 'Our favourable conditions are the suitable climate, the just-sufficient rain supply, the enormous extent of virgin soil, and the relative abundance and cheapness of native labour.'[10] Against these assets could be set the formidable difficulties involved in transporting bulk goods to the coast by means of the Shire-Zambezi waterway. But Johnston refused to be discouraged. All that was required, he wrote in a later despatch, was for 'the Administration to act as friends of both sides, and introduce the native labourer to the European capitalist'.

> Given abundance of cheap native labour, and the financial security of the Protectorate is established. The European comes here with his capital, which he is ready to employ to almost an unlimited extent if he can get in return black men who will, for a wage, work with their hands as he cannot do himself, in a tropical sun. It only needs a sufficiency of native labour to make this country relatively healthy and amazingly rich.[11]

Johnston's first step was to give legal title in the form of official 'certificates of claim' to almost all of the land acquired, or at least claimed, by Europeans up to 1891. Johnston and, later, his biographer presented this exercise as a rigorous one, involving the rejection of a substantial number of fraudulent claims but the reality was rather different. In the Northern District, for example, a huge area of 2,700,000 acres was transferred to the British South Africa Company as a result of a series of spurious deals transacted by the ALC and almost entirely lacking in documentary backing.[12] More than 30 years later, a government commission confirmed that 'there appears to be substantial support for the view of many of the native chiefs [in the area] that they never sold or in any way transferred their land to Europeans.'[13] Further south, in the Shire Valley and High-

7   Johnston, *British Central Africa*, p. 424; Johnston to FO, 1 June 1895, TNA FO 2/88.
8   See William Gervase Clarence-Smith, 'The Coffee Crisis in Asia, Africa and the Pacific, 1870–1914' in Clarence-Smith and Steven Topic (eds), *The Global Economy in Africa. Asia and Latin America, 1500–1989* (Cambridge, 2003), p 101.
9   *LWBCA* April, August 1891.
10 Johnston, *First Three Years*.
11 *Report by Commissioner … Johnston on the Trade and General Conditions of the British Central African Protectorate, 1895–1896*, Cmd. 8254.
12 Bridglal Pachai, *Land and Politics in Malawi, 1875–1975* (Kingston, Ontario, 1978), pp. 155–71.
13 *Report of the North Nyasa Native Reserves Commission*, 1929, quoted in Pachai, *Land and Politics*, p. 170.

lands, where a further one million acres were alienated to some 25 individuals or partnerships, the situation was rather different. Chiefs had normally signed documents transferring large amounts of land in exchange for small quantities of trade goods – 60,000 acres, in one case, for goods valued at £50. As White has noted, a partial explanation, at least in the Shire Highlands, may have been that Yao chiefs disposed of land that was temporarily largely unoccupied and uncultivated following the devastation caused by the famine of the 1860s and the movement of villagers into places of refuge.[14] But to this must be added an older explanation: that, in giving Europeans rights to cultivate, chiefs failed to recognise the extensive rights to ownership that planters claimed as a result of the transaction. Johnston went out of his way to include in most certificates of claims 'non-disturbance' clauses designed to protect the occupancy rights of villagers living on alienated land. However, these clauses proved to be almost entirely worthless. No attempt was made to designate what land within estate boundaries remained in African possession. Consequently landlords came to treat all Africans living on estates as tenants at will, whether they were the original inhabitants or incomers from Mozambique (described collectively by the British as 'Anguru') who arrived in the Shire Highlands in increasing numbers from around 1892.

Thus, by the mid-1890s, a massive shift in the structure of landholding had occurred that was to profoundly influence the character of Malawi's political economy. In the far north, after lengthy negotiations, the BSAC transferred over 51,000 acres to the Livingstonia Mission but otherwise left the land allocated to it almost entirely neglected, neither exploited directly nor sold to others.[15] In the Shire Highlands, however, the impact was immediate. Johnston's settlement not only alienated over 800,000 acres, nearly half the total area of the Highlands to Europeans, it also confirmed a distorted pattern of land holding that was to act as a drag on the Protectorate's economy for the next half century – as the most able of Johnston's successors was later to note.[16] A dozen settlers shared 133,000 acres between them. But their landholdings were dwarfed by those of the three leading planters of the early colonial period: John Buchanan, the Perthshire gardener and disgraced missionary; Eugene Sharrer, the archetypical outsider, 'a forceful German trader, of Jewish appearance if not of Jewish origin', according to an unfriendly colonial official; finally Alexander Low Bruce, wealthy son-in-law of David Livingstone and a pillar of the Edinburgh establishment. By 1893, John Buchanan and his brothers David and Robert had obtained certificates of claim for 167,823 acres, almost all in the Zomba, Blantyre and Cholo districts. Eugene Sharrer had acquired a vast area of 363,034 acres of which some 290,000 were in the Shire Highlands. Alexander Low Bruce had obtained 176,000 acres, all but 7,000 acres located in a large sweep of land south of Zomba, which he named 'Magomero' in honour of the pioneer UMCA missionary settlement. Bruce died in 1893 and Buchanan in 1896 but this did not result in the fragmentation of their landholdings. The A. L. Bruce Trust (later A. L. Bruce Estates Ltd) remained a family firm with most shares owned by two of Bruce's sons, Alexander Livingstone and David Livingstone Bruce. By contrast,

---

[14] White, *Magomero*, pp. 78–81.
[15] McCracken, *Politics and Christianity*, pp. 135–6; Pachai, *Land and Politics*, p. 167.
[16] See Colby to Sir Sidney Abrahams, 28 Feb 1949, TNA CO 525/207 44332/1948.

the Buchanan estates were taken over in the late 1890s by a group of fellow Scottish landowners, including John Moir and R. S. Hynde who, in 1901, formed the giant Blantyre and East Africa Company with a capital of £60,000. A year later, in 1902, Eugene Sharrer also transferred his holdings into a limited company, the British Central Africa Company with an expanded acreage of 372,536 acres, more than twice that of its nearest rival. Over the next two decades, settlers purchased a further 139,000 acres in freehold but the basic character of Johnston's land settlement remained untouched. In the Shire Highlands a small number of companies and estate owners owned far more land than they had the capital or labour to cultivate. On the largest estates, as White has noted, 'the big proprietors employed managers to open up small plantations, leaving the bulk of their holdings unused.'[17] Even during the height of the coffee boom, from 1895 to 1900 the total acreage under cash crops rose to a peak of only 16,917 acres, probably more than was being cultivated by Europeans in Southern Rhodesia at this time, but a tiny proportion of the whole.

Johnston's decision to ratify the overwhelming majority of land claims was accompanied by a further initiative intended to assist the expansion of the plantation sector. As he was quick to recognise, if land was available in abundance to settlers, labour certainly was not. By 1889 some Ngoni/Chewa cultivators from the Southern Highlands had been persuaded to take work clearing land on European estates in the dry season. However, they returned home to their gardens during the rains, leaving the cleared land choked with weeds. A partial solution was provided by Tonga workers recruited by the ALC and brought down by steamer from Bandawe but never in sufficient numbers to cope with the problem.[18] Johnston's answer was the introduction in 1891 of a six shilling hut tax (quickly reduced to three shillings) as a means both of raising revenues and of forcing men in the Southern Province into wage employment. However, by the time of his departure from the Protectorate in 1896 the limitations of this policy were becoming clear. Rather than turning to agricultural wage labour, a deeply unpopular option, villagers in the Shire Highlands increasingly opted for the sale to settlers of chickens, fish, maize and other foodstuffs to meet their tax demands.[19]

Estate owners, in consequence, embarked on a new strategy, initially with the full approval and cooperation of the government. From 1897 freelance labour recruiters, black and white, several of them former ivory hunters, turned their attention to 'Central Angoniland', the uplands north and west of Dedza, which had been opened to European penetration in November 1895 by the defeat of the Maseko Ngoni kingdom of Gomani. Armed with guns and actively collaborating with the government Collectors and *boma* askaris, these men carried out a series of raiding expeditions, loosely defined as a search for tax defaulters, which involved the widespread burning of villages, destruction of food crops, rape of women and occasional murder of men. The contradictions in this policy came to a head in 1900, when the intense popular dislike of forced labour recruitment was compounded by near famine conditions over much of southern Malawi. An experienced administrator wrote that in the central region, men who had once

---

[17] White, *Magomero*, p. 82.
[18] *LWBCA*, April 1889; John Buchanan, 'Coffee: Its Position and Prospects', *CAT*, Oct 1895.
[19] Report on Blantyre District for 1895, *BCAG*, 1 March 1896.

gone voluntarily to the south, fled 'into B.S.A. (North-eastern Rhodesia) into Forest Hills, anywhere but Blantyre', where the shortage of labour had become acute.[20] Meanwhile, in the Shire Highlands, Lomwe/Nguru labourers brought by the recruiters Tom Walker and John Sinderam from Mozambique, died in their hundreds on the road between Blantyre and Mulanje, having been provided with neither food nor shelter.[21]

The subsequent enquiry led by the recently appointed Chief Judicial Officer, Joseph Nunan, uncovered incontrovertible evidence that some of the worst atrocities had been committed on the orders of the Central Angoniland Collector, H. J. Morris, acting under direct instructions from the Acting Commissioner, Lt-Col William Manning.[22] However, in a politically shrewd judgement, Nunan ignored their culpability and put the blame on less privileged groups: askaris, black labourer recruiters and 'foreign Jews', who were punished with considerable severity. Three askaris found guilty of murder were summarily hanged. Donald Malota, a former mission teacher and ivory hunter employed by Sharrer as a labour recruiter, was also sentenced to death, although he later escaped from custody and was subsequently reprieved. In a remarkably frank talk to members of the settler-run Labour Bureau, Nunan made clear that 'raiding expeditions (for they were nothing less) of irresponsible labour recruiters' had to cease and that instead the Bureau should provide proper shelters and rations for migrants making their way to Blantyre.[23]

This measure by no means halted the use of force by state officials to propel tax defaulters into European employment but it did contribute to a re-evaluation of policy. In January 1902 Alfred Sharpe, Johnston's successor as Commissioner, responded to pleas from the settler-controlled Labour Bureau by doubling the tax rate from three shillings to six with the introduction of a three shilling rebate for men who could prove they had worked 30 days for Europeans. Increased pressure was thus placed on peasant farmers to enter the plantation economy. However, a more important development, starting in the early 1890s, was the migration of a variety of people, described by the British as 'Nguru' but speaking a number of interconnected languages including Mpotola and Lomwe, across the Mozambique border between Lake Chilwa and the Ruo valley. In the early 1890s, the movement was relatively small scale and often involved former slaves fleeing from chiefly stockades. But in 1899 it grew to mass proportions in response to Portuguese attempts to impose compulsory labour in an area previously little affected by colonial rule. Initially, many Lomwe/Nguru obtained access to land from Mang'anja and Yao headmen and chiefs who welcomed the opportunity to increase their dependents at a time when they were moving back to the lower ground of the plain. Others, however, took up residence on European-owned estates such as that of John Moir near Mulanje, attracted by the offer of good, well-watered land. In exchange, they were required to work on the estate for one month each year, a form of labour rent described by the settlers as *thangata*. By 1903 some 18,000 Nguru were living in the Blantyre district and many more in

---

[20] A. J. Swann to J. Nunan, 15 March 1901, MNA J2/9/1.
[21] *CAT*, 14, 21 July 1900.
[22] See Manning to Morris, 15 Oct 1900, MNA J2/9/1; Manning to Nunan, 19 Dec 1900, MNA J 1/2/1.
[23] *CAT*, 16, 23 Feb 1901. This episode is discussed in McCracken, 'Marginal Men', pp. 548–50.

1 African Lakes Company ivory store with carriers, c.1889, photographed by Frank Moir, joint manager of the ALC

2 Commercial agriculture on the march: the first consignment of peasant-grown cotton produced for the export market in the Upper Shire District is brought for sale at Liwonde, 1905

the Mulanje, Cholo and Zomba districts. On Moir's estate, the Lomwe migrants were regarded as a 'labour reserve' to be hired out on commission to neighbouring estates when the latter required more workers.[24]

The development of *thangata* came at a time of transition when officials were beginning to question whether Nyasaland's economic future should rely on the plantation economy sector alone. In 1893 ivory valued at £18,253, some of it drawn from the elephant-rich Luangwa Valley to the east, accounted for more than 80% of Nyasaland's exports. Three years later, ivory still accounted for 59% of exports; from that year, however, the trade went into steep decline as a result of the high customs duties, gun and game taxes, and a fall in the number of elephants. By 1900, the value of ivory exports was down to £2,500; elephant hunting was being re-branded as a rich man's sport. Over the same period, coffee, which had an export value of only £2,996 in 1893, grew rapidly to £22,413 in 1898 and on to £62,245 in 1900, when it constituted 79% of the Protectorate's exports. In that year 1,000 tons of coffee were exported as compared with just ten tons in 1891. Some 100 European planters, all but twelve of them British, most of these Scots, were said to be working on estates in the Shire Highlands and nearly 17,000 acres had been planted with coffee. A future Governor claimed that the protectorate was 'as yet the solitary instance of a successful agricultural colony within tropical Africa'.[25]

The collapse of the coffee industry in 1901 brought the settler dream to an end. One factor was a sharp fall in world prices, down from over 100 shillings a cwt in 1897 to 55 shillings in 1901, caused by the expansion of coffee growing in Brazil.[26] Even more important was a decline in the quality of Malawian coffee as a result of insect pests and the unchecked growth of weeds. The latter was linked to the crisis in the labour supply, exacerbated by the failure of estate owners to feed their workers at a time of drought and famine. 'On every side he saw his own and his neighbour's coffee dropping off the trees because of the growth of weeds, which they had not the labour necessary to keep down', one planter complained in 1900.[27] The reason was that men were 'naturally afraid to risk their lives in a starving country', as the Labour Bureau reported.[28] Several coffee estates were sold; others were abandoned. In 1902, the value of coffee exported fell to £14,751, a decline of 76% over the previous year; aggregate commerce fell by 51%.[29] In a gloomy editorial, the *Central African Times* noted: 'We have failed to attract the attention of capitalists from other parts. We have likewise failed to produce any capitalists of our own.'[30]

In a frenzy of anxiety, estate owners turned to alternative crops: tea in Mulanje, tobacco near Blantyre, cotton over much of the Shire Highlands. This time, however, they did so in a context in which their claim to monopolise export production was being challenged from two directions. By the end of 1903 about

---

[24] Alexander Hetherwick to James Inglis, 20 July 1903, Inglis to Hetherwick, 20 July 1903, Hetherwick Papers, MNA; White, *Magomero*, pp. 87–89; Boeder, *Silent Majority*, 17–23.

[25] *Report by Consul Sharpe on Trade and General Conditions of British Central Africa 1896–97*, Cmd. 8438; Alfred Sharpe, quoted in *The Central African Planter*, Dec. 1895.

[26] *Handbook of Nyasaland* (Zomba, 1908), pp. 182–83.

[27] *CAT* March 1900, 6 April 1901.

[28] *CAT* 6 April 1901.

[29] *CAT* 6 July 1901, 13 July 1901, Jan 1902; Baker, 'Malawi's Exports', p. 80.

[30] *CAT* 18 June 1901.

8,000 acres of cotton had been planted on estates but collectors had also started to distribute cotton seeds to peasants in the Shire Highlands, the Upper and Lower Shire Valley and at the south end of Lake Malawi.[31] Moreover, it was in that year that Alfred Sharpe, the new Commissioner, once one of the most enthusiastic supporters of settler agriculture, gave permission for the Witwatersrand Native Labour Association to recruit Malawians for work in the Transvaal mines. His explanation for the decision, made to the Chamber of Commerce in March 1903, was notably blunt. 'The Commissioner…said that ever since he had been in the country they had been endeavouring to get some paying exportable product.' Two years before, Harry Johnston, newly retired from Uganda, had proposed that recruitment for the mines should be permitted but Sharpe had objected for fear that in consequence less labour would be available for the estates. Now, however, conditions had changed. 'He thought…that the export of coffee having declined year after year that there was very little hope of building up an export in that product as several plantations had been abandoned and opinion was not so hopeful.'[32]

Settler influence was by no means at an end. In 1908 the first unelected, non-official representative was appointed to the newly formed Legislative Council. In 1911, this representation was increased to six non-officials (one of whom was usually a missionary) who sat alongside an equal number of officials. *The Central African Times* and its successor, *The Nyasaland Times* continued to trumpet settler views. The Associated Chamber of Agriculture and Commerce, founded in 1895 and enlarged in 1907, operated as an important pressure group, both through its role in nominating candidates for the Legislative Council and in its representations to the colonial government.[33] Nevertheless, Nyasaland had by now become the scene of a lengthy and often confused debate between the proponents of three types of export production. European farmers were challenged from within the government both by supporters of peasant agriculture and by those who believed that Nyasaland's most valuable economic function would be as a supplier of labour for the more developed economies of the south.

The origins of labour migration

In the early years of the twentieth century, it was this latter view that predominated. Labour migration from northern Malawi can be dated from the mid-1880s when Tonga villagers from west of the Lake were actively encouraged by Scottish missionaries of the Livingstonia Mission to take up employment as head porters and field labourers with the African Lakes Company. Workers were gathered together at Bandawe in groups of 20 or 30, issued with six month contracts and then transported by steamer to the Upper Shire and from there to Blantyre and beyond.[34] In 1886 the London Missionary Society agent, Alexander Carson observed some 30 Tonga porters at Katunga on the Lower Shire, employed to

---

[31] *Report on Trade and Conditions, 1903–04*, Cmd. 2242.
[32] *CAT* 21 March 1903.
[33] Simon S. Myambo, 'The Shire Highlands Plantations: A Socio-economic History of the Plantation System of Production in Malawi, 1891–1938', MA University of Malawi, 1973, pp. 4–8,12.
[34] John McCracken, 'Underdevelopment in Malawi: the Missionary Contribution', *African Affairs*, 76, 303 (1977), pp. 198–99.

carry loads to Blantyre. They were being paid by the month rather than by the job, as was the practice with Yao and Mang'anja carriers also working at the port. Carson noted that their services 'can be commanded at any time, for being away from their homes they are quite dependent upon their masters.'[35] Already by 1894, three years before taxation was introduced in their district, 5,500 Tonga were said to have been working for settlers or the ALC in the Shire Highlands.[36] Confronted by low wages and irregular food supplies (sometimes no food supplies at all), increasing numbers began to look for alternative places of employment. Precisely when and how the first migrants made the long trek of 500 or 1,000 miles to Southern Rhodesia and South Africa remains unknown although it is likely that pioneers were recruited in the mid to late 1890s by labour touts operating on behalf of Rhodesian mining companies.[37] In 1901 an official noted that in recent times some 2,000 Malawians a year had crossed the Zambesi at Tete on their way home following the expiry of their contracts.[38] Many, although not all of these, were Tonga. By 1903, the Collector at Nkhata Bay was commenting on the yearly exodus of men from the district to Salisbury. A year later they were said to be going 'by the hundred' for work south of the Zambesi. Few, if any, signed on with labour recruiters in the government-approved tours made from 1904. By that time, most had come to recognise the comparative advantages in terms of wages and of labour conditions gained by independent workers who chose their own employers.[39]

Where Tonga migrants led, others soon followed. By the turn of the century, men from 'Central Angoniland' had begun to make the hazardous trek from Fort Jameson, down the mail route along the Mozambique border to the ferry crossing at Feira on the north bank of the Zambesi, and from there via Zumbo to Salisbury and beyond. At the southern extremity of the country, labour migrants from the Lower Shire crossed the Zambesi at Tete. In the north of the country, young Ngoni and Tumbuka men either took the Feira road or cut across to Broken Hill in Northern Rhodesia, where they might work for a time before moving on to the south.

Motives for migration varied from district to district. Among the Tumbuka and Ngoni of northern Malawi the central feature would appear to have been the undermining of their indigenous economy, the end of raiding and the severe blow struck by the spread of rinderpest in 1893 which decimated Ngoni cattle for some years. Initially it was to the Livingstonia Mission that young men turned for work and wages but, by 1899, Ngoni workers were said to have transferred their interest away from the mission to better paid employment outside the country. In 1901, they were reported to be departing 'in all directions' from Salisbury to Tanganyika and in such strength that the missionaries did not believe that the introduction of a labour tax would significantly alter the numbers

[35] A. Carson, 'Journey from Quillimane to Niamkolo, March 28–July 4 1886', London Missionary Society Papers Box 3/35, SOAS Library.
[36] Laws to Dr Smith, 10 Sep 1894, NLS 7878.
[37] See B.S. Krishnamurthy, 'Economic Policy, Land and Labour in Nyasaland, 1890–1914' in Pachai, *Early History*, p. 396.
[38] Boeder, *Builder of Empire*, p. 78.
[39] Report of Collector, West Nyasa District, 1902–03, MNA NNC3/1/1; Monthly Reports, West Nyasa, August, November 1904, MNA NNC3/4/1; Annual Report West Nyasa, 1903–04, MNA NNC3/1/1.

involved.[40] 'Scarcely any of the Angoni of Mombera's country visit the Shire Highlands', Alfred Sharpe noted, on the eve of the extension of hut tax to the kingdom: 'Of late years, however, large numbers of them have annually gone in search of work to Salisbury, Beira, Umtali, and other industrial centres south of the Zambezi river.'

Further south, the impact of the state was more directly felt. Following the imposition of hut tax over most of the area in 1895, 'Central Angoniland', the Dowa-Dedza area, was exposed to the full brunt of government-inspired labour recruiting campaigns but with very different results from those that the government envisaged. In 1897, between 4,000 and 5,000 men from the area were said to be working as porters and labourers in the Shire Highlands but many more crossed the border into North-east Rhodesia as a form of escape and signed on with labour recruiters there.[41] Hut tax, in particular the differential labour tax introduced in 1902, was thus an important factor in propelling men into the labour market. However, in many areas it gave strength to an existing movement rather than creating it from scratch.

The shift in policy concerning labour migration throws light on the complex inter-relationship between metropolitan and colonial interests. In the early years, the colonial Government used various means to stem the flow with the aim of ensuring an adequate labour supply for local settlers. Sharpe pressed unavailingly for the introduction of a pass system and, when this was rejected by the Colonial Office, demanded that labour agents should receive official permission before they signed up workers.[42] The dramatic change in 1903 involved a shift both in imperial and colonial attitudes. From the metropolitan perspective, the central development was the acute labour crisis confronting the Transvaal gold mines following the end of the South African war. Both the Transvaal Chamber of Mines and the High Commissioner Lord Milner made appeals to the Colonial Secretary Joseph Chamberlain, who in turn pressurised the Foreign Office to permit the Witwatersrand Native Labour Association (WNLA or, more popularly, Wenela) to recruit in Nyasaland and Northern Rhodesia.[43] Alfred Sharpe and the Nyasaland Government were initially opposed to the proposal but, with the collapse of the coffee-based plantation sector in 1902, they withdrew their objections on condition that Nyasaland benefited financially from the arrangement. An outbreak of famine early in 1903 in the notoriously drought-stricken Lower Shire Valley provided the pretext for action. Following representations from Sharpe and the Acting Governor, Major Pearce, the Foreign Secretary Lord Lansdowne gave permission on 19 March for 1,000 labourers to be recruited for the Transvaal mines at wages of 30 shillings a month – nearly eight times more than they could hope to receive in their homeland. It was agreed in addition, that 10 shillings per migrant would be paid to the Administration, a useful supplement to its perilously low revenues, and that the mines would pay the annual hut tax of six shillings a man as well as paying four shillings for the maintenance of each family. There would be a system of deferred pay with three-

---

[40] McCracken, *Politics and Christianity*, pp. 115–16.
[41] *BCAG, 15 May 1897;*
[42] Krishnamurthy, 'Economic Policy', p. 396; Boeder, *Sharpe,* p. 78.
[43] Krishnamurthy, pp. 396–97. This is expanded in B. S. Krishnamurthy, 'Land and Labour in Nyasaland, 1891–1914', Ph.D. dissertation, University of London, 1964, pp. 232–39.

quarters of the wages being paid back in Nyasaland at the end of the contract.[44]

On 17 June 1903, the first group of 380 workers, all drawn from the humid Lower Shire Valley, arrived on the Rand after an arduous steamer journey to Delagoa Bay and from there by train to Johannesburg. Exposed to the extremes of a raw South African winter above ground and the intense heat of the mines below, 20 workers died of pneumonia and related diseases in the first six weeks and more than 100 were treated in hospital. Eighty-five more refused to go underground, were tried, found guilty of breach of contract and punished by fines and imprisonment.[45] This did not deter WNLA which in the course of the year sent a further 556 men to the Rand.[46] They were pioneers in a movement by which, between 1903 and 1907, 1,500 Malawians a year were recruited for the Transvaal gold mines, most of them drawn from the Dowa-Dedza area and from the north. Mortality rates among them, mostly resulting from pulmonary diseases, averaged 140 per thousand per annum, figures that compare with the carnage of the First World War.[47] Nevertheless, it was only in 1907 that the Colonial Office intervened by requesting that Malawians should not be made to work underground until three months after they had arrived on the Rand.[48] With the labour crisis beginning to ease, the mine-owners rejected this demand and suspended the formal recruitment of labour from the Protectorate. However, in 1908, in an important development, the Nyasaland government reached agreement with the Southern Rhodesian authorities for the Rhodesian Native Labour Bureau to recruit 1,000 Malawians for the Rhodesian mines on terms that allowed for deferred payment of wages.[49] Over the next two years, the RNLB recruited several thousand workers in the protectorate while WNLA, deprived of its rights to formal, government-approved recruitment, continued to sign on large numbers of Malawian workers at its base across the Mozambican border south of Dedza, prior to the resumption of organised recruiting in 1909.

It was therefore not until 1910–1911 that a determined effort was made to reverse the policy of the previous decade and suppress recruiting entirely. The first step was taken in 1910 by Alfred Sharpe who, in response to pressures from the Nyasaland Chamber of Commerce, abrogated the agreements with WNLA and the RNLB, thus ending all formal external recruiting in Nyasaland. A year later, Sharpe was replaced as Governor by Sir William Manning, a bluff soldier and staunch supporter of settler interests, who injected a new tone of urgency into proceedings. On Manning's instructions, in 1911 a circular was sent to all government officials:

> There are the most ample grounds for believing that the exodus of local natives from their own homes to South Africa is as seriously inimical to the interests of the emigrants themselves and of their families as to those of the Protectorate generally. It is therefore the

---

[44] Sharpe to Lansdowne, 11 March 1903; Lansdowne to Sharpe, 19 March 1903; Pearce to Lansdowne, 25 March 1903 in *Correspondence relating to the Recruitment of Labour in the British Central Africa Protectorate for Employment in the Transvaal*, 1903, Cmd. 1531.

[45] Boeder, *Sharpe*, p. 79.

[46] *Nyasaland Report for 1903–04.*

[47] Government of Transvaal to Col. Sec,. 6 Aug 1906; Sharpe to Col. Sec,. 29 Oct 1906, *Correspondence relating to the Recruitment of Labour in the Nyasaland Protectorate for the Transvaal and Southern Rhodesian Mines, 1908*, Cmd. 3993.

[48] Col. Sec. to Gov. Transvaal, 28 Sep 1907, ibid.

[49] Col. Sec. to Acting Gov. Nyasaland, 2 March 1908, ibid.

settled intention of this Government to discourage such emigration by every just and lawful means in its power, and District Officers should lose no legitimate opportunity of giving effect to this policy.[50]

Efforts were made to force WNLA and the RNLB, now operating on Nyasaland's borders, to abandon their activities and in an energetic campaign 1,368 migrants were fined and 167 imprisoned for leaving Nyasaland without permission.

Changes in policy, however, had little effect on a practice that, for northern Malawians in particular, had become a virtual necessity. Most of the 25,000-odd men believed to be working outside the Protectorate in 1911 had gone as voluntary workers. There was no chance of reducing their numbers significantly as long as Nyasaland's neighbours refused to place an embargo on the employment of migrants without passes. In fact, as an official at the Colonial Office pointed out:

> The truth is that Sir W. Manning is too late. The Nyasaland Government first encourages the natives to go ahead and get rich, and then hopes to be able to compel them to stay at home against their wills and the wishes of their former or future employers. It has set in motion a force which it cannot control without the help of those who have no interest in helping it to get control.

Recruitment by WNLA came to a halt in 1913, when concern about the continued high death rates from pneumonia and tuberculosis suffered by 'tropical' miners resulted in the British and South African governments banning the recruitment of labour from north of Beit Bridge (22° S). Some Malawians, however, continued to travel illegally to South Africa and many others made the journey to Southern Rhodesia, either through the auspices of the RNLB, which continued to operate from Northern Rhodesia and Mozambique, or else as independent travellers. In 1912, there were estimated to be 20,000 Malawians working in Southern Rhodesia, about 10,000 in the mines and the rest on farms and as domestic servants, clerks and policemen.[51] Salisbury, one observer claimed, was 'over-run by Nyasaland natives'.

> In the public offices, in the shops, in the factories, in private houses and hotels the better services were invariably performed by these natives. The common native language in the streets was Chinyanja.[52]

Not until 1936 was the ban on the recruitment of Nyasa labour formally lifted but during much of the intervening period, Malawians provided approximately a third of the labour on Rhodesian mines (an average of 20,000 in 1934) as well as thousands of workers on Rhodesian farms.[53]

---

[50] Governor's circular, 12 October 1911, TNA CO 525/41.
[51] Minute by J C Casson, 16 Dec 1913, TNA CO 525/56. An alternative estimate, provided by the Southern Rhodesian *Report on Public Health,* is that there were 5,000 Malawians in Rhodesian mines in 1912.
[52] C. Knipe to Acting Governor, Zomba, 11 June 1908 enclosed in *Correlating to the Recruitment of Labour… for the Transvaal and Southern Rhodesian Mines,* 1908.
[53] *Report of the Committee appointed by His Excellency the Governor to enquire into Emigrant Labour, 1935* p. 14.

Peasant production

West of the Lake, and up to the mid-1920s, most Malawians became involved in the colonial economy as migrant labourers. Further south, commercial agriculture in a variety of forms offered a viable alternative. In the 1870s and 1880s, British Indians, many of them from Gujarat or Bombay, had traded extensively in Lower Zambezia with African producers of oilseeds or sesame (used in Europe largely for cooking).[54] In this period, the ALC also purchased a limited amount of oilseeds in the Lower Shire Valley but it was not until 1892 that the trade took off. Confronted by the collapse of the peasant economy in Zambezia, Indian merchants took advantage of the armed peace enforced by the British and pushed up the Shire Valley into Nyasaland. They opened up stores in Port Herald, Chiromo, Chikwawa and (in 1894) Blantyre, providing markets for a range of cultivated and gathered items: oilseeds, groundnuts, wild rubber, beeswax and strophanthus.[55] At first it was oilseeds, cultivated by Kololo rulers and peasant farmers alike, that attracted the greatest attention. Between 1897 and 1903, the average annual value of oilseeds, almost all grown in the Lower Valley and exported by traders through Port Herald, was about £600 and more may have been carried by dugout canoe down river to Portuguese territory. By the turn of the century, however, other, mainly gathered raw materials became of greater importance. Buoyed by rising prices in Europe, there was a sudden expansion in the collection of wild rubber, again mainly from the Lower Shire, with the value exported rising from a negligible £276 in 1895–96 to £1,626 in 1901–2 and on to over £8,000 in 1910–11. By this time, wild rubber ranked third in the Protectorate's exports, behind cotton and tobacco but ahead of the old settler staple, coffee. Other items of importance were beeswax, sold by Indian traders predominantly to German companies and strophanthus, the flowering plant traditionally employed in Africa as an arrow poison but used in European hospitals as a drug to stimulate the heart. So vigorously did villagers respond to demand for these items that, in 1905, their aggregate value of £16,211 was slightly higher than that of the two leading cash crops, coffee and cotton. Not until the First World War, when the near-exhaustion of wild rubber resources coincided with the loss of the German market for beeswax, did the trade in gathered items fall away.

If the fruits of the forest were now incorporated into the expanding capitalist economy, so too was a range of foodstuffs. Trade in food in pre-colonial Malawi took place only on a restricted scale; although this was less the case in commercial centres like Nkhotakota and Mponda's which regularly supplied provisions to passing caravans. By 1892 however, peasants around both Blantyre and in the Lower Shire Valley were responding to the early introduction of hut tax by selling maize and other foodstuffs to European employers. This trade expanded in later years as a consequence of the increase in the number of carriers employed by transport companies in the Shire Highlands – up to 20,000 in 1901. As Euro-

---

[54] Newitt, *Mozambique*, pp. 318–20; Vail and White, *Capitalism and Colonialism*, pp. 64–7.
[55] Johnston to FO, 29 March 1892, TNA FO 84/2/197; *Johnston, First Three Years; Report on Trade and General Conditions… 1895–96.*

pean settlers concentrated almost entirely on the growing of cash crops, it was left to peasants to meet the new demand, sometimes by recruiting workers from more marginal areas. By the turn of the century, Yao cultivators in the Blantyre district were employing Ngoni migrants from the southern highlands to grow surplus grain; a few years later, Mang'anja chiefs in the Mulanje district were employing Lomwe women in a similar capacity.[56] By 1907, Blantyre had the largest daily food market in the country, attracting producers from miles around.[57] However, probably more surplus foodstuffs were being cultivated in Mulanje district as a result of the influx of workers building the railway. Large amounts of maize, beans, millet and cassava were grown for sale in the fertile Chiradzulu district, 'the granary of the Shire Highlands', as one official described it.[58] Further north, villagers in the Ntcheu area sold grain to workers from the Shire Highlands during the worst of the famine in 1900–1901.[59] Also, from 1895, cultivators inland from Nkhotakota grew rice to pay for their taxes. In 1904 they produced nearly 980 tons of rice, of which 500 tons went on feeding Malawian soldiers and labourers in public works, with the remainder being purchased by transport firms, planters and the railway company.[60]

Peasant production of food went largely unnoticed in colonial circles; peasant production of cotton was a matter of serious official concern. The production of cotton and of cotton cloth was still being undertaken sporadically in the Lower Shire Valley in the mid-1870s, according to John Buchanan but, in the next decade, local production of cotton declined in the face of competition from European imports. This process accelerated in the early 1890s following the establishment of colonial rule.[61] By 1894, Harry Johnston noted: 'The intro-duction of European calico has practically killed the native manufacturers, and the cultivation of cotton is now almost abandoned.' He added: 'Curiously enough, the native-manufactured cotton cloth is far superior to the European introduction, and the pattern occasionally woven a hundred degrees higher in taste than the Manchester criteria.'[62]

It was Manchester, however, both in the supply of cotton goods and in the demand for the raw material that was to dominate the cotton regime in colonial Malawi. Sporadic efforts had been made in the late 1890s to grow cotton on European estates, but it was not until the founding of the British Cotton Growing Association [BCGA] in Manchester in 1902, with the avowed aim of stimulating the growth of raw cotton in Britain's dependent empire to meet the demands of Lancashire mills, that the matter was given serious attention. Nyasaland, in the aftermath of the collapse of coffee prices, was one of the first territories to be targeted.[63] In the initial stages, the BCGA concentrated on supplying generous financial advances to settlers, leaving support for African

[56] *LWBCA*, March 1899; *CAT*, March 30 1901.
[57] Blantyre District Book, Volume 1, 1907; *Handbook of Nyasaland*, 1908, p. 51.
[58] Ibid., p. 47; S.S. Murray, *Handbook of Nyasaland* (1922), p. 96.
[59] *CAT*, 23 Feb 1901.
[60] *Report on Trade and Conditions, 1896–97; 1904–05*, Cmd. 2684.
[61] Buchanan, *Shire Highlands*, p. 127–28.
[62] Johnston, *First Three Years, March 1894*.
[63] For the most detailed account of the BCGA and it is operations in Nyasaland see Jennifer Ann Dawe, 'A History of Cotton-Growing in East Central Africa: British Demand, African Supply', PhD, Edinburgh, 1993.

growers to a small cluster of enthusiastic district officers, notably F. J. Whicker and C. A. Cardew in the Upper Shire district, who gave Egyptian cotton seed to headmen near the river to distribute to local villagers. In 1904–05 they produced a meagre 24 tons of cotton which the government bought up at a penny a pound.[64]

The arrival from Egypt in May 1905 of Samuel Simpson, an officially designated 'cotton expert', trained at Edinburgh University and sent out by the Colonial Office, led to a partial change in policy. Appointed to advise settlers on cotton growing, Simpson responded by castigating European farming practices with a professional acerbity that was to make him deeply unpopular among settlers both in Nyasaland and later in Uganda. On his first day in Blantyre he visited the plantation of the African Lakes Corporation. 'A more desolate picture was never seen', he reported. 'This was not an isolated instance, but hundreds of acres in the Highlands were in a similar deplorable state.' He related the failure of the crop directly to the inefficiency of settlers anxious to make a quick killing out of the sudden rise in cotton prices and supported by over-generous loans from the BCGA.

> Coffee prices fell, crops failed, when suddenly tempted by the high price of cotton everyone rushed into big acreages under this product. It was a general belief that no experience was essential to its cultivation and as to the most suitable varieties for the different situations, that important point does not appear to have been considered at all…. All and sundry received large grants for putting in cotton and no discrimination as to the capabilities of the applicants appeared to have been practised. In a country like this at least 75 per cent of the planters have no experience of agricultural work whatever, and would absolutely starve in most countries.[65]

Simpson's advice, that the BCGA should stop supplying settlers with loans and instead provide peasants with reliable seed and markets, was accepted only partially in colonial circles. Not until 1913 did the government come out firmly against the provision of loans and, even then, the association continued the practice for a further year.[66] By 1906, however, African cotton growing had been extended to the Lower Shire, Mulanje, and South Nyasa districts and, from the same year, the BCGA had begun to take responsibility for distributing seed. In the Upper Shire district, where markets and ginneries were in short supply, peasants tended to invest scarce family labour in food production, thus reducing cotton growing to a secondary activity.[67] In the Mulanje district, however, Yao chiefs and headmen overcame the labour problem by employing Lomwe immigrants from Mozambique to grow cotton for them. Meanwhile, in the Lower Shire Valley, peasants devised effective means of integrating cotton into their agricultural systems first by planting cotton away from the river on the same land used for food crops; later by growing cotton on the flood land exposed following the end of the rains.[68] New government-approved markets were

[64] Vaughan, 'Social and Economic Change', pp. 241–52.
[65] Simpson to C.O., 11 July 1906, TNA CO 525/13.
[66] Dawe, 'Cotton-Growing', p. 274; John Percival, Report on work of BCGA in Nyasaland, 1914, sent to Director of Agriculture, Zomba, 16 Feb 1915, TNA CO 525/65.
[67] Megan Vaughan, 'Food Production and Family Labour in Southern Malawi: the Shire Highlands and Upper Shire Valley in the Early Colonial Period', *JAH*, 23, 3 (1982), pp. 351–64.
[68] Mandala, *Work and Control*, pp. 134–35.

opened at Chiromo and at the railway terminus, Port Herald, where the BCGA built a ginnery in 1910 and production in the Valley increased, from 134 tons of seed cotton in 1910 to 705 tons in 1913 out of a total of nearly 1,200 tons produced by peasants in Malawi. There could be little doubt, as the Acting Governor, Major Pearce, asserted, '…if cotton is to be a permanent success in this Protectorate that end is much more likely to be achieved through the native cultivator than through the European planter.'[69]

Where peasant and settler agricultural interests directly clashed, however, it was still the settler who came out on top. As late as 1914, the government actively discouraged peasant production of cotton in the Blantyre and Zomba districts, the main area of European production, on the grounds that 'there is plenty of employment on the European plantations and the Native Cotton industry undoubtedly interferes with the local labour supply'.[70]

For the settler community, the decade following the collapse of the coffee industry was a period of turbulence which demonstrated just how difficult it was to establish capitalist agriculture in Malawi. The initial reaction, to rush into cotton, resulted in another devastating collapse. By late 1904 over 18,000 acres of cotton had been planted on European estates as compared with only 580 acres two years earlier. But, as Simpson described, by the time of the harvest in 1905, 'in many instances nothing remained but dead and dying remains of cotton plants.'[71] 'We all know that the past year has, for various reasons, been a disastrous one as regards the cultivation of cotton', the chairman of the Chamber of Commerce commented.[72]

Recovery, when it came, drew on separate initiatives taken by three of the most controversial settlers in the country. William Jervis Livingstone, the manager of A. L. Bruce's Magomero estate, was a short-tempered, violent man, notorious even among his fellow-planters for his brutality to estate workers, but he was also a dedicated agriculturalist who made an important contribution to the development of cotton growing in the country. In the 1890s he had been one of the pioneers in growing coffee and, when this failed, had joined with other planters in the first doomed attempt at cultivating Egyptian cotton in the highlands. The initial failure was followed by gradual success. Between 1905 and 1908 Livingstone, aided by the government cotton expert, Simpson, developed a new variety of cotton, Nyasaland Upland, well suited to Malawi's climatic conditions, which obtained a premium price on the British market. Other planters in the Shire Highlands made use of his seed and the acreage under plantation cotton expanded to 12,752 acres in the 1910–11 season (well under the acreage of 1904) and to 23,337 acres in 1911–12, by which time cotton (well over 80% grown by white farmers) had become Nyasaland's largest single export. On the main Magomero estate Livingstone opened 16 plantations, none of them large, with a total area under cotton of 5,000 acres.[73]

[69] Pearce to C.O., 13 Sep 1913, TNA CO 525/50.
[70] Minutes of meeting of the council of the BCGA with Stewart J. McCall, Director of Agriculture, Nyasaland, 19 Oct 1914, TNA CO 525/60.
[71] Simpson, 'Report on Agricultural Resources of Nyasaland, Oct 1908', enclosed in Sharpe to CO, 14 Oct 1908, TNA CO 525/24.
[72] CAT 19 Nov 1904.
[73] White, Magomero, pp.108–13; Nyasaland Protectorate Annual Reports, 1910–11; 1911–12.

With the market for cotton expanding, the question of how was it to be grown and harvested remained. Livingstone's answer, again followed widely across the Shire Highlands, was to intensify use of the quasi-feudal *thangata* system by which tenants, many but by no means all Lomwe settlers, were forced to work during the rainy season when other forms of labour were scarce. In theory, tenants were required to work for two months only, one to meet their hut tax obligation and a second in paid labour as a form of rent. No written agreements were made, however and, in practice, planters and their *capitaos* often extended the period of work by several weeks by delaying issuing the necessary tax vouchers or by increasing the number of days that a tenant had to labour. Workers were given specific daily assignments. If they were not completed to the satisfaction of the *capitao* no credit would be given for the work that had been done. On the larger estates capital was invested in ginning machinery and in ox wagons to transport cotton to the railhead. But in the fields, no machinery of any type was used; instead labourers worked with hoes and axes to clear the land and then sowed and picked the cotton by hand.

Human labour, however, while still widely employed in transporting cotton from the field to the ginnery, offered no solution to the long-term problem of shifting cash crops from the Shire Highlands to the coast. Proposals to build a railway linking the Highlands to the Lower Shire Valley went back to the mid-1890s but, in the absence of tangible government support, they failed to reach fruition. Eugene Sharrer, the classic colonial outsider, was not to be deterred. As the founder of the Zambesi Traffic Company, which ran a fleet of steamers on the Zambesi and Shire rivers in competition with the ALC, Sharrer was well aware of the benefits that a railway could bring. In December 1902, after lengthy negotiations, he obtained a concession for his newly created Shire Highlands Railway Company and the next year work on the track began. Under-resourced, it was not completed until 1908 when the first train ran from Port Herald (Nsanje) over a bridge at Chiromo and then up the steep escarpment to Blantyre, four miles from the newly created township of Limbe, where the headquarters of the railway company were based. Shoddily built, subject to frequent delays and still linked through steamers and barges to the sandbank that was Chinde rather than to an East African port such as Beira or Quelimane, the 113 mile rail line created almost as many problems as it solved. Yet with its opening, a major obstacle to the export from the Shire Highlands of cotton and, even more, of the new cash crop, tobacco, was removed.[74]

Like cotton, tobacco had been widely grown and consumed in the Malawi region prior to colonial rule, but its export had been dependent on the intro-duction of imported seed by John Buchanan in the early 1890s. However, the fledgling industry went into decline following his death in 1896. It was left to Robert Hynde, General Manager of the Blantyre and East Africa Company from 1901, to revive production, making use of curing techniques borrowed from African farmers. At first the tobacco was sold in South Africa but, in 1903, Hynde, a pugnacious Scot and outspoken critic of government policy, persuaded his Board to send out two Americans from Virginia to provide technical advice.

---

[74] Vail, 'Railway Development', pp. 366–69; C.A. Crosby, 'Railway Development in Malawi; the early years, 1895–1915' in Macdonald, *From Nyasaland to Malawi*, pp.124–32; 'History of the British Central Africa Company', TNA CO 525/208/44332.

In the same year he despatched his first consignment of tobacco to Britain.[75]

It was not until 1908 and the arrival of the Imperial Tobacco Company in Nyasaland that tobacco was launched as a major export crop. The initial impetus behind the ITC's involvement came in 1906 when it was persuaded by the British Central Africa Company to send out the young American tobacco expert, A. W. Boyd, to report on the state of the industry. Boyd was critical of the quality of tobacco marketed by the Blantyre and East Africa Company and recommended that the Imperial Tobacco Company establish its own buying organisation and factory at Limbe, close to the headquarters of Eugene Sharrer's British Central African Company – its major tobacco-growing ally – and also of Sharrer's newly completed railway. In 1908, the Imperial factory opened for business. Thereafter many planters sold their tobacco at Limbe rather than risk sending it to a broker in London. For the first time, an important international company – Imperial was by far the largest British producer of tobacco and cigarettes – had located a major part of its activities in Nyasaland. It was not until 20 years later that it would construct a comparable repacking factory in Southern Rhodesia. Meanwhile, the ITC encouraged planters to produce flue cured tobacco, although it also purchased a small amount of air and fire cured tobacco, some grown by tenants on the B&EA's estates, others by independent growers in the Zomba district.[76]

In 1908 the export value of tobacco, £9,239, was well behind that of coffee and cotton and only slightly in advance of the combined value of gathered items such as wild rubber, beeswax and strophanthus. By 1911, however, tobacco exports were valued at £42,627, still less than the value of cotton at £58,687, but much more than that of any other export. Prior to the First World War, the acreage under European-grown cotton far exceeded the acreage under tobacco (24,155 acres under cotton in 1912 as compared with just 7,441 acres under tobacco). But it is an indication of the good returns achieved by European tobacco farmers that, in almost every year from 1912, tobacco had the highest monetary value of Nyasaland's export crops. It is not surprising then that, by 1914, planters in the Shire Highlands were already beginning to move out of cotton into tobacco, although this was a process that would accelerate markedly in the immediate post-war period.

Regional responses

The new economic order affected communities in Malawi unevenly. Particularly badly hit by the colonial occupation were the most prominent members of the long-distance trading community: Yao entrepreneurs from the Lake Malawi region whose prosperity during the late nineteenth century had been based on the sale of slaves and ivory. For them colonial rule meant not only the suppression of the slave trade but also the strangulation of the trade in ivory, hastened by restrictions imposed on Africans' use of firearms and by the imposition of

[75] Colin Wilshaw, *A Century of Gold: Malawi's Tobacco Industry, 1893–1993* (Central Africana Ltd, Blantyre, 1994), pp. 7–20.
[76] Wilshaw, *Century of Growth*, pp. 21–28; W. Twiston Davies, *Fifty Years of Progress: An Account of the African organisation of the Imperial Tobacco Company, 1907–1957* (Bristol, 1957), pp. 13–17, 26–31.

customs duties. With the collapse of the caravan trade went the fall of once busy commercial and agricultural chieftaincies like Makanjira's and Mponda's which had been cosmopolitan centres of technical and cultural innovation in the 1880s when they were firmly linked to the still vibrant East African coastal economy. Twenty years later, they were impoverished rural backwaters: the construction of colonial boundaries had divided them from their markets on the coast and reoriented trade south to Southern Rhodesia and South Africa. Makanjira's chieftaincy, for example, was reconstituted on the Malawi side of the border with Mozambique by Chief Chimatilo [Makanjira VI] following the death in 1915 of the arch-resister, Makanjila V. Isolated from the new commercial centre of Blantyre, it was a shadow of its previous eminence.[77]

Some attempt was made to introduce new economic activities to the area – notably cotton growing – but with very limited results. In 1904 officials distributed cotton seed to Yao and Nyanja farmers round the south end of the lake. But within a couple of years cotton had been abandoned in this area owing to both prohibitive transport costs and the natural reluctance of households to divert family labour into the production of an inedible crop at a time when food production was less than certain.[78] In the vicinity of Mponda's (although less so in Makanjira's chieftaincy which was further from the markets), fishing for profit expanded as an alternative occupation.[79] More commonly, however, young Yao men resorted to wage labour, first as *tengatenga* porters and subsequently as policemen and as soldiers with the Central African Rifles (from 1902 the King's African Rifles). Normally they provided at least half of Nyasaland's two-battalion strength. In 1912, 344 out of 455 soldiers in the First Battalion were reported to be Yao. Many of these askaris in the earlier years may well have been ex-musketeers utilising experience they had gained on Yao raiding expeditions. But a more persuasive feature propelling them into military service was the limited range of alternative opportunities open to them, combined with the colonial stereotyping of the Yao as Nyasaland's 'martial race' par excellence, a process begun by Harry Johnston in 1896.[80]

Access to military employment, however, did little to prevent the marginalisation of Yao lakeside communities, particularly once water levels began to rise in the 1920s, inundating previously fertile land on which rice and maize had been grown. In the once prosperous chieftaincy of Makanjira, famine (*njala*) had become a yearly occurrence by the 1930s, culminating in the official designation of the district as a 'distressed area' in 1935.[81] 'The unfortunate inhabitants seem to move in a vicious circle', it was reported in 1936. 'Not only were they unable to procure a sufficiency of food but many were too weakened by hunger to cultivate their gardens and so they are again faced with the likelihood of shortage.'[82]

The Ngoni kingdoms of Mbelwa and Gomani also suffered from the colo-

---

[77] 'Tribal History', 1936, Fort Johnston District Book Vol I Part II; Abdallah, *The Yaos*, pp. 40–49.

[78] *Report on Trade and Conditions, 1903–04;* Vaughan, 'Social and Economic Change', p. 245.

[79] *Fort Johnston District Book.*

[80] McCracken, 'Authority and legitimacy in Malawi', pp. 164–66; Risto Marjomaa, 'The Martial Spirit: Yao Soldiers in British Service in Nyasaland (Malawi), 1895–1939', *JAH* 44, 3 (2003), pp. 413–32.

[81] *Fort Johnston District Book* entries for 31 March, 30 Dec 1930; 1934; South Nyasa District Report, 1925, 1930, 1933, 1939; MNA NSF 3/1/1, NSF 4/1/1–4; NSF 4/1/5.

[82] Annual Report of the Southern Province for 1936, MNA NS 3/1/6.

nial occupation, although they were equally affected by a series of natural disasters dating from the early 1890s as they were by the direct impact of colonial policies. Recent research has done much to undermine the once classic view of the Ngoni kingdoms as essentially parasitic military states. Records of early European travellers in the Kasitu valley and on the Kirk range refer to well-tended fields of maize and millet grown by Chewa and Tumbuka cultivators living under Ngoni political control.[83] Nevertheless, the over-grazing of cattle, the creation of centralised villages and the cutting down of large numbers of trees in the northern kingdom from the early 1890s resulted in the gradual movement of Ngoni settlers away from their exhausted maize fields to new land in the Mzimba district. These pressures were increased by the spread of rinderpest into northern Malawi in 1892 and the subsequent decimation of Ngonde and Ngoni cattle.[84] Much of southern Malawi was untouched by the pandemic which had spread south from Ethiopia where it had been introduced by cattle from India imported by the invading Italians.[85] But in northern Ngoniland the impact was devastating. Travelling through the area in September 1894, Robert Laws was 'very much struck by the changed attitude of the people. …The cattle plague coming southwards from Masailand has emptied many of their kraals and destroyed at one sweep their most cherished possessions.'[86] Herds recovered within a matter of years but in the interval northern Malawi was afflicted by a further succession of disasters: smallpox, killing many people, and locusts, destroying three harvests in succession.[87] Of particular concern was the impact of the woodland-based tsetse fly which carried parasites, some fatal to cattle and horses and some to humans. Up to the mid-1890s, tsetse-fly belts in the Malawi region were confined north of Dedza to the Luangawa Valley and the Vwaza Marsh. However, with wild animals recovering from the rinderpest epidemic faster than cattle, and with the movement of village populations back onto land that had reverted to bush, tsetse began to spread from the Luangwa Valley towards Kasungu. The cattle died, forcing cultivators to retreat and, in 1908 sleeping sickness was carried to Nyasaland.[88]

The colonial occupation, therefore, hit economies that were already in a state of disrepair and wrought further damage upon them. Defeated by the British in 1896, Gomani's Ngoni suffered the looting of many of their cattle after which thousands of Ngoni migrants moved into the Shire Highlands plantation economy. Although their northern cousins were spared military defeat, they too were affected by the suppression of raiding, an important activity for young

[83] Laws to Convenor, Livingstonia Committee, Feb 1879, FCSMR, 2 June 1879; J. L. Nicoll, 'Notes on a Journey to Angoniland', BCAG, 20 Feb 1894. See also Thompson, 'Origins, Migration and Settlement of the Northern Ngoni', pp. 23–6.
[84] The argument is most strongly argued by Vail, 'Making of the "Dead North"', pp. 230–65. For an alternative analysis suggesting that the extent of environmental degradation may have been exaggerated, see McCracken, 'Conservation and Resistance in Colonial Malawi', pp. 157–63.
[85] Kjekshus, Ecology Control and Economic Development, pp. 126–7.
[86] Laws to Smith, 10 Sep 1894, NLS Mss. 7877.
[87] BCAG, 2 Feb, 23 May 1894, 15 Sep 1896; Aurora, 1 April 1898; Crawshay to H.H. Johnston, 23 Sep 1893, TNA FO 2/55; Livingstonia Mission Report, 1897–98.
[88] John McCracken, 'Colonialism, Capitalism and Ecological Crisis in Malawi: a reassessment' in David Anderson and Richard Grove (eds), Conservation in Africa: People, Policies and Practice (Cambridge, 1987), pp. 63–8.

Ngoni men. In addition, in 1906 they suffered the delayed introduction of hut tax, enforced with a good deal of violence by *chikoti*-bearing policemen.[89] Like the Yao, many northern Malawians were thus forced into migrant labour. Yao Muslims from the south end of Lake Malawi possessed few readily marketable skills other than those of the warrior; whereas Tumbuka, Tonga and Ngoni migrants gained from their contacts with the Livingstonia Mission which, by 1910, was operating 446 schools in the north – nearly 40 per cent of all schools in the protectorate – as well as the influential training centre, the Overtoun Institution.[90] Thus, at least some northern migrants had access to skills of language and literacy which they were able to use to obtain positions of comparative privilege in the labour markets of Northern Rhodesia, Southern Rhodesia, South Africa and Katanga as clerks, 'boss boys', storekeepers and the like. Mission-sponsored schemes for agricultural advance were largely unsuccessful, but, by remitting money home to buy education for their families, northern Malawians were able to maintain a certain freedom of choice in places to work that was denied to most other Central Africans.[91] As 'foreign aliens' in the main urban centres, however, these northerners were particularly vulnerable to fluctuations in employment opportunity. When labour was shed from the mines of Katanga in 1915 or again on the Zambian Copperbelt in the early 1930s, it was 'foreign' Nyasas who were targeted for dismissal.[92]

Where conditions permitted, notably in the Shire Highlands, a few Africans entered the new economy as small-scale capitalist entrepreneurs. With one or two exceptions, notably that of the ivory-hunter Kumtaja who flourished in the early 1890s as a land speculator as well as a coffee-planter and brick-maker, 'the careers of these individuals showed little continuity with pre-colonial economic entrepreneurship.'[93] Most were products of the Blantyre mission, often initially employed as teachers or as *capitaos* on European estates. They invested their savings in leasehold land, made available to them by Harry Johnston against the wishes of settlers. They grew coffee and vegetables through wage as well as family labour, and speculated in retail trade.[94] By the time of his downfall in 1900, Donald Malota, a Blantyre school teacher-turned ivory hunter-turned labour recruiter had 80 acres under coffee on his Nguludi estate as well as a fine herd of cattle and a substantial amount of land under maize.[95] Joseph Bismarck, a fellow former student and teacher at Blantyre, also initially cultivated coffee on his Namwali estate before turning his attention to a range of fruit and vegetables grown especially for the European and Indian market.[96] He also operated a trading store, as did Duncan Njilima, owner of a 150 acre estate at Nsoni, near Chiradzulu, an area where several African businessmen had land. Two of these, the brothers Gordon and Hugh Makata, in 1913 employed 50 workers on a 250 acre block dedicated largely to tobacco.[97] One businessman, Paton Somanje, a

---

[89] Vail, 'Agricultural Production, Labour Migrancy and the State'.
[90] Report of the Third Nyasaland Missionary Conference, 1910.
[91] McCracken, 'Underdevelopment', pp. 202–04; McCracken, *Politics and Christianity,* pp. 132–56.
[92] Charles Perrings, *Black Mineworkers in Central Africa* (London, 1979), pp. 157–8.
[93] Vaughan, 'Social and Economic Change', p. 157.
[94] Vaughan, ibid.: pp. 157–60; Myambo, 'The Shire Highlands Plantations', Chap. 2.
[95] *CAT* 20 April 1901.
[96] Bandawe, *Memoirs of a Malawian*, pp. 60–61.
[97] McCracken, 'Marginal Men', pp. 551–2.

first generation migrant from Mozambique who farmed 200 acres near Zomba, was successful in passing on his inheritance intact to his immediate children. However, in many cases, the demands of an individual's kin group plus discriminatory tax policies and the imposition of measures restricting African access to credit or leasehold land ensured that the death of the original entrepreneur was swiftly followed by the disintegration of his estate. A distinct bourgeois class was therefore slow to form in the Shire Highlands although, as will be shown in the next chapter, a handful of African landholders continued to operate up to the First World War and beyond.

For all the transforming effects of colonialism, many Malawians from outlying districts were only marginally affected by its impact prior to the 1920s. The payment of tax was frequently avoided, particularly in areas such as the South Rukuru valley where the national boundary with Northern Rhodesia could be used to facilitate evasion. 'The open nature of the country, the facility with which natives can cross the border and the apathy of the headmen, all contribute to make tax collecting very difficult', the Resident for the Mzimba district reported in 1927.[98] Few administrators and African policemen were appointed to the Northern Province: in the early 1930s there were seven administrators and perhaps 70 policemen to cover the whole vast area from Karonga to Kasungu. Many people regularly took refuge in their garden huts whenever the tax collectors passed by.[99] Local industries, cloth, iron and salt, were all seriously affected by competition from cheap manufactured imports sold in the growing network of stores, many of them Indian-owned. The extent of the impact varied between industries and in different parts of the country, but virtually everywhere cotton cultivation and weaving collapsed, not to be replaced even at times of acute economic distress. However, iron hoes continued to be made in a few scattered districts, notably in the Chimaliro hills of the Kasungu District where new furnaces were being built as late as 1926.[100] More common was the experience of the Lower Shire Valley where iron smelting ceased at the beginning of colonial rule but ironworking continued in the hands of immigrant Mwenye artisans from the Lower Zambesi who produced hoes and other items, making use of the remains of imported iron goods.[101] Salt production as a village-organised activity declined but individual women continued to produce salt for local markets both on the shores of Lake Chilwa and along the banks of the Shire River.[102] As early as 1888, enterprising traders were bringing 'caravans of fish from Lake Chilwa' for sale at the Blantyre mission.[103] Fishing techniques appear to have been largely unaffected by the introduction of colonialism as was the vigorous trade in fish for foodstuffs between the Shire Valley and the Shire Highlands. It was not until the First World War with the emergence of a new extended market in Blantyre that significant changes in the organisation of fishing and fish trading began to take place.[104]

98 Northern Province Annual Report, 1927. MNA S1/542/28.
99 Mzimba District Book.
100 Kasungu District Book.
101 Mandala, *Work and Control*, pp.. 90–91.
102 Mandala, ibid. p. 91; Ernest Gray, 'Notes on the salt-making industry of the Nyanja people near Lake Chirwa', *South African Journal of Science*, XLI, Feb. 1945, pp. 465–75.
103 *LWBCA*, Aug. 1888.
104 McCracken, 'Fishing and the Colonial Economy', pp. 414–21.

Conclusion

In some respects, the dozen years prior to the First World War formed a period of sustained colonial economic advance, marking the increased integration of the territory into the wider capitalist system. Between 1902 and 1914 the value of Nyasaland's exports rose over 900%, from a negligible £21,739 to a still very small £200,734. Local revenues more than doubled: hut tax increased three fold, from £21,235 to £69,809, a demonstration of the still patchy extension of colonial influence. In 1914, for the very first time, the Protectorate became self-supporting in the sense that, with revenues now roughly in line with expenditure, it did not receive any imperial or BSAC subsidies.[105] By that date British sterling, first introduced in 1894, had largely replaced calico and the Indian rupee as the dominant currency. Over one hundred Africans held accounts in one or other of the four branches of the Post Office Savings Bank now open.[106]

Selective statistics, however, tell only one side of the story. With the decline in the value of gathered items, settlers in 1915 dominated the production of export crops more fully than they would ever do again. In that year 89% of all cotton and 94% of all tobacco was produced on European farms. White farmers, however, remained few in number (only 107 in 1911), lacked capital and were so plagued by the continuing problems of inadequate communications and high transport costs that they were able to survive only through a variety of desperate and ultimately self-defeating expedients. Monthly wages for adult farm workers were kept at a level lower than anywhere else in southern Africa: 3 to 4 shillings as compared to 15 to 30 shillings in Southern Rhodesia and 45 shillings in the Transvaal. Head porterage remained the main means of transport away from the railway and the lake. Tobacco, like cotton, was grown continuously on the same soil without fertilisers, with the result that, by 1914, yields per acre had fallen to 347 lbs as compared to 458 lbs in 1909: some 200 lbs less than would be regarded a reasonable yield on tobacco farms in Virginia.[107] No doubt there were exceptions to the overall trend. The Italian, Ignaco Conforzi, who arrived in Nyasaland in 1907, was an exceptionally shrewd if uncompromisingly ruthless entrepreneur with a good understanding of tobacco cultivation. But in a high proportion of cases, Simpson's judgement that 'at least 75 per cent of the planters have no experience of agricultural work whatever, and would absolutely starve in most countries' remained disconcertingly true.[108]

Other aspects of the economy also gave grounds for concern. With the exception of a small amount of cotton grown near Karonga, in the northern two-thirds of the country hardly any cash crops had been produced by 1914. Minerals, a key capital earner in neighbouring territories, were conspicuous by their absence. Small amounts of mica found in scattered surface deposits were mined by prospectors in the Dedza and Upper Shire districts in 1911, but after a brief

[105] Vaughan, 'Social and Economic Change', Table 1, 'Total Revenue and Expenditure, 1900–1918', p. 326.
[106] Murray, *Handbook*, 1922, p.185; *Nyasaland Annual Report for 1913–14*.
[107] *Report of the Nyasaland Department of Agriculture, 1914–15*, TNA CO 626/3.
[108] Simpson to C.O., 11 July 1906, TNA CO 525/13

flurry of activity, operations had come to an end by 1915.[109] In most parts of Africa during the early colonial period government revenues were drawn in large part from customs duties which expanded dramatically in line with the growth of international trade. In Nyasaland, however, this growth was so modest that customs revenues constituted only a small part of the whole. Much more important was hut tax – a direct tax on the poorest and most vulnerable members of society – which increased as a proportion of locally raised revenues from 34 per cent in 1900 to 61 per cent in 1914.[110] Major Pearce, the most strongly anti-settler of all of Nyasaland's early administrators, was in no doubt as to the unfairness of this state of affairs:

> The natives at present contribute no less than 70% of our revenue and they contribute it largely by direct taxation from which the European community is almost wholly exempt …On the other hand the great bulk of local expenditure is devoted to purposes which may or may not be incidentally useful to natives but which primarily serve the needs of Europeans.[111]

As in the rest of British Africa, about half the revenue was spent on the salaries and pensions of colonial officials. Much also went on military expenditure. Public works and medical services both made growing demands on public revenues. But as yet there was no expenditure on African education or welfare. Indeed, in an ironic twist, the pioneering investment made by Scottish missionaries in education – the one area where Nyasaland clearly outpaced its neighbours – brought little immediate returns to the Protectorate. Confronted by low wages and limited local opportunities, Malawian graduates from Livingstonia's Overtoun Institution (at this period the leading centre of post primary education in south-central Africa) were more likely to find employment in neighbouring territories such as Tanganyika, Northern Rhodesia and Southern Rhodesia than they would in the country of their birth. Early Nyasaland was not, as a recent historian has described it, a 'failed state': the government had not lost the monopoly of legitimate force, nor was it unable to carry out decisions.[112] Only in the most rudimentary manner, however, did it deliver public services.

[109] *Nyasaland Protectorate Reports, 1913–14; 1914–15.*
[110] Vaughan. 'Social and Economic Change', p.327.
[111] Pearce to CO, 14 July 1913, TNA CO 525/47.
[112] Mandala, 'Feeding and Fleecing', p. 524.

4

Religion, Culture & Society

Introduction

The large-scale adoption of Christianity, accompanied in parts of the south by the large-scale adoption of Islam, is a major theme in the history of colonial Malawi. Not only did it involve an enormous increase in the number of Malawians who identified themselves as Christians, it also resulted in the emergence of new, vibrant religious communities, authentically African in ethos yet closely linked ideologically and institutionally with Christian churches in the West. As Schoffeleers, in particular, has shown, central to the process was the growing interaction between indigenous and external religious systems and beliefs.[1] But also important was the pervading influence of Christian missions, political, social and economic, as providers of colonial education and of Western medicine. All over Africa, as Peel, the Comaroffs and others have abundantly demonstrated the engagement between agents of the new religions and African peoples had profound and complex results.[2] In Malawi, however, the exceptional weakness of the colonial state combined with the exceptional responsiveness of some indigenous societies gave a special importance to Christian missions and churches – an importance which has continued up to the present day. Partly in consequence, the changing nature and evolving role of Islam in Malawi has, until recently, been largely ignored by historians but its importance should not be underestimated. By 1928, it has been estimated that there were some 105,000 Muslims in Malawi, some living in and around Nkhotakota but the great majority situated south of the Lake, particularly in the South Nyasa (modern Mangoche) and Upper Shire (modern Machinga) districts.[3] It is with their history that this chapter will begin.

---

[1]   Schoffeleers, *Rivers of Blood;* Schoffeleers, 'The Interaction of the M'bona Cult and Christianity, 1859–1963' in T.O. Ranger and John Weller (eds), *Themes in the Christian History of Central Africa* (London, 1975), pp. 14–29.

[2]   J.D.Y. Peel, *Religious Encounters and the Making of the Yoruba* (Bloomington, 2001); John and Jean Comaroff, *Of Revelation and Revolution* (Chicago. 1991 and 1997), 2 vols.

[3]   Pachai, *Malawi*, p.179.

Islam

There is a certain paradox in the fact that the popular spread of Islam took place at a time when the secular advantages of becoming a Muslim were fast disappearing.[4] As has previously been noted, Islam in Malawi had its origins in the expansion of long-distance trade and the growing tendency of Yao chiefs to identify themselves culturally and economically with their Swahili partners from the coast. By the early 1880s, small, court-based Muslim centres complete with their mosques and *waalimu* existed not only at Nkhotakota but at Makanjira's town, where Makanjira III is believed to have been converted around 1870. Other centres were established at the towns of Mponda and Jalasi. Mponda I was buried according to Muslim rites in 1885 by which time several of his elders were said to be believers. No fully convincing explanation has been provided for why they became Muslims. But Alpers is probably right to emphasise the attraction to chiefs of Islam as a supplementary source of ritual authority and also as a means of obtaining access to Muslim teachers, literate in Arabic script, who could be employed as scribes in communications with their coastal rivals.[5] It is noteworthy that Mponda I and II both went out of their way to seek technical and medical support from Christian missionaries while ultimately turning for assistance to Islamic teachers who could be relied upon to facilitate their continued involvement in long-distance trade. By 1891 there were no fewer than twelve Qur'anic schools at Mponda's head town and perhaps an equal number of *waalimu*.[6]

As these numbers suggest, Islam was now beginning to advance as a popular movement, at precisely the time when the Swahili/Yao trading empire was beginning to collapse. One factor that may have facilitated conversion at this period was popular armed opposition to the British, evinced most spectacularly by the lengthy resistance mounted by the followers of Makanjira III between 1891 and 1895. But against this must be placed the vacillating behaviour of virtually all other Yao chiefs as well as the readiness of many young Yao Muslims to join the colonial army.

A more important factor appears to have been the gradual extension of religious syncretism involving the growing Islamisation of Yao rites of passage and, eventually, the increasing self-identification of the majority of Yaos as Muslims. In the initial phase, Muslim chiefs took the initiative in incorporating Islamic elements into the traditional *lupanda* initiation ceremony for boys and transforming it into *jando* as a gateway both to adulthood and to Islam. However, by the early years of the twentieth century, the lead was being taken by itinerant *sheiks* or teachers, such as Abdullah bin Haji Mkwanda, who travelled throughout the southern lake region, as Bone has noted, 'giving instruction

---

[4] This section is largely based on the following: David S. Bone, 'Islam in Malawi', *Journal of Religion in Africa*, 13, 2, 1982, pp. 128–138; Edward A. Alpers, 'Towards a History of the Expansion of Islam in East Africa: the Matrilineal Peoples of the Southern Interior' in Ranger and Kimambo, *Historical Study*, pp. 172–201; David S. Bone (ed.), *Malawi's Muslims: Historical Perspectives* (Kachere, CLAIM, Blantyre, 1900). See also Augustine W.C. Msiska, 'The Spread of Islam in Malawi and its Impact on Yao Rites of Passage, 1870–1969', *SOMJ*, 48, 1 1995.

[5] Alpers, 'Towards a History of Expansion of Islam', pp. 186–7.

[6] McCracken, *Politics and Christianity*, pp. 39–41, 55.

about Islamic belief and practice, teaching people how to transliterate Arabic in order to read the Qur'an, disseminating literature, establishing mosques and training up young men as *mu'allims* and *sheiks*.[7] As in some Christian communities, Yao practices in inheritance, divorce and marriage continued virtually unchanged. But by 1910 Islam had become fully rooted as a popular religion with mosques established in most Muslim villages and Ramadan regularly observed. Many Yao men had now taken to wearing caps and robes as a demonstration of their Islamic identity; few if any women, however, had adopted the *hijab*. At this time, Islamic brotherhoods (*tariqua*) had only recently reached Lake Malawi from the East Coast. Over the next two decades, however, they spread widely, first in the form of the Shadiliya and later of the Qadiriya, Islam's oldest and largest *tariqua*. It was through the disciples of these brotherhoods that the esoteric ritual of *sikiri* (known in East Africa as *dhikr*) was carried to southern Malawi where it was regularly performed at funerals, marriages and other festivals.[8]

At Nkhotakota, meanwhile, religious expansion took a slightly different course. There, right through the 1890s, Islam had remained largely the preserve of Swahili and Yao traders who made little attempt to proselytise among their Chewa neighbours.[9] From the early years of the twentieth century, however, Islam began to spread as a result of the growing popularity of the Muslim *jando* initiation ceremony.[10] The crucial event appears to have been the introduction of the Qadriya by a remarkable woman, Sheikh Mtumwa binti Ali. The daughter of a slave mother and Swahili father, Sheikh Mtumwa built up a large and enthusiastic following at Nkhotakota on her return from Zanzibar in the late 1920s.[11] In 1931 it was estimated that there were 4,000 Muslims in the district. However, this was a modest number in comparison with the roughly 70,000 Muslims, almost all of them Yao, recorded in the South Nyasa and Upper Shire districts in the same year or in the smaller but still significant number of Muslims recorded in the Zomba and Chiradzulu districts.[12]

In Malawi, in contrast to the situation on the Tanganyikan coast, converts to Islam tended to become economically and educationally marginalised within the emergent colonial society.[13] Muslim teachers continued to operate *madrassas* (elementary Quranic schools) in a number of villages. But the rudimentary education provided did not equip pupils with the basic skills, including literacy in the western script, now in demand in the new Western-dominated economy. In Tanganyika, the German government went out of its way from 1892 to open secular, Swahili-speaking government schools to which coastal Muslims flocked.[14] But in Nyasaland, Western education remained a monopoly of the Christian missions right up to 1928 when the government acceded to pressure

7   Bone, 'Outline History of Islam, p. 17.
8   Alan Thorold, 'The Yao *Tariqa* and the *Sukuti* Movement' in Bone (ed.), *Malawi's Muslims*, pp. 90–112.
9   R.G. Stuart, 'Christianity and the Chewa: the Anglican Case 1885–1950'. PhD dissertation, University of London, 1974, pp. 112–13.
10   Stuart, 138–39.
11   Thorold, 'Yao *Tariqua*', p. 93.
12   S.S. Murray, *Handbook of Nyasaland* (Zomba, 1932), p. 154. See also Bone, 'Development of Islam and Response of Christian Missions' in Bone, *Malawi's Muslims*, p. 135.
13   Bone, 'Modernists and Marginalisation' ibid., pp. 70–75.
14   Iliffe, *Modern History*, pp. 208–9.

from several Yao chiefs by establishing small experimental schools in the Liwonde and Fort Johnston districts. These, however, failed to recruit competent teachers and did not succeed in overcoming the suspicions attached to any institution thought to be connected with Christianity. In 1930, for example, the average attendance at the government school at Jalasi's village was only 21; two years earlier fewer than 1,000 pupils, almost all of then non-Muslims, were attending officially recognised schools in the Liwonde District. The District Resident reported that the standard was 'so poor that it is worse than useless and most disheartening to any who aspire to enlightenment'.[15] Muslims accordingly remained disadvantaged in terms of access to jobs requiring education such as those of teacher and clerk. It was to be as policemen and soldiers, house servants and watchmen, fish traders and tailors that they would find a place within the colonial economy.[16]

The emergence of Christian communities

It was of crucial importance to the later history of Malawi that significant Christian communities emerged there earlier than anywhere else in British-controlled Central Africa. Livingstonia's involvement in Tongaland and northern Ngoniland dates back to the early 1880s when permanent stations were established at Bandawe (1881) and Njuyu (1882). Among the lakeside Tonga, fear of the Ngoni combined with the internal competitiveness of their society led headmen to compete with each other in seeking to cement an alliance with the mission by attracting schools and teachers to their villages. In northern Ngoniland, however, relations between the paramount chief Mbelwa and the mission were often strained, with the Ngoni seeing Livingstonia both as a potential ally and also as a source of instability. As interpreter and negotiator, the Lovedale evangelist William Koyi won the respect and affection of Ngoni councillors. However, it was not until 1890 that the first Ngoni converts were baptised, by which time there were only four schools in the district with some 300 pupils enrolled.

The subsequent expansion of popular Christianity can be related in part to the changing economic and political circumstances facing the Ngoni but it also involved attempts to adapt Christianity to Ngoni religious values and needs.[17] Confronted by new epidemic diseases such as rinderpest, by the enforced ending of raiding, the threat from Johnston's army, and the growth of labour migration, Ngoni and Tumbuka alike in the 1890s sought out new sources of spiritual power but did so in terms that did not involve a wholesale abandonment of traditional beliefs. An early example of Christian adaptation came in the drought-stricken rainy season of 1885–86, when the pioneer missionary Walter Elmslie acceded to requests from councillors that he should pray for rain, only to find himself acknowledged by the Ngoni then and for several years to come as one of their most prestigious rain-callers. This initiative, however, was overshadowed in the

[15] File entitled 'Educational Facilities for Mohammedans', MNA S1/1067/28; Fort Johnston District Book; Resident Liwonde to Director of Education, 7 June 1928, MNA S1/1067/28.
[16] Bone, 'Development of Islam', p. 138.
[17] The analysis here follows Thompson, *Christianity*, pp. 30–99 and McCracken, *Politics and Christianity*, pp. 73–99, 114–31.

1890s by the remarkably rapid spread of schools and teachers throughout the kingdom, signifying not only a popular demand for the skills associated with Western education but also a growing interest in the new religious concepts that the teachers had to offer. Between 1893 and 1899 the number of schools in Ngoniland grew from 10 to 45 and the highest attendance from 630 to 7,766. There and on the lakeshore, indigenous evangelists such as Yakobe Msusa Muwamba and Stefano Mujuzi Kaunda conducted preaching tours in villages where they answered many inquiries concerning Christianity.

The breakthrough came in Tongaland, the area of greatest social dislocation, not long after missionaries preached for the first time in the local language Chitonga rather than the Chinyanja they had brought from Cape Maclear. Writing from Bandawe in July 1895, Alexander Macalpine reported: 'The most striking feature in the past half year has been the awakening of the people around to a deepened interest in the Gospel message.' Six months later, he noted: 'The very remarkable religious revival … is still with us.'[18] More than 1,000 people, men and women alike, regularly participated in church services at Bandawe and, as in Ngoniland, there was a dramatic increase in numbers attending school: from 1,600 in 1895 to perhaps 5,000 in 1898. The number of catechumens seeking admission to full church membership increased to over 300 in 1895 and over 600 a year later. Meanwhile, Christianity spread to villages in the northern part of the district where the only contact with the mission was through itinerant evangelists. By 1897, when more than 2,000 people gathered at Bandawe to take part in a sacramental convention, Christianity had become established as a genuinely popular movement inspiring a further wave of evangelical expansion almost entirely pioneered by Tonga Christians. Within a matter of years, Tonga teachers and evangelists had made their way to Kasungu, where they opened a school in 1897, three years before the arrival of the first European missionary. They had travelled to Mwenzo in Northern Rhodesia, first visited by John Afwenge Banda in 1895. They had also trekked into the Luangwa Valley where from 1899 Tonga, Tumbuka and Ngoni evangelists worked for several months each year among the Senga people. They were followed by David Kaunda, father of Kenneth Kaunda the first President of Zambia, who began preaching to the Bemba people in the Chinsali district of North Eastern Rhodesia in 1904, inaugurating a long ministry that was to last until his death in 1932.[19]

Meanwhile, a popularly rooted Christian community was in the process of creation in Ngoniland. Donald Fraser, an exceptionally sensitive and innovative missionary, arrived at the recently-opened station of Ekwendeni in January 1897, by which time the popular movement in Tongaland was already well under way. Fraser's contribution was to give his blessing to the proliferation of schools as instruments of evangelisation while, at the same time, giving cautious encouragement to the emergence of an indigenous church, drawing at least in part on traditional religious sources. From May 1898 he held annual sacramental conventions, conducted in an atmosphere of high emotion, lasting five days at a time and drawing congregations several thousand strong. As Thompson has

---

[18] Livingstonia Mission Report, Jan–June 1895, p. 5; July–Dec 1859, p. 8.
[19] For the most comprehensive account of Kaunda see At Ipenburg, *'All Good Men': the Development of Lubwa Mission, Chinsali, Zambia, 1905–1967* (Frankfurt am Main, 1991).

suggested, Fraser's model was probably the Scottish Highland communion conventions he had witnessed in his youth. But to the Ngoni, these annual celebrations of baptism and communion may well have brought back memories of the Nguni *incwala* First Fruits ceremony during which the Chief had been ceremonially washed.[20] At all events, these years marked a remarkable expansion in the church. As late as 1892 there were only eleven converts in Ngoniland, but in 1898 no fewer than 196 adults and 89 children were baptised in a day and by 1899 this figure had increased to 309 adults and 148 children. In that year, 662 church members took communion at the climax of the convention. They did so in the presence of more than 6,000 of their fellow tribesmen, many of whom had travelled from a distance to be present. By this time, hymns composed by local Christians, some of them set to traditional Ngoni tunes, were being regularly used in church services.[21] They contributed to the creation of an Ngoni/Tumbuka church, Presbyterian in form yet incorporating certain elements of Ngoni culture. By 1909 this church had been divided into two kirk sessions, Ekwendeni in the north and Loudon (modern Embangweni) in the south, linked to no less than 238 village schools, by far the largest number of schools in any single district in Malawi. Bandawe, also under Livingstonia's control, came second with 138 schools, more than the total number of schools (121) run by the Blantyre Mission in the south. Figures for Christian adherence, always highly problematic, suggest that in Tongaland and Ngoniland by 1914 there were over 6,700 church members with a claimed Christian community of 25,000, far greater than in anywhere else in Malawi.[22] Although men monopolised official positions in the church, both as ordained ministers, from 1914, and as elders elected to kirk sessions and the presbytery, the role of women was not insignificant. From 1901, in response to Fraser's promptings, female elders, later known as *bararakazi*, took an active part in Ngoniland in settling disputes and supervising morals among women.[23] They acted as a model for subsequent communities of Christian women, notably the body, Chigwizano cha Amayi a Chikristu, founded by the Dutch Reformed Church Mission in 1939.[24]

The emergence in northern Malawi of Christian communities, Scottish Presbyterian yet African, universal yet local, coincided with a second wave of missionary expansion which resulted in the undermining of the Scots' Christian monopoly. By the early 1890s two additional missions had entered the region. One was the UMCA, initially in the person of W. P. Johnson who began evangelising on the east coast of Lake Malawi in 1881. Four years later, in 1885, the mission launched a steamer, the *Charles Jansen*, on the lake and established a port, station and diocesan centre on Likoma Island. From there the steamer functioned as a key instrument of evangelisation, connecting the mission to a chain of lakeside villages and stations, many in increasingly Islamised areas, including Nkhotakota (opened in 1894), Mponda's (1896) and Malindi (1898).[25] A second steamer, the *Chauncey Maples*, was launched in 1901.

[20] Thompson, *Christianity*, pp. 88–94.
[21] Ibid., pp. 147–50.
[22] Fraser, *Livingstonia*, p. 85.
[23] Thompson, *Christianity*, pp. 162–3.
[24] Isabel Apawo Phiri, *Women, Presbyterianism and Patriarchy: Religious Experience of Chewa Women in Central Malawi* (Kachere Monograph, Limbe, 1997), pp. 71–90.
[25] Goode, *Steamer Parish*, pp. 77–78; 81–91; 107–22.

One special feature of the Nyasa diocese was the role of African teachers and priests, several of them freed slaves, most non-Malawians, who had been trained at Kiungani, the UMCA college on Zanzibar. By 1885 the first four Kiungani teachers were at work on Likoma. Later they opened schools and evangelised in several lakeside villages. Muslim resistance in Yao chieftaincies ensured that progress was slow but new converts were made. Among them was Leonard Kamungu, a Mang'anja born on the east coast of the Lake, 30 miles south of Likoma, who spent several years at Kiungani before being ordained deacon in 1902. In 1909, after further training at St Andrew's College, Likoma, opened in 1905, Kamungu became the first Mang'anja priest (Nyasaland's first indigenous Christian minister)[26] with a parish north of Nkhotakota. The next year he volunteered to set up a new station at Msoro, near Fort Jameson (later Chipata), Northern Rhodesia. By the time of his premature death in 1913 he had established a thriving local Christian community built through Malawian missionary support.[27]

Kamungu's example was followed by other local UMCA priests, most notably Petro Kilekwa, whose life story illustrates in a particularly dramatic form the transitions experienced by many of the first generation of Christian evangelists. Enslaved as a child in about 1870 near Lake Bangweulu in Zambia, Kilekwa was marched via Lake Malawi to the East African coast, put aboard a slave-trader's dhow and then freed by a British naval vessel. After various adventures, he arrived at Zanzibar and trained as a teacher at Kiungani. In 1899 he began teaching in the Nyasa diocese before being made deacon in 1911 and priest in 1917. In the 1920s he and a group of African teachers pioneered the evangelisation of the people in the Ntchisi hills. Later, as priest-in-charge at Mkope, on the western lakeshore north of Mangoche, Kilekwa became the first African Anglican to head a mainland mission station. By the time of his death in 1966 he had witnessed the entire sequence of events leading from the era of the slave trade to British colonisation and on to the establishment of the Republic of Malawi.[28]

Relations between the UMCA and Livingstonia were predominantly those of cooperation and so too, initially, were relations between Livingstonia and the mission established in 1888 by the Cape Colony branch of the Dutch Reformed Church in opposition to those DRC clergymen who wished to confine their preaching to Afrikaner-speaking congregations. Indeed, for over a year the first DRC missionary, Andrew Charles Murray based himself at Livingstonia's stations. In 1889, however, Murray and T. C. B. Vlok founded the first DRC station at Mvera, close to the head village of the Ngoni chief Chiwere. Further new DRC stations were then opened in central Malawi, at Kongwe in 1892 and at Nkhoma in 1896, signalling the first systematic attempt to evangelise among the Chewa people. By 1899 these three stations were home to 18 missionaries,

---

[26] Kamungu, like many other Anglicans who served subsequently in the UMCA's Nyasa diocese, spent most of his working life in Nyasaland, although he was born in what later became part of Portuguese East Africa.

[27] John C. Weller, *The Priest from the Lakeside* (Blantyre, 1971). See also G.H. Wilson, *The History of the Universities' Mission to Central Africa* (UMCA, London, 1936).

[28] Petro Kilekwa, *From Slave Boy to Priest: The Autobiography of Padre Petro Kilekwa*, trans. from Chinyanja by K. H. Nixon Smith (UMCA, London, 1937); *Nkhani Zaulere: the Malawi Chatterbox*, Feb. 2007, p. 3.

81 DRC schools and nearly 400 adult church members.[29]

The colonial conquest provided the opportunity for further mission expansion. Ironically, the leading protagonist was the radical, anti-colonial pacifist, Joseph Booth, a man blessed with exceptional powers of persuasion but cursed by his inability to work with others.[30] Taking advantage of the newly established transport system, Booth travelled from England to the Shire Highlands in 1892 to found the interdenominational Zambezi Industrial Mission at Mitsidi, five miles from Blantyre, on a 26,000 acre estate purchased from the ivory-hunter, Kumtaja. In 1894 he left Mitsidi after disagreements with colleagues. But this only stimulated him to found two further missions: the Nyasa Industrial Mission, established at Likhubula in 1893 and the Baptist Industrial Mission, established at Gowa, near Ntcheu in 1895. After further disagreements, Booth turned his attention in 1897 to American churches, black as well as white, as potential new sources of funds and religious inspiration. Support came from the Seventh Day Baptist Church in Plainfield, New Jersey which financed the establishment of the Plainfield Industrial Mission near Cholo (later Thyolo) in 1900. However, when it fell into difficulties Booth switched his allegiance again, this time to the American-based Seventh-day Adventist Church which in 1902 sent him and the African-American, Thomas Branch, to take over the Plainfield Mission. The arrangement lasted only until February 1903 when, following the breakdown of relations between himself and Branch, Booth departed from Nyasaland, never to return. His legacy was four small Protestant churches or sects (three more sects inspired by Booth were to appear in the next decade) along with a network of Malawian converts who had been influenced by his personal example of non-racial behaviour along with his strongly anti-colonial teachings. In the long run, this legacy was probably less important in the shaping of Malawi than the activities of the Protestant South African General Mission, established in the Lower Shire District in 1900 and, even more, of those of the Roman Catholic White Fathers and Montfort Fathers from 1901 onwards. But, as is demonstrated in Chapter 5, in the years up to 1915 Booth's ideas and enthusiasm played a formative part in the shaping of the first wave of Malawian anti-colonial protest.

Roman Catholic missions arrived relatively late in Nyasaland but they did so with considerable energy. From his base in Bembaland, where the White Fathers had established a presence in 1896, the Apostolic Vicar, Bishop Joseph Dupont viewed the growth of 'the Protestant menace' with considerable alarm. His response was to persuade the Montfort Order, based in France and with no previous experience in Africa, to send out three priests to Nyasaland in 1901. The next year, they were followed by a contingent of White Fathers who quickly set to work among the Chewa of the Central Region. By 1905 there were five Roman Catholic stations with a combined total of 20 priests. These were Nzama, south of Ntcheu, and Nguludi, close to Blantyre, worked by the Montforts and the White Fathers' stations of Likuni, Kachebere and Mua.

Initial responses of local people to the two missions varied according to their

[29] J. L. Pretorius, 'An introduction to the history of the Dutch Reformed Church Mission in Malawi, 1881–1914' in Pachai, *Early History*, pp. 36–69.
[30] For details of Booth's career in Malawi see Harry Langworthy, *"Africa for the Africans": The Life of Joseph Booth* (Kachere, Blantyre, 1996).

particular circumstances. At Nzama, Kachebere and Mua, Ngoni chiefs went out of their way to establish good relations with the missionaries, partly as a means of using them as a protection against the abusive actions of government labour recruiters and tax collectors; partly to strengthen their authority against their Chewa subjects. At Likuni, by contrast, where Chewa village headmen dominated, the White Fathers faced an uphill task. Confronted by the hostile influence of *Nyau*, the missionaries did not make their first converts until 1909 and had to make do with catechists from other stations.[31] Catechists, often equipped with only the most basic education, took the lead at a village level in evangelisation and teaching and as leaders of the African Church. Whereas at Livingstonia, Blantyre and in the UMCA a number of African ministers were ordained prior to the First World War, it was not until the 1930s that the first African Roman Catholic priests were ordained.[32]

On the eve of the First World War, missionaries in Nyasaland numbered around 200, compared with only 107 planters and 100 government officials. The Scots Presbyterians, with their substantial congregations and impressively constructed stations, remained the dominant group. But they now had to coexist with missionaries of many nationalities and beliefs: French and Dutch priests of peasant stock, High Church Anglican scholars, Afrikaans-speaking sons of the soil, Evangelical Americans from the Bible Belt and many others as well. Although little about them appears in the literature, mission-based women were now playing increasingly important roles: as 'missionary wives', officially over-looked 'helpmeets' to their husbands but sometimes very much more, as teachers, nurses and, in the Catholic missions, as nuns.[33] The first nuns, almost all of them French, reached the Montfort stations of Nguludi and Nzama in 1904. Thereafter they taught in mission schools and used their medical training to good effect, visiting women in neighbouring villages with a freedom not open to the priests. Livingstonia's short-lived experiment in appointing a woman doctor, the redoubtable Jane Waterston, in 1879 quickly foundered on the refusal of Dr Laws to accept her as an equal colleague. However, by 1914 the UMCA had appointed 21 European women as nurses and the two Scottish missions had appointed 24.[34] At Livingstonia the first European woman teacher was not appointed until 1894. However, over the next decade nine women teachers joined the mission and only one man.

Mission education

Mission schools were important as instruments of evangelisation but even more as the purveyors of new skills and ideas that would be of fundamental importance

---

[31] Linden, *Catholics*, pp. 55–61.

[32] Ibid., p. 138.

[33] The frustrations experienced by an educated 'missionary wife' are well documented in Margaret Sinclair (ed.), *Salt and Light: The Letters of Jack and Mamie Martin in Malawi, 1921–28* (Kachere, Blantyre, 2003). For the particularly dramatic life story of a pioneer woman missionary see John McCracken, 'Class, Violence and Gender in Early Colonial Malawi: The Curious Case of Elizabeth Pithie' in *SOMJ*, 64, 2, 2011.

[34] Agnes Rennick, 'Church and Medicine: the Role of Medical Missionaries in Malawi 1875–1914', PhD dissertation, University of Stirling, 2003, pp. 332–337.

in the shaping of twentieth-century Malawi. Education in the Blantyre and Livingstonia missions consisted initially of little more than memorising the first few letters of the alphabet as a prelude to reading portions from the Bible.[35] And this was also true of the village schools opened by the DRC and the Roman Catholics with the important proviso that, among the Catholics, attention focused on memorising the catechism and on selected stories from the Scriptures rather than on the Bible itself.[36] Although Livingstonia, in 1910, thanks to its early involvement in education, still ran far more schools than any other mission (446 out of a total of 1,116), the DRC, with 244 schools, had decisively outpaced Blantyre's 121, while the Catholic missions with 105 schools between them were not far behind.[37]

Blantyre's relatively modest investment in village schools, however, must be set alongside the mission's pioneering role in providing a handful of adherents with exceptional educational opportunities. The process began as early as 1878, when Duff Macdonald sent five young men from Blantyre for training at the Free Church Lovedale Institute, the most prestigious centre of African education in South Africa. In the early 1880s further scholars were sent to Lovedale and others accompanied missionaries back to Scotland where two (Donald Malota and Kapito) spent a year at the board school in Muthill, Fife, while a third, Mungo Murray Chisuse, entered elementary classes at Stewart's College, one of Edinburgh's leading schools. Back in Blantyre, under the tutelage of David Clement Scott, these young men and others like them emerged as the male half of Malawi's first consciously 'modern' community: Christian, literate, using European names (often those of mission benefactors) and wearing European clothes, sometimes with considerable distinction. Most married Christian wives trained at Blantyre in domestic skills, and lived on the mission site in cottages 'kept clean and tidy and decorated in a most wonderful manner'.[38] Several left the mission early for higher paid employment elsewhere. But seven (one a woman, Majonenga) were set apart in 1894 as 'deacons' and received intermittent instruction from Scott in Church History, Biblical Criticism and Metaphysics as well as in Civilization, English Grammar and Maths. Their training came to an end around 1898, following Scott's departure, when the deacons' course was closed.[39]

However, by this time they were already embarked on a remarkably varied set of careers that exemplify the opportunities and hazards confronting the first generation of educated African Christians in the settler-dominated Shire Highlands. Harry Kambwiri Matecheta worked for years as an evangelist among the southern Ngoni before being ordained in 1911 as the first Malawian Presbyterian minister. Mungo Murray Chisuse spent six months back in Scotland in 1897 before returning to Blantyre where he ran the Printing Department for over a decade and became Malawi's first and still most distinguished African photographer.[40] Joseph Bismarck became an independent businessman and

35 Dr Stewart to Dr Duff, 26 Oct 1876, published in the *Daily Review*, 6 Feb 1877.
36 Linden, *Catholics*, pp. 101, 105, 139–40.
37 Memo on education enclosed in Smith to CO, 27 Nov 1916, MNA S1/1494/19.
38 *CSHFMR*, Nov 1887, p. 57.
39 Ross, *Blantyre Mission*, pp. 152–3.
40 John McCracken, 'Mungo Murray Chisuse and the Early History of Photography in Malawi', *SOMJ*, 61, 2 (2008), pp. 1–18.

3 Girls' tea party, Blantyre Mission, c.1888. David Clement Scott presides at the far end. Fine china and various Scottish delicacies are laid out before the children; education, according to the missionaries, involved the acquisition of cultural as well as academic skills.

4 Ordination of Livingstonia's first Malawian ministers, May 1914.
Front row (l – r): Yesaya Zerenje Mwasi, Hezekiah Tweya, Jonathan Chirwa.
Back row: A.G. Macalpine, Walter Elmslie, Robert Laws

estate-owner from the late 1890s. John Gray Kufa left mission employment to work as hospital assistant on the Bruce estates at Magomero, a move that was to bring him into contact with the worst excesses of settler colonialism. From there it was a short step to involvement with John Chilembwe and his Providence Industrial Mission and participation in the 1915 rising.

Scott's visionary but largely unstructured initiative was important for the provision of new forms of educational opportunity in the Shire Highlands. But it was in the north that the major institutional advance took place. Protestant missionaries in the 1890s were divided on the desirability of introducing Western 'civilisation' to Africa alongside Christianity. Some, like Bishop Smythies of the UMCA, emphasised the need 'to distinguish very clearly between Christianising and Europeanising. What we want is to Christianise them in their own civil and political conditions; to help them develop a Christian civilization suited to their own climate and their own circumstances.'[41] Others, like Robert Laws at Livingstonia, took the alternative view. In the Overtoun Institution, founded at Khondowe in 1894, Laws set out to create a tech-

---

[41] Gertrude Ward, *The Life of Charles Allan Smythies* (London, 1898), p. 4.

nical and educational college comparable with the best in Scotland and composed both of industrial departments providing training in engineering, telegraphy, carpentry, building and printing and also of a school to train teachers, medical assistants and theology students.[42] By 1904, 130 apprentices were being trained in the industrial departments on five year contracts. Three years later, there were 218 students taking full-time classes at the college, of whom 70 were being trained in the Upper School as certificated teachers. Others were being trained on the theological course, designed for prospective ministers. There were also courses in Medicine and Commerce for medical assistants and office workers and one in Arts, aimed at the most academically successful students, providing instruction in Greek and Latin as well as in English Language and Literature, History, Psychology, Philosophy and Mathematics.

All this did little to stimulate the rural economy of the north. But it did mean that Livingstonia graduates were much in demand by European employers, both in Nyasaland and beyond. From 1897, when the first two trained telegraphists took up employment in Zomba, there was a steady flow of skilled workers to the south. Livingstonia-educated clerks were regularly recruited by the Northern Rhodesian government. Others, including the future trade union leader, Clements Kadalie and the Watchtower evangelist, Eliot Kamwana, obtained employment in such administrative and commercial centres as Bulawayo, Salisbury and Cape Town.[43] Much of the education they had received was culturally biased and involved the excessive acquisition and regurgitation of facts. Nevertheless, it equipped the most able with skills of language and literacy open to few other Africans in the southern African interior.

By 1914, most of the major features that were to distinguish Western education in Malawi throughout the colonial period were already in place. First, as in much of colonial Africa, education remained the preserve of Christian missions, consisting in 'religious instruction in preparation for baptism', as the historian of the Catholic missions has noted, provided through a network of simple bush schools. As in Islamic schools, teaching was predominantly 'a matter of chanting after the teacher', who himself would quite often have had only the most rudimentary training.[44] In 1905 the Dutch Reformed Church had 14,000 pupils on its rolls but spent only £100 on them.[45] Government grants-in-aid date from 1907 when a grant of £1,000 was paid, of which £250 went to Livingstonia and £250 to Blantyre. But government-authorised curriculae and inspections were only introduced later, in 1926, following the appointment of the first Director of Education.

Literacy, perhaps the most sought-after aspect of education, therefore remained inseparably associated with the Christian story. At Livingstonia, Laws was insistent that:

> The Bible, blackboard, note book, diagrams, and pictures should be the means of study; to know the Bible, rather than to know about it, the aim of study; while to use it in the

[42] McCracken, *Politics and Christianity*, pp. 132–56.
[43] For Kadalie, the founder of the mass-based Industrial and Commercial Workers Union of South Africa, see Clements Kadalie, *My Life and the ICU: The Autobiography of a Black Trade Unionist in South Africa* (London, 1970).
[44] Linden, *Catholics*, p. 139.
[45] Iliffe, *Africans*, p. 222.

closet, the class-room and in the village should be the purpose and object of such study.[46]

One consequence of this Bible-focused approach was the remarkable emphasis placed by Protestant missionaries, often working closely with African intellectuals, on the transcription of dialects into written languages and the provision of translations of appropriate texts. As early as 1884 Robert Laws produced a version of the New Testament in Chinyanja, although this was to be replaced in 1907 by an improved new version, composed by the DRC missionary William Murray, who also played a large part in the first complete translation of the Old Testament into Chinyanja, published in 1922.[47] Alexander Hetherwick published an early version of the Gospels in Yao, while in the north, Noa Chiporupa, one of the most distinguished of Malawians actively involved in this task, translated St Mark's Gospel into Chitonga.[48] Livingstonia missionaries were slow to encourage the use of Chitumbuka with the result that Bishop Colenso's famous Zulu Bible continued to be bought and read by older Christians well into the 1920s. In the early 1930s, however, Charles Chinula's influential Tumbuka translation of John Bunyan's *Pilgrim's Progress* was published to be followed, many years later, by Samuel Hara's translation into Tumbuka of the Zulu Bible.[49]

The result, as it related to Malawian intellectual influences, is difficult to overestimate. At Blantyre and Livingstonia, from the early 1890s onwards, Christians made considerable financial sacrifices to purchase English and Zulu Bibles as well as portions of the Scriptures in local languages but read virtually nothing else. By 1910 a total of 21,036 copies of the new Nyanja New Testament had been sold; sales of mission-produced indigenous-language newspapers had been derisory. In 1917 only 17 copies of *Pilgrim's Progress* were sold at Blantyre.[50] As was strikingly revealed in the aftermath of the Chilembwe Rising of 1915, educated Christians, whether members of the Scottish churches or of smaller missions, drew on an encyclopaedic knowledge of Biblical texts in justifying their political behaviour but, with few exceptions, had little knowledge of socialist or pan-Africanist ideologies. Even in the 1930s, Malawi was exceptional in the extent to which political activists drew inspiration from the Bible rather than from secular ideologies.

A second feature of missionary education as experienced by the 1920s was the marginal position allocated to women. Pioneer missionaries like Robert Laws were convinced that Christianity, with its prohibition of polygamy, would have a particularly liberating impact on women; however, this proved to be far from the case. During the years of violence in the 1870s and 80s, mothers with children and single women, cut off from their kin, frequently found in mission stations the security denied to them elsewhere. But the education they received was essentially domestic in nature, aimed at ensuring that they would become good wives for Christian husbands. At Cape Maclear, under Margaret Laws's instruction, women were trained in making dresses and washing pots (although

[46] Robert Laws, 'Memorandum regarding the Organisation and Development of the Livingstonia Mission', 1892, printed in *The Livingstonia Mission, 1875–1900*, NLS.
[47] Retief, *William Murray*, pp. 96–104.
[48] A.G. Macalpine, Account of Experiences with the Livingstonia Mission, EUL.
[49] D.D. Phiri, *Malawians to Remember: Charles Chidongo Chinula* (Blantyre, 1975), pp. 19–20.
[50] Article on 'Literature for the Native', *LWBCA*, April-July 1918.

Laws admitted that, in their villages, pots, other than the *nsima* pot, were kept scrupulously clean).[51] At Blantyre, resident women were employed in washing clothes in the laundry and in making bedcovers and petticoats.[52] Girls filled up to 30–40% of places in village school elementary classes. But many were withdrawn during the rains to help in hoeing; most, as they grew older, were denied school fees by their families. At the Overtoun Institution only 27 girls were examined out of 193 pupils in 1900, five out of 110 in 1905 and none at all in the next four years. In the years up to 1914, nine out of 19 Scottish teachers employed by the mission were women; Nyasa women teachers, by contrast, were rarely recruited. In 1927 only 13 women were so employed as compared to 1,403 men.[53] As late as 1911, the only fully trained woman teacher in the UMCA's Nyasa diocese was the Tanzanian Kathleen Mkwarasho, who had been educated at the girls' school on Zanzibar before coming with her husband to Likoma. Around 1900, Mkwarasho spent some time as schoolmistress in charge at Likoma after the only European woman teacher had departed. Other UMCA women teachers were said to lack 'the small amount of knowledge really necessary to teach even our elementary scholars'.[54]

Women's education in the Roman Catholic missions was also undeveloped. In 1924 the White Fathers founded a boarding school at Kachebere but no girls from Nyasaland could initially be persuaded to attend. In a striking development, the first religious order for women in Nyasaland was started in the 1920s by the Montforts at Nguludi. Women proved easier to attract to a life of celibacy than men but numbers at first were small. Taught to read, write and sew, seven Sisters took their religious vows in 1928. Four of them stayed at Nguludi, to cook and care for orphans. The remaining three, so Linden notes, 'were sent to the new European girls' boarding school at Limbe to perform menial tasks'.[55] By this date some African churchmen associated with the leading Protestant missions had begun to comment on the absence of training facilities for women. But there is little evidence to suggest that they were committed to significantly extending opportunities.[56]

The third distinctive feature of missionary education in Nyasaland was the extent to which it varied in both quantity and quality in different parts of the territory. Raw statistics on the number of schools must be treated with considerable caution. But what the figures for 1915 collected by the government suggest is that the greatest number of schools was in the Ngoni/Chewa heartland of the Central Region, where competition between the Dutch Reformed Church and the Montforts and White Fathers was intense. This was followed by the 500 schools run by Livingstonia in the north, the area probably with the highest school to population ratio, and then by the Shire Highlands, where Blantyre was now exposed to competition from over half a dozen other missions. By contrast, there were relatively few mission schools in the Lower Shire Valley, although

---

[51] Robert Laws, *Women's Work*, pp. 8, 18–20.
[52] *LWBCA*, May 1889.
[53] Donald Fraser, *Livingstonia* (Edinburgh, 1915), pp. 86–88; McCracken, *Politics and Christianity*, p. 253.
[54] Dora Williams, *What We Do in Nyasaland* (Westminster, 1911), pp. 33–4, 192.
[55] Linden, p. 174.
[56] Resolutions of the Native Session in attendance at the 5th General Conference of the Federated Missions of Nyasaland, 1926, MNA Liv. Corr.

this was to begin to change from 1921 when the Catholics established a mission at Nsanje in competition with the South African General Mission. In areas where Islam was strong, round the south of Lake Malawi and in the hills to the east, mission schools also remained few in number, despite the best efforts of the Anglicans. From the mid-1870s onwards, Mponda's chieftaincy was subjected to Christian evangelisation, first from Scottish Presbyterians, then from French White Fathers and later from English members of the UMCA. Yet in 1914 it was described as 'almost the hardest station in the Mission', with hardly a pupil at school.[57]

Table 4.1
Nyasaland: Number of Schools, 1910 and 1915

Mission	1910	1915
Livingstonia	446	514
Blantyre	121	239
DRCM	244	610
UMCA	61	108
Marists	44	217
White Fathers	63	160
SAG Mission	3	23
7th-day Adventists	3	40
Nyasa Indus Mission	28	41
Baptist Ind Mission	25	33
ZIM	78	79
	1,116	2,064

For the most ambitious Malawian Christians, quality was more important than quantity and quality, even at this time, was seen above all as proficiency in English. The various factors which contributed to the influence of the Overtoun Institution at Livingstonia and, from 1909, of the Henry Henderson Institute at Blantyre have already been discussed. They included a commitment to a high standard of academic education, a belief in the importance of English, not held prior to 1914 by the DRC and the Roman Catholic missions, the provision of a structured system of village and district education, out of which the best students and teachers came, and a growing recognition among such students of the tangible advantages of proficiency in language and literacy to migrants entering the southern African labour market. A further feature that would appear to have grown in importance between the wars, at a time when both Scottish missions were suffering a decline in educational ambition and resources, was the tenacity demonstrated by individuals educated at Livingstonia and Blantyre in passing down to the next generation of family members some of the skills that they had acquired. More research is required on the subject but it looks to be the case that, where educational resources were limited, advantages accrued to fami-

---

[57] Memo on education enclosed in Smith to CO, 27 Nov 1916, MNA S1/1494/19; A.G. Blood, *The History of the Universities' Mission to Central Africa*, Vol. II (UMCA, Westminster, 1957), pp. 62–63.

lies with a tradition of literacy where English was regularly spoken.[58] In that sense, mission education in Malawi, as in many other places, both created opportunities for the marginalised and reinforced advantages for the relatively privileged.

Missionaries, medicine & disease

Missionary education had an immediate and tangible impact on Malawi; missionary medicine did not.[59] Among church-goers in Britain in the late nineteenth century, the missionary doctor was often depicted as a Christ-like figure, dissolving ignorance and superstition through the application of Western science; the reality, however, was different. Sixteen out of the 70 European staff employed by Livingstonia between 1875 and 1900 were medically qualified. However, far from carrying Western medicine into outlying villages, most pioneer doctors, confronted by a hostile disease environment, were predominantly employed in largely unsuccessful attempts to maintain the health of their missionary colleagues. In the quarter century up to 1900 no fewer than 21 Livingstonia missionaries died, the great majority from malaria and its complications, and eleven were invalided home. Those Scottish missionaries who survived often owed their lives to the care and support of their Malawian associates, a circumstance that could result in the narrowing of the social divide between them but which was hardly conducive to an enhanced respect among Africans for the efficacy of the medicine Scots missionaries had to offer.[60] At Cape Maclear, Laws dressed tropical ulcers, handed out simple medicines, pulled a number of teeth and conducted a few cases of minor surgery, at least one involving the use of chloroform. Overwhelmingly, however, Africans treated Western medicine as a last resort among a variety of approaches, one normally not resorted to until other healing systems had failed. Diseases continued to be regarded as falling into two broad categories: those that resulted from human malice or breach of custom, normally investigated by a witchcraft specialist, and those diseases regarded as 'natural' which could be treated by a herbalist (ng'anga) making use of a wide range of herbal medicines or, by extension, by a western doctor.

The character of missionary medicine changed significantly from the late 1890s as a consequence of the development of bacteriology and the emergence of the new science of 'tropical medicine'. A key feature was the discovery of the role of mosquitoes in the spread of malaria, followed by advances in the use of quinine prophylaxis. As so often with medical advances, the consequences were far from straightforward. This was a period when a variety of new epidemics, related at least partly to colonialism, among them rinderpest, sleeping sickness,

---

[58] For an example of one such family, the Muwambas, see McCracken, *Politics and Christianity*, pp. 149–50.

[59] This section is based predominantly on Markku Hokkanen, *Medicine and Scottish Missionaries in the Northern Malawi Region, 1875–1930* (Lampeter, 2007) and on Rennick, 'Church and Medicine'. See also Charles M. Good, *The Steamer Parish;* Michael and Elspeth King, *The Story of Medicine and Disease in Malawi* (Blantyre, 1992); Vaughan, *Curing Their Ills: Colonial Power and African Illness* (Cambridge, 1991).

[60] Hokkanen, *Medicine*, pp. 193–230.

plague, influenza and tuberculosis, entered Central Africa to take their place alongside endemic disease such as malaria, smallpox, bilharzia and hookworm. What the consequences were is difficult to determine but it is generally accepted that across East and Central Africa mortality rates increased up to the 1920s although they seem to have declined thereafter.

If new developments in medicine were of little consequence to the great majority of African people, they did, however, have an effect on European immigrants, including missionaries, and on the Africans most associated with them at mission stations. The first signs of a new approach came around 1900 when doctors began insisting that Europeans should be segregated from their African neighbours, on the grounds that they, and particularly African children, were prime sources of malarial infection. Even on Likoma Island, where UMCA priests had gone out of their way to live simply in close proximity with Africans, the station was reorganised under Dr Howard to separate European houses from those of Africans.[61] In a related development, European missionaries, like Europeans in general, came to obtain access to new drugs which were too expensive to be made widely available to Africans. The consequence can be seen in the dramatic improvement in health at all three pioneer missions. In contrast to the high death toll of the last quarter of the nineteenth century, only three Europeans associated with Livingstonia, all of them missionary wives, died between 1901 and 1929. In the UMCA's Nyasaland's Diocese, where there were 22 European deaths and 22 invalidings between 1887 and 1903, there was an immediate improvement in health following the arrival of Dr Howard at Likoma in 1899 and the introduction of a wide-ranging programme involving the introduction of mosquito nets, the draining of swamps and the regular use of prophylactic quinine, a measure which W. P. Johnston opposed. By the 1920s, mission stations, like European settlements more generally, had become much more healthy environments. But they also tended to become more racially divisive, with even African ministers not being invited to share meals with Europeans.

A further development was the growth of mission hospitals, the most visible examples of the new Western scientific medicine in practice.[62] Temporary rooms had been set aside to provide shelter for the critically ill in all missions during the 1880s. But it was not until 1896 that the first genuine hospital in Malawi was constructed by Dr Neil Macvicar at Blantyre.[63] A man of unorthodox religious views, forbidden to preach or evangelise, Macvicar represented a new generation of professional missionary doctors, trained in tropical medicine, who refused to allow themselves to be seriously diverted from their medical duties. His Blantyre Mission hospital, constructed in brick with cement floors and, by 1903, with 43 beds, became a model for other mission hospitals, notably the Livingstone Memorial Hospital, founded in Zomba in 1903 with financial assistance from David Livingstone's daughter, Agnes Bruce, and the David Gordon Memorial Hospital, opened at Livingstonia in 1911, 17 years after Livingstonia's industrial and educational departments.

Similarities in layout, however, did not imply similarities in function. All

61   Good, *Steamer Parish*, pp. 267–9.
62   The argument in this paragraph follows the analysis of Rennick, 'Church and Medicine', pp. 220–239.
63   The best starting point for a study of Macvicar's remarkable career in Nyasaland is R.H.W. Shepherd, *A South African Medical Pioneer: The Life of Neil Macvicar* (Lovedale, 1952).

mission hospitals provided the opportunity for a limited number of surgical operations to be performed along with in-patient treatment. But whereas at Livingstonia and Likoma patients were normally rural villagers, referred by senior members of their lineage group, at Blantyre most patients were casualties of the new settler economy. Many in the early years were malnourished Ngoni or Lomwe carriers, far from family support and abandoned by the transport companies for whom they worked. Most, from 1901, were migrant workers on estates or with the railway company, referred to the hospital by their employers under a medical insurance system pioneered by the mission which involved employers paying a limited amount each year to have their workers treated when they were ill. At Blantyre between 1908 and 1914, an average of around 400 patients were treated at the hospital each year. Elsewhere, however, hospitals struggled to convince potential patients of the value of in-patient treatment. In 1913, Nurse Cole at the David Gordon Memorial Hospital confessed: 'Although all have a free invitation, I am sorry to say we can seldom get our two wards full. The women's ward has not had more than three or four in it, and at present there is only one woman.'[64]

The creation of hospitals made possible the training of African medical assistants. Here again, the key figure was Neil Macvicar who initiated the systematic training of medical assistants at Blantyre in 1896. Unlike the first 'dispensary boys' of the UMCA who were recruited from the ranks of patients and school boys on the assumption that the tasks that they would perform would be limited to little more than bottle-washing, Macvicar's medical assistants included some of Blantyre's best educated students, Harry Kambwiri Matecheta and John Gray Kufa among them.[65] By 1897 five assistants were employed at Blantyre, dressing ulcers, giving out medicines and taking temperatures. The next year, John Gray Kufa, following his achievement in obtaining 90 per cent in his surgical exam, established a dispensary at Mlumba in Lomweland where, within a matter of months, he had treated more than 500 patients, dressing ulcers, extracting teeth and, in a few cases, opening abscesses.[66] When the station was closed as a result of the aggressive actions of the Portuguese authorities, Kufa became chief dispenser and chloroformist at the Blantyre mission hospital before taking up employment at Nsoni.[67]

Other missions were slow to follow Blantyre's example. At Bandawe Stefano Potifar Kaunda provided simple medical assistance from 1899 on the basis of the instruction he had received from individual missionaries. However, it was not until 1904 that the first systematic medical course was opened at Livingstonia, and then only two men were enrolled. One withdrew but the second, Yoram Nkata, graduated in 1907 to embark on a long career, including a period in the 1920s in sole charge at Bandawe Hospital. Numbers, however, remained very low. Only two medical assistants were in training at Livingstonia in 1910 and four in 1926.[68] Even at Blantyre, there were only 12 medical assistants being trained in 1912 as compared with 376 trainee teachers enrolled at the Henry

[64] Annual Report, Livingstonia Mission 1913, quoted in Rennick, 'Church and Medicine' p. 231.
[65] Vaughan, Curing, pp. 64–5; Mills, What We Do, pp. 137–8.
[66] LWBCA, August 1898.
[67] LWBCA Apr–June 1901.
[68] Hokkanen, Medicine, pp. 412–19.

Henderson Institute.[69] Male African medical assistants had begun to interact with local populations over a wide area rarely visited by doctors, but there were too few to make a significant impact. Even when they were reinforced by European female nurses, of whom there were usually at least six spread over the Nyasa diocese of the UMCA as compared to a single male doctor, the results were limited.[70] Western medicine, in the 1920s as now, was concentrated in a limited number of centres, one of them being the well-equipped hospital opened in 1908 by the Seventh-day Adventists at Malamulo near Cholo. Much of the country remained untouched, despite some growth in the medical services provided by government.

Government medical support in the 1890s was almost entirely focused on its own military and administrative staff, although, by the turn of the century, it had begun to take over responsibility for the health of the settler population, with European-only hospitals being opened at Blantyre, Zomba and Fort Johnston. By 1908, the recognition that epidemic diseases could easily spread from Africans to Europeans resulted in the Government's first venture into public health. Initially on its own, and later in collaboration with the leading missions, the government responded to the spread of smallpox by embarking on a number of mass vaccination campaigns, conducted largely by African assistants. From 1908, it also put serious money into monitoring the movement and investigating the causes of sleeping sickness in the area bordering on Northern Rhodesia, a task given added urgency as a consequence of the large numbers of deaths, in excess of 200,000, incurred from sleeping sickness around Lake Victoria up to 1905. Under Dr Henry Hearsey, Principal Medical Officer from 1902, the government opened African hospitals in Zomba and Blantyre along with a number of dispensaries to supplement those provided by the missions. As late as 1919, however, only 5,222 cases were treated, almost all of them through the agency of medical assistants.[71]

With such limited facilities, the impact of Western medicine was necessarily slight. Given that malnutrition was a key underlying cause of chronic ulcers, there was no possibility that they could be entirely eradicated. However, there is some evidence to suggest that the extensive use of aseptic dressings had reduced the incidence of severe ulcers among villagers close to missions by the late 1920s.[72] Of equal significance were the campaigns against smallpox, first launched on a large scale in 1901 by Blantyre Mission medical assistants and resulting by 1903 in the vaccination of some 60,000 people in the Blantyre District alone. Waged in a highly coercive manner, involving the compulsory vaccination of villagers and the burning of huts believed to have been inhabited by those suffering from the disease, smallpox campaigns provided vivid demonstrations of colonial violence in action. But they also contributed to a reduction in the number of deaths from smallpox in the interwar years.[73] In the 1920s, improved drugs, notably the arsenical compounds, salvarsan and neosalvarsan,

[69] Rennick, 'Church and Medicine', p. 296.
[70] Agnes Rennick, 'Mission Nurses in Nyasaland: 1896–1916' in John McCracken, Timothy J. Lovering, Fiona Johnson Chalamanda (eds), *Twentieth Century Malawi: Perspectives on History and Culture* (Centre of Commonwealth Studies, University of Stirling, Occasional Paper No. 7, 2001), p. 23.
[71] Nyasaland Medical Report for 1927, TNA CO 626/7.
[72] Nyasaland Medical Report for 1928, TNA CO 627/7; Rennick, 'Church and Medicine', pp. 272–4.
[73] Rennick, 'Church and State', pp. 300–04.

proved highly effective in treating syphilis and yaws, thus resulting in an influx of people to dispensaries to demand injections. But while ultimately these drugs were to be effective in reducing the incidence of yaws, between the wars they were regarded by a number of leading missions as too expensive to use.[74]

Efforts to combat other endemic diseases were largely unsuccessful. Outside urban centres and mission stations, malaria went untreated. The significance of bilharzia first became apparent in 1910, when Dr Howard reported that about half the males in some of Malawi's lakeside villagers were infected, but doctors did little to combat the disease other than to call for improved village latrines and water systems.[75] From as early as 1882, Livingstonia medical missionaries were periodically summoned to assist in cases of difficult childbirth, almost always those where African medical specialists had been previously unsuccessful.[76] But both at Livingstonia and in other missions, midwifery services remained underused. In 1912, there were only 18 confinements at Blantyre.[77] Meanwhile, new diseases proved almost impossible to treat. The devastating influenza pandemic of 1918–19 killed more than 1,400 people in the North Nyasa district alone and perhaps 50,000 in the whole of the country.[78] Tuberculosis was virtually unknown in the country in 1900, according to Dr Howard. But after 1910 it became increasingly prevalent as the result of the return to their homeland of labour migrants who had contracted the disease while working in South African and Southern Rhodesian mines. In 1912, Dr Hearsey commented on the high percentage of returned workers suffering from tuberculosis. A preliminary investigation a year later suggested that more than three per cent of mineworkers might be affected.[79] Thereafter, the disease increased 'relentlessly', immune to any drugs available at the time. Between 1928 and 1948 notifications of cases of tuberculosis rose threefold; the total number of sufferers remained unknown. By the 1950s it had become one of the most common causes of deaths in Nyasaland.[80]

It was in the struggle against leprosy that medical missions had their greatest disappointments. The earliest leprosy settlements in Malawi were founded by the UMCA on Likoma and at Likwenu. Further settlements were subsequently developed by the Seventh-day Adventists at Malamulo, the While Fathers at Mua and the Montfort Fathers at Utale. At an early stage the government made clear that it lacked the resources to intervene directly. But from 1924, it and the British Empire Relief Association provided small grants to mission leprosaria in the belief that the drugs they provided, involving the injections of hydnocarpus oil, would cure or stabilise leprosy. With the subsequent recognition that the drugs did not work, the leprosy settlements degenerated. At Likwenu during the early 1904s Electra Dory noted that the patients 'called themselves the Dead ... Those who progressed did so slowly, often with many relapses.' Her descrip-

[74] Good, *Steamer Parish*, pp. 387–88; Hokkanen, *Medicine*, pp. 18081.
[75] Michael Gelfand, *Lakeside Pioneers* (Oxford, 1964), pp. 291–2; Goode, *Steamer* Parish, p. 231; Hokkanen, *Medicine*, p. 488.
[76] Ibid., *Medicine*, pp. 285–90.
[77] Rennick, 'Church and Medicine', pp. 283–84.
[78] For further information see Chapter 6.
[79] Nyasaland Medical Report for 1912, PRO CO 626/1; Good, *Steamer Parish*, p. 253; Gelfand, *Lakeside Pioneers*, p. 291.
[80] King, *Story*, pp. 78–80.

tion of the method of treatment through injections was equally bleak: 'We rammed – I fear that is the only word that describes the treatment – we rammed in the oleaginous product of the hydnocarpus wightiana, causing more pain and destruction than the lepra bacilli.'[81] It was not until the introduction of sulfone drugs in the 1950s that the treatment of leprosy improved.

African encounters with Christianity

When mission doctors entered the Malawi region they discovered that 'medicine', *mankhwala*, had a double meaning. *Mankhwala* was applied to the herbs and lotions that these doctors would also describe as medicines. But it was also used as a term for magical charms bringing individuals health or harm or else providing protection or success in warfare, farming, hunting or any other activity.[82] On his first meeting, in 1879, with a member of the Livingstonia Mission, the Ngoni chief Mtwalo asked '...that I should wash his body with medicine to protect him from his enemies who wished to kill him'.[83]

The ambiguity contained within the meaning of *mankhwala* was also present in the wider issue of early converts' responses to Christianity. As Iliffe has noted, nineteenth-century mission Christianity was 'an individualised, intellectualised faith which regarded many human problems – sickness and misfortune and death – either as soluble only by faith and prayer or as beyond the scope of religion and explicable only by science or chance.'[84] Indigenous religions, by contrast, were this-worldly, in that they provided the means by which the causes of unexpected misfortune or unusual prosperity could be identified and remedied. For Malawi's pioneer Christians, the growing recognition of those areas where mission Christianity could not provide specific solutions to problems resulted in the growth of eclecticism, the tendency for converts to adapt Christianity to meet their particular needs. Linden oversimplifies the process in his claim that 'Christians simply chose in the Christianity presented to them the elements that were meaningful and helpful to them, and ignored the rest.'[85] There are many accounts in the story of the growth of Christianity in northern Malawi of male converts who agonised over giving up all but one of their wives in order to become baptised, or who spoke out against the use of charms. One pioneer Malawian evangelist in the Luangwa Valley called on the local magistrate 'to seize the dancers of a village because they refused to give up dancing when requested to do so'. Another announced that if villagers continued to tend their gardens on the Sabbath, 'I shall go and take their hoes that they may not dishonour God's day.'[86]

Nevertheless, if converts sometimes took the lead in their condemnation of heathen practice, they also tended to forge for themselves an indigenous Christianity which accepted its central tenets without abandoning belief in the malevolent power of witches or the value of indigenous healing practices and of local

[81] Quoted in Iliffe, 'Poor in the Modern History of Malawi', pp. 256–8. See also Good, *Steamer Parish*, pp. 337–45; Vaughan *Curing*, p. 87.
[82] Hokkanen, *Medicine,* pp. 54–7.
[83] Kaningina Station Journal entry for 1 Oct 1879, NLS 7910.
[84] Iliffe, *Modern History*, p. 236.
[85] Linden, *Catholics*, p. 205.
[86] Quoted in McCracken, *Politics and Christianity*, p. 130.

medicines. As Hokkanen has demonstrated, in a series of discussions, starting in 1912 and lasting for several years, African ministers on the Livingstonia Presbytery succeeded in widening the debate on the issue of the proper relationship of Christians to African healing to at least tolerate the use of certain traditional medicines, whether worn for protection or consumed.[87] It was reported in 1926 that large numbers of Christians, including several elders at Elangeni, continued to wear charms as a protection against witchcraft. Many more were caught up in the anti-witchcraft movement, *mchape*, in 1933.[88] There is no means of knowing whether the missionary-anthropologist, Cullen Young was correct in his assertion, made in 1931, that teachers, civil servants and clergymen were among those northerners who were practising as *wang'anga* (defined by Young as 'dealers in drugs and charms'). But, given Young's intimate knowledge of northern Malawi, it is by no means unlikely.[89]

Popular concern over the ability of mission churches to provide answers to ordinary people's spiritual concerns was one of the features that explain the emergence of the first wave of Christian independency in Nyasaland. In those missions where the tradition of church authority was strong, as most notably in the Roman Catholic missions, independent breakaways rarely took place.[90] However, where the history of the European church was one of frequent division and reunion, as in the two Scottish Presbyterian missions, breakaways were not uncommon. At Livingstonia, disputes over church control and the slow pace of African ordination created the tensions which led to the departure from the mission of Charles Domingo in 1908. Born in coastal Mozambique, as were several other pioneer Christians in Malawi, Domingo was recruited to the Livingstonia mission as a child by William Koyi. He was educated at Lovedale, completed his theological education at Livingstonia in 1900, won a glowing reputation as a schoolteacher and in 1907 was sent to Fraser at Loudon to prepare for the ministry. The next year, however, he left the mission at the start of a journey of spiritual self-discovery which was to lead him into contact with Joseph Booth. The latter encouraged Domingo to return to northern Malawi where he and other pastors set up a network of Seventh Day Baptist churches and schools.[91]

Domingo's experiences as minister of the church would be painfully familiar to many Malawians today. A strong advocate of self-sufficiency, he was almost entirely dependent financially on the funds sporadically provided to him through Booth by the Seventh Day Baptists of Plainfield, New Jersey. His efforts between 1910 and 1914 to create a genuinely self-governing church, free from white control and yet rivalling Livingstonia in the quality of its schools, demonstrated a yawning gap between aspiration and achievement. Teachers went unpaid; school supplies were negligible; Domingo and his wife lived in penury. A critical visitation by two white Americans from Plainfield in 1912 only increased his

---

[87] Markku Hokkanen, 'Quests for Health and Contests for Meaning: African Church Leaders and Scottish Missionaries in the Early Twentieth Century Presbyterian Church in Northern Malawi', *JSAS*, 33, 4, 2007, pp. 733–50.

[88] McCracken, *Politics and Christianity*, pp. 288–82.

[89] Quoted in M. Hokkanen, 'Scottish Missionaries and African Healers: Perceptions and Relations in the Livingstonia Mission, 1875–1930', *Journal of Religion in Africa*, 34, 3, 2004, p.339.

[90] Linden, *Catholics*, pp. 180–81.

[91] The most detailed account of the Seventh Day Baptists in northern Malawi is contained in Langworthy, *Africa for the Africans*, pp. 224–73.

sense of frustration. Writing to Booth, a sympathetic ally, Domingo drew upon the Bible to develop a scathing indictment of colonial society in all its elements, economic, administrative and religious. The key passage, written in September 1911, has become one of the most frequently quoted political statements made by a Malawian:

There is too much failure among all Europeans in Nyasaland. The Three Combined Bodies: Missionaries, Government – and Companies or Gainers of money do form the same rule to look on a Native with mockery eyes. It sometimes startles us to see that the Three Combined Bodies are from Europe and along with them is a title 'CHRIST-NDOM'. And to compare or make a comparison between the MASTER of the title and His Servants it pushes any African away from believing the Master of the title. If we had power enough to communicate ourselves to Europe, we would have advised them not to call themselves 'CHRISTNDOM' but 'Europeandom'. We see the title 'CHRISTNDOM' does not belong to Europe but to future BRIDE. Therefore the life of the Three Combined Bodies is altogether too cheaty, too thefty, too mockery. Instead of 'Give' they say 'Take away from' – from 6 am to 5 or 6 pm there is too much breakage of GODS pure law as seen in James' Epistle V:4. Therefore GOD's vengeance is upon The Three Combined Bodies of Nyasaland.[92]

For all its stylistic idiosyncrasies, the passage, as Hastings notes, 'presents a quite remarkably powerful analysis of the colonial situation'.[93] Yet it is important to note that it appeared in a private letter, subsequently published by Booth in a leaflet, and not in a public manifesto. Domingo, as his most recent biographer has stressed, was activated primarily by religious rather than political convictions and by 1912 had significantly moderated his earlier radicalism.[94] It is not altogether surprising that in later years he was recruited into government service as one of the two first-grade clerks in the Northern Province.[95]

Domingo's departure from Livingstonia took place in the same year, 1908, in which his fellow student from the Overtoun Institution, the Tonga Eliot Kenan Kamwana, began preaching in the West Nyasa District. One distinction that historians have drawn in comparing the two is to note that Domingo fits most easily into the 'Ethiopian' tradition of Christian independency and Kamwana into the 'Zionist'. Domingo believed in development along Western lines but under African control. Kamwana sought to abandon conventional Western models in favour of a new radical spiritualism which reached out to popular African concerns. The paradox was that just as Domingo received financial support from the Seventh Day Baptists, so Kamwana operated as an evangelist for the Watchtower Bible and Tract Society, the forerunner of Jehovah's Witnesses and the largest and most wide-ranging of the American-based fundamentalist religious movements that spread to Africa around the turn of the century. Based on an absolute adherence to Biblical precepts and a belief in the imminent second coming of Christ, Watchtower was introduced to South Africa in 1907 by the same Joseph Booth who was to inspire Charles Domingo. The next year he was joined at Cape Town by Kamwana, who had worked for four years as a hospital assistant at the Main Reef Mine, Roodeport, near Johannes-

[92] Domingo to Booth, 20 Sep 1911, Domingo Papers, University College Library, Zomba.
[93] Adrian Hastings, *The Church in Africa, 1450–1950* (Oxford, 1994) p. 484.
[94] Langworthy, *Life of Booth*, pp. 328–58; 400–04.
[95] McCracken, *Politics and Christianity*, p.218.

burg. After four brief months receiving tuition in Watchtower doctrine, Kamwana returned to his home district, one of those most heavily evangelised by the Livingstonia Mission. There he preached an Africanised form of Watchtower millennialism: 'The advent of Christ was to take place at the end of 1914. The whites were all to leave the country. There would be no more oppression from the tax gatherers.'[96] Of special attraction to his hearers was the offer of immediate, unconditional baptism and hence entry into Christian life for the community as a whole in contrast to Livingstonia's emphasis on individual conversion, achieved only after a lengthy period of study. Among scenes of enthusiasm, no fewer than 10,000 people were baptised by Kamwana in a matter of months. For government officials, these baptisms were not in themselves a cause of concern. But they grew alarmed when news reached them that Kamwana taught that Christ's Coming would result in the ending of colonial rule. In April 1909 he was arrested and deported from the district at the start of a long period of exile that was not to end until 1937 when he was finally allowed to return to his home village. There he founded the Watchman Healing Mission, a church that rejected Western medicine in favour of spiritual healing.[97] Meanwhile, following his deportation, the number of adherents in the West Nyasa district sharply declined. Over the next couple of years, however, labour migrants carried the Watchtower message south both through word of mouth and also through the circulation among Protestant Christians of all denominations of a host of vividly illustrated pamphlets and periodicals published by the Watchtower Bible and Tract Society. By 1914, therefore, throughout much of Nyasaland, millennial expectations were high.

The growth of Christian independency was only one aspect of the complex process of religious adaptation that took place in Malawi in the early decades of the twentieth century. Another was the change that occurred in indigenous religious institutions confronted by the twin forces of Christianity and colonialism. Unlike the Evangelicals who ruled India in the 1830s and 40s, British colonial officials in Nyasaland had no desire to provoke unnecessary confrontations with traditional religious authorities whom they tended to find less troublesome than disputatious missionaries. Nevertheless, the colonial state struck at indigenous beliefs in at least two ways: first, by ignoring the interconnections between secular and religious authority integral to traditional societies but denied under indirect rule and second, by rejecting the existence of witchcraft. Under legislation introduced in 1911, anyone attempting to identify witches was committing a punishable offence.[98]

In the Malawi area, in contrast to the situation in Southern Rhodesia, the deepest damage appears to have been experienced by territorial cults, several of which had suffered badly at the time of the Ngoni invasions. Both the Chisumphi cult, influential among the Chewa, and the cult of Chikangombe among the southern Tumbuka fragmented into local units in the early decades of the twentieth century.[99] Even the influence of the Mbona cult contracted significantly

[96] McMinn, 'The First Wave of Ethiopianism in Central Africa', *Livingstonia News,* Aug 1909, pp. 56–9.

[97] The most recent discussion of Kamwana is provided by Henry Donati, 'A Very Antagonistic Spirit: Elliot Kamwana', *SOMJ,* 64, 1, 2011, pp. 13–33.

[98] Nyasaland Government Gazette, Summary of Proceedings of 7th Session of Legislative Council, 9–12 May 1911.

although, as Schoffeleers has demonstrated in a series of path-breaking articles, this cult succeeded over time in adapting itself to the new challenge of Christianity, thus ensuring that it would continue to play an important part in the cultural life of the Lower Shire Valley. Based on two main shrine centres, Cholo and Khulubvi, close to present-day Nsanje, the Mbona cult by the 1860s had come to represent the cultural integrity of the Mang'anja people in the sense that the martyred male prophet, Mbona, who spoke periodically through a medium and was served at his shrines by a spirit-wife and a priestly hierarchy, was believed to act as a guardian of the land, protecting it from epidemics, droughts and floods. In their very first contacts with Christianity, as represented by David Livingstone and the UMCA, officials of the cult responded with hostility, alarmed at what they saw as a 'violent attempt to invade Mang'anja society'.[100] But with the growing influence of the Catholics and the South African General Mission from the early 1920s, the response was very different. Drawing on the concept of Mbona as a prophet and martyr, the cult came to incorporate biblical elements in its message, thus extending its appeal to the wider non-Mang'anja population. At the same time, baptised Christians began to take up roles at its shrines.[101]

If Mbona demonstrated the capacity of indigenous religious institutions to adapt to the new order, *Nyau* is normally seen as illustrating their ability to resist. *Nyau* secret societies, comprising masked dancers who perform at initiation ceremonies for girls and at mourning rites, have been a central feature of Chewa culture for centuries and probably increased in importance in the nineteenth century at a time when the territorial rain shrines weakened. Following the arrival of Christian missions, *Nyau* responded to what their adherents saw as an assault on Chewa village-based values by encouraging children to boycott mission schools in a campaign that came to its head in the 1920s. At the same time Catholic and Anglican missionaries made a series of largely unsuccessful attempts to persuade colonial officials to take action against cult officials.[102] As Kachapila has noted, the outcome of this conflict was not a blanket resistance among Chewa villagers to the advent of new ideas. Despite the efforts of *Nyau* adherents, many Chewa became Christians and large numbers of mission schools were successfully established in the Central Region.[103] Nor should the role of *Nyau* be reduced to that of anti-colonial resistance. In a remarkable wave of inventiveness, *Nyau* adherents throughout the twentieth century produced an extraordinary range of face masks and structures, some of them representing ancestral figures and animals, others European officials, motor bicycles and cars. Although these masks were regarded by their makers as ephemeral objects, normally constructed for a performance and then burnt, there are good grounds for seeing them as among the finest achievements of Malawian indigenous art,

---

[99] Schoffeleers, *Guardians*, pp.37, 138–40, 171–3, 201.

[100] Schoffeleers, 'Interaction of the M'Bona Cult and Christianity', pp.14–19.

[101] Schoffeleers, *Guardians*, p. 175.

[102] Schoffeleers, *Rivers,* pp. 33–41; M. Schoffeleers and I. Linden, 'The Resistance of the Nyau Societies to the Roman Catholic Missions in Colonial Malawi' in Ranger and Kimambo, *Historical Study*, pp. 252–73; I. Linden, 'Chewa Initiation Rites and *Nyau* Societies' in Ranger and Weller, *Themes*, pp. 30–44.

[103] Hendrina Kachapila, '"Remarkable Adaptability": Gender, Identity and Social Change among the Chewa of Central Malawi, 1870–1945', PhD dissertation, University of Dalhousie, 2001, pp.3–12.

items that have found their place in some of the greatest galleries in the world.[104]

Communal rituals were on the retreat in the face of Christianity in the first half of the twentieth century; witchcraft idioms were not. Whether witchcraft increased under colonial rule it is impossible to tell but this certainly was the belief of many Malawians who blamed the colonial government for seeking to suppress the *mwavi* poison ordeal which had previously been widely used to identify and kill witches. One consequence, as Soko has argued, was the sharp rise in spirit possession cults, notably *vimbuza*, *virombo* and *vyanusi* in the north. The other was the emergence of witchcraft eradication cults, centred around influential prophets, who dispensed medicine to whole villages with the aim both of removing witchcraft from the community and of killing those witches who refused to mend their ways. Notable early witchcraft eradicators included Mgwede Mhoni at the beginning of the century and Lameck Chirongo, known as Mzimu, who dispensed medicine throughout the Karonga district in the 1920s. They, however, were overshadowed by *mchape*, the major movement, discussed in Chapter Eight, which spread through Nyasaland and beyond between 1932 and 1934; by the movements initiated by Bwanali in the Chikwawa district from 1946; and by Chikanga in the Rumphi district from 1954.[105] By 1959–60, the period when the nationalist struggle was at its peak, Chikanga, who was now at his most influential, attracted pilgrims in their thousands from southern Tanganyika and Northern Rhodesia as well as from Nyasaland. The two leading Ngoni chiefs, Mbelwa and Mtwalo, both ordered that all the villages under their control should be purified by Chikanga. When the Revd George Mawafulirwa, the CCAP minister at Deep Bay, attempted to forbid his parishioners to visit him, his manse and church were burnt to the ground.[106] Remarkably, at a time when the clash between nationalists and government forces had made northern Nyasaland little short of a war zone, many northerners were at least as much caught up in Chikanga's crusade for spiritual cleansing as they were in the struggle for political independence.

The episode is a reminder both of the tenacity with which some committed Christians rejected compromises with traditional religious beliefs and also of the readiness of others to combine their Christian faith with indigenous explanations of misfortune. It also demonstrates that, even in the 1950s and early 1960s, when the fight for nationalist liberation was at its height, many Malawians remained equally concerned with another, spiritual, battle, the on-going struggle against evil, represented most potently by those forces believed to threaten the wellbeing of the village community.

---

[104] Schoffeleers, *Rivers*, pp. 34–41; Birch de Aguilar, *Inscribing the Mask*.

[105] *Mchape* is discussed in greater detail in Chapter 8. For Bwanali, see G. Marwick, 'Another Modern Anti-Witchcraft Movement in East Central Africa', *Africa*, 20, 1959, pp. 100–12. Chikanga is discussed from different angles by Boston Soko and Gerhard Kubik, *Nchimi Chikanga: The Battle against Witchcraft in Malawi* (Kachere Series, Zomba, 2008) and by Bill Jackson, *Send Us Friends*, pp. 184–90. See also R.G. Willis, 'Kamcape: an anti-sorcery movement in south-west Tanzania, *Africa*, 38, 1968, pp. 1–15.

[106] Jackson, pp. 185–6; Samson K. Msiska and Wallace G. C. Muntali to Synod Clerk, Livingstonia, 20 Nov 1960, Helen Taylor Papers, EUL.

5

The Chilembwe Rising

Introduction

On the night of Saturday 23 January 1915 a party of armed men made their way the eight miles from Mbombwe near Chiradzulu, the headquarters of the Revd John Chilembwe's Providence Industrial Mission, to Magomero, the headquarters of the A.L. Bruce Estates. There they killed two Europeans, including the estate manager, William Jervis Livingstone. They then cut off his head and carried it back to Chiradzulu where it was displayed on a pole at the Sunday service conducted next day by Chilembwe. Livingstone's wife Katherine, two other European women and their children were escorted across the Phalombe plain towards Mbombwe before eventually being released unharmed. Meanwhile, a further contingent of men attacked the ALC headquarters at Mandala.[1]

Within a fortnight the revolt had been suppressed. Three Europeans had died; two had been severely wounded, 36 convicted rebels had been executed, many others had been killed by the security forces. 'For a rebellion against foreign rule, it had been, on the face of it, singularly ineffective' noted Shepperson and Price in their authoritative account of the rising. Yet, as they also commented, the importance of the rising was far greater than its immediate, quantifiable, impact.[2] A leading historian has claimed that this was the only significant rebellion in the whole of Africa to be inspired by Christianity prior to the First World War.[3] It provided Malawi with its one unproblematic hero, John Chilembwe; his image is now depicted on Malawian bank notes.[4] Furthermore, the Governor, Sir George Smith believed that it opened 'a new phase in the existence of Nyasaland'. In the view of Shepperson and Price, 'Chilembwe's was the first Central African resistance to European control which looked to the future,

---

[1]   The major study remains George Shepperson and Thomas Price, *Independent African* (Edinburgh, 1958). This, however, should be supplemented by White, *Magomero;* Ian Linden and Jane Linden, 'John Chilembwe and the New Jerusalem', *JAH* 12, 4 (1971), pp. 629–51; Ian Linden and Jane Linden, 'Chiefs and Pastors in the Ncheu Rising of 1915' in Macdonald, *Nyasaland to Malawi;* D.D. Phiri, *Let Us Die for Africa* (Blantyre, 1999).

[2]   Shepperson and Price, *Independent African*, p. 267.

[3]   Iliffe, *Africans*, p. 196.

[4]   For a discussion of the making of this image see McCracken, 'Mungo Murray Chisuse'.

not to the past' and was aimed at 'founding a nation rather ... than restoring the fortunes of the tribes'.[5]

The thangata *regime*

It was no mere accident of timing that the 'Chilembwe Rising', the name normally given to this short-lived revolt, took place only five months after the outbreak of the First World War and only four months after Malawian troops had been heavily involved in the engagement at Karonga where a British-officered but almost entirely African force had defeated a German contingent.[6] Coming in 1914, the very year that the Watchtower leader, Elliot Kamwana, had prophesied would bring the Second Coming in which the just would inherit the earth, the advent of war gave fresh impetus to the mounting tide of apocalyptic expectations that were to influence the behaviour of many of the participants. In a letter to the *Nyasaland Times*, written only a couple of months before the Rising began, John Chilembwe publicly protested against the shedding of African blood for ends that were unrelated to African interests. Once the decision to resort to violence had been taken, he appealed to the German authorities in East Africa for arms, although he delayed so long in requesting assistance that his letter did not reach them until after the rising had been suppressed.

If the war contributed to the timing of the Rising, however, other factors were of greater importance in explaining its origins and character. Historians have been reluctant to situate the Rising within the context of peasant politics, suggesting in one instance that 'it is wrong to argue that Chilembwe acted on behalf of, or was in the vanguard of an aroused peasantry.'[7] But if 'the peasantry' as an undifferentiated mass played no significant part in the Rising, labour tenants on certain European estates – many but by no means all of them 'Anguru' or Lomwe immigrants from Mozambique – were actively involved. It is in the precarious alliance established by these most wretched and exploited of Malawi's inhabitants with sections of the Southern Province's emergent African bourgeoisie that the origins of the Rising can be found.

The evolution of the estate sector in the Shire Highlands has been described in Chapter Three. By the 1890s, over 800,000 acres of land in the area had been alienated to a handful of white settlers. The major problem they faced in the early years was the shortage of labour but, from the late 1890s, this was considerably eased as thousands of refugees, escaping the harsh forced labour regulations introduced in Mozambique in 1899, fled across the border in search of land and security. Some settled under Yao chiefs on Crown land where they 'were kept in a certain degree of mild subjection and occasionally perform a little menial labour';[8] others were given permission to settle on unutilised land on European estates on condition that they paid a labour tax (*thangata*) of so many weeks' work each year (See Chapter Three). By 1912 the Governor was

---

5 Shepperson and Price, pp. 396, 409.
6 For Malawi and the First World War see Chapter 6.
7 Robert I. Rotberg, 'Psychological Stress and the Question of Identity: Chilembwe's Revolt Reconsidered' in R.I. Rotberg and Ali. A. Mazrui (eds), *Protest and Power in Black Africa* (New York, 1970), p.373.
8 White, *Magomero*, p. 88.

convinced that 'without the Anguru immigration ... the extension of plantations in the Shire Highlands would not have been possible, and no European
would have ventured to have risked capital where a labour supply was only exis-
tent when it was least required'.[9]

It was the limited number of opportunities available to them that made the
Lomwe immigrants, in the Governor's words, 'the backbone of our labour
supply'.[10] Although indigenous peasant communities were deeply affected by
the establishment of a settler economy in their midst, a range of economic
options remained open to them. Some could earn money in the dry season by
working on European estates, returning to their own fields during the rains.
Others entered the market economy through the production of food crops;
others again made use of the escape hatch of migrant labour to the higher-wage
economies of Southern Rhodesia or South Africa. For immigrants from Mozambique, however, the options were considerably narrower. One alternative, extensively employed by family groups, was that of internal migration, moving from
one location to another in search of permanent places of settlement. As the
number of immigrants grew, however, fertile, well watered land became increasingly scarce with the result that more and more Lomwe were forced to turn to
the estates. By 1915 they comprised nearly half of the 4,926 hut-owners on the
162,000 acre Magomero estate, nearly all of the 4,000 tenants on the Nachambo
estate and the great majority of the 4,617 hut-owners on the British Central
Africa Company estate at Mikalongwe. As tenants at will, they lacked security of
tenure. Not only could estate owners call upon their labour in the wet season,
they also could enforce the continued residence of Lomwe men by threatening
to burn their homes and evict their families if they attempted to seek work as
migrant labourers. Only on the estates of the Blantyre and East Africa Company
from 1908 was the tenant production of fire-cured tobacco encouraged. Elsewhere, the peasant option was specifically excluded, with tenants being expressly
forbidden to grow cash-crops. Under a draft ordinance prepared by the Government in January 1914, tenants would have had the option of paying their rent in
cash.[11] In practice, on virtually all estates, *thangata* could be paid only in labour.

For many immigrants in the early years of the twentieth century, the
constraints involved in labour tenancy were more than compensated for by the
advantages on offer. One was the freedom enjoyed from the exactions of the
government askaris. Whereas in southern Ngoniland, as late as 1900, armed
police and labour recruiters regularly carried out raiding expeditions on villages,
the settler estates were regarded as 'no-go areas' which the police entered only
with caution. To send out askaris on a manhunt for carriers was a 'perfectly
harmless move, which in any other district would be perfectly normal', the Blantyre Resident explained to his assistant at Chiradzulu in 1913. But when the
Assistant recruited in this manner in the Shire Highlands he was informed that
this was an error of judgment which on no account should be repeated. 'I expect
that it is my fault for not sufficiently rubbing it in to you that Blantyre district
is not Angoniland.'[12]

[9]   Manning to CO. 2 Oct 1912, TNA CO 525/44.
[10] Ibid.
[11] G. Smith to C.O. 17 Jan 1914, TNA CO 525/55.
[12] Resident Magistrate to Cruise, Chiradzulu, 27 April 1913, MNA NSB 2/1/1.

Protection from the police was not the only attraction. Refugees settling on the A.L. Bruce estates around 1900 had access to an abundance of land, water and firewood, the three basic necessities for trouble-free farming. At that time the duties imposed upon them were not too onerous, comprising only a month's *thangata* labour paid for at the current rate of tax with, in addition, a further month's labour to meet hut tax demands. In comparison with the violence and insecurity of colonial Mozambique, the Shire Highlands were viewed as a haven of good order. 'This place is wonderful', women still sang in the early 1980s in the almost forgotten language, Mihaveni, used by the original immigrants to Magomero, a sentiment which conjured up distant recollections of what life had been like before *thangata* came fully into its own.[13]

The increased exploitation of tenant labour can be related to changes in the settler economy. Following the collapse of coffee prices in 1900, the estate sector went into a decline from which it was temporarily rescued in 1903 by a dramatic shift into cotton. By 1906, however, it had become apparent that the Egyptian cotton extensively grown on Shire Highland estates could be cultivated success-fully only in the hotter, lower-lying Shire Valley. Acreage under cotton cultiva-tion was halved and renewed attention was paid to a hardier variety, named Nyasaland Upland and developed by W.J. Livingstone, the manager of the Magomero estate owned by the A.L. Bruce Trust. By 1908, Livingstone had 1,000 acres of the estate under cotton; by 1914 this figure had increased to 5,000 acres. Total European cultivation of cotton increased from 7,000 acres in 1907 to 25,600 acres in 1914 although by that time, tobacco, which was less subject to disease, was rivalling both the acreage and the value of cotton planted. Some enterprises, notably the A.L. Bruce Estates and the British Central Africa Company, remained wedded to cotton; others, among them the Blantyre and East Africa Company, gave higher priority to tobacco.

The expansion of land under cultivation resulted in an intensification of the *thangata* system. Given that only 55,000 acres – little more than five per cent of the total amount of land alienated to Europeans – had been brought under culti-vation by 1914, it might appear that landlords would have no difficulty in finding labour. But cotton is a highly labour intensive crop; labour saving machinery was conspicuous only by its absence; and there was little hope of attracting wage labourers to estates which paid wages of only four to five shillings a month without food, 'a record for any settled part of Africa', as a colonial official noted in 1912.[14]

The consequence was that the opening of new plantations was accompanied by an increase in the number of weeks that tenants were forced to work. Quite how Livingstone ensured that approximately 5,000 tenants worked for five or six months of the year remains unclear, although the often contradictory evidence supplied to the Commission of Inquiry held in 1915 offers a number of useful insights. Legally, tenants were required to provide one month of paid labour each year in lieu of rent, plus a further month (defined as 26 days) in order to meet their hut tax obligations. Most agreements with tenants were verbal rather than written, however, and hence could easily be manipulated to the land-lord's advantage. *Thangata* labour was frequently extended to two or three

---

[13] Quoted in White, *Magomero*, p. 108.
[14] W.C. Bottomley, 23 Dec 1912, TNA CO 524/44.

months. Work for hut tax was increased well over the legal month by the simple expedient of refusing to provide workers with the vouchers required to demonstrate to the government that they had met their obligations. A month's labour was counted as 28 days and was frequently extended to as much as five weeks. Widows and single women were compelled to perform *thangata* and children too were frequently rounded up by the estate rangers and forced to work. If a tenant failed to complete the task allocated to him 'no credit was given to him for the time he had worked, and occasionally he had to work several days extra to make up for the day that was lost'.[15] Labour roll books were not properly maintained and methods of payment were haphazard. Captain Thorburn, who spent a year on the Magomero estate, concluded that Livingstone 'was not fair to the boys in their pay. ...A boy comes for his pay and expects 3/- or so and gets 1/6d ... and I thought that a little boy getting 3d for a month's work was very mean.'[16] The Church of Scotland pastor, Stephen Kundecha, was equally critical of the methods that Livingstone employed. Workers frequently received part of their wages in rolls of tobacco, he alleged. Men seeking to obtain tax certificates 'were all grumbling' at being forced to work '12 or 13 weeks for 1 Hut Tax paper and 2/- of which they did not understand at all'.[17]

On estates where demands for labour were less pressing, *thangata* was not so rigorously imposed, although nowhere did it fail to provoke resentment. On virtually all estates by 1914 tenants were required on pain of eviction to work for a minimum of two to three months a year at wages that never rose higher than 5 shillings and much more frequently were pegged at 4 shillings a month. Yet while there are grounds for arguing that conditions on the Bruce Estates mirrored those in the Shire Highlands as a whole, in two respects they were at least marginally different. With its emphasis on cotton and its 16 separate plantations, Magomero's labour requirements were of a different order from those of many of its competitors; while in both the joint owner, Alexander Livingstone Bruce, and the general manager, W. J. Livingstone, the estate possessed an obsessively ruthless management team even by the uncertain standards of the day.

Historians have focused most of their attention on the insecure, short-tempered W.J. Livingstone, a man given to alternating acts of brutality and personal kindness. But it is worth stressing that it was Livingstone Bruce, grandson of David Livingstone and a member of the Legislative Council, who set the tone of management on the estate. Wounded in the South African War and capable of walking only with sticks, Bruce was a somewhat distant figure to the tenants, whereas Livingstone was ever present, settling disputes and distributing food in times of famine but also urging on workers with kicks and blows and extending the tasks that the capitaos had allotted to them. Nevertheless, it was Bruce who was responsible for banning all schools from the Magomero estate and Bruce again who personally refused to allow Chilembwe's followers to build a church on his land. As Bruce explained to the Commission of Inquiry, he had absolute control over the making of policy on the estates. If Livingstone

---

[15] *Report of the Commission appointed ... to inquire into Various Matters and Questions concerned with the Native Rising within the Nyasaland Protectorate* (Zomba, 1916).
[16] Evidence of Capt Charles Thorburn to Commission on Enquiry, 5 July 1915, TNA CO 525/66.
[17] Evidence of Revd Stephen Kundecha to Commission of Enquiry, 8 July 1915, TNA CO 525/66.

was the rough instrument in carrying these policies out, he could not have acted without Bruce's approval.[18]

In his evidence to the 1915 Commission of Inquiry, the cotton planter, A.C.J. Wallace-Ross concluded a remarkably detailed description of the violence he had seen Livingstone inflict on his workers by indulging in a little comparative anthropology. 'I think the native of Nyasaland is a very dangerous boy to play the fool with', he told the no doubt startled commissioners.

> The West Indian negro if you hit him would knock you down with the hoe or anything that was handy straight off. The Gold Coast native would go to the Boma at once. The Nyasaland boys sit down and think of it, and I think a man is apt to take liberties with them which he should not do. The Nyasaland native has only one idea of reparation, and that is to get up and kill.[19]

Setting aside the colonial stereotypes reflected in this statement, Wallace-Ross's words reflect the dilemma that labour tenants faced. Desertion, the classic strategy employed by abused workers on plantations all over the world, was an unattractive option for refugees who had fled from the even greater abuses inflicted on workers in Mozambique. Yet there was little prospect of the distant Boma providing justice, particularly as it had transferred responsibility for tax collection almost entirely to the estate owner.[20] 'I always looked upon Magomero as far as the natives were concerned as rather like a Boma', Thorburn commented; 'They tried all their cases there.'[21] Hidden forms of resistance, such as deliberately working slowly, were of little utility in a work environment where they resulted in the loss of pay. By 1910, evidence of workers 'grumbling', 'sulking' and otherwise expressing their dissatisfaction was beginning to accumulate. Yet without leadership or inspiration there was little they could do. It was at this point that some tenants turned to John Chilembwe.

John Chilembwe

The emergence of the short-sighted, asthmatic pastor of the Providence Industrial Mission at the head of a violent, peasant-based rebellion is one of the more puzzling episodes in the history of African resistance.[22] For much of his career, Chilembwe appeared the very model of non-violent African advancement. He was educated in a Church of Scotland school near Blantyre before, in February 1893, becoming the protégé of the radical, independent-minded Baptist missionary, Joseph Booth. In 1897, Chilembwe accompanied Booth to the United States on a fund-raising expedition. In America he was befriended by Dr Lewis Jordan, secretary of the Afro-American National Baptist Convention, who arranged for him to be enrolled in the Virginia Theological Seminary and

---

[18] Evidence of A. Livingstone Bruce, 30 June 1915, TNA CO 525/66.
[19] Evidence of A.C.J. Wallace-Ross to Commission of Enquiry, 5 July 1915, TNA CO 525/66.
[20] Resident, Blantyre to Ass. Resident, Chiradzulu, 19 Dec 1913, MNA NSB 2/1/1; evidence of E. Costley-White, Resident Zomba, 2 July 1915, MNA COM 6 2/1/2.
[21] Evidence of Capt Thorburn, 5 July 1915, TNA CO 525/66.
[22] The best and most detailed account of Chilembwe's early career remains Shepperson and Price, pp. 7–147.

College at Lynchburg. In 1900, he returned to Nyasaland as an ordained minister, supported by the National Baptist Convention, and bought land in the Chiradzulu district at Mbombwe where he founded the Providence Industrial Mission. By 1910, he had seven assistants helping him minister to 800 church members. Two years later, more than 900 pupils were in attendance at the P.I.M.'s seven schools and work had begun on an impressively large brick church, rivalling that of the Blantyre Mission in size if not in intricacy of decoration.

Compared to Watchtower, with its network of congregations extending throughout Nyasaland and beyond to the mining centres of Southern Rhodesia, Chilembwe's mission might seem small and narrowly focused. But for sections of the tenant population, as for most members of the local *petit bourgeoisie*, it appeared as a symbol of hope. By 1911 an increasing number of the *capitaos* or foremen employed on the Bruce estates had begun to attend services at Mbombwe. The next year, 1912, a P.I.M. church was secretly opened on the estate, in direct defiance of Bruce, who had ordered that no such church should to be built. The discovery and burning of the church by Livingstone in November 1913 only strengthened the resolve of Chilembwe's followers; it was followed by the baptising of large numbers of Lomwe immigrants in 1914.

Chilembwe's appeal derived from three separate and contradictory elements: a concern for African advancement; a dislike of British colonialism; and, last but not least, a belief in the imminence of the Second Coming when the poor and exploited could expect to come into their own. In the early years, it was as a successful African moderniser in a white dominated society that Chilembwe made his mark. Even before his return from America, a small group of Blantyre-educated entrepreneurs, including Duncan Njilima, Gordon and Hugh Mataka, John Gray Kufa and Joseph Bismarck, had begun to challenge settler assumptions of white racial superiority by growing cash crops with wage labour on freehold land in the Chiradzulu district; with Chilembwe's arrival their cause was considerably strengthened. Whether building his church or growing cash crops like cotton, founding the African Industrial Society with fellow-businessmen, or dressing himself and his family in formal European clothes, Chilembwe threatened the prevailing belief in European hegemony. His attitude to women was particularly revealing. Concerned, as he wrote in 1912, that 'The ordinary African woman in her heathen state is ignorant, uninteresting and unlovable', he encouraged his wife, Ida, to teach girls sewing and deportment, and lectured teachers, pastors and businessmen on the need to clothe their wives in elaborate European dresses.[23]

The standards he required of his male followers were equally demanding. 'He exhorted people from keeping themselves into strong drinks, and such like', Chilembwe's earliest African biographer reported. 'He taught adults and children to keep on work, not to lounge about ... He liked to see his country men work hard and prosper in their undertakings, also to see them smart, such as negro fellows he had seen in America and other countries.'[24]

This emphasis on improvement was specifically related to an insistence on

[23] *Journal of the Thirty-Second Annual Session of the National Baptist Convention*, 11–16 Sept. 1912 quoted in Shepperson and Price, *Independent African*, pp. 174–5.
[24] George Simeon Mwase, *Strike a Blow and Die* (Cambridge MA 1967), p. 27.

*5 John Chilembwe, his wife, Ida and daughter Emma, photographed
by Mungo Murray Chisuse*

racial equality which drew at least part of its inspiration from Chilembwe's experiences in the American South. On a visit to the P.I.M. central school, where for five years up to 1906 Chilembwe was assisted by two African-American missionaries, Landon Cheek and Emma DeLany, the pioneer Blantyre minister Harry Kambwiri Matecheta noted that children answered such questions from 'a little English Catechism', such as 'Did God say that white people should be superior over the black people?' The answer was 'No, God made all alike, we are the same before God.' They were also being taught that 'God gave Africa to the Africans and Europe to Europeans ... also about colour, that colour is from the climate of the country.'[25] Matecheta observed, not unjustly: 'Such kind of teaching brings the question of the colour line and is purely American, an African native does not want to be white, and when he is alone does not say that he is black.' But he added that while Africans were not normally affected by issues of colour, they were when they found themselves racially abused. So regular was the use of the 'foulest language' by whites in the settler-dominated cultural environment of the Shire Highlands, according to Matecheta, that Africans came to regard their behaviour as synonymous with vulgar discourtesy: 'When young boys insult big men, the big men say, "this is Chizungu [European behaviour], which has no politeness."'[26]

By 1910 Chilembwe had begun to add to his assertion of the social and economic equality of all races vigorous denunciations of British colonialism. Although they were sometimes critical of individual acts of government policy, Scottish missionaries and their African staff were in no doubt that the colonial impact was essentially beneficial in that it had ended the slave trade and created new economic and educational opportunities. Chilembwe took the alternative view, expressed most clearly by his former mentor, Booth, that 'Africa [was] for the Africans; Europeans have come only to take away your land.' The different approaches were well spelt out by Matecheta in his account of two discussions he had held with Chilembwe, the first at the time of the coronation of King George V in 1910 and concerning Matecheta's sermon in the Zomba church:

> He asked me about the Coronation at Zomba, and I told him about the text I chose at Zomba. And then he said "No – you were mistaken in saying – 'Honour the King'. The King is not our King, he is the Azungu's King" and he said "Even the Governor is not our King. He came here for the interests of the Europeans, not of the natives, because he has not corrected our grievances."

When they met again in 1913, Chilembwe expressed his views in openly millenarian terms. 'Sin', he suggested to Matecheta, 'was what the Europeans were doing here, coming and taking away the land':

> And then another thing which he asked me about was if I knew about the first and second resurrection. I could not tell him about it, and then he brought in a blue book, and read from it, and said the first resurrection is freedom from bondage and slavery. And then he said the second resurrection is the future resurrection, and then he said all the Europeans have risen from the first resurrection, and that the natives have not risen from it. I asked

---

[25] Revd Harry Kambwiri, 'The Origin of John Chilembwe Rising', paper submitted to the Nyasaland Rising Commission of Enquiry, 13 July 1915, TNA CO 525/66.
[26] Ibid.

him "How", and he said "Because we are ruled by Europeans." Then he said "When we shall be free from their rule then we shall have risen."[27]

Chilembwe's language reflects the influence in Malawi of Watchtower with its insistence on the imminent second coming of Christ. Watchtower was introduced by the prophet Eliot Kamwana to the Nkhata Bay area in 1908. A year later Kamwana baptised some 10,000 people in the district before being deported south, eventually ending up in detention at Mulanje.[28] In the aftermath of his departure, the millenarian Watchtower message was carried to southern Nyasaland and later to Southern Rhodesia, both through the efforts of Tonga labour migrants and through the circulation among Protestant Christians of all denominations of a host of pamphlets and periodicals produced by the American-based Watchtower Bible and Tract Society. It was from this period, in the build up to the Battle of Armageddon and the triumph of God's Kingdom on Earth, predicted by Watchtower teachers for October 1914, that Chilembwe began preaching about 'Noah's Ark' and 'the great deluge of wars', saying that 'the people were safe who stayed with him, but if they remained with the Azungu they would perish.'

The outbreak of the First World War at precisely the time that millennial expectations were reaching a peak inflamed the situation further. Appalled by the loss of African life in the engagement at Karonga, Chilembwe reverted to a more orthodox political stance. In a courageous letter to the *Nyasaland Times* of November 1914, written 'in behalf of his countrymen', he complained:

A number of people have already shed their blood, while some are crippled for life.... If this were a war ... for honour, Government gain of riches, etc., we would have been boldly told: Let the rich men, bankers, titled men, storekeepers, farmers and landlords go to war and get shot. Instead the poor Africans who have nothing to own in this present world, who in death leave only a long line of widows and orphans in utter want and dire distress are invited to die for a cause which is not theirs.[29]

To his adherents in Ntcheu, however, he continued to proclaim a message of messianic hope: 'My dear brethren be strong, preach the true Gospel trusting that our Heavenly Father will help us. Strengthen all weak brethren. Preach the Kingdom of God is at hand.'[30]

Two months later, on Friday 22 January, he convened a meeting of his supporters at Mbombwe where plans for the insurrection were finally revealed. Three groups of fighters were to attack Mandala, the African Lakes Company headquarters at Blantyre, with the intention of seizing ammunition and guns. Meanwhile two further columns of men were to kill all male Europeans on the Bruce Estates at Magomero and at the sub-station, Mwanje. Either that evening or on the Saturday morning, emissaries were given letters to take to Chilembwe's close associates, Stephen Kadewere in Zomba and Phillip Chinyama in Ntcheu announcing that the rising had begun and calling upon them to lead their

---

[27] Evidence of Kambwiri, 13 July 1915, TNA CO 525/66.
[28] Langworthy, *Africa for the Africans*, pp. 195–209; McCracken, *Politics and Christianity*, pp. 184–208.
[29] Quoted in Shepperson and Price, pp. 234–35.
[30] Chilembwe to Kusita, 22 Dec. 1914, MNA NCN 4/2/1 quoted in Linden, 'John Chilembwe and the New Jerusalem', p.640.

followers in attacks on the neighbouring bomas. Finally, on Sunday 24 January, Chilembwe despatched a messenger to Tunduru in Tanganyika seeking an alliance with the German authorities.

By this time, however, the hopes of the rebels were rapidly receding. Although the attacks on the Bruce Estates had been successfully accomplished, leaving three of the four European managers dead and the other seriously wounded, only five rifles had been taken in the attack on Mandala and four fighters had been captured in the ensuing flight. With the loss of surprise and in the absence of any large-scale popular rising, Chilembwe's supporters were forced onto the defensive. Some accounts of the sermon he delivered that Sunday in his brick church at Mbombwe suggest that he remained focused on the millennium: 'I was told that the kingdom of God was at hand', one his adherents recollected. 'John Chilembwe said, "You will hear the bugles sounding."' Others related that he preached resignation and the need to face certain defeat with courage.[31]

At all events, as the days passed, government forces took the initiative. Most British troops were now stationed at Karonga, far to the north, but a contingent of about 100 African troops from the KAR Reserve at Zomba was mobilised, as were divisions from the European-manned Nyasaland Volunteer Reserve. On Monday 24 January, the rebels succeeded in ambushing the KAR reserve near Mbombwe, forcing it to retreat. However, the next day the soldiers entered the PIM headquarters unchallenged, only to find that Chilembwe had fled. (They did, however, discover a War Roll containing 175 names, forming what was to be an uncanny parallel with the list of 300 names abandoned by Henry Manoah Chipembere following his abortive coup almost exactly 50 years later.) Meanwhile, the attempted risings of Kadewere near Zomba, and Chinyama with some 200 armed followers at Ntcheu, were quickly brought to an end, in part through the intervention of chiefs supportive of the government. Early on Tuesday morning, some of the rebels attacked the Roman Catholic Marist Fathers' mission at Nguludi, burning several of the houses and leaving the priest in charge severely beaten. Thereafter, they scattered, seeking safety as best they could. John Chilembwe fled towards the Mozambique border with his brother Morris, moving cautiously from one village to another. On 3 February, they were spotted by a military patrol and shot by askaris as they tried to escape. Chilembwe's body was examined by Henry Vassall, assistant magistrate. 'He was wearing a dark blue coat, a coloured shirt and a striped pyjama jacket over the shirt and grey flannel trousers. With the body was brought in a pair of spectacles, a pair of pince nez, and a pair of black boots.'[32] Even in his last, most desperate hours, Chilembwe had attempted to maintain the appearance of a civilised gentleman.

Marginal men

It is a good deal easier to understand why sections of Nyasaland's most marginalised population rose in armed revolt than it is to explain why they were joined

---

[31] White, *Magomero*, p. 138; Shepperson & Price, p. 285; Mwase, *Strike a Blow*, pp. 42–3.
[32] Evidence of Henry Holland Vassall, Enquiry into the death of John and Morris Chilembwe, Mlanje, 4 Feb 1915, MNA J 2/9/3.

by members of the new entrepreneurial class. Certainly, men like Duncan Njilima and John Gray Kufa, two of Chilembwe's closest associates, were prevented by the government's discriminatory policies from signing the labour tax papers of their workers and were refused easy access to credit. Yet as relatively prosperous landowners, growing cotton, tobacco and maize on up to 150 acres apiece, they appear unlikely candidates for political martyrdom. Part of the answer may relate to their ambiguous social position as salaried employees who were also labour-employing capitalist farmers. John Gray Kufa owned 140 acres of freehold land at Nsoni, yet he was also a Blantyre Mission-trained hospital assistant who had spent two years or more working as hospital dispenser and *capitao* on the Bruce estates. He was therefore in close touch with the other *capitaos* (or foremen), men like Wilson Zimba, Yotam Lifeyu, Johnston Latis and Henry Kolimbo, most of whom had been educated alongside Njilima and Kufa at the Blantyre mission and were fellow members of Chilembwe's church. As White has noted, over much of southern Africa, estate workers derided *capitaos* as collaborators. But on the Bruce estates, although *capitaos* were paid much more than ordinary workers, up to 30 shillings a month, they were treated in the same abusive manner by the estate managers – sometimes being flogged – and hence maintained a common identity of interest. When the rising began on 23 January, it was Wilson Zimba, at one time head *capitao* at Chiradzulu, who led the assault on W.J. Livingstone at Magomero, and Yotam Lifeyu and Johnston Latis who launched the subsidiary attack on the Mwanje plantation of the Bruce Estates.[33]

Yet if personal contacts and economic discrimination played their part in explaining why Kufa and his associates were drawn towards desperate revolt, two other factors were also important. First, as has been demonstrated with Chilembwe, several of this group, among them Njilima, were influenced by the mounting tide of millennial expectations associated with Watchtower. In the initial stages, it is likely that the adoption of these views encouraged them to develop other-worldly, pacifist attitudes, as was the case with most Watchtower adherents. David Kaduya, however, the most militant of Chilembwe's supporters, was constant in proclaiming what the Lindens have described as a 'singularly martial doctrine of salvation'; his activist views appear to have gained increasing influence in late 1914, following the widespread disappointment felt at the failure of the predicted Second Coming to materialise.[34]

Fundamentalist beliefs of this kind, however, fed on a second form of conflict arising from the particular character of colonial relations in the Shire Highlands. As Dane Kennedy has elegantly demonstrated, European settlers in Kenya and Southern Rhodesia were driven by a combination of arrogance and anxiety to form 'islands of white', aimed at isolating themselves culturally from the much larger indigenous population with whom, economically, they were inextricably involved.[35] In the Shire Highlands, settlers were few in number – under 400 in 1911 – most of them drawn from Scotland and England, rather than the somewhat more segregationist South Africa. Nevertheless, they demonstrated a

---

[33] White, *Magomero*, pp. 125–7; evidence of Moffat Kanchanda, 7 July 1919; evidence of Mwalimu, 7 July 1915, MNA Com 6 2/1/2.

[34] Linden, 'John Chilembwe', pp.640–41.

[35] Dane Kennedy, *Islands of White* (Durham 1987)

similar determination to create artificial boundaries, separating themselves materially and symbolically from people of other races. Outbreaks of 'black peril' hysteria, the public fear that African men might sexually threaten white women, were almost, although not entirely, absent from Nyasaland. However, while informal liaisons between European men and African women were tacitly accepted prior to the 1920s, and were relatively common, marriages between Europeans and Africans were rejected out of hand, as was demonstrated in 1903 when a young European, Albert Storey, attempted to have his marriage to Alice Ndumei formally registered, only to have his plea dismissed by Judge Nunan, to the approval of the white community.[36]

In this context, the all-too-visible presence of the first generation of literate Blantyre-educated Christians came as an intolerable affront to settler sensibilities, challenging the assumption that Africans were morally and intellectually inferior to Europeans. The wearing of western clothes, notably hats, was a particularly explosive issue, bringing the two parties into direct confrontation. As the thoughtfully posed portraits taken by Mungo Chisuse, Malawi's first African photographer, testify, Chilembwe, John Gray Kufa and their wider circle of acquaintances all gave high priority to the wearing of smart, European clothes, quite different from those worn by settlers, in shaping their image of the new African man (or woman): civilised, Christian and free. For the average settler, by contrast, Africans wearing such clothes were guilty of transgressing racial boundaries and hence of striking at the very roots of colonial social order.[37]

In his evidence to the Commission of Inquiry, Joseph Bismarck, an economic ally and social acquaintance of Chilembwe, who ignored the call to arms and came through the rising unscathed, provided a vivid account of the passionate emotions that the wearing of hats could arouse. In carefully chosen language, he noted that he and his friends regarded the wearing of a hat as an outward sign of civilisation, indicating: 'Now I am educated and am a freeman.' Yet Africans wearing hats, walking in Blantyre or Limbe, were treated with disrespect by whites who either refused to acknowledge their salutes or else threatened to whip them for their arrogance in aping European manners. In one encounter, an Italian planter had pulled a revolver on him with the words: 'You are a blackman and I am a white man, and you must take off your hat.' To Bismarck, and one may assume to Chilembwe and his associates, confrontations of this type were 'war', leading them to 'say that that is not liberty, and that we are just treated as slaves'.[38] If the settlers' jibes struck at the new men's sense of honour and identity, their own response was to challenge the conventional justification for British colonial rule by asserting that rather than bringing liberty to an enslaved people, the colonialists had imposed their own form of slavery, one just as degrading as that which had preceded it.

---

[36] *CAT*, Nov 1903. This case gave rise to a considerable amount of discussion among missionaries, most of whom were critical of the Judge's decision. See Hetherwick to W. P. Johnson, 18 Nov. 1903; W. A. Murray to Hetherwick, 2 Dec 1903, MNA, Hetherwick Corr., Church of Scotland. Papers.

[37] McCracken, 'Mungo Murray Chisuse'.

[38] Evidence of Joseph Bismarck to Nyasaland Rising Commission of Enquiry, 14 July 1914, TNA CO 525/66.

Interpretations

What turns people with grievances into active insurgents? In the case of Chilembwe, a variety of explanations have been suggested. Did despair at his failing health and mounting debts lead him to seek to 'strike a blow and die'?[39] Was the outbreak of the First World War the last straw, precipitating him into action? Was it frustration at the failure of the millennium to dawn that turned him from pacifism to violence? Was his resentment personal, against the anti-Christ W. J. Livingstone? [40] Or were all these elements combined with a further concern: the desire to repudiate settler racialism by seeking to create a new political order, in part nationalist, in part Africanist but always drawing on Christianity for its basic ideological message?

In responding to these questions, three observations can be made. The first is that while Livingstone was the principal victim and the Magomero Estate the main venue of the Rising, the intention of the rebels was to operate on a very much wider scale. As has been noted, the principal target on the night of 23 January appears to have been the African Lakes Company's store at Blantyre where arms and ammunition could be found. Attacks were also planned on the bomas at Zomba and Chiradzulu and also at Ntcheu, the home of large numbers of migrant labourers with extensive experience of working on the Shire Highlands estates. Incompetent planning and early failures prevented the rising developing significant momentum. However, there is no reason to doubt that in intention this was a 'general uprising' – a term much used at the time – even though in practice it operated predominantly on a local level.

The second observation, however, is that to describe the 1915 Rising as 'nationalist' is to strain the meaning of that admittedly ambiguous term. As Shepperson and Price convincingly argued 50 years ago, the Rising was of a distinctively different nature from earlier forms of resistance. Not only was it a response to colonial oppression rather than an attempt to preserve the independence of pre-colonial states, it was also led by 'new men' (the term is entirely appropriate), drawing on Christian ideology to proclaim, as Landeg White has noted, that the new colonial society, far from being itself Christian, was in fact 'based on expropriation and deep racial injustice'.[41] Chilembwe, as we have seen, wrote in protest against the war on 'behalf of his countrymen', a term that he appears to have used both of Africans in Nyasaland and of Africans more generally, but his concept of the new society which he was seeking to create contained a strong element of Christian Utopianism as well a belief in the need to extend authority and control to Africans. Chilembwe should be perceived not simply or even predominantly as a secular leader but rather as a prophet, albeit one for whom religion and politics were inextricably mixed. It is in this context that we should place the most disturbing element in the revolt: the service at Mbombwe conducted by Chilembwe with Livingstone's head displayed beside him. As Shepperson and Price, and D.D. Phiri have correctly emphasised, there are occa-

[39] See Rotberg, 'Psychological Stress', pp. 337–376.
[40] White, *Magomero*, pp. 127–33.
[41] White, *Magomero*, p. 130.

sions dating from the 1890s when both Malawian traditional rulers and European military commanders cut off and then displayed the heads of their enemies.[42] In that sense, Chilembwe was by no means unique in his action. Nevertheless, the deed was more consistent with a personalised form of religious fundamentalism than with a commitment to national liberation.

The third observation concerns the nature of the leadership provided by Chilembwe and his fellow African landowners. Shepperson and Price suggest that one reason for the failure of the rising was the reliance of the small African *petit bourgeoisie* on 'what has been called "the worst of all possible allies", the violent, vacillating "lumpenproletarians" [sic].' [43] But it can be argued that the reverse was true: that Lomwe and other labour tenants demonstrated remarkable courage and self-discipline but were let down by vacillating leaders.[44] For all his qualities of eloquence and conviction, Chilembwe, like the Irish patriot Roger Casement, who was executed for his part in an attempted insurrection against British rule a year after the Nyasaland Rising had been crushed, combined hatred of injustice with a total lack of capacity for the detailed logistical planning required for successful insurrection in the twentieth century.[45] How far Chilembwe was propelled into premature action by the news that the government was planning to deport him is uncertain; what is clear is that, by failing to give adequate advance warning of the outbreak of the Rising to his supporters at Zomba and Ntcheu, he condemned them to certain defeat. Certainly, the ability to maintain secrecy among his followers in the build-up to the attacks suggests a measure of effective internal discipline. However, no prior systematic attempt appears to have been made to establish an alliance with the Germans or to seek to coordinate tactics with them.

Once the Rising began, the business elite showed little stomach for action. John Gray Kufa disobeyed orders and took refuge in the bush rather than leading the contingent under his command – perhaps 500 strong – in an attack on the African Lakes Company store at Blantyre; Duncan Njilima, although getting as far as Blantyre, failed to carry out the task allotted to him, that of setting fire to the Boma. With Chilembwe inactive at Mbombwe – where he is said to have spent much of the time in prayer – practical leadership reverted to the Lomwe evangelist, David Kaduya, a militant millenarian and former KAR askari, and the only rebel of proven military quality. With Kufa absent, Kaduya took responsibility for leading the assault on the A.L.C. store at Blantyre on the night of Saturday 23 January, personally breaking into the ammunition store and carrying off boxes of ammunition and rifles. He then withdrew to Mbombwe where, on the Monday, he inflicted the one reverse suffered by government troops, ambushing them as they tried to cross the Mbombwe river and forcing them to retreat. The next day, according to some accounts, he led the attack on the Roman Catholic mission station at Nguludi, suffering a leg wound in the process.

---

[42] Shepperson and Price, pp. 262–63; Phiri, *Let us Die for Africa*, pp. 76–77.

[43] Shepperson and Price, p. 402.

[44] A point made by Vail and White, *Capitalism and Colonialism*, p.177.

[45] G. S. Mwase was the first writer to specifically compare Chilembwe to Casement. See Mwase, *Strike a Blow*, p. 80. Sir Roger Casement, after a distinguished British consular career in which he played a significant part in exposing the atrocities committed by King Leopold of the Belgians' government in the Congo, took part in an abortive rising against British rule in Ireland in 1916. He was later executed for treason.

When Kaduya was captured and then publicly executed in front of the workers on one of Magomero's cotton plantations, effective military resistance was brought to an end, although it was not until 3 February that Chilembwe was tracked down and shot. By that time government reprisals were fully under way, resulting in the destruction of Chilembwe's fine church, the execution by firing squad or hanging of dozens of his supporters, and the flogging and imprisonment of many more.

The collapse of the Rising throws light on its character. Elsewhere in East and Central Africa, centralising religious institutions and African political authorities were at the heart of large-scale resistance to incorporation in the colonial economy, but in the Chilembwe Rising this was not the case. With few exceptions, Yao chiefs and headmen in the Southern Province actively opposed Chilembwe rather than giving him their support. Officials of the Mbona cult remained uninvolved. A couple of Muslim headmen allied themselves to the fighters but overall, Islam, which had expanded rapidly in southern Malawi in the previous decade, was not utilised as an ideology of resistance, despite fears among colonial officials that it represented their greatest threat. On the other side, Christian capitalists proved half-hearted and unreliable revolutionaries. Catholic peasants failed to unite with Protestants. Immigrant labour tenants, lacking leadership, had difficulty carrying their message beyond the confines of the estates to independent peasants beyond. If the mounting tide of millennial expectations swept some Protestant Christians into militant action, for others, Watchtower teaching, with its emphasis on the imminence of the Second Coming, functioned as an obstacle rather than as an incentive to revolt. Neither Eliot Kamwana, who had been detained by the authorities at Mulanje, nor many adherents of Watchtower and Churches of Christ, took an active part in the Rising.

The initial defeat did not suppress all forms of resistance. In the eight weeks following, dissident villagers near Magomero kept the embers of revolt alight by repeatedly cutting the telegraph line between Blantyre and Zomba. However, so rigorous were the punishments imposed by the government that even this action was soon brought to an end.[46] Meanwhile, up to 30 of the most wanted supporters of Chilembwe took refuge on the Mbugwe stream in Mozambique close to the Nyasaland border. They were still there a year later when their presence was said to have resulted in 'a mild epidemic of alarmist rumours' among the Protectorate's settler population.[47]

Consequences

Even if the Chilembwe Rising was, in the short run, a political failure, it continued to resonate in the minds of Malawians and remained of concern to colonial officials. By the 1920s Malawian contemporary opinion tended to divide between that of the many disillusioned villagers living in the Shire Highlands who had come to explain the Rising as the consequence of nothing more important than a quarrel between Livingstone and Chilembwe over a bell and those

[46] Smyth to Chief Sec., 22 March 1915; Duff to Resident Blantyre, 8 April 1915, MNA NSB 1/2/1.
[47] Report of Chiradzulu Sub-District for 1915–16, MNA NSB 7/3/3.

members of the educated elite who were beginning to see in Chilembwe the self-sacrificing proto-nationalist hero. 'Yes, I heard more of that African patriot John Chilembwe and I am indeed proud of his name. It was a few days ago that I was relating his adventure to my staff at this office and they were indeed inspired', wrote Clements Kadalie, the Malawian founder of the most powerful trade union in South Africa, in 1925. It was as a patriot, although also as a self-sacrificing martyr that George Simeon Mwase, the Tonga intellectual and tobacco grower, depicted Chilembwe in his unpublished biography, written in about 1932.[48] A very different Chilembwe was discussed by peasants at independent Watchtower assemblies in the Lomagundi district of Southern Rhodesia in the late 1920s. 'I have heard the name Chilembwe. Those who dip us say they do his work. They say when Chilembwe comes we will fight with the White People', one participant recorded.[49] 'It is believed that Reyi, John Chilembwe and Mariya will rise out of the water and come to the people in the "Mbudzi" moon', another witness explained. 'They will give the people a potent to drink from a cup... When they awake they will be white and have massed wealth... All people will be on an equal footing financially and socially.'[50] Peasant populism, radical millenarianism and modernising nationalism were interrelated elements within the movement associated with Chilembwe; it is hardly surprising that they contributed to the various legends associated with him after his death.

Colonial responses varied nearly as widely as African ones. Faced by what he initially feared to be a widespread rising with substantial popular support, Sir George Smith, aided by the Chief Secretary, Hector Duff, insisted on the speedy trial, conviction and punishment of suspected rebels and encouraged the large-scale burning of villagers' huts. All firearms, whether breech-loading or muzzle-loading, were confiscated from Africans in the affected areas. Headmen were called together at special meetings where they were lectured on the need for 'implicit obedience' to the colonial government and reminded 'how signally' the attempt at insurrection had failed and 'with what swiftness and severity retribution has fallen on the ringleaders'.[51] In addition, collective fines of four shillings per male adult head were imposed over parts of the Chiradzulu, Zomba, Mulanje and Ntcheu districts as a punishment for 'colluding with, or harbouring, or failing to take reasonable means to prevent the escape of rebels'.[52]

As authority was re-established, the targets became more selective. So great was initial government suspicion of educated Africans that one teacher came to believe that 'the English had determined after the late fighting to kill off all the well-to-do natives.'[53] Roman Catholic and Anglican missions were perceived by the government as inculcating a suitably hierarchical mode of education but, according to Hetherwick, the 'godless' Governor and Chief Secretary displayed an 'openly hostile attitude' to the Scottish missions as well as to the smaller Protestant sects, all of whom were judged guilty of allowing their scholars un-

48 Mwase, *Strike a Blow*, pp. 69–74.
49 Statement by 'Buka', 20 Jan 1929 enclosed in Chief Native Commissioner Jackson to Commissioner, BSA Police, 29 Jan 1929, Zimbabwe National Archives, S 138/226.
50 Native Commissioner, Sinoia to CNC, 3 Jan 1929, ZNA S 138/226.
51 Duff to Resident, Blantyre, 12 Feb 1915; 23 Feb 1915, MNA NSB 1/2/1.
52 Duff to Residents, Southern Province, 8 June 1915, MNA NSB 1/2/1.
53 W.P. Johnson to Hetherwick, 23 Feb 1915, MNA Church of Scotland Papers.

supervised access to the Bible.[54] In the Legislative Council, Livingstone Bruce introduced a motion demanding that 'all schools in charge of native teachers in the Protectorate be closed at once'.[55] But this time he had gone too far. Hetherwick and Laws mobilised the support of Church interests in Scotland and with their help were successful in repelling this threat to their educational work. Similar protection, however, was not available for smaller, predominantly American-based missions such as the Churches of Christ and the Watchtower Society. In a series of panicky measures, the government deported Eliot Kamwana and other leading members of the Watchtower Society to Mauritius and thence to the Seychelles, where they were to languish until 1937. It also imposed a ban on the importation into Nyasaland of all Watchtower literature as well as a variety of other publications. African-organised churches were ordered to suspend their operations and Residents were instructed that 'Natives are not to be permitted to assemble in any considerable numbers for the discussion of religious topics or of the social and political questions which are often associated with native preaching.' [56]

Not until 1919 were government restrictions relaxed, and then only because it had become apparent that labour migrants were continuing to smuggle the banned literature into the country undetected. In the belief that 'it was less dangerous to allow the movement limited recognition than to drive it underground where its development could not be watched', the Government therefore gave permission for limited numbers of Watchtower churches to be built on condition that services should not be held between sunset and sunrise. Residents were instructed that they should no longer feel compelled to confiscate all Watchtower literature.[57] Nevertheless, and as a legacy of the Rising, the Government continued to pursue censorship polices that were even more illiberal than those in operation in most other Southern African territories. Between the wars, Marcus Garvey's *Negro World* and Clements Kadalie's *Workers' Herald* were both banned in Nyasaland, although they remained legal publications in South Africa.

Repressive measures would only be effective, Smith recognised, if they were accompanied by administrative reforms. One initiative taken as early as 1915 as a means of controlling the 'shiftless, unruly Nguru' who were perceived as forming the rank and file of the rebels, was the attempt to force peasants out of their scattered homes into concentrated villages where they could be more effectively controlled.[58] Another was to establish closer links with the predominantly non-Christian, non-educated Yao chiefs and headmen who had stood by the British during the time of crisis, although not at the expense of limiting the authority of estate owners. It would be many years before the provisions of the 1912 District Administration (Native) Ordinance, granting chiefs minor administrative powers would be extended to the Shire Highlands.[59] For a brief moment in July the alliance appeared to be threatened when a German agent was captured

---

54 Hetherwick to Laws, 27 March, 30 April 1915, MNA Church of Scotland Papers.
55 Quoted in Shepperson and Price, p. 365.
56 Duff to Residents, 22 July 1917 MNA *Confidential File.*
57 Acting Chief Secretary to PC Northern Province, 12 March 1923, MNA NN1/20/2.
58 Duff to Resident Blantyre, 22 March 1915; 23 April 1915, MNA NSB 1/2/.
59 Duff to Resident Blantyre, 22 March 1915, TNA NSB 1/2/1; L. White, "'Tribes" and the Aftermath of the Chilembwe Rising', *African Affairs,* 83, 333, (1984), pp. 511–41. For a modification to White's analysis see Chapter 9.

carrying dynamite and letters calling on Muslim chiefs to rise alongside the Germans in an attack on the infidel British. However, Yao leaders responded in a public demonstration of support by offering 'full expressions of loyalty and contentment with British rule' at a party hosted by the Governor at the close of Ramadan.[60] With fears of a Muslim rising dissolved, the charm offensive accelerated. In July, at the Zomba depot of the KAR, three hapless Christian recruits were flogged when they petitioned for a church to be built alongside the existing mosque.[61] Thereafter, colonial officials tended to emphasise the value of the Yao: 'good physically, intelligent and amenable to discipline' in contrast to the Nguru, who were said to be 'represented among the idle and criminal classes to a disproportionate extent'.[62] It was still the case that British administrators regarded Nguru immigrants as 'a very considerable asset to the country as agricultural labourers'.[63] But politically, it was Yao chiefs, exercising their authority over Lomwe/Nguru commoners, with whom they preferred to work.[64]

Further proposals were aimed at the creation of 'something more powerful than the present police force' to cope with Nyasaland's 'dangerous class', defined by the Resident at Chiradzulu as composed of 'discharged capitaos, houseboys, mission teachers etc., returned emigrants to South Africa, professional criminals, and generally natives who have become dissatisfied with the state of life in which they were born, but are unprepared to improve it by honest industry'.[65] Nothing could be accomplished during the war, but with the return of peace, action was finally taken. The old system of relying on district residents to recruit their own askaris was abandoned. In the Southern Province a professional, European-officered force was established, complete with a Criminal Investigation Department, set up in 1922 to investigate activities liable to threaten the security of the state. Insufficient funds were available, however, to allow European police officers to be posted to the Central and Northern Provinces, as Smith had hoped. The Governor was equally unsuccessful in his attempt to persuade the Colonial Office of the need to form a European Defence Force, composed of all adult male settlers, such as existed in Southern Rhodesia, as an insurance 'against native risings and revolt'.[66] Internal security in Nyasaland therefore remained precariously balanced. It would be more than 30 years before it became clear quite how fragile were the foundations upon which it was based.[67]

One final area of concern related to the character of the *thangata* regime. Although the Commission of Inquiry emphasised the central importance of the political notions imbued by Chilembwe from Joseph Booth and from his African-American colleague in bringing about the Rising, it also stated that 'the treatment of labour and the system of tenancy on the Bruce Estates ... were in several respects illegal and oppressive.'[68] Bruce's response, White has charitably

---

[60] Smith to CO, 15 Nov 1915, TNA CO 525/63.
[61] Hetherwick to Elmslie, 21 Aug 1915, MNA, Church of Scotland Papers.
[62] 'Information for military handbook of Nyasaland, 1922', MNA S2/6/27; S.S. Murray, *A Handbook of Nyasaland* (Zomba, 1922), p. 56.
[63] Murray, *Handbook*, p. 57.
[64] Vail and White, 'Creation of Tribalism', pp. 168–71.
[65] Ann Rep of Chiradzulu Sub-Dist for 1915–16, MNA NSB 7/3/3.
[66] Smith to CO, 24 Jan 1921, MNA S2/10/20.
[67] For a fuller discussion see McCracken, 'Authority and Legitimacy in Malawi', pp. 166–68.
[68] *Report of the Commission ... concerned with the Native Rising.*

suggested, was to bring to an end the 'brand of casual brutality' associated with Livingstone and instead to initiate a new regime in which wages were paid at the official rate and a month's work was measured at 28 days. For the next 30 years, 'dull attrition', associated only sporadically with naked violence, was to characterise labour relations on the estates.[69]

A more intractable problem concerned the system of tenancy. Responding to a recommendation from the Commission of Inquiry, the Government introduced a radical new ordinance in 1917 which made it illegal for landlords to exact services in lieu of rent from tenants living on their estates. Had this measure been obeyed, *thangata* would have ceased to exist, with profound consequences for the subsequent history of landlord-tenant relations in the Shire Highlands. Instead, in an intervention that was to be frequently repeated in subsequent years, estate owners, led by Livingstone Bruce, threatened to evict their tenants in large numbers unless they were allowed to continue to exact *thangata*. Faced by the prospect of having to settle these people on Crown Land, the Government backed down. By 1920, when a further Commission of Inquiry met, the 1917 ordinance was being uniformly ignored. As the Commission noted: 'the general practice on agricultural estates in the Districts of Blantyre and Zomba is that the tenant works for a certain period for his landlord in return for his right of residence.'[70] Its conclusion was that *thangata* was there to stay: 'We do not see how this practice can be abolished, nor, in our opinion, is it objectionable if it is regularised by law and strictly supervised in its operation.'[71]

In consequence, grievances were to continue to fester from 1915 into the 1950s.

[69] White, *Magomero*, p. 146.
[70] *Report of a Commission to enquire into and report upon certain matters connected with the Occupation of Land in the Nyasaland Protectorate'* (Zomba, 1920), p. 14. See also White, *Magomero*, p. 152.
[71] *Ibid.*

6

Malawi & the First World War

European politics were exported to Africa in a particularly oppressive form
during the First World War. In military terms, the East African campaign was
a sideshow, a distraction from the titanic struggle being conducted on the
Western Front in France. Yet for millions of Africans (and many thousands of
Malawians) the war marked the high point of colonial violence: a period in
which the compromises of the colonial state fell away to reveal a naked demand
for manpower, both as soldiers and even more as porters, and for supplies of
grain and cattle. Nyasaland was largely spared the horror inflicted on German
East Africa – its use as a battlefield – but, in other respects, the impact of the
war on the territory was exceptionally disruptive. No other British dependency
in Africa suffered the loss to the military of such a high proportion of its
manpower and this in turn had profound consequences both for the health and
wellbeing of many Malawians and for popular attitudes in the Protectorate. The
war, moreover, was paradoxical in its effects in that it demonstrated not only the
extent of European power but also its ultimate fragility. Imperial supplies on an
unprecedented scale poured into Nyasaland. Yet, from 1917, the conduct of the
campaign was dependent almost entirely on the endeavours of African soldiers
and porters.

The campaign

When Britain and Germany went to war in August 1914, the forces available to
the colonial government of Nyasaland were remarkably small. Earlier in the
century the two battalions of the Kings African Rifles had numbered over 1,400
men, but 2 KAR had been disbanded in 1911 following the decision of the Imperial General Staff to downgrade the use of African troops for imperial defence
and in 1912 the last Indian troops had left the territory. By June 1914 fewer than
300 troops were available, along with a further 300 time-expired veterans in the
reserves. There were three old-fashioned maxim machine guns in support, six 7–
pounder muzzle loading cannons dating from the campaign against Mlozi, and
no field artillery at all. The Nyasaland Volunteer Reserve (180 British subjects 'of

European race') was almost totally lacking in discipline or military training.[1]

If the British forces were limited, however, those available to the German authorities in Tanganyika were even more so. With a Defence Force consisting of 218 Europeans and 2,542 askaris, Colonel von Lettow-Vorbeck, the brilliant German military commander, might appear to have had the advantage. But Lettow-Vorbeck's troops were far outnumbered by those of his opponents, not only in Nyasaland with its short land boundary with Tanganyika, but in Kenya, Uganda, the Belgian Congo and Mozambique as well. It was apparent to him that he could best serve Germany's interests by fighting a long defensive war, attracting as many British troops as possible away from more vital theatres of action.[2]

The campaign that followed was fought largely on Lettow-Vorbeck's terms. Hostilities began on 8 August 1914 when a British warship opened fire on a wireless station at Dar es Salaam, the capital of German East Africa. Five days later Nyasaland forces also became involved when the British gunboat *Guendolen* demobilised the German ship *Hermann von Wissmann* in dry dock at Spinxhaven (a task eased by the fact that the *Wissmann's* captain had not been alerted to the outbreak of war).[3] With British control of Lake Malawi now established, the Nyasaland Field Force, consisting of 480 African soldiers plus 17 British officers and 30 European volunteers, was despatched north to Karonga, near the border with German East Africa. There, in September, it succeeded, through a combination of good fortune and courage, in defeating a German force some 400 strong in the short but bloody battle which was to be the only significant military engagement of the war on Nyasaland soil.[4]

With the preliminaries out of the way, the campaign moved into the first of three phases, each more destructive than its predecessor and each involving Malawians on a larger, more costly, scale. The initial stage was distinguished by a lack of military action. British rejoicing over the victory at Karonga was quickly dispelled in October when news reached Nyasaland of the devastating defeat by German-led askaris of an expeditionary force at Tanga on the Tanganyikan coast, an event which forced the British onto the defensive for the next 18 months. 'Business as usual' became the motto at Blantyre, with work at the Church of Scotland mission continuing as before.[5] On the frontier separating Nyasaland and Northern Rhodesia from Tanganyika, both sides made occasional raids into enemy territory but significant contact was avoided. The Chilembwe Rising at

---

[1] Note by Lt.Col. R.W. Baldwin, OC Nyasaland, June 1913, MNA KAR 1/1/1.
[2] This account of the campaign is based largely on the following sources: Iliffe, *Modern History, pp.* 240–72; C.P. Lucas, *The Empire at War* (London, 1921), Vol. IV; H.L. Duff, 'Nyasaland in the World War 1914–1918', Imperial War Museum; H. Boyse-Barlett, *The King's African Rifles* (Aldershot, 1956). For the impact of the war on Malawians the key study is Melvin E. Page, *The Chiwaya War. Malawians and the First World War* (Westview Press, 2000). In this chapter I also make use of Page's postgraduate dissertation, 'Malawians in the Great War and after, 1914–1925', Ph.D, Michigan State University, 1977 and of Page, 'The War of *Thangata*: Nyasaland and the East African Campaign, 1914–1919', *JAH*, 19, 1 (1978). Hew Strachan, *The First World War in Africa* (Oxford University Press, 2004) is excellent on the campaign overall but has little to say on Nyasaland.
[3] Jonathan Newell, '"How the English Gentleman Makes War in the Colonies": Securing Naval Supremacy on Lake Malawi, 1914–1916', *SOMJ*, 46, 2 (1993).
[4] There is a racy account of these developments in Oliver Ransford, *Livingstone's Lake. The Drama of Nyasa* (London, 1966), 237–52.
[5] *LWBCA*, Sept–Dec 1914; Jan–Mar 1915.

Chiradzulu and Blantyre in January 1915 (discussed in the previous chapter) resulted in the rapid deployment from Karonga to the Shire Highlands of two companies of the KAR, but otherwise was of limited military significance. Indirectly, however, it contributed to a shift in the pattern of military recruitment. Although no serving askaris took part in the rising, the Governor, Sir George Smith, convinced himself that it would be dangerous to rely unduly on the continuing loyalty of African soldiers and appealed for European reinforcements.[6] With the German surrender in South West Africa in July 1915, white South African troops became available for service. In an unusual intervention, King George V, who was concerned by reports of German raids on the Northern Rhodesian frontier, asked 'whether it would not be possible to induce the Union Government to increase the Nyasaland contingent and to send a contingent to East Africa instead of carrying out their proposal to send a contingent to Europe', and this was speedily approved.[7] On 16 August, J. C. Davidson, a junior minister at the Colonial Office, informed the King's private secretary that the South African government had agreed to reinforce the garrison in Nyasaland.[8] By January 1916, more than 750 white South Africans were serving on the frontier as compared with 730 askaris. Meanwhile, the decision had been taken to reconstitute the 2nd battalion of the KAR to serve, not in Nyasaland but, rather, along with Ugandan and Kenyan battalions in the army now being constructed at Nairobi. The South African General Smuts, however, as overall commander, took care to ensure that the enlarged army was predominantly white. In March 1916 Africans comprised only one in seven of the 48,750 soldiers under his command.[9]

The arrival of Brigadier-General Edward Northey at Karonga in February 1916 as the commander of the Nyasaland-Rhodesian forces marked the end of the phoney war and the beginning of the second phase of the military campaign. As a professional soldier, previously commander of a brigade in France, Northey was shocked by the incompetence he uncovered. Constant friction existed between the local officials and South African officers. Arrangements for the transport of supplies had been so neglected that there was a serious shortage of food, with askaris and carriers receiving only starvation rations: 1.25 pounds of maize each day. German patrols had been allowed to wander at will on the border, raiding British territory with impunity.[10]

With the invasion of Tanganyika imminent, Northey swung into action, liaising with Governor Smith on the reorganisation of the transport system between the railhead at Limbe and Karonga and sending military recruiters through the villages in search of both carriers and soldiers. Military camps were established at Blantyre and Zomba; men and supplies were funnelled into the lake port of Fort Johnston. For the next two years, this port was to function as a vital link on the communications chain running from South Africa to Chinde on the Zambezi mouth and from there for up to 700 miles to wherever the front columns were operating.

[6]   G. Smith to Colonial Secretary, 19 July 1915, TNA CO 525/62.
[7]   Lord Stamfordham, Windsor Castle, to Colonial Secretary, 14 August 1915, TNA CO 525/62.
[8]   J.C. Davidson to Lord Stamfordham, 16 August 1915, TNA CO 525/62.
[9]   Iliffe, *Modern History*, 243. For Smuts' views see Charles Miller, *Battle for the Bundu. The First World War in East Africa* (London, 1974), p. 259.
[10] War Diary of Major-General Sir Edward Northey, 29 Jan, 16 Feb 1916; summary 4 Dec 1915–8 April 1916. Imperial War Museum.

In the middle of March, Smuts began his cautious advance from Kenya into German East Africa while on 25 May, Northey crossed the Nyasa-Tanganyika border in a subsidiary thrust designed to encircle the German forces. Neu Langenburg, the German district headquarters, was occupied on 29 May and on 29 August so too was Iringa, more than 200 miles from the Lake, convincing the senior command that victory was imminent. On 11 September Northey noted in his diary: 'The enemy's morale is quite broken, and their Europeans are in poor health, short of proper food, and mostly thoroughly sick of the war, considering that the continuance of the campaign out here is a useless waste of life.'[11]

Lettow-Vorbeck, however, was far from beaten. Avoiding Smuts's attempt to entrap him at Morogoro, he moved southwards with the main body of German troops while smaller detachments doubled back north-west to the east of Lake Malawi, harassing Northey's supply columns. By late November the rains had begun to fall. Newly constructed motor roads were impassable and many carriers were already dying of cold. So high was the incidence of malaria and dysentery among British and white South African troops that they had to be invalided home in their thousands and replaced from the beginning of the year by African soldiers, most of them from the KAR and up to half recruited in Nyasaland.[12] Reviewing the forces at his disposal in March 1917, Northey noted that the 1st South African Infantry numbered only 60 men, most of them unfit; the 2nd South African Rifles were also nearly all suffering from malaria. The men of the 5th South African Infantry, who had only just arrived, were so untrained, inexperienced and lacking in morale that their commanding officer refused to lead them in the field.[13] In July the last European contingents were disbanded and most remaining South African and Southern Rhodesian troops were distributed among KAR companies as machine gunners. Meanwhile, total numbers in the KAR increased from 4,338 at the beginning of 1916 to 30,658 by the end of the war. Nyasaland's share rose from two battalions to eight, totalling some 15,000 men in 1918. In addition, 3,000 troops were in training at depots and as many as 1,000 Malawian migrant workers had been recruited into the Rhodesian Native Regiment.[14] During the last year of the war approximately 123,000 Malawian porters were employed: nearly 32,000 as front-line carriers alongside the troops; 35,000 on the lines of communication, transporting, food, ammunition and supplies for 200 miles or more from the nearest depot; and 56,000 making roads, carrying foodstuffs to the military camps, and cutting down and transporting firewood.[15]

It was therefore predominantly Nyasa troops and porters who were involved in the final, most exhausting stage of the war: the grim pursuit of Lettow-Vorbeck as he feinted towards Nyasaland in May 1917, thus forcing Northey to move his headquarters temporarily to Zomba, crossed into Mozambique in November and then doubled back north into Tanganyika in September

[11] Northey War Diary, entry for 11 September 1916. IWM.
[12] Lucas, *Empire at War*, 275; Duff, 'Nyasaland in the World War', Chap. 6; Northey War Diary, entry for 4 Feb 1917, IWM.
[13] Northey War Diary, entries for 3 Feb, 4 March, 1 April 1917, IWM.
[14] Page, 'Malawians in the Great War', pp. 49–50, 103–4; G.W.T. Hodges, 'African Manpower Statistics for the British Forces in East Africa, 1914–1918', *JAH*, 19, 1 (1978) pp. 103–4.
[15] Lucas, *Empire at War*, Vol. IV, p. 270.

1918. They were still following in Lettow-Vorbeck's wake when he turned south-westwards into Northern Rhodesia in October, close to the spot from which Northey had begun his advance nearly two and a half years earlier. When the war ended, on 18 November, a week after the armistice in Europe, Lettow-Vorbeck's army remained in the field and was heading south to Broken Hill.

The impact of war: death, dearth & disease

The impact of the war on Nyasaland was highly disruptive. According to official figures, 19,000 soldiers were recruited in the territory compared with 10,500 recruited in Kenya, a country with a population twice Nyasaland's size; 1,740 died on active service with a further 2,200 being wounded.[16] Nyasaland also supplied between 200,000 and 197,000 porters for periods lasting officially between six months and a year although often, in practice, for very much longer. All soldiers and the great majority of porters were men, but some women and children were also employed in carrying food supplies to the lake.[17] According to one, admittedly impressionistic estimate, over 83 per cent of all able-bodied men served at some time or another.[18]

'Of all natives who were recruited for military work, whether as combatants or otherwise, the "tenga-tenga" (carriers) undoubtedly had the hardest time', Hector Duff noted in his unpublished history of the war.[19] The askaris, at least, had the benefit of relatively high wages: 10 shillings a month for members of the 1st Battalion KAR, rising in March 1917 to £1 1s 4d, following a wave of complaints. This was the sum paid to members of the 2nd Battalion billeted alongside soldiers from the higher wage economies of Kenya and Uganda.[20] The carriers, by contrast, had to make do with 5 shillings per month and a blanket. Military recruits were medically inspected with many being rejected. But in the case of porters, 'old men who are not really fit to work' were recruited along with men who had failed the soldiers' medical examination. Every effort was made, by no means always successfully, to ensure that the askaris were adequately fed. However, as early as April 1916, many of the carriers returning from Karonga were described by a local official as appearing to be 'in a starving condition' and once the invasion of Tanganyika began, conditions deteriorated further.[21] By January 1917, Northey noted that many of those employed carrying supplies across the 9,000 feet high Livingstone Mountains to Songea or Lupembe were either deserting on the road or else dying of the intense cold. A few months later

[16] Chief Sec to Colonial Secretary, 23 Feb 1922, PRO CO 534/9; Hodges, 'African Manpower Statistics', 116. Murray, in *Handbook* (1922) p. 271, estimates that 18,920 were recruited for service with the KAR. Hodges provides a lower figure of 15,000 on the grounds that the remainder was still in training at the Namidi depot when the war ended.
[17] Page, 'Malawians in the Great War', p. 83; Lucas, *Empire at War,* p. 270; Duff, 'Nyasaland in the World War'. Murray, *Handbook* (1922) gives the lower figure of 191,200. For further details, see Acting Chief Sec to Governor, 28 June 1918, MNA NSB 1/2/5 and Duff, Acting Governor, to Colonial Secretary, 27 January 1919, TNA CO 525/82.
[18] Hodges, 'African Manpower Statistics', p. 113.
[19] Duff, ' Nyasaland in the World War', chap 11.
[20] Northey War Diaries, summary 1 April 1917, IWM; Page, 'Malawians in Great War', pp. 41–2.
[21] Resident, Chinteche, to Chief Sec, Zomba, 26 April 1916, MNA NNC/1/1/1.

they were dying of malaria in the plains.[22] Tonga porters returning to the West Nyasa district late in 1917 brought back stories of 'ill treatment, frequent floggings and loads far in excess of their strength'. Similar reports came from other parts of the country.[23] Clothing supplied to porters by 1918 consisted of little more than 'an occasional worn dunny bag'; medical attention was virtually non-existent; agreements made by labour recruiters were widely ignored.[24] At a district council meeting held at the south-east of Lake Malawi in October, 'All the chiefs and headmen stated they had originally persuaded their people to sign labour contracts for definite periods, e.g. 4 or 6 months but in most cases no notice of this had been taken by the authorities and consequently they were now laughed at by the people and told to their faces they were liars'.[25]

According to official statistics, deaths among carriers from Nyasaland amounted to 4,400, only 2.25 per cent of the total. This does not take account of those who were believed to have deserted or of the starving, disease-ridden survivors who succumbed only after they had been officially discharged.[26] Dr Laws in February 1918 wrote of the 'terrible mortality' among carriers, averaging 300 a month at least.[27] Sir George Smith estimated their losses at four or five per cent in 1917 and 1918, although, as he indicated in a chilling aside, this rate did not compare unfavourably with the fatalities among migrants in the South African mines.[28]

The drain of labour varied considerably between different parts of the country. Worst hit throughout the war were the Upper Shire, Liwonde and South Nyasa districts. This area was of marginal economic importance on the direct line of communications from Blantyre to Fort Johnston and, hence, particularly open to military recruiters. In 1918, according to the administrative census of that year, between 59 and 81 per cent of adult males normally resident in these districts were employed in war work, a significantly higher proportion than anywhere else.[29] At Makanjila's village, 'all present stated that their people had considered they had been unduly called up for "Tangata" work and hence demanded a rest and leisure to cultivate their gardens'. The chief 'pointed out how his people had been harassed in meeting the military demands' and asserted that 'many of them were now living away from the villages, having taken refuge in the bush.'[30]

By contrast, the plantation areas of the Shire Highlands – Blantyre, Chiradzulu, and Mulanje – produced substantial numbers of carriers in the early years of the war but much fewer later. Settler complaints against the disruption of their resident labour supply forced the military recruiters to turn their attention elsewhere. In the Chiradzulu sub-district, Yao chiefs seeking to demonstrate

22 Northey War Diaries, Entries for 30 Nov, 13 Dec 1916, 1 Jan 1917, IWM.
23 Resident, Chinteche, to Chief Secretary, Zomba, 16 Nov 1917, NNC 1/1/1. See also Linden, *Catholics, Peasants and Chewa Resistance*, pp.110–11.
24 Annual Report West Nyasa District for year ending 31 March 1918, MNA NNC 3/13.
25 Summary of proceedings of District Council, 29 October 1918. Fort Johnston District Book, Vol. II.
26 Page, 'Malawians in the Great War', p. 154.
27 Laws to James Reid, 13 February 1918, Church of Scotland papers, MNA.
28 Sir George Smith to Colonial Secretary, 13 August 1917, TNA CO 525/74.
29 1918 Administrative Census, MNA NSB 1/2/5 reproduced in Page, 'Malawians in the Great War', 50, 82.
30 Summary of proceedings of District Councils, 29 Oct 1918; Section Council meeting, August 1918, Fort Johnston District Book Vol 2.

their loyalty to the British furnished over 3,000, predominantly Lomwe, porters in 1915 in the aftermath of the Chilembwe Rising; European estates, however, went virtually untouched. Only 149 military labourers were recruited in the Mulanje district in 1918.[31]

Also partially spared, in consequence of its privileged economic position as the main centre of cotton growing in Nyasaland, was the Lower Shire Valley. It survived largely unscathed up to the final year of the war when some 2,500 men were pressed into service. No such protection was extended to the Central and Northern provinces, although in this great area where colonial control was still only lightly established, substantial numbers of men were successful in avoiding recruitment. Some took refuge in the bush and others (Hastings Kamuzu Banda among them) migrated to South Africa.[32]

The techniques utilised in obtaining labour became increasingly coercive as the war progressed. KAR recruiters were able to offer potential askaris wages up to three times higher than those prevailing locally but similar financial inducements were not available to carriers. At first the government attempted to work through chiefs and headmen who were called upon to produce carriers on pain of being deposed. But once the push into German East Africa began, policemen and messengers were also employed in hunting down military labour. In scenes reminiscent of the worst days of the slave trade, police patrols raided villages at night, seizing adult men, tying them up, and leading them off into service.[33] Policemen who failed to produce sufficient carriers were fined. District residents ordered the destruction of the houses of men who had failed to come forward for recruitment.[34] Members of the educated elite were almost as much at risk as ordinary villagers. So many of Livingstonia's teachers were recruited as interpreters, guides and hospital orderlies that it became necessary to close most of the mission schools.[35] In 1918 every able-bodied Watchtower teacher in the West Nyasa district that the resident could lay his hands on was enrolled as a military carrier.[36]

The intensity and persistence of the war affected families far from the battle-front. With imported goods in short supply, bark cloth replaced mass-produced textiles in many homes and locally smelted hoes reappeared.[37] The demand from the military for cattle and foodstuffs created short-term opportunities but also longer-term hazards for peasant producers in what had previously been marginal areas. At Fort Johnston, the major entrepot for the lake, 7,600 bags of rice were sold to the military in 1916–17 at £4 a ton but only

---

[31] Resident, Chiradzulu to Wade, 8 Feb 1916, MNA NSB 7/3/3; Chief Sec to Resident, Blantyre, 2 Feb 1916, MNA NSB 1/2/3; Acting Chief Sec to Governor, 28 June 1918, MNA NSB 1/2/5.

[32] Standard accounts explain Banda's departure from Kasungu in 1915 as a consequence of his determination to acquire a better education in the south following his failure to obtain entrance to Livingstonia. It would hardly be surprising however, if like many other Malawians from his district, he was also influenced by his wish to avoid military service. This undoubtedly would have been his fate had he enrolled at Livingstonia. All teacher training courses there were suspended in February 1916 with the students being recruited by the army.

[33] See Page, 'The War of *Thangata*'.

[34] Resident, Chinteche, to Chief Sec, 16 Nov 1917.

[35] McCracken, *Politics and Christianity in Malawi*, 222–23.

[36] Annual Report for the West Nyasa District for year ending 31 March 1918, NNC 3/13. MNA.

[37] Nyasaland Annual Report, 1916–17, draft. CO 525/75; Resident, Chinteche, to Chief Sec, 1 Feb 1917, MNA NNC 1/1/1.

2,360 bags in 1917–18 as a consequence of the drain of agricultural manpower.[38] The enterprising headman, Mwamadi Matewere, took advantage of the expanded market for fish by erecting a reed barrier with traps across the Shire River at the Bar and selling his catch to the newly constructed camps at Zomba and Blantyre.[39] Several thousand head of cattle from the Mzimba and North Nyasa districts were also sold to the military. By the end of the war more than 10,000 tons of maize and millet had been requisitioned, some of it from the Lilongwe plain which had not previously featured as a significant producer of cash crops.[40] With prices buoyant, African cotton output in the Shire valley increased up to 1916–17, only to fall away in the following year as the demand for military porters took its toll.[41]

By 1918 the drain of manpower combined with the export of foodstuffs was creating a crisis in the local food supply, worsened by drought in the northern half of the territory. Fear of famine surfaced late in 1917 and spread during the rainy season as reports came in from various quarters showing that 'the present scarcity of foodstuffs among the native population is leading to great hardships and that already a number of deaths have occurred.'[42] Along the northern lakeshore little rain fell and the maize crop failed, while in the Shire Highlands the maize crop was described as 'light' in consequence of the reduced acreage of foodstuffs that the depleted labour force had managed to plant.[43] Government relief measures were hampered by the unavailability of imported grain and could not prevent deaths taking place among the most vulnerable sections of the population: children and the old.[44]

Lack of food reduced resistance to disease which spread along the lines of supply. Six thousand cases of smallpox were recorded in 1918 and bubonic plague broke out at Karonga, as it had done previously on several occasions.[45] Most serious of all was the worldwide influenza pandemic. It swept through Southern Rhodesia in September and October 1918, killing seven per cent of black mine-workers, many of them from Nyasaland, before reaching Blantyre in November.[46] Within a matter of weeks all hospitals in the Shire Highlands, military and civilian alike, were filled to overflowing with victims. However, there was hardly a doctor, nurse or orderly to treat them as they too had contracted the disease.[47] With European medicines ineffective, witchcraft accusations flourished and rumours that headmen were administering *mwavi* were reported from several districts in the protectorate.[48] The pandemic spread with astonishing speed, breaking out in village after village and, in some cases, carrying whole

---

38 Fort Johnston District Book Vol II.
39 McCracken, 'Fishing', 420.
40 Duff to Col Sec, 27 Jan 1919, MNA CO 525/82; Annual Report of Department of Agriculture for year ending 31 March 1918, 18.
41 Duff, Acting Governor, to Col Sec, 27 Feb 1919, TNA CO 525/82.
42 J.W. Stratton, Nyasaland Chamber of Commerce, to Acting Chief Sec, 9 Jan 1918, MNA NSB 1/2/5.
43 Laws to James Thin, no date [late 1919]. Thin papers, Edinburgh; *LWBCA* April–June 1918, 2.
44 Hector Duff, 'Nyasaland in the World War'; Duff to Col Sec, 14 April 1919, TNA CO 525/82.
45 Page, 'Malawians in the Great War', 182–3; Laws to Thin, no date, Thin Papers.
46 Terence Ranger, 'The influenza pandemic in Southern Rhodesia: a crisis of comprehension' in David Arnold (ed.), *Imperial Medicine and Indigenous Societies*, (Manchester, 1988), 173–5: Van Onselen, *Chibaro*.
47 *LWBCA*, July 1918– June 1919, 1–2.
48 Resident, Blantyre, to Resident, Chiradzulu, 17 Dec 1918, MNA NSB 2/1/1.

families away. In January 1919 it reached Karonga; by April 1,400 deaths were reported in the North Nyasa district.[49] According to the Acting Governor, writing in February, 1,700 deaths and 16,000 cases had been reported in or near the principal European stations. To this should be added the thousands of further deaths (in excess of 8,000 in the Dowa and Lilongwe districts alone) that went unrecorded by the medical authorities.[50] The best estimate available is that up to 50,000 people, perhaps five per cent of the population, died: a similar proportion to the death rate suggested by Ranger for Southern Rhodesia but somewhat higher than in neighbouring Tanganyika.[51] At all events, as in many other countries, it seems likely that more Malawians died from influenza in the 12 months after the ending of the First World War than died on military service over the whole of the previous four years.

The impact of war: memory & dance

It is difficult to generalise about the effect of the war on African attitudes. Soldiers and civilians alike complained at the sheer length of the campaign and, in the latter stages, vehemently called for peace. 'Petition received from "C" Company to return to Nyasaland', recorded the commanding officer of 2/1 KAR in May 1918 after months of forced marches and short rations.[52] A village headman wrote to the Chief Secretary, Duff: 'Now this war has lasted perhaps three years... and many men are dying, so we are wondering when the war will end, because the women are alone, and there is hunger in our villages.'.[53] For some askaris, however, the hardships of war were in part compensated for by the camaraderie and professionalism engendered. Evidence on this point is necessarily indirect but it is suggestive that at no time after 1918 did the KAR have difficulty in attracting recruits. As a consequence of their performance in the war, the reputation of Malawian troops in military circles grew and so did their sense of self-esteem. 'Troops composed of natives of this Protectorate have been much sought after by the adjacent Protectorates in East Africa', the Nyasaland Military Handbook recorded in 1926.[54] Reverting to ethnic stereotype, the Intelligence Officer in 1937 commented:

> The Yaos have a magnificent war record, and it is safe to say that they could be employed satisfactorily for warfare in any tropical or semi-tropical country. They were found during the Great War to be more satisfactory in conditions in East Africa than white South African troops.[55]

If the askaris could point to a job well done, porters were more likely to be conscious only of the terrible sacrifices involved. 'Mtengatenga is thangata', an

[49] Laws to Mrs Kirkwood, 18 April 1919, Kirkwood Papers, Inverness.
[50] Duff to Colonial Secretary, 27 Feb 1919, CO 525/82; Hut tax summary, Lilongwe District Book.
[51] Page, 'Malawians in the Great War', 222; G. Coleman, 'The African Population of Malawi: An Analysis of the Censuses between 1901 and 1966', *SOMJ*, 27, 1 (1974), 32; Ranger, 'The influenza pandemic in Southern Rhodesia', 175; Iliffe, *Modern History of Tanganyika*, 270.
[52] Page, 'Malawians in the Great War', 128.
[53] Duff, 'Nyasaland in the World War'. See also Hector Duff, *African Small Chop* (London, 1932), 187.
[54] Nyasaland Military Handbook, 1926 MNA S2/6/27.
[55] Intelligence Report for half year ending June 30 1937, MNA S2/6/27.

informant insisted to Professor Page. 'We used to call it thangata in those days. We were forced to work.'[56] By 1918, in Makanjila's chieftaincy, as in other parts of the country, many people 'were now living away from the villages lest they be caught for "Tangata" work'. When attempts were made to pressgang them into service, they reacted by assaulting the recruiters or by taking refuge in the neighbouring hills.[57] The experience of porterage was not easily forgotten. When I KAR carried out an exercise in the Mulanje district in 1924, men fled en masse from their villages 'largely due to the fear that they might be seized as tenga-tenga'.[58]

Other reactions to the war took a wide variety of forms. Chiefs and headmen called upon to recruit faced an agonizing dilemma. Those like the Ngoni chief, Kachindamoto, who complied with government demands reaped the hatred of their subjects.[59] Those who refused to supply porters risked being deposed. In a notorious incident, Chief Chimtunga, paramount of the northern Ngoni, was deprived of office and deported for his refusal to recruit.[60] Most white missionaries, whatever their denomination, were actively involved in furthering the war effort. Thus, Watchtower teachers like Sam Amanda, imprisoned as a result of his anti-war preaching in 1917, emerged as the most consistently eloquent critics of the military campaign. In words reminiscent of Kamwana's, Amanda preached that 'both the Government and the Chiefs were doing very wrong in collecting and sending the people away as military carriers and road labourers, and that such as were sent would only die.'[61] Hymns sung at Watchtower assemblies in 1919 were full of references to the losses sustained: 'Fire burns in Sodom. Your children are thrown into it. The white man too gave their teacher and they are finished', went one version, vividly conjuring up the plight of the young men of the village and of mission teachers, consumed by the flames of war. 'The white men say the war is finished, where are your children?' went another Watchtower hymn, with the grim refrain: 'You may shave your heads', that is, 'you may go into mourning.'[62] Some Malawians in the Central and Southern provinces looked to the village-based *Nyau* secret society to defend them against alien cultural influences, but others turned to mainstream Christianity.[63] The latter suffered badly from the disruption of schools and the loss of external finance but may have gained in popularity as a consequence of the increased responsibilities given to African pastors and evangelists during the war when many white missionaries were absent.[64] The true crisis of authority for Livingstonia, for example, came not when pastors like Hezekiah Tweya, Yesaya Zerenje Mwasi and Patrick Mwamulima were running congregations unsupervised by Scottish missionaries but rather when the Scots returned.

The spread of the military-style *beni*, *malipenga* and *mganda* dance societies

[56] Page, 'The War of *Thangata*', 93.
[57] Summary of proceedings of District Councils, 29 October 1918, Fort Johnston District Book, Vol 2.
[58] Lt-Col Dobbs to Chief Sec, 2 Jan 1924, MNA S2/8/20.
[59] Linden, 'Catholics', 109–10.
[60] Agnes R. Fraser, *Donald Fraser* (London, 1934), pp. 226–29.
[61] Resident, Chinteche, to Chief Sec., 2 May 1918, MNA NNC 1/1/1.
[62] Resident, Chinteche, to Chief Sec, Zomba, 3 July 1919, MNA S2/11/19.
[63] Melvin Page, 'The Great War and Chewa Society in Malawi', *JSAS*, 6, 2 (1980)
[64] McCracken, *Politics and Christianity*, 224–230; Blood, *History of the Universities' Mission to Central Africa*, pp. 126–30.

is particularly revealing of the ambiguous and paradoxical emotions that the war aroused.[65] *Beni*, a costumed dance parodying military activities, had its origins among urban Swahili communities on the Kenyan coast in the 1890s. It spread to Tanga and Dar es Salaam around 1914 and followed the tradition of earlier dance modes by dividing into competing associations, the *marini* for the 'haves' and the *arinoti* for the 'have-nots'. During the war, *beni* was danced in both armies with askaris tending to join *marini* bands and porters and more generally 'rougher people' joining the *arinoti*. By 1918 it had been introduced to Nyasaland, first by prisoners of war dancing in the detention camp at Zomba and later by detachments of the 2nd KAR on their return from Nairobi.[66] In 1921 it still remained strongly identified with those who had served in the war. Men danced with particular enthusiasm in the garrison town of Zomba and in the major recruiting areas around the south end of the Lake. By this time, however, *beni* was being challenged in the northern half of the country by *malipenga*. In one view, *malipenga* is a direct derivative of the *marini* bands that had previously played in the area, in another, a variant type of military-style dance owing its origin to civilian imitation of wartime parades.[67] By 1927 *malipenga* bands were described as 'very numerous' all over the Northern Province. By the same period, Nyasa migrants had carried the dance under the name *mganda* to the mining compounds of Northern Rhodesia, Southern Rhodesia and Katanga as well as back into Tanganyika, where it had originated.[68] Aspects of *beni*, notably the enthusiastically loyal tone of a number of the songs (one line went: 'By whose orders do we fight the enemy? By the orders of the King in London'), have convinced some historians that the movement can best be understood as an example of the 'adjustment to absolute power' made by Africans traumatised by the intensity of the colonial impact.[69] But this would be too simple an explanation. *Beni* was indeed a response to the European impact and particularly that of the First World War. It appropriated many of the symbols of colonial authority: military drill and uniform and elaborate hierarchies involving Kings, Governors, Generals and Sergeant Majors. However, it was also an expression of popular culture, drawing not only on European but also on indigenous African idioms. Its significance lies not in the particular political message it conveyed, which could range from pride in wartime achievement to resentment at the suffering involved, but rather in the demonstration it provides of the ability of African people to internalise the calamitous violence of the war in a way that also provided competitive enjoyment for subsequent generations.

[65] The key study is T.O. Ranger, *Dance and Society in Eastern Africa 1890–1970* (London, 1975). For *beni* and its derivatives in Nyasaland, see D. Kerr and M. Nambote, 'The Malipenga Mime of Likoma Island', staff seminar paper no.26, Chancellor College, University of Malawi, 1982; C.F. Kamolengera, '"A species of pantomime to be depreciated": The Case Against the Beni Dance in Colonial Malawi', unpublished paper, University of Malawi, n.d; J.C. Mitchell, *The Kalela Dance, Aspects of social relationships among urban Africans in Northern Rhodesia*, Rhodes-Livingstone Papers, no.27 (Manchester, 1956).

[66] Major Stephens to Chief Sec, 17 Feb 1921, MNA S2/1/21.

[67] Kerr and Nambote, 'The Malipenga Mime of Likoma Island', 2–3.

[68] PC Northern Province to Chief Sec, 1 Sep 1927, MNA S2/1/21.

[69] Major Stephens to Chief Sec, 17 Feb 1921, MNA S2/1/21.

The aftermath

The spread of *beni* took place within a colonial state that had been altered in four distinct ways by the impact of the First World War. Economically, the most significant long term impact was the introduction of motor transport and the gradual undermining of the *tengatenga* system which had been so vital during the course of the war itself. Prior to 1914, head porterage provided virtually the only form of transport, except in that small part of the country, from Port Herald to Limbe, served by the railway. During the course of the war, however, thousands of labourers were employed in the construction of motor roads, notably the road linking Blantyre to Fort Johnston. Hundreds of lorries and cars were introduced as a means of speeding up the movement of supplies.[70] The coming of peace gave a new impetus to the shift in patterns of communications. In 1919 nearly every planter and firm in the neighbourhood of Blantyre was said to have acquired a car, although at that time they could still be most usefully employed only in the Shire Highlands.[71] Over the next five years, the ALC disbanded almost all of the large gangs of carriers which it had previously employed to transport goods to the furthest parts of the country. Lorries began using the newly opened dirt road to Lilongwe, at least in the dry season. By 1929 more than 450 lorries and 600 cars were licensed in the protectorate, a tiny number in comparison with modern figures yet sufficient to release into agriculture and migrant labour several thousand men who had previously worked as porters.[72]

Equally important, if less easy to quantify, was the coercive legacy of the war. Coercion had always been a characteristic of the colonial state but during the course of the war it began to be applied more systematically throughout the length and breadth of the Protectorate, even in those remote areas where previously colonial rule had been experienced only to a limited extent. In the Lilongwe District, for example, the number of hut taxes paid (always a useful index of colonial penetration) rose from 19,600 in 1913 to 37,900 in 1917, remaining well over 30,000 in the early 1920s. This is all the more significant given the probable fall in population at this time, resulting partly from the influenza epidemic.[73] Large increases in hut tax paid were also recorded in the Mzimba and Dowa districts, among others, although by 1920 wages were conspicuously failing to keep pace with prices for imported goods which had risen by at least 70 per cent compared to the rate for 1914. 'It is unquestionable to everybody that natives since the hideous war broke out, find great difficulty in supporting themselves and find that goods in stores are beyond their means', the Mombera Native Association noted in 1921.[74]

Forced labour, once routinely employed for military work, was now utilised in building roads for the Public Works Department or to provide seasonal labour for Europeans, a policy justified by Smith on the grounds that 'the native was war

[70] Philip Mitchell, *African Afterthoughts* (London, 1954), pp. 38–9; Nyasaland Military Handbook, 1922, MNA S2/6/27.
[71] *LWBCA* July 1918–June 1919, 23–4.
[72] Nyasaland Military Handbook, 31 Dec 1929, MNA S2/6/27.
[73] Hut tax summary, Lilongwe District Book, MNA.
[74] Minutes of Mombera Native Association, 26 Sept 1921, MNA S1/210/20.

weary and lazy and so needed forcible measures to come out to work.'[75] It was officially noted in 1922 that in several districts, 'the monthly seizure of men for Zomba causes resentment and bad feeling.'[76] Two years later, gangs of prisoners in chains and handcuffs, escorted by policemen, had become a regular sight on roads leading from the Central Province to the Shire Highlands estates from which they were said to have deserted.[77] It was a bitter reward for people who had sacrificed so much for Britain in a war which they had so little interest in fighting.

The third change in the nature of the colonial state relates to the shift in educational priorities demonstrated most markedly in the two Scottish Presbyterian missions. As Hastings has noted, the Protestant missionary movement probably reached its height at the time of the Edinburgh Missionary Conference of 1910 only to gradually decline, at least in relative terms, in the decades following the outbreak of the First World War.[78] Events at Blantyre and Livingstonia mirrored this decline. In 1914 northern Nyasas had access to one of the liveliest educational systems then existing in Central Africa. But in the next few years, Malawian and Scottish teachers were recruited into the army, external financial support fell, and school work at the Overtoun Institution and in many district and village schools was brought to a halt. With the coming of peace schools were reopened, albeit in a climate where Robert Laws's ambitious aim, initially revealed in 1922, of establishing the nucleus of a university at Livingstonia came under increasing opposition.[79] One obstacle was financial: the recognition that although Scottish donations to Livingstonia might increase, there was little prospect, in the aftermath of the war, that they would do so at a pace which would allow the mission to meet all its expanding commitments. So limited were Livingstonia's resources that in 1924, in the face of opposition from many local Christians, it handed over its Kasungu schools and churches to the DRC. A second obstacle was intellectual: the growing belief, emphasised by Fraser, that what was required was 'mass education … rather than the intensive education of a few'.[80] Building on an influential report from the American-based Phelps-Stokes Commission, which visited Nyasaland in 1924, Fraser criticised the Overtoun Institution for giving too much attention to training in Western skills and not enough to assisting rural communities.

For a time, Laws's vision of an embryo 'Overtoun College of the University of Livingstonia', drawing students from Northern Rhodesia and Tanganyika as well as from Nyasaland, attracted favourable official attention.[81] But as the financial realities hit home, enthusiasm rapidly diminished. Without large-scale government support the project could not get off the ground. Yet, in 1924 the Nyasaland Government spent only £3,000 in total on mission education, nearly seven times less than the sum spent by the Government of Uganda and ten times less than was spent by the settler government of Southern Rhodesia – a colony with a near iden-

---

[75] L.S. Norman to Colonial Secretary, 4 October 1920, CO 525/94; G. Smith to Colonial Secretary, 21 February 1921, TNA CO 525/95.
[76] Central Province Annual Report for 1921/22, MNA NC 2/1/1.
[77] Major Stephens to PC, Southern Province, 18 July 1924, MNA POL 2/19/4.
[78] Hastings, *Church in Africa*, pp.550–51.
[79] McCracken, *Politics and Christianity*, pp. 227–38.
[80] Donald Fraser, *The New Africa* (London, 1927), p. 163.
[81] McCracken, *Politics and Christianity*, pp. 234–5.

tical population to Nyasaland's.[82] With Laws's retirement in 1927, therefore, the project was brought to a close, being replaced by a less ambitious scheme for the training of primary school teachers. Livingstonia continued to function as one of the very best centres of education in Nyasaland. However, it was now far surpassed by secondary schools such as the Alliance High School in Kenya, and King's College, Budo in Uganda. It was not until 1940, and after considerable prevarication by missionaries anxious to preserve their monopoly over post-primary education, that Nyasaland's first secondary school was opened at Blantyre.

One final factor deriving from the First World War must be considered. The expansion of tsetse fly, killing cattle with trypanosomiasis and threatening humans with sleeping sickness, began well before 1914 but was accelerated by military demands for labour and cattle and by the influenza epidemic.[83] In northern Ngoniland, where tsetse had not previously been noted, a veterinary officer reported in April 1915 that:

> [T]rypanosomiasis was found to occur among the cattle in villages along the course of the Rukuru river as far north as the main road. The spread of the tsetse fly is taking place from N.E. Rhodesia and is gradually extending along the water courses to the east. The infections among cattle as one passes to the west are found to be more extensive, a great number of the animals having died and in some cases all that remains to indicate that cattle were kept is the khola which once sheltered the animals.[84]

In 1921 the fly had spread over the whole of the Nkhamanga plain and as far east as the Njakwa hills. By 1926 the belt had extended at least four miles further south along the Kasitu valley although most of the Mzimba district remained clear.[85]

The spread of tsetse in the Central Province was even more alarming. When W.A. Lamborn, the government's single medical entomologist first visited the area in 1914, he found that tsetse had crossed into the north-west corner of the Kasungu district from the Luangwa Valley and had occupied the area between the frontier and the Lingadzi River as far as Mpembe Hill.[86] Five years later the fly was spreading rapidly through the close canopy brachystegia woodlands towards the Rusa River about 20 miles south of their 1914 limits. Several cases of sleeping sickness were detected on the Kasungu Plain in 1922, leading to the forced evacuation of 58 villages and the establishment of Kasungu Game Reserve (now National Park) adjacent to an area where the free shooting of animals was now permitted. This did nothing to halt the advance of the fly. Moving at a speed variously calculated at between seven and five and a half miles a year, a tsetse belt more than 40 miles wide progressed southwards towards Lilongwe, crossing the Rusa River in 1924, reaching the Ludzi River in 1926 and approaching Fort Manning (Mchinji) in 1927.[87] In 1923 cattle died of trypanosomiasis in no less

[82] Thomas Jesse Jones, *Education in East Africa* (London, 1925).
[83] McCracken, 'Colonialism, Capitalism and the ecological crisis', pp. 63–7.
[84] Department of Agriculture, Annual Report, 1914–1915.
[85] R.F. Fairfax-Franklin, Resident Mzimba, to P.C., Northern Province, 15 July 1926, MNA M2/23/4.
[86] Lamborn, 'The Tsetse Fly Problem in the Northern Province'.
[87] Lamborn, 'Tsetse Fly Problem'; Annual Report on the Northern Province for 1922–23, MNA N2/23/3; Kasungu District Book, vol. 1, 'Sleeping Sickness'; B.D. Burt, 'A brief investigation of the country in the neighbourhood of the advance of Glossina Morsitans to the Bua River in Nyasaland', June 1937, MNA M2/23/2.

than eight districts in the Protectorate although, in comparison with Tanganyika, human deaths from sleeping sickness remained remarkably few.[88] 'We have more to fear from this disease as a hindrance to the development of the Protectorate as a whole than any other disease, political condition or change in market values of the raw products which we can produce', the Chief Veterinary Officer commented. Substantial economic damage had resulted from the 'constant necessity for the movement of the population of the affected areas and the losses of livestock'. The Officer claimed that the fly was responsible for the reversion to bush of at least one-third of the uninhabited land in the territory.[89] It was not until 1928, when the expansion of tobacco-growing on the Lilongwe Plain led to the cutting back of bush, that the threat posed by the tsetse fly began to diminish.

[88] Violet Jhala, 'Human Sleeping Sickness in Nyasaland, 1908–1945', History Seminar paper, December 1985, Chancellor College, University of Malawi.
[89] Annual Reports of the Department of Agriculture for 1923 and 1925.

7

Planters, Peasants & Migrants
The Interwar Years

Introduction

In his political history of Southern Rhodesia, Lord Blake describes the inter-war years as a 'not very interesting' period in the colony's history, when little of significance took place.[1] In Nyasaland, by contrast, the interwar years were marked by profound although unspectacular changes, resulting in the creation of economic structures that continued virtually unaltered into the 1960s. Estate agriculture, once seen as the leading sector in the territory's economy, went into steep decline, while peasant communities emerged into more active participation in the cash economy, only to run headlong into the Great Depression. On a political level, the fierce dramas of 1915 and, again, of the 1950s were conspicuous by their absence. But Nyasas were involved in the forging of new forms of identity, forms that were to remain of considerable importance well into the post-war era.

Peasant & planter

In Southern Rhodesia the 1920s were marked by the consolidation of the white farming sector and the decline of the African peasantry; in Nyasaland this pattern was reversed. Following the declaration of peace, 'there was an influx of new settlers', most of them ex-servicemen, 'with some, if not too abundant a supply of capital' bringing the number of white farmers in the territory from 154 in 1916 to 399 in 1921.[2] No soldier settlement schemes of the type employed in Kenya and Southern Rhodesia were sponsored by the Nyasaland Government. But land was made available in the hitherto unexploited Cholo district by the British Central Africa Company which brought out 56 ex-officers, paid them salaries of £12–15 a month for three years and then sold them 1,000–acre farms at inflated prices.[3] Fourteen plots of 500 acres each were leased to prospective

---

[1] Robert Blake, *A History of Rhodesia* (London, 1977), p. xiii.
[2] R. Rankine to Colonial Office, 10 Nov 1922, TNA CO 525/102.
[3] History of the British Central Africa Company, 1949, TNA CO 525/208/44332; Robin Palmer, 'White Farmers in Malawi: before and after the Depression', *African Affairs*, 84, (1985), pp. 222–23.

cotton planters in the Ndindi marsh in the Lower Shire Valley, and further lease-hold grants amounting to over 100,000 acres in all were made by the government in the Mulanje District, in the Upper Shire Valley and in the Central Province, where little land had been alienated previously.[4]

The collapse of the estate sector was almost as rapid as its expansion. In the Ndindi marsh the first crop grown by European planters was swept away in the floods of 1918–19 and the second was destroyed by drought.[5] Elsewhere in the Lower Shire Valley, landlords attempting to exact *thangata* labour from their tenants were frustrated by widespread peasant resistance involving the flight of tenants onto Crown land, into the sparsely populated Chikwawa district or, in some cases, across the international boundary into Mozambique.[6] With local labour in short supply, landlords recruited Lomwe migrants instead, only to be faced from the early 1920s by increased competition from rich peasants for this form of labour. By 1923 estate production was on the brink of collapse. Many plantations were choked with weeds owing to the difficulty of attracting workers. 'European efforts to develop this area of the Protectorate have been conspicuously unsuccessful', the Director of Agriculture noted in that year, adding that, in consequence, no further land in the Lower Shire Valley should be alienated to European or Asian farmers.[7] By 1930 almost all leasehold estates in the area had been returned to the government and plantation produc-tion of cotton was virtually at an end. Production had moved decisively into the hands of Mang'anja and Sena peasants who, by combining the use of family with emigrant labour, had increased production of seed cotton in the Valley from 217 tons in 1920–21 to 2,226 tons in 1928 (91 per cent of Nyasaland's total output) and to 4,733 tons by 1930. The European share of cotton produc-tion had fallen from 88 per cent in 1922, to 7 per cent in 1928, and to 2 per cent in 1930.[8] By this time almost the only tangible evidence of European cotton growing in the area was the rusting remains of the large ginnery erected by the British Central Africa Company at Mitole, not far from the boma at Chik-wawa.[9]

Changes in tobacco production followed a similar path. Up to the mid-1920s almost all tobacco was grown on European plantations in the Shire Highlands. Exports fell during the First World War but, with the introduction of imperial preference in 1919, local prices temporarily soared from 4d to 1s.2d per pound for graded tobacco.[10] There was an immediate increase in production: land under tobacco on European estates more than doubled to 25,000 acres in 1927. Exports of flue-cured tobacco (cured in brick barns by hot air conducted through metal flues and produced almost entirely under European supervi-sion) also more than doubled to 10,488,464 lbs. On the Bruce Estates, where previously cotton had been king, tobacco production expanded to 8,000 acres

4   Murray, *Handbook* (1922), p. 68; *Report of a Commission to enquire into and report upon certain matters connected with the occupation of land in the Nyasaland Protectorate* [The Jackson Report] (Zomba, 1921).
5   Murray, *Handbook of Nyasaland*, 1922, pp. 68–69.
6   Mandala, *Work and Control*, pp. 118–24.
7   Annual Report of the Agricultural Department for 1923.
8   See Palmer, 'White Farmers', Table 1 p. 236.
9   History of the British Central Africa Company, TNA CO 525/208/44332.
10 Sir George Smith to C.O., 31 May 1920, TNA CO 525/89.

grown on 31 separate plantations in 1925.[11]

The sudden rise of the industry was followed by as sudden a decline. As early as 1924 a visiting expert warned that Nyasaland planters made no distinction between flue-cured and fire-cured tobacco in the types they grew, used barns that were much too big, and in consequence produced largely nondescript leaf that would be vulnerable to external competition.[12] With Southern Rhodesian growers also rushing onto the market, the worst fears were justified. A glut resulted in 1928, prices collapsed and, at the end of the season, much of the Nyasaland crop remained unsold. Unable to bear the exceptionally high freight charges levied by the Nyasaland Railways, several planters left the country, following a stream of ex-servicemen who had already departed. Others switched to tenant production of dark fire-cured tobacco (cured by being suspended over open fires) which did not require the expensive brick barns used in the flue-curing process. Responding to an appeal from the Nyasaland Planters Association, Smith's successor as Governor, Sir Charles Bowring (1924–9) agreed to make loans available to indigent tobacco planters as a means of keeping them in the country. But, in view of Nyasaland's straitened financial circumstances, an annual ceiling of only £8,000 was set by the Colonial Office, too small a sum to halt the downward drift.[13] By 1935 land under tobacco on European estates had declined to 6,144 acres. Flue-cured tobacco exports had fallen from 5,419,595 lbs, valued at £232,579 in 1928 to 1,020,107 lbs, valued at £29,982. Only 82 tobacco farmers were still in business, compared with 229 seven years earlier.[14] As little as 19 per cent of Nyasaland's tobacco was being produced by direct labour on European estates as compared with 94 per cent in 1922.

The decline of the European flue-cured industry was preceded by the rise of African fire-cured production. Before the First World War, the Blantyre and East Africa Company had pioneered the production of tobacco by some tenants working on their own account rather than as wage labourers on its enormous 130,000 acre estate. This scheme was extended in a small way to other estates in the Southern Province in the early 1920s.[15] The major breakthrough, however, came with the extension of tobacco growing to the gentle slopes and fertile soils of the Lilongwe plain. In May 1920 A.F. Barron and R.W. Wallace, two planters from the Zomba district, obtained leasehold rights over 2,000 acres of land on the Mbabzi stream, some ten miles from the tiny settlement of Lilongwe. At first they attempted to grow tobacco directly through the use of wage labour. But faced 'with only limited success', in 1922, Barron turned to his tenants to whom he distributed seedlings in exchange for the right to purchase their crop.[16] A year later he extended the scheme to Crown Land growers not only in the Lilongwe

[11] White, *Magomero*, p. 150.
[12] Report on a visit to Nyasaland by H.W. Taylor, Tobacco Expert, 15 April 1924, MNA A2/95/26.
[13] See MNA S1/575I/28.
[14] Minutes of the Executive Committee of the Nyasaland Tobacco Association, 4 January 1935, MNA S1/126A/1929; Annual Report of the Nyasaland Agricultural Department for 1935.
[15] History of the Blantyre and East Africa Company, 1949, TNA CO 525/208/44332; Annual Report of the Agricultural Department for 1917.
[16] Lands Officer to Chief Sec, 21 May 1924, MNA S1/2010/29; P. Foster, 'A Brief History of the system inaugurated by Mr. A.F. Barron in the Central Province', 6 August 1932, MNA S1/2461/23. For an account of the Central Province tobacco industry, see John McCracken, 'Planters, Peasants and the Colonial State: the Impact of the Native Tobacco Board in the Central Province of Malawi', *JSAS*, 9, 2 (1983).

district but west, into Fort Manning and north, through the western portion of Dowa district as far as Ngara, south of Kasungu. Tobacco nurseries were established in numerous localities and six Europeans and 120 African instructors were employed to provide advice to prospective growers. Roads were built to link the Lilongwe interior to the main road from Zomba to Dedza, completed in 1925, and from that year lorries were used to transport the crop to the Imperial Tobacco Company's factory at Limbe.[17] Other settlers followed Barron's example. New buyers, most prominent among them being an Italian, Ignaco Conforzi, opened up additional markets, competition intensified, and with prices rising, the number of peasant growers in the Central Province increased from 900 in 1923 to over 33,000 in 1926. In the Lilongwe and Dowa districts production soared from 24 tons of tobacco in 1924 to 1,244 tons in 1927. By 1932 these two districts were producing 3,879 tons of tobacco between them, more than 50 per cent of all tobacco grown in Malawi.

The rapid growth of peasant production in the Central Province owed as much to the favourable circumstances affecting the Chewa inhabitants of the plateau stretching north and west from Lilongwe as it did from Barron's initiative. The land here, covered by combretum-acacia woodlands, much of which was subsequently used as firewood for tobacco curing, is mainly fertile and well-drained. Although variable, rainfall is higher than in the dry brachystegia woodlands further north. Accordingly, the Chewa of the Lilongwe plain needed to invest less labour to ensure subsistence than did a number of their less fortunate neighbours, and found it easier to produce surpluses to sell. Even in the nineteenth century, surplus foodstuffs from this area were traded down to Senga Bay and across to Ngombo on the eastern shore of Lake Malawi. As late as the 1920s, indigenous tobacco was widely cultivated and was traded locally.[18] The result was that, once the formidable transport and marketing problems had been overcome, there were no insuperable obstacles to the growth of peasant production. With tax collection beginning to be widely and harshly enforced in the Lilongwe district from 1915–16, increasing numbers of people came to yearn for 'a method of earning money without having to work for somebody else' and hence were extremely receptive to the opportunities that Barron provided.[19] By contrast with the situation in the south, land shortage was not a major problem even in the mid-1930s, by which time some 30,000 acres in the Lilongwe district had been alienated to Europeans. Over a million mostly fertile and well watered acres remained in African hands. Nor was labour a major constraint: although a substantial increase in the number of young men seeking work in the Rhodesias was reported from 1910 onwards, many returned to their homeland once tobacco growing began.[20]

The initial success of the industry attracted the attention of the state. In theory, free market exponents should have welcomed the increased competition among buyers which undermined Barron's monopolistic marketing arrange-

[17] R.M. Antill, 'A History of the Native Crown Land Tobacco Industry of Nyasaland', *Nyasaland Agricultural Quarterly Journal*, 5, 3 (1945), 53–55; W.H.J. Rangeley, 'A Brief History of the Tobacco Industry in Nyasaland', *Nyasaland Journal*, 10, 1 and 2 (1957).

[18] Kings Phiri, 'Precolonial Economic Change', pp. 19–20; Fort Manning District Book Vol III, 1923–28.

[19] P.C., Northern Province, to Chief Sec, 27 June 1924, MNA S1/1879/24.

[20] Lilongwe District Book, Hut Tax summary.

ments and pushed up the prices paid to producers. As peasant production expanded, however, white farmers became alarmed at the ability of independent peasants to produce fire-cured tobacco at a lower cost than they could and called for a system of control. 'The reasons given for the necessity of control differ', W. Tait Bowie, the manager of the Blantyre and East Africa Company, explained:

> On the one hand independent planters fear that a large development of peasant agricul-turalists might affect the labour supply, and the control wanted, and the legislation asked for is for the purpose of restricting peasant development. On the other hand certain large owners, who are developing portions of their estate by means of native peasant agricul-turalists, wish control for the object of securing to them the full benefit of the work they are doing.[21]

Paternalistic colonial officials, distrustful of African initiative, were glad to lend their support. Barron's request that he should be granted a monopoly over the purchase of African-grown tobacco on the Lilongwe plain was rejected by the Governor. Instead, in 1926 the parastatal Native Tobacco Board was founded with the aim at once of improving the quality of the Crown Land crop and of restricting smallholder production in the interests of European planters. As a means of reducing the gap in production costs between African and European growers, the work of the Board was financed, not from central government funds, but rather from a cess of two shillings and sixpence per 100 lbs of tobacco, levied on the buyers although in fact provided indirectly by the growers. A further safe-guard was the appointment to the Board, which was chaired by the Director of Agriculture, of a succession of prominent estate owners, among them Barron, Conforzi and W. Tait Bowie, whose Blantyre and East Africa Company had the greatest experience of tenant production in the Southern Province.

Under their aegis, all African tobacco growers were registered and the size of their holdings limited to half an acre each. The number of markets was reduced from a maximum of nine in 1928 to three in 1934 in a successful attempt to restrict peasant production to the Lilongwe and Dowa districts. This left peas-ants in Kasungu, Dedza and Nkhotakota districts without any outlet for their tobacco.[22] No support was initially given to tobacco-growing peasants in the Shire Highlands. However, under pressure from African associations and government officials, the NTB modified its stance and from 1931 agreed to distribute seed to Southern Province growers and to provide a skeleton support service in the area.[23] A year later, there were 5,757 registered growers in the Shire Highlands as compared to 39,042 in the Central Region. Despite the Board's attempts at control, peasant production continued to rise, reaching 10,509,402 lbs of tobacco in 1932 compared with 4,201,818 lbs in 1926, the year when the NTB began operations. This was 54% of all tobacco grown in the country. It was a figure that would increase to 62% by 1937.[24]

The rapid growth of peasant production on the Lilongwe plain was accom-

[21] W. Tait Bowie to E.E. Colville, 7 Oct 1924, MNA S1/1879/24.
[22] McCracken, 'Planters, Peasants and the Colonial State', pp. 178–79.
[23] Minutes of the Native Tobacco Board, entries for 19 Jan, 8 Sep 1930, 18 Feb, 29 April 1931, MNA S1/720/26.
[24] Figures calculated from NTB annual reports, MNA S1/720/26 and from Report of the Commission into the Tobacco Industry, 19 July 1939, MNA COM 7 4/21.

panied from the late 1920s by three significant changes in the character of the plantation economy. The first of these was the growth of the tea industry in the Cholo and Mulanje districts of the Shire Highlands. Tea-planting in the Mulanje district goes back to 1891 when seedlings obtained from the Blantyre Mission were planted on John Moir's Lauderdale Estate, owned from 1898 by what became known as the Blantyre and East Africa Company.[25] Under the direction of R.S. Hynde, a shrewd and pugnacious Scot, the Company increased its acreage under tea to some 800 acres in 1918, by which time it was contributing significantly to the B&EA Company's profits. Other planters gradually followed its example, with the result that, between 1921 and 1926, some 5,000 acres were under tea, almost all in the Mulanje district.

The dramatic fall in tobacco prices from 1927 transformed the prospects for tea. The first steps were taken by the B&EA Company which followed the building of a well-equipped tea factory at Lauderdale in 1925 by opening new plantations in the Mulanje district and at Zoa in the Cholo district, thus bringing the Company's holdings under tea to 2,400 acres by the early 1930s.[26] Lack of capital and expertise prevented the majority of European tobacco farmers from following this example. But such was not the case with Ignaco Conforzi who switched from tobacco to tea on his extensive Cholo estates with such rapidity that, by 1933, he had over 2,000 acres in production, making him the largest single independent producer of tea in Nyasaland.[27] By that time, Nyasaland's acreage under tea had increased to some 15,400 acres, almost as much as the total grown in Kenya, Tanganyika and Uganda. Nyasaland was thus excellently placed to take advantage of the International Tea Regulation Scheme introduced in 1933. It limited the amount of tea that could be exported from the three main producing states, India, Ceylon and the Dutch East Indies, thus ensuring that world prices for tea remained buoyant.

The emergence of tea as a significant export earner for Nyasaland benefited only a minority of planters. A demanding crop, capable of production only in areas of heavy rainfall and high altitude, tea was restricted for climatic reasons to the wetter parts of Mulanje and Cholo districts alone and could not be grown in the rest of the Shire Highlands. Furthermore, tea is a perennial crop whose bushes are not ready for plucking for a minimum of four years. Thus it involves long-term investment rather than the speculative raids that had characterised the settler approach to cotton and tobacco. Malcolm Barrow, Nyasaland's leading settler politician of the 1950s, was exceptional in investing the huge sum of £60,000 in his 1,000 acre Naming'omba estate in the Cholo district, which he opened in May 1929.[28] Since a medium-sized tea factory cost £15,000 to build, planters lacking capital or expertise were unlikely to succeed. A few individuals, such as the capable Arthur Westrop with his experience of Malaya and Ceylon, were able to sustain the cause of the small proprietor into the early 1950s.[29] Much more frequently, however, ownership of tea plantations moved in the 1930s into the hands of a tiny

[25] History of the Blantyre and East Africa Company, TNA CO 525/208/44332.
[26] Ibid.
[27] John McCracken, 'Economics and Ethnicity: the Italian Community in Malawi', *JAH*, 32, 2, 1991, p. 319.
[28] Evidence by M.P. Barrow, 25 June 1938, Foreign and Commonwealth Office Library, Record of Oral Evidence heard before the Rhodesia-Nyasaland Royal Commission, Vol III [Bledisloe Commission].
[29] Arthur Westrup, *Green Gold* (Bulawayo, n.d. [c1964]).

group of large and relatively well-capitalised companies based in Britain and with connections to India and Ceylon. One such was J. Lyons and Co. Ltd.[30]

The second change in the character of the plantation economy involved a shift from direct to tenant farming in those districts of the Shire Highlands, above all Zomba and Chiradzulu, where lack of sufficient rainfall prevented tea being grown. Production by tenants has a long history in Malawi, going back at least to 1912 when the Blantyre and East Africa Company, in contravention of what subsequently was believed to be possible, began encouraging tenants to produce flue-cured tobacco on plots of about 1.5 acres in extent.[31] During much of the 1920s production through direct labour remained dominant, constituting between 94 and 95 per cent of all tobacco grown on European estates.[32] However, with the down turn in prices from 1928, it became increasingly common for planters to abandon the production of flue-cured tobacco through wage labour, which was now seen as too costly. Instead they chose to look to their tenants to produce fired-cured tobacco with labour supplied by their families. On the Bruce Estates, the new manager, Major Kincaid-Smith, fought a rear-guard action against tenant production but even he eventually had to admit defeat, as he described in 1938:

> On behalf of this Company I held out as long as I could against native production, contin-uing the cultivation of Flue-cured as long as possible. This market failed, however, in 1932, and with the steady decline in prices each year received for Fire-Cured, we were eventu-ally forced to take the line of least resistance, and come on to a policy of native tenant-production similar to that of the Government.[33]

In the Zomba and Chiradzulu districts combined, the number of registered tobacco growers on estates grew from a few hundred in the 1920s to 4,926 in 1932–3, and to 7,330 in 1933–34. By that time, tenant production of tobacco was fast overtaking production by direct labour on the Shire Highlands estates, several of which were only able to survive through the deliberate flouting of the law.

No issue in the colonial history of Malawi was more subject to bitterness and confusion than the relationship between landlords and tenants on the estates of the Shire Highlands. In the wake of the Chilembwe Rising, an attempt was made in the 1917 Native Rents Ordinance to modify *thangata* by prohibiting landlords from extracting services from their tenants in lieu of rent without the specific agreement of the tenant. This was widely ignored, however, with the result that, by 1926, virtually all estates demanded service from their tenants in lieu of rent, many for as much as six months in a year, some for four months and some for only two.[34] Furthermore, tenants remained deprived of even the vestiges of secu-rity of tenure, leaving landlords with the option of responding to the renewed influx of Lomwe peasants from Mozambique in the 1920s by expelling thou-sands of their tenants onto over-crowded Crown Land.

---

[30] Robin Palmer, 'The Nyasaland Tea Industry in the Era of International Tea Restrictions, 1933–1950', *JAH*, 26 (1985), pp. 218–20.
[31] Department of Agriculture Annual Report for 1917.
[32] Report of the Commission into the Tobacco Industry, MNA COM 7 4/21.
[33] Memorandum by Captain M. Kincaird-Smith to the Commission into the Tobacco Industry, 1938, MNA COM 7 2/3/1.
[34] R.S. Hynde to Chief Sec, 8 May 1926, MNA S1/596/26.

It was this threat to the social fabric of the Shire Highlands that led the administration to introduce the Natives on Private Estates Ordinance of 1928, a measure that, in theory at least, was to regulate landlord-tenant relations for the next two decades. Under the Ordinance, limited and temporary security of tenure was provided to tenants through provisions which stipulated that evictions could take place only every five years and that the number of people evicted should not exceed 10 per cent of the African population of the estate. On the other hand, the attempt to restrict *thangata* was abandoned and, instead, three forms of rent were legalised. First, a cash payment fixed at average wages in the district for between two or three months (in practice anything between six and 20 shillings); second, *thangata* labour of three months in the rainy season or six months in the dry; and third, the production of a cash crop, almost always tobacco, which the landlord was required to buy at rates fixed by the local District Rent Board. No consideration was given to the rights of those African residents whom Harry Johnston's non-disturbance clauses had been intended to protect. However, in a significant concession, barely discussed at the time, the Ordinance ruled that a landlord's right to exact rent from a tenant would be forfeited if he or she were unable to offer work or provide facilities for the growing of cash crops.[35]

The passing of the 1928 Ordinance deepened the divide between law and practice in landlord-tenant relations. Landlords assumed, almost to a man, that the Ordinance permitted them to take tenants' tobacco in lieu of rent. They were, therefore, appalled when they were informed by district officers, acting on the instructions of the new Governor, Sir Shenton Thomas, in 1931, that *thangata* tobacco had to be paid for at market rates and that failure to purchase nullified the requirement of tenants to pay rent.[36] Thereafter, most landlords did pay tenants for tobacco. However, up to 1939, prices were lower than those paid to independent peasants on Crown Land and the whole transaction was open to innumerable abuses. On the Bruce estates virtually no technical advice was provided to growers, 'overage' was commonly exacted (a polite way of saying that the purchaser cheated over weights) and a deferred credit system was introduced which resulted in growers being paid several months in arrears.[37] Elsewhere, landlords took advantage of a loophole in the Ordinance to change the legal status of tenants who had defaulted on their rents. They were stripped of their privileges and made tenants at will, subject to a cash rent as well as to service.[38] Tenants, in their turn, exploited the opportunities created by the growth of independent peasant production of tobacco on Crown Land to smuggle their tobacco across estate boundaries and into the newly opened markets. Shire Highland estates thus remained zones of confrontation, providing tenants with the opportunity, previously denied them, to become cash-crop farmers but also placing various arbitrary and sometimes illegal obstacles in their path. It is from this period that allegations of *chifwamba* began to spread, allegations that some British landlords were in the

[35] H.W. Young, 'Notes on the position of natives and non-natives on freehold land', 27 Dec. 1933, MNA NC 1/15/7.
[36] H.D. Kittermaster to C.O., 15 Dec 1934, PRO CO 525/156; Annual Report for the Southern Province, 1931, MNA NS 3/1/2. The best published account of landlord-tenant relations at this period is White, *Magomero*, pp. 152–77.
[37] D.C. Chiradzulu to Chief Sec, 10 June 1936, MNA S1/411/33; evidence of Kincaird-Smith, G.D.N. Bartlett and E.C. Barnes to the Tobacco Commission, 1939, MNA COM 7 2/1/1.
[38] D.C. Cholo to Chief Sec, 13 June 1936, MNA S1/411/33.

habit of prowling their estates in the search of African victims whom they would kill and eat in order to give them strength.[39] There could be no better metaphor for the fear-ridden character of social relationships in the Shire Highlands.

The visiting tenant system on the Lilongwe plain shared many similarities with tenant production in the Shire Highlands. At a deeper level, however, the two were distinct. In the early 1920s A.F. Barron and the other European pioneers in the Central Region were concerned mainly with buying tobacco from Crown Land growers to whom they provided seedlings and technical advice in exchange for the exclusive right to purchase their crop. The influx of new buyers into the region undermined these monopolistic arrangements, however. After the government in 1926 had founded the Native Tobacco Board to take responsibility for the production and marketing of Crown Land tobacco, Barron, Wallace and the other pioneers began to increase production on their own estates, where their monopoly over buying remained unimpaired. Fifteen new leases were taken up in 1926–27, 12 in the Lilongwe District alone. During the next decade new leases continued to be granted on the Lilongwe plain, most notably to Ignaco Conforzi, the principal buyer of tobacco in the Central Province. By the late 1930s Conforzi had acquired some 12,000 acres in the Lilongwe and Fort Manning districts on which he had pioneered the production of sun-cured tobacco, a variety much used in hand-rolled cigarettes.[40] Not till 1941 did the government call a halt to the alienation of land and, by that time, over 60,000 acres in the Lilongwe, Dowa and Fort Manning districts had been leased to some 20 European farmers. These were divided into three distinct groups: a tiny planting aristocracy, consisting of Barron, Wallace and F. D. Warren known as the 'Big Three' of the Central Province, with over 20 estates between them; a rather larger group of 'working farmers' headed by D.W.K. Macpherson and T. W. Bradshaw; and, finally, a close-knit Italian community, less than a dozen strong, whose aggressive farming methods were often criticised by their British neighbours. Most came from Conforzi's home town, Poggio Mirteto, north of Rome, and were linked to him by ties of kinship and employment.[41]

The attempt to create a viable estate sector in the Central Province involved a much more subtle approach to the acquisition of labour than was the case in the Shire Highlands. In the Southern Province, white settlers had been able to use their control of over nearly a million acres to force their tenants to pay *thangata*, either as a labour rent or else through the production of cash crops. In the Central Province, however, independent peasants retained access to much good soil and no captive labour force existed comparable with the thousands of Lomwe migrants who worked on the Shire Highlands estates. Some estate owners attempted to recruit farm labourers in the early 1920s but the wages offered were too low to attract more than a handful of takers. The result was that, by the mid-1920s, Central Province landlords began to recruit tenants as share-

[39] C.Z. Chidzero, 'Thangata in Northern Thyolo District: a socio-economic study in Chimaliro and Bvumbwe areas', History Seminar paper, Chancellor College, 1980–81; Westrop, *Green Gold*, pp. 343–45.

[40] Annual Report for the Central Province, 1926–27, MNA S1/1003/27; McCracken, 'Economics and Ethnicity', pp. 318–20. For an overview of the visiting tenant system see John McCracken, 'Share-cropping in Malawi: the Visiting Tenant System in the Central Province, c. 1920–1968' in Centre of African Studies, *Malawi: an Alternative Pattern of Development*.

[41] McCracken, 'Economics and Ethnicity', pp. 320–26.

croppers on short-term verbal contracts renewed on an annual basis. Five hundred strong in 1927, these 'visiting tenants' increased in number to 2,650 in 1930 and to 4,981 by 1935. By 1938, 7,531 tenants were working in the Province, over 5,000 of them in the Lilongwe district alone.[42] Up to 1931 most of these were Chewa peasants from the Lilongwe plain, drawn to the estates by the superior returns over independent peasant production that successful sharecroppers achieved. In that year, however, Crown Land tobacco showed a marked improvement in quality and price with the consequence, as the Provincial Commissioner noted, that 'many natives who, for several years, have been growing on private estates have this year gone back to their villages and the great majority of those now growing on private estates are natives of districts where tobacco cannot be grown.'[43] Most tenancies in the Fort Manning district, where outlets for peasant production were negligible, continued to be taken by local residents. But in the Lilongwe district, by 1934, over 90 per cent of tenants were said to be migrants, many of them accompanied by their wives and children, who spent from four to six months on the estates during the tobacco season, returning to their villages on Crown land during the rest of the year.[44] In 1938 the majority of these tenants were Chewa peasants from those marginal areas no longer served by the Native Tobacco Board, in particular Fort Manning, Kasungu and Nkhotakota districts. However, they were joined by 1,200 migrants from the Shire Highlands, most from the congested Chiradzulu district from which Conforzi, Barron and Wallace had recruited 600 growers. Smaller numbers came from the South Nyasa and Mzimba districts and from across the border in Mozambique.[45]

Compared with growers on the estates of the Shire Highlands, the visiting tenants were in a relatively fortunate situation. They and their families were not registered under the 1928 Ordinance and hence possessed no security of tenure.[46] But they were not subjected to demands for *thangata*, and were paid for their tobacco. They also received adequate technical advice which allowed them to achieve yields significantly higher than on Crown Land: 350 to 400 lbs per acre in the late 1930s as compared to 150 lbs achieved by independent peasants.[47] Further, they were permitted to grow considerably more tobacco than was allowed by the N.T.B: normally 1.25 acres but occasionally up to ten.[48] In most years, therefore, their cash incomes tended to be higher than those of independent peasants, but their expenses were also higher as most foodstuffs had to be purchased from neighbouring Crown Land growers, usually with the aid of loans provided by the estate.[49] Pressure on family labour was thus intense with many women and children earning a subsidiary income as tobacco graders during the buying season, and others hiring themselves out for work on those portions of the estate retained for flue-cured production.[50] Most tenants were

[42]   Report by R.M. Antill to Secretary, NTB, 9 Feb 1938, MNA NN 1/3/9.
[43]   Annual Report for Northern Province, 1931, MNA S1/61/32.
[44]   Annual Report for Lilongwe District, 1934, MNA S1/89A-E/35.
[45]   Report by R.M. Antill, Feb 1938, MNA NN 1/3/9.
[46]   R.W. Mulliner to D.C. Lilongwe, 24 Dec 1946, MNA NCL 2/2/2.
[47]   Report of Commission into the Tobacco Industry, 1939, COM 7 4/2/1.
[48]   Evidence of R.M. Antill to the Tobacco Commission, MNA COM 7 2/3/1.
[49]   Ibid., and evidence of A.G.O. Hodgson to the Tobacco Commission, MNA COM 7 2/1/1.
[50]   Evidence of D.W.K. Macpherson, Dr.W.H. Watson and T.W. Bradshaw to the Tobacco Commission, MNA COM 7 2/3/1.

permanently indebted to the estate owners who supplied them with maize and equipment on credit on the security of the next season's crop. It was frequently asserted that the estate owners made a very good profit on these advances when they purchased their tenants' tobacco.[51]

The expansion in export crops was accompanied by changes in the domestic economy. By the early 1920s many independent peasants in the Blantyre and Chiradzulu districts were selling maize on a regular basis at the produce markets that had sprung up at Blantyre, Limbe and Lunzu or else direct to European estates.[52] They were joined in the 1930s by Lomwe settlers in the hills to the south of Cholo district who grew food crops 'in considerable variety and far in excess of local consumption' which they sold both to the tea estates and to cotton-growing peasants in the Shire Valley below.[53] On the Lilongwe plain, the introduction of tobacco growing among independent peasants represented only one aspect of the complex process of agricultural change. Substantial, although at present unquantifiable, increases in the amount of land placed under production occurred in the 1930s. There was also a rapid increase in cattle population and, from the late 1930s, a tendency to move cattle onto land which had only recently been cleared of tsetse fly.[54] Virtually all households remained self-sufficient in foodstuffs; many sold maize to neighbouring estates.

Technological change was less evident than change in what was grown. On the Lilongwe plain, several peasant farmers were said to have gone in for ploughing by 1922, while in the Dowa district Headman Mashambodza cultivated large fields of wheat in the same manner, as did other headmen for maize cultivation.[55] Elsewhere, however, ploughs and oxen were notable only by their absence and technological change was restricted to the use of iron rather than wooden hoes, most of them of European make.[56] Iron smelting continued to take place in the Chimalira hills of the Kasungu district as late as 1926. But by the early 1930s the market had been flooded by imported hoes and the industry was said to be moribund.[57]

The collapse of iron working took place at a time when African commercial fishing and fish trading was expanding.[58] Up to the First World War, this trade was confined largely to the exchange of dried fish for foodstuffs from the more agriculturally productive highland regions adjacent to Lake Malawi and the Shire River and to the sale of fish from Lake Chilwa to the markets established at Blantyre and Zomba. In the 1920s, however, the expansion of markets in the Shire Highlands and the growth of a money economy resulting from the increase in cash-cropping in areas like the Lilongwe plain led to an increased demand for fish, the only significant source of animal nutrition in a country notably short of

---

[51] Evidence of Bradshaw, Antill and A.F. Barron to the Tobacco Commission.
[52] Southern Province Annual Report to March 1924, MNA NS 3/1/1.
[53] P. Topham to Director of Agriculture, 29 Jan 1938, MNA NS 1/2/4.
[54] See McCracken, 'Experts and Expertise', p.110.
[55] Central Province Annual Report for 1922/23, MNA NC 2/1/1.
[56] Adams D. C. Banda, 'Agricultural Change in Northwestern Kasungu during the Colonial Period'. History seminar paper, Chancellor College, University of Malawi, 1982.
[57] Kasungu District Book; Northern Province Annual Report for 1933, MNA S1/112/34.
[58] The most useful accounts of fishing in this period are John McCracken, 'Fishing and the Colonial Economy: the case of Malawi', *JAH*, 28 (1987) 413–429, and Wiseman C. Chirwa, '"Theba is Power": Rural Labour, Migrancy and Fishing in Malawi, 1890s-1985', Ph.D. dissertation, Queen's University, Kingston, Ontario, (1992), 175–86.

meat. In the Upper Shire Valley, some labour was initially diverted away from fishing as a result of the renewed growth of the cotton industry. This was stimulated by the drying up of Lake Malombe, which made it possible for cultivators to plant their food gardens on the floor of the lake while growing cotton around its edges.[59] In 1925, however, Lake Malombe was flooded as a result of the inexorable rise in the levels of Lake Malawi and the Shire River. With their food gardens inundated, many cultivators switched from cotton growing to the fishing industry in order to obtain the money required both to purchase maize and to pay for hut tax.[60] By 1931 at least 10,000 people were involved in the trade, the great majority being hawkers carrying dried fish on long poles slung over their shoulders. Some individuals took to bicycles, whose relative cheapness, carrying capacity and mobility were of crucial importance in extending sales of fish beyond the main lorry arteries into the southern Malawian hinterland.[61] Most fishermen remained near subsistence, utilising family labour and achieving average earnings of no more than £10 a year. But some fishermen at Nkhotakota made between £20 and £30, while Mwamadi Matewere, the pioneer commercial fisherman near Fort Johnston, made considerably more. By 1932, at the sand bar near the outlet of Lake Malawi, Matewere had constructed a set of fish weirs so impenetrable, according to one observer, that 'it is literally impossible for any fish of even medium size to enter the Shire river at all'.[62] Several Indian and European lorry-owners purchased fresh fish from him at a rate of up to 2,000 a day which they transported to Blantyre and Zomba.[63] Lake Chilwa and the adjacent Phalombe river were hives of activity during the dry season fringed by 'hundreds of grass shelters ... covered with fish drying in the sun, many tea booths, in fact a large settlement under temporary lodging'.[64]

Transport & traders

Two central features shaping the extent and character of commercial relations were the role of immigrant traders and the uneven spread of transport facilities. Until 1914 goods were carried by a combination of head porterage, the Blantyre-Port Herald railway which was extended in 1915 to Chindio on the Zambesi, and by the lake and river service reaching in the south to the British concession of Chinde on the Zambesi mouth and in the north to Karonga on Lake Malawi. As in much of Africa, motor transport, and in particular the growing use of lorries, constituted a mini transport revolution in the 1920s, making redundant the large scale use of *tengatenga* labourers and opening up the Lilongwe plain to cash crop production. From 1924 the track from Dedza to Fort Manning was officially designated an all-weather Class III main road, although in 1937 it was noted that there were very great restrictions on mechanised transport in the wet season during which the main road beyond Lilongwe

[59] South Nyasa District Annual Report for 1931, MNA NSF 4/1/3.
[60] South Nyasa District Annual Report for 1931, MNA S1/1307/30.
[61] Nyasaland Protectorate Report of the Census for 1931, MNA S1/1307/30.
[62] Minute by R.C. Wood, 26 April 1930, MNA S1/437i/30.
[63] D.C., Fort Johnston to P.C., Southern Province, 14 Nov 1932, MNA S1.437i/30
[64] Southern Province Annual Report for 1931, MNA NS 3/1/2.

was impassable.[65] Motor transport, in consequence, was concentrated very largely on the Southern Province and the Lilongwe plain, although a few motor cycles were in use further north. Most lorries were owned by Europeans and Asians but by the early 1930s a growing number of Africans were employed as motor drivers and mechanics. Some had achieved the widely held ambition of purchasing a lorry of their own: Yotam Takemana in 1934 had one, as well as running five stores in the Ntcheu and Dedza districts.[66]

The opportunities created by the expansion of motor traffic were in part nullified by the distorting consequences of Nyasaland's railway policy.[67] Historians have noted that the Shire Highlands Railway from Blantyre to Port Herald had the disadvantage, compared with most railways elsewhere in British tropical Africa, in not being funded through an imperial grant. The extension of this railway for 61 miles to the northern bank of the Zambesi at Chindio in 1915 and, even more, the opening in 1922 of the Trans-Zambesia Railway from Beira to the southern bank of the Zambesi, imposed further burdens on Nyasaland which it was ill equipped to bear. On the positive side, the journey from Blantyre to the East African coast was reduced from ten days to two, a blessed relief for those who had suffered the mosquito-ridden misery of the steamship service to Chinde. But by rejecting the alternative, shorter route to Quelimane, the authorities were left with the major problem of how to bridge the Zambesi at one of its widest parts. In a deal worked out between the British Government and the TZR, Nyasaland was made responsible for guaranteeing interest payments on the railway company's loan. Yet, with the elimination of the steamer service and the closure of the British concession at Chinde in 1922, rates actually rose.[68] During the 1930s, so Palmer notes:

> the rate for sending tea from Luchenza, the nearest railhead to the estates in Cholo and Mlanje, to the port of Beira in Portuguese East Africa was 0.97d per lb, which was generally thought to be excessive and which compared with rates of 0.23d and 0.38d per lb from North-West India's tea estates to the port of Calcutta.[69]

Figures presented to the Tobacco Commission in 1938 told a similar story. In that year, tobacco charges from Limbe to Beira were more than five times those facing Southern Rhodesian growers shipping their tobacco the slightly longer distance from Salisbury to Beira. Total transport costs to Britain from the Central Province were even greater: 2.39d per lb as compared to 1.7d per lb from Uganda.[70]

The financial implications for Nyasaland of building the huge bridge, 2.3 miles long, across the Zambesi in 1935 were the subject of much debate among British politicians and officials. In the preceding two decades, a total of £233,000

---

[65] P.A.Cole-King, *Lilongwe. A Historical Study*, Department of Antiquities Publication no. 10 (Zomba, 1971), pp. 37–38; Intelligence report for half year ending June 1937, MNA S2/6iii/27.

[66] Ncheu District Annual Report for 1934, MNA S1/89 A-E/35.

[67] The key, pioneering studies are Leroy Vail, 'Railway Development and Colonial Underdevelopment: the Nyasaland Case' in R. Palmer and N. Parsons (eds), *The Roots of Rural Poverty in central and Southern Africa* (London, 1977) and Vail, 'The Making of an Imperial Slum: Nyasaland and her Railways, 1895–1935', *JAH* 16 (1975), 89–112. These, however, must now be read in conjunction with Landeg White, *Bridging the Zambesi. A Colonial Folly* (London: Macmillan, 1993).

[68] White, *Bridging the Zambesi*, p. 59.

[69] Palmer, 'White Farmers in Malawi', p. 230.

[70] Report of the Commission into the Tobacco Industry, MNA COM 7 4/2/1.

had been paid from the Nyasaland government's slender revenues as its contribution to Trans-Zambesia Railway Guarantees (the British Government had provided £1,543,000).[71] Now, however, even the Treasury recognised that Nyasaland could not be expected to meet the full £1.74 million cost of the bridge. It was financed instead by a combination of a direct British grant plus a large loan to Nyasaland, which in later years was serviced through annual Treasury grants-in-aid.[72] Therefore, rather than being a major financial drain on Nyasaland's public funds, as Vail suggests, the Zambesi Bridge cost the Protectorate relatively little.[73] However, the completion of a direct rail link from Nyasaland to the coast, more than 30 years after the first sleeper had been laid, had little immediate impact on the territory's agricultural economy. No doubt the elimination of the arduous process by which goods were loaded and unloaded onto barges for the crossing of the Zambesi reduced damage and wastage but there was no reduction in freight charges and hence no stimulus to increased production. In the short run at least, as White has noted, the most obvious beneficiaries were the minority of Malawian migrants who used the line on the first stage of a journey that would take them to Salisbury and Johannesburg.[74]

The concern with pouring money into the southern, Mozambican, section of the railway stands in striking contrast with the half-hearted and equally unsuccessful efforts made to develop transport facilities further north. The colonial vision for Nyasaland, going back to the days of David Livingstone, was of a steamer service, penetrating as far as the north end of Lake Malawi and providing cheap and reliable outputs for the export of agricultural produce. In the event, investment in lake services shrank to a trickle in the 1920s. Not a single port was provided with shore facilities. The only vessels available to transport passengers or bulk cargoes prior to the building of the unreliable *Mpasa* in the late 1930s were the government steamer, the *Guendolen*, launched in 1898, and one or two ageing missionary vessels.[75]

In theory at least, the construction of the northern extension of the railway from Blantyre to Salima between 1931 and 1935 marked a dramatic reversal of policy aimed at revolutionising transport facilities in the north. In practice, however, as the Governor, Geoffrey Colby was to argue in 1948, its impact on export production was negligible and the opportunity costs associated with it were high.[76] Built with the aid of a grant of nearly £900,000 from Britain's Colonial Development Fund (the first example of Britain providing significant development funds for Nyasaland), the railway traversed some of the least productive areas of the Zomba, Ntcheu and Dedza districts before reaching the lake terminal, Chipoka, an open roadstead, infinitely inferior as a port to Monkey Bay. Beneficiaries of the northern extension included cotton growers on the

[71] R.D. Bell, *Report of the Commission appointed to enquire into the Financial Position and Further Development of Nyasaland,* HMGO, 1938, p.310.
[72] CO to Governor, 12 Apr 1948, PRO CO 525/213/44425; memo by Duncan Watson on Nyasaland Railway, 12 Feb 1949, PRO CO 525/214/4443.
[73] Vail, 'Railway Development' draws a different conclusion but without supplying any information on the real costs of the bridge for Nyasaland. My analysis is informed by an unpublished paper by Stephen Smith entitled 'Was Nyasaland Impoverished by its Railways 1908–1953?'.
[74] White, *Bridging the Zambesi*, 196–98.
[75] Murray, *Handbook* (1932), p. 405; Colby to Cohen, 10 Dec 1951, TNA CO 1015/350.
[76] Colby to Creech-Jones, 18 Dec 1948, TNA CO 525/214/44443.

south western shore of the Lake and rice-growers from the Nkhotakota district. Most northerners, however, were too distant from the railhead at Salima to profit from its construction, and tobacco-growers in the Lilongwe/Fort Manning and Dowa/Mponela areas also lost out.[77]

Anxious to maximise traffic on a line in which it had invested heavily, the Government introduced a Motor Traffic Ordinance in 1934 which effectively banned road transport for general services between the Central and Southern Provinces. Following representations by Conforzi, special permission was given for him to use his fleet of lorries to transport air cured tobacco to Cholo, although not to carry goods in the other direction. All other buyers from Lilongwe were forced to carry their tobacco by lorry down the escarpment 60 miles or more to Salima where it was transferred to the railway for despatch to the south.[78] Investment in the road from Blantyre to Lilongwe and beyond was accordingly halted, despite the widespread recognition, noted by Colby in 1948, that 'if the present motor restrictions were lifted, all traffic from Lilongwe and Fort Jameson to Limbe would go by road all the way.'[79] Colby himself took the view:

> ...if the Northern extension had not been built and if the capital cost had been available for other purposes not only could practically all the goods traffic carried by the Northern extension since its opening have been carried by road transport, at little if any extra cost, but both this Government and His Majesty's Government would have been saved considerable losses.[80]

Had the railway been extended to Lilongwe, a feat not accomplished until 1979, the Northern Extension might have performed a useful role in Malawi's communications network. With the railhead stranded at Salima, however, investment was diverted away from the potentially more productive road system while transport costs remained high.

Investment in transport, however limited, created opportunities for commercial expansion; the opening of markets made it possible. In the interwar years, European and Indian traders competed with each other for access to produce markets and control over retail trade with significant consequences for the subsequent shape of Nyasaland's commercial economy. In 1921, 361 Indian traders were already at work in the Protectorate out of a total Indian population of 563, of whom about half were resident in the Blantyre district.[81] Further immigration followed in the next two decades, despite opposition from the Commissioner of Police. The Indian population rose to 1,591 in 1931 and to 2,804 in 1945, by which time there were more Indians than Europeans in Nyasaland.[82]

---

[77] 'History of the Northern Extension' enclosed in Colby to Creech Jones, 18 Dec 1948, TNA CO 525/214/44443. See also *Report on an Economic Survey of Nyasaland 1958–1959* (Federation of Rhodesia and Nyasaland, C. Fed 132) [The Jack Report].
[78] See file 'Transport of Tobacco for Mr. I.C. Conforzi 1935–1939', Malawi Railway Archives.
[79] P. C. Central Province quoted in Colby to Creech Jones, 18 Dec 1948, TNA CO 525/214/44443.
[80] Colby to Creech Jones, ibid.
[81] Nyasaland Census for 1921, MNA. Since the partition of India in 1947, people originating from the sub-continent have usually been described in East Africa as 'Asian'. Historically, however, 'Indian' is the more accurate term for the years before 1947, even although some people originated from what has become Pakistan. I revert to the term 'Asian' for the post-1947 period.
[82] Floyd Dotson and Lillian O. Dotson, *The Indian Minority of Zambia, Rhodesia and Malawi* (New Haven, 1968), p. 48; Evidence of Major F.T. Stephens to the Bledisloe Commission, 20 June 1938, FCO.

A small but significant minority of Indians, 80–odd strong in 1931, were recruited from Bombay to work on the Shire Highlands Railway in skilled positions such as engine driver, station master and inspector.[83] More numerous were the 1,000–plus traders, the great majority Gujarati speakers from Western India, most of whom were initially brought to Nyasaland by well-established members of their extended families to serve as shop assistants and clerks.[84] The most successful of these followed the pioneer, Osman Adams, in becoming wholesalers and general merchants in the busy Indian shopping quarters of Blantyre, Limbe and Zomba. Others set up retail stores throughout the Shire Highlands and the Lower Shire Valley, selling sugar, salt, paraffin and cotton cloth. Others again made their way north in search of new commercial opportunities.[85] By the early 1930s, 20 Indian stores had been opened in the dusty market town of Lilongwe, 16 Indian traders had established shops in the Kasungu district and a handful of others had spread into the Mzimba and West Nyasa districts. Their presence in the last two provoked considerable opposition from African shopkeepers, most of them returned migrants from southern Africa who had invested their savings in trade.[86]

For much of the colonial period, government officials vied with members of the Malawian elite in denouncing Indian traders as unscrupulous adventurers, who practiced usury, exploited a credulous peasantry and exported their profits abroad. In more recent times these accusations have been repeated by Malawian historians.[87] Yet, while it is true that there were structural tensions between Indian traders and Malawian peasants (as between middlemen and peasants elsewhere), exemplified by the development of a credit system in which traders in the Lower Shire valley made loans to cotton-growing peasants on the security of next year's crop, these did nothing to diminish the general effectiveness of their role. Alert to peasant tastes and highly mobile, Indian traders pushed more deeply into Malawi's rural hinterland and operated on significantly lower profit margins than did their European rivals. Time and again they took the lead in purchasing peasant-grown produce, switching, after they were excluded from cotton markets in 1923, into a range of items ranging from maize and fish to tobacco and groundnuts. In the absence of government loans, which were not made available to African farmers until the 1950s, they were almost the only source of credit available to independent peasants. Although the interest they demanded was often high, so too were the risks they took. When the credit system collapsed during the Depression many of the smaller Indian traders became bankrupt.[88]

The growing prominence of Indian merchants influenced European commerce in two distinct ways: the trend towards concentration on the one

[83] See file entitled 'Shire Highlands Railways – Letters to Bombay Agents', Malawi Railway Archives.
[84] Nyasaland Protectorate. Report on the census for 1931, S1/1309/30 MNA; Dotson and Dotson 33, 66–8.
[85] Ibid., and Mandala, *Work and Control in a Peasant Economy*, 143–4.
[86] Cole-King, *Lilongwe*, 39; Report on the census for 1931; minutes of meetings of the West Nyasa Native Association, 1–2 May 1929, MNA S1/2065/19; the Central Province Native Association, 16 June 1928, MNA NC 1/3/2; the M'Mbelwa Native Association, 24 July 1935, MNA NC 1/3/6.
[87] Chanock, 'Political Economy of Independent Agriculture', 115, 126; Mandala, 142–45, 162–3, 169–70.
[88] Joey Power, 'Race, Ethnicity, and Anglo-Indian Trade Rivalry in Colonial Malawi, 1910–1945', *International Journal of African Historical Studies*, 26, 3, 1993, pp. 593–95.

hand, and the greater involvement of the state in the marketing of cash crops on the other. In 1911 nine European firms were involved in general trade including the oldest and largest, the African Lakes Corporation (Mandala), which by this time had opened 50 village shops in the rural areas in addition to its wholesale and European business in the towns.[89] The disappearance of the German firm L. Deuss and Co. as a result of the First World War strengthened the position of the ALC in relation to its European competitors, particularly as its main rival, Kubula Stores, failed to penetrate the rural market with any degree of success.[90] Some competition came from the London & Blantyre Supply Co, founded in Blantyre in 1906. In the 1920s it extended its activities from wholesale to retail trade under the title 'Kandodo' by seizing the assets of a number of bankrupt Indian traders to whom it had provided credit.[91] Otherwise, European firms remained confined to the towns with the important exception of those involved in the purchase of cash crops. Even here, however, a process of concentration was at work. For whereas in the mid-1920s dozens of European and Indian middlemen were employed in buying tobacco from Crown Land growers, by 1938, under the auction system introduced in that year, there were only 16 buyers, of whom two, the Imperial Tobacco Company and I. Conforzi, purchased 65 per cent of all tobacco sold.[92]

Labour migration & the making of the 'Dead North'

The growth of cash cropping on the Lilongwe Plain and in substantial areas of the Southern Province took place at a time when much of the Northern Province was being restructured as a labour reserve. Labour migrants wending their way from Northern districts to the labour markets of Katanga, Southern Rhodesia and South Africa were already numerous in 1913 when more than 25,000 Malawians were estimated to be working abroad.[93] The decision of the Government in 1919 to permit the Trans-Zambezi Railway Company to recruit workers in Nyasaland enlarged the market for labour. A further impetus was provided by the famine of 1924–25 which the Kasungu District Resident in 1926 identified as the cause 'for the excessive emigration last year.'[94] Wartime inflation, more than doubling the cost of goods in stores, imposed further pressure as did the rise in the rates of hut tax in 1912–13 from three shillings with a labour certificate and six shillings without to four and eight shillings respectively. This was replaced in 1921 by a flat rate poll tax of six shillings a year, the sum initially charged by Harry Johnston 30 years earlier.[95] Henceforth, the annual tax demand remained a potent force but only as one among a number of financial burdens afflicting

---

[89] Macmillan, 'Origins and Development of the African Lakes Company', 435–6; John Donaldson, 'The African Lakes Corporation – an analysis of its role in the economy of East Central Africa c.1878–1913', BA dissertation, University of Stirling, 1995, 52–54.

[90] History of British Central Africa Company, 1949, TNA CO 525/208/44332.

[91] Leishman and Cole-King, 'History of Blantyre'.

[92] Report of the Commission into the Tobacco Industry, 1939, MNA COM 7 4/2/1.

[93] See Boeder, 'Malawians Abroad', Appendix C, p.287.

[94] Northern Province Annual Report for Year ending 31 March 1926, MNA S1/920/26.

[95] Eric Smith, *Report on the Direct Taxation of Natives in the Nyasaland Protectorate*, Government Printer, Zomba, 1937, p. 7; Pachai, *Malawi*, p. 114.

peasants in the north. Equally important was the need to provide bride-price and school fees, and also the growth of consumer demand for a widening range of imported commodities such as cotton cloth, kerosene, salt, and iron hoes.[96]

Obstacles to the cultivation of cash crops interacted with the growth of financial pressure to propel northerners into the Southern African labour market. The attempt to develop cash-cropping in the north dates from 1905–1906 when Ngonde peasants began growing small quantities of cotton on the Karonga-Songwe alluvial flood plain. Their efforts were boosted in 1912 by the intervention of the British Cotton Growing Association which opened a ginnery at Vua, 28 miles south of the market at Karonga, agreeing to purchase the crop.[97] Because of the high freight charges incurred carrying cotton bales to the south, prices paid to northern growers were two-thirds or less of those paid to growers in the better placed Lower Shire valley.[98] Nevertheless, growers continued to increase production of cotton to a peak of 158 tons in 1925 at which time the discovery of the invasive pest, the pink bollworm, at Karonga brought cotton growing to a halt.[99] Anxious to prevent the spread of the pest to the more lucrative southern cotton-growing districts, the Government banned northern cultivation of the crop, a prohibition that lasted up to 1930. By that time world prices for cotton had plunged so low that the BCGA refused to purchase the crop, leaving Karonga growers with no outlet.[100] Not until 1934 was the industry revived, and then only as a marginal activity providing a modest return for up to 3,000 growers.

Market-related problems were also central to the collapse of tobacco growing in northern Malawi. In the early 1920s, A.F. Barron reached the shrewd conclusion that the sandy loams covering much of the Kasungu district and spreading into southern Mzimba were well suited for the growing of tobacco. The poor standard of roads discouraged him from penetrating further north than the Dwangwa River but, south of that, peasants were encouraged to plant tobacco which they sold at a market newly opened at Ngara.[101] By 1928 there were 1,100 registered growers in the southern portion of the Kasungu district plus many others further north who had begun to petition the Government for assistance in cultivating and selling their tobacco.[102]

The subsequent decision of the NTB to concentrate peasant production on the Lilongwe plain thus came as a major blow to northern producers. In 1930 the market at Ngara was closed, condemning Kasungu peasants to a long 43-mile trek to Mponela in order to sell their tobacco. Not surprisingly, the number of registered Crown Land growers in the district fell to 563 in 1931 and to 180 in

---

96   Contrasting views on the financial pressures forcing Malawians into labour migration are provided in *Report of the Committee appointed to enquire into Emigrant Labour, 1935* (Zomba, 1936) and in Smith, *Report on Direct Taxation*. For a lucid summary of the evidence see Richard Gray, *The Two Nations* (London, 1960), pp. 125–27.
97   Report on operations of the BCGA for the year ending 31 December 1912, TNA CO 525/47.
98   E.B. Pearce to Colonial Office, 26 April 1913, TNA CO 525/48.
99   Annual Report of Department of Agriculture for 1935; 'Cotton, North Nyasa, 1925–40', MNA S1/1751/25.
100 T.G. Thomas to Colonial Office, 23 January 1931, TNA CO 525/140/34029/1931.
101 P.C. Central Province to Chief Sec, 19 March 1924, MNA S1/2461/23; Kasungu District Book, District Council minutes, 7 October 1925.
102 Kasungu District Annual Report for 1931, MNA S1/61/32; Kasungu District Book, District Council minutes, 4 June and 20 December, 1926.

1933.[103] Some of those squeezed from the market became visiting tenants on European estates but others were forced into seeking employment beyond Nyasaland's borders

The collapse of cash cropping was only one aspect of the restructuring of Northern Province economies. Up to the First World War about two thirds of the cattle in Malawi were owned by Northern Ngoni and Tumbuka in the sparsely wooded highlands of the Mzimba district and by Ngonde on the Karonga lakeshore plain. Sales to the military created the prospect of a growing internal market in cattle to the estates of the Southern Province which would allow owners to pay their taxes at home. Following the end of the war, however, the government banned the export of cattle from these districts following an outbreak of the tick-borne East Coast fever.[104] A further blow came with the renewed spread of tsetse fly in the 1920s which killed off some 6,000 head of cattle in the Karonga District and penetrated from North Eastern Rhodesia deep across the whole of the Nkhamanga plain in the Mzimba district.[105] Northern herds of cattle survived and by the mid-1920s were even beginning to increase. But from 1926 they were cut off from prospective markets in the south by the meeting of the eastern and western tsetse belts between Kasungu and Nkhotakota.[106] In the 1930s a brisk trade in cattle to the Southern Province was opened up by cattle owners from Dedza and Ntcheu. But further north, so the Mzimba District Commissioner commented in 1934, Tumbuka/Ngoni peasants were 'in an almost impossible position in regard to the exportation of their surplus stock... Their country is surrounded by fly with the exception of a short stretch of the Lake Shore.'[107]

By the 1930s some Livingstonia-trained farmers, headed by the redoubtable Yacobe Harawa, were still cultivating coffee and tea on the margins of the mission's 50,000 acre estate.[108] On the Karonga lakeshore Ngonde peasants were selling beans, rice and maize in considerable quantities at the nearby Lupa Goldfields in Tanganyika.[109] There was a handful of pioneer coffee growers in the Misuku hills, a few hundred fishermen and fish traders on the western shore of the lake and some 1,300 schoolteachers, virtually all of them men, employed part-time by the Livingstonia mission. A few dozen northerners worked for the two or three solitary European farmers who attempted to scratch out a living in the hills of the North Nyasa district. Nearly a thousand more were employed up to 1932 on the ALC's Vizara and Chombe rubber estates south of Nkhata Bay.[110]

For an increasing proportion of northerners, however, migrant labour became

103 Kasungu District Annual Reports for 1931 and 1933, MNA S1/61/32 and S1/112/340.
104 McCracken, 'Experts and Expertise', pp. 114–15; Annual Report of Agricultural Department for 1914–15; Minutes of District Council Meeting, 2 September 1920, Mzimba District Book.
105 Resident, Karonga to P.C. Northern Province, 17 June 1926; Resident, Mzimba to P.C. Northern Province 15 July 1926, MNA M2/23/4.
106 P.C. Northern Province to Chief Sec, 10 September 1926, MNA M2/23/4.
107 Annual Report on Mzimba District for 1934, MNA S1/89 F-J/35.
108 McCracken, 'Underdevelopment in Malawi', p.208; A.C. Caseby, 'Livingstonia Mission Estate', written evidence submitted to North Nyasa Lands Commission, June 1929, MNA COM 4/1.
109 Annual Report on North Nyasa District for 1934, MNA.
110 Annual Reports on the Northern Province for 1927, MNA S1/542/28 and 1932, MNA S1/54/22; Chrispin S. Mphande, 'An Aspect of the Colonial Economy in Nkhata Bay District: the Case of Vizara and Chombe Rubber Estates', History Seminar Paper No. 5, 1990/91, Chancellor College, University of Malawi.

the major means of satisfying economic demand. By 1930, at least 80 per cent
of hut tax revenue in the Mzimba District was provided directly or indirectly by
migrants and the District Commissioner noted, that it was 'now unusual to find
any young men in the villages'.[111] Labour statistics must be treated with very
great caution but it is worth noting that the first major qualitative study, the
Lacey Report of 1935, suggested that in 1934 between 60 and 65 per cent of able
bodied men were absent from the West Nyasa (Chinteche) and Mzimba districts
as compared with 10 per cent or less from the southern districts, where cash
cropping opportunities were greater.[112] Some district figures provided by Lacey
are clearly inaccurate, but overall they were broadly confirmed by a labour census
conducted in 1937. It showed that 60.9 per cent of adult men were absent from
the West Nyasa District, 45.4 per cent from the Mzimba District and 43.8 per
cent from the Kasungu District. By comparison, an average of only 8 per cent
of adult men were absent from the six major cash cropping districts (Lilongwe,
Dowa, Lower Shire, Chikwawa, Mulanje and Cholo).[113] In the view of the Lacey
Committee, a total of 120,000 Malawians were working abroad in 1934, an estimate which the labour census downgraded to 90,000 in 1937. As Gray notes,
however, this revised figure probably erred on the conservative side and it is more
than likely, as the Government acknowledged, that by the mid-1930s at least
110,000 Malawian workers were absent from their homeland.[114] Two estimates
of how they were distributed, the second the more reliable, are set out in Table
7.1:

Table 7.1
Estimates of Number of Malawian Labour Migrants

Place	Labour Census 1937	Government estimate 1937
Southern Rhodesia	64,078	75,000
South Africa	13,938	25,000
Northern Rhodesia	4,108	4,300
Tanganyika	5,792	6,000
Belgian Congo	599	600
Other countries	1,582	2,000
Total	90,097	112,900

As these figures demonstrate, Southern Rhodesia attracted at least two-thirds
of all Malawian migrants, as it had from the early 1920s onwards. The number
of Malawians working in the mining industry increased from an average of

[111] 'Suggested application for a system of Indirect Rule to the Mombera District', D.C. Mzimba, 27
January 1930, MNA NNM1/14/6.
[112] *Report of the Committee to Enquire into Emigrant Labour, 1935* (Zomba, 1936) p. 36.
[113] Bell, *Report*, 1938, Appendix A. Useful additional discussion of labour statistics is provided in G.
Coleman, 'International Labour Migration from Malawi, 1875–1966', *Malawi Journal of Social
Science*, II (1973), pp. 31–46 and in G. Coleman, 'Regional and District Origins of Migrant Labour
from Malawi to 1966', *Malawi Journal of Social Science*, VI (1970), pp. 45–59. For this period, however,
the most authoritative account remains Gray, *The Two Nations*, pp. 120–27.
[114] Gray, *Two Nations*, p. 121. See also Memo from the Nyasaland Government to the Standing
Committee on Migrant Labour, 3 December 1937, TNA CO 525/161, cited in Boeder, 'Malawians
Abroad', p. 137.

12,500 between 1920 and 1926 to 30,700 in 1937, about 33 per cent of the total work force.[115] Some 25,000 Malawians worked on Rhodesian farms and a further 20,000 in Rhodesian towns, including at least 10,000 in Salisbury, on one estimate, nearly half the city's African population.[116] It was there, in the township of Harare, and in Johannesburg, that a Malawian urban culture was born.

For many Malawians, including the two most famous, Clements Kadalie and Hastings Kamuzu Banda, Southern Rhodesia was a staging post on the road to the higher wage economy of South Africa. Banda worked for eighteen months in a hospital at Hartley before taking employment at the Maronjeri colliery in South Africa early in 1917. Kadalie worked as a clerk on the Rhodesian Railways and on two Rhodesian gold mines before heading south to Kimberley almost exactly a year later.[117] A major obstacle was the ban on the employment of migrants from territories north of latitude 22 degrees south imposed in 1913 as a consequence of the appalling death rate from pneumonia suffered by 'tropicals' in the deep-level mines and lasting up to 1932. However, while this measure was largely effective in excluding Malawians from those mines federated to the Chamber of Mines, it failed to prevent them taking employment illegally in non-federated mines such as the Zaaiplaats Tin Mine near Nylstroom and the Consolidated Gold Mine at Leydsdorp, or in a range of non-mining industries.[118] By the late 1930s some Malawians were employed in near slavery conditions as low-paid farm labour in the Bethal District of Northern Transvaal. Others were better placed, working in hotels in Cape Town and Durban. Others again were domestic workers, shop assistants and warehousemen. Following WNLA's resumption of recruiting in Nyasaland in 1936 the number of Malawians employed in the Rand mines grew to 6,600 in 1939.[119]

Additional smaller labour markets existed north and west of the Protectorate where the talents of Malawians were in particular demand. Perhaps 2,000 Nyasas were employed in the copper mines controlled by the Union Minière Company in Katanga in the boom years of the 1920s, many of them 'in jobs where the skills of language and literacy were at a premium – particularly low level supervision, clerical, store-keeping and minor hospital posts.'[120] Numbers fell following the introduction of a policy of stabilisation favouring local workers on contract. But new opportunities for semi-skilled Nyasas emerged with the development of the Northern Rhodesian Copperbelt from 1928. In 1930, Nyasas constituted 38.5 per cent of the total work force at the Roan Antelope mine, although this proportion decreased later as state restrictions on the employment of 'alien' (i.e. non-Northern Rhodesian) workers began to bite. In 1937 only 1,050 Malawians were recorded as working on the Northern Rhodesian mines. On the Lupa Goldfields in Tanganyika, a sudden surge in demand for labour in 1935 resulted in the employment on short term contracts of as many as 15,000 Malawians. Once

---

[115] Kuczynski, *Demographic Survey*, p.558 cited in W.C. Chirwa, 'Rural Labour, Migrancy and Fishing', p.160; Gray, *The Two Nations*, p.92.
[116] G.N. Burden, *Report on Nyasaland Native Labour in Southern Rhodesia* (Zomba 1938).
[117] Philip Short, *Banda* (London 1974), pp. 14–15; Kadalie, *My Life and the ICU*, pp. 34–7.
[118] Boeder, 'Malawians Abroad', pp.73; G.N. Burden, *Report on Nyasaland Native Labour in South Africa* (Zomba, 1940); J.C. Abrahams, *Report on Nyasaland Natives in the Union of South Africa and in Southern Rhodesia* (Zomba, 1937).
[119] Burden, 1940, p.19.
[120] Perrings, *Black Mineworkers in Central Africa*, pp. 157–8.

again, however, numbers fell rapidly in the next few years, to a low of 2,200 in 1939.[121]

A number of common patterns can be distinguished in the experience of labour migrants. Even in the Mzimba district where the volume of absentees was particularly high, young men took pains to limit the damage done to village economies, for example by postponing their departure until at least April or May after planting and weeding had taken place.[122] Most carried charms to protect them on their journey and travelled in small groups of five or more. Some signed contracts with the recruiting agents who operated on Nyasaland's borders with Northern Rhodesia and Portuguese East Africa. But by the 1930s contract labour or *chibaro* had become synonymous throughout the Protectorate with forced labour or slavery with the result that the great majority rejected the greater ease of travel that labour touts could offer in order to preserve their freedom of action.[123] More than 90 per cent made the long and dangerous journey south on foot rather than by rail. From the early 1930s, some began to travel by lorry at rates of between 15 shillings and £1 from Blantyre to Salisbury, increased to 25 shillings and £2 for the return journey.[124] Up into the 1920s migrants faced the danger of being attacked and robbed by armed gangs while passing through Mozambique and they were also frequently subjected to extortion from policemen and messengers there and in Rhodesia.[125] The illegal crossing into South Africa was a further hazard because those arrested were frequently consigned as labourers to the low-wage farms of Bethal in Northeastern Transvaal.[126] Migrants were particularly vulnerable on the journey home when they were laden with possessions, and travel by rail did not eliminate the risk. In the mid-1930s, Blantyre station was a favourite haunt of sneak thieves on the lookout for luggage to steal.[127]

The common image of the labour migrant is of the single young man oscillating at relatively regular intervals between his rural village and urban place of employment. In practice, prior to the major expansion of contract labour in the 1940s and 50s, migrants were more likely to move to a variety of jobs taking them ever further south before eventually returning home.

Zinthani Shaba's experiences conform to the general pattern.[128] Born near Ekwendeni around 1913, Shaba went south with a group of friends in 1934, travelling through the bush by day in order to avoid contact with *magalachani*, the dreaded labour recruiters. For four months he worked as a milkman in Salisbury at 15 shillings a month before walking to Pretoria and from there to Johannesburg, where he obtained a post as factory labourer at £3 a month, four times

---

[121] Annual Report on the Northern Province for 1938, MNA NC 2/1/9.
[122] Joseph H.C. Mfuni, 'Labour Migration from Northern Mzimba', History Seminar paper No. 11, 1981/82, Chancellor College, University of Malawi.
[123] *Report of the Committee to Enquire into Emigrant Labour*, 1935, p.28. For a valuable discussion see also Charles Van Onselen, *Chibaro. African Mine Labour in Southern Rhodesia, 1900–1933* (Pluto Press, London, 1976) pp. 99 and 119–23.
[124] *Report on Emigrant Labour*, 1935, pp. 24–5.
[125] E.P. Makambe, 'The Nyasaland African Labour "Ulendos" to Southern Rhodesia and the Problem of the African "Highwaymen", 1903–23', *African Affairs*, 79, 317, 1980, pp. 548–66.
[126] Mfuni, 'Labour Migration'. For a vivid depiction of conditions in the late 1940s, see Michael Scott, *A Time to Speak* (Faber, London 1958), pp. 169–90.
[127] Blantyre Monthly Police Report, May 1935, MNA POL 5/2/1.
[128] Joseph Mfuni interview with Zinthani Shaba, T.A. Mtwalo, Mzimba, 23 September 1981.

what he had been getting previously. In 1936 he moved to a better paid job on a neighbouring coal mine; some time later he returned to Nyasaland. Overall, he was absent from his village for over three years, a period not dissimilar to the average length of absence (three years and seven months) among migrants from 110 Northern Province villages studied by Margaret Read in the mid-1930s.[129]

These figures, however, conceal wide variations. Some migrants, including the majority of Malawians on the Lupa Goldfields, were absent for only two or three months. Others were away for over six years. In the opinion of the Emigrant Labour Committee, between 25 and 30 per cent of all migrants were *machona* or 'lost ones': people who had severed their connexions with their homeland and were unlikely to return.[130] Some of these formed permanent Nyasa communities at Rhodesian mines, such as Shamva, complete with their wives and children.

Their presence indicates that single men were not the only players in the labour market. Each year, as many as 5,000 youths aged between 10 and 18 accompanied older relations abroad, particularly to the Lupa Goldfields where child labour was actively encouraged.[131] Emigration by women remained uncommon, although less than is often assumed.[132] Writing of the Northern Province in 1939, Margaret Read noted:

> In the dowry districts it is almost unknown for women to leave the village and go off on their own. In other areas it is becoming common. Some manage to get to S. Rhodesia, others to Blantyre, Lilongwe, Kotakota, Mponela, to any place in fact where money is plentiful and a prostitute's trade is a paying one.[133]

Influx control was designed to prevent migrant workers settling permanently with their families in Southern African towns. But with the growth of urbanisation, these controls were frequently evaded. By the 1920s Southern Rhodesian officials were commenting on the significant number of women from Nyasaland who had entered the territory, sometimes with their husbands and sometimes alone.[134] Twenty years later they were also becoming numerous in South Africa. In 1942 it was noted that 'several hundred Northern women were resident in South Africa and that the number continually was being increased by further clandestine entries.'[135] Some government officials in Nyasaland were now convinced of the merits of women joining their husbands although others remained opposed.[136] Government thus continued to ally itself with chiefs, headmen and male guardians in seeking to prevent women migrating to the south

[129] Margaret Read, 'Migrant Labour in Africa and its Effects on Tribal Life', in *International Labour Review*, XLV, 6 (1942), p.621.

[130] *Report of the Committee on Emigrant Labour*, 1935, p. 29.

[131] Ibid., p. 16 and Appendix 6, 'Report by the Hon. and Rev. W.P. Young on a visit to the Lupa Goldfield Area, Nov 1–6'; Chirwa, 'Rural Labour, Migrancy and Fishing', pp. 164–5.

[132] For a pioneering discussion see Zoe Rebecca Groves, 'Malawians in Colonial Salisbury: a social history of migration in central Africa', PhD dissertation, University of Keele, 2011, pp. 62–103.

[133] Margaret Read, 'Emigration from Nyasaland: its effects on village life. Preliminary Report', June 1939, MNA S36/1/4/2.

[134] Diana Jeater, *Marriage, Perversion, and Power. The Construction of Moral Discourse in Southern Rhodesia 1894–1930* (Clarendon Press: Oxford, 1993), pp. 232–3.

[135] E.H. Warner, Nyasaland/Northern Rhodesia Labour Office, Johannesburg to Acting Labour Officer, 26 September 1942 MNA S 36/1/2/6.

[136] See 'Native Female Immigration to South Africa', 1942, MNA S 36/1/2/4.

although, by the late 1950s, these measures had been relaxed. In 1958, 1,733 women travelled to Southern Rhodesia from Nyasaland on the free, 'ulere' bus service provided by the Southern Rhodesian Government, along with 17,813 men.[137]

The effects of labour migration depended on how it interacted with local economies. Where labour requirements for the production of foodstuffs were low, the absence of even 60 per cent of able-bodied young men was not an economic catastrophe. By concentrating on the cultivation of cassava, carried out largely by women, and the netting of fish, Tonga communities in the West Nyasa District were able to sustain a viable economy with a fair measure of success.[138] Access to education, acquired through the Livingstonia Mission with its base at Bandawe, was a further positive factor, for it meant that most migrants going abroad carried with them skills of language and literacy that were attractive to potential employers. Tonga workers often took the lead in obtaining white-collar jobs at higher than average wages; this meant that returning migrants frequently had money to spend. Remittances from abroad were significantly larger than in any other district, as the table below demonstrates, with the result that cloth and other possessions were relatively abundant. 'I have never seen men or women better dressed in Nyasaland', an official noted of the Chinteche district in 1937.[139] Little or no capital was reinvested in agriculture. But a number of the more successful Tonga migrant workers invested in stores and, from the 1940s, in fishing and fish trading.

Table 7.2
Remittances from Abroad: Northern Province[140]
Postal and Money Orders in £s

District	1937	1938
Chinteche	13,677	16,010
Mzimba	9,223	12,052
Karonga	697	1,477
Kasungu	2,219	2,451
Kota-Kota	1,688	1,891
Ft Manning	759	1,065
Lilongwe	1,162	3,553
Dowa	2,302	3,889
Dedza	6,758	8,865
Ncheu	5,555	8,888

[137] Teresa Barnes, 'Virgin Territory? Travel and Migration by African Women in Twentieth-Century Southern Africa' in S. Geiger, J.M. Allman and N. Musisi (eds), *Women in African Colonial Histories* (Bloomington, Indiana, 2002), *p*. 165.
[138] J. Van Velsen, 'Labour Migration as a Positive Factor in the Continuity of Tonga Tribal Society' in I. Southall (ed.), *Social Change in Africa*, (London, 1961), pp. 230–41.
[139] Agricultural Survey, 'Chinteche' by J.W. Pryor in 'Interim Report of the Agricultural Survey of the Five Most Northerly Districts of Nyasaland'. 1937, MNA Liv Corr Box 1.
[140] Annual Report on the Northern Province for 1938, MNA NC 2/1/2.

Where labour requirements were higher, however, the impact of migration could be damaging. The Kasungu district, with one of the lowest population densities in the country, was particularly susceptible to the drain of manpower, as the local Resident noted. In some villages, by 1926, 'hardly a single able-bodied man [was] left at home'. Gardens were no longer cultivated and fields had reverted to bush.[141] This resulted in turn in an upsurge in the animal population, the spread of tsetse and an increase in the incidence of sleeping sickness. In 1922, fifty-eight villages were evacuated from what is now the Kasungu National Park but the tsetse still continued to spread.[142] Not till 1928 was the trend reversed. By that time, there was 'so little inducement to return to this poverty-stricken area' that Chewa migrants were spending on average six years away from the district, nearly twice the length of absence of labour migrants from elsewhere.[143] Furthermore, as educational opportunities were limited, migrants from the Kasungu district tended as a rule to go to less well-paid jobs and hence to have significantly less capital to invest. This meant that standards of housing were inferior to those elsewhere as were standards of diet.[144] Thus, by the 1930s much of the Kasungu District was little more than a rural slum with few prospects available for its inhabitants.

If Chinteche and Kasungu represent extremes in the variety of responses to labour migration, the large Mzimba district comes somewhere between the two. An area of marginal soils, negligible transport facilities and limited economic opportunities, this district was in some respects the classic labour reserve during the interwar years. Yet it also possessed one of the most comprehensive networks of schools in Nyasaland, and a high proportion of men who had passed Standard I and were literate in Tumbuka or English. In consequence a substantial number gained access to skilled or semi-skilled employment when working abroad in Katanga, Northern Rhodesia and Southern Rhodesia.[145]

The effect of their involvement in the migrant labour system is a contentious issue dividing both participants and observers. Looking back from the early 1980s on their experiences between the 1930s and the 1950s, former labour migrants from northern Mzimba were often surprisingly positive about what they had gained.[146] Most pointed to the material possessions they had brought back from Southern Africa: blankets, clothes, hats and shoes; and sometimes sewing machines and bicycles. Several had acquired cattle for *lobola* with the money they saved. Others brought back knowledge of new languages: Afrikaans, Zulu and Xhosa. One returned from Johannesburg with an enthusiasm for ballroom dancing which he had learnt as a waiter at the Royal Hotel. Another admitted, "What I learnt from there is drinking

---

[141] Annual Report on the Northern Province for the year ending 31 March 1926, MNA S1/920/26.

[142] W.A. Lamborn, 'The Tsetse fly Problem in the Northern Province', paper read to the Blantyre branch of the British Medical Association, 1936, MNA M2/23/3; Annual Report for the Northern Province, 1922/23, MNA S1/1712/23. See also McCracken, 'Colonialism, capitalism and the ecological crisis', pp. 63–77.

[143] Read, 'Migrant Labour in Africa', p. 16.

[144] Ibid.

[145] Read, 'Migrant Labour'; McCracken, *Politics and Christianity in Malawi*.

[146] Mfuni, 'Labour Migration from Northern Mzimba'; John D. Nkosi, 'Labour Migration and its effects on Rural Life: a case study from Mzimba district, c.1930s-1950s', History Seminar 1981/82, Paper no.12, Chancellor College, University of Malawi.

beer and fighting."[147] As in Chinteche, only a minority invested their savings in commercial agriculture, most often in the production of food crops. But several others purchased maize mills and opened groceries and stores.

The material prosperity of the few, however, must be set against the pressures exerted on the many. Several of the more extravagant assertions made by the Lacey Committee in 1935 can be confidently discounted. There is no evidence to suggest that the 'whole fabric of the old order of society' was 'undermined' as a consequence of the removal of large numbers of able-bodied men from the villages, that the integrity of the tribal community was threatened, that 'immorality' was rampant or that the long term effect was to bring about a fall in the birth rate.[148] In fact, the take-off in population growth and the expansion of labour migration occurred virtually simultaneously from the late 1920s. As Van Velsen has noted with reference to the Tonga, migrants tended to respond to urban insecurity by seeking to maintain and build on relationships with the rural community from which they came.[149] In the 1930s, for example, members of a Tonga Association in Katanga regularly remitted money to pay the school fees of their younger kinsmen.[150]

Yet, if labour migration did not result in the collapse or disintegration of indigenous institutions, it did bring to the surface tensions implicit in the relations between men and women in rural communities. Although the debate was focused on such issues as marriage, divorce and public morality, Chanock is right to insist that control over labour and resources were underlying issues.[151] A particular problem was the pressure on marriages that resulted from the prolonged absence of men from their families. As early as 1912, the Mzimba District Officer noted that 31 out of 36 women recently granted divorces were the wives of labour migrants who had left for the south between four and eight years previously.[152] With divorces proliferating in the 1920s, chiefs combined with members of the educated elite to counter the growing independence of women. Customary law was interpreted as giving the husband's family control over the children of broken marriages. Yet women were often made responsible for paying back *lobola*, even though it was their husbands who had deserted them.[153] As women also found themselves liable for the payment of hut tax, whether their husbands supported them financially or not, they were placed in a highly vulnerable position. The emergence of *vimbuza* spirit-possession in the North may derive from its origins in the Ngoni assault on the status of Tumbuka women back in the mid-19th century. But it is likely, as Vail and White note, that its rapid growth in the 1920s reflects the severe psychological and economic pressures that labour migration imposed upon them. Condemned by mission-

[147] Interviews by Joseph Mfuni with Zinthani Shaba, Kaibanthe Mchisi and Mchona Honde, September 1981.
[148] *Report of the Committee on Emigrant Labour*, 1935, pp. 30–38.
[149] Van Velsen, 'Labour Migration as a Positive Factor'.
[150] *Report on Emigrant Labour*, 1935, p. 21; McCracken, *Politics and Christianity*, p.284.
[151] Martin Chanock, *Law, Custom and Social order. The Colonial Experience in Malawi and Zambia* (Cambridge, 1985), p.12–16.
[152] Mzimba District Book, 1910–1913.
[153] Notes on district council meetings held on 2 September 1920, 9 February 1921, Mzimba District Book, 1918–23; notes on district council meetings held on 31 December 1928, 31 March 1930, Mzimba District Book, 1923–30; minutes of the Mombera Native Association, 1–2 September 1920, MNA S1/210/20.

aries, educated Christian men and chiefs alike, *vimbuza* and related forms of spirit-possession, *virombo* and *vyanyusi,* continued to spread as vehicles of women's resentment and anxiety.[154]

Famine, disease & demographic change

Developments in migrant labour and in cash-cropping constitute the most important structural changes in the 1920s and 1930s. But for most Malawians they took second place to the ongoing struggle for survival. Drought and disease remained potent enemies, but they were now compounded by the ambiguous and contradictory impact of capitalism and colonialism. Well into the 1920s they continued to have a predominantly destructive effect on food production in Malawi. Thereafter, some of the more extreme pressures were reduced with important consequences for demographic trends in the region.

The early 1920s must count as one of the most miserable periods in the colonial history of Malawi. Hard on the heels of the influenza epidemic of 1919–1920 came a prolonged drought in the Southern Province in 1920–1921, broken only at the beginning of February, several weeks after the rains normally began. With crops already in short supply as a result of the demands of the war, famine quickly struck throughout the Lower Shire, Upper Shire and South Nyasa districts. As so often in times of drought, Mulanje was largely unaffected but in many districts there was 'an exceedingly heavy death rate', lasting well into 1923 with 'the deaths among the adolescent population' of Chikwawa district being 'far heavier than was realized at the time'.[155]

The partial recovery in the Southern Province was followed by the outbreak of a new famine in the north which started late in 1924 and came to a climax in 1925. The Mzimba plain was particularly badly affected. 'The famine became more and more acute during February and March and was particularly severe in Chinde's section and in the Loudon area', the Provincial Commissioner reported. Near Loudon, many people died 'of slight illness from which they would have recovered had food been available'.[156] Over the whole of the plain, people could be seen making their way across the border into Northern Rhodesia or into neighbouring districts in a desperate search for food. Those who travelled to the Karonga lakeshore plain were generally successful, but women heading for the Kasungu district, which was also badly affected, were turned away empty handed. Men were forced to slaughter their cattle and sheep in an attempt to obtain the wherewithal for grain. With people absent from their villages searching for food, many fields were left neglected. Not till the maize crop had been harvested in 1926 did food supplies become relatively abundant again and then surpluses had to be shipped down to the Southern Province which was now

---

[154] Leroy Vail and Landeg White, *Power and the Praise Song: Southern African Voices in History,* London, 1991, pp.231–70. See also B.J. Soko, 'An Introduction to the *Vimbuza* Phenomenon', *Religion in Malawi,* 1, 1 (1987), pp. 9–13; B.J. Soko, 'The *Vimbuza* Possession Cult: the Onset of the Disease', *Religion in Malawi,* 2, 1 (1988), 11–15.

[155] Annual Reports on the Southern Province for years ending March 1924 and April 1925, MNA NS 3/1/1. For a brief pioneering discussion of changes in the food supply, see Iliffe, 'Poor in the Modern History of Malawi', pp. 258–59.

[156] Annual Report on Northern Province, April 1924 – February 1925, MNA S1/993/25.

suffering from a new famine, caused this time by excessive rainfall and flooding.[157]

It is an indication of the contradictory character of colonialism and capitalism that the same forces that brought about rural Malawi's post-war crisis were in part responsible for its alleviation. As Iliffe notes, it is probable that 'early colonial economic changes exacerbated the long standing problem of seasonal shortages in bad years, but that the problem was then relieved by more effective government.'[158] Distressed areas where seasonal food shortages regularly occurred in the late 1920s and 1930s included the Lower Shire River, particularly after the floods of the late 1930s, and the Fort Maguire area at the south-east arm of Lake Malawi, whose 'unfortunate inhabitants' were described in 1936 as seeming 'to move in a vicious circle. Not only were they unable to procure a sufficiency of food but many were too weakened by hunger to cultivate their gardens and so they are again faced with the likelihood of shortage.'[159] From 1922, however, when over 700 tons of maize was imported into the Lower Shire Valley, the worst affected area, the government took upon itself responsibility for providing famine relief by transporting maize from surplus districts, notably Cholo, Mulanje and Lilongwe, to deficit ones: the South Nyasa district in 1931 and 1936 and the Mzimba district in 1938.[160] In most cases, the maize provided had to be purchased by villagers, but free issues were made 'to the old, the children, infirm and destitute', i.e. to those social categories particularly at risk as a consequence of lack of family support.[161] However, Mandala is almost certainly correct in arguing that these limited initiatives played only a minor part in the prevention of famine in the country. Of greater importance was the role played by the British as 'keepers of social peace', providing the circumstances in which villagers could move in search of food from areas of hunger to those with surpluses: something they had been unable to do during the great famine of 1862–63.[162] Low-level malnutrition continued to deepen, not least in those areas where absentee rates among able-bodied men reached 50 per cent or more. In the Lower Shire Valley, as in certain other districts, *njala*, seasonal hunger, was a regular occurrence.[163] However, there were no further 'famines that kill' prior to 1948, despite the dramatic variations in rainfall that took place over this period.[164]

The easing of the crisis in the food supply was accompanied by a contraction in tsetse fly belts. In the previous decade, medical experts charged with halting the spread of tsetse had employed two main strategies with equal lack of success. Free shooting of game, attempted briefly in the early 1920s, had simply scattered wild animals to new regions at considerable expense. But W.A. Lamborn, the government entomologist, had been no more successful with his ambitious

---

[157] Annual Report on the Northern Province for year ending 31 March 1926, MNA S1/920/26.

[158] Iliffe, 'The Poor in the Modern History of Malawi', p. 258.

[159] Annual Report on the Southern Province for 1936, MNA NS 3/1/6.

[160] 'Famine conditions in Nyasaland, 1922', MNA S1/244/22; Annual Report on the Northern Province for 1938, MNA NC 2/1/9; Elias C. Mandala, *The End of Chidyerao: A History of Food and Everyday Life in Malawi, 1860–2004* (Heinemann, Portsmouth NH, 2005) pp. 49–51.

[161] Annual Report on the Southern Province for 1936, MNA NS 3/1/6.

[162] Mandala, *End of Chidyerano*, pp. 47, 62–66.

[163] Ibid., pp. 73–99.

[164] Iliffe, 'Poor in the Modern History of Malawi', pp. 258–59.

scheme for a vast anti-tsetse fly barrier constructed with great labour in the Dowa district in 1926.[165] Less than a year later, tsetse flies in significant numbers were discovered south of the barrier. Lamborn had begun to contemplate the likelihood 'that the whole countryside – mile after mile of Lilongwe, the western part of Dedza and much of Ncheu – will be successively and rapidly occupied by the fly which has made an advance so phenomenal during the present rains.'[16]

Help came from an unexpected source. By 1927 the expansion of African tobacco growing in the Central Province was beginning to take effect. Barron, Conforzi and other settlers purchased leasehold estates on the tsetse-infested land in the vicinity of the Bua, Mudi and Ludzi rivers. As immigrants flooded in to take up tenancies, the bush was cut back, increasing amounts of land were put under cultivation, and the advance of tsetse was halted. If the impact of capitalism, by forcing the withdrawal of labour from lightly inhabited areas, had contributed to the original expansion of the fly, its influence now worked in the opposite direction. Visiting the Dowa and Fort Manning districts in 1929, Lamborn was

> ...greatly impressed at the great economic development of the region to the immediate south of the tsetse area that has taken place during the late rains, on the Dowa side of the Bua in particular.... The tobacco patches become larger and larger annually and in the train of development has come the conversion by the Tobacco Board of more tracks into motor roads... and the institution of large buying centres.[167]

Two years later, the retreat of tsetse was well under way and Lamborn's report was a veritable hymn to commercial agriculture:

> The economic opening up of the country within the past few years has been prodigious. Patches cleared by natives for the cultivation of tobacco have become noticeably larger and more numerous even within the past eighteen months, and the rapid deforestation that is proceeding has become more and more evident, the demand for fuel for curing purposes being considerable. More and more motor roads and tracks are being developed and more natives are coming in as tenants to assist in opening up European-owned estates... Furthermore there is general agreement among Europeans and natives alike that the game is fast vanishing south of the reserve and has actually gone in the vicinity of the tobacco-growing centres. This accords with my own recent experiences, for I saw very few evidences indeed of the presence of game. Such is the combination of factors that seem to be determining the withdrawal of the fly.[168]

By 1937, 400 square miles of previously infested land had been cleared; none existed south of the Ludzi and Mudi rivers and, with the exception of a couple of small patches, none could be found up to ten miles north of the Ludzi.[169] In both the Lilongwe and Dowa districts, cattle were being cautiously reintroduced to land from which they had previously been removed. Subsequent progress was erratic, but the trend towards the withdrawal of tsetse was maintained. When a

---

[165] For further details see McCracken, 'Experts and Expertise', pp. 107–09.

[166] W.A. Lamborn, 'Further Report on the Tsetse Control Scheme', 22 April 1927, MNA GFT 1/5/1.

[167] Lamborn, 'First Report on the Tsetse Fly problem in Dowa and Fort Manning Districts, 9 May 1929', MNA GFT 1/5/1.

[168] Lamborn, 'First Report on the Tsetse fly Problem, 1931', MNA M2/23/3.

[169] Lamborn, 'Report No.1 on Tsetse Problem in Lilongwe, Dowa and Fort Manning Districts for 1937', MNA M2/23/3.

committee investigated the distribution of the fly in Nyasaland in 1954, it was found that in the Central and Northern provinces tsetse was confined to the Kasungu Game Reserve and to three substantial patches near the lakeshore, with a thinner subsidiary area further north spreading out from the Vwaza Marsh.[170] 'Tsetse belts in Nyasaland are limited in extent and there is evidence that they have contracted during the last fifty years from an area of about 5,000 square miles to possibly some 3,000 square miles at the present time', wrote a veterinary officer in 1959, in apparent ignorance of the dramatic fluctuations that had occurred in the intervening period. 'In this period also the problem of human trypanosomiasis has decreased to the point where it can be regarded as of being of negligible importance.' [171]

From our perspective today, it is possible to see that the most important, although at the time the least appreciated development of the 1930s was the gradual take off in population growth. Population censuses, giving the results shown in Table 7.3, were conducted in 1921, 1926, 1931 and 1945, although all were deeply flawed. It is not until the census of 1966 that the figures can be accepted with any degree of confidence.

Table 7.3
Nyasaland Census Returns, 1921–1966

1921	1,201,983
1926	1,293,291
1931	1,603,454
1945	2,183,220
1966	4,305,583

What they appear to reveal when corrections are made for obvious errors is that any increase in population up to the mid-1920s came largely from the extensive emigration of Lomwe from Mozambique into the Southern Province. Thereafter, however, as in other parts of Eastern and Central Africa, the decline of natural disasters and of famine, the suspension of warfare and the emergence of a colonial peace, along with the growth of a slightly more effective central government, resulted in a marginal fall in the death rate and hence a natural increase in the population. Absolute figures must be treated with caution. Yet it is not unreasonable to suppose on the basis of the available evidence that the decennial increase between 1931 and 1945 was in the region of 26 per cent, of which less than 10 per cent came from immigration. Population growth was therefore still relatively slow but it was on an accelerating curve which was to rise with increasing steepness in the years after 1945 when the average increase was 3.3 per cent per annum.[172]

[170] B.L. Mitchell and B. Steele, *A Report on the Distribution of Tsetse Flies in Nyasaland and Some Recommendations for Control*, Zomba, 1956.

[171] Annual Report of the Veterinary Department for 1959, p. 12.

[172] The most detailed and authoritative study of demographic change in this period is Kuczynski, *Demographic Survey*, Vol. II, pp.522–639. See also Coleman, 'The Censuses of Malawi', SOMJ, 27, 1 (1974), pp. 27–35, and *Malawi Population Census 1966 Final Report* (Zomba, 1967). My analysis of demographic change in historical perspective here and elsewhere is influenced by the account provided in John Iliffe, *Africans*.

Up to the 1920s the population of Malawi was virtually stagnant. Thereafter, however, the inexorable increase in the number of people in a country where population density was already higher than anywhere else in the region was to have profound consequences both for African pressure on land and for the growth of labour migration. In certain areas, notably in the Northern Province, the rate of increase remained relatively slow but in the Southern Province the rise in population, fuelled in part by continued immigration from Mozambique, took on dramatic proportions. Significant changes in regional population resulted, strengthening the numerical dominance of the south, as is demonstrated in Table 7.4

Table 7.4
Percentage of Population by Regions: 1921–1966[173]

Province	1921	1931	1966
Northern Province	18%	14%	12%
Central Province	39%	39%	36%
Southern Province	43%	47%	52%

This in turn reflected sharp variations in population density in different parts of the country. As late as 1966 there were only 48 people per square mile in the Northern Province as compared to 108 per square mile in the Central Province and 169 per square mile in the South. District variations were even more dramatic. In the Chiradzulu district the population density in 1945 was a spectacular 310 per square mile, rising to 482 in 1966. By contrast, in the Mzimba district (divided now into Rumphi and Mzimba) the figure was 27 in 1945 rising to 47 in 1966. By that time Malawi's population density at 111 persons per square mile of land area was surpassed on the African mainland only by Rwanda, Burundi and Nigeria. Zimbabwe, by contrast, had a density of 28, Mozambique 23, and Zambia only 13.[174] As these figures suggest, there was no simple link between population density and the growth of popular unrest. Nevertheless, it is important to recognise that it was in precisely those areas where pressure on land was greatest that, in the early 1950s, peasants began turning to violence.

[173] *Malawi Population Census 1966*, p. vi.
[174] Ibid.

8

The Great Depression & its Aftermath

Historians are divided on the impact of the Great Depression on third world societies. One view, expressed most eloquently by John Iliffe for Tanganyika, is that the period originating with the onset of the world depression in 1929 and continuing up to 1945 was a turning point, marking both the emergence of colonial society in its most complete form and the beginning of its dissolution.[1] The alternative argument, advanced most vigorously in a collection of essays edited by Ian Brown, is that the impact of the depression on non-Western societies was much less damaging than is conventionally believed. Peasants suffered from the world-wide fall in prices for primary products between 1929 and 1933 but they benefited from the admittedly shallower fall in the price of manufactured imports and were often better equipped than settlers to adapt to the new economic conditions.[2]

In this chapter, I follow Iliffe in suggesting that the depression was an event of great importance, exposing in a particularly vivid manner the contradictory interests that were involved in the shaping of Nyasaland's economy. But I also suggest that its effects tended to be muted, partly because, in many instances, peasants were able to ride out the storms to which they were exposed; partly because the new policies to which the colonial government resorted in the 1930s could not be put effectively into practice because of a shortage of funds. The 1930s, therefore, mark the beginnings of important new developments, economic and political, in the relations of Malawians with their colonial rulers. But it was not until the late 1940s and the early 1950s that the real crisis of colonial society emerged.

Malawi & the world Depression

The sudden contraction in world commodity trade that began with the collapse of share prices on the New York stock exchange in 1929 had its immediate effects

---

[1] Iliffe, *Modern History of Tanganyika*, pp. 4 and 342.
[2] Ian Brown (ed.), *The Economies of Africa and Asia in the Inter-War Depression* (London, 1989), esp. pp. 1–6.

on Nyasaland's precarious economy. On the Lower River, prices for first grade cotton, which had been between 1.75d and 2d in 1928, fell by half to between 0.75d and 1d in 1930. In 1931 they fell again to an average of 0.62d, a figure that did not begin to improve significantly until 1934. Even then, prior to the Second World War, cotton prices did not begin to approach those of the mid to late 1920s.[3] Tobacco prices paid to producers also fell steeply between 1928 and 1934 and so too did prices for tea, to a low of 6d per pound in 1932, before rising to 1 shilling or more from 1933 following the implementation of the International Tea Restriction scheme in that year. With profits falling, agricultural wages were cut to as low as 5 shillings a month in the Mulanje District as compared with 6 shillings in the 1920s. With the Central African mining industry also temporarily in recession, thousands of Malawians were thrown out of work in South Africa and the Rhodesias and despatched back to their homeland, thus inflicting unemployment on the Protectorate for the very first time. 'I think there is a great deal of discontent among the natives and that their lot has not been a happy one during the last year', the Provincial Commissioner for the Southern Province noted in his annual report for 1931.[4]

With money in short supply, the domestic economy was also adversely affected. Many storekeepers, both Indian and African, were forced to close their shops; fish traders suffered a serious decline in sales; prices for cattle collapsed: in the Lilongwe district from £4 a head in 1931 to as low as 8s a head in 1934.[5] Production on the Vizara and Chombe rubber estates was temporarily halted in 1932, leaving nearly 1,000 people redundant. Not until 1935 was a slight improvement in the economy recorded, with new stores being opened and bicycles being imported in substantial numbers.[6] There was also an expansion in the trade in fish, greatly facilitated by the increased use of bicycles, and some improvement in conditions on the Cholo estates where planters seeking to build up a permanent labour force began providing better housing for wage labourers, along with protective raincoats for pluckers. Wages also rose slightly to 8 or 9 shillings a month in 1938.[7] Government revenues, which had dropped significantly, from £325,500 in 1929 to £302,000 in 1932, recovered strongly to £379,000 in 1937.[8]

White farmers & the Depression

In Malawi, as in many parts of Africa, white farmers were among the most spectacular casualties of the depression. The sudden fall in flue-cured tobacco prices in 1928 marked the beginning of the crisis; this was followed in the next three years by the collapse of the market for sisal, grown on plantations in the Shire Valley, and by the temporary decline in tea prices which led to the laying off of ten European managers in 1932 and to cuts in wages and capital equipment.[9]

---

3   Figures drawn from *Agricultural Department Annual Reports*.
4   Annual Report on the Southern Province for 1931, MNA NS 3/1/2.
5   Annual Report on the Lilongwe District for 1934, MNA S1/89 A-E/35.
6   Annual Reports on Southern Province for 1935 and 1936, MNA NS 3/1/5 and NS 3/1/6.
7   Annual Report on Southern Province for 1938, NS 3/1/7.
8   Bell, *Report*, 1938, p. 123.
9   Palmer, 'Nyasaland Tea Industry', pp. 224–5; *Annual Report of the Agricultural Department for 1931*.

With the sector in disarray, support was sought from the Government but with very mixed results. Shenton Thomas, the bright new broom brought in as Governor in 1929 to galvanise the administration, demonstrated his opposition to government assistance for lame duck farmers, white as well as black, by bringing Bowring's modest loan scheme to an end in 1931 in the face of furious settler protests.[10] His successors, Hubert Young (1932–4) and Harold Kittermaster (1934–9), were much more sympathetic to settler interests but the direct support they provided was of limited effectiveness. Through Kittermaster's initiative, the loan scheme was restarted in 1935 with the aim of fostering the European tobacco industry, but by 1939 only £20,044 had been lent to 77 farmers, a tiny sum in comparison with loans made by the Land Bank in Southern Rhodesia, and one that was too small to halt the flight of settlers from the land.[11] Between 1926 and 1945 the number of white farmers in Nyasaland fell from 324 to 171. Seventy-one leasehold estates, many of them located in the Shire Valley and the Namwera region in the South Nyasa District, were surrendered to the Government between 1929 and 1931.[12] In the same period, responsibility for the production of export crops on most of the freehold estates in the Shire Highlands was transferred to African tenants. The majority of the casualties were individual settlers, under-capitalised and often inefficient. But some of the largest companies also found profit-making beyond them. On the A.L. Bruce estates, accumulated losses stood at more than £60,000 by 1932 and all 31 plantations on the Magomero estate had been abandoned.[13] Losses in the British Central Africa Company increased to £150,000 by 1930, at which time none of the Company's three sisal estates were operating and very few of its tobacco plantations.[14] Even the tightly-controlled African Lakes Corporation ran into difficulties, although it is a tribute to the ALC's managers that the small losses it sustained in 1933 and 1934 were more than compensated for by the modest profits it achieved during the remainder of the decade.[15]

In his pioneering account of white farmers in Malawi, Robin Palmer has suggested that the effect of the depression was to hasten 'the virtual demise of the settler family farm so characteristic of "white" Southern Africa at the time' and to consolidate 'a few large and relatively well capitalized company estates run by expatriate managers'.[16] This was particularly the case of the tea industry, whose origins in the high-rainfall Cholo and Mulanje districts has already been discussed. The crucial breakthrough, differentiating tea from other export crops, came in 1933 with the introduction of the International Tea Regulation Scheme which, by restricting exports from the world's leading producers, was successful in stabilising prices. As the largest producer in Eastern Africa with 15,700 acres already planted in 1934, Nyasaland was well placed to benefit from a scheme which severely restricted the number of additional acres that a country was

[10] For details see MNA S1/575B/28.
[11] Kittermaster to Colonial Office, 18 June 1935, MNA S1/575II/28; W.J. Roper to Chief Secretary, Northern Rhodesia, 4 November 1938, MNA S1/575v/28; Palmer, 'White Farmers', p. 240.
[12] Ibid., pp. 242–43.
[13] White, *Magomero*, p. 171.
[14] 'History of the British Central Africa Company', TNA CO 525/208/44332.
[15] Donaldson, 'The African Lakes Corporation', Appendix A.
[16] Palmer, 'White Farmers', p. 214.

allowed to plant.[17] As the table below demonstrates, between 1930 and 1938 acreage under tea nearly doubled, exports by weight increased five times and exports by value increased nearly tenfold, making tea the Protectorate's largest export earner in 1938–39.

Table 8.1
Nyasaland Tea Production Statistics[18]

Year	Acreage	Exports(lbs)	Exports(£)
1930	9,686	1,939,756	56,543
1932	12,595	2,573,871	42,898
1934	15,414	4,624,111	171,470
1936	16,346	7,706,088	256,870
1938	17,516	10,218,821	448,477
1940	18,284	12,794,314	481,688

British-based companies – Blantyre & East Africa, J. Lyons & Co. and Cholo Highlands Tea Estates – were among the leaders in the field. But it is important to stress, in opposition to Palmer, that certain individuals bucked the general trend by prospering at a time when the majority of farmers were in economic distress. Some of these, like the redoubtable Malcolm Barrow, were high-profile settler politicians in possession of considerable economic resources. But others, notably Ignaco Conforzi, had little or no purchase upon the colonial state.

Conforzi's case is of particular interest. An Italian immigrant in a British protectorate, he neither expected nor received special favours from the Government.[19] As the son of a land-owner and possessed of a diploma in agriculture, Conforzi brought an understanding of farming to Malawi in 1907 that was largely lacking among other settlers. For nearly 20 years he followed a conventional career, first as a manager for the Blantyre and East Africa Company and then, from 1909, on his own tobacco estate in the Cholo district. The breakthrough in his fortunes can be traced to 1923 when he established links with the Belfast-based tobacco company, Gallaher Ltd, the principal rival of the Imperial Tobacco Company. The following year, he began purchasing tobacco direct from independent peasants in the Central Province with such success that by 1935 he had cornered 54 per cent of the market. In 1928 he switched with remarkable speed from tobacco to tea on his Cholo estates. In the same year he began to acquire substantial leaseholdings in the Lilongwe and Fort Manning districts on which he pioneered the cultivation of sun-cured tobacco, required by Gallaher's for hand-rolled cigarettes.

In common with other settlers, Conforzi was hit by the initial impact of the depression. But in contrast to most, he rode the storm, assisted by a growing network of fellow Italians whom he employed as estate managers and motor mechanics. As others faltered, his fortunes prospered, making him by the late

[17] For details see Palmer, 'Nyasaland Tea Industry', pp. 221–31.
[18] Ibid., p. 234.
[19] The account of Conforzi that follows is drawn from McCracken, 'Economics and Ethnicity: the Italian Community in Malawi' where a full list of references is provided.

1930s the proud owner of ten tobacco estates in the Central Province, six tea plantations in the Cholo District, a flourishing tobacco purchasing business and a fleet of a dozen lorries. In 1939, with typical foresight, he converted his private empire into a British-based company, I. Conforzi (Tea & Tobacco) Ltd, with the result that, when war broke out between Britain and Italy in June 1940, the Conforzi estates, alone among those owned by Italians, were not expropriated by the colonial government. During the next six years, annual profits ranged from £41,000 to £61,000, an indication that, for at least one family-based company, Nyasaland was not the graveyard of economic ambitions that it has often been depicted.

Much more typical of the settler experience was the case of Conforzi's compatriot, Alberto Sabbatini, a charming, innovative, endlessly resourceful man, owner in the early 1920s of a 17,000–acre tobacco estate on the outskirts of Limbe, several estates producing sisal in the Lower Shire Valley and a fine castellated mansion at Mapanga, its grounds embellished by avenues of cypress trees. With the advent of the Depression, however, Sabbatini's fortunes went into decline. Plagued by low prices, high freight duties and falling yields on land that had been under tobacco continuously for more than 20 years, he was forced to close down his Limbe estates in 1929. Two years later, production on his sisal estates ended at a personal loss to him of £50,000. His later schemes for the introduction of a steamer service on the Lower Shire River and for a rope and twine factory at Chiromo proved equally unsuccessful. By 1939, Sabbatini was reduced to selling his beloved Mapanga estate and concentrating on the buying and shipping of tobacco. Not until economic conditions improved in the aftermath of the Second World War was he able to return to estate farming.[20]

Peasants: the Lower River

African cultivators also suffered from the impact of the Depression, although in their case too there were important gradations and exceptions within the overall pattern of rural deprivation. Across the cash-cropping areas of the country, the dramatic fall in prices elicited an immediate response. At Mponela in the Dowa District, for example, the District Officer in 1930 was inundated by complaints about the low prices paid for tobacco while, in the same year, the Dedza District Officer was informed by Chief Kachindamoto that 'the people say the price [for cotton] is too little.'[21] Some peasants threatened to abandon the market entirely. But it is an indication of how fully integrated into the capitalist economy they had become that most cultivators reacted by seeking to increase production further to compensate for the fall in prices. It was for this reason that record crops of cotton and tobacco were produced by Malawian peasants in 1935 and 1937 respectively.

[20] McCracken, 'Economics and Ethnicity', pp. 316–7; Mario Sabbatini, 'Life with Father', *Society of Malawi Journal*, 40, 2 1987.
[21] Dowa District Book, note on section council meeting, 18–20 August 1930; Martin Chanock, 'The Political Economy of Independent Agriculture in Colonial Malawi: the Great War to the Great Depression', *Journal of Social Science*, University of Malawi, 1, 1972, p. 124.

Superficial similarities, however, concealed substantial differences, as the contrasting stories of Lower River cotton growers and Lilongwe Plain tobacco farmers reveal. By 1929 Mang'anja and Sena cultivators had created a peasant economy of considerable complexity in the Port Herald and Chikwawa districts.[22] Two separate agricultural systems were employed, the rain-fed or *mphala* system, involving the utilisation of the dryland or *munda* some distance from the river, and the river-fed or *dimba* system involving the use of the rich alluvial soils of the flood plain or *dambo*, exposed each year following the ending of the rains. Both were utilised in the cultivation of cotton which was often intercropped with food crops such as maize, sorghum and pear millet. In general, higher yields were achieved on the fertile flood plain than on the dryland, a factor that benefited Sena peasants in the Port Herald district, with its large extent of marshland, as compared to Mang'anja peasants in the Chikwawa district who grew most of their cotton on the *munda*.[23] Both groups, however, benefited from their easy access to markets, over which the British Cotton Growing Association had a monopoly between 1923 and 1927. They also gained from the proximity of the valley to the railway, a factor which ensured that minimum prices there were always higher than those obtained in less fortunately situated cotton-growing areas further north. The Lower Shire Valley, in consequence, dominated Nyasaland's production of cotton, with sales rising from 1,131 tons of seed cotton in 1927 (81.5 per cent of the total) to 3,057 tons in 1929, 87.2 per cent of Nyasaland's cotton exports (see Table 8.2).

Table 8.2
Peasant Cotton Export Figures[24] *(seed cotton in tons)*

Year	Port Herald	Chikwawa	Ruo[25]	Total Shire Valley	Total Nyasaland	Valley exports as % of total
1910–11	310	8	60	378	692	54.6
1914–15	264	100	293	656	867	75.7
1918–19	56	103	155	314	365	86.0
1922–23	253	4		257	387	66.4
1924	732	128		860	1,367	63.0
1927	779	352		1,131	1,387	81.5
1929	1,809	1,248		3,057	3,505	87.2
1931	1,126	1,040		2,166	2,477	87.4
1934	2,870	2,074		4,944	5,377	92.0
1935	3,776	3,079		6,855	9,737	70.4
1939	455	829		1,284	3,168	40.5

The expansion of cotton growing had profound consequences for social relations in the Valley. As Mandala has demonstrated, most growers were small peasants, utilising the labour resources of monogamous households and involving women equally with men. During the 1920s, however, several hundred *zunde*

22 The analysis which follows is largely based on Mandala, *Work and Control in a Peasant Economy*.
23 Ibid., p. 139.
24 Figures drawn from Mandala, p. 137.
25 Ruo District was abolished in 1922.

owners emerged, well-off, usually polygamous men, who established their own separate cotton gardens (*zunde*) on which they employed hired labour. Little is known of their origins, but the available evidence suggests that a significant proportion of the *zunde* holders were government employees, several of whom had been educated in schools run by the South African General Mission, one of only two missions of significance operating in the area.[26] Some may have replicated the experiences of Simon Likongwe, the leading cotton grower at Lisungwe north of Chikwawa, who was both a former labour migrant to South Africa and the principal headman of his area.[27] Several had 'quite large farms of native cotton running into 40 and 50 acres'.[28] Most employed a combination of Lomwe migrants from across the Shire River and dependent children. These latter were recruited through the institution of *nomi*, a youth association involving both boys and girls, which provided labour to anyone prepared to pay.[29] Co-wives of *zunde* holders might also work on their husbands' cotton fields. But in their case, unlike the majority of married women in the area, they had no claim to the proceeds of the cotton when it was sold.

The dramatic restructuring of economic and social relations in the Lower Shire Valley that took place from 1930 owed as much to ecological factors as it did to the Great Depression. When cotton prices collapsed from a high of 2d in 1929 to 1d in 1930, and then down to 0.75d in 1931, the most prominent casualties were the *zunde* holders, several of whom were taken to court by migrant labourers from Mozambique in 1931 for failure to pay their wages. The number of hired workers in the Lower Shire district declined dramatically, from 1,109 in 1931 to 514 in 1932, and over the same period the number of 'large gardens' was said to have dropped by 61.3 per cent.[30] By 1933, barely one per cent of gardens in the Port Herald district and just over two per cent in Chikwawa were cultivated by hired labour and it was noted that there were few cotton gardens over three acres left.[31] No permanent decline in the total number of growers took place, however, with the result that sales of seed cotton, which had fallen sharply in 1931, rose to new levels in 1934 and 1935 as prices showed signs of recovery [see Table 8.2].

By this time, however, Lower Shire valley cultivators were under threat from a different direction. Even in the 1920s, their fragile economy had been repeatedly threatened by drought and the damage caused by insects. But these hazards were as nothing compared to the devastation of the 1930s. In 1932 a new infestation of locusts began, causing havoc to dryland crops. Further damage was caused by the red bollworm which attacked cotton bolls and seriously reduced average yields.[32] This, however, was merely a prelude to the destruction caused

[26] Mandala, *Work and Control in a Peasant Economy*, p. 138; Report by E. Lawrence, District Agricultural Officer for July 1930, MNA A 3/2/200.
[27] Sir William Himberg, 'Northern Rhodesia, Southern Rhodesia and Nyasaland as Sources for Increasing our River Cotton Supplies', Diary Notes, 15 July 1927, TNA CO 525/119; Report by E. Lawrence on Lisungwe Cotton Area, October–November 1930, MNA A 3/2/200.
[28] Himburg, Diary Notes, 14 July 1927, TNA CO 525/119.
[29] For a lengthy contemporary account on *nomi* see Annual Report on Southern Province for 1931, MNA NS 3/1/2.
[30] Monthly Agricultural Reports, August 1931 and July 1932, MNA A 3/2/200.
[31] Monthly Agricultural Reports, June and July 1933, MNA A 3/2/201, Report of Agricultural District Officer, Lower Shire and Chikwawa in *Annual Report of the Agricultural Department for 1933*.
[32] E.O. Pearson and B.L. Mitchell, *A Report on the Status and Control of Insect Pests of Cotton in the Lower River Districts of Nyasaland* (Zomba, 1945).

from 1936 onwards by the waters of the Shire River, whose relentless rise resulted in the permanent inundation of thousands of acres of marshland in the Lower Shire district and brought the *dimba* system virtually to a halt. Flooding took its toll in 1936, and again in 1938, when more than 2,500 gardens were damaged. Further flooding on a still larger scale took place in 1939, covering 120,000 acres and leaving thousands of people homeless.[33]

Thereafter, cotton production on the *dambo* was brought virtually to an end with dire consequences for Port Herald growers. Cultivation now became increasingly centred on the Chikwawa district where surplus *mphala* land was still available. Production improved after the disastrous year of 1939, when low prices combined with flooding to reduce the valley crop to 1,284 seed tons, the lowest it had been since 1927. But it was not until 1942 that sales reached the levels of the mid-1930s. By the 1950s, Port Herald no longer featured as a major producer of cotton, although it is worth emphasising, in contrast to the general impression, that cotton cultivation remained a major occupation in the Valley, involving over 34,000 growers in 1944, and that sales from the Chikwawa District continued to rise, reaching a peak of 9,153 tons in 1960.[34]

The Valley thus remained a major centre of peasant agriculture with the qualification that the *dimba* system no longer functioned effectively and that, in consequence, increasing pressure was being placed on available dryland. By 1945, average yields of cotton had fallen to 165 lbs per acre as compared with 623 lbs per acre on the *dimba* in 1932.[35] Cash incomes tended to remain depressed with the consequence that a growing proportion of young men from the area turned to the escape hatch of labour migration to meet their economic demands. Of little importance up to the late 1930s, the migration of males from the Port Herald district took off in the years between 1937 and 1940: it was estimated that between 3,000 and 4,000 men were absent from the district at any one time. This figure grew between 1941 and 1946 when nearly a fifth of all taxes collected in the district was paid by migrants working in Southern Rhodesia.[36] It was still high in 1947, when the District Commissioner commented on the large number of people from the area now employed in Southern Rhodesia and South Africa.[37] Other former cotton growers had switched to commercial fishing whose expansion in the 1940s can be explained both by the growing markets for dried fish in Blantyre and Limbe and by the increase in volume of the Shire River.[38] There was also some movement by former *zunde* holders into the ownership of cattle bred for the Blantyre meat market, although the significance of this development prior to the 1960s should not be over-emphasised. During the 1940s the number of African-owned cattle in the Port Herald District remained small, rising from 367 in 1939 to 1,345 in 1948.[39] Further increases in the 1950s took

---

[33] Mandala, *Work and Control*, pp. 185–7; Annual Report of the Southern Province for 1939, MNA NS 3/1/8.

[34] Southern Province Annual Report for 1944, MNA NS 3/1/10.

[35] Pearson and Mitchell, *Report*, p. 7. In Uganda, by contrast, the average yield between 1934 and 1943 was 298 lbs of seed cotton per acre.

[36] Mandala, *Work and Control*, pp. 241–2.

[37] Lower River District Report for 1947, MNA 3/1/18.

[38] Mandala, *Work and Control*, pp. 249–53.

[39] *Annual Report of the Agricultural Department for 1939*; Lower River District Report for 1948, MNA NS 3/1/18.

the figure to between 4,000 and 5,000 cattle in the Lower Shire Valley as a whole, less than two per cent of the total head of cattle in Malawi.[40] It was not until after Independence that the major expansion took place, propelling a small elite of cattle-owners to a position of considerable economic and political power, and increasing the cattle population of the valley to as much as 75,000.[41]

Meanwhile, many women, who had previously retained a fair measure of economic independence through the sale of cotton, found their position undermined as a consequence of the contraction of their earning opportunities and their growing reliance on labour remittances from male relatives on the one hand and on the production of food crops on the other. Women, therefore, were particularly affected by the growing crisis of the food supply resulting from the enforced dependence on dryland crops in an area notoriously susceptible to droughts. In 1941 and almost annually up to 1949, people in the Nsanje district suffered seasonal shortages of food, giving rise to endemic malnutrition among young and old alike. Only by resorting to the consumption of water lily bulbs, gathered from the river banks and to the bartering of fish for maize were people able to survive.[42]

Peasants: the Lilongwe Plain

Chewa peasants on the Lilongwe Plain also suffered from the Great Depression but in their case it was the way in which the tobacco crop was marketed that attracted most concern. Peasant resentment against the Native Tobacco Board goes back to the late 1920s, when many growers became disillusioned with the advice proffered by supervisors and their African assistants, several of whom were chased from their gardens by irate growers in the Fort Manning district in 1929.[43] With the fall of tobacco prices from the early 1930s, discontent spread, aggravated by the Board's decision to reduce the number of markets on the central plain from seven to three and by its attempts to limit, if necessary by compulsion, the amount of tobacco that independent peasants could grow. Prices paid to growers in the Central Province fell from an average of 3.5d in 1929–31 to 2.5d per pound in 1932–34. There was a slight improvement in 1935–36. But in 1937 the production of a record crop of 4,315 tons of tobacco in the Lilongwe and Dowa districts was followed by a collapse in demand and by a further fall in prices to an all-time low of 1.67d per pound.[44] Visiting the market at Tembwe on 4 June, the Provincial Commissioner found 'only five persons buying and hundreds of natives returning home with full baskets after having refused the prices offered'.[45] Elsewhere, the senior supervisor reported 'widespread discon-

[40] *Annual Reports of the Veterinary Department for 1956 and 1959.*

[41] For brief introductions to this development see Matthew Schoffeleers, 'Economic Change and Religious Polarization in an African Rural District' in *Malawi: An Alternative Pattern of Development*, pp. 193; Mandala, *Work and Control*, pp. 254–57.

[42] William Beinart, 'Agricultural Planning and the Late Colonial Technical Imagination: the Lower Shire Valley in Malawi, 1940–1960', in *Malawi: An Alternative Pattern of Development*, pp. 100–01; Annual Report for the Lower River District, 1949, MNA NS 3/1/18.

[43] Fort Manning District Book, District Council meeting, 8 April 1929.

[44] Report by Financial Secretary on the Native Tobacco Board, 24 July 1939, MNA S1/275/39.

[45] A.O. Hodgeson, P.C. Northern Province to Chief Sec., 4 June 1937, MNA S1/437/34.

tent amongst the natives, many of them turning their tobacco out of their baskets by the side of the road and setting fire to it'.[46] Indignant demands were made for the existing system of marketing to be abolished, and the NTB, acutely conscious of the malpractices resorted to by some buyers, stirred itself into action.

In August 1937 the NTB reached an agreement with the Executive Committee of the settler-run Nyasaland Tobacco Association to institute an auction system similar to that successfully introduced in Southern Rhodesia in 1936.[47] Competitive buying of Crown Land tobacco was abandoned; instead, from 1938, the Board took responsibility for purchasing all tobacco grown by independent peasants and transporting it to the auction floors constructed by the newly founded company, Tobacco Auctions (Nyasaland) Ltd, at Lilongwe and Limbe, where it was sold to the major exporters. The cess paid by the growers was abolished and a new scheme was instituted by which the Board drew its revenues from its 'working margin', the difference between the price it paid to the growers and the price it received at the auction.[48]

Changes in marketing, however, did little to ameliorate the wretched position of the growers. Because of the high levy exacted by the Board, the marked improvement of world market prices at the end of the decade was not passed on to the producer. In 1938, 44.27 per cent of the auction price of tobacco went in expenses to the Tobacco Board while, a year later the proportion had risen to nearly 53 per cent, with a miserly 47 per cent of the auction price for their tobacco actually reaching the people who had grown it.[49] With average earnings from Crown Land tobacco declining by more than half in four years, from £2.9.8d in 1935 to £1.3.9d in 1939, the dissatisfaction of growers reached a head. In 1938 riots broke out in the vicinity of Nathenje, led by the Native Authority, Kalumbu, himself a large-scale tobacco grower. Peasants set fire to the homes of NTB instructors and used sticks and stones to drive them from their villages.[50] The following year, up to 10,000 growers abandoned the industry in disgust. Crown Land production fell by no less than four million lbs.[51]

The year 1939 was something of a turning point in the tangled politics of tobacco. Up to then, the major exporting companies had given their tacit approval to the policy pursued by the NTB of seeking to restrict production by independent peasants while making no objection to the continued expansion of tenant-grown tobacco, much of it produced on estates owned by members of the Board. With the collapse in Crown Land production, however, exporters, who were now worried that the estate sector was incapable by itself of meeting their requirements, called for a drastic change in policy and the General Manager of the Imperial Tobacco Company added his voice to the chorus of discontent.[52] One exporter publicly alleged that 'The interests of the unofficial members of

[46] Antill, 'History of the Native Crown Land Tobacco Industry', pp. 60–61.
[47] Colin Wilshaw, A Century of Growth. Malawi's Tobacco Industry 1893–1993 (Blantyre, 1994), pp. 62–3.
[48] Minutes of meetings of N.T.B., 10 Aug, 27 Nov 1937, 8 Feb, 18 March 1938, MNA S1/720/26.
[49] Report by Financial Secretary on N.T.B., 24 July 1939, MNA S1/275/39.
[50] R. Antill to Secretary, N.T.B., 24 July 1938, MNA A6/1/37.
[51] Wilshaw, Century of Growth, p. 65.
[52] Secretary, Nyasaland Tobacco Exporters Association to Chief Sec., Zomba, 27 July 1939; C.A. Barron to Chief Sec., 20 June 1939, MNA S1/275/39.

the Board ... are, as large tenant growers, in direct competition with Trust Land production.' Calls were made for 'a thorough overhauling of the Board's expenditure and overhead charges, the personnel of the Board's staff and their system and methods of buying'.[53]

In June 1939, the newly-appointed Governor, Mackenzie-Kennedy, authorised the Financial Secretary to carry out an investigation. His report, presented on 24 July, justified most of the charges made by critics of the Board. Summarising its conclusions, the Financial Secretary emphasised that, unless reforms took place, the tobacco industry would be doomed to a lingering death:

> The present position is precarious. The native does not understand why his tobacco sells for 4.48d per lb. while he gets only 2.27d: and it would be folly to tell him that the difference is needed to support a body of Europeans whose salaries and expenses (excluding transport of the produce and auction fees) absorb 1.8d per lb... The essential thing is to obtain and retain the confidence of the grower and that can only be done by giving him a better return for his labours. If we fail in this we stand the risk of the total collapse of the industry.[54]

Major reductions in the size of the European staff were therefore ordered. Both senior supervisors resigned; allowances paid to members of the Board were abolished; and in 1942 the Department of Agriculture took over responsibility for supervising the production of Crown Land tobacco, leaving the NTB to concentrate on purchasing and marketing. Not until 1946 were the first African members appointed to the Board, and they were substantial capitalist farmers by no means representative of smallholder opinion. Almost the first action taken by Chief Mwase on his appointment was to ask that African farmers employing workers should be paid higher prices than those employing family labour alone.[55] Nevertheless, with African members such as the energetic J. R. Chinyama involved, openly discriminatory policies became more difficult to pursue, particularly because the Colonial Government by the early 1940s had come to recognise the value to government revenues of a healthy smallholder tobacco industry.

There are a number of reasons for regarding the crisis of the late 1930s as a watershed in the history of cash-crop production in Nyasaland. In itself, the establishment of an auction system, initially used for the sale of smallholder and flue-cured tobacco alone but extended in 1946 to cover tenant-produced tobacco, appears little more than a technical change. However, the emergence of the Native Tobacco Board as sole purchaser of some 75 per cent of Nyasaland's total crop was a significant development, comparable to the creation of the Cocoa Marketing Board in the Gold Coast: it extended the powers of the state into control over marketing in a much more comprehensive manner than had occurred earlier in the marketing of peasant-grown cotton. In this sense, Wilshaw is right to detect in the Board's action the seed of the system that was to be adopted after independence by the Agricultural Development and Marketing Corporation (ADMARC).[56]

53 Minutes of a meeting of the Nyasaland Tobacco Exporters Assn, Limbe, 26 July 1939, MNA S1/275/39.
54 Report by Financial Secretary on N.T.B., 24 July 1939, MNA S1/275/39.
55 Minutes of meeting of the N.T.B., 5 April 1946, MNA LA/293 AGR 33/vi.
56 Wilshaw, *Century of Growth*, pp. 63–4.

What is more, the suspicions fuelled among growers by the Board's performance in the face of dramatic fluctuations in prices created a legacy of resentment
which could not be easily dispelled. In their evidence to the Bledisloe Commission in July 1938, chiefs from the Northern and Central Provinces were unanimous in declaring that 'we are not satisfied' with the working of the NTB.[57] A
year later, growers questioned by the Commission into the Tobacco Industry
repeated their complaints at the low prices paid by the Board, adding that 'the
NTB capitaos at the receiving stations had refused to accept a lot of tobacco
which was perfectly good and well graded'.[58] Throughout much of the Central
Province, such circumstances were leading to the perception of the Tobacco
Board as an instrument of government-inspired exploitation, whatever its intentions.

By 1942 independent peasants on the Lilongwe plain had begun to emerge
from the dark tunnel of economic depression. In the previous decade, they had
suffered many frustrations in their dealings with the NTB, but they had retained
access to land and control over family labour. Thus, they were well-placed to
take advantage of the improved conditions for cash-crop growers that were to
occur later in the 1940s. It is an indication both of their resilience and of the
limited impact of the Board's restrictive policies that tobacco production in the
Lilongwe district increased nearly six-fold between 1926 and 1937, and that the
number of registered growers also rose despite the sharp fall that took place in
1939. In 1942, 58,755 Crown Land growers were registered in the major Central
Province tobacco districts as compared to 34,147 in 1933.[59]

To a significant extent, the policies of the Board acted as a brake on the accumulation of capital and hence on the growth of a rural bourgeoisie. But they
could not prevent the emergence of a number of substantial farmers (virtually
all male), some of whom by 1938 had succeeded in bypassing the limitations
imposed on the amount of tobacco an individual might grow. They had taken
up tenancies on neighbouring estates, usually farmed by wage labourers, in addition to the gardens they cultivated through family labour on 'traditional' land.[60]
Several of these men accumulated large herds of cattle. Others, such as Chief
Kalumbu's councillor, Kefa, specialised in the sale of maize.[61] In a few cases –
notably that of Kalumbu himself – officially-designated Native Authorities were
able to become successful large-scale growers through the astute manipulation
of the perquisites of office. Chief Kalumbu possessed four large gardens, each
approximately 24 acres in size. He cultivated his considerable holding by using
prisoners convicted in his court and tax defaulters whose debt was paid in
exchange for their labour. Further, he benefited from tribute labour supplied by
local headmen.[62] More commonly, however, successful farmers were former
wage-earners, some of them labour migrants, who used their savings to obtain
access to five or more acres in the sparsely-populated frontier lands to the north-

[57] Evidence of Native Authorities, Northern Province, 1 July 1938, Bledisloe Commission Papers.
[58] Evidence of the Lilongwe Native Tobacco Committee and of Natives from Dowa and Ncheu, 1939,
MNA COM 7 2/1/1.
[59] Figures calculated from NTB notes on natives registered as tobacco growers, 1933–34 season and
1942–43 season, MNA S1/72/26; 1A/293 AGR 33/vi.
[60] Evidence of Lilongwe Native Tobacco growers, 1938, MNA COM 7 2/2/1.
[61] Lilongwe District Book, 'Chiefs and Headmen', 1939.
[62] Interview with Chief Kalumbu, Nathenje, 21 July 1982.

west of Lilongwe. Here they employed permanent workers from such areas as Nkhoma, Dedza and Ntcheu.[63] Several of the most prosperous farmers were non-Chewa incomers to the region, among them Ralph Chinyama who had been born at Domwe and educated at the Blantyre mission school at Domasi. In 1927 Chinyama founded the 120-acre Kaimbe estate with the proceeds he had obtained from working as a teacher at the Henry Henderson Institute in Blantyre and, later, as a general clerk and typist for the North Charterland Exploration Company at Fort Manning.[64] For several years, in the 1930s, Chinyama combined the management of his farm with working on a seasonal basis as a tobacco buyer for A.F. Barron. Later, in the 1940s, he was promoted manager of one of Barron's estates while continuing to grow tobacco and maize in considerable quantities on his own farm.[65]

The Depression & the colonial state

In Malawi, as in other African countries, the Depression contributed to the growth of government intervention, although the forms it took were limited, prior to the late 1940s, by the sparse financial and human resources available to the colonial state. The mid to late 1920s witnessed some relaxation in government policies of coercion. Forced labour was almost brought to an end by pressure from Britain. The number of troops stationed in Nyasaland was reduced from 1,125 in 1921 to 250 in 1930. Plans were set in train, culminating in the official introduction of indirect rule in 1933, to create new, more effective, collaborative mechanisms by extending the powers and privileges of colonial chiefs.

With the alarming reduction in government revenues brought on by the depression, these attempts to enhance the legitimacy of the state were brought to a halt. Elsewhere in Africa, customs duties had largely replaced hut tax as the main source of government revenues by the 1920s. In Malawi, however, external trade was so sluggish that, in 1929, hut tax remained the major source of revenue, constituting 34 per cent of the total. With many Africans now too poor to pay, the amount collected in the enlarged Northern Province spiralled downwards from £73,541 in 1931 to £51,747 two years later. Government circles feared that, if the shortfall was allowed to continue, 'the financial position, which is already sufficiently serious, will become precarious.'[66] Vigorous tax drives in 1931 and again in 1934 resulted in the arrest of thousands of defaulters, many of whom were housed in a temporary prison camp erected at Zomba airfield.[67] District officers who failed to meet tax targets were removed from office (the fate suffered by the

---

63 These findings are drawn from a study of over 100 interviews conducted under my supervision by five students, J. Kazembe, J.A. Juma, C.C. Kamcholoti, Mary Mpanje and Mercy Thawe, with tobacco growers in the Lilongwe District in July 1982.

64 Biographical note attached to Chinyama Papers, MNA. See also Jessie Sagawa, 'J.R.N. Chinyama: profile of a political and economic entrepreneur', History seminar paper, Chancellor College, 1982/83.

65 Testimonial to Mr. Ralph Chinyama by M.G. Barron, 25 Aug 1947, MNA Chinyama Papers 19/JRC/3.

66 Annual Report on the Northern Province for 1933, MNA S1/112/24; Keith Tucker, Act. Chief Sec., circular letter, 4 June 1934, MNA NS 1/2/3.

67 K.R. Tucker to Governor, 30 Jan 1934, MNA S1/1379/27.

unfortunate H.N. Vassall in Lilongwe in 1933).[68] Headmen were threatened with reductions in pay if arrears were not eliminated.[69]

As the crisis deepened, the Government launched an abortive 'grow more crops' campaign during which peasants were informed that 'whatever the price, increased production is to be aimed at as a duty.'[70] Several unemployed European farmers were enlisted to encourage the cultivation of 'alternative crops', notably cotton and groundnuts. But with prices for the latter at an all-time low, this initiative quickly collapsed. The result was that, in the mid-1930s, government officials came to regard the sale of labour abroad as an increasingly attractive option. Nothing could be done as long as external demand remained low. However, with the rapid revival of the southern African mining industry, the demand for Nyasa migrant labour expanded, particularly in South Africa where the ban on the employment of 'tropicals' in deep level mines was lifted in 1932. Hints at a change of policy came in 1934 when, in his annual report, the Mzimba District Officer frankly confessed that the district's 'economic future in regard to internal production and export is nil' and called for a system of 'organised recruiting'.[71] The first step came a few months later when the Governor, Kittermaster, authorised a Nyasaland-based company to recruit labour in the Northern Province for clients in Southern Rhodesia and South Africa. It was the first time for 25 years that such recruiting had been permitted.[72] This was followed in June 1935 by the appointment of a committee under the chairmanship of the Director of Education, Travers Lacey, to report on the causes and impact of labour migration and to recommend changes in policy.

The report, published in 1936, is a remarkable document, deeply embarrassing to the government in its dramatic account of 'the extent and deep rooted nature of the evils resultant from the uncontrolled emigration of our Natives'. However, it was broadly supportive of Kittermaster's new approach.[73] Building on its recommendations, the Nyasaland Government signed conventions in Salisbury and Johannesburg in 1936, regularising the recruitment of labour. In return for an agreement on the payment of deferred wages and the regular repatriation of workers, the Nyasaland Government gave permission for up to 4,000 Nyasas to be recruited by the Witwatersrand Native Labour Association (WNLA) in 1936–37, as well as promising to facilitate the passage of workers to Southern Rhodesia. This was accomplished through the construction by the Southern Rhodesian government in 1938 of the free labour transport system popularly known as *ulere* (the Chichewa term for 'free'). Workers making use of the system were transported to their southern destinations in lorries, free of charge, although on the homeward journey a fare of 10s had to be paid. In 1938, 13,000 workers were transported to Southern Rhodesia in this way.[74] Depots were constructed in Nyasaland both by WNLA and by its Rhodesian rival, *Mthandizi*, 'the helper', (established in 1947 under the official title of the

---

[68] Lilongwe District Report for 1933, MNA S1/112A-E/34.
[69] Note of district council meeting, 28 Dec 1932, Fort Johnston District Book, vol. 4 1929–32.
[70] Keith Tucker, Act. Chief Sec., circular letter, 6 June 1934, MNA NS 1/2/3.
[71] Annual Report on the Mzimba District for 1934, MNA S1/89 F-J/35.
[72] Kittermaster to Col. Sec., 25 Feb 1935, PRO CO 158/44053; 1 June 1935, TNA CO 525/158.
[73] *Report of the Committee appointed to enquire into Emigrant Labour*, 1935, p.37.
[74] Boeder, 'Malawians Abroad', pp. 146–54; Chirwa, 'Rural Labour, Migrancy and Fishing', pp. 384–5.

Rhodesia Native Labour Supply Commission). Competition for labour at the regional level intensified, resulting, as Chirwa has noted, in Malawian migrants gaining greater freedom of movement and more choice in their access to labour markets.[75]

Prior to 1947, no significant increase in the total number of migrants appears to have taken place. Most of them, as M.C. Hoole noted in 1948, continued to go as independent workers rather than on contract.[76] Some shift occurred, however, in the districts from which migrants were drawn, with proportionally more coming from the Central and Southern Provinces and fewer from the Northern Province.[77] This reflects, in part, the collapse of the Lower Shire cotton industry but it can also be related to the acceleration in population growth that the two southern provinces were experiencing, as well as the greater facilities for contract workers that WNLA and later *Mthandizi* provided.

In his contribution to the standard history of Central Africa, Leroy Vail argues that by 1944 'the administration had long since abandoned plans to foster peasant production and had accepted the position of Nyasaland as a labour reserve for the rest of central and southern Africa.'[78] The reality is different. Much colonial policy in the interwar years consisted of balancing the varied interests of peasants, planters and metropolitan producers. But in the crisis of the depression it became clear, even to the most pro-settler officials, that a healthy peasant sector was essential for both the social stability and economic wellbeing of the state. Far from abandoning plans to stimulate peasant production, therefore, the administration was poised in the early 1940s to enter this area more vigorously. Changes in labour policy should not be misconstrued. What Kittermaster and his successors were concerned with achieving from the mid-1930s was not a dramatic expansion in the number of labour migrants but rather a measure of control. Their aim was an increase in the proportion of migrant wages that would be spent in Nyasaland itself, along with some influence over the way in which migration from Nyasaland was conducted. In that sense, the new labour policy reflected the more general tendency of the state to take on responsibilities over a wide range of affairs which previously it would have shunned. Not until the early 1950s did the tensions stirred by this new enthusiasm for economic and social engineering result in the emergence of a popular backlash, putting the authority of the state at risk.

State intervention in the labour market was more than matched by the intervention of the state in soil conservation issues. Conservationist anxiety has a long history in Malawi, going back to the early 1890s when Harry Johnston expressed his concern that desiccation was proceeding rapidly as a consequence 'of the ravages of the bush-fires and the destruction of the forests'.[79] Schemes aimed at stream bank protection and the establishment of forest reserves were developed

---

[75] Chirwa, 'Rural Labour, Migrancy and Fishing', pp. 379, 391–4.
[76] M.C. Hoole, 'Memorandum on Labour Migration from Nyasaland to other Territories in Africa', 26 Oct 1948, Hoole Papers, Rhodes House Library Oxford, Mss. Afr. S 997. The number of Malawians abroad was estimated at 120,000 in the Lacey Report of 1936. In 1946, the estimate was 121,700. See Boeder, 'Malawians Abroad', Appendix C3, p. 287.
[77] Vail, 'Malawi's Agricultural Economy', p. 71.
[78] Vail, 'The Political Economy of East-Central Africa', p.243.
[79] Johnston, *First Three Years*.

by the Forestry Department from the early 1920s. These were dwarfed in the 1930s by the more interventionist approaches that resulted from the development of the tobacco industry in the Southern and Central Provinces. In the initial stages, A. J. Hornby, the Assistant Director of Agriculture, was particularly concerned with encouraging planters to grow their tobacco on terraced ridges.[80] In a further initiative, from 1934 the Native Tobacco Board turned its attention to African tobacco-growers, who were instructed to cease from growing their crops on mounds or *matutu*, which were believed to be susceptible to erosion, and to cultivate on terraced ridges, like the planters. Efforts were also made to get tobacco growers to construct contour bunds, 'large ridges with a base of a few feet which contour the fields at a grade of one in four hundred and are spaced on an average forty yards apart', designed to prevent the rains sweeping away topsoil. In 1935 it was claimed that 'Under the direction of Capt. Antill of the Native Tobacco Board 2,500 acres of gardens have been protected against erosion.'[81] A year later, 6,454 acres of land in the Lilongwe District were said to have been bunded and, in addition, several 'village demonstration plots' had been opened, designed to demonstrate the advantages that fertilising and crop rotation would bring.[82]

From the mid-1930s concern over erosion was heightened as a consequence of official reactions to the 'dust bowl' disaster of the American plains which had been caused by a combination of drought and the ruthless application of capital-intensive farming methods.[83] Up to then, Nyasaland officials had largely drawn their ideas on conservation from their contacts with agriculturalists in South Africa and Southern Rhodesia.[84] Now, however, the American example was brought to the fore and administrators and agriculturalists reacted with alarm. In October 1935 the Colonial Advisory Council on Agriculture and Animal Health, meeting at the Colonial Office in London, called for the appointment of full-time soil erosion officers in each of the East African colonies to take preventive measures against erosion 'with the minimum of delay'.[85] The Governor in Nyasaland was glad to concur. The result was that, in May 1936, approval was granted for the secondment of Paul Topham from the Forestry Department to act as Soil Conservation Officer.[86] On 1 January 1937 Topham took up his post at the start of a three-year campaign involving increasingly coercive methods of intervention. Emphasis was placed on 'mass education and compulsion in respect of a few very simple points at first'.[87] But in 1938 Topham launched the first of a series of campaigns in hilly areas in the Ntcheu, Zomba, Cholo [Thyolo], and Lower Shire districts, designed to impose the construction of ridges and bunds on increasingly hostile local populations.[88] In what was to become a familiar pattern, Native Authorities were induced to pass orders

---

[80] Annual Reports of the Nyasaland Agricultural Department, 1930 and 1931.
[81] Annual Report of the Nyasaland Agricultural Department, 1935, p.17.
[82] Annual Report of the Nyasaland Agricultural Department, 1936, pp.46–7.
[83] McCracken, 'Experts and Expertise', pp. 110–14. For a more detailed discussion which highlights the role played by the Imperial Forestry Institute at Oxford University in propagating conservationist ideas, see Mulwafu, *Conservation Song*, pp.59–80.
[84] See Beinart, 'Soil Erosion, Conservation and Ideas about Development'.
[85] See file on Soil Erosion, MNA FE 1/4/1.
[86] H.B. Kittermaster to J.H. Thomas, Secretary of State for Colonies, 26 March 1936, MNA FE 1/4/1.
[87] P. Topham, 'Soil Conservation Policy', 8 Aug. 1939, MNA NS 1/2/4.
[88] P. Topham to PC, Southern Province, 15 September 1937, MNA NS 1/2/4.

enforcing the construction of ridges, which they then avoided enforcing in the face of the opposition of their people. Topham demanded that District Commissioners should overrule these Authorities and issue supplementary orders themselves.[89] 'It is my considered opinion', he stated, 'that, to enforce the orders already given, either every offender must now be prosecuted and heavily punished, or else supplementary orders setting a near time limit must be issued.'[90]

Confrontation subsided in most areas following the outbreak of the Second World War and the secondment of a number of members of the agricultural staff to military duties. But this was not the case in the North Nyasa district, where the Misuku Land Usage Scheme emerged as the flagship of the agricultural department's conservation policies.[91] It was based on the widely accepted belief, shared by Scottish missionaries and agricultural officers alike, that the *visoso* system of cultivating millet, involving the cutting down and burning of trees, was both morally and environmentally destructive. The scheme was launched in 1938 by Major Dennis Smalley in the remote Misuku Hills overlooking the Tanganyikan border. Organised by the Major with military precision, the scheme involved an ambitious attempt to halt deforestation in an area targeted for coffee growing and vulnerable to soil erosion. It thus prohibited peasants from growing millet except under strict supervision; restricted cattle to designated grazing zones; and pursued the construction of contour ridges and bunds.[92] At first, so Smalley wrote, many Sukwa people strongly resented this massive interference with their methods of farming and fled across the border into Tanganyika and Northern Rhodesia rather than submit to the new demands. But by the mid-1940s, according to his optimistic reports, these doubts had been largely overcome. Contour bunding and ridging had been widely accepted; virtually no millet was being grown, and soil erosion had been almost halted. In what was almost an aside, Smalley admitted that, in 1947, several offenders against agricultural rules had been punished in Native Authority Courts. But he added: 'Today the Asukwa people marvel at their past stupidity and praise what has been done for them.'[93] Less than a year later, the intelligence report for the Karonga district reached a different conclusion in its assessment that 'there is still great opposition to agricultural policy in the area... The opposition is not against contour ridging so much as against the rules which make millet cultivation from their point of view so difficult.'[94] But this dissident note was disregarded by colonial strategists for whom the Misuku Scheme served as an outstanding example of successful conservationist planning. It was, in part, with Smalley's achievement in mind that the planners entered on a new and infinitely more dynamic phase of colonial intervention in the aftermath of the Second World War.

[89] Topham to DC, Cholo District, 29 November 1938, MNA NS 1/24.
[90] Ibid.
[91] For more detailed discussions of this scheme see McCracken, 'Conservation and Resistance in Colonial Malawi', and Mulwafu, *Conservation Song*, pp. 112–17.
[92] Smalley's accounts appear in three forms: in an article entitled 'The Misuku Land Usage Scheme' published in the *Nyasaland Agricultural Quarterly Journal*, 4, 3 (1944) and in two unpublished papers with similar titles although rather different forms, entitled 'The Misuku Land Usage Scheme North Nyasa District, Nyasaland 1938–1943' and 'The Misuku Land Usage Scheme, 1938–1947', Rhodes House Library Oxford [RHL], Mss. Afr. S. 918.
[93] Smalley, 'Misuku Land Usage Scheme, 1938–1947'.
[94] Intelligence Report, Karonga District for 1948, MNA NN 4/2/11.

Popular responses to the Depression

Nothing better illustrates the complexity of African responses to the depression than the dramatic spread of the witchcraft eradication movement, *mchape*, throughout Nyasaland between 1932 and 1934.[95] Prior to the twentieth century, generalised attempts to eradicate witchcraft appear to have occurred occasionally in a number of societies as alternatives to more conventional procedures of detecting individual witches. The outlawing by the colonial government of the *mwavi* poison ordeal, used by chiefs to test individual cases, undermined confidence in these procedures but did nothing to weaken the widespread belief, held by Christians and non-Christians alike, in the power of witches (*mfiti*) as an ever-present force in everyday life. 'This ufiti is still being believed by all sections of people irrespective of any creed, religion or doctrine', Charles Matinga, the secretary of the Blantyre Native Association and a future President of Congress, wrote in 1932.[96] The advent of the depression, leading to the return home of streams of young men, male unemployed labour migrants, many of whom found difficulty in reconciling the achievement-oriented assumptions of the new economic order with the community-oriented morality of the village, created further tensions. These were often made manifest in the attempts of young men to challenge the authority of chiefs and elders. The result was the emergence throughout Central Africa of a number of witchcraft eradication movements, among which *mchape* was by far the largest, directed, so it has been suggested, 'not so much against individual sorcerers … but against sorcery as a frame of reference and an institution'.[97]

The medicine, *mchape,* appears to have been first dispensed in June 1932 by one Maluwa in Mulanje district. Information concerning the movement did not reach colonial officials until August when several young men were found selling the medicine at large meetings in the Chiradzulu district at which they called upon everyone present to give up their instruments of witchcraft. Within a few weeks *mchape* was carried from Cholo to Port Herald and from Chiradzulu to Zomba, Liwonde and Fort Johnston.[98] At first the authorities attempted to suppress the movement by arresting the vendors and throwing them into gaol. But as its introduction spread, the popular conviction among all sections of the community, educated and non-educated, that *mchape* was an essentially beneficial force that would eliminate witchcraft and cure disease grew so strong that the police were reduced to impotence. By January 1933 the Attorney General had come to the conclusion that 'if the law is strictly enforced…the prisons could not hold the offenders.'[99] Emissaries, therefore, continued with impunity in their triumphant tour through the Northern Province and beyond into Zambia and

[95] For a general introduction see T.O. Ranger, 'Mchape and the study of witchcraft eradication', Conference on the history of central African religious systems, Lusaka, 1972.
[96] Charles J Matinga to DC Blantyre, 22 Sep 1932, MNA NS 1/23/2.
[97] W.M.J. van Binsbergen, 'The dynamics of religious change in western Zambia', *Ufamu*, 1976, 6, 2, pp. 81–2.
[98] This account is drawn from material in the following two files: MNA S1/522/32 and NS 1/23/2.
[99] Minute by Attorney General, 4 Jan 1933, S1/522/32. See also McCracken, 'Coercion and Control in Nyasaland', pp. 136–37.

Tanganyika in 1933–34. On Likoma Island, UMCA missionaries recorded in July 1933, *mchape* 'spread like wild fire' among the predominantly Christian villagers. Similar scenes were recorded in the Bandawe district where at least 365 members and catechumens of the Presbyterian Church were suspended for agreeing to drink the medicine.[100] One Livingstonia graduate noted that African Christians were singled out by the vendors as hypocrites on the grounds that 'they are the people who are hiding in this religion and are great wizards more than anyone else.' Edward Shaba, who witnessed a *mchape* ceremony at Chief Samuel Jere's village, estimated that 2,000 people attended. The young man in charge told his audience: 'What we are here for is to purge the country and save the people by casting away all evils which have been in force for many days.'[101] Those who gave up all charms and drank the medicine were promised freedom from witchcraft, with the threat that those who attempted witchcraft thereafter would suffer instant death. In village after village a sense of communal purification was achieved. Inevitably, it failed to last for long.

Mchape's appeal is likely to have been enhanced by a growing disenchantment with some aspects of the major mission churches that affected many Malawian Christians in the 1930s. Throughout this period, the number of converts and schools continued to grow. This was in part a result of the new-found drive and confidence apparent in the Catholic missions stemming from the visit to Nyasaland in 1928 of the inspirational Visitor-Apostolic, Arthur Hinsley. In a series of meetings, Hinsley made clear that missionaries should abandon their long-held suspicion of all but the most elementary education and seek to improve their schools, even if that meant neglecting their churches.[102] While Livingstonia's school network slowly shrank from 514 schools in 1915 to 399 in 1927 and 353 in 1937, the number of schools run by the White Fathers and Montfort Marists dramatically expanded: 377 in 1915, 792 in 1927 and 1751 in 1937. By that time there were more Catholic schools in Malawi than those run by the three combined synods of the Church of Central African Presbyterian (CCAP), founded in 1924 through the union of the Blantyre, Livingstonia and DRC synods.[103]

The increase in the number of under-equipped and poorly staffed village schools did nothing, however, to dispel the nagging conviction of many Malawians that Nyasaland was being left behind in the competition for educational advantage. Reflecting on the situation in the Lower Shire Valley, a Catholic missionary in 1940 complained that 'a serious mistake has been made by applying for too many schools, 150 in all, which nobody could possibly supervise.'[104] But these concerns were overshadowed by the complaints of northern Presbyterians, nostalgic for the days of Livingstonia's ascendancy and resentful at the poor standards of education now provided by the mission. 'The standard of education given by the Mission in which he was educated was lower now than it had been twenty years ago', declared Levi Mumba, a senior government clerk and leading

---

[100] Ranger, 'Mchape'; McCracken, *Politics and Christianity*, p. 280.
[101] Edward Shaba, 'A Brief History of the Proposed Visit of the "Mchape" People', 3 March 1934 quoted in McCracken, *Politics and Christianity,* p. 281.
[102] Linden, *Catholics*, p. 157; Hastings, *Church in Africa*, p. 562.
[103] Figures taken from Sir George Smith to CO, 27 Nov 1916, MNA S1/1494/19; *Annual Report of the Education Department for 1927*; Steytler, *African Village Schools*, pp. 15–16.
[104] Quoted in Schoffeleers, *Pentecostalism and Neo-Traditionalism*, p. 7

political activist, at a meeting of the Advisory Committee on Education in 1938. Six years previously he had started his campaign to persuade the Government to build Nyasaland's first secondary school, with no result. Northern chiefs shared the sense of disillusionment. 'It is generally said that the Nyasaland Protectorate was second to South Africa in receiving education... It is clear that the Protectorate is now far behind comparing the education which neighbouring territories are obtaining,' the Atonga Tribal Council of Chiefs noted in 1943.[105] Eight years earlier the Council had deplored the failure of the Nyasaland Government to establish industrial schools of a type similar to those already in existence at Tjolotjo and Domboshawa in Southern Rhodesia.[106]

It was in part with the intention of filling this gap that Yesaya Zerenje Mwasi in 1934 unveiled his plans for a Nyasaland Black Man's Educational Society. Founded on the premise that it could attract funds from Malawian migrants working in Northern and Southern Rhodesia, the society aimed 'to improve and develop the impoverished condition of the black man, religiously, morally, economically, physically and intellectually by starting a *Purely Native Controlled high school or college*'.[107]

Little came of the scheme, which attracted opposition from Malawian chiefs and colonial officials alike. But other attempts to provide African alternatives to European-dominated structures met with greater success. Between 1928 and 1934, four new independent churches were founded in northern Malawi, all of them led by former graduates of the Overtoun Institution. The earliest of these, The African National Church, reflected the views of educated Christians, several of whom had been excommunicated from the Livingstonia Church for making polygamous marriages. Formed in the Karonga district in 1928, it attracted over 3,000 members by 1940 through teachings which emphasised the divisive impact of mission churches and particularly their exclusion of the elderly:[108]

> The aim of this Church is the uplifting of the African *en masse*, taking in its rise the old people who are at present being left out by religions of the North and is civilization, as well as winning those who are considered bad because of polygamy and drink, and are refused any latent qualities for doing good any more, to try and restore an atmosphere of a deeply, naturally religious life as prevailed in the days of long ago which was manifest in words as well as deeds.

In a moving prayer, composed by the former ICU activist, Robert Sambo, members confessed:

> We have done wrong in our village, Father. Witchcraft, adultery, and hatred, all these are in our villages ... Our chiefs do not love one another in their hearts ... The old worship is broken down; we have come as wild animals which are without God. Call us again to worship, Father.[109]

---

[105] Petition by Tribal Council of Atonga Chiefs to the Governor, 6 Oct 1943, MNA NNC5/1/1.
[106] Minutes of Atonga Tribal Council, 30 Sep 1935, MNA NNC 5/1/1.
[107] Y. Z. Mwasi, 'Submission of an Application to Government for adoption and sanction of the Scheme entitled: "The Nyasaland Blackman's Educational Society"', 18 Aug 1934, MNA NN1/20/4.
[108] Quoted in Kenneth R. Ross (ed.), *Christianity in Malawi. A Source Book* (Kachere Series, Zomba, 1996), pp. 162–3. For a discussion of these churches see McCracken, *Politics and Christianity*, pp. 273–83.
[109] Quoted in Ross, *Christianity in Malawi*, p. 167–8.

Sambo's concern was echoed in the lengthy statement produced by Yesaya Zerenje Mwasi when he broke from Livingstonia in 1933 to create The Blackman's Church, which is in Tongaland. One of the mission's most senior clergymen, an ordained minister from 1914 and Moderator of the Presbytery in 1918, Mwasi was a fiercely independent individual who had clashed with Scottish missionaries on several occasions before he finally left the church. The issue of missionary authority was thus a serious one for Mwasi, as it was for his fellow ministers, Yaphet Mkandawire, who founded the African Presbyterian Church in 1932 and Charles Chinula, who founded the Eklesia Lanangwa (Church of Freedom) in 1934. But an even more important matter was the creation of a genuinely African church:

> An exotic Christianity will never take vital roots in the life of the natives. It is a mistaken view to think that the measures of introducing initiative force of indigenous Church shall be done by the missionaries themselves... The time has now come for the Native Church to take up its responsibilities alone as the individual churches planted by the Apostle Paul did, without fear that absence of mission is death of the Christianity of the soil.[110]

In 1935, Mwasi joined forces with the other two ministers in a federated church divided into three clearly defined sections: the *Mpingo wa Afipa wa Africa*. Five years later, in 1940, it had acquired some 3,500 adherents. Mainstream mission-based churches thus continued to dominate the institutional expression of Malawian Christianity. But in several areas, the Shire Highlands as much as the north, they faced keen competition from independent African competitors. The Ana A Mulungu (Children of God) Church, established in 1935 in the Cholo District by Wilfred Gudu, a former Seventh-day Adventist teacher, was only one, although probably the most controversial, of ten religious denominations working in that district. A charismatic figure, Gudu presided over what has been called a 'total community' of some 60 convinced believers. He got into a dispute with colonial officials from 1937 as a result of his refusal to pay government taxes.[111]

In a lecture he delivered to the Atonga Tribal Council in August 1935, Uriah Chirwa, senior assistant at the Overtoun Institution, told his audience of chiefs and teachers: 'Our country belongs to the Crown and we must be loyal to our King ... You should always trust the Government and ask it to understand your questions accordingly.'[112] Chirwa's words remind us that, well into the 1930s, the cult of royalty employed by the British as a means of legitimising their rule still retained some purchase in Nyasaland. In the same year, even in remote Fort Manning [now Mchinji], King George V's Silver Jubilee was celebrated with a wealth of calculated symbolism: a flagstaff ceremony, drill display, *mganda* dancing and a play performed by children at the Kachabere school 'depicting ancient conditions in Nyasaland – warfare, slavery, etc. and [the] peace and contentment of today.'[113] When George V died in 1936, Native Authority Kawinga, anxious (so he claimed)

---

[110] Ibid., pp. 169–78.
[111] J.C. Chakanza, *Voices of Preachers of Protest. The Ministry of Two Malawian Prophets: Eliot Kamwana and Wilfred Gudu* (Blantyre, 1998), pp. 58–76.
[112] Lecture by Uriah Chirwa to Atonga Tribal Council, Aug 1935, MNA NNC 5/1/1.
[113] Annual Report for the Northern Province, 1935, MNA S1/80/36. See also McCracken, 'Authority and Legitimacy', pp. 170–71.

'to dry the tears of the Queen', collected money for the purchase of a wreath, which was later placed on the King's tomb at Windsor.[114]

The continued practice of rituals of loyalty cannot, however, disguise the reality that the network of local alliances so carefully woven in the early years of the century was becoming frayed prior to the Second World War. African policemen and soldiers appear to have been largely untouched by the erosion of confidence in the colonial order that spread through the ranks of African inter-mediaries. But many chiefs, upon whose shoulders responsibility in the local areas had been placed, were not immune to the infection. Even before the First World War, the rise of Watchtower, 'first of the twentieth-century mass movements to demonstrate the collapse of chiefly power', gave warning of the paradox that the more authority colonial officials transferred to chiefs, the less respect they could expect from their African subjects.[115] By the early 1930s, *mchape* vendors organ-ised village ceremonies whether chiefs cooperated or not. As government inter-vention became more active in the aftermath of the depression, so the weakness of their agents was exposed. When, in 1938, Chiefs Ntondeza and Nsabwe issued soil conservation orders to some 300 cultivators in the Cholo area on the instruc-tions of Topham, the orders were almost entirely ignored.[116]

Neither the depth of disenchantment nor the radicalism of response should be exaggerated. Among the varied ideological movements that spread through southern Africa in the interwar years, Communism appears to have made little or no headway in Nyasaland. Sporadic efforts of the Communist Party of South Africa to establish links with a variety of individuals believed to be associated with 'the labour and peasant movement' proved ineffective.[117] Christian socialist and Garveyite ideas of social justice and racial solidarity continued to appeal to certain northern intellectuals, notably Yesaya Mwasi. Perhaps the most signifi-cant development, however, was the growing tendency of 'dependent intellec-tuals', senior clerks and civil servants, to become disenchanted with what the British had to offer. Levi Mumba's rise, to a seat on the Advisory Committee on Education in 1933 and to the position of Interpreter on the Emigrant Labour Commission of 1935, did nothing to reduce the concern he felt at the disinte-grating effect of the European presence.

> The European came with his individualism and thrust it on the native... I hate individu-alism because it has suddenly torn the son from the father, or one man from another... So we see that freedom and justice which was supposed would result from the disintegration of tribal communal life has not yet been achieved.[118]

Mumba's anxiety, ironically shared by many colonial officials, was combined with a healthy appreciation of the benefits to be obtained from individual advancement. But it did suggest the existence of a widespread disaffection with the colonial order that would grow in the post-war era.

---

[114] Annual Report for the Southern Province, 1936, MNA NS 3/1/6.
[115] T.O. Ranger, *The African Voice in Southern Rhodesia*, London, 1970, p. 212; Karen E. Fields, *Revival and Rebellion in Colonial Central Africa*, Princeton, 1985.
[116] P. Topham to DC, Cholo, 29 Nov 1938, MNA NS 1/24.
[117] See Supt CID Zomba to DC Karonga, 30 July 1932, NC 1/23/4.
[118] Quoted in M. L. Chanock, 'Ambiguities in the Malawian Political Tradition', *African Affairs*, 74, 296, 1975, p.335.

9
Contours of Colonialism

Introduction

Three features distinguish the colonial power structure that emerged in Nyasa-land in the inter-war years and which continued to influence patterns of rural government up to the coming of independence. The first was the creation of a 'prefectural administration', as Berman describes it, 'staffed by an elite cadre of political officers acting as direct agents for the central government, and exercising diffuse and wide-ranging powers'.[1] The central element was the secretariat in Zomba which engaged both with the Colonial Office in London and with the provincial and district administration spread across the Protectorate. This basic structure came into force as late as 1921, with a Chief Secretary as the main administrative officer directly below the Governor, linked with three Provincial Commissioners (reduced to two between 1931–1946). These gave instructions to district officers, each of whom had a specified area of territory directly under his control.

The second feature was the network of official chiefs, 105 in 1949, designated as Native Authorities from 1933, and working in tandem with the district officers.[2] The role and character of official chieftaincies is one of the issues most disputed among Central African historians. One view, widely held until recently, is that by incorporating chiefs within the colonial structure of authority, the British condemned them to a lingering decline resulting in the collapse of chiefly authority and the emergence in their place of 'new men' more 'modern', better educated, and less 'tribal' than the chiefs, and better placed to exploit weapons of constitutional change when these eventually became available. A second view, espoused most vigorously by Mamdani for sub-Saharan Africa as a whole, is that through the introduction of indirect rule official chiefs were able to consolidate their control as 'decentralised despots', freed from the limitations on tyrannical rule exercised in pre-colonial times by the threat of challenges from below, yet possessed of a remarkable range of administrative, legislative and judicial powers. It is Mamdani's thesis that official chiefs, supported to the hilt by white admin-

---

[1] Bruce Berman, *Control and Crisis in Colonial Kenya* (London 1990), p. 73.
[2] Paper on 'Native Administration in 1949', RHL, Oxford Mss. Afr S/210.

Map 4 Administrative Districts, 1932

istrative officers, were thus able to maintain a peculiarly brutal and tyrannical form of governance in rural areas, one which confronted major challenge at the time of the rise of nationalism, yet frequently survived, basically unreformed, well into the post-colonial period.[3] How these broad theses relate to the reality of power on the ground in rural Nyasaland is a central concern of this chapter.

The third feature concerns the consequences of indirect rule. How far did it result in the hardening of distinct and antagonistic tribal identities? How far should the shifting character of 'tribal', 'regional' and 'national' identity be seen less as a consequence of administrative diktat imposed from above, and how far as an expression of indigenous concerns? Further, how did the new administrative structure, in particular the establishment of officially-sanctioned Native Courts, affect marginalised groups within rural communities, notably the fifty per cent of the population: women?

District officers

As in many British colonies, the shift from what has been called the politics of conquest to the politics of consent was marked by a change in the composition of the provincial administration. By the early years of the twentieth century virtually all representatives of the colourful, sometimes brutal band of locally appointed white officials had been weeded out. Instead, Residents (later, District Commissioners) were recruited by the Colonial Office, predominantly from the ranks of upper-middle-class candidates, educated in fee-paying public schools. Both the Colonial Office and successive governors favoured graduates from Oxford and Cambridge who were alleged to possess qualities of leadership not enjoyed by men (not women) from other universities. However, Nyasaland, as a relatively unfashionable colony, was compelled to draw its recruits from a somewhat wider social and educational spectrum. Out of the 15 appointments made between April 1920 and September 1921, there were only six university graduates: two from Cambridge, two from Glasgow, one each from Durham and Trinity College Dublin and a mere three who, in the opinion of the Governor, Sir George Smith, had attended 'schools of repute'.[4] Smith himself, despite his insistence that officials should have the most privileged education, was unusual among governors in that he had not been educated at a public school or a university. Oxbridge dominance became more marked in the 1930s by which time the two universities were running a one-year training course for newly appointed recruits. Even at this later stage, Nyasaland drew its junior administrators from a field slightly wider than the colonial norm. The 'rough-hewn' Bill Rangeley, for example, grew up in Northern Rhodesia, where his parents were pioneer settlers, although he later gained respectability in Colonial Office eyes by winning a Rhodes Scholarship to Oxford.[5]

The main characteristics of these officials can be briefly noted. First, there

[3] Mahmood Mamdani, *Citizen and Subject: Contemporary Africa and the Legacy of Late Colonialism* (London, 1996), pp. 37–61.
[4] Smith to Colonial Office, 25 August 1921, TNA CO 529/97.
[5] Obituary of W-H.J. Rangeley, *Nyasaland Journal,* 11, 2 1958, p. 7; Patrick Mullins, *Retreat From Africa* (Edinburgh, 1992), p. 53.

were remarkably few of them: 40 at the time of the outbreak of the First World War; 51, including two Provincial Commissioners, in 1937.[6] Numbers rose after the war, as they did in the colonial agricultural, educational and police service but only on the eve of self-government in 1961, to a sparse 120 (including three African Assistant DCs). They were generally young and frequently on the move from one district to another. The North Nyasa District had four residents over a twelve-month period in 1925–26;[7] between 1948 and 1956 there were nine district commissioners at Fort Johnston.[8]

The knowledge of Malawian locations and languages, particularly Chinyanja, possessed by district officers was incomparably superior to that of all but a handful of the infinitely larger body of expatriates working for non-governmental organizations who flocked to post-colonial Malawi. But they themselves and their superiors in the secretariat in Zomba were constantly frustrated by the superficiality of their understanding of Malawian societies: by the sense that they were not sufficiently in touch. Time and again, in the late 1920s and again in the late 1940s, instructions went out that district officers should spend more time on *ulendo*, travelling from village to village, talking with headmen and hearing complaints rather than remaining stuck in their district offices. Yet the paradox was that the more they travelled, the greater appeared their social distance from those they governed. Even in the early 1950s, 'Europeans lived their own lives, with no direct contacts with Africans', according to Patrick Mullins, the District Officer at Mzimba. On *ulendo*, an officer would camp near to a village rather than staying in a village house, as happened in Ghana at this time.[9] Social distance resulted in the assertion of stereotypical views. Writing in 1942 on the relationship between the Council of Lilongwe Chiefs and the District Officer, the Provincial Commissioner, P. C. Ellis claimed: 'The scene is reminiscent of that of a headmaster with his sixth form boys between whom there is mutual respect and regard.'[10] It was in order to challenge paternalistic attitudes of this kind that in the late 1950s, Dr Banda contemptuously dismissed district officers as little boys in shorts.

District officers, like the technicians of empire also employed by the colonial state (foresters, agricultural officers, geologists and others) were generally well-meaning and hard-working, anxious to ameliorate poverty and improve the lot of local people. But while they were capable of displaying genuine concern and even admiration for subsistence cultivators, they were often ill at ease with the consequences of social change, critical of the growing influence of mission-educated Malawians, and suspicious of individual success. 'The product of the advanced schools is inclined to be an ill-mannered fellow with an exaggerated idea of his own importance' announced J. D. Locker within months of his arrival in the territory on his very first appointment at Karonga.[11] His preference was for the Ngonde, a gentlemanly, conservative people who 'wish to advance as a tribe and, not like the neighbouring Henga people, as individuals.'[12]

6   Anthony Kirk-Green, *Symbol of Authority: The British District Officer in Africa* (London, 2006), pp. 4–5.
7   Northern Province annual report for year ending 31 March 1926, MNA S1/920/26.
8   Reply to question in the House of Commons by Lennox-Boyd, 2 May 1956, TNA CO 1015/1095.
9   Mullins, *Retreat*, pp. 24 and 38–39.
10 Lilongwe District Report for 1941, MNA NCL 4/1/5.
11 North Nyasa Annual Report for 1933, MNA S1/112 F-J/34.
12 Ibid., North Nyasa Annual Report for 1934, MNA S1/89 F-J/35.

Although they were promoters of capitalism in the sense that a central part of their responsibility was to propel Malawians into the money economy, most district officers came from non-commercial backgrounds and were often hostile to entrepreneurs, whether African, Asian or European. In a remarkable insight into their contradictory beliefs, the DC for the Lower Shire District, where government agents had been promoting the growing of cash crops for over 40 years, responded to the 1948 famine with the hope that it would demonstrate the worthlessness of money. Instead, so he ruefully noted:

> The gentleman with long trousers, jacket, pork-pie hat and bicycle, making a living entirely as a middleman was able to find food at all times with money in his pocket, while his honester harder working brother who laboured on the land was left without subsistence should his crops fail from causes beyond his control.[13]

The early 1950s brought the growing sense of unease among district officers to a head. Their numbers expanded at the time of 'the second colonial occupation' (see Chapter 10). But with the increasingly intrusive involvement of the government in enforcing agricultural rules, they often found themselves relegated to a supporting role alongside agricultural officers who were seeking to implement ambitious soil conservation measures with which many had little sympathy. Griff Jones, the District Officer at Nkhata Bay in 1952, was by no means unique in his concern that, by imposing unpopular measures on resistant cultivators, the Government risked undermining public order, the very thing which administrators saw as their first duty to preserve.[14]

Further frustration came with instructions to promulgate the values of the much disliked Federation of Rhodesia and Nyasaland – a policy which, if followed through to its logical outcome, would have put them out of a job.[15] They were now confronted by the emergence of politicians, gentlemen with long trousers, jackets and pork-pie hats, with whom they had little sympathy or understanding. Some of the new generation of administrators had fought in the Second World War, an experience that may have made them more liberal-minded than their predecessors. But overwhelmingly, as their memoirs demonstrate, they had virtually no social contact with the new generation of politically active, educated Malawians and little or no respect for their aims. Masauko Chipembere, one of the first African Assistant DCs as well as one of Nyasaland's most radical politicians, found himself regularly frustrated by unsympathetic British seniors, although he made an exception for the Rhodesian, Bill Rangeley (Nyasaland's foremost amateur historian), whom he found both friendly and helpful.[16] A minority of administrators were subsequently to achieve a rapprochement with nationalist leaders when they came to power. But most, when faced in the 1950s by the rise of militant nationalism, demonstrated little or no understanding of the phenomenon with which they were confronted.

---

[13]   Annual Report for the Lower Shire District, 1948, MNA NS 3/1/18.
[14]   McCracken, 'Conservation and Resistance', pp. 168–70. See also Henry Phillips, *From Obscurity to Bright Dawn* (London, 1998), p. 22.
[15]   Griff Jones, *Britain and Nyasaland* (London, 1964), pp. 171–89.
[16]   Robert I. Rotberg (ed.), *Hero of the Nation: Chipembere of Malawi* (Kachere, Blantyre, 2002), pp. 171, 179, 213–4.

Towards indirect rule

The creation of a professional elite of white administrators was accompanied by the more gradual emergence of 'official chiefs', designated specific powers by the colonial government. In theory, these chiefs would be 'legitimate' in that they had the hereditary right to rule over a particular group of people, either a tribe or the portion of a tribe. More often than not, however, this claim to legitimacy would be contested so that it was not uncommon for rulers to be challenged by rival claimants.

There are many factors that explain the slow drift towards indirect rule from the 1920s. One was practical necessity. Given its limited resources and the small number of white district administrators employed, there was every reason for the state to seek to enlist the support of African intermediaries in preserving social order and enforcing its basic demands. Some of these intermediaries were recruited directly into the colonial service as policemen, interpreters and clerks. But with the government's growing demand for African labour, first as porters during the First World War, and later to build roads and work on European estates, the administration made a concerted effort to impose on selected chiefs the responsibility for recruiting labour by extending the 1912 District Administration (Native) Ordinance beyond the nine districts where it was in force in 1913. Six years later, the powers of the ordinance had been extended all over the country. The significant exception was of the Shire Highlands where, for more than two decades, the estate owners were successful in blocking any measure that might weaken their control over their workers.[17] As White has shown in an influential article, Yao Muslim chiefs, anxious to demonstrate their loyalty to the colonial government in the aftermath of the Chilembwe Rising, went out of their way during the war to recruit Lomwe subjects for the war effort.[18] But while officials welcomed this development, they had no hesitation in giving priority to settler interests. Rather than seizing 'the opportunity of the Yao chiefs' goodwill...to proceed years in advance of anywhere else in the Southern Province, with the implementation of the DANO and with the appointment of Principal Headmen', as White has argued, the government in 1919 acceded to the settlers' demands that DANO should not be applied to the Shire Highlands.[19] Thereafter, for over a decade, the estate owners exercised a virtual veto over the transfer of administrative responsibilities to chiefs, whether predominantly Yao in the Blantyre, Zomba and Chiradzulu districts, or Mang'anja in Cholo and Mulanje. Not until 1930 were Principal Headmen recognised in the Shire Highlands and even then their role was restricted to what the estates allowed them to do.[20]

Elsewhere, indigenous authorities or prominent individuals appointed Principal Headmen under DANO received little reward for their exertions other than the prestige that came with an official title and a small annual stipend, fixed in

[17] Murray, *Handbook*, 1922, pp. 89–97.
[18] White, '"Tribes" and the Aftermath of the Chilembwe Rising', pp. 526–33.
[19] Vail and White, 'Tribalism in the Political History of Malawi', pp. 169–73; Murray, *Handbook*, 1932, pp. 133–34.
[20] Murray, *Handbook*, 1932, pp. 135–39.

1918, based on the number of huts under a chief's control. In return, they were called upon in the 1920s to assist the colonial government in its insatiable demand for labour. The Central Province, not yet a significant centre of tobacco-growing, was the major focus of attention. Each year, up to the late 1920s, Principal Headmen were coerced into sending around six or seven thousand men south to the Shire Highlands where they were employed on basic wages either on settler estates or else in building roads for the Public Works Department or carrying timber from Mulanje.[21] When men deserted from this bitterly unpopular work, they were subjected to the full rigour of Nyasaland's draconian employment laws. As late as 1929, Nyasaland was second only to Kenya in the number of people charged under Masters and Servants legislation. What is more, if comparative populations are taken into account, Nyasaland equalled Kenya in the number of convictions.[22]

Government demands for forced labour played a key part in the shift to indirect rule. By the mid-1920s district administrators had become thoroughly disenchanted with their role in coercing labour; however, in Zomba, the new Governor, Sir Charles Bowring (1924–29), pursued the policy with enthusiasm. Shortly before he arrived in the Protectorate, the 1912 ordinance was revised to extend the powers granted to Principal Headmen to compel villagers to work unpaid on local projects. In 1928 Bowring returned to the issue, demanding that villagers should be forced to work on projects such as the motor road from Blantyre to Lilongwe, whether they were local or not.[23]

The Colonial Office response was to signal both the end of forced labour and the beginning of a new approach to chiefly authority. Concerned by the furore aroused in humanitarian circles in Britain over the scandal of forced labour in Kenya, the Colonial Secretary, Leo Amery, vetoed Bowring's proposals and instead demanded that he consider the introduction of indirect rule in Nyasaland and the establishment of 'native administrations' along with 'native courts' and 'native treasuries'.[24] Bowring was unconvinced. As he explained to the Hilton Young Commission in 1928, he believed that tribal organisation in Nyasaland was in a state of disintegration. He was therefore 'sceptical as to the possibility of continuing to make use of Native chiefs'.[25] In the Colonial Office, patience with Bowring, widely regarded as someone who 'only cares about his planting friends', was now exhausted.[26] In 1929 his tour of duty was cut short and 'a younger and more energetic man', Thomas Shenton Thomas, Chief Secretary in the Gold Coast and a former administrator in Nigeria, was appointed in his place.[27] In an early circular, sent to all administrative officers,

---

[21] Annual Reports for the Central Province for 1922–23 and 1923–34, MNA NC 2/1/1; Annual Report for 1927, MNA S1/482/28.

[22] Bruce Berman and John Lonsdale, *Unhappy Valley: Conflict in Kenya and Africa,* Book One, (London, 1992) footnote 49, p. 125. In 1929 there were 755 convictions in Nyasaland, 1,492 in Kenya and only 190 in Uganda.

[23] Governor Sir George Smith to Colonial Office, 9 Aug 1922, TNA CO 525/96; Governor Bowring to CO, 30 Nov. 1925, TNA CO 525/112; Bowring to CO, 30 May 1928, TNA CO 525/112.

[24] Amery to Bowring, 17 May 1928, TNA CO 525/123.

[25] Notes on interview with Sir Charles Bowring, Governor, 19 March 1929, Evidence to the Hilton Young Commission, Foreign Office Library.

[26] Note by J.G. Green, 23 Oct 1929, TNA CO 525/1230.

[27] Confidential note by S. H. W. to Colonial Secretary, 19 March 1929, TNA CO 525/131; note by J. F. Green, 23 Oct 1929, TNA CO 525/123.

Thomas made clear his intention 'to strengthen or to restore where it no longer exists, the native authority which is not alien to the people.'[28]

Native Authorities

Indirect Rule was the creation of Frederick Lugard, the Indian Army officer who had led the abortive expedition launched by the ALC against Mlozi and his slave-trading allies at the north end of Malawi in 1887. By the early years of the twentieth century he had become Sir Frederick Lugard, the conqueror of the Muslim emirates of Northern Nigeria. The system of government devised by Lugard for this large area was created for pragmatic reasons but, by the 1920s, had been transformed into political dogma. There would be a single colonial administration in which indigenous rulers would be incorporated. They would possess 'legitimacy', not just in the sense that the Governor had appointed them but also in that they were recognised by the people of their tribe as the rightful traditional rulers. These rulers had the executive power to make laws and carry through projects, and would have Native Courts, operating according to 'customary' rather than to colonial law. Native Treasuries collected taxes. Under indirect rule, ultimate authority was conceived as residing in the person of the British monarch (George V for much of the period covered in this chapter). He, in turn, was represented by the Governor and then through the colonial hierarchy to the most junior British officer. For all the power and status attached to Northern Nigerian emirs, it was the white man who was ultimately supreme.[29] In 1925 Sir Donald Cameron, fresh from Nigeria, introduced indirect rule to Tanganyika: it was this system that Shenton Thomas determined to extend to Nyasaland.

The fate of indirect rule in Nyasaland in the two decades from 1930 provides a striking demonstration of the law of unintended consequences. Thomas's intention was to introduce Lugard's model as quickly and as thoroughly as possible. His arrival in the Protectorate, however, coincided with the initial impact of the Great Depression and a sharp decline in government revenues which made immediate administrative reform impossible. He returned to the issue in 1932, only to be almost immediately promoted to the Governorship of the Gold Coast, leaving the matter unresolved.[30] It was thus left to Thomas's successor, Sir Hubert Young, a much more conservative figure, to introduce a watered-down version of the policy in 1934. Anxious to placate settler interests in the country, Young labelled the new system as one of 'local government' rather than 'indirect rule'. He insisted that Native Courts should have no jurisdiction in areas, including estates, where non-Africans predominated. He also made clear, in a fundamental rejection of Lugard's views, that Native Authorities should have no responsibility for the administration of government revenues or for the collection of taxes.[31] It was not until 1940 that Native Authorities were entrusted, in theory, with the collection of tax. Even then, chiefs played only a

---

[28] Quoted in Timothy Keil Barnekov, 'An Inquiry into the Development of Native Administration in Nyasaland, 1888–1937', MA thesis, Syracuse University, 1967, p. 71.
[29] For an eloquent exposition of this view see Christopher Fyfe, 'Race, Empire and the Historians', *Race and Class*, 33, 4 (1992).
[30] Barnekov, 'Native Administration' p. 71.
[31] Barnekov, 'Native Administration', pp. 72–5.

nominal role in the process. Tax collection continued to be carried out by government clerks, although they now resided in chiefs' villages.[32]

As in Tanganyika, the central issue facing the colonial administration was what criteria should be used in appointing Native Authorities. Broadly speaking, the government approach was to confirm principal headmen appointed under the 1912 ordinance in office but with two exceptions. First, where local pressure was greatest (usually articulated by leading educated Christians), the government was prepared to acknowledge 'traditional legitimacy' over the preferences of colonial officers. This was the case in the Northern Province. Ngoni pride had suffered a severe blow in 1915 as a result of the government's action in removing Paramount Chief Chimtunga from office and banishing him to the south. In the 1920s the Mombera Native Association mounted a major campaign to have Chimtunga's son, Lazaro Jere, appointed as paramount chief. In 1927 the Provincial Commissioner, A. J. Brackenbury, rejected the claim and threatened to send in troops to suppress the movement.[33] The following year, however, the government relented to the extent of making Lazaro Jere, one of the seven Ngoni principal headmen. This failed to satisfy Ngoni activists, who argued in 1930 that 'the desire to have a paramount chief in Mombera still rings in the hearts of the people, for the present policy of equalizing all Principal headmen is contrary to the law of the country.'[34] The compromise offered by the government in 1933 was that principal headmen should become Native Authorities, each independent in his own section, although federated in a council under Lazaro Jere's chairmanship. However, the Ngoni chiefs combined in rejecting this solution. With no other option open to them, the colonial authorities accepted defeat and instead appointed Lazaro Jere as Native Authority and paramount chief for the whole Ngoni-Tumbuka area, with the other six chiefs as his subordinates.[35] In addition, Lazaro Jere was permitted to revive the title of Mbelwa which had been suppressed in 1915. Ironically, through pressure from below and in contradiction of colonial policy, a unified Ngoni polity had been created.

In similar vein, albeit in the face of less official opposition, the authorities accepted another claim to paramountcy, this time over the southern Ngoni. The successor, Gomani, was a direct descendant of the chief killed by the British in 1896. His official status under the 1912 ordinance was restricted to that of one of nine principal headmen in the Ntcheu District, although officials recognised that in practice his influence was much greater than that. His elevation in 1933 to the position of the single Native Authority with six subordinate authorities below him was in many respects the *de facto* acceptance of the existing state of affairs.[36]

Second, where chiefs were weak or non-existent, an alternative strategy was employed. Pre-colonial authority among the Tonga had been divided amongst a substantial number of fiercely competing clan heads. In 1917, with the extension of DANO to the area, the British recognised five Tonga Principal Headmen. With the imminent arrival of indirect rule, conflict broke out over which men

---

[32] Lilongwe District Annual Report, 1940, MNA NCL 4/1/5; Mzimba District Book, Vol. 1; Lord Hailey, *Native Administration in the British African Territories, Part II* (HMSO, London, 1950) p. 43.

[33] Annual Report for Northern Province for year ending 31 March 1927, MNA S1/955/27.

[34] Quoted in Vail and White, 'Tribalism', p. 163.

[35] Annual Report for Northern Province for 1933, MNA S1/112/34.

[36] Ibid.

among a myriad of chiefs, should be chosen as native authorities. The government's solution, repeated on Likoma Island, was to construct a conciliar system, by which the powers of the Native Authority were vested in the Atonga Tribal Council, consisting of 32 Tonga chiefs and headmen[37]. As Power has noted, this set the scene for a protracted debate, lasting for almost two decades, in which leading Tonga intellectuals ceaselessly discussed the validity of the conciliar system and who or what could best replace it.[38]

Elsewhere, the adoption of indirect rule, with the enhanced benefits that it brought to officially-appointed chiefs, encouraged rival contenders to use alternative versions of history to bolster their claims for legitimacy. The central problem, deriving from the political upheavals of the late-nineteenth century, was that in many areas, no single, universally accepted traditional ruler existed. Even in the far north, where the authority of the Kyungu, Peter Mwakasungulu, as Native Authority in Ungonde went virtually unchallenged, there was still considerable opposition among minority communities to being incorporated under Ngonde rule.[39] Elsewhere, divisions intensified, in several cases erupting in violence at the time of the rise of nationalism in the 1950s. Thus at Nkhotakota, many Chewa headmen were resentful of the appointment in 1933 of Chief Msusa as Native Authority, as he was the Nyamwezi/Yao descendant of one of the Jumbe's leading supporters and hence regarded as being unsympathetic to Chewa interests.

It was in the Southern Province, however, that the issue of legitimacy was most widely contested. J.C. Abrahams, the Provincial Commissioner at the time that indirect rule was introduced, flirted with the idea of making widespread changes in the composition of officially-recognised chiefs to reflect popular acceptability but instead opted for continuity.[40] Thus, in the Chikwawa district, all five Makololo principal headmen were recognised as Native Authorities, as were all seven Mang'anja principal headmen in the Port Herald District despite the fact that, by the 1930s, Sena immigrants were in a clear majority in the district. Four out of six officially approved chiefs in the Cholo district described themselves as Mang'anja, yet three-quarters of the population were Lomwe. Equally significant, deep-rooted divisions occurred within the indigenous Mang'anja population. At the time of the British occupation, the Lundu chieftaincy had long since dwindled into insignificance and Tengani was recognised as the senior Mang'anja ruler. With the introduction of indirect rule, however, Saizi Lundu, then a village headman, combined with officials of the Mbona cult to make a renewed bid for recognition as the senior spiritual and political force in the area. Thwarted in 1936 by the elevation of the Christian moderniser, Molin Tengani, as native authority, Lundu retreated to his village where he became a focus of opposition to the Tengani dynasty. When an attempt was made to overthrow Tengani in 1953, the Lundu was imprisoned as one of the ringleaders.[41]

[37] Annual Report for the West Nyasa District, 1931, MNA S1/112 F-J/34.
[38] Joey Power, *Political Culture and Nationalism in Malawi: Building Kwacha* (University of Rochester Press, Rochester NY, 2010), pp. 35–43.
[39] Owen Kalinga, 'The British and the Kyungus: A Study of the Changing Status of the Ngonde Rulers during the Period 1891–1933', *African Studies*, 38, 2, 1979.
[40] J. C Abrahams, Annual Report for the Southern Province for 1934, MNA NS 3/1/4.
[41] Schoffeleers, *River of Blood*, pp. 106–07; Mandala, *Work and Control*, pp. 204, 231–33; Annual Report for Southern Province, 1931, MNA NS 3/1/2; Native Affairs Report for 1953, TNA CO 626/30.

Indirect rule, as it emerged in Nyasaland, took a number of distinctive forms. First, in comparison with Northern Nigeria or even with much of Tanganyika, the financial resources made available to Nyasaland's native authorities were strikingly slim. Under the new system, Native Authorities initially received 2d out of every six shilling hut tax raised, significantly more than had been paid to principal headmen. Mbelwa, for example, who presided over the largest authority in the territory, received £50 in 1934 as compared with £16 two years earlier; the Tumbuka Chief, Chikulamayembe received only £24.[42] With the establishment of Native Treasuries and Courts, officially appointed chiefs could levy rates, dues and fees and collect rents from the lease of land – a particularly valuable source of revenue in the Central Province where European demand for land was increasing. But given the poverty-stricken nature of Nyasaland's rural economy, the sums raised were always likely to be small. Whereas the Kano emirate in the mid-1930s had an annual revenue of £206,000 out of which the Emir's personal salary amounted to £6,000, in 1935, Native Authority treasuries in the Southern Province had a revenue of about £880.[43] In Ntcheu and Lilongwe, where rents on leased land were successfully charged, Native Treasury revenues amounted to £1400–1500 in the same year. In Kasungu, by contrast, little over £200 was raised.[44] Chiefs in Bukoba in Tanganyika had salaries of over £2,000, thus ensuring that almost all of them could afford a car. In Nyasaland, the chiefs, though generally wealthier than their subjects, were more likely to own a bicycle.

Lack of funds directly affected the role played by Native Authorities. Chiku-lamayembe introduced an ambitious scheme for compulsory primary education in his district, but in most chieftaincies, schemes for social and economic devel-opment were limited to the upkeep of district roads, the provision of commodity markets and, in some cases, to the construction of dispensaries.[45] More impor-tant was the provision permitting Native Authorities to make rules subject to the Governor's approval. In an excess of enthusiasm, Mbelwa, fresh from his triumph in being officially recognised as paramount chief, introduced a series of orders seeking to enforce Ngoni culture on the area under his control. His subjects were forbidden to take part in a variety of dances, including *vimbuza*, because 'they are of foreign origin and not in accordance with Ngoni and local custom.' Only Ngoni clan names were allowed to be used; no one could 'tattoo face or/and body with tribal marks other than Angoni Tribal marks'.[46] In the Nkhotakota District, Msusa issued orders in 1934 and 1935 forbidding gambling and controlling *vinyau*.[47] Ten years later, however, neither these orders nor Mbelwa's prohibition of *vimbuza* had been enforced.[48] Just as the colonial police were unsuccessful in their repeated attempts to suppress *kachasu* drinking, so official chiefs were unable to impose their authority in matters of public behav-iour where they failed to carry popular opinion with them.[49]

[42] Mizimba District report for 1934, MNA S1/89 F-J/35.
[43] Lord Hailey, *An African Survey* (OUP, London, 1938), pp. 426–7; 464–65.
[44] Annual Report for Northern Province, 1935 MNA S1/80/36.
[45] Hailey, *Native Administration* Part II, p.44.
[46] Mzimba District Annual Report for 1934, MNA S1/89 F-J/35.
[47] Kota Kota District Report for 1934, MNA S1/89 F-J/35.
[48] Native Affairs Report for 1946, PRO CO 262/24.
[49] See McCracken, 'Coercion and Control', pp. 135–37.

With the growing recognition of the practical limits of chiefly power, native authorities increasingly confined themselves to introducing rules aimed at providing additional sources of revenue. Most popular were beer licences, focused directly at women brewers, which became an important source of revenue, particularly in the Southern Province. But licences were also imposed on bicycles and even, from the 1940s, on dogs, although the latter provoked considerable opposition from those individuals asked to pay. In the Northern Province, by the early 1950s, it was noted that 'no chief whether his sympathies lie with Government or not, wishes to incur unnecessary unpopularity for himself by enforcing such unpopular legislation.'[50]

Even more unpopular were the many rules foisted on Native Authorities by the colonial government. In the mid-1930s, these largely concerned measures to prohibit cultivation near streams and to prevent the needless cutting down of trees. By 1939, however, they were being extended to cover almost every aspect of peasant activity from the compulsory ridging of gardens to the uprooting of cotton and tobacco, and from there to the construction of officially approved latrines. In all these cases, the rules were drawn up in colonial agricultural or health departments and then passed to Native Authorities for implementation. Robert Moffat, who carried out a survey of Native Authority Courts in 1949, noted that courts rarely possessed copies of the rules and orders that they were supposed to administer. Instead, offenders were brought to court by colonial officials. There was usually a flat rate punishment and the accused were rarely permitted to defend themselves.[51]

Native Courts were in many respects the most important innovation introduced under indirect rule. In theory, in the early decades of the Protectorate, the administration of justice was carried out by a handful of white administrators, untrained in the law, acting as magistrates. In practice, however, as Hynde has noted, over the greater part of the territory, 'cases that reached the magistrates' courts were normally brought on appeal by the plaintiffs themselves, and the role of dispensing justice remained the preserve of chiefs and headmen acting on an informal basis'.[52] Most disputes were settled at village level by headmen and their advisers.

The establishment of Native Courts from 1934 brought a number of changes. Not only were disputes now increasingly dealt with by chiefs' courts rather than by village headmen, but these courts were empowered to impose punishments of up to six months in gaol, fines of up to £5, and corporal punishment of up to 12 strokes with a cane. In Nigeria and Kenya, where similar punitive sanctions were combined with the creation of locally recruited Native Authority police forces and fearsome Native Authority gaols, official chiefs were able to exercise their powers with considerable brutality. But in Nyasaland, where a handful of 'native messengers' constituted the only coercive force available to official chiefs, the situation was very different.[53] In the absence of designated 'tribal policemen',

50 Native Affairs Report for 1953, PRO CO 626/30.
51 R.L. Moffat, 'Report on Native Courts in Nyasaland', 30 June 1951, TNA CO 1015/639.
52 Stacey Hynd, 'Law, Violence and Penal Reform: State Responses to Crime and Disorder in Colonial Malawi, c. 1900–1959', *JSAS*, 37, 3, 2011, p. 435.
53 Evidence of Major F. T. Stephens, Commissioner of Police, 20 June 1938, to Bledisloe Commission, Foreign Office Library. In 1943 the Governor proposed introducing 'tribal police' under the control of Native Authorities but the next year the proposal was abandoned. See file on Tribal Police, MNA NC 1.291.

chiefs were forced to rely on what limited support they could obtain from the central government's tiny police force which was largely concentrated in areas of European settlement. In 1945, out of 500 African policemen only 66 were stationed in the Northern Province.[54]

The result was that, with very few exceptions, chiefs were notably cautious in using their new powers. Government statistics must be treated with a measure of scepticism: court clerks were by no means infallible in filling in official forms. But the figures from across the Protectorate tell a similar story. Corporal punishment, frequently imposed by colonial magistrates in the early colonial period, was used only infrequently in Native Courts. In the Southern Province in 1935, only two sentences of flogging were ordered out of 6,785 cases tried.[55] There was an increase in this form of punishment at the time of the serious famine of 1949, when Chief Tengani in the Lower Shire Valley ordered several young men convicted of stealing food to be flogged. Such orders were prohibited later in the year as a result of a High Court decision that it was not in accord with native custom.[56] Similarly, imprisonment, while used more frequently than whipping, remained very much a minority option, imposed only 96 times in the Southern Province in 1935. In 1947, by contrast, it was imposed only 37 times out of 8,218 criminal cases in the Central Province.[57] In general, fines, paid into the Native Treasury, were the preferred means of dealing with breaches of Native Authority rules and orders. More frequently still, cases brought to Native Courts were treated as civil rather than criminal matters, nearly all of them being settled by the payment of compensation.[58] Despite frequent complaints from Provincial and District Commissioners, Native Courts, at least up to the late 1940s, demonstrated a marked preference for conciliation over punishment, except in cases brought directly to them by agricultural or forestry officers where they acceded to colonial government demands for punitive action.[59]

Where Native Courts played a particularly important role was in the settling of matrimonial cases. In 1934 such cases or, more specifically, those dealing with adultery, constituted fifty per cent of the cases heard in the Nkhotakota district.[60] In 1945, matrimonial cases involving both husbands deserting their wives and wives committing adultery presented by far the largest number of cases discussed in Northern Province courts. In 1947, they also constituted a large number of the cases considered in Southern and Central Province courts. As such cases were almost always brought by injured parties, overwhelmingly women, these numbers demonstrate that, whatever the shortcomings of Native Courts, they were seen by women as providing the best hope for justice that they were likely to obtain. This is not to deny, however, that, as courts were dominated by male elders apprehensive as to the domestic consequences of labour migration, women's sexual misbehaviour was treated more severely than that of men. Indeed, adultery by women tended to be regarded as a criminal offence. In Dowa and Kasungu, courts normally imposed the maximum fine, irrespective of

[54] McCracken, 'Coercion and Control', p. 131.
[55] Hynd, 'Law, Violence and Penal Reform', p. 437.
[56] Lower River District report for 1949, MNA NS 3/1/18.
[57] Hailey, *Native Administration* Part II, p. 46.
[58] Moffat, 'Report on Native Courts' 1951, TNA CO 1015/639.
[59] Ibid.
[60] Kota Kota District report for 1934, MNA S1/89 F-J/35.

the behaviour of the husbands.[61] What is more, so Moffat noted, courts in the Central Province frequently bowed to the wishes of Roman Catholic and UMCA missionaries in refusing to grant divorces to Christian women, even in cases where they would be entitled to divorce under customary law.[62]

In the 1930s and early 1940s, there was no fundamental contradiction between support for chiefly authority and a desire for modernisation. Indeed, a number of mission-educated Christians found valuable opportunities to exercise their talents in the space created by indirect rule. Peter Mwakasungulu is the outstanding example. A one-time Livingstonia teacher, later a polygamist, Mwakasungulu used his experience as a store capitao with the ALC to found three of his own stores as well as investing in cattle and in cotton growing. When his brother, the Ngonde Kyungu fell sick in 1927, Peter stepped in as Regent. On his brother's death in 1932 he inherited the title which he continued to hold until 1965.[63] One of the very few chiefs in Malawi regarded by his subjects 'with anything approaching a superstitious veneration', Mwakasungulu, while abandoning all claims to divinity, was active in promoting many indigenous practices.[64] At the same time, he won the respect of the local DC for the skill with which he promoted the interests of his people.[65]

Other chiefs who embodied this tradition of 'progressive traditionalism' included Chief Mwase at Kasungu, and the Ngoni chief, Philip Gomani at Ntcheu. Samuel Mwase, a regular reader of the *Manchester Guardian Weekly*, subscribed for him by his kinsman, Hastings Banda, took up the position of Native Authority in 1936, following a spell as sergeant in charge of compound police at Shambani Mine in Southern Rhodesia. In subsequent years he encouraged the protection of water supplies and forests while pushing for improvements in village sanitation.[66] An inveterate self-improver with a taste for travel, Mwase visited Southern Rhodesia in 1938 and London in 1939, where he spent six months courtesy of the Nyasaland Government, assisting in a project on Chinyanja being carried out at the School of Oriental and African Studies. Lauded by the PC for the Central Province for his 'personality, influence and a genuine desire to improve his area and the lot of his people', Mwase went out of his way to promote his vision of Chewa culture. But he was also a pioneer nationalist, actively involved in the Nyasaland African Congress from its foundation in 1944.[67]

Phillip Gomani was an equally enthusiastic moderniser and, like Mwase, a man who found no difficulty in combining the burden of traditional office with involvement in modern political organisations. Educated at the Blantyre Mission and a member of the Dutch Reformed Church branch of the CCAP, Gomani was one of the first chiefs to attend the special course for Native Authorities and

---

[61] Chanock, *Law, Custom and Social Order*, pp. 39,180–90, 193–200.
[62] Moffat, Report on Native Courts, TNA CO 1015/639.
[63] Wilson, *Constitution of Ngonde*, pp. 68–69; Owen Kalinga, 'The 1959 Nyasaland State of Emergency in Old Karonga District', *JSAS*, 36, 4, 2010, p. 757.
[64] Annual Report for Northern Province, 1931, MNA S1/61/32.
[65] North Nyasa Annual Report for 1934, MNA S1/89 F-J/35.
[66] Northern Province Annual Report for 1938, MNA NC 2/1/9.
[67] Native Affairs Report for 1949, TNA CO 262/25; Tony Woods, 'Chief Mwase and the Kasungu Chewa: Ethnicity, Nationalism and Political Rhetoric in Colonial Malawi', (unpublished paper, University of Malawi).

their families introduced at the Jeanes Centre, Domasi in 1934.[68] In subsequent years he was praised by the colonial authorities for the 'dignity and efficiency' with which he administered his area, as a result of which he and Mwase were selected to represent the Central Province at the royal *indaba* held at Salisbury in 1947, presided over by King George VI.[69] At the same time, Gomani took an active part in the meetings of the Angoni Highlands Association, a body dominated by commoners, which raised various issues with the Native Authority.[70] It thus came as a considerable shock to the government that in 1953, as a protest against the introduction of the Central African Federation, Gomani, at the prompting of his son Willard, ordered his people to disregard a wide range of colonial rules concerning the dipping of cattle, soil conservation and the protection of trees.[71]

Gomani's remarkable *volte-face* after two decades of close association with the colonial authorities was one among a number of ways in which official chiefs reacted to the changing political and economic circumstances of the late 1940s and early 1950s, a time during which indirect rule virtually dissolved. One potential response to government attempts to impose far-reaching conservation measures on an increasingly hostile peasantry was for Native Authorities to take the lead in imposing coercive measures on their people. This was the policy pursued in the Port Herald District of the Lower Shire Valley by Molin Tengani, a former teacher with the South African General Mission, who succeeded his uncle as Native Authority in 1936. An energetic moderniser, Molin Tengani differed from fellow modernisers like Peter Mwakasungulu both in his open assault on traditional religion (in his case the spirit mediums of the Mbona cult) and also in his ferocious insistence that gardens should be cultivated in ridges. When the local District Officer, Lewis, embarked on a compulsory ridging campaign in 1946, Tengani became his leading enforcer. Acting with a ruthlessness that made him deeply hated, in 1948, Molin Tengani fined or imprisoned more than 400 peasants for offences relating to ridging – far more than in any other district in the country. This in turn led local members of Congress to call upon headmen and villagers to oppose these actions.[72] It was only through the direct intervention of the colonial authorities in punishing those Congress members involved that Tengani's authority was restored.[73]

Molin Tengani stands out as a chief in the Mamdani image, a local tyrant, largely oblivious to pressures from below and fusing in his person judicial, legislative and executive powers. But perhaps his special importance lies in the fact that, in Nyasaland, he was the exception rather than the rule. Most official chiefs, confronted by the twin pressures of increasing government authoritarianism and nationalist agitation, rejected both Tengani's and Gomani's responses. They involved themselves, instead, in a delicate set of manoeuvres through which they attempted to avoid risking the displeasure of the government while, at the same time, retaining the support of their subjects.

[68]   Ncheu Annual Report for 1934, MNA S1/89 A-E/35; Barbara Morrow, 'Indirect Rule in Nyasaland: Preconceptions and Problems', MA University of Malawi, 1987, pp. 48–51.
[69]   Annual Report on Native Affairs for 1947, TNA CO 262/24.
[70]   Hailey, *Native Administration*, p. 43; Annual Report on Native Affairs for 1949, TNA CO 262/25.
[71]   Annual Report on Native Affairs for 1953, TNA CO 265/25.
[72]   Lower River District Report for 1948, MNA NS 3/1/18.
[73]   Annual Report for Southern Province, 1948, MNA NS 3/1/13.

By the late 1940s these strategies looked increasingly threadbare. Frustrated by the failure of most Native Authorities to provide more than minimal assistance in imposing agricultural rules, the Government embarked on a number of piecemeal reforms. Native Treasuries were grouped together as larger financial units. 'Indirect Rule' was replaced in official rhetoric by 'Local Government'. Attempts were made to widen the constitution of District and Chiefs' Councils through the inclusion of educated commoners.[74] But with chiefs suspicious of these innovations and many commoners refusing to become involved, tangible results were few. In 'many cases', according to a report of 1951, local government institutions were 'proving unequal to the strain'.[75] The rural crisis that erupted in violence only two years later (described in Chapter 12) would confirm the veracity of these views. Many rural people, as has become increasingly clear in recent times, continued to respect the judgement of chiefs on local issues such as the allocation of land. But from the early 1950s, they ceased to operate with credibility as agents of central government. Barely two decades after indirect rule had been introduced, it had virtually collapsed.

Tribal identity & Native Associations

The introduction of indirect rule is often associated with the strengthening of tribal identities in the colonial period, although this is probably less true in the case of Nyasaland than it is of several other territories. Most pre-colonial Malawians could be identified as members of broad ethnic groupings – Mang'anja, Yao, Chewa, Ngoni, Tumbuka, Tonga and Ngonde, among others. But these groupings were flexible and did not preclude individuals possessing further identities related to clan, village or chieftaincy. In areas where Ngoni conquest states had been recently established and Ngoni men had married Chewa or Tumbuka women, the identity of their children was problematic. This was also the case in the Shire Highlands, where immigration and inter-marriage had resulted in a particularly fluid set of relationships.

It was in the northern Ngoni kingdom where belief in pre-colonial authority remained strong that tribal identity was first asserted in modern political form. Faced in the early 1920s by the removal of their paramount chief, the disintegration of their economy, the expansion of migrant labour and the growing influence in their midst of the Tumbuka language and culture, it was not surprising that members of the Ngoni elite should seek to reassert Ngoni values through the campaign to restore the paramountcy. What is more surprising is the prominent role played in this campaign by educated Christian members of the Mombera Native Association. Founded in 1920, the MNA drew its members from teachers, clerks and clergymen educated at Livingstonia. In addition, it established a close association with Jere chiefs and headmen, several of whom had also received mission education, including Amon Jere, who became President of the Association in 1921. Its meetings were normally held the day before the main meeting between Ngoni chiefs and the district officer, thus providing chiefs with an opportunity to rehearse their arguments. Later, the two bodies came

---

[74] Annual Report for Southern Province for 1947, MNA NS 3/1/12; for 1948, MNA NS 3/1/12.
[75] Memo on 'Native Administration in 1949', RHL Mss. Afr 1210.

together informally, with the result that on at least one occasion, in 1936, the district officer intervened, asking which body was in session.[76]

Central to this alliance was the Reverend Charles Chinula, one of Livingstonia's leading intellectuals, whose career exemplifies the varied stances taken by pioneer Malawian politicians in seeking to assert their independent identities within the colonial context. Although he was a Tumbuka commoner, Chinula played an active part, as secretary of the MNA, in fighting for the reestablishment of a unified northern Ngoni state under Mbelwa's leadership. Subsequently, he acted as adviser to Mbelwa in his relations with the government. But, through his writings, Chinula also contributed to the growth of a sense of wider Tumbuka identity that covered the greater part of the Northern Province. In the mid-1940s, he widened his political vision to actively embrace the cause of Nyasa nationalism while maintaining his keen interest in the politics of region and of tribe.[77] For him, as for other politicians of his generation, political identity was not exclusive; rather it involved stressing one identity over another at different times, depending on what seemed most likely to be effective.

The revival, albeit in a new form, of pre-colonial chieftaincies was accompanied by the emergence of new types of ethnic identity. One of these involved the growth of Tumbuka consciousness. In pre-colonial times, the Tumbuka had been a heterogeneous people, sharing a common language but lacking any overall political and cultural unity. In the aftermath of the Ngoni invasion, some Tumbuka went out of their way to identify themselves with the Ngoni kingdom, but others sought to assert Tumbuka identity, most particularly through the use of the Tumbuka language in preference to ChiNgoni. Initially, the Livingstonia mission, by teaching in Chinyanja and making translations in Ngoni, impeded this process. But when the mission switched to employing the Tumbuka language in schools and churches, the move to assert Tumbuka consciousness increased. In 1907, anxious to reduce Ngoni political influence, northern Tumbuka teachers succeeded in having Chilongozi Gondwe, an educated policeman, appointed Chief Chikulamayembe IX. Although the authority of the Chikulamayembe chieftaincy had been effective only in the northern part of Tumbuka country prior to its destruction during the Ngoni conquest, this did not deter the new chief and his supporters from claiming a more glorious heritage. Livingstonia-educated intellectuals, starting with the telegraph clerk Saulos Nyirenda, wrote histories of the Tumbuka, exalting the role of the Chikulamayembes. These accounts were given wider circulation in numerous publications written by the missionary, Cullen Young. His analysis was taken up by the Livingstonia pastor, Edward Bote Manda, whose ambition, as the local DC claimed, was to create 'a united Utumbuka without the stigma of subserviency to Angoni rule'. At first, the colonial authorities opposed the scheme but in 1933 relented to the extent of recognising the Chikulamayembe as native authority over a circumscribed area north of the Ngoni sphere. Although it was much smaller than Mbelwa's kingdom, this area provided a tangible focus for Tumbuka identity, one that was to grow in the 1930s as a consequence of the near-universal use of the Tumbuka language in Livingstonia's schools.

---

[76] Notes on Proceedings at a meeting of the District Commissioner with the Jere Council, 19–20 March 1936, MNA 1/15/2. This account draws on the analysis of Vail and White, 'Tribalism', pp. 160–63.

[77] The best account is Phiri, *Chinula*.

Pressures from chefs and rural intellectuals played a significant part in the re-imaging of tribal identities but so did colonial administrative initiatives. Pioneer administrators such as Harry Johnston made use of simple ethnic stereotypes in discussing their new African subjects and these were utilised in recruiting Malawians to the colonial army and police forces. By 1922, the Nyasaland Military Handbook was solemnly listing the 'Military Value of Tribes', starting with the Yao who were considered 'Excellent. Good physically, intelligent and amenable to discipline' and ending with the Chewa, whose military value was considered 'only slight'.[78] Administrators in Nyasaland, in contrast to those in Tanganyika, were less ready to assume that tribes should be utilised as units of administration, partly because of the belief that southern Malawi at least had become relatively 'detribalised' but also because of the conviction that in the Shire Highlands, the authority of European estate owners should be preserved. Eric Smith, the Cholo DC in 1934, saw little point in native authorities in the area receiving special training as they would have few opportunities to put their plans into action.[79] Nevertheless, the central thrust of colonial policy in the 1930s involved an emphasis on the tribal unit, both because of the assumption that Africans were tribal people and also as a matter of political calculation. At a time when nationalism was taking root all over the colonial empire, indirect rule was perceived as providing a system of self-government that might deflect African political ambitions into local, non-nationalist channels. In a measure designed to weaken the influence of native associations founded by educated Christians, the government, from 1935, demanded that all complaints and proposals from Malawians should be channelled through native authority councils.[80]

The establishment of administrative structures, however, was less important in the making of tribes than the experiences of Malawian migrants – around 120,000 in number in 1936. Many thousands of Lomwe and Sena immigrants, who entered Nyasaland in the first three decades of the twentieth century, might be added to this number. Much research is still required on the migrant experience in all its complexity, but three points can be made with some confidence. First, as George Shepperson noted in 1960, the experience of working abroad in the Rhodesias and South Africa appears to have stimulated a sense of national consciousness, among at least some migrants by the 1930s.[81] One influence came from above: the tendency of employers to group together Malawians from diverse ethnic backgrounds under a single label: usually 'Blantyrers' or 'Blantyre Boys', up to the First World War; 'Nyasas' or 'Nyasalanders' thereafter.[82] The second came from below: the shared antipathy of Malawians working south of the Zambesi to the profusion of pass-laws and the rigidity of racial divisions.

---

[78] 'Information for Military handbook of Nyasaland', 1922, MNA S2/6/27. For further details see McCracken, 'Authority and Legitimacy', pp. 165–66.

[79] Morrow, 'Indirect Rule', pp. 44–45.

[80] See discussion in MNA NC 1/3/6.

[81] George Shepperson, External Factors in the Development of African Nationalism, with Particular Reference to British Central Africa', *Phylon*, 22,3 1961, pp. 207–225.

[82] As late as 1937, however, J.C. Abrahams noted that 'Nyasaland Natives are [still] commonly known in the Union [of South Africa] as "Blantyre boys, but the term "Blantyre" includes practically any native from north of the Zambesi.' Abrahams, *Nyasaland Natives in the Union of South Africa and in Southern Rhodesia*, p. 2

The visit to Central Africa in 1938 of the Bledisloe Commission, set up to consider closer association between the Rhodesias and Nyasaland, provides early evidence of this sentiment. Given the opportunity to express their feelings, a wide range of Malawian witnesses, many of them present or former migrants, combined in common opposition to amalgamation and, tacitly, in support of the embryo nation state of Nyasaland.[83] It is not surprising that when the Nyasaland African Congress began to build a following in the 1950s, much of its financial and popular support came from migrants living in Southern Rhodesian urban locations.

The second point is that urban residence brought in its wake an awareness of cultural diversity. Confronted both by the uncertainties of urban living and also by the belief that ultimate security was most likely to be found back in one's rural village, migrants sought refuge in a host of cultural associations, among them ethnic, burial and mutual aid societies, linking them with their kinsfolk in the cities as well as with their rural homes. In Harare Township in Salisbury, Yao Muslims were attracted to the Mponda Yao Burial Society; there and elsewhere, Sena migrants from the Lower Shire took refuge with the Port Herald Burial Society.[84] Religious bodies were also used to bring together members with similar interests while reinforcing contacts with their home community. Presbyterians from Blantyre and Livingstonia established dozens of semi-independent congregations as far afield as Broken Hill, Bulawayo and Salisbury. Chewa migrants carried *Nyau* to Southern Rhodesia and joined in performances of *Gule Wamkula*.[85] Not all such associations were specifically tribal in character: the Nyasaland Burial Society aimed to involve workers from across the territory. However, confronted in the work market by regional and district discrepancies in skill and experience, some Malawians responded by emphasising tribal solidarity. The Achewa Improvement Society was founded in Johannesburg in 1946 by a group of Chewa migrants and intellectuals who were anxious to ensure that fellow Chewa would not lose out to better educated Tumbuka and Tonga workers in the struggle for employment.[86]

Back in Nyasaland, the recognition of a specific Lomwe tribe drew on similar frustrations. As has been previously noted, migrants from Mozambique taking up residence in the Shire Highlands early in the twentieth century were collectively identified by settlers and administrators as 'Nguru', despite the fact that they came from different clans and spoke different dialects or languages. Initially dependent for access to land on the approval of Yao chiefs and European settlers, the Nguru suffered as a marginalised people, condemned by settlers for their destruction of woodlands and denied chiefly authority under indirect rule. What a minority of Nguru had to their increasing advantage was access to western education as supplied by the Blantyre Mission. A key consequence, stressed by Vail and White, was the intervention of Lewis Bandawe, the outstanding Lomwe intellectual of his generation. Born in Mozambique, where he received his first education at a school run by John Grey Kufa, Bandawe was sent to Blantyre as a child in 1899. By 1910 he had become one of the two best educated Africans

[83] Gray, *Two Nations*, pp. 175–7.
[84] Groves, 'Malawians in Colonial Salisbury', pp. 120–137'; Van Onselen, *Chibaro*, pp. 198–99.
[85] Groves, 'Religious Lives'; McCracken, *Politics and Christianity*, p. 200.
[86] McCracken, 'Ambiguities of Nationalism', pp. 70–71.

in the mission. In 1913 he returned to Mozambique as a teacher at the newly-opened station of Mihecani. He remained there until 1928, acting for several years as head of the mission and translating the New Testament into Lomwe – the first edition published in 1930 an important step in the strengthening of Lomwe identity. On his return to Blantyre, he left the mission and became a clerk in the High Court. He was promoted to head clerk and interpreter in 1934, a post he held for 26 years. For much of this period he was the highest paid African in the civil service and the confidante of a succession of judges.[87]

Bandawe's pivotal position within the colonial order made him an ideal advocate for his people. By the early 1940s descendants of migrants from Mozambique had increasingly resented the use of the derogatory term, 'Anguru' by their neighbours. Their occasional resort to verbal and physical violence met with little sympathy from the authorities. Bandawe, by contrast, embarked on a more sophisticated strategy, designed to appeal to the British, and involving a reinterpretation of the immigrants' history to demonstrate that they were all part of a larger Lomwe tribe. His initiative led to the Lomwe Tribal Society, founded in Blantyre in 1943, with branches in Chiradzulu, Cholo and Mulanje. Two years later, the society called on the government to replace the name 'Anguru' with the word 'Alomwe' in all official correspondence; at precisely the same time Bandawe persuaded the Southern Provincial Council, of which he was a member, to pass a resolution making the same demand. In November of that year, the government acceded to the request, although this did not in itself bring to an end the frequent use by historians and others of the name 'Nguru'.[88] Nevertheless, from this time Lomwe identity was asserted with increasing confidence, not just by Lomwe intellectuals but by many villagers who had suffered the stigma of inferiority.

The third point to note about the interaction between labour migrancy and tribalism concerns the influence of returned migrants on their rural localities. In sharp contrast to contemporary assumptions that migrants might become 'detribalised' through their experiences in Southern African cities, most migrants were acutely concerned with preserving their interests at home during the period when they were working outside Nyasaland.[89] Many of the discussions in chiefs' courts and native association meetings focused on issues near to the heart of male migrants – female adultery, the failure to consult *Nkhoswe* in divorce cases, and the payment of bridewealth.[90] Migrants were thus drawn into a *de facto* alliance with chiefs. However, by the 1940s, as Moffat noted, it had become an uneasy relationship, often transformed into mutual hostility and suspicion.[91] Access to land and claims to traditional office were also matters of great importance to many migrants, including some of the best educated, most professionally successful Malawians of their time. Ernest Alexander Muwamba, for example, was a senior clerk and interpreter with the Northern Rhodesian Government for many years before returning to Nyasaland to become one of the first African members of the Legislative Council in 1949. Yet Muwamba was

[87] Lewis Mataka Bandawe, *Memoirs of a Malawian* (Blantyre, 1971).
[88] Bandawe, *Memoirs*, pp.22–23; 128–9; White, *Magomero*, pp. 193–4.
[89] The classic pioneering study is Van Velsen, 'Labour Migration'.
[90] Chanock, *Law, Custom and Social Order*, pp. 192–216.
[91] Vail and White, *Tribalism*, p. 159; Moffat, 'Report on Native Courts'.

also a passionate tribalist who fought a long campaign to have his kinsman, Chief Chiweyu, recognised as the Tonga paramount chief.[92]

It took Muwamba's cousin, Clements Kadalie, charismatic leader of the Industrial and Commercial Workers Union of South Africa, to put this campaign into perspective. Writing to his cousin in 1923, Kadalie supported the move 'to reclaim the throne now temporarily with Marenga'. But he emphasised that this was not enough:

> I frankly confess that that family and its throne ought to be maintained but what will that be when speaking after modern civilization? It is the white man that is ruling Nyasaland and not Marenga or any black chief. … What we require is that we shall send men to sit as legislators at Zomba where laws are made to govern Nyasaland.[93]

Kadalie recognised that liberation required obtaining power at the centre of the territory and not just at the locality. This was not a view held by most educated Malawians between the wars. Instead, the native associations they founded were essentially hybrid bodies, closely associated to the politics of tribe but also with aspirations to combine at a regional or territorial level. Historians in recent years have tended to minimalise the importance of this aspiration, yet it is striking how many of these leaders were to play influential roles in the first, in some respects, most attractive, stage of Nyasa nationalism.

It was among teachers, ministers and clerks educated at the Livingstonia Mission that native associations in Nyasaland had their origin. The first, the North Nyasa Association, was formed as early as 1912 with Peter Mwakasun-gulu, the future chief, as president and Levi Mumba, a senior clerk in mission and later in government employment, as secretary. With the outbreak of war and the recruitment into the army of 38 members of the association, almost all of them as interpreters or clerks, meetings were temporarily halted. But in 1919 the North Nyasa Association was revived, to be joined early in 1920 by the Mombera Native Association and the West Nyasa Native Association. On Levi Mumba's promptings, the Southern Province Native Association was founded at Zomba in 1923, to be followed by further associations based at Chiradzulu and Blantyre. In addition, in 1929, the key inspiration behind many of these bodies, Levi Mumba, established the Representative Committee of Northern Province Native Associations in Zomba. An umbrella group, drawing for its membership on northern civil servants, the Committee gave tangible political form to northern regionalism although it frequently took up territory-wide issues.[94]

From the first, the methods employed by the associations were strictly consti-tutional. Complaints were forwarded to the central government concerning a wide range of issues including the need for local development, concern over the use of forced labour, racial discrimination, and the quality of education. Where government or mission employees constituted the majority of their member-ship, their criticisms tended to be muted, but where, as in the Central Province, shopkeepers and tobacco farmers dominated the meetings, criticisms of the

[92]   McCracken, *Politics and Christianity*, pp. 149–50, 289–90.
[93]   C. Kadalie to E.A. Muwamba, 29 April 1923, MNA S2/71/23.
[94]   J. Van Velsen, 'Some Early Pressure Groups in Malawi', in Stokes and Brown, *Zambesian Past*, pp. 376–411; Gray, *Two Nations*, pp. 170–75; McCracken, *Politics and Christianity*, pp. 257–73.

Native Tobacco Board and calls for government assistance were expressed with a vehemence that attracted the tacit support of many of the smaller farmers.[95] The weakness of the Central Province Native Association, founded in 1927, was that its principal architect, George Simeon Mwase, was a maverick Tonga intellectual whose attempts to interfere in Chewa succession disputes left him deeply unpopular. Its strength was that it brought Chewa tobacco-growers into a temporary alliance with the Blantyre-educated Ngoni, Ralph Chinyama, the leading independent African farmer in the district and a future President of the Nyasaland African Congress.

Confronted by the growing hostility of government, the Central Province Native Association had, like several other rural associations, fallen into abeyance by the 1930s. But this did not prevent those associations that remained active from achieving a distinct success on a major issue. Under pressure from settlers in Southern and Northern Rhodesia, Britain appointed a Royal Commission in 1937 under the former Governor General of New Zealand, Lord Bledisloe, to report whether closer cooperation between the three Central African states was desirable. In 1938 it took evidence from whites in all three territories and also from African groups north of the Zambezi, although not in Southern Rhodesia. The response in Nyasaland was particularly well organised. At Blantyre, in June, about 200 members of the Blantyre Native Association informed the commission of their unanimous opposition to amalgamation. A few days later at Lilongwe, native authorities from the Northern Province submitted a memorandum, prepared by the indefatigable Levi Mumba, expressing hostility to any form of closer union with the Rhodesias.[96] Through Mumba's efforts, chiefs and civil servants, Northerners and Southerners, had combined in expressing near identical views. The impact of this opposition deeply influenced the commissioners. In their report, they concluded that 'the striking unanimity...of the native opposition to amalgamation...are factors [sic] which cannot in our judgement be ignored.'[97] White settler hopes for amalgamation remained high but with the outbreak of the Second World War a year later, plans were put on hold. At the very least, Levi Mumba and the native associations that he had initiated and encouraged had won some precious breathing space for a Nyasaland, under colonial as opposed to settler control.

---

[95] Martin Chanock, 'The New Men Revisited' in Macdonald, *From Nyasaland to Malawi*, pp. 234–53.
[96] Gray, *Two Nations*, pp. 174–77.
[97] Quoted Gray, p. 177.

10
The Age of Development

Introduction

In May 1949 Col. Laurens van der Post visited Malawi on behalf of the Colonial Development Corporation to investigate the economic potential of the two main mountainous areas in the country, Mulanje and the Nyika Plateau. In *Venture to the Interior*, the immensely popular account of his expedition – still in print and with sales of over a million – van der Post recorded his impressions of a territory on the cusp of economic and political change. Blantyre was a disappointment, its buildings 'drab and insignificant… dumped by the side of a road full of dust'. But of even greater concern was the attitude of the colonial officials he met, several of them individually charming, but many 'with set, sallow, lifeless, disillusioned faces under wide-brimmed hats', killing time before their retirement to Britain.[1] In passage after passage, colonialism is depicted as an inoffensive but superficial phenomenon, as deeply alien to Africa as the English sweet peas and roses that its representatives cultivated in their gardens, and as doomed, ultimately, to fail.[2]

It is ironic that van der Post's depiction of a colonial state still to recover from the lethargy into which it had sunk during the Second World War should have been written at a time when the transformation of Britain's relationship with her African colonies was already well under way. All over colonial Africa, the post-war decade witnessed a 'second colonial occupation' designed to restructure African economies in the interests of the British consumer and involving the large-scale investment of men and money.[3] In Malawi, however, the form it took had a number of distinctive features. First of all, in contrast to the situation in Nigeria and the Gold Coast, where a number of important new initiatives were taken during the war, neither Sir Donald Mackenzie Kennedy, Governor from 1939 to

---

[1] Laurens van der Post, *Venture to the Interior* (London, 1952), pp. 77–79, 89–90.
[2] Ibid., pp. 84–86, 173. For a more detailed discussion see John McCracken, 'Imagining the Nyika Plateau: Laurens van der Post, the Phoka and the Making of a National Park', *JSAS*, 32, 4, 2006, pp. 812–85.
[3] D.A. Low and J.M. Lonsdale, 'Introduction' in D.A. Low and Alison Smith (eds), *History of East Africa*, III (Oxford, 1976), p. 12.

237

1942, nor his successor, Sir Edmund Richards (1942–48) demonstrated any enthusiasm for the task of economic or social regeneration. It was therefore not until the arrival in Zomba of the energetic Sir Geoffrey Colby in March 1948 that the new colonialism was effectively launched.[4] Second, Colby's ambitious programme of economic and social engineering was given heightened urgency by fears of a growing agrarian and security crisis – a crisis that was to erupt in open violence during the 'troubles' of 1953. In an influential study, Terence Ranger has compared the outbreak of the Mau Mau revolt in Kenya in 1952 with later eruptions of peasant violence in Zimbabwe and Mozambique.[5] A better comparison, however, would have been between the position of the White High-lands of Kenya and the Shire Highlands of Malawi, both of them areas where, in the 1940s, the already fraught relationship between planters and tenants deteri-orated beyond control. Finally, the strategies for constitutional change that were an essential, although at times an apparently contradictory, element in the new colonialism, took different forms in Malawi from those in most of British Africa. In the Gold Coast and Nigeria, post-war plans for constitutional change involved the expectation that, in a generation or less, political authority would be trans-ferred to friendly African successors.[6] In Nyasaland, by contrast, British metro-politan strategies focused on the incorporation of Nyasaland into a federation with Southern and Northern Rhodesia – a development of which the effect would be to transfer authority into the hands of a settler minority.

The Second World War

The Second World War is one of the least studied periods in the history of colo-nial Malawi but its significance should not be discounted. In the absence of a demand for carriers, far fewer people were commandeered for service in the war than in the period 1914–18 and the disruptive impact on local economies was correspondingly less. Nevertheless, it is important to note that more Malawians were recruited as soldiers during the Second World War than during the First and that the experiences they gained – of different countries, peoples, skills and ideas – were infinitely more varied. Colonial violence was less extreme than it had been in 1916–17. Nevertheless, the war imposed strains on African loyalties to the imperial project – strains that were to grow in intensity during the next decade.

From the perspective of Britain, the value of Malawi to the war effort was related almost entirely to manpower, although opinion was divided as to whether military recruits for the KAR or labourers for southern African mines were of greater strategic importance. On the outbreak of hostilities in Europe in September 1939, Acting Governor Hall banned all labour recruitment to the south in the belief that the needs of the military would be paramount. A month later, however, the British Government reversed this measure under pressure from Southern Rhodesia and the South African Chamber of Mines.[7] From then

---

[4]   Colin Baker, *Development Governor. A Biography of Sir Geoffrey Colby* (London, 1994), pp. 77–96.
[5]   Terence Ranger, *Peasant Consciousness and Guerrilla War in Zimbabwe* (London, 1985).
[6]   For a level-headed introduction see, John Hargreaves, *The Decolonization of Africa* (London, 1988).
[7]   John Martin to Malcolm Macdonald, 11 December 1939; Hall to CO, 27 April 1940, TNA CO 525/185/440531/1.

on labour recruitment to the south continued to take place, although, with the entry of Italy into the war in 1940, priority was given to the 'enlistment of as many fit men as possible in the KAR'.[8] Outright compulsion was largely avoided. Instead, provincial and district officers threatened Native Authorities and Headmen with the loss of privileges if they failed to provide sufficient numbers of recruits.[9] In the early years, alarmingly large numbers of the men thus provided either deserted or were rejected on medical grounds. But by August 1942 a total of 16,400 Nyasas were serving with the KAR as compared with fewer than 2,000 at the beginning of the war.[10] Altogether 12 Nyasaland battalions were raised out of a total of 43 KAR battalions. Other Nyasa soldiers were recruited into the Artillery, Engineers, Service Corps and Medical Corps, bringing the total of those enlisted by 1945 to around 27,000 as compared with fewer than 19,000 Malawian askaris recruited in the First World War.[11]

At first there were fears that the high reputation gained by Malawian troops during 1914–1918 would not be sustained. Writing in July 1940 the Governor warned: 'If your military commanders expect the type of fighting man we raised in the last war, they will be grievously disappointed.'[12] But following the success of the 1st Battalion KAR in resisting an Italian attack on the border post of Moyale in Kenya, this opinion rapidly changed. During 1941 Nyasa contingents played an active part in the rout of the Italian army in Somaliland and Ethiopia; the next year, a Nyasa battalion took the lead in the defeat of pro-German French forces in Madagascar. Faced now by the capitulation of its south east Asia empire to the Japanese invaders, Britain turned to Africa for support in the gruelling Burma campaign. In 1944, four Nyasa battalions out of a total of 17 KAR units were posted to Burma. In the next few months they advanced down the Chindwin in the face of determined Japanese opposition, fighting their way through dense jungle and across precipitous ridges in the teeth of a heavy monsoon.[13]

There can be little doubt of the vivid impact of their war-time experiences on the African troops demobilised from the Army in 1945 and 1946. In the preceding years they had lived in as many as half a dozen countries – Ethiopia, Somaliland, Madagascar, Ceylon, India and Burma – and had fought alongside people of different races and cultures – British, Indian, American, Nigerian and Ghanaian. It is hardly surprising that, to the colonial authorities, they appeared as an unsettling and slightly dangerous group, expert in modern weapons, open to new political ideas of socialism or nationalism, and in receipt of substantial

8 Circular to all officers of Nyasaland Civil Service to Governor, 25 October 1940 enclosed in Kennedy to CO, 26 October 1940, TNA CO 525/185/44053/1.
9 'Notes of a Meeting with N.A. M'Mbelwa and Other Chiefs at Mzimba on 19th July', No date [1940], MNA S 41/1/8/1. [I owe this reference to Tim Lovering]. See also Mapopa Chipeta, 'Labour in a Colonial Context. The Growth and Development of the Malawian Wage Labour Force during the Colonial period', Ph.D. dissertation, University of Dalhousie, 1986, pp. 239–40.
10 Kennedy to CO, 17 April 1942, TNA CO 525/189/44053/24.
11 Figures provided by Tim Lovering who has studied the relevant files in MNA S33/2/1/1 and S33/2/2/1. See also Memo by T.D. Thomson on 'African Demobilisation: Progress to 31 August 1946', MNA LB 8/2/4–5. It was estimated that a further 7,000 Malawians enlisted in South African, Southern Rhodesian, Northern Rhodesian and Tanganyikan units bringing the total number involved to some 34,000. Richards to Stanley, 17 Jan 1944, MNA S33/2/2/1.
12 Kennedy to Major General D.P. Dickinson, 24 July 1940, MNA S 41/1/8/1.
13 Moyse-Bartlett, *King's African Rifles*, Part V; Gerald Hanley, *Monsoon Victory* (London, 1946).

balances of pay calculated at £468,000 in total in 1946.[14] More than 3,000 askaris were trained as lorry drivers by the army, and some of these carried this skill into civilian life. Lali Lubani, for example, joined the Central African Transport Company in Blantyre on his demobilisation from the KAR in 1946, later bought his own lorry, and moved into self-employment as a transporter.[15] Several former soldiers, including Lubani, also participated in new political organisations. Ex-askari delegates were active at the annual conferences of the Nyasaland African Congress in 1945 and 1946, complaining, in the latter year, about 'the little payments given to them and also that all promises made by Government about pensions, bonuses etc. have not been fulfilled'.[16] Most, it would appear, were content to return to their villages, their gratuities invested in cattle or in fish trading.[17] But many of these shared with home-based peasants a growing discontent at the acute shortage of land in the Southern Province. The main item for discussion at the Ntondwe demobilisation camp was said to be the desire for land among the inhabitants of Zomba, Blantyre and Mulanje districts. The camp commandant noted that 'In the last connection, the King Charles's Head of Magomero monotonously obtrudes itself.'[18] It is intriguing to note that the young George Shepperson, Malawi's most eminent historian, gained his first knowledge of John Chilembwe from the askaris he commanded in the Burmese jungle.[19]

For those who remained in Malawi the impact of the war was less dramatic. With demand now growing again, African producers were able to benefit from an increase in prices for tobacco although the sharpest rises came from 1946 in the immediate post-war decade. Tea planters also benefited from a rise in prices, brought about in part through the fall of the Dutch East Indies to the Japanese in 1942, but in their case production remained virtually static throughout the period of the war.[20] Wartime disruption of shipping, moreover, led to a shortage of imports. Iron hoes were in such short supply that the Government attempted to encourage a revival in their making from scrap iron.[21] Fish trading suffered from a lack of tyres for bicycles.[22] Cotton goods were also in very short supply. For the three years ending in 1945 an annual average of less than 10 million yards of cotton goods were imported into Nyasaland as compared with 12.5 million yards in 1938 and 16.5 million yards in 1947 when the shortage began to ease.[23] As elsewhere in Africa, the Government intervened to set prices for staple commodities and to introduce a much-ignored monthly minimum wage (10 shillings per 30–day ticket in the Southern Province in 1946). Overall, however,

[14] Thomson, 'African Demobilisation'.
[15] Joey Power, 'Individual enterprise and enterprising individuals: African entrepreneurship in Blantyre and Limbe, 1907–1953', Ph.D. thesis, University of Dalhousie, 1991, pp. 275–76; Colin Baker, 'Civil Responses to War: the Nyasaland Civil Service 1939–1945', *SOMJ*, 38, 1 (1985), pp. 44–45.
[16] Minutes of the Third Annual General Meeting of the Nyasaland African Congress', 23–26 September, 1946, MNA PCC 1/4/1
[17] Phyllis Deane, *Colonial Social Accounting* (Cambridge, 1953), p. 87
[18] Thomson, Progress Report on African Demobilisation to 31 December 1945, MNA LB 8/2/4–5.
[19] George Shepperson, 'Edinburgh and Nyasaland', in A.H.M. Kirk-Green (ed.), *The Emergence of African History at British Universities* (Oxford, 1995), pp. 143–45.
[20] Palmer, 'Nyasaland Tea Industry', p. 233.
[21] *Annual Report on the Southern Province* for 1940, MNA NS 3/1/9.
[22] *South Nyasa District Report*, 1942, MNA NSF 4/1/6.
[23] Deane, *Colonial Social Accounting*, p. 85.

wages failed to keep pace with the rise in the cost of basic foodstuffs and merchandise with the result that, by the late 1940s, many workers on estates and elsewhere were even more impoverished than before.[24]

White settlers generally benefited from the rise of cash crop prices. But this was not the case for members of the innovative Italian community, their status transformed in June 1940 to that of enemy aliens, whose estates were expropriated by the newly created Custodian of Enemy Property and sub-leased to their British rivals. Not until 1944 were the first Italians allowed to repossess their farms. In the intervening period, the land had been mercilessly exploited by the British leaseholders, several of whom took advantage of the rise in prices to produce the largest possible amount of tobacco at the smallest possible cost.[25]

As the war progressed, new sources of imperial funding became available but with disappointingly meagre results. Malawi benefited to the tune of about £100,000 from Britain's Colonial Development and Welfare Act of 1940, an imaginative measure designed at once to stimulate the economies of the poorest colonies and to stave off American anti-imperial pressure. But with internal revenues increasing only slowly, funds for development remained very tight. By 1944 Government expenditure on education was a miserly £36,096 as compared with £21,405 five years earlier (see Table 10.1). No government secondary school had yet been opened. Instead, the entire provision for education remained in the hands of the missions with the aid of small government grants in aid – a total of £24,000 in 1944.[26] Only two secondary schools existed in the country – Blantyre Secondary, a Protestant institution, opened by the Federated missions in 1940 and Zomba Catholic Secondary opened in 1942. Their joint enrolment in 1945 was 71, all boys.[27]

Table 10.1
Nyasaland Government Expenditure: Selected Departments
Value in £s

Date	Agric.	Education	Medical	Native Admin.	Police	Prov & Dist Adm	PWD
1934	12,655	17,492	49,138	–	20,552	53,673	31,733
1939	21,812	21,405	51,993	11,145	22,112	48,418	66,377
1944	36,253	36,096	69,999	22,094	27,738	45,845	82,698
1946	63,531	94,441	91,112	25,906	36,195	6,016	146,993
1948	103785	133,333	142,750	272,997	51,202	92144	3253,243
1950	183,302	184,598	167,569	450,840	110,388	133,429	1,044273
1952	209,334	246,449	232,586	490,094	131.884	157,189	972,705
1954	285,291	304,067		580,195	293.268	203,847	958,755
1956	343,614	362,633		994,898	366,278	254,115	1,400652

[24] Chipeta, 'Labour in a Colonial Context', p. 263; John McCracken, 'Blantyre Transformed: Class, Conflict and Nationalism in Colonial Malawi', *JAH*, 39, 2 (1998), p. 254.

[25] McCracken, 'Italian Community in Malawi', pp. 326–27.

[26] *Annual Report of the Nyasaland Educational Department for 1949*, p. 1.

[27] Isaac C. Lamba, 'The Nyasaland Post-War Development Plan: A Historical Examination of African Education Development Strategies up to 1961 with particular reference to the Primary and Secondary Sectors' in Centre of African Studies, *Malawi: An Alternative Pattern of Development*, p. 174.

Other government activities were equally starved of funds. Despite its importance to the maintenance of colonial order, the police force in the mid-1940s remained an ill-trained body, made up of 18 European officers, all based in the Southern Province, and 494 mainly illiterate African policemen, many of them dressed in ragged uniforms.[28] The Agricultural Department, according to its Director, was badly understaffed. Health provision was inadequate despite the fact that more money went to the Medical Department than to any other spending department in the territory. Even the passage of a new Colonial Development and Welfare Act in 1945, with its promise of a further £2 million to Nyasaland, failed to bring the transformation required. Under its auspices an extra £345,000 was pumped into primary and secondary education in the next five years, resulting in the opening of the first government secondary school at Dedza in 1951.[29] But other developments were slower to take shape. Writing in 1948, shortly after his arrival in the protectorate, Sir Geoffrey Colby noted: 'We are now reaping the harvest of the parsimony of the past forty years... and it is obvious that the neglect of forty years cannot be repaired in a matter of months.' In Colby's view, 'the years that have passed have produced an attitude of helplessness and frustration among a considerable proportion of the Service' with the result that 'standards here are definitely lower than in Nigeria.' What was required, he argued, was a complete overhaul of the machinery of government combined with the investment of still more funds.[30]

Colonial planning

In his aptly entitled study, *Development Governor*, Colin Baker portrays Sir Geoffrey Colby as laying 'the economic foundation upon which independence was later built'.[31] The claim is a controversial one, ignoring the contribution both of colonial planners in Britain and of African producers in Malawi, but it is accurate in two important respects. Having spent much of the war as government controller of imports, exports and prices in Nigeria, Colby was a passionate developer, convinced of the virtues of state intervention in transforming economic structures.[32] Yet he was also, unwittingly, a liberator in the sense that, by 1956, colonial rule in Nyasaland had been weakened, perhaps fatally, as a result of policies he had pursued. Large in stature and generous of heart, Colby was a natural autocrat, very hard working, decisive in judgement and unwilling to countenance alternative views. As a result of his drive, roads, houses and schools were built in abundance between 1948 and 1956, the civil service more than doubled in size and the government's ordinary revenues increased from £1.625 million to £5.664 million, a rise of 248 per cent.[33] Yet Colby's blindness to the nature of African political developments contributed to the crisis in which his successor, Sir Robert Armitage, was to find himself engulfed.

[28] *Annual Report of the Police Department for 1945*; Geoffrey J. Morton, *Just the Job: some experiences of a Colonial Policeman* (London, 1957), pp. 232–40.
[29] *Reports of the Nyasaland Educational Department*, 1945–51.
[30] Colby to C.E. Lambert, 13 Dec 1948, TNA CO 525/214/4445.
[31] Baker, *Development Governor*, p. xiv.
[32] Ibid., pp. 48–54, 80–96.
[33] Ibid., p. 96.

Colby's strategy was predicated on the extension of government control over the marketing of African cash crops. During the Second World War it had become common for independent peasants to sell their tobacco to estate owners rather than to the Native Tobacco Board.[34] No sooner had he arrived in Nyasaland, however, than Colby brought this practice to a halt. An amended Tobacco Ordinance was passed in 1948 re-establishing the legal monopoly of the NTB over the purchase of Trust Land Tobacco. In the same year Colby signalled that he intended to use this monopoly to increase government revenues by extending the already large gap that existed between the prices obtained on the auction floor for tobacco and those paid to African smallholders.[35] With world prices now rapidly rising, surpluses quickly accrued. In 1945 growers had obtained an average of 3.70 pence per lb for their tobacco, 66 per cent of the auction price. By 1952 the price they obtained had risen to 6.39 pence per lb but the percentage of the auction price had fallen to just 38.4.[36] Some of this, in theory, went to the fund introduced by the Government in 1945 in an effort to stabilise prices. But on Colby's instructions, the greater part was invested in employing a vastly increased number of European and African agricultural supervisors to spearhead 'a great drive to improve the industry, particularly by an improvement of yield, cultivation methods, curing and grading'.[37] Additional marketing boards were established for cotton in 1951 and for maize, peanuts and pulses in 1952; these in turn were amalgamated with the NTB in 1956 to form a single organisation. Designated the Agricultural Produce Marketing Board, this monster body was made responsible for marketing all significant African-grown cash crops. Prices paid to peasants were kept artificially low while the funds made available to government correspondingly increased. It was the marketing boards (and hence Malawian peasants), even more than CDWF grants-in-aid, that paid for the remarkable growth in the number of staff employed by the Agricultural Department – from 628 in 1948 to 1,417 eight years later.[3] In all, up to March 1956 some £1,381,000 was channelled from marketing boards to the Government-controlled Native Development and Welfare Fund.[39]

As funds increased, aided by the growth in customs duties, taxation and loans, so Colby's developmental strategy unfolded. Priority was given to infrastructural development with the result that expenditure by the Public Works Department soared: from £147,000 in 1946 to nearly £1,401,000 ten years later. Much of this expenditure was spent on housing for European and African staff. But there was also substantial investment in restructuring and tarring roads (particularly those radiating from Blantyre to Zomba, Cholo, and the airport now open at Chileka), in constructing hospitals and schools, and in erecting public buildings. By 1958 the council chamber and Government Press buildings in Zomba had been completed, as had the first stage of the large Queen Elizabeth Hospital in Blantyre, and the High Court and Post Office in Limbe.[40] Colby, however,

[34] McCracken, 'Share-Cropping in Malawi', pp, 47–48.
[35] Minutes of meeting between the Governor and the Nyasaland Northern Province Association, Lilongwe, 23 Nov 1948, Central Province Association Papers [CPA], MNA.
[36] Report of the Nyasaland Agricultural Production Marketing Board for 1960, p. 15.
[37] NTB Minutes for 26 Nov 1949, MNA 1C/88 NTB/1.
[38] Baker, *Development Governor*, pp. 86–87.
[39] Colby to Lennox-Boyd, 24 March 1956, TNA CO 1015/1133.
[40] *Annual Reports of the Public Works Department*, 1951–1958.

was unsuccessful in his protracted attempts to bring Nyasaland Railways under government control. Nor was he able to significantly reduce the annual loan charges on the railways of some £140,000 a year that the Protectorate was required to bear.[41] Deficiencies in transport thus continued to hamper the efforts of Nyasaland's producers, although there was at least the consolation that in 1953 the Federal Government took over responsibility for servicing the loans.

Infrastructural investment was accompanied by large-scale developmental planning, much of it targeted on the north. With the coming of peace, politicians in Britain had begun to look to Africa for support in reviving the war-torn imperial economy. The Colonial Development Corporation, founded in 1948, was seen as the vehicle for this purpose. In the next few years CDC money was poured into a variety of highly speculative, capital-intensive schemes in the sparsely populated highlands of northern Malawi with the joint aim of invigorating the economy of the 'dead north' and, more importantly, of producing precious raw materials for Britain's hard-pressed consumers. The Vipya Development Scheme was the largest and most ambitious example. Originating in 1946 with the establishment on the Viphya Plateau by the Nyasaland Government of an experimental tung plantation (tung oil was an essential ingredient in certain types of paint), the scheme took off from 1948 when the CDC took over the experiment with the intention of extending the area under cultivation from 500 to 20,000 acres.[42] With British politicians anxious to find a source of tung oil other than the leading producer, China, capital was easy to find. In 1949, the unusually large sum of £1,410,000 was set aside for the project along with a further sum of £149,000 to be used to grow rice and maize on the marshlands near Nkhata Bay (the Limpasa Dambo) to feed the workers on the tung estates. Large numbers of Europeans were brought in to run the scheme and Mzuzu township was founded as the headquarters of the project.[43] By 1953, however, the scheme had run into serious difficulties. Rice growing had proved to be beyond the capability of the inexperienced European managers. Only 3,200 acres of tung had been planted, far fewer than was projected in the plan and, with China poised to re-enter the market, prices had begun to fall. The painful decision was therefore taken to scale down the project at a loss of well over £700,000.[44] Tung continued to be grown on the Viphya but on a much smaller scale than previously envisaged. Instead, by 1964 the first fateful steps had been taken to cover the Viphya with softwood plantations to be grown under the auspices of the new Malawi government.[45] Meanwhile, in the mid-1950s many of the CDC's offices and houses were sold off to the Government, which now made Mzuzu the administrative capital of the north.

The failure of the Vipya Development Scheme was matched by the fate of other CDC projects. Given past experience, there were good reasons for seeking to develop the production of flue-cured tobacco in the Kasungu district but not

---

[41] Baker, *Development Governor*, pp. 143–79; Phillips, *Obscurity to Bright Dawn*, pp. 51–56.
[42] The best and most detailed account is Canaan R. K. Phiri, 'The Viphya Tung Scheme, 1945–1968: a futile strategy to "awaken the dead north"', History Seminar Paper, 1987/88, Chancellor College.
[43] CDC Annual Reports for 1951 and 1952, PRO CO 1015/674; Report by Walter Baumann on Tung Oil from Nyasaland, 3 May 1948, MNA 10170; S.G.B. Williams, 'The Beginnings of Mzuzu with some biographical notes of some Vipya Tung Project managers', *SOMJ*, 22, 1. 1969, pp. 46–50.
[44] Quarterly Report of CDC to 30 June 1953, TNA CO 1015/674.
[45] Pike, *Malawi*, pp. 198–9; 204; Phiri, 'Viphya Tung Scheme'.

when the contribution of African producers was systematically ignored. The capital-intensive scheme started early in 1950, with the large-scale use of bull-dozers in order to clear the land. It quickly ran into difficulties. By the end of the 1953 season £193,000 of capital had been invested in planting 500 acres with tobacco, yet losses stood at some £54,000. Costs of production were estimated at 46.5 pence per lb, more than twice the price at which Kasungu tobacco was selling.[46]

Developments on the Nyika Plateau took a similar form.[47] One of the remotest parts of Malawi, only sparsely populated by the Phoka people, the rolling grasslands of the Nyika had been targeted as a possible site for European settlement, initially for Jewish refugees, from as early as 1938.[48] Two expeditions, one of them led by Laurens van der Post, investigated the area in 1949 and recommended that it should be colonised by stock farmers.[49] In 1951, however, the CDC sent out a further expedition headed by the forestry expert, Dr Ian Craib, who reported that the Nyika was 'the finest stretch of afforestable land I have ever seen'.[50] The CDC, in consequence, set up the Nyika Forestry Syndicate in 1952 in partnership with a British-based firm of paper manufac-turers. A pilot plot of pines and eucalypti was planted at Chelinda as the first stage in what was envisaged as a massive operation, leading to the planting of 250,000 acres of cedars producing 380,000 tons of paper a year.[51] Pine growth, however, was slower in the early years than had been expected and there were growing fears of 'of political opposition by the local African population – arising from a jealous regard for land rights...and suspicion that the new enterprise would involve considerable European immigration'.[52] In 1957, therefore, the CDC withdrew, leaving the Nyika virtually undisturbed. By this time more than £24,000 had been spent on the project, an 'almost unbelievable sum' given the smallness of the Chelinda plot, but one that shrinks into insignificance compared with the overall costs of at least £1 million (not much short of the entire internal revenue for Nyasaland in 1947) incurred by the CDC's schemes between 1948 and 1954.[53] It could no longer be claimed that the north was starved of funds although, with the exception of the construction of Mzuzu and the building of a jetty at Nkhata Bay, it was difficult to see what northerners had gained from them. By November 1950, educated Malawians were reported as being 'critical of the CDC because it acted for its own benefit, did not train Africans, and employed a growing army of European supervisory workers'.[54]

Large scale planned development was not confined to the CDC. Following the

[46] R.E. Brooks to A. Creech Jones, 1 Feb 1950, TNA CO 525/221; CDC Annual Report for 1950; CDC Quarterly Reports to March and June 1953, TNA CO 1015/680.
[47] For an overview see McCracken, 'Imagining the Nyika Plateau'.
[48] Governor of Nyasaland to CO, 12 Nov 1945, TNA CO 525/199/44362/1945.
[49] E.G. Barnes, 'Report on the Nyika Plateau with special reference to its suitability for stock', 12 May 1949; G. Fowler, 'Report on the Nyika Plateau', 9 Sept 1949, MNA NN 1/15/14.
[50] Dr Ian Craib, 'The Afforestability of the Nyika Plateau', 17 Sep 1951, TNA CO 1015/479.
[51] Notes by J.E. Rendall, 1 Oct 1951 and R. Terrell, 20 April 1953, on CDC Quarterly Reports, TNA CO 1015/479.
[52] Note by I.H. Harris, 12 April 1960, TNA CO 852/1785.
[53] Note by E.S. Collier, 29 Dec 1953, TNA CO 1015/479.
[54] Michael Cowen, 'Early Years of the Colonial Development Corporation: British State Enterprise Overseas during Late Colonialism', unpublished paper, Institute of Commonwealth Studies, London, 1982/83.

permanent flooding in 1939 of extensive marshlands in the Lower Shire Valley, colonial officials had been concerned to find ways of improving conditions in the area.[55] Fluctuations in the levels of the Shire River and the Lake were perceived as the fundamental problem to be tackled. It was believed that if stabilisation were to be achieved, the waters of the Shire could be harnessed to irrigate thousands of acres of fertile land, thus boosting the production of cotton. The experts were divided on how best to achieve this aim, so in 1948 Colby took the initiative by appointing the British engineering company, Halcrow, to come up with recommendations. As Beinart has noted, the resultant Shire Valley Project was 'by far the most ambitious and potentially most expensive proposal for planned development on the government's agenda'.[56] Involving the construction of a barrage to control the outflow of the lake, the scheme, in Colby's words, was a 'gigantic project' which would 'revolutionise the whole life of the Southern Province and, indeed, the economic life of the Protectorate as a whole'.[57] Costed at a colossal £78 million in 1954, it included plans for the building of hydro-electric power stations and the reclamation of up to 320,000 acres of land in the Lower Shire Valley. This would be used in the development of large-scale sugar plantations under European control and also in the provision of land for smallholders on which they would grow cotton and rice. CDC funding was not forthcoming. But, after protracted negotiations, Colby persuaded the Federal Government to fund the first stage of the project, the building of a temporary bund across the Shire River in 1956. The following year, nature, in the shape of an unexpected further rise in the levels of the lake, then took a part, breaching the bund in 1957 and flooding riverside villages. This brought to an end all hopes of a comprehensive scheme, although several of the constituent parts remained to be revived later. Both the power station built after independence at Nkala Falls and the sugar plantation opened by Lonrho at Nchalo in the 1960s were scaled-down versions of what Colby had planned, but with the modification that Lonhro's project, unlike its colonial predecessor, allowed no role for African smallholders.[58]

The cash crop boom

The succession of disappointments suffered in the 1950s by a variety of capital-intensive schemes stands in contrast with the expansion of the export economy as a whole. Fuelled by a growth in international prices for a wide range of primary products in the post-war years, Nyasaland's cash crop boom benefited both African peasants and European planters. Between 1945 and 1953 the total value of agricultural produce increased nearly four times from £1,805,000 to £7,040,000.[59] Thereafter, the increase was smaller, but still significant – to nearly £10,000,000 in 1960.[60] Rising tea prices linked to a doubling of production

---

[55] Mandala, *Work and Control*, p. 208.
[56] William Beinart, 'Agricultural Planning and the Late Colonial Technical Imagination: the Lower Shire Valley in Malawi, 1940–1960' in Centre of African Studies, *Malawi*, p. 130.
[57] Colby to Huggins, 13 Nov 1954, quoted in Beinart, 'Agricultural Planning', p. 133.
[58] Ibid., pp. 141–42.
[59] A. G. Irvine, *The Balance of Payments of Rhodesia and Nyasaland 1945–1954* (London, 1959), p. 159.
[60] R.W. Kettlewell, 'Agricultural Change in Nyasaland: 1945–1960', *Food Research Institute Studies*, 5, 1965, p. 264.

between 1945 and 1960 meant that tea planters were the largest beneficiaries. From 1954, tea began to provide nearly 40% of Nyasaland's export earnings, as compared with around 33% in the late 1940s. Tobacco, however, now a predominantly African crop, also regularly contributed 37% or more of export earnings and there were also significant advances in the export of groundnuts and maize, two crops that had not previously featured in the export market (see Table 10.2).

Table 10.2
Values of export crops (£ thousand)

Year	Tea	Tobacco	Cotton	Groundnuts	Maize	Total
1945	686	845	117	28	–	1,769
1946	750	1,252	128	35	–	2,239
1947	849	1,526	192	1	–	2,622
1948	1,350	2,250	369	20	15.7	4,097
1949	1,171	3,151	218	19	4.5	4,610
1950	1,691	2,767	335	22	5.2	4,889
1951	2,029	2,773	330	40	372.9	5,591
1952	1,912	2,134	744	230	798	6,042
1953	1,570	2,878	788	455	967	6,958
1954	2,728	2,776	557	325	449	7,124
1955	3,128	2,395	728	421	691	7,743
1956	2,957	3,064	245	1,134	664	8,497
1957	3,456	3,232	299	916	307	8,616
1958	2,944	2,234	354	468	82	6,874
1959	2,843	3,165	594	882	88	7,960
1960	3,806	3,514	802	1,008	190	9,761
% of total	35.5	41.8	7.1	6.3	4.9	100

(*Source:* R.W. Kettlewell, 'Agricultural Change in Nyasaland', p. 264)

Some previously marginal districts, notably Kasungu, became actively involved in the growing of cash crops, both tobacco and groundnuts, which was strongly encouraged by the Department of Agriculture from the early 1950s. More generally, however, it was districts with a lengthy history in the production of export crops that benefited the most. Thus, despite the considerable investment that took place in the north involving the production of rice in the Karonga district and groundnuts in the Mzimba district, cash receipts remained tiny compared to the very much larger sums earned in the Central Province and the South.[61] As late as 1963, for example, 91.5 per cent of all tobacco purchased from independent peasants by the Agricultural Produce Marketing Board came from the Central Province (15,194 tons out of a total of 16,779 tons) and 88.9 per cent of all seed cotton purchased came from the Southern Province, most from the Chikwawa district. Groundnuts were the Northern Province's most successful crop in this period. Yet between 1960 and 1963 the proportion from the north sold to the Marketing Board never rose

[61] For a detailed breakdown on export crops grown on customary land, see *Compendium of Agricultural Statistics 1977* (Zomba, 1977), pp. 8–34.

above 13.6 per cent and in most years was as low as 6 or 7 per cent.[62]

It was among tobacco growers in the Central Province that the cash crop boom had its most marked effects. The process began during the Second World War when the Native Tobacco Board responded to demands from British manufacturers, concerned by the disruption of supplies from America, by abandoning its long-held policy of restraint and embarking on a programme of expansion. Growers were informed of the need 'to produce as large a quantity of tobacco as possible on Native Trust Land'; four new markets were opened, including one at Kasungu (in 1944) operated entirely by Chief Mwase and his followers, and a search began for additional field staff.[63] Auction room prices for fire-cured tobacco, as for all other types, began to rise and, although sharp variations took place from one year to another, the general trend was decisively upwards until 1949, followed by a more gradual rise until 1958 when conditions temporarily deteriorated.

Production also substantially increased, with NTB purchases of Northern Division fire-cured tobacco rising from a low of 3,437,698 lbs in 1939 to 9,623,559 lbs in 1945 and 24,767,718 lbs in 1958. Average yields, however, remained disappointingly low, rising only slowly to a little over 200 lbs per acre, less than half what was achieved by the best tenants on European-owned estates.

Two main phases can be detected in the evolution of the tobacco industry from the early 1940s. The first involved the uncontrolled expansion in Trust Land production, which reached a peak in 1947 when 'the Central Province crop was by far the largest ever produced but one of the poorest in quality.'[64] Little supervision was provided by the Department of Agriculture, several of whose members had been recruited into the army. The registration of growers was allowed to lapse, and NTB marketing facilities proved so inadequate that many growers began to sell their crop to neighbouring estates in contravention of government directives. The effect, according to the Acting Director of Agriculture, was a serious decline in the quality of dark-fired tobacco.[65] Colby agreed. 'During the last two or three years...the situation has deteriorated rapidly', he noted, less than a year before the outbreak of the 1949 famine, the most severe in Malawi's history since the famine of 1861–63.

> This would be serious enough if the adverse effect was on the tobacco crop alone but, in fact, these high prices paid to producers have had the effect of unbalancing the whole of our agricultural production. Indeed, if some remedial action is not taken, a serious shortage of food will result in a very short time.[66]

From 1948, therefore, Colby placed his formidable weight behind a new policy of government intervention designed to reduce the acreage under tobacco while increasing quality and yield. Reversing the policy of his predecessor, E.C. Richards, who had instructed the Native Tobacco Board in 1945 to work to a very small profit margin, 'not more than 1/4d per lb. profit for the whole crop',[67]

[62] All these figures are drawn from *Compendium of Agricultural Statistics 1977.*
[63] Minutes of meetings of the NTB, 8 October 1940 and 15 July 1942, MNA 1A/291/AGR33/iv and 1A/293/AGR33/vi.
[64] *Annual Report of the Agricultural Department, 1947*, p. 5.
[65] E. Lawrence, 'The Control of Tobacco Growing on Native Trust Land', 30 March 1948, MNA 2–30–8R/3498/10061.
[66] Colby to C.W. Anson, 29 May 1948, MNA 2–30–8R/3498/10061.
[67] Secretariat notes, 27 and 30 June 1945 on NTB minutes, MNA 1A/293 AGR 33/vi.

Colby asked for 'a substantial overall reduction in prices to the grower, with proportionally higher reductions in the lower grades'.[68] He was opposed by representatives of the local buying associations who feared that growers would emigrate in large numbers to Southern Rhodesia if prices were pushed too low. He responded by having a clause inserted into the 1948 Tobacco Ordinance giving the Governor, in consultation with the Director of Agriculture, the final authority to determine the price paid by the Board.[69] Thereafter, up to 1957, a wide gap was deliberately maintained between prices obtained on the Auction Floor and those that were paid to the grower. In the nine years of Colby's governorship, £900,000 was diverted from NTB profits into a Price Fluctuation Fund designed to protect growers from market fluctuations, and a further £800,000 was paid into the Native Development and Welfare Fund to stimulate rural development.[70] Annual contributions of £13,500, increased from 1952 to £16,000, were also paid direct to the Government as a charge on the service that the Department of Agriculture provided. It was not until 1957 that the combination of increasing grower discontent and the arrival of a new governor, Sir Robert Armitage, led to a temporary change of policy (to be quickly reversed once Dr Banda came to power), with the Board committing itself to pay the producer 'as nearly as can be foreseen the full market value for his cotton and tobacco'.[71]

With the Trust Land smallholder tobacco industry established as a major source of government funds, the way was open for the NTB to reassert its control over production and marketing. Prior to 1948, many of the wealthier, labour-employing African growers on the Lilongwe Plain had sold their crop to private buyers rather than at NTB markets where they were restricted to the sale of a basket a day.[72] In that year, however, the amended Tobacco Ordinance re-established the legal monopoly of the NTB over the purchase of Trust Land tobacco. And this was followed over the next three years by the opening of a substantial number of new markets, considerably alleviating delays and, by 1950, bringing the total in the Northern Division (mainly the Central Province) to 26.

At the same time, Colby attempted to stimulate improvements in yields, cultivation methods and curing through 'a substantial increase in NTB staff – greater perhaps than the D/A [Director of Agriculture] anticipated.'[73] At his urging, plans were adopted in 1949 to increase the European staff to 44, including seven who would be employed full time in field work. And it was also at his request that the Board took on responsibility for providing selected farmers with fertilisers and ox-carts at subsidised rates and for encouraging the building of barns.[74] The resulting technological changes have left their mark on the Lilongwe district to today. By 1958 a modest annual total of 458 tons of fertiliser was being sold in the Central Province and 2,500 sturdy wooden ox-carts were

[68] Colby to Anson, ibid.
[69] Ibid.; Tobacco (Amendment) Ordinance, 1948.
[70] The total amount channelled from all marketing boards into this fund during Colby's governorship was £1,300,000.
[71] Report of the Working Party on Cotton and Tobacco Bonuses, Zomba, 1958, MNA 3–15–3R/9725/34049.
[72] D.C. Lilongwe to P.C. Central Province, 23 August 1948, MNA 2–30–8R/3498/10061.
[73] Minute by Colby, 15 July 1948, MNA 2–30–8R/3498/10061.
[74] Minutes of meetings of the NTB, 29 Aug and 26 Nov, 1949, MNA 1C/88 NTB/1.

being used in the area – a number that rose to close on 3,700 by 1960.[75] Agricultural officials believed that limited improvements had taken place in land use and mixed rotation farming. But much tobacco was still lost at the curing stage and yields remained disappointingly low. Ox-ploughs, which were by now widely employed in parts of Southern Rhodesia, Northern Rhodesia and Tanganyika, remained largely unused in Nyasaland, despite the fact that the Agricultural Department subsidised their sale for some years to farmers in the Mzimba district seeking to open up virgin land.[76]

The growth of NTB staff was accompanied by a return to restriction. During the late 1940s, a major debate took place within the Agricultural Department between the Director, P. B. Garnett, who did not believe 'that any real progress in agricultural methods and techniques can be sought through legislative control and regulations' and E. Lawrence and R. W. Kettlewell, who argued in favour of restriction.[77] Taking advantage of Garnett's absence on leave in March 1948, Lawrence circulated a lengthy memorandum on the need for control in the tobacco industry which advocated the reintroduction of registration as a means of ensuring 'the exclusion of all those who have proved themselves to be grossly unfit and improper persons to grow tobacco'.[78] Garnett replied from his holiday home in Bournemouth that the proposed legislation was 'neither suitable nor practical'. But in an era when the transforming role of the state was being accepted as the prevailing orthodoxy in government departments all over Africa, there was little support for his far-sighted comment that 'the rate of development of the African people must be highly dependent on the attitude and goodwill of the people themselves.'[79] In March 1950, having lost the confidence of the Governor, Garnett left Nyasaland for the Gambia; and with Lawrence and Kettlewell in the ascendant, coercion was given full reign.[80] In the early 1950s the registration of tobacco growers was reintroduced, first in the Southern Province and in certain marginal areas of the Central Province and then throughout the country.[81] By 1955 nearly 2,000 families a year were being refused registration in the hope that they would grow food crops instead; several markets had been closed in the Southern Province where Trust Land tobacco growing was now actively discouraged. By such means the number of families involved in tobacco growing in the Southern Province was reduced from 10,485 to 5,935 between 1951 and 1953; in the same period the number of registered growers in the Central Province dropped from well over 70,000 to 57,489.

By the late 1950s the structure of the Central Province tobacco industry had been modified in three major respects as compared with twenty years earlier. First, it is clear that for all the disappointment of agricultural officers at their failure to bring about a fundamental transformation in production, modest improvements in real cash incomes did take place in the major tobacco-growing areas. Despite the depressing effects of the NTB's pricing policy, the average

---

[75] *Annual Report of the Agricultural Department*, 1958, pp. 3, 15; Kettlewell, *Agricultural Change*, p. 246.
[76] Kettlewell, p. 247.
[77] Garnett to Chief Secretary, 9 April 1948, MNA 2–30–8R/3498/10061.
[78] Lawrence, 'Control of Tobacco Growing', 30 March 1948, MNA 2–30–8R/3498/10061.
[79] Garnett, ibid.
[80] Garnett's enforced departure from Nyasaland is described in Baker, *Development Governor*, pp. 112–13.
[81] *Annual Reports of the Agricultural Department*, 1951 and 1952.

returns to tobacco growers in the Central Province rose from a little over 25 shillings a year in 1937–39 to 126 shillings a year in 1947–49 and to 363 shillings a year in 1956–58. This was an increase significantly higher than the cost of living, but still lower, so a working party noted in 1958, than the daily rate for labourers.[82] Added to this, there was a dramatic increase in the sale of maize and groundnuts from 1949, explained by the sharp rise in prices for food crops guaranteed by the government following the famine, and by the establishment of numerous markets. In the Lilongwe district, maize sales at government markets rose from 900 tons in 1945 to a peak of 25,032 tons in 1954. Official sales then declined as a result of the government decision to cut the price offered for maize in its markets. African traders, however, purchased much of the surplus at the old price and groundnut sales also rose to a peak of 9,803 tons in 1962. The marked increase in the value of such imports as cotton goods and bicycles that took place between 1945 and 1953 is above all an indication of improved living standards among tobacco growers.[83]

A second feature of the post-war boom in cash crops was the emergence of a distinct group of 'progressive' farmers who employed wage labour, both permanent and casual, and cultivated up to twenty acres of land. No detailed research has yet been conducted into this group but it is apparent from the fragmentary evidence available that a significant minority were incomers to the Lilongwe district, like J.R. Chinyama (see pp. 205) and the Mozambican, Esau Gomiwa, foreman and large tenant grower on Bradshaw's Kachawa Estate. Both men used the capital they had acquired by working in supervisory positions for European estate-holders to expand into cash-crop production.[84] Lacking government loans, which were not made available to African producers on any substantial scale until 1958, these farmers were faced by considerable difficulties in their efforts to expand their activities. But by banding together in organisations such as the African Farmers Association, founded at Lilongwe in 1948, they were able to establish regular contacts with the Agricultural Department which supplied them with subsidised fertilisers and ox-carts and, from 1954, appointed individual members as agents of the Produce Marketing Board.[85] By 1951, Chinyama was selling over 1,100 baskets of maize a year. Other successful farmers had an average income from cash crops in 1957 of over £250, with profits estimated at £130.[86] Even among the most entrepreneurial of these rural capitalists, however, kinship ties were an important source of labour. In his detailed study of Chewa Master Farmers in the Lilongwe District in 1958, R.W.M. Johnson noted that, 'The general picture is one of mutual help in village marriage customs.' Several of these farmers had married virilocally in defiance of Chewa custom, but all made extensive use of wives, daughters and sons-in-law in cultivating their land.[87]

---

[82] Average returns are calculated from Report by Financial Secretary on NTB, 24 July 1939, MNA S1/275/39 and from annual reports of the Agricultural Department. See also 'Report of the Working Party on Cotton and Tobacco Bonuses', 1958, MNA 3–15–3R/9725/34049.

[83] Irvine, *Balance of Payments*, pp. 168–71.

[84] For details on Gomiwa see D.C. Lilongwe to P.C. Central Province, 29 March 1945, MNA NCL 3/1/2.

[85] For the activities of the African Farmers Association see MNA 17B/42.

[86] *Annual Report of the Agricultural Department*, 1957, p. 15.

[87] R.W.M. Johnson, 'Some Economic Aspects of African farming in the Lilongwe District, Central Province, Nyasaland' (unpublished paper, 1958), MNA 18–6–6–R/7008.

The gradual emergence of some African farmers 'to whom tobacco growing is a business from which a maximum financial profit should be wrenched' was accompanied by changes in the influence and structure of the estate sector.[88] During the 1930s, a few powerful estate-owners, among them Barron and Conforzi, had dominated the production and marketing policies pursued by the NTB but, by the late 1940s, this was no longer the case. Under Colby's direction, central government took tight control of agricultural strategies. The more progressive peasant farmers were actively supported and with up to four Africans, including Chinyama, appointed as members of the Board from 1947, openly discriminatory policies became more difficult to pursue. Colby went out of his way in November 1948 'to correct the impression that Government was trying to kill the tobacco industry for European planters'. But he did not disguise his belief that the economic future of the Protectorate lay predominantly in African hands.[89] It is an indication of the reduced attention that the government paid to estate owners that they were not consulted in 1957 over the decision to pay Crown Land growers what amounted as near as possible to world market prices although, as the estate owners complained, the action was one that threatened to undermine their profit margins and put their very future at risk.[90]

Tenant production of fire-cured tobacco in consequence declined, from a weight of 7,616, 000 lbs sold at auction in 1948 down to 1,579,500 lbs in 1952. But the estate sector responded by demonstrating resourcefulness in adversity and was thus able to survive and prosper. Starting from the late 1940s, Marjorie Barron, A.F. Barron's widow, abandoned the short-term approach that had previously characterised much tenant production and, with the assistance of her estate manager John Foot, reorganised the Mbabzi estates on more environmentally friendly yet also more productive lines.[91] Plots were standardised, with each tenant being given a minimum of six acres of land: two for tobacco, two for food crops, and two that were allowed to remain fallow. A regular system of crop rotation was introduced; tenants were provided with fertilisers on credit; and, as a means of improving efficiency, the length of tenancy was extended from six to ten months or even more.[92] Similar reforms were carried out on a number of other estates, notably that of D.W.K. Macpherson at Namitete, with the result that yields improved and with them the returns achieved by tenants. By 1963, according to a report commissioned by Dr Banda, tenants were producing on average 540 lbs of tobacco per acre as compared with 212 lbs produced by Trust Land growers.[93]

Most of the tenants by this time were growing burley, a mild-flavoured type of tobacco, introduced into Malawi in the late 1940s when it was grown by independent peasants and tenants alike. In 1952, however, burley was set aside as a

---

88 D.C. Lilongwe to P.C. Central Province, 23 Aug 1948, MNA 2–30–8R/3498/10061.
89 Minutes of a meeting between the Governor and the Nyasaland Northern Province Association, 23 Nov 1948, MNA Central Province Association Papers.
90 See file on 'Relationship between Tenant and Trust Land Tobacco Production, 1958', MNA 3–15–3R/9725/34–49.
91 Marjorie Barron to C.W.F. Footman. 27 July 1948, MNA 10704; interview with Bruce Barron, Mbabzi Estates, 20 July 1982.
92 Ibid.; Note by John Foot, 20 June 1948, MNA NCL 2/2/2.
93 Report of the Burley Tobacco Industry Commission [The Watson Commission], 1964, Central Province Association Papers

tenant monopoly on the instructions of the Department of Agriculture. A seemingly minor measure, designed to provide some temporary assistance to estate-owners in the face of Colby's new marketing strategy, the decision to confine the growing of burley to the estates was to prove to be of fundamental importance. In 1963, the 5,900 tenants on Central Province estates produced nearly 4,500,000 lbs of burley, more than 13 per cent of Malawi's tobacco exports, and well over twice the amount of air-cured tobacco they grew. Average net returns (taking into account the advances paid by estate owners earlier) were 747 shillings (over £37), only a half of what Chagga coffee growers had achieved in Tanganyika in 1955, but still almost double the average return of Trust Land growers.[94] Tenant farming in the Central Province was here to stay, although this was still by no means apparent in 1962 – the year in which Dr Banda launched a vituperative attack on the visiting tenant system in the Legislative Council, accusing it of being a form of *thangata*.[9] It was not until 1966, when Banda and other leading Malawians began to develop their own Central Province estates, making use of tenants in the production of burley, that it became clear that the visiting tenant system would survive the transition to political independence.[96]

In the Southern Province the cash crop boom took an altogether more ambiguous form. It was there, in the Shire Highlands, that population pressure on land became increasingly apparent to colonial officials by the mid-1940s, and there too that the alarm was first raised at what was seen as the worrying rush into tobacco with a consequent decline in the production of food crops. The outbreak of famine in 1949 in much of the Southern Province and along the lakeshore areas of the Central Province, which reached a peak in January 1950, was thus significant for its effects not only on the local population (up to 200 people died from starvation) but also on government policy.[97] Officials were agreed that the immediate cause of the famine lay in the catastrophic failure of the rains from Christmas 1948, following the poor harvest of the previous season which had reduced local reserves to a minimum. Nevertheless, they also believed that longer term factors were at work, including population growth in a region where large areas of land had been alienated to private estates, and a sharp rise in the price paid for tobacco at a time when the price of maize, as fixed by the Maize Control Board, was kept very low.

One consequence was that, in the aftermath of the famine, the government moved to restrict the growing of tobacco on Native Trust Land in the Southern Province while encouraging greater emphasis on the production of food crops. Registered Southern Province growers declined in number from 17,724 in 1948 to between 6,000 and 8,400 between 1956 and 1962, the numbers oscillating year by year. Marketing Board purchases fell from almost 3 million lbs of tobacco in 1948, 19.38 per cent of its total purchases, to between 500,000 and 900,000 lbs between 1953 and 1959, something between 2.0 and 4.7 per cent of the total.[98]

[94] Report of the Burley Tobacco Industry Commission; Iliffe, *Modern History*, p. 453.
[95] Speech by Dr Banda, 1 June 1962, Proceedings of the 4th Meeting of the 76th Session of the Legislative Council.
[96] See McCracken, 'Share-Cropping in Malawi', pp. 55–59.
[97] An excellent discussion of the causes and consequences of the famine is contained in Vaughan, *Story of an African Famine*.
[98] Figures drawn from *Annual Report of the Agricultural Production and Marketing Board*, 1960, Appendix C and *Compendium of Agricultural Statistics, 1977*.

Such figures, however, take no account of the expansion in the domestic food market consequent upon the increase of wage employment in the Southern Province. This had benefited many Trust Land growers and resulted in the emergence of an important group of African maize traders. Often returned migrants or former soldiers, these men purchased maize mills and lorries and played an active part in transporting surplus food from the Central Province for sale in the urban areas of the south.[99]

Estate farming in the Southern Province also experienced oscillations in fortune in the post-war period, although with a marked contrast between the tobacco-growing estates of the Zomba and Blantyre districts and the tea plantations grouped around Mulanje and Cholo. Land resettlement and the break-up of the giant Shire Highland estates are discussed in Chapter Twelve. Here, suffice to say that major changes in landownership took place from the late 1940s, involving the sale in 1950 of the greater part of the huge Bruce estates to a total of fourteen new landlords (most of them owners of tea estates, anxious to acquire land for food crops) and the further sale to the government of some 460,000 acres of land by 1958.[100] Tenant farming of the type that dominated in the Central Province thus tended to decline and instead the remaining landlords focused on two distinct activities: flue-cured production by direct labour, one of the oldest forms of European farming in the country, and the highly specialised production of dark-fired tobacco for the West African trade. Flue-cure production experienced a temporary boom in 1946 when average auction prices rose to 22.04d per lb, almost double the price for the previous year.[101] Thereafter, however, the old problems of low yield and indifferent leaf re-emerged, accentuated by the fact that Southern Rhodesian farmers were now becoming markedly more efficient and hence were obtaining better prices for their tobacco.[102] In 1956 over 8,000 acres were planted with flue-cured tobacco and some four million lbs of it were sold at auction. Over the next few years, however, as political unrest grew, production declined to a low in 1963 of 3,200 acres producing 2,666,000 lbs of tobacco; the numbers of farmers also fell to a low of 68 in 1959.[103] It was not until after Ian Smith's fortuitous Unilateral Declaration of Rhodesian Independence in 1965 and the subsequent international boycott of Rhodesian exports that Malawi's flue-cured tobacco industry was able to achieve a modest recovery.

For some estate owners, notably those in the Zomba district, it was the West African trade that allowed them to survive. This had its origin in the early 1930s when Captain Kincaid-Smith, the manager of the infamous Bruce estates at Magomero, opened up a new market for Nyasaland by signing a contract with the United Africa Company to provide dark-fired tobacco finished in a very precise manner for sale in West Africa. Other growers, led by Roy Wallace, followed his example. A direct route to West Africa was opened up in 1938. Thereafter, thousands of women and children were employed in the painstaking task of tying bunches of tobacco into 'heads', each of them five or six leaves in number and measuring 19 to 20 inches long, before they were sent off to Sierra

[99] Vaughan, *African Famine*, pp. 96–98, 104.
[100] White, *Magomero*, pp. 209–13.
[101] Wilshaw, *Century of Growth*, p. 71.
[102] *Annual Reports of the Department of Agriculture*, 1950–1959.
[103] *Annual Report of the Agricultural Department*, 1959.

Leone, Liberia and Nigeria to be traded up-country as currency by Creole and Lebanese merchants.[104] In 1943, exports to West Africa exceeded two million lbs, 14.8 per cent of Nyasaland's total tobacco exports.[105] Thereafter, the West African trade remained buoyant – a striking early example of the way in which, from the 1940s, Nyasaland's tobacco exports began to diversify away from the British market to outlets in other parts of Africa and beyond.

Tea planting

For tea planters, the late 1940s was a period of particular anxiety. First, they were burdened by the usual difficulties facing the tea sector – the mediocre quality of Nyasaland leaf, unpredictable rainfall and the high cost of transport. Second, they were also faced by new uncertainties: an acute shortage of labour and the imminent dissolution both of the International Tea Regulation Scheme under which the industry had flourished in the 1930s and of the cosy wartime marketing arrangements by which the British Ministry of Food made bulk purchases of all tea at prices set in advance. In the event, the reestablishment of the London Auctions in 1951, combined with the exposure of the tea industry to free market conditions, proved much less disastrous to Nyasaland's fortunes than many tea planters had predicted.[106] Good prices in 1951 were followed in the next two years by a fall brought about by over production for the British market, which was still restricted by wartime rationing. However, while some planters were pushed into serious financial difficulties at this time, the industry as whole recovered and began to flourish.[107] Prices per pound of tea exported remained at least 150 per cent higher than in 1945; average yields per acre increased steadily from around 700 lbs in the mid-1940s to close to 1,000 lbs in 1960, the result, in part, of a greater use of fertilisers. Acreage under tea more than trebled between 1945 and 1962, and average sales rose from £686,000 in 1945 to £1,691,000 in 1950 and on to £3,810,000 in 1960.[108]

Crucial to this expansion was the ability of the estates to attract labour at a period when the ending of *thangata* meant that planters could no longer automatically rely on Lomwe tenants coerced into work by the fear of eviction. Tea was a particularly labour-intensive industry involving over 30,000 workers at periods of peak demand in the early 1950s, a time when over one million lbs of tea were said to be lost each year as a result of the shortage of pluckers.[109] Some improvement could be made through raising minimum wages, among the lowest paid on tea plantations worldwide, from 6 shillings in the late 1930s for a 30 day ticket, to 17s. 6d. in 1950 and up to 20 shillings in 1953. But this was still significantly lower than minimum farm wages in Southern Rhodesia: 27–30 shillings for newcomers in 1949.[110]

[104] White, *Magomero*, p. 172; Wilshaw, *Century of Growth*, pp. 67–68.
[105] *Annual Report of the Agricultural Department*, 1943.
[106] Palmer, 'Nyasaland Tea Industry', pp. 235–37; Westrop, *Green Gold*, pp. 300–302.
[107] Westrop, *Green Gold*, pp. 306–16.
[108] Irvine, *Balance of Payments*, 162; *Report on an Economic Survey of Nyasaland, 1958–59*, pp. 219–220.
[109] Much of this paragraph is drawn from Robin Palmer, 'Working Conditions and Worker Responses on Nyasaland Tea Estates, 1930–1953', *JAH*, 27, 1 (1986), pp. 105–126.
[110] *Nyasaland Labour Department Annual Report*, 1949.

From the late 1940s, tea planters, therefore, began to make improvements in the housing supplied to workers from a distance and also to ensure regular food supplies, or *posho*, often now including dried fish as well as maize. New strategies were also developed to recruit labour, so that by the 1950s the solid core of local workers, Lomwe and Mang'anja villagers from trust land adjacent to the estates, were reinforced by three other categories of worker. The first and longest established were Lomwe seasonal migrants from Mozambique who crossed over during the hoeing season every year before returning to their homeland. These were joined by two other groups: internal migrants from the Central Province and single women, who were employed as daily, *ganyu*, workers in increasing numbers from the mid-1950s onwards.[111] Those recruited to Cholo from the marginal areas of the Central Province participated in a complex network of internal migration designed to reduce the problems created by widespread absenteeism among local workers who frequently took time off to work on their own gardens. By the 1950s, thousands of short-term workers from the most congested districts of the Southern Province travelled by rail and lorry each year to work as graders on Central Province tobacco estates. Thousands more travelled in the opposite direction from the more marginal districts of the Central Province to work in the tea estates at Cholo.[112]

Much of this process seems to have been master-minded by the Conforzi empire, which included tea estates in the south and tobacco estates in the centre as well as a fleet of lorries. Allowed to return to Nyasaland in 1947, having spent the war in exile in Italy, Ignaco Conforzi once more injected into the tea industry that element of ruthless entrepreneurship which the territory conspicuously lacked.[113] In 1950 he acquired a further 40,000 acres of land from the Bruce estates with the intention of using it in part to grow maize for his 5,000 workers, thus allowing him to maximise the land under tea on his Cholo plantations. Later he extended his tea factory to make it the largest in Africa. Later still he stood firm against any attempt to unionise his workforce, an attitude that in 1960 provoked a full scale strike in which 5,167 employees were involved.[114] In all this, Conforzi was representative of the more productive elements within the tea sector: often abrasive and exploitative yet also energetic and risk-taking, with a readiness to reinvest profits in the industry.

Labour migration

Changes in the rural economy must be considered in relation to changes in the pattern of labour migration. On the surface, it might have been expected that the signing of the Salisbury Agreement in 1936 and the reopening of WNLA recruiting operations the following year would have given a significant boost to labour migration from Malawi. With the coming of the Second World War, however, no such increase took place. In fact in 1945 only 98,500 male migrants

[111] *Labour Department Annual Reports,* 1955, 1959.
[112] McCracken, 'Share-Cropping in Malawi', pp. 40, 49; Palmer, 'Working Conditions and Worker Responses', p. 110.
[113] McCracken, 'Economics and Ethnicity', pp. 328–31.
[114] *Labour Department Annual Report,* 1960.

were recorded in the census as compared with an estimated 113,000 in 1937.[115] The 1945 figure, however, does not include the 22,000 Malawians temporarily serving in the army, many of whom might otherwise have been working abroad. With the soldiers demobilised, numbers grew to an estimated 143,000 in 1947, according to the annual Labour Report, an increase far short of the rise in population over the previous decade.[116]

This, however, was only the prelude to a further increase from the early 1950s, caused partly by the growth of competition for Nyasa labour from other territories in Southern Africa and partly by developments within the rural economy itself. WNLA led the way, increasing its annual number of recruits for the South African gold mines from Malawi from 7,828 in 1951 (less that the quota of 8,000 permitted) to 12,600 in 1955, 20,000 in 1959 and 25,960 in 1960, a time when the quota had been temporarily removed. *Mthandizi* (the Rhodesian Native Labour Supply Commission), founded in 1947, followed WNLA in establishing a network of depots in the Southern and Central Provinces but proved less successful in recruiting labour for Southern Rhodesian farms. In 1951 it provided only 3,742 recruits as against a quota of 8,000. Seven years later, in 1958, the number of recruits had risen to 8,647 as against a quota of 14,000.[117] Thus, if the Federal Prime Minister, Godfrey Huggins, intended to use the incorporation of Nyasaland into the Federation as a means of diverting labour from South Africa to Southern Rhodesia, as has often been suggested, he did not succeed in his aims.

An additional impetus to migration came with the abandonment of *thangata* on some Shire Highlands estates, joyously recorded in the pounding songs dating from the 1950s collected by Landeg White.[118] Further stimuli were provided by the restrictions on tobacco growing, imposed in the Southern Province and in parts of the Central Province from 1949 and, in some areas, by pressure on land. Many migrants, including virtually all from the Nkhata Bay district, continued to travel independently, thus ensuring that the precise number remains unknown, but the general trend is not in doubt.[119] In 1958, according to Labour Department figures, at least 169,000 male Malawians were working abroad. By 1966, following the sharp downturn in the economy that had taken place from 1959, the figure had risen to 229,000, to which could be added 22,000 women and 33,000 men over 50 who had settled permanently outside Malawi. Of these, 139,000 were in Rhodesia and 68,000 in South Africa.[120] As Vail has noted, this overall rise was accompanied by a change in the balance of districts from which migrants came: the Central Province and in particular the Southern Province now produced a much higher proportion of migrants than in the past; the proportion from the Northern Province had fallen to little over 17 per cent. (See Table 10.3).

Unlike earlier in the century, labour migration had thus become a Malawi-

[115] Coleman, 'Regional and District Origins of Migrant Labour', p. 55.
[116] *Annual Report of the Labour Department*, 1947.
[117] *Annual Reports of the Labour Department*, 1951–58; Chirwa, '"Theba is Power"', pp. 393–95.
[118] White, *Magomero*, pp. 221–30.
[119] According to official statistics only nine men from the Nkhata Bay District signed on as contact labourers between 1952 and 1956, by far the lowest number in the country. Acting PC, Northern Province to DC, Mzimba, 15 June 1957, MNA PC N1/21/4.
[120] Boeder, 'Malawians Abroad', p. 289; *Malawi Population Census 1966*, pp. x–xi.

Table 10.3
Migration by Region: 1966

Region	Population	% of Population	Migrants	% of Migrants
Northern Region	497,491	12.3	46,000	17.29
Central Region	1,474,952	36.5	94,000	35.39
Southern Region	2,067,140	51.2	126,000	47.37
MALAWI	4,039,583	100.0	266,000	100.0

(*Source: Malawi Population Census 1966. Final Report.*)

wide phenomenon. This is not to say that its impact on the rural economy was totally destructive, as some historians have argued. Certainly, the number of migrants grew substantially in the late colonial period. But the rise of popula-tion at this time meant that the proportion of Malawians abroad actually fell from around 6.8 per cent in 1937, before large-scale labour recruiting began, to about 6.2 per cent in 1966.[121] Low wages meant that tea estates suffered from labour shortages up to the mid-1950s but, in the Central Province in particular, new land continued to be brought into production as the growing number of young peasant farmers cut back the bush as the first stage in opening up new farms in more marginal parts of the country. Furthermore, the apparently dramatic shift in the areas from which migrants were drawn appears much less striking if comparisons between districts are made over time. In 1966, it was still the case that a significantly higher proportion of northerners became labour migrants than did men and women from the Central and Southern Provinces. The Nkhata Bay District, which had the highest proportion of adult male migrants in the country in 1937 (46.6%) continued to have the highest propor-tion in 1966 (44.6%). A dramatic five-fold increase in the proportion of labour migrants took place in the Lower Shire District from where, in 1966, some 25.7 per cent of adult men went abroad as compared with only 4.6 per cent in 1937. However, as Mandala and Schoffeleers have demonstrated, this arose from exceptional circumstances: the permanent flooding of thousands of acres of fertile floodplain from 1938 and the collapse of cotton-growing in Nsanje (Port Herald).[122] A significant increase in migration also took place from the Chiradzulu District where population density in 1966 reached 482 per square mile, four times the Malawi average. Elsewhere, continuity was more striking than change. In 1937 an estimated 11.7 per cent of male adults from the Lilongwe District were working abroad. In 1966 the figure was 11.6 per cent.[123]

The final point to be made concerns the impact of labour migration in the post-war period. Caution is required in generalising from the very different experiences of thousands of migrants. But it is important to stress that, with the increase in competition for Malawian labour from the late 1930s, conditions tended to improve. By the late 1940s both WNLA and *Mthandizi* were providing

[121] This estimate is based on the assumption that there were 112,000 migrants abroad in 1937 out of a population of 1,634,000 and 266,000 migrants abroad in 1966 out of a *De Jure* population of 4,305,000. (Figures taken from Kuczynski, p. 534 and *Census 1966*).

[122] Mandala, *Work and Control*; Schoffeleers, *Pentecostalism and Neo-Traditionalism*, pp. 2–5.

[123] *Malawi Population Census 1966*, Figures 3 and 1. Chiradzulu's population density was 482 per square mile as compared with 111 for the whole of Malawi.

free transport by lorry and train to and from the south and arrangements for family remittances and deferred pay were in place.[124] By comparative world standards, wage levels in the South African gold mines remained very low although, in comparison with local Malawian wages, they were distinctly attractive. In 1949 minimum wages on the Rand ranged from 70 shillings to 100 shillings a month, plus free rations and quarters; minimum wages on Cholo tea estates remained stuck at around 15 shillings.

Resistance to WNLA, therefore, dissolved almost everywhere other than in the Nkhata Bay district and the tangible rewards of migration grew, as is demonstrated by the increased value of remittances paid out in Nyasaland. In 1951, the total value of remittances, postal orders and money payments from South Africa and Southern Rhodesia was estimated at £397,744; by 1958 this figure had increased to £1,765,385.[125] Part of this went in family remittances, thus helping to sustain women and children in Nyasaland when men were absent. Part also was received in deferred payments at the end of contracts, thus providing returned migrants with access to limited capital resources. Historians have tended to dismiss the items purchased, notably bicycles, sewing-machines and clothes, as 'unproductive' consumer goods of no value to the rural economy.[126] But it is worth noting that the bicycle, the single most desired item sought by migrants in 1949, was in fact an exceptionally cost-effective, flexible means of transport, of great value in transporting a range of items throughout the rural hinterland, yet not requiring the expensive investment in roads and fuel needed by lorries and tractors.[127] In the mid-1950s, fish traders using bicycles were able to make their way to the Cholo and Mulanje tea estates during the rainy season over roads that were impassable to European-owned lorries.[128]

Returned migrants, in consequence, were active during the post-war era in a range of entrepreneurial occupations. Many involved themselves in retail trade and, although the casualty rate was high, some succeeded in making their businesses going concerns. In the Northern Province, as Chirwa has noted, migrants owned about 90 per cent of all shops.[129] Elsewhere, they faced keen competition from Indian shopkeepers but achieved some success in ancillary occupations as maize traders, millers and transporters. Richard Chidzanja, later a well-known politician, was one of several returned migrants in the Central Province who acquired lorries through the savings they had made in South Africa.[130]

Fishing and fish trading also offered opportunities. Starting in the 1930s and continuing at a greater level in the 1950s, Tonga labour migrants from Nkhata Bay used the capital they had saved in Southern Africa to set up as commercial fishermen along the south-east arm of Lake Malawi, a much more productive area for

[124] Chirwa, "'Theba is Power'".
[125] Annual Reports of the Labour Department, 1951, 1958. For a useful discussion of remittances see Chirwa, "'Theba is Power'", pp. 436–440.
[126] Vail, 'Malawi's Agricultural Economy', p. 69.
[127] In a survey conducted in the Southern Province in 1949 on the reasons for migration, 35.33 per cent of people questioned said 'to obtain money necessary to buy bicycles'. 'Report of a Labour Survey undertaken in the Southern Province of Nyasaland concerning emigration of Nyasaland natives in search of work', 1949, MNA LB3/3/3 quoted in Chirwa, "'Theba is Power'", p. 408.
[128] Chirwa, ibid., pp. 459–61.
[129] Chirwa, ibid., p. 441. For a full discussion of African retail trade see E.C. Wright, African Consumers in Nyasaland and Tanganyika (London, 1955).
[130] McCracken, 'Blantyre Transformed', p. 264.

fishing than their rocky northern homeland.[131] By the mid-1950s they had been joined by other former labour migrants who 'set up fisheries on a real business basis', employing workers (*alovi*) and investing in imported nets and boats. 'They are all African business men, some from other parts of the country and have spent most of their lives in South Africa and Southern Rhodesia and have come back to set up businesses', the Fisheries Officer noted in 1956.[132] Some of the problems they faced are illustrated by the example of Crispo Gwedala, who began fishing in the Mangochi area in 1954 after a four-year spell in South Africa. Helped by a government loan, Gwedala bought a canoe, a second-hand lorry and a large nylon net with which he caught fish worth over £300 in a season. But as his business grew, his profits evaporated as a result both of the dishonesty of his workers and the frequent accidents in which his lorry was involved.[133]

Yet if the risks were great, so were the opportunities. In the 1950s Amos Charles, who had worked in Southern and Northern Rhodesia as well as Tanganyika, employed twenty men at Nkhotakota and Lake Malombe who between then caught nearly 5,000 fish at each casting.[134] At the south-east arm of Lake Nyasa, two African fishermen caught 100 tons of fish each year. For those with capital, fish trading could also be a profitable venture. 'Some of the bigger African fish businessmen have got the idea of having agents along the road between here and Blantyre selling fish for them while they themselves proceed with the remainder of the fish to the towns', reported Masauko Chipembere, then a member of the Legislative Council and himself an active fish-trader, in 1956.[135] At least sixteen African-owned lorries were licensed to carry fish from Fort Johnston to the Central Province in 1961. Lake Chilwa was served by 'numerous' lorries as well as 'innumerable' traders on bicycles.[136]

Most of these were able to eke out only a meagre living from an arduous occupation. Nevertheless, their resilience is a reminder that the link between migrancy and rural poverty was not direct. Labour migration may have contributed little to the wealth of Malawi as a whole, but many rural households benefited directly from it in terms both of capital and goods, as the testimony of former migrants makes clear. As their experience since the ending of recruitment in the mid-1970s has demonstrated, if there was one thing worse than working in South Africa, it was being deprived of the opportunity of doing so.[137]

Medicine & disease

For Colby, economic development took precedence over the expansion of social services. But even he was affected by the changing character of the late colonial

[131] McCracken, 'Fishing and the Colonial Economy', p. 427.
[132] Evidence of A.D. Sanson, Fisheries Officer, to the Commission of Inquiry into the Fishing Industry, Fort Johnston, 8 June 1956, MNA COM 9/4/2.
[133] Evidence of Crispo Gwedala to the Commission of Inquiry, ibid.
[134] Evidence of Amos Charles, ibid.
[135] Evidence of H.B. Chipembere, ibid.
[136] H.B.H. Borley, 'Notes for the working party on the development of the fishing industry', 1961, MNA 4-6-8.
[137] W.C. Chirwa, '"No TEBA… Forget TEBA": The Plight of Malawian Ex-Migrant Workers to South Africa, 1988–1994', *International Migration Review*, 31 (1997), pp. 62–85.

state and its tendency to give greater emphasis than previously to questions of social provision. As we have seen, medical provision in the early decades of colonial rule was met largely by the missions and by traditional African medical practitioners. In 1930, however, over £100,000 (62 per cent of the total) of the funds allocated to Nyasaland under the Colonial Development Act of that year were targeted at medical services. The result was that, by 1937, 93 government rural dispensaries had been opened, staffed by African dispensers and supplementing the better equipped government hospitals maintained in Zomba, Blantyre, Fort Johnston, Lilongwe and Nkhotakota.[138] Little expansion took place during the war but, in its aftermath, the Colonial Office pressed for an improvement in social services. This call was taken up by the Post-War Development Committee which in 1946 recommended that the number of Government rural dispensaries should be increased to 400 over the next decade.[139]

The subsequent growth of medical provision, however, was much slower than the planners had envisaged. Colby agreed in principle that there was a connection between productivity and health. But with the costs of medicine rapidly rising, neither he nor the Federal Government, which took over responsibility for medical services in 1954, was willing to commit the resources requested. Government funds spent on medical provision in Nyasaland rose from £142,750 in 1948 to £232,585 in 1953 and to an impressive-looking £892,000 in 1961. But this sum was far less than the Federal Government spent on medical provision in Northern and Southern Rhodesia, both with similar populations to Nyasaland; less too than might have been expected in absolute terms given the rapid rise of the population at this period [see Table 9.4]. Official statistics are not always accurate but it would appear that the number of rural dispensaries and government hospitals rose only very slightly – from a combined total of 115 in 1949 to 129 in 1960 as compared with the figure of 400 envisaged by post-war planners. The construction of the Queen Elizabeth Hospital in Blantyre (opened in 1958) was evidence of a new emphasis on a limited number of large-scale hospitals with modern facilities and improved access to drugs. But even in this area, expansion was remarkably modest. In 1961 only 64,813 African patients were treated in government hospitals as compared with 30,173 in 1948. Beds available in all hospitals, government and mission combined, rose from a mere 2,752 in

Table 10.4
Trends in Expenditure on Medical Services Actual expenditure in £000

Year	Nyasaland	N. Rhodesia	S. Rhodesia	Nyasaland's share as % of total
1954–5	395	1,255	2,368	9.83%
1956–7	543	1,761	2,983	10.27%
1958–59	766	2,153	3,856	11.72%
1960–61	892	2,360	4,270	11.71%

(Source: *Federation of Rhodesia and Nyasaland Annual Report for 1961*)

[138] *Annual Reports of the Nyasaland Medical Department for 1930 and 1937.*
[139] *Report of the Post-War Development Committee, 1946*, TNA CO 525/198 44334.

1955 to only 3,520 in 1960. Staffing shortages were even more of a problem than shortages of beds. The number of government medical officers increased from a low of 12 in 1949 (three less than the figure for 1938) to an establishment of 38 in 1953 and 48 in 1959. These figures, however, mask a shortfall in recruitment explained by the unpopularity among colonial doctors of Federal terms and conditions.[140] Only 19 medical officers were employed in Nyasaland in 1955, a figure that fell to a low of 14 in 1963, on the eve of the break-up of the Federation.[141]

Medical missions, moreover, were unable to fill the gap. Government grants in aid to missions rose nearly six-fold between 1953 and 1960 but, with Scottish missionaries now tending to downplay the importance of their medical role, growth as measured in hospitals, beds and doctors was even slower than growth in the government section. Much of the expansion that did take place was carried out by Catholic missions who, by 1964, had 1,036 beds in their hospitals compared with the 580 beds provided by the Presbyterian missions.[142]

With its growth curtailed, the medical service atrophied. Segregation by race and gender had been a key feature of its structure in the 1930s and this pattern continued into the post-war period at a time when, in West Africa and Uganda, Africans were beginning to take an increasingly prominent role in the medical profession.[143] Staff were divided by race and gender into four categories: white male medical officers, Asian sub-assistant surgeons, white female nurses and, at the bottom, African hospital assistants and dispensers. This structure survived virtually unchanged to the eve of independence, despite the Federation's multiracial pretensions. As only British qualifications were recognised, doctors with degrees from American or Indian universities were disqualified from practising as medical officers. Yet, when Dr Hastings Banda made good this omission by obtaining British qualifications in Edinburgh and Liverpool, steps were taken to reject him. After lengthy discussions in the Colonial Office as to whether Banda could be offered a job at a lower level of pay than European officers, or perhaps in a situation in which he would not have to treat European patients, the Nyasaland Government noted in 1941 that 'he is not the right sort of man for Government employment and it has been agreed not to employ him.'[144]

African involvement in the service thus remained restricted to those men and women employed as hospital assistants, dispensers and midwives. Educated predominantly at Blantyre and Livingstonia, these auxiliaries were as important in the spread of biomedicine in the rural areas as evangelists were in the spread of Christianity. Frequently castigated by their superiors for their inefficiency and lack of discipline, they nevertheless maintained medical services in district hospitals with virtually no supervision during the Second World War, and ran

---

[140] Dr J.C.R. Buchanan, 'Observations on the Process of Federating the Medical and Health Services of the Rhodesias and Nyasaland', 5 Jan 1954, TNA CO 1015/1090.
[141] *Annual Reports of the Nyasaland Medical Department, 1949–53*; *Annual Reports on Public Health, Federation of Rhodesia and Nyasaland, 1954–63*, TNA DO 123/26–8.
[142] Iliffe, 'Poor', p. 256.
[143] John Iliffe, *East African Doctors* (Cambridge, 1998) pp. 92–113.
[144] *Nyasaland Legislative Council Proceedings*, 57th Sessions, First meeting, 1941 quoted in Colin Baker, 'The Government Medical Service in Malawi: An Administrative History, 1891–1974', p. 308; 'Medical Department, African Personnel – Hastings Banda', TNA CO 7031/19(1938) 44034/4. I owe this reference to Andrew Fairweather-Tall.

rural dispensaries unaided well into the 1950s.[145] Dan Ngurube, one of the assistants at Zomba African Hospital in the 1930s, regularly corrected the diagnoses made by doctors in South Africa and Rhodesia on men invalided from the mines.[146] From the late 1940s, medical training was provided at Zomba African Hospital and, from 1951, at Lilongwe African Hospital, but many auxiliaries objected to serving under the Federal Government and were ultimately forced to resign. Only 44 per cent of African staff in service in 1953 transferred to the Federal Service despite the absence of alternative employment. Total numbers of Nyasaland staff fell sharply from 1,241 in that year to 599 in June 1958.[147]

The staffing crisis highlighted gaps in medical provision. Christian missions still remained active in the 1950s in providing care for patients suffering from leprosy and the blind. But despite the opening of a Government leprosarium at Kochirira in 1956, demand continued to outpace supply. In 1962 eleven leprosaria treated 2,000 inpatients, but the estimated number of lepers in Malawi had risen from 30,000 in 1950 to 80,000 in 1965. Blindness – due to smallpox, trachoma and other causes – was exceptionally common, with rates in parts of Malawi being among the highest in the world. Yet, training for the blind was considered so expensive that for most of the post-war period the Government deliberately left it to voluntary agencies.[148]

Public health measures designed to control disease were even more conspicuously unsuccessful. Federal health improvement campaigns against malaria, bilharzia and smallpox had some success from the mid-1950s in Southern Rhodesia where adequate financial and staffing resources existed. But, with only 6 per cent of the medical budget going on preventive medicine in Nyasaland, its impact was inevitably slight.[149] Almost no action at all was taken to reduce the incidence of bilharzia, despite the recognition that it was very common along the lake shore and in the Shire Valley. Measures designed to combat malaria were equally ineffectual. For a brief period, starting in 1956, the Medical Department conducted an experimental anti-malarial spraying campaign in the Zomba – Lake Chilwa area. But this was brought to a halt in 1959 and the staff dispersed elsewhere.[150]

Measures taken against smallpox were particularly contentious because of the tendency for villagers to interpret compulsory vaccination campaigns as expressions of state coercion.[151] Few tangible successes appear to have been achieved by the intensive vaccination campaign launched in the Central and Southern Provinces in 1948, with the result that scepticism concerning the efficacy of vaccination grew.[152] When a new smallpox epidemic broke out in 1956, therefore, the campaign against it provoked considerable unrest. In the following year,

[145] King, *Story of Medicine and Disease*, pp. 136–137.
[146] W.C.T. Berry, *Before the Wind of Change* (Suffolk, n.d.[1985], p. 5).
[147] Baker, 'Government Medical Service', p. 306.
[148] Iliffe, 'The Poor in the Modern History of Malawi', pp. 272–73.
[149] *Annual Reports on Public Health, Federation of Rhodesia and Nyasaland*, 1955–1962; Baker, 'Government Medical Service', p. 308.
[150] *Annual Reports on Public Health, Federation of Rhodesia and Nyasaland*, 1956, pp. 6–7, 1957, 2–3, 1959, 6–7.
[151] Megan Vaughan, 'Health and Hegemony: representation of disease and the creation of the colonial subject in Nyasaland' in Dagmar Engels and Shula Marks (eds), *Contesting Colonial Hegemony. State and Society in Africa and India* (London 1994), pp. 185–87.
[152] *Annual Report of the Nyasaland Medical Department*, 1949, p. 6.

federal authorities seized the opportunity to launch a large-scale programme in Nyasaland involving the forced vaccination in 1960–1961 alone of nearly 1,400,000 people. In response, peasants refused to cooperate with the vaccinators and in some cases drove them from their villages.[153] Federal politicians entered the dispute, blaming Dr Banda and the Malawi Congress Party for the failure of the campaign. But there can be little doubt that the opposition was more an expression of popular mistrust than the result of political action.[154]

Education

For most of the post-war period, education was an even more contentious issue than public health. The Bell Report of 1938 had reinforced Nyasaland's reputation in colonial circles for outstanding educational provision through its exaggerated claim that between 50 to 60 per cent of the population were literate in the vernacular and that 6 per cent were learning English.[155] During the course of the war, however, criticisms of the Nyasaland system grew, coming to a climax with the publication of the 1945 census, which appeared to demonstrate that only 7.2 per cent of the population were literate, less than a fifth of those who had attended schools.[156] Charles Matinga, as President of the Nyasaland African Congress, called for a commission of enquiry into education. His view was supported by such members of Congress as M. Q. Chibambo (the son of one of Livingstonia's earliest ministers) who reported that 'the education his father received was far better than the one he has taken.'[157] Dr J. C. Dougall, who, in 1947, carried out an educational survey in Nyasaland on behalf of the Church of Scotland, reached a similar conclusion. So too did the Advisory Committee on Education in the Colonial Office. After a lengthy discussion in February 1948 of the Gwilliam-Read Report into women's education, the committee noted that

> it has found the educational problems in Nyasaland unusually urgent and intractable; urgent because in spite of its long history and early promise, education has yielded such meagre results, intractable because after years of discussion, Government has not succeeded in giving a firm direction to education policy.[158]

The structure of education was distorted, with over 98% of all pupils being enrolled in low-level junior primary or village schools. Wastage rates were colossal. Teachers were badly paid and untrained. Only a handful of pupils, a mere 116 in 1948, had qualified for entry to secondary school. Only two of these were female: a reflection of the fact that an overwhelming proportion of the girls

---

[153] *Annual Report on Public Health, Federation of Rhodesia and Nyasaland*, 1961, p. 8.
[154] Short, *Banda*, pp. 140–41.
[155] *Bell Report*, p. 13.
[156] *Nyasaland Census of 1945*; Hailey, *Native Administration, Part II*, p. 22.
[157] Charles Matinga to Sir Edmund Richards, Governor of Nyasaland, 15 May 1945, TNA CO 525/199/44379/1946; Minutes of the meeting of the Second Annual Conference of the Nyasaland African Congress, 16–19 Oct 1945, MNA NS 1/3/10.
[158] Minutes of Advisory Committee on Education: African Sub Committee, 19 Feb 1948, TNA CO 525/203/44070/10 quoted in I. C. Lamba, 'The History of Post-War Western Education in Colonial Malawi, 1945–61: A Study of the Formulation and Application of Policy', Ph.D. dissertation, University of Edinburgh, 1984, p. 155.

who received any education at all withdrew before they had completed the first two years of school.

Subsequent attempts to improve educational provision demonstrate how 'intractable' Nyasaland's educational problems had become. In the initial stage, Government support was focused on improving the quality of primary education by increasing the number of senior primary schools and improving conditions and the training of teachers. Expectations of moving to universal primary education, contained in the Report of the Post-War Development Committee, were tacitly ignored. Instead, missions went out of their way to reduce the number of unassisted village schools they maintained while significantly increasing the number of senior primaries – to 149 in 1957 as compared with 27 ten years earlier. The overall number of pupils in schools rose only from 217,222 in 1948 to 265,678 in 1957, an increase that barely kept pace with the growth in population. But, over the same period, the number of pupils in senior primaries swelled from 190 to 13,311, with a consequent growth in the numbers in Standard VI, the gateway to secondary education.[159] As in medicine, government expenditure increased rapidly, from £36,000 in 1944 to £304,000 in 1954 – at which time education counted for 8.4% of the government's total recurrent expenditure. Thereafter, the figure spent on education increased year by year, dwarfing the amount provided by missions and rising in 1960/61 to £918,775, 13.4% of total government expenditure.[160] By this time the number of pupils approached 330,000, although numbers dipped in the next few years during a period of recession, when Dr Banda's majority-rule government was forced into economy cuts. In 1966, two years after independence, 305,851 students were recorded in the national census as attending school, 7.5 per cent of the total population. This was the lowest percentage recorded since records were taken, and only 23.9 per cent of the optimum school age group: those aged between 7 and 19.[161] About 36 per cent of the population aged five and over were recorded as having spent at least a year at school, a figure which suggests that numbers dropping out early remained very large.

In one respect, however, the increased expenditure on education over the previous two decades had achieved tangible results. No reliable figures exist on changes in the literacy rate. But by 1966 some 81,000 Malawians had reached Standard 8 or higher, thus successfully completing their primary education, whereas, in the mid-1940s, Blantyre and Zomba secondary schools had between them only 71 students on their rolls.[162] The subsequent expansion of secondary education from 1948 to 1952 under the initial direction of an energetic new Director of Education, D. S. Miller, was slow by comparison with developments in neighbouring territories, but an improvement on the previous state of affairs.[163] In 1951 the first government secondary school was opened at Dedza, to be followed in the next few years by a variety of missionary–controlled junior secondary schools, most of them with less than 100 pupils apiece, at Malamulo, Nkhoma, Mtendere, Livingstonia and elsewhere. Secondary school enrolments

---

[159] *Report on an Economic Survey of Nyasaland 1958–59*, pp. 168–173.
[160] *Report of the Committee of Inquiry into African Education* [The Phillips Report] (Zomba, 1962), p. 20.
[161] *Malawi Population Census 1966 Final Report*, p. xii.
[162] *Malawi Population Census 1996*, p. xii.
[163] Lamba, 'History of Post-War Western Education', p. 80.

grew from 408 in 1953 to 1,189 in 1958.[164] But, as late as 1961, there were only four secondary schools in the country offering full school certificate courses: Blantyre, Zomba, Dedza and Mzuzu Government School, this last opened in 1959. Secondary education in the run up to independence thus remained the privilege of a tiny minority, almost all of them male. Only 32 girls as compared with 277 males took the Cambridge School Certificate course in 1962. Sixteen men and no women took the higher school certificate course, required for entry to university education.[165]

Educational expansion reduced regional diversity but by no means eliminated it entirely. Many of the new schools founded in the 1950s were established by Roman Catholic missions responding to a new drive within the Catholic Church aimed at improving educational standards. Nevertheless, areas exposed at an early stage to Scottish Presbyterian influence tended to keep their lead. In 1959, according to figures produced by the Department of Education, the Northern Province, with a population of 379,644 had 304 primary schools (a ratio of 1:1,239). By comparison, the Central Province with a population of 983,814 had 258 primary schools (1: 3,813) and the Southern Province with a population of 1,296,522 had 303 schools (a ratio of 1: 4,279).[166] In 1966, 55 per cent of the Northern population had attended school as compared with 35% from the Centre and 32% from the South. More striking still was the evidence of variations between districts. Whereas in that year only 6.8 per cent of children in the predominantly Muslim Fort Johnston district were at school, the percentage in the Blantyre district was a respectable 34.3 and that in the Rumphi district, Livingstonia's heartland, 54.9.[167] It is hardly surprising that when the University of Malawi was opened in 1965 the Northern Province, with less than a fifth of the population, produced the highest proportion of eligible candidates.[168]

For all but a tiny handful of Malawians, higher education remained an unattainable dream. In the mid-1920s, Robert Laws had planned to found a University of Livingstonia but with his retirement, the vision was allowed to fade.[169] In 1941, however, the Governor, Edmund Richards, decided to provide bursaries for Malawians to attend Makerere College at Kampala in Uganda.[170] With secondary education in its infancy in Nyasaland, no qualified candidates were available but, in 1943, three students (two from Blantyre Secondary School and one from Zomba) were accepted for a preliminary year at the college; the next year four candidates took the entrance exam although only one was successful.[171] This was the prelude to a lively debate on higher educational provision which was not to be resolved until the founding of the University of Malawi after independence. While Makerere had its advocates, some Malawians, led by the senior government clerk, James Sangala, argued in favour of Fort Hare in South

[164] *Report of the Advisory Commission on the Review of the Constitution of Rhodesia and Nyasaland* [The Monckton Report], (London, 1960), p. 208.
[165] Lamba, 'History of Post-War Western Education', p. 180.
[166] Jack Report, p. 172. See also Lamba, pp. 39–40.
[167] *Malawi Population Census 1966*, p. xii.
[168] R. J. Macdonald, 'A History of African Education in Nyasaland, 1875–1945' PhD. dissertation, University of Edinburgh, pp. 542–3.
[169] John McCracken, 'The University of Livingstonia', *SOMJ*, 27, 2 (1974), pp. 14–23.
[170] Lamba, 'History of Post-War Western Education', p. 101.
[171] *Reports of the Nyasaland Educational Department*, 1943, p. 9; 1944, p. 6.

Africa's Eastern Cape as a cheaper and culturally more attractive alternative. Two students at Fort Hare could be educated for the price of one at Makerere, Sangala asserted in 1944.[172] Others, even at this stage, argued in favour of a University of South Central Africa, to be located in Northern or Southern Rhodesia. And others again asserted that only by admitting Africans into multiracial universities could the required standards be achieved. 'To speak frankly the Africans wish all what is called a European education', Sangala informed a Scottish missionary in 1949.[173] Responding to such concerns, the Nyasaland Government widened its range of approved institutions, giving scholarships in 1945 to three students: S.V. Bhima, taking medicine at Makerere; G.T. Kamanga, taking the Arts course at Fort Hare; and J.G. Chingattie, taking a social welfare course at the Jan Hofmeyr School of Social Work in Johannesburg.[174]

The subsequent struggle of Malawians to gain access to university education provides an indication of how far standards had declined in the territory in comparison with Nyasaland's neighbours. Both Blantyre and Zomba Secondary schools were modest institutions, operating at lower levels than such schools as Tabora in Tanganyika, Munali in Northern Rhodesia and Goromonzi in Southern Rhodesia, and offering their students a more restricted syllabus. It was not until 1948 that the first two locally educated Malawians, John Msonthi and Dyson Chona, were provided with the opportunity of taking and passing the Cambridge School Certificate and not until 1958 that the Cambridge Higher School Certificate was introduced at Dedza. With secondary provision limited, university entrance remained the preserve of a few. By 1950, as Table 10.5 demonstrates, students from Southern and Northern Rhodesia had been conspicuously more successful than those from Nyasaland in obtaining places at Fort Hare.

Table 10.5
Africans in Higher Education 1943–1950

University	Northern Rhodesia	Southern Rhodesia	Nyasaland
Fort Hare	13	87	3
Makerere	11	–	5
Other	4	9	2
Total	28	96	10

(*Source: Report of the Commission on Higher Education for Africans in Central Africa* (Central African Council, Salisbury, 1953), p. 11.)

What is more, several students who did gain access to universities owed their success to the secondary education they received in schools outside Nyasaland. The gifted Orton Chirwa, perhaps the most talented Malawian student of his era, was educated up to Standard 6 at Livingstonia but went on to study for three

---

[172] Minutes of a General Meeting of the Parents and Guardians Educational Association, 15 Jan 1944, MNA NSB 3/3/6.
[173] Sangala to Andrew Doig, 18 July 1949, MNA AFR 231 Box 140, quoted in Lamba 'History of Post-War Education', pp. 110.
[174] Annual Report of the *Nyasaland Education Department*, 1945, p. 4.

years at St Francis College, Marianhill, Natal before gaining admission to Fort Hare in 1947.[175] There he joined Champion Ngoma, one of the students supported financially by Dr Banda. Ngoma was the son of a labour migrant from the Nkhotakota district, educated entirely in Northern Rhodesia and at the Wilberforce Institute in the Transvaal before entering Fort Hare in 1945.[176] Several Malawian students at Makerere followed similar, if more exalted routes. Kanyama Chiume left Usisya in the Nkhata Bay district at the age of nine, following the death of his mother, and was educated at Dar es Salaam Secondary School and Tabora before gaining admission to Makerere in 1949.[177] One of his classmates there was David Rubadiri, the son of a respected senior clerk, who had received his secondary education at King's College, Budo, one of East Africa's oldest and most distinguished schools.

With the rise of university admission levels from the early 1950s, the difficulties facing Malawian students worsened. University entrance now increasingly depended on the candidate obtaining a Higher School Certificate, something not offered by any school in Nyasaland prior to 1958. As an emergency measure, therefore, government bursaries were given to a small group of students – up to ten a year – to complete their secondary education in Northern and Southern Rhodesia, either at Goromonzi or Munali secondary schools.[178] Several of these went on to universities, including Henry Masauko Chipembere, a product of Blantyre Secondary School, who spent the academic year 1950–1951 at Goromonzi (where he became 'obsessed' by the notion of behaving like a 'gentleman') before entering Fort Hare in 1952.[179]

As the son of an Anglican archdeacon devoted to the education of his children, Chipembere was typical of the majority of post-war university graduates in coming from a background of relative educational privilege. Some of these, like Orton Chirwa and his fellow Tonga, Manoah Chirwa, received their initial education from Livingstonia teachers. Others, such as the Makerere-educated Augustine Bwanausi and his brother, Dr Harry Bwanausi (educated at Fort Hare and at medical school in Johannesburg), were products of the Blantyre Mission and of well-established Blantyre families. By the mid-1950s a few had begun to emerge from areas where no long history of educational provision existed; these, however, tended to be drawn from the ranks of the more privileged. John Tembo, the first graduate from the Dedza district, was the son of 'a prominent minister of the Nkhoma Synod of the Church of Central African Presbyterian' and a member of 'one of the most progressive families in the District'.[180] Twenty-one out of the 23 graduates recorded up to 1959 were men. But it is worth noting that, as early as 1953, Roseby Kazembe proceeded to Bath College in England to take a Domestic Science diploma and that, in 1957, Sarah Chavunduka

---

[175] Chirwa, O.E., Personal File, Fort Hare Student Records, *Malawi News,* 19 October 1962.

[176] Dr Alexander Kerr to Director of African Education, Northern Rhodesia, 28 August 1946; Dr Hastings Banda to the Principal, Fort Hare, 3 April 1946; Ngoma, C.K, Personal File, Fort Hare Student Records.

[177] M.W.K. Chiume, *Kwacha. An Autobiography* (Nairobi, 1975), pp. 3–51.

[178] Lamba, 'History of Post-War Western Education', 123; *Annual Report of the Nyasaland Education Department,* 1957, p. 4.

[179] Anon., *Mr Masauko Chipembere* (Limbe, 1961?); Chipembere, H.B., Personal File, Fort Hare Student Records.

[180] *Malawi News,* 19 October 1962, 9. For other brief biographies see *Malawi News,* 20 July 1961.

(Rhodesian educated but Malawian connected) became the first African woman to attend the University College of Rhodesia and Nyasaland in Salisbury.[181]

As the 1950s progressed, higher educational opportunities diversified. Malawi has a long history of overseas educational contacts, particularly with the United States but, by the 1940s, these had been largely brought to an end.[182] In 1948, however, the anthropologist Margaret Read persuaded the Department of Education to send six Malawians to study for the one-year Professional Teachers' Certificate at the Institute of Education in London. Thereafter, the number of students studying in Britain on degree or, more commonly, sub-degree courses grew, rising to 18 in 1960.[183] They included among their number Augustine Bwanausi, who obtained a teacher's diploma at Bristol University in 1955, and Orton Chirwa, who was called to the English Bar on 6 May 1958, returning as Nyasaland's first African lawyer. After considerable debate, the Government permitted John Msonthi to take up an Indian Government scholarship in 1950 to study at St. Xavier's College, Bombay, thus inaugurating a trend for Malawians (including Bingu wa Mutharika, later President of the country) to study for university degrees in India. However, it refused to issue a passport to Flax Katoba Musopole in 1957, thus preventing him from taking up a scholarship in Moscow.[184] During his years in South Africa, Musopole had developed close links with Communist Party members in Cape Town and had also contributed to *The New Age*, one of the most radical of South African journals.[185]

The opening of the University College of Rhodesia and Nyasaland in 1957 provided a further opportunity for Malawians, although one that tragically few were able to seize. Born out of lengthy discussions, going back to the 1940s, the University College was designed as a racially integrated institution, drawing students of all races from the three Central African territories and thus providing a substitute for Fort Hare, which in 1953 had reluctantly closed its doors to new non-South African students on the orders of the Nationalist government. Sited in the affluent white suburb of Mount Pleasant in Salisbury, the Federal capital, the College was equipped with excellent facilities and a talented staff, including some exceptionally able academics. In that sense it was admirably well prepared to meet Sangala's demand for 'all what is called a European education'. But with admission standards high, the initial African enrolment was small – numbering 38 (only seven from Malawi) out of 168 students in 1960. Racial incidents, including the short-lived and unsuccessful attempt by some white girls to bar Sarah Chavunduka from the women's hall of residence, increased Malawian popular suspicion of its character. But the crowning blow was the extent to which it was identified in Malawian perceptions as a Federal institution; despite the fact that it was planned and largely financed by Britain through the agency of the Central African Council before the Federation began.[186] It was understandable,

[181] Lamba, 'History of Post-War Western Education', pp. 122, 128–9, 180.
[182] Kings Phiri, 'Afro-American Influence in Colonial Malawi, 1891–1945: a case study of the interaction between Africa and Africans of the diaspora', in J.E. Harris (ed.), *Global Dimensions of the African Diaspora* (Washington D.C., 1982), pp. 251–67.
[183] Lamba, p. 141, D.D. Phiri, *Malawians to Remember: James Frederick Sangala* (Lilongwe, 1974), p. 28.
[184] Nyasaland Intelligence Report, August 1957, TNA CO 1015/1748.
[185] Nyasaland Intelligence Report, October 1957, TNA CO 1015/1748.
[186] Thomas M. Franck, *Race and Nationalism. The Struggle for Power in Rhodesia-Nyasaland* (London, 1960), pp. 129–31.

although ironic, that in the early 1960s, at the very time that UCRN gave promise of becoming one of the liveliest African centres of higher education, Dr Banda made clear that university education in independent Malawi would take a territorial rather than regional route.

Constitutional change: initial stirrings

By the end of the war, ministers and officials in the Colonial Office were convinced of the need for the devolution of authority in Africa but the form that it should take in Nyasaland remained a matter of debate. Indirect rule in its original form was no longer perceived as providing a satisfactory instrument for the expression of African views. But the question remained as to what should be the place of Africans – and particularly educated Africans – in the new political dispensation. What should be the position of the European and Asian communities? What should be the relationship of the territory, Nyasaland, to the wider Central African region? Behind these issues lay an equally pertinent question: would the authoritarianism of the colonial state provide a model for the new political order or would democracy flourish in the post-colonial state?

The position of educated Africans in the political process was directly related to the future of indirect rule. Introduced in Nyasaland as a comprehensive system only in 1934, indirect rule was intended as a device to deflect African political energies from territorial into tribal channels through the construction of a network of Native Authorities with their own Native Courts and Treasuries. The war-time Governor, Richards, was an enthusiastic advocate of the system and in the early 1940s supported measures to transfer responsibility for tax collection entirely to chiefs and to equip them with their own tribal police contingents.[187] From the end of the war, however, pressures for reform grew, stimulated by changes in the Colonial Office. In 1947, in an important initiative, Arthur Creech Jones, the new Labour Colonial Secretary, called on African governors to develop 'an efficient and democratic system of local government' through the incorporation of 'the growing class of educated men' into local councils.[188] Lord Hailey, who visited the Protectorate in 1948, was highly critical of the performance of Nyasaland chiefs'.[189] Colby, on a visit to the Colonial Office, took a similar line: 'His Native Authorities were generally speaking apathetic and very little useful work was being done by the Native Treasuries whose funds were largely devoted towards paying the salaries of their staffs.'[190]

An administrator to his roots, contemptuous of politicians of all colours, Colby was convinced 'that however desirable progress in the reorganisation of Local Government might be, the reorganisation of the economic life of the territory was of first priority.'[191] Nevertheless, if the Colonial Office required consti-

---

[187] File, 'Reduction of Nyasaland Police Force and Appointment of Tribal Police', MNA NC 1/29/1; See also Mzimba District Book Vol 1. Supplement to 1 Jan 1942.
[188] Creech Jones to African Governors, 25 Feb 1947, TNA CO 525/214/44446/1949.
[189] Colonial Office minute by R.E. Robinson, 17 June 1949, TNA CO 525/214/44446/1949.
[190] Colonial Office minute on discussion with Colby, 4 Aug 1949, TNA CO 525/214/44446/1949.
[191] Ibid.

tutional change he was not disposed to object. Even before his arrival in Nyasa-land, the government had created a pyramid of councils in which handpicked commoners discussed issues alongside chiefs. At its base lay Chiefs' councils, proceeding through District and Provincial councils to the Protectorate Council, introduced in 1946. From 1949 tentative measures were taken to make this system more efficient and ostensibly democratic by grouping Native Treasuries together as larger financial units and by devising indirect systems of election to local councils.[192] Certain of these bodies, notably the Dowa Council of Chiefs, are said to have worked with reasonable efficiency. But 'in many cases', so a report noted in 1951, local government institutions were 'unequal to the strain'.[193] In much of the Southern Province attempts to organise Group Coun-cils were largely unsuccessful. Chiefs saw them as a threat to their authority. Educated commoners refused to take part.

The path to devolution led through the Legislative and Executive Councils in Zomba. Set up in 1907, the Legislative Council was a consultative body, composed of an equal number of administrators and nominated unofficials, which discussed legislation submitted to it by the Governor. In the early 1940s there were six unofficials, all of them Europeans, five representing the interests of the settler community and one, a missionary, the Bishop of Nyasaland, appointed by the Governor to represent African interests. Not until 1944 was the issue of direct African representation considered, following an approach by James Sangala and Charles Matinga of the newly formed Nyasaland African Council (soon to be re-named the Nyasaland African Congress); and when it was, the Government proved reluctant to act.[194] Richards, although, as he informed the Colonial Office, not in principle opposed to the appointment of Africans to the council, recommended delay until the new local government system had come into being. Four years later, Colby took a similar stance.[195] Arriving from Nigeria in 1948, he was 'naturally surprised that…there was no African representation in the Legislature', he confided to a senior official at the Colonial Office. But he quickly convinced himself of 'the backward state of development of Africans in general' in Malawi and of 'the paucity of candidates capable of playing a useful part in the Legislative Council in particular'.[196] With Colonial Office support, he therefore rejected any direct involvement of the Nyasaland African Congress, falling back instead on an expanded Legislative Council. This had two African members, appointed by the Governor from nomi-nations made by the Protectorate Council and one Asian representative, nomi-nated through the Asian Chamber of Commerce as well as three administrators to ensure that an official majority was maintained. In 1953, the two original African nominations, Alexander Muwamba and Ellerton Mposa, were joined by a third African, Herbert Gondwe, but the balance of power in the Legislative Council remained unchanged. Europeans had six unofficial representatives. The Governor retained his majority.

For Colby, in the early years of his governorship, the place of immigrant

[192] See Memo on 'Native Administration in 1949', RHL Mss. Afr S 1210.
[193] Memo on 'African Local Government', 25 May 1951, RHL Mss. Afr S 1210.
[194] Memo prepared by Mr C.J. Matinga and presented to the Bishop of Nyasaland, 28 Jan 1944; J.F. Sangala to Chief Secretary, 24 Feb 1944, TNA CO 525/199/44379/1946.
[195] Colonial Secretary to Governor, 19 April 1944, TNA CO 525/44248/1944.
[196] Colby to A.B. Cohen, 23 July 1948, TNA CO 525 205/44248/1948.

communities in the new political order was an even more pressing issue than the role of the African majority. As Table 10.6 demonstrates, the number of Asians living in Nyasaland increased threefold between 1945 and 1956, at which time the Asian population of 8,504 was significantly higher than the European population of 6,732.

Table 10.6
Europeans & Asians in Nyasaland 1901–1961

Year	European Population	Asian Population
1901	314	115
1911	766	481
1921	1486	563
1926	1656	850
1931	1975	1591
1945	1948	2804
1956	6732	8504
1961	8750	10630
1966	7395	11299

(*Source*: Dotson, *Indian Minority*, p. 48; *Malawi Census 1966*, ix.)

Such an increase might have been expected to result in a demand for greater constitutional rights but, in fact, the Asian political voice was muted. Pranlal Dayaram sat as a nominated member on the Legislative Council from 1949. But divisions among Asians ensured that no concerted campaign was launched to press for further representation. Split on religious grounds between the majority Muslim community, based centrally in Limbe and Zomba, and the minority Sikh and Hindu communities, based in Blantyre and elsewhere, Asians in Nyasaland became further divided as a consequence of the partition of India in 1947. Some Muslims, such as the barrister, Sattar Sacranie, retained their links with India and, in the early 1950s, played an active part alongside Apa Pant, the Indian High Commissioner to East and Central Africa, in providing financial and ideological support for the NAC. Other Muslims identified themselves with Pakistan and denounced Sacranie to the Government for his anti-European activities.[197]

As Asian numbers rose, European politicians led by Malcolm Barrow called for action to neutralise what they saw as a growing political threat.[198] The franchise system devised by the Nyasaland Government for the first federal elections in 1953 and subsequently used in the territorial elections of 1956 provided the answer to their prayers. Only British citizens literate in English were allowed the vote, a measure which had the effect of disqualifying the great majority of Asians in Nyasaland, many whom were British-protected subjects, not citizens. Both Asian candidates were overwhelmingly defeated in the 1953 elections with all four seats going to European representatives of the Federal Party and in 1956

[197] Nyasaland Political Intelligence Reports, June 1952, July–October 1953, TNA CO 1015/404 and 465. See also Dotson, *Indian Minority*, pp. 53–4, 324.
[198] J.R.T. Wood, *The Welensky Papers* (Durban, 1983), p. 329; Nyasaland Political Intelligence Report, August 1953, TNA CO 1015/465.

the outcome was even worse.[199] Colby had considered retaining a reserved seat for Asians in the Legislative Council but abandoned the proposal under pressure from the Federal Government with predictable results. Only 338 Asians were admitted to the voters' roll compared with 1,866 Europeans. White candidates won all six non-African seats. One of the two Asians who stood forfeited his deposit.[200] Asian involvement in the Council was thus brought to an end, with the result, as a report noted later that year, that 'the Asian community is now taking little interest in politics.'[201]

European settlers were a more formidable force but they too were afflicted by weaknesses. Small in number – with a population of only 6,700 in 1956 – the European community was divided in a variety of ways. Many missionaries no longer felt any common identity with white farmers. But farmers were themselves divided: by nationality into British and 'others' (the Italians and the Greeks); by occupation into the salaried employees of British-based tea companies and the small minority of genuine settlers who were permanent residents of Nyasaland; and by geography into the comfortably situated inhabitants of the Shire Highlands and the more self reliant tobacco farmers of the Lilongwe Plain. It is notable that while the Blantyre-based Convention of Associations was accepted by Europeans in the Southern Province from 1928 as the appropriate body to nominate individuals as unofficial representatives on the Legislative Council, this claim was regularly challenged by farmers from Ntcheu northwards who, in 1936, founded the Northern Provinces Association to represent their interests.[202]

Furthermore, whereas successive governors in the 1930s had been broadly persuaded of the economic and strategic value of the settler community to Nyasaland, Colby, in the late 1940s and early 50s, was altogether more tepid in his views. Like Shenton Thomas before him, Colby approved of the well-run tea plantations in Cholo and Mulanje districts but he was less supportive of the white tobacco farmers in the Central Province and he had no time at all for the huge land-owning companies in the Shire Highlands which he regarded, with some justification, as 'a serious brake on the development of this territory' and a major cause of Nyasaland's poverty.[203] In consequence, Colby, while prepared to work with European politicians, was opposed to transferring any further authority to them. By 1948, when he took up the Governorship, six European unofficials sat on the Legislative Council, two of whom also served on the inner cabinet, the Executive Council. Colby admired the abilities of the senior Executive Councillor, Malcolm Barrow, a wealthy tea planter, who was later to become deputy Prime Minister of the Federation of Rhodesia and Nyasaland. But he was critical of the 'reactionary' nature of most Europeans in the country and argued that, if they were granted an unofficial majority in the Legislative Council, it would be 'used to stifle African development and progress on the southern model'.[204]

[199] Political Intelligence Reports for November and December 1953, TNA CO 1015/455.
[200] Pachai, *Malawi*, p. 240; Wood, *Welensky Papers, pp.* 433–35.
[201] 'The Political Situation in Nyasaland at the end of 1956', TNA CO 1015/961.
[202] Minutes of the Northern Provinces Association for 12 April 1945, 31 May 1947, 26 Jan 1952, MNA.
[203] Colby to Sir Sidney Abrahams, 28 Feb 1949, TNA CO 525/207 44332/1948.
[204] Colby to Cohen, 23 July 1948, TNA CO 525 205/44248/1948.

With the introduction of the Federation in 1953, Colby was reluctantly forced to agree to the creation of an electoral system by which Europeans and Asians on a common roll could vote directly for members of the Legislative Council. But he demonstrated his continued preference for direct rule by largely ignoring the views of Barrow's successor, A.C. Dixon, the general manager of the BCA Company, and of those of other European members on the Executive Council.[205] Not until 1956 when Sir Robert Armitage, an old Kenya hand, took over from Colby were settler politicians to be regularly consulted by the Governor and even Armitage was acutely conscious of their limitations.[206] Soon after his arrival in the Protectorate, Armitage made clear his belief that members of the European community were too limited in ability as well as too few in numbers to be considered for ministerial office.[207] Through their London boards and extensive political contacts, large institutions such as the BCA Company were capable of obstructing the implementation of colonial policies – as they demonstrated in the 1950s over the attempt to end *thangata*.[208] In the post-war period, however, their ability to initiate change was almost non-existent. If Nyasaland's Europeans were to secure their position in an increasingly uncertain climate, their only hope of doing so was to forge an alliance with the far larger settler minorities of Southern and Northern Rhodesia.

The origins of Federation

As Lord Blake has noted, the Federation of Rhodesia and Nyasaland 'now looks like an aberration of history – a curious deviation from the inevitable course of events, a backward eddy in the river of time'.[209] Yet for more than a dozen years prior to its formal dissolution at midnight on 31 December 1963, the Federation was a subject of intense passions, vehemently condemned by the overwhelming majority of Malawians, supported with almost equal fervour by white settlers in Central Africa, and giving birth to an immense scholarly literature, very little of which, unfortunately, is relevant to the history of Malawi. In particular, the central question of why Nyasaland was incorporated into the Federation against the strenuous opposition not just of many Malawians but also of the Nyasaland Governor has barely been addressed.

The background to the emergence of the Federation can be found in the periodic initiatives taken by settlers in Southern and Northern Rhodesia between the wars to amalgamate the two territories under a single government. In the initial stages, Nyasaland was only marginally involved but in the mid-1930s some settlers in the territory became convinced of the political and economic advantages to be gained from the creation of a British Central African Dominion of which Nyasaland would be a part, a view which the then Governor, Harold Kittermaster, shared.[210] Nyasaland's constitutional future was, therefore, one of

---

[205] Colby to Gorell Barnes, 24 Dec 1953 TNA CO 1015/549; Baker, *Development Governor*, pp. 342–45.
[206] Colin Baker, *Retreat from Empire: Sir Robert Armitage in Africa and Cyprus* (London, 1998), pp. 184–85.
[207] Record of Informal Discussion between Colonial Secretary and Governors of Northern Rhodesia and Nyasaland, 30 Dec 1956 TNA CO 1015/1604.
[208] See Chap. 12.
[209] Foreword by Lord Blake to Wood, *Welensky Papers*, p. 15.

the issues considered by the Bledisloe Commission, set up by the British Government in 1937 to examine proposals for closer association of the Central African territories. The evidence it received, however, revealed deep divisions between the majority of white farmers, who were generally favourable to the establishment of closer links with the settler-controlled colony of Southern Rhodesia, and a variety of African groups – native authorities, native associations and others – all of whom were emphatically opposed.[211] The commissioners, therefore, although attracted to the idea of closer union, recognised that it would be prudent to delay. On their recommendation, an inter-territorial body, 'The Central African Council', was founded in 1944 to discuss such issues as transport and agricultural research. Otherwise, the coming of war brought discussion of amalgamation to an end.

The resurgence from the late 1940s of interest in closer union can be explained in a number of ways. For Sir Godfrey Huggins, prime minister of Southern Rhodesia, and Roy Welensky, leader of the elected unofficials in the Northern Rhodesian Legislative Council, the key new factor was the growing evidence of Britain's readiness to contemplate a transfer of power within her African possessions. Faced by the possibility that Northern Rhodesia might in time follow the Gold Coast on the path to majority rule, Welensky looked to the creation of a Central African dominion that the white minority would continue to dominate. By 1948 he had become convinced that neither the Labour Government nor the Conservative opposition in London would contemplate a simple transfer of power to white settlers – the inevitable consequence of amalgamation – and instead had fallen back on the lesser option of federation where the distinctive characteristics of the northern protectorates would continue to be preserved. This would have the virtue of complying with the Colonial Office requirement that educated Africans would be progressively involved in government while ensuring that in practice power passed to – or in the case of Southern Rhodesia, remained in – settler hands.[212] In Huggins's view the presence of Nyasaland was an optional extra: desirable in the sense that labour from Nyasaland was of value to the Southern Rhodesian economy but of much less importance to his constituents than were Northern Rhodesia's booming copper mines.

Andrew Cohen, head of the Colonial Office's African division, took a different, although complementary position. One of the architects of Britain's post-war decolonisation strategy, Cohen was a man of left-wing tendencies, critical of white segregationist attitudes and an advocate of African advancement as long as it resulted in the emergence of stable and politically pro-Western successor states.[213] The election of Dr Malan's National Party government in South Africa in 1948, however, reinforced his belief that South Africa was a hostile, expansive power, seeking to pull Southern Rhodesia and possibly Northern Rhodesia into its orbit. His conclusions were summarised in a memorandum he wrote in 1950, discussing the arguments for and against federation: 'From the broad Commonwealth point of view the creation of a solid British

---

[210] Quoted in Robert Rotberg, *The Rise of Nationalism in Central Africa* (London, 1966), pp. 105–06.
[211] Palmer, 'White Farmers in Malawi', pp. 218–21; Gray, *Two Nations*, pp. 177–193.
[212] Sir Roy Welensky, *Welensky's 4000 Days* (London, 1964), pp. 21–25.
[213] Blake, 'Foreword', in Wood, *Welensky Papers*, pp. 24–25; R.E. Robinson, 'Sir Andrew Cohen: Proconsul of African Nationalism', in L.H. Gann and P. Duignan (eds), *African Proconsuls: European Governors in Africa* (Cambridge, 1978), pp. 353–64.

bloc of territories in Central Africa would make it easier to resist economic and political pressure from the Union of South Africa and to prevent the undue spreading of South African ideas northwards.'[214] Moreover, Federation would also be economically advantageous. 'From the strategic, economic, and communications points of view there would be great practical advantages in establishing a stronger inter-territorial organisation in Central Africa.' As long as a formula could be found that would protect the interests of the African peoples of Northern Rhodesia and Nyasaland in their association with settler-ruled Southern Rhodesia, Federation seemed the ideal option.

Arthur Creech Jones, the Colonial Secretary from 1948 to 1950, remained sceptical of this plan. Perhaps he was influenced by the coherent arguments against Federation contained in a pamphlet written by his friend and correspondent, Dr Hastings Banda, in May 1949.[215] But when Creech Jones lost his post in the Cabinet reshuffle of 1950 the case against Federation diminished. James Griffiths, Creech Jones's successor, gave his assent in November 1950 for a conference of officials to examine the practicalities of the scheme, although he remained committed in principle to not going ahead in the face of African opposition. When the Conservatives won the 1951 election, however, this reservation was immediately dropped. Oliver Lyttelton, the new Colonial Secretary, persuaded the Cabinet to endorse the scheme and then convened the Lancaster House Conference of April 1952. Boycotted by African delegates, the conference saw the settlers' representatives further advance their cause. In both Britain and Central Africa, a heated campaign followed during which supporters and opponents of Federation attempted to influence public opinion, but by this time the political decision had been made.[216] After a series of lengthy debates in the British parliament, the Federal Constitution Order in Council was approved on 27 July 1953. A little over a month later, on 3 September 1953, the Central African Federation was formally inaugurated with Huggins as its first prime minister. The views of Malawians and their supporters in the Church of Scotland had been disregarded. So too had the views of the Governor, Colby, who in repeated messages had warned the Government of the dangers that Federation was likely to bring. A natural autocrat, happy to welcome the Federation in 1948 if it succeeded in preventing 'considerable areas of Africa developing as African states with all the attendant disadvantages', Colby became convinced in the early 1950s that Federation had no economic or strategic advantages for Nyasaland and was politically dangerous in that it would be likely to give rise to African unrest.[217] As late as March 1952 he was still providing the Colonial Office with detailed arguments against Nyasaland's involvement, including the not unjustified assertion that, were it to be introduced, Federation 'would place this Protectorate, in so far as federal subjects are concerned, largely in the hands of

[214] Memorandum by A. B. Cohen on 'Relations of the two Rhodesias and Nyasaland', 15 March 1950 in R. Hyam (ed.), *The Labour Government and the End of Empire, 1945–1951*, 4 vols, (London, 1992), vol. IV, pp. 267–72.

[215] H.K.Banda and H.M. Nkumbula, *Federation in Central Africa* (London, 1949). See also Short, *Banda*, pp. 56–60.

[216] The most detailed account is Gavin A. Ross, 'European Support for and Opposition to Closer Union of the Rhodesias and Nyasaland with special reference to the period 1945–1953', M.Litt. dissertation, University of Edinburgh (1986).

[217] Colby to Lord Milverton, 23 Dec 1948; Colby to CO, 30 Nov. 1051, RHL Colby Papers.

the European elected members of Northern and Southern Rhodesia.'[218]

It is a curious feature of the historiography of decolonisation that, for all the hundreds of pages that have been written on the introduction of the Federation, no convincing explanation has yet been provided as to why Whitehall insisted on the inclusion of Nyasaland, even against the advice of one of its most respected governors. Several suggestions made at the time do little to clarify the matter. As Colby was at pains to demonstrate, there was never any likelihood of Nyasaland being absorbed into the South African bloc.[219] Nor can Whitehall have seriously believed that Southern Rhodesian access to Nyasaland labour was dependent on the two territories being part of a single state. Both before the Federal period as well as after it, many thousands of Malawian workers found employment on Rhodesian farms and mines. Greater credibility can be given to the argument, touched on by Lord Blake, that in insisting on Nyasaland's involvement British officials were seeking to rid Whitehall of financial liability for debts – debts, it should be added, that their predecessors in the 1920s and 1930s had been responsible for incurring in the first place.[220] Certainly, the Colonial Office was insistent that the Federal Government take over responsibility for the railway guarantees which Nyasaland and, in particular, the British Treasury had previously met. CDW loans to Nyasaland, however, continued to be made, so that if Britain did save financially the gain was very slight.

Financial considerations, therefore, must be related to a wider agenda. Fear of apartheid South Africa concentrated the Colonial Office mind but not to the exclusion of its long-term decolonising objectives. British politicians and officials were by no means clear about the precise form that decolonised states would ultimately take. But it was the general assumption in the Colonial Office in the early 1950s (an assumption so deep that it was hardly worth putting into words), that there were a number of colonial territories – including Nyasaland, Sierra Leone, the Gambia, and the individual West Indian islands – that were more likely to become politically and economically viable as part of a wider political community than if they remained confined to the borders of the colonial state. Big might not always be beautiful but there were certain attractions in size. Similarly, the involvement of over two and a half million Malawians in a federation initially dominated by Southern Rhodesian whites could only shift the balance of power and make a 'multiracial' solution including Southern Rhodesia more likely rather than less. Left to itself, there seemed little likelihood that the settler government of Rhodesia would agree to share power with Africans to any significant extent. As part of the Federation that was a possible outcome although – as events were to demonstrate – not one that actually transpired.[221]

---

[218] Memorandum by Sir G. Colby on 'Central African Federation', 19 March 1952, RHL Colby Papers.
[219] Ibid.
[220] Blake, 'Foreword', in Wood, *Welensky Papers*, pp. 20, 26. For the creation of these debts see Vail, 'Making of an Imperial Slum'.
[221] Philip Murphy (ed.), *British Documents on the End of Empire: Central Africa* (London, 2005), Part I, pp. xlviii-li.; Murphy, p. li, minute by W.L. Gorell Barnes, 28 March 1952, PRO CO 1015/65.

Federation & Nyasaland, 1953–63

Few events in the history of Malawi have attracted such widespread condemnation as did the introduction of the Federation of Rhodesia and Nyasaland. Yet for most Malawians, the direct consequences of Federation in the ten short years of its existence were remarkably small. Nyasaland remained a protectorate ruled by a Governor responsible to the Colonial Office and the government of the day in London, and served by a familiar small band of British-based colonial officials, all members of the Colonial Service and hence liable to be posted elsewhere. Most of the matters 'predominantly or exclusively affecting Africans' remained territorial responsibilities, including native and provincial administration, African education, agriculture, fisheries and labour. European agriculture, a Federal responsibility in the other two territories, remained under territorial control in Nyasaland. So too did responsibility for law and order and hence the police, despite the strenuous opposition of Huggins, who had been anxious to create a unified federal police force. The Legislative and Executive Councils continued to function ostensibly unchanged.[222]

Superficial continuity, however, masked three major changes, all of importance in the operation of the state. First, a Federal Government now existed, based in the new Federal capital of Salisbury, with its own locally-based set of civil servants and its own extensive powers. External affairs, immigration, import and export controls, railways, posts and communications and health were all designated Federal responsibilities, creating considerable difficulties for doctors, nurses and dispensers who were forced to choose between transferring to the Federal civil service or moving elsewhere. Responsibility for defence was also vested in the Federal Government, with the result that the two Nyasa battalions of the KAR were transferred from the East Africa Command to the Federal Defence Force and, in consequence, became 'completely divorced from the British Army' with which they had been associated for more than 50 years.[223] British officers were replaced almost entirely by white Rhodesians, a process that was not completed until 1959. African NCOs found their promotion prospects dented, with no Africans being promoted even to the controversial and unsatisfactory rank of Native Officer (*Effendi*), a position held by 35 members of the East African Command in 1959.[224] Not until the eve of independence were the first steps taken to appoint African officers.

Changes in administration were accompanied by changes at a political level. As many Africans had feared, the creation of a federal parliament, most of whose members were elected on a restricted franchise, increased the status and power of white politicians while providing few opportunities for Africans. Under the immensely complicated constitutional system approved by Britain, the Federal Government was made responsible to a parliament consisting of thirty-five members. Seventeen of these were drawn from Southern Rhodesia, eleven from

[222] 'Proposal for the unification of the police services of Central Africa, 1952', TNA CO 1035/370; Wood, *Welensky Papers*, pp. 176–7, 257–8, 325–7.

[223] Timothy Lovering, 'The Role of the Nyasaland Colonial Armed Forces' (unpublished paper, 2000).

[224] Timothy Parsons, *The African Rank-And-File* (Oxford, 1999), pp. 109–110.

Northern Rhodesia and only seven from Nyasaland, a formula designed to reflect the special economic and political significance of Europeans in Southern Rhodesia and bearing no relation to population ratios. Twenty-six of the total (four from Nyasaland) were Europeans elected on a common roll consisting almost entirely of European voters along with a few hundred Asians. Nyasaland was also represented by a European (the Church of Scotland missionary, Andrew Doig) selected by the Governor to represent African interests and by two Africans nominated by the Governor following elections in the Protectorate Council (Wellington Manoah Chirwa and C.R. Kumbikano, both of them active members of Congress).

Power, in consequence, was firmly located in the hands of white Rhodesian politicians, members of the United Federal Party, founded in November 1953 and led by Huggins and, from November 1956, by Roy Welensky. Virtually all European politicians in Nyasaland became members of this party and in so doing found themselves adopting a set of policies and beliefs developed by their more powerful neighbours in the south. White political attitudes tended to become more intransigent, a development exemplified in the career of Malcolm Barrow who, in his rise to the position of Federal Minister of Home Affairs and Deputy Prime Minister, jettisoned the caution and moderation of his early years in favour of an altogether more confrontational approach. By 1960 Barrow had become one of the most extreme as well as one of the most powerful of Federal politicians, a man who berated senior British politicians for their 'criminal folly' in planning to release Dr Banda from gaol and who demanded instead that Banda should be banished from Nyasaland for life.[225]

For African politicians, by contrast, the Federal Parliament proved ultimately unrewarding. A lively and effective debater, regarded by Welensky as his most formidable parliamentary opponent, Wellington Manoah Chirwa spoke regularly in the Federal Assembly. But, treated by his fellow parliamentarians at best with condescension and at worst with scorn, he was in a permanent minority and incapable of influencing events.[226] From 1956, opposition within Congress against his continued participation in the Assembly mounted rapidly, leading to his expulsion from Congress in August 1957. Whether, as Blake has suggested, a radical change in the franchise bringing many more seats to Africans could have gone some way to reconcile Malawians to Federation is highly unlikely. In practice, the various constitutional changes that were undertaken, culminating in the Federal Electoral Act of 1958, actually reduced the proportion of Africans in parliament directly elected by Africans, thus demonstrating that Welensky's European-dominated government had no intention of diluting, far less of transferring, power.[227] 'The Federal and Southern Rhodesian Governments play lip service to the need to give opportunities to Africans but have shown no signs of action so far', Colby wrote in January 1956, pointing out that it had failed to employ Africans as firemen on the Rhodesian Railways or as clerks in post offices in Salisbury.[228] Hardly a Federal minister paid a visit to Nyasaland prior to 1956.

---

[225] 'Record of a meeting between the Federal Cabinet and the Secretary of State for the Colonies', 25 March 1960, TNA CO 1015/2547; Wood, *Welensky Papers*, pp. 751–52.

[226] Wood, *Welensky Papers*, pp. 406, 418–19; Phillips, *Obscurity to Bright Dawn*, pp. 80–81.

[227] Blake, 'Foreword' in Wood, *Welensky Papers*, pp. 31–2.

[228] Colby to Lennox Boyd, 24 Jan 1956, RHL, Colby Papers, Box 1, Folder 2.

Both Huggins and Welensky treated it as a distant and potentially hostile province.[229]

Finally, the economic and fiscal consequences of Federation affected Nyasaland in a number of ways, although it is by no means easy to disentangle the developments brought about by federation from those linked to the cash crop boom, to the growth in production and to the increased investment of CWD funds. Under the fiscal scheme drawn up in 1952, the federal government was assigned control of income tax and customs revenues with the proviso that an agreed share of taxes on profits and incomes should be returned to the territories. As significantly the poorest of the three territories, Nyasaland was allocated only 6 per cent of these revenues but this represented a sum substantially larger than Nyasaland's contribution to federal taxes. The result, when additional federal expenditures in Nyasaland were taken into account, was that, in every year from 1954 to the dissolution of the Federation in 1963, Nyasaland gained considerably from these arrangements – made possible by net transfers from Northern Rhodesia where copper prices were temporarily buoyant.[230] As Colby emphasised, this expansion in revenues had been preceded by the earlier increases that had taken place in Nyasaland from 1948.[231] Nevertheless, as even its sternest critics conceded, 'Federation...brought substantial fiscal gains to Nyasaland', although the same authors also made the relevant point that 'There can be few if any federations elsewhere in which a distinctive and conspicuously poorer region, containing over one-third of the population, would receive so small a share of public funds.'[232] Henry Phillips, who returned to Nyasaland as financial secretary in 1957 after four years' absence, was in no doubt that the impact of the federal fiscal arrangements up to that point had been 'phenomenal', noting that estimated territorial expenditure had doubled from around £4 million to over £8 million between 1953 and 1957/58, despite the fact that the Protectorate no longer had responsibility for two of the largest spending departments, telecommunications and health.[233]

Other economic consequences of federation are more difficult to determine, partly because the issue became highly politicised in the late 1950s and 1960s, spawning a number of partisan accounts. As Hazlewood has demonstrated, Nyasaland's involvement in a new protective customs union with Northern and Southern Rhodesia artificially increased the costs of textiles and utensils from India and Hong Kong to the advantage of Southern Rhodesian manufacturers but at the expense of Malawian consumers.[234] Nyasaland probably benefited from the greater credit-worthiness on the London market of the Federation as compared to the Protectorate. However, by far the largest proportion of loans raised by the Federal Government went on the Kariba dam project and on other

[229] Philips, *From Obscurity to Bright Dawn*, p. 85.
[230] The most useful sources on this topic are: Arthur Hazlewood and P.D. Henderson, *Nyasaland: The Economics of Federation* (Oxford, 1960) and Arthur Hazlewood, 'The Economics of Federation and Dissolution in Central Africa' in A. Hazlewood (ed.), *African Integration and Disintegration* (London, 1967), pp. 185–250. For an admirable summary, see T.D. Williams, *Malawi: the Politics of Despair* (London, 1978), pp. 148–60 with accompanying tables.
[231] Colby to Lennox-Boyd, 24 March 1956, PRO CO 1015/1133.
[232] Hazlewood and Henderson, *Nyasaland*, pp. 49, 58.
[233] Phillips, *Obscurity to Bright Dawn*, p. 91.
[234] Hazlewood, 'Economics of Federation', pp. 217–221. It should be noted that the new tariff was only fully applied to Nyasaland as from May 1957.

developments in Southern and Northern Rhodesia, with Nyasaland's share being less than 5 per cent.[235] Overall, as the Jack Commission reported in 1959, the early years of the federation was a period of marked economic growth for Nyasaland, although this growth had its origins back in the 1940s, prior to the period of federation, and was influenced only marginally by it.[236] Hazlewood's admittedly scanty figures on GDP suggest that Nyasaland's Net Domestic Product, valued at constant prices, rose by 120 per cent between 1950 and 1954 and by a further 43 per cent between 1954 and 1958.[237] This was followed by a slow-down in economic growth in the last years of the federation, caused both by declining export prices and a falling off in investment. Nevertheless, it is worth emphasising that Nyasaland's economy grew faster in the fifteen years leading up to the dissolution of the federation than at any time previously and, other than in the period 1964 to 1978, at almost any time since.[238] Much of this growth was fuelled, as we have seen, by substantial increases in the value of agricultural exports, notably tobacco and tea, the former grown largely by African farmers and the latter on European-owned estates. By contrast, the growth of manufacturing, however statistically impressive, took place from such a small base that the impact on Nyasaland's economy as a whole was very small. By 1958 Nyasaland's manufacturing output was valued officially at only 5 per cent of Southern Rhodesia's.[239] Tobacco processing, a cigarette factory, a cotton factory (David Whitehead & Sons Ltd., opened in 1957), a cement factory, a canning plant and a bottling plant constituted virtually all of Nyasaland's industrial base. Several initiatives, such as the cigarette factory opened by the United Tobacco Company at Chichiri, Blantyre, in 1949, had been established before federation and were not influenced by it.[240] More generally, the overwhelming attraction of Salisbury to investors probably deprived Nyasaland of some import-substitution industries which, in other circumstances, would have been established in Blantyre or Limbe.

Federation, it seems safe to conclude, was, on balance, of some economic benefit to Malawi, bringing the country capital that would not otherwise have been raised at the time and hence contributing to an expansion of agricultural exports that was already under way. Politically, however, it was a disaster. Whatever the faults – and they were many – of the colonial administration in the postwar period, they shrink into insignificance when compared with the behaviour of Federal politicians and civil servants. Smug, incompetent and totally lacking in vision, they would, from 1956, be prime targets for a revitalised Nyasaland African Congress.

[235] Hazlewood and Henderson, pp. 55–59.
[236] Jack Report, pp. 18–27; Hazlewood and Henderson, p. 13.
[237] Hazlewood, 'Economics of Federation', pp. 205–206.
[238] On one estimate, the gross domestic product (GDP) grew by 4.6 per cent annually between 1954 and 1963; by 6.8 per cent annually between 1964 and 1972; and by 6.4 per cent between 1973 and 1978. D. Ghai and S. Radwan, 'Growth and Inequality: rural development in Malawi, 1964–78', in Ghai and Radwan (eds), *Agrarian Policies and Rural Poverty in Africa* (Geneva, 1983), pp. 73–75.
[239] *Federation of Rhodesia and Nyasaland Economic Report for 1958*, p. 69.
[240] For a discussion of tobacco manufacturing in Nyasaland, see Wilshaw, *Century of Growth*, pp. 85–90.

11
The Urban Experience

At the time of independence in 1964 over 95 per cent of Malawi's population lived in the countryside and the economy was almost entirely agricultural in character. Nevertheless, the importance of Malawi's colonial towns should not be underestimated. In their different ways, settlements like Blantyre, Limbe, Zomba and Lilongwe epitomised the colonial imagination at its most vivid in the way that urban space was ordered into precisely designated functions, normally involving the segregation of the European zone from Asian and African sections. Although towns were thus perceived as strong points in the colonial system of control the reality was often rather different. In the years after 1945, Blantyre and Limbe witnessed the emergence of a group of independent African businessmen, several of whom also played a part in a short-lived but comparatively militant labour movement. At the same time, Africans living in the vicinity of Blantyre, most of them in peri-urban villages such as Ndirande not directly under colonial control, forged a distinctive urban-rural culture. This involved both a continued commitment to the rural village as the place of ultimate identity to which most Malawians expected to return, and exposure to a variety of predominantly urban experiences – in sport and in leisure as well as at the work place.

New towns for old

With few exceptions, indigenous towns were casualties of the colonial occupation. Commercial settlements such as those established by Mlozi near Karonga and by Makanjira were destroyed by the British during the anti-slave trade campaign, and although a new Makanjira's was constructed on the lakeshore it was a shadow of what had existed before. Mponda's village retained a population of over 3,000 as late as 1931 as compared with 820 living within the township boundaries in the capital, Zomba.[1] By that time, however, it had lost most of its administrative and commercial functions to neighbouring Fort Johnston and made little contribution to the economy of the country.

---

[1] Kuczynski, p. 536.

Of the pre-colonial commercial settlements it was therefore only Nkhotakota that retained any dynamism during the colonial period and it did so by taking on some of the aspects of a colonial town. One of the largest Islamic centres on Lake Malawi in the 1880s with a population of about 6,000, a small mosque and an Arab school, Nkhotakota suffered from the collapse of the slave and ivory trades but benefited from the establishment of an administrative *boma* there in 1894 as well as an Anglican mission station complete with church and school.[2] For two decades before the construction of a motor road beyond Lilongwe, it served as the port for Fort Jameson with both the government steamer, the *Guendolen*, and the Lakes Company ship, *Queen Victoria*, calling at least once a month. But while dhows were able to sail into the dhow harbour, half a mile from the main market where quantities of rice and cassava were traded, steamships had to anchor a mile offshore in the large shallow bay open to north-easterly winds and rely on lighters to handle cargo. For a time Nkhotakota served as the base for a highly cosmopolitan community consisting of descendants of the original Swahili and Nyamwezi settlers, Chewa ex-slaves, Indian traders, Anglican priests, British administrators, African boatmen, fishermen and farmers. But by the 1940s, it had become largely bypassed as a communications centre, with Nkhata Bay emerging as a more important port. Nevertheless, the town retained its role as an important entrepot for the distribution of foodstuffs with a 'tremendous trade' being carried on in cassava, transported in dhows up and down the lakeshore and a further trade in rice, several hundred tons of which were sold each year to the government.[3] In the 1920s and 30s Nkhotakota consisted of 3,000 to 4,000 huts extending along the harbour and for about half a mile inland, joined by a 'fine avenue' to the market place, near which were the mosque, the government office and the house of Chief Msusa, a descendant of one of the first Jumbe's lieutenants. Further off were the UMCA compound with its distinctive church and school, a government hospital and a collection of Indian and European-owned stores.[4] From 1938, these were joined by the offices of the Kota Kota Rice Society, a cooperative society established through the efforts of the district commissioner, which by the mid-1950s was selling over 2,000 tons of rice a year.[5]

A place afflicted by appallingly high levels of hookworm and bilharzia, Nkhotakota had a reputation for 'immorality' of a type frequently associated with ports.[6] Both *Nyau* societies and *mganda* dance groups flourished in its cosmopolitan atmosphere, the reflection of increasing tension between the Islamised elite clustered around Chief Msusa and his Chewa subjects who became increasingly assertive in the early 1950s in challenging the authority of their ruler. By 1955 the intellectuals associated with the Achewa Improvement Society had succeeded in making the removal of Msusa one of the key aims of the local branch of Congress.[7]

[2]   Lawrence Goodrich to FO, 19 Feb 1885, TNA FO 84/1702; *Life and Letters of Arthur Fraser Sim*, pp. 98–118.
[3]   Annual Reports for Northern Province, 1927, MNA S1/542/28; 1931, S1/61/32.
[4]   Murray, *Handbook*, 1922, p. 135–37.
[5]   Annual Report for Northern Province, 1938, MNA NC 2/1/9; Frank Debenham, *Nyasaland. Land of the Lake* (London, 1955), pp. 83–6, 208–10.
[6]   Annual Report on Kota Kota District, 1934, MNA S1/89 F-J/35.
[7]   Political Intelligence Report, Oct 1953, TNA CO 1015/465; 'The Political Situation in Nyasaland at the end of April 1956', PRO CO 1015/961; *Annual Report on Native Administration for 1956*.

The survival of Nkhotakota was of less importance for the emergence of an urban culture than the founding of a handful of new colonial towns, Zomba, Lilongwe, Blantyre and Limbe, the last two united as the municipality of Blantyre in 1959. Small in size and lacking in many basic amenities, these towns reflect the limited impact of settler colonialism in Malawi up to the 1950s. Yet in the striking contrasts between the administrative capital, Zomba, and the commercial centre, Blantyre, a number of distinctive features in Malawi's colonialism can be seen.

The emergence of Zomba as one of the smallest and most beautiful colonial capitals in Africa is indicative of the fissures that existed below the apparently smooth façade of British colonial society. By the late 1880s, Blantyre had become the leading European settlement in the area, centred on the Blantyre Mission, founded in 1876, and the African Lakes Company headquarters at Mandala constructed in 1882. Harry Johnston, however, was anxious to avoid too close a contact with the disputatious Scottish missionaries and pioneer settlers and instead made his base at the turreted Residency built for Consul Hawes by John Buchanan on the lower slope of Zomba Mountain and completed in 1887. By 1895 only five houses, one of them a post office, existed alongside the Residency. But over the next few years, the settlement gradually expanded to include a military cantonment, a new Government House, a Gymkhana Club, a central prison, two hospitals – one for Europeans and one for Africans – and a collection of wide-verandahed, high-ceilinged bungalows set back in terraces on the side of the mountain, with spectacular views to Mulanje. Racial segregation was carefully maintained through the construction of a golf course which acted as a *cordon sanitaire* between the European residential area and the native township and commercial area on the plain.[8] At the same time, Zomba was endowed with its own Indian-style hill-station through the construction of a road up the mountain (built at a time when hardly another road existed in the country) leading to a dozen or more rustic cottages, perched at an elevation of 6,000 feet, to which officials regularly retreated in the hot season. Here, images of an imaginary English countryside could be contemplated – rolling grasslands set off by vivid green patches of forest and a rushing stream. The latter was stocked with brown trout brought from Scotland at considerable expense and effort in 1907 in order to provide sport for dryfly fishing enthusiasts.[9]

Visitors in the early decades of the twentieth century described Blantyre as Nyasaland's Glasgow, 'the seat of its trade and enterprise', and Zomba as its Edinburgh, the elegant although rather languid seat of government, and this comparison can be made in more than one respect.[10] Edinburgh, so a popular aphorism goes, is 'all fur coat and nae knickers', ostentatious gentility masking a seedier underside, and Zomba too combined superficial charm with an altogether less appealing reality. The first town in East Africa to be equipped with electricity, supplied from the Mulungusi river, Zomba boasted in the Old Residency 'the finest European dwelling…north of the Zambezi' up to the 1920s as

[8]   Murray, *Handbook*, 1922, pp. 163–64; *Report of Land Commission*, 1920.
[9]   Charles Seed, 'Trout in Nyasaland', *Nyasaland Journal*, 2, ii (1949), 23–4. Earlier attempts to introduce brown trout to Zomba Plateau are described in Letters to J. McClounie, 1898–1901, MNA 1/3/1.
[10] Norman Maclean, *Africa in Transformation* (London, 1914), p. 59.

well as an abundance of carefully-tended gardens, bright with jacaranda blossom and shaded by avenues of cedar and eucalyptus.[11] Yet it also lacked any public system for the disposal of sewage with the result that all human excrement had to be buried in pits in the householders' gardens, contributing at once to the vividness of the flowers and the prevalence of amoebic dysentery among officials and their families. Not until 1934, with the aid of a CD grant, was a scheme for water-flushed sewage and pipe-born drinking water begun. Before that, as the Medical Officer noted, residential Zomba was 'practically a block of decomposing animal organic matter 4 or 5 feet thick' with its water being drawn 'from irrigation ditches'.[12]

As Zomba grew during the period of post-war government expansion from a tiny scattered settlement only some 4,500 strong in 1945 to a modest-sized town of over 19,000 inhabitants 20 years later, new colonial suburbs were built but the essential character of the capital remained unchanged. European officials and their families, of whom there were nearly 1,000 in 1961, continued to live a remarkably isolated life with their whites-only club, their whites-only hospital and their whites-only cottages on the mountain, insulated almost as much from the small settler community as they were from their African and Asian neighbours. It was not until the Governor, Sir Glyn Jones, had resigned in protest at its antediluvian policy in 1961, that the club admitted its first African member. Racial solidarity, however, was combined, as always, with an almost obsessional concern for social hierarchy. Housing was allocated precisely by rank with staff literally rising, as they were promoted, from 'Misery Farm', the junior officers' bleak new estate on the plain, to ever more spacious residences set higher and yet higher on the mountain slope where the most senior officials lived. Even in the mid-1950s, hardly a single African was invited to the constant round of sundowners, dinner-parties and balls, although a partial exception was made in the case of the well-educated Orton Chirwa, even before his success in becoming a qualified lawyer.[13]

Blantyre

The leisurely expansion of Zomba in the post-war years may be contrasted with the much more explosive growth of Blantyre, the one Malawian settlement where an unambiguously urban culture emerged during the colonial period. Blantyre, dating from 23 October 1876 when the pioneer Blantyre Mission party took up residence in the area, has claims to be regarded as the oldest colonial settlement in South Central Africa. Little progress in constructing the station was initially made but, in April 1877, James Stewart, a civil engineer from India, took over the settlement and in the next few months laid out the mission on a plan that still survives today: centred on a wide square, fringed by Indian-style bungalows and with an ambitious terraced garden irrigated by a channel from a neighbouring

[11] Murray, *Handbook*, 1932, pp. 163–64; Maclean, p. 62.
[12] *Annual Report on the Social and Economic Progress of the People of Nyasaland*, 1931, TNA CO 626/10; *Annual Medical Report*, 1934, TNA CO 626/13.
[13] Mullins, *Retreat from Africa*, pp. 24–27. See also Phillips, *Obscurity to Bright Dawn*; Ann M. Davidson, *The Real Paradise: Memories of Africa 1950–1963* (Edinburgh, 1993).

stream. As Stewart was quick to note, Blantyre's site, healthy, fertile and on the main route from Quelimane to Lake Malawi, was well placed to make it 'the market place of the district' and an important 'commercial and agricultural centre'.[14] Within a matter of years, John and Fred Moir had constructed Mandala House and compound, the African Lakes Company's ambitious headquarters, on a neighbouring ridge, while Eugene Sharrer, a rival transporter and land speculator, had built his own headquarters on Kabula Hill. In 1894 plans for a township in the hollow bordering these three settlements were approved by local landowners. Over the next decade the town gradually took shape with 'none of the wide streets running at right-angles, typical of Bulawayo, Johannesburg, Nairobi and other African towns', but rather as a collection of 'hamlets in a circle of four or five miles', joined by dusty roads in a spectacular state of disrepair.[15] Indian traders, the first being the Muslim, Osman Adams, opened stores in what became known as 'the Asiatic Ward', a flourishing 'native market' was started, and in 1901 a 'native location' was opened to provide temporary accommodation for the large number of porters employed in carrying loads – although this was closed following the opening of the railway in 1908 and the consequent reduction in the number of carriers.

The opening of the railway proved less of a boost to Blantyre than its inhabitants had hoped. Already weakened by the Administration's preference for Zomba as the colonial capital, the township suffered from the decision of the Shire Highlands Railway Company to locate its workshops and headquarters at the tiny settlement of Limbe, five miles distant, particularly as the Imperial Tobacco Company immediately followed suit, opening its new factory at Limbe in August 1908.[16] Indian traders flocked to the township, further tobacco factories were built and, in 1938, the Auction Floor was opened, reinforcing Limbe's position as the tobacco marketing centre of Malawi. Meanwhile, Blantyre stagnated in the 1920s and 1930s, during which time Nyasaland's white farming community fell by nearly half. By 1945 there were still fewer than 4,500 inhabitants living in and around the township compared to over 7,000 in Limbe. Approximately 280 Europeans were living in each settlement, compared with over 1,000 Asians, 400 in Blantyre and 600 in Limbe. Blantyre could boast the only hotels of substance in the territory, the High Court, a couple of banks, lawyers' offices, a weekly cinema and a flourishing whites-only club. But it remained remarkably thin on basic amenities, lacking tarred roads or a water-born system of sanitation. However, the European area was now the proud possessor of electric lighting, introduced in 1926, and of a piped supply of drinking water, in operation from 1933.

From the first, as John Iliffe has noted, Blantyre 'exemplified that combination of colonial poverty and Southern African racialism that was Nyasaland's particular misfortune.'[17] Male Europeans only were permitted to stand for the pioneer town council elected in 1897 and it was they who were to define the racially segregated character of the settlement. Repeated efforts were made to confine Indian traders to the centrally located but increasingly crowded 'Asiatic

---

[14] James Stewart to Dr Macrae, 21 May 1878, *Missionary Record*, 21 May 1878.
[15] L S Norman, *Nyasaland Without Prejudice* (London, 1934), p. 32; *CAT*, 26 Sep 1903.
[16] Twiston Davies, *Fifty Years of Progress*, pp. 38–40.
[17] Iliffe, 'Poor', p. 260.

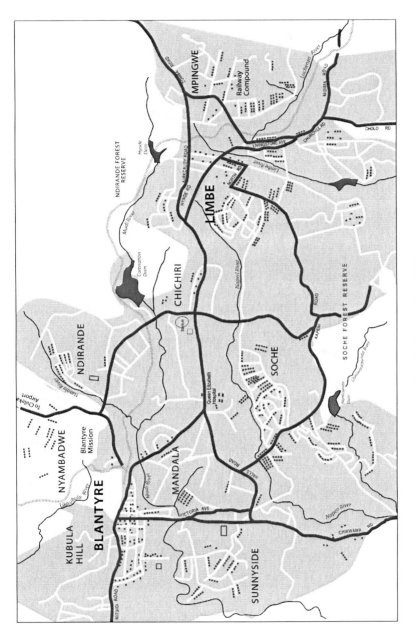

Map 5 Blantyre, late 1950s

Ward'. Africans were banned from providing housing for themselves – in contrast to the situation in Dar es Salaam where African-owned houses were common – through the stipulation in the bylaws 'that only buildings of brick, wood or iron be allowed, and that such houses should be of no less value than £50'.[18] Europeans were housed in leafy suburbs, one of the earliest being the aptly named Sunnyside.

With the passage of time, bylaws discriminating against Asians were gradually relaxed under pressure from Government but Africans were subjected to further segregationist measures. Following the appointment in 1899 of a township police force, financed by the ratepayers, a curfew was imposed on Africans who were forbidden to remain in the township between 9 p.m. and 5 a.m. without a pass provided by their employers.[19] Only domestic servants and night watchmen were allowed to live in the township; no Africans, accordingly, were permitted on the electoral roll – a situation that continued right up to the eve of independence. As late as the early 1950s, Africans were served through a window in most European-owned shops; hardly a single hotel would accept African custom.[20]

Yet, while at one level Blantyre conformed to Southern African type, at another the town diverged from it as a consequence of the negligible resources available to the local council. Faced in the 1920s by the growing demand for African accommodation, both Blantyre and Limbe councils produced plans for native locations modelled loosely on those in Bulawayo and Pietermaritzburg.[21] But with neither the European ratepayers nor the Government prepared to pay, progress was agonisingly slow. Not until 1936 were the first 30 houses constructed on the Blantyre Council location at Naperi and they, according to a later report, were of an 'unbelievable' standard, consisting of 'windowless brick and thatch hovels in poor repair'.[22] A few private companies in Limbe followed the lead of the Imperial Tobacco Company and Nyasaland Railways in providing basic housing for their employees on their own locations.[23] But the great majority of workers was forced to find accommodation elsewhere – a few in illicit shacks constructed with the tacit approval of employers within the township; others on the back verandahs of Indian-owned shops. Most African urban residents, however, lived in villages fringing the town, some of these close to Blantyre at Ndirande, on the lower slopes of the mountain of that name; others at Chichiri, mid-way between Blantyre and Limbe, at Mpingwe, Michiru and even, by the 1950s, at Chiradzulu, twelve miles or more from town.

Much useful information on the character of Blantyre-Limbe's peri-urban villages is provided in the series of surveys carried out under the supervision of

---

[18] Blantyre Town Council Minutes, 21 September 1897, MNA BL 2/1/1/1.
[19] *CAT*, 12 December 1903; Blantyre Township Bye-Laws, February 1913; Blantyre and Limbe Township Ordinances, 1930, MNA S1/392/19. See also McCracken, 'Coercion and Control', pp. 132–3.
[20] Morton, *Just the Job*, p. 234; Power, 'Individual Enterprise', p. 35; Blantyre Town Council minutes, 28 February 1922, 30 May 1922, 30 May 1923, 1 Aug. 1923, MNA BL 2/1/1/2.
[21] Blantyre Town Council minutes, 28 February 1922, 30 May 1922, 30 May 1923, 1 Aug. 1923, MNA BL 2/1/1/2.
[22] *Annual Report of the Nyasaland Medical Department for 1936*, PRO CO 626/15; 'Report by the Advisory Board of Health on the Sanitary Services in Blantyre and Limbe', 1951, MNA PC 53/5/1.
[23] Davies, *Fifty Years of Progress*, pp. 38–40.

David Bettison in the mid-1950s.[24] All of the 17 villages studied possessed a pronounced rural-urban hybrid quality: women retained access to land on which they cultivated maize and a variety of other crops; most men worked in town. In 1957, 73 per cent of adult males resident in villages lying within four miles of Blantyre were working there, as were 66 per cent of those living between four and eight miles from the town. In striking contrast to the shifting population of Salisbury, where labour migrants from Nyasaland and Mozambique formed a majority of the African population up to the mid-1950s, the population of Blantyre's peri-urban villages was 'remarkably stable', with some 71 per cent of adults in 1957 having been born in or close to the villages in which they lived.[25] According to the somewhat dubious statistics collected on 'tribal affiliation', 36 per cent designated themselves 'Yao', indicating that they were descended from the communities that had established political dominance in the district in the 1860s, while a further 15 per cent described themselves as 'Lomwe', meaning that they were descended from incomers from Mozambique. No less than 34 per cent described themselves as 'Ngoni', meaning in this context that their relatives had come from the Ntcheu and Dedza districts of the Central Province, a trend that originated in the late 1880s and early 1890s when many Ngoni came to work for the ALC and other companies. Virtually no Tumbuka or Tonga labour migrants from the Northern Province were recorded as living in these villages. Some northerners, however, worked in the railway workshops and lived in the compound at Limbe which had been opened in 1947; others were employed in Blantyre as clerks, although these were few in number when compared with the growing community of Livingstonia-educated civil servants in Zomba. Overwhelmingly however, Blantyre, in contrast to Zomba with its communities of northern clerks and Yao Muslim domestic servants, was a town of stabilised southerners, over 75 per cent of them Christians, who lived with their wives and families in a semi-rural environment which was largely independent of colonial control.

The particular character of Blantyre's urban culture is best represented by Ndirande, a sprawling settlement which had its origins in the proliferation of villages formed by former slaves and others in the vicinity of the Church of Scotland mission from the late-1870s. By the 1950s, Ndirande had become the home of more than 3,000 inhabitants but it remained officially invisible – absent, for example, from any town map prior to the 1960s – and saved by its Trust Land status from council interference. A place of exceptional poverty, it also provided some Malawians with exceptional opportunities. The poorest townsfolk resident here had less to eat than rural villagers, according to Platt's nutritional survey in 1938.[26] But Ndirande's proximity to the centre of Blantyre ensured that it was also home to members of a new urban elite, men like the Blantyre Mission-

[24] David G. Bettison, 'The demographic structure of seventeen villages, Blantyre-Limbe, Nyasaland', *Rhodes-Livingstone Communications,* XI (Lusaka, 1958); Bettison, 'Migrancy and social structure in peri-urban communities in Nyasaland', in R.J. Apthorpe (ed.), *Present Interrelations in Central African Rural and Urban Life* (Rhodes-Livingstone Institute, 11th Conference Proceedings, Lusaka, 1958); D.G. Bettison and P.G. Rigby, 'Patterns of income and expenditure, Blantyre-Limbe, Nyasaland', *Rhodes-Livingstone Communications* XX (Lusaka, 1961).

[25] Bettison, 'Demographic structure of seventeen villages', pp. 73–4.

[26] Veronica Berry and Celia Petty (eds), *The Nyasaland Survey Papers 1938–1943* (London, 1992). pp. 138–43.

educated clerk James Frederick Sangala, one of the founders of the Nyasaland African Congress in 1944, and independent African businessmen such as the locally-born Lawrence Makata, a successful transporter and bar owner, known in the 1950s as 'the king of all African businessmen'.[27] By the 1950s men like these frequently built and rented out rooms and houses in Ndirande, adding to its increasingly cluttered appearance.[28]

The rise of Makata is an indication that certain limited opportunities had long existed for entrepreneurial African businessmen in the Blantyre area, despite the many formidable restrictions to which they were subjected. As early as 1901, two enterprising 'native tailors' were working on their own account at Kabula Hill, making jackets and trousers for Europeans.[29] These were the fore-runners of the 180 tailors, the 42 butchers, the 12 bicycle and gramophone repairers and the 25 blacksmiths that the District Commissioner, Ion Ramsey, counted in the environs of Blantyre in 1931.[30] There were also four laundry owners, one of whom, Charles Thomas Mtemenyama, employed a staff of 14 and netted profits of £90 a year, and several dealers in foodstuffs, timber and furniture.[31] Some women traded in foodstuffs either in Blantyre or Ndirande market; many more were involved in the production and selling of beer and particularly of the illegal spirit *kachasu*. According to one estimate, in the early 1930s successful beer brewers from villages close to Blantyre were making profits of from £8 to £10 a year.[32]

The story of the growth in the production and sale of drink is inextricably linked to the changing fortunes of urban women. Back in the 1870s, when the pioneer Blantyre missionaries arrived in the Shire Highlands, beer brewed from maize, millet or sorghum was widely consumed; but locally distilled spirits were rarely drunk – chiefs and headmen instead preferring imported spirits, notably brandy obtained from Portuguese traders, to which they applied the Brazilian name, *kachasu*.[33] From 1892, however, an international tariff aimed at limiting the sale of European spirits in the Zambesi basin reduced imports and hence gave rise to an increase in the sale of locally distilled *kachasu* which quickly attracted the disapproval of the colonial authorities.[34] In 1911 distilling of this type was made illegal and residents were instructed to 'sharply punish' those involved.[35] Meanwhile, with the spread of money, beer brewing as a commercial activity took off, with beer being 'sold to all-comers at a penny a jug' in the vicinity of Blantyre in 1905.[36] Four years later, in 1909, both Blantyre and Limbe Councils proscribed its sale and consumption within the townships, following a campaign led by the Presbyterian missionary, Alexander Hetherwick. The women brewers, however, simply moved their activities to the outer boundaries

[27] Obituary of L.M. Makata by O.E. Chin'oli Chirwa, *Malawi News*, 19 Apr. 1962.
[28] Power, 'African Entrepreneurship', p. 43; D.G. Bettison and R.J. Apthorpe, 'Authority and Residence in a Peri-Urban Social Structure – Ndirande, Nyasaland', *Nyasaland Journal*, 14, 1 (1961), pp. 7–39.
[29] *CAT*, 30 Nov. 1901.
[30] Blantyre District Annual Report, 1931, MNA NSB 7/1/2.
[31] Power, 'African Entrepreneurship', pp. 173–93.
[32] Power, ibid., pp. 199–200.
[33] Duff Macdonald, *Africana*, I, pp. 90–92.
[34] Suzanne Miers, *Britain and the Ending of the Slave Trade* (London, 1975), pp. 174 and 277.
[35] *Nyasaland Protectorate The Resident's Handbook*, 3rd edition, (London, 1914), p. 29.
[36] *LWBCA*, Dec. 1905.

and continued as before.[37] In 1915, the government responded by introducing a licensing system by which only certain, predominantly male, Africans – usually chiefs or headmen – were given the legal right to sell beer at designated places. This, however, had the unintended effect, so a missionary ruefully complained in 1917, of creating 'bars', run by women, who paid a fee to the license-holder, with the aim of '"raising the wind" by cooking and selling beer' and hence of making money for themselves.[38]

By the 1920s, therefore, women brewers were already involved in a lengthy rearguard action designed to ensure their right to produce and sell alcohol in the face of a series of measures aimed either at ending the drink trade or of bringing it under male control. Chiefs were quick to use the enhanced powers they obtained from the introduction of indirect rule to enforce the payment of beer licences by women, at an annual cost of over £3,000 in the Southern Province by 1948.[39] Meanwhile, police regularly raided distillers of *kachasu* in the area, arresting over 100 individuals per year. With few alternative means of making money in sight, however, women traders were undeterred. In 1946 *kachasu* distillers were said to have no difficulty in paying the £5 fines, and when the fines were increased, several combined together to ensure that the money could be found. As in cities elsewhere, some policemen in Blantyre were quietly induced not to pursue their investigations too rigorously, with the result that the number of cases reported bore no relation to the number of offenders.[40] In 1951 groups of men and women intoxicated through *kachasu* drinking could be found at any hour of day or night within two miles of the Blantyre post-office.[41] At one village adjacent to Blantyre, 11 out of 17 houses contained stills in 1957. In another village, 56 per cent of the total village income accrued from *kachasu* sales.[42] By 1948, so Rangely noted, Chichiri had emerged as 'the gin palace and brothel area of the district', the haunt of hundreds of young men drawn there to drink beer and *kachasu*, to dance with bar girls (prostitution was an alternative source of income) and to listen to South African music.[43]

The two decades from 1945 marked the transformation of Blantyre and Limbe. Even during the war the population began to grow, stimulated by a substantial increase in the number of Asian traders, who more than trebled in number between 1937 and 1945. It was the peacetime boom, however, that brought matters to a head. With prices rising for most commercial crops, new tobacco processing factories were opened in Limbe and by the United Tobacco Company at Chichiri, leading in turn to the expansion of European-owned transport and commercial companies and to the further immigration of Asian traders. The boundaries of the townships were sharply expanded in 1948 and a new rating system was introduced, significantly increasing the revenues available to

37 Power, 'African Entrepreneurship', p. 8. See also Blantyre Township Bye-Laws, 1912, MNA S1/392/19.
38 *LWBCA*, July-Dec 1915; April-Dec 1917.
39 Annual Report for Blantyre District, 1949, MNA NS 3/1/14.
40 Blantyre Monthly Police Reports, Sep 1944, May 1946, June 1946.MNA POL 5/2/2.
41 Report of Social Welfare Officer, Southern Province, 1951, MNA 2/28/7F 2525. I owe this reference to Megan Vaughan.
42 H.D. Ng'wane, 'Economics of Kacasu distilling and brewing of African beer in a Blantyre-Limbe Village', in Apthorpe, *Present Interrelations in Central African Rural and Urban Life;* Vaughan, *African Famine*, p. 130.
43 Rangeley to Ellis, 24 April 1948, quoted in Power, 'African Entrepreneurship', p. 304.

the councils.[44] New building funds were made available by the government, anxious to diversify government buildings away from Zomba in the aftermath of the destructive landslide that hit the town in December 1946, leading a commission of enquiry to recommend that, if the funds could be found, the capital should be transferred to Blantyre.[45] With the European population at last beginning to grow, two British-based building contractors set to work in the townships, providing opportunities by the score for African sub-contractors. By 1948 fifteen African businessmen, working independently but combining to share the hire of a lorry, supplied lime from Lirangwe in the Shire Valley to European builders in Blantyre and Limbe. Dozens more, employing many hundreds of workers, were hard at work in the brickfields that had suddenly sprouted at Chirimba, Ndirande and the Midima road areas. Others were involved in the sale of charcoal, the price of which trebled in 1949. Over twenty Africans owned maize mills in the Blantyre district as compared with just two in 1947. Many more had entered the timber industry and were supplying sawn planks to European customers.[46]

As the economy expanded, new jobs were created and many more Africans flocked to town, bringing the total population of Blantyre-Limbe to close on 55,000 in 1956, and to 110,000 ten years later. Between 1948 and 1956, Blantyre's dusty and pot-holed roads were surfaced, hundreds of houses were built, and work began on a number of major projects including the 400-bed Queen Elizabeth Hospital, completed in 1958, the High Court Buildings at Chichiri and the Rangely (later Kamuzu) Stadium. Factories producing soap, cement and other goods were opened, marking Nyasaland's first faltering venture into the manufacturing sector. Many new buildings were erected by, among others, the Nyasaland Transport Company which inaugurated a bus service in Blantyre in 1947.

Negotiations aimed at amalgamating the two councils began in 1948 but progress was slow and it was not until 1956 that a new combined Town Council was created, consisting of six European elected members for a European population of 2,500, two elected Asian councillors for an Asian population of 2,700 but leaving the 50,000 African urban residents unrepresented.[47] African opinion, therefore, went largely unconsulted with the result that, when the government in 1951 introduced a radical new plan involving the division of the town into high, medium and low density areas, it provoked a strong negative response. By 1955–6 more than a thousand houses were being constructed for African government employees at the locations opened at Soche and Naperi. But, at the same time, active steps were taken to destroy the lively settlement of independent householders, businessmen and prostitutes that had grown up along the main road at Chichiri, now designated an industrial zone.[48] Evictions continued sporadically in the face of protests from African householders, reaching a climax

[44] Blantyre Town Council minutes, 8 March 1948, MNA B2/1/1/13.
[45] Report of the Committee appointed to examine the advisability of removing the capital from its present site, 22 March 1947, TNA CO 525/213/44398/1947. This proposal was blocked by the Colonial Office.
[46] Blantyre District Annual Reports, 1948, 1949, MNA NS 3/1/14.
[47] Blantyre Town Council minutes, 1 Jan 1956, MNA BL 2/1/1/15.
[48] *Annual Report of the Labour Department, 1955; Annual Reports of the Public Works Department, 1955–56.*

in 1959 when the Government took advantage of the presence of Rhodesian troops during the Emergency to destroy 'well over a thousand huts of unlawful squatters' at Chichiri.[49] New sites were opened at Bangwe east of Limbe and Michiru west of Blantyre. But with the influx to the city accelerating, the housing crisis grew more severe. By 1962, according to one study, Blantyre was in urgent need of at least 7,500 additional houses of the cheapest, most basic type.[50]

Population growth was only one aspect of a much wider set of changes influencing the behaviour of working people in Blantyre. With imported goods in short supply, prices for hoes, cotton goods, bicycles and tyres rose rapidly between 1939 and 1947, leading to the doubling of the cost of living for many urban Africans.[51] Food prices also rose with a particularly sharp increase in the market price for maize flour, the staple food, from 0.5d per lb in 1939 to 1d in 1945, and up to 4d or 5d during the worst months of the famine of 1948–49.[52] With labour in short supply in the years after 1946, pressure on wages was intense and they too rose, although from a very low base and probably at a slower rate than the cost of living up to the late 1940s. Basic wages for unskilled male workers, exclusive of rations, rose from 6 shillings per month in 1939 to 10 shillings in 1946 and 12s 6d in 1947 – a figure that remained unchanged until 1950.[53] In certain occupations, however, much lower rates of increase were recorded. Unskilled railway workers received 9s 6d a month in 1938 but only 10–15 shillings in 1947, plus a cost of living allowance of 5 shillings a month for Blantyre and Limbe. Senior domestic servants were paid an average 20 shillings a month in 1938; some of them were still being paid only 25 shillings in 1947. This was in contrast with the wages of 40 shillings or more commanded by Malawian cooks working in Southern Rhodesia.[54]

For those workers unfortunate enough to live in town, wages were only part of the problem. Even in the 1930s, housing conditions were bleak but with the growth of population they deteriorated further. Some temporary alleviation of Blantyre's dreadful sanitary conditions had taken place in the early 1930s with the installation of a piped supply of drinking water to the town, paid for through a CDW grant.[55] No waterborne system of sewage disposal was constructed, however, and little effort was made by the Town Council to keep pace with the growing population. A survey carried out by the Government Health Inspector in 1949 'revealed a deplorable state of affairs.'[56]

In the central areas of the Township over-crowding was rife and subdivision of trading plots up to 1/40th of an acre was recorded. Shop assistants were sleeping in shops, their beds being screened off by temporary partitions. African servants were sleeping on the back verandahs of shops, in bath rooms and even in disused latrines...Waste water latrine

[49] *Annual Reports on African Affairs*, 1959, TNA CO 624/36.
[50] Iliffe, 'Poor', p. 275.
[51] Blantyre District Annual Report for 1947, MNA NS 3/1/4.
[52] *Annual Reports of the Nyasaland Labour Department*, 1946–49. Vaughan, *African Famine*, pp. 29–49 provides a graphic account of changes in the price and availability of food during the famine.
[53] *Annual Report of the Labour Branch of Provincial Administration*, 1938, TNA CO 626/18; *Annual Reports of the Labour Department*, 1946–1951.
[54] Southern Province Annual Report for 1947, MNA NS 3/1/12.
[55] *Annual Report on the Social and Economic Progress of the People of Nyasaland*, 1931, TNA CO 626/10.
[56] Secretary, Advisory Board of Health to PC Southern Province, 26 Apr. 1951, MNA PC 53/5/1.

washings and liquid excrement were disposed of from plots by earth or broken concrete drains to the main road drains in the townships, which are open and flow through the main streets to the nearest river bed. The water in the river beds was thus grossly polluted and this water was the main source from which African domestic supplies were drawn and in which ablutions and the washing of laundry took place... Night soil disposal sites were situated dangerously in the centre of built up areas and were maintained in a shockingly filthy state.

Some improvements in the collection of night-soil (human excrement) were introduced in Blantyre in 1950, but the situation in Limbe 'was not so fortunate.' Writing in 1951, a board of experts noted: 'There is a rapidly increasing African urban population for which no provision is made in the way of sanitary services.' The only water supply available, the streams running through the townships, continued to be heavily polluted. 'The advent of serious epidemic disease', they concluded, 'is only a matter of time...'[57]

Workers & businessmen

It is against this background of urban deprivation and rising prices that the first wave of worker militancy in Blantyre emerged. Labour unrest in Malawi has a long history, going back at the Blantyre mission to the 1880s when 'The wages question was a vexed one...strikes were a common occurrence several times in one day.'[58] Nevertheless, while Malawian migrants had been deeply involved in worker protest in the interwar years in places as far apart as Cape Town, the Shamva mine in Southern Rhodesia and the Copperbelt, there is little evidence that the experience they gained in the south was directly employed in labour disputes in their homeland. Tales of 'Kerementi' (Clements Kadalie), the visionary Malawian trade union leader who fought to ensure 'that black men are allowed to have a union so that they can speak to the whites as one clan speaks to another', circulated widely in Malawi during the 1920s.[59] Yet even the return of Kadalie's right-hand supporter, Robert Sambo, to Nyasaland in 1929 did not result in the founding of a branch of the powerful Industrial and Commercial Workers Union of South Africa [ICU] in the country from which they came. As Palmer has noted, 'manifestations of the kinds of hidden local, day-to-day and passive resistance appropriate to the conditions of American slave plantations [and] Southern Rhodesian mining compounds' were common on Nyasaland tea estates during the 1930s.[60] But evidence of more overt action in Blantyre is very largely lacking prior to the ending of the Second World War when labour shortages and inflation provided the potent combination out of which the labour movement was to grow.

The emergence of an urban-based workers' movement may be dated from October 1945 when members of the recently established Nyasaland Teachers' Association met in Blantyre to press for higher wages.[61] Little appears to have

---

[57] Ibid.
[58] *LWBCA*, March 1913.
[59] T Cullen Young, 'The native newspaper', *Africa*, 11 (1938), p. 60.
[60] Palmer, 'Working conditions and worker responses,' p. 119.
[61] Minutes of a meeting of the Nyasaland Teachers' Association, 7 Oct. 1945, MNA NSB 3/3/6.

been achieved at this meeting but, in 1946, 'there were symptoms of dissatisfaction among labour' caused, it was said, 'by the rise in the cost of living'.[62]
And over the next two years a series of further protests took place, involving
transport workers, domestic servants and council workers, among others, and
demonstrating the growth, if not of unambiguous class consciousness, at least of
group solidarity. Domestic servants were the earliest to act. In 1946 they solicited
the support of the Blantyre branch of the Nyasaland African Congress in order
to press their case with European employers. Calls were made for a significant
increase in the wage rate to bring it closer into line with wages in Southern
Rhodesia where many Malawian servants had worked and demands were made
that long-service workers should receive pensions or gratuities. Mr Solijoli, a
cook, complained 'that we are not treated as human beings'; Mohomed Matola,
noted 'that we work from 4 or 4.30 a.m. up to 8 or 9.30 p.m. daily, yet our pay is
too little'. James Gunde added: 'Our maize and everything is where we are
employed because we have no time to go home to open garden and to feed our
family.' Moses Sangala returned to the basic question: 'Why Nyasaland servants
cannot get better pay? Every servant in Rhodesia is better paid.'[63] The threat of
strike action was openly employed although, in the event, neither domestic
servants nor the leaders of Congress were prepared to risk confrontation. Using
the excuse that 'we have not enough time and it is difficult to meet', the domestic
servants' leaders rejected suggestions from Congress that they should form a
union. In the absence of such a body, the Congress President, Charles Matinga,
was unwilling to push the issue to a showdown. By September 1946 he was
boasting that it was through his conciliatory advice that a strike by servants had
been averted.[64]

While domestic servants talked, Blantyre's night soil workers acted. A
despised group, only a few dozen strong in comparison with the army of more
than 1,000 servants employed in the town in the late 1940s, night soil workers
were responsible for maintaining Blantyre's antiquated sewage system which
depended on the daily emptying of buckets.[65] When they went on strike in May
1947, demanding increased wages, protective clothing and an additional soap
ration, the Council was stung into action. Within a day wages had been increased
to a modest 18s 6d a month and it had been agreed that soap would be issued
weekly rather than monthly. As waterproof coats were expensive, the Council,
with characteristic miserliness, ruled that they would not be allowed.[66] But this
decision was rescinded in 1951 when, following the threat of a further strike,
wages for night soil workers were increased to 35 shillings and mackintoshes
were finally provided.[67]

As in many parts of Africa, transport workers were at the heart of Blantyre's

[62] *Annual Report of the Nyasaland Labour Department*, 1946.
[63] Meetings of the Nyasaland African Congress, Blantyre branch, with domestic servants, 23 Mar. and
2 June 1946, MNA NS 1/3/10.
[64] Charles Matinga, President's Address to the 3rd Conference of the Nyasaland African Congress, 23
Sept. 1946, MNA PCC 1/4/1.
[65] For a vivid description of the operation of sewage disposal in Blantyre see Morton, *Just the Job*, pp.
244–46. By 1957 the number of domestic servants employed in and around Blantyre had increased to
3,500. David G. Bettison, 'The private domestic servant in Blantyre-Limbe', *Nyasaland Journal*, XII
1 (1959), p. 36.
[66] Blantyre Town Council Minutes, 22 May 1947, MNA BL 2/1/1/13.
[67] Blantyre Town Council Minutes, 23 Apr. 1951, MNA BL 2/1/1/14.

labour movement, although fundamental distinctions existed between free-booting, entrepreneurial, lorry drivers and the railway workers who constituted the core of Blantyre's proletariat. The presence of railwaymen as the largest occupational group in Blantyre dates from 1908 when the Shire Highlands Railway Company (renamed in 1930, the Nyasaland Railway Company) established its headquarters and major workshops at Limbe. In the late 1940s the company employed about 4,800 men, the majority of whom were housed with their wives and children in the large location it opened at Mpingwe in 1947 and extended in subsequent years.[68] Railwaymen were thus in a very different position from the majority of wage-earners in Blantyre who retained regular access to land and lived in Ndirande or in peri-urban villages five miles or more from the town.

Like workers elsewhere, the railwaymen were affected by the Company's racially segmented recruitment policy under which Europeans, Asians, Coloureds, Mauritians and Africans were employed on separate wage scales and under separate conditions of employment. However, they had the advantage over black railway workers in the Rhodesias in that the proportion of non-African workers employed was comparatively small (approximately 1:16 as compared to fewer than 1:3 in Southern Rhodesia in 1957).[69] In consequence, a number of skilled jobs barred to Africans on the Rhodesian railways, notably those of driver and fireman, were filled by African railwaymen in Nyasaland. Significant differentiation, accordingly, existed among Malawian railway workers who were divided in 1955 into 3,200 low-paid unskilled workers, 300 clerks and 850 artisans, including drivers, senior foremen and firemen, some of whom by this time were earning up to 23s 6d a day, more than twenty times as much as many of their fellows.[70]

The existence of this relatively small group of skilled workers, many of them former apprentices with more than five years on the railway, was an important factor influencing the development of the labour movement in the 1940s. The first signs of trouble came in February 1946, when African drivers and firemen took advantage of their crucial strategic position to press the management for a substantial rise in wages.[71] This occurred only four months after the outbreak of a major strike on the Rhodesian railways in which Malawians were believed to constitute about half of the 1,200 strikers, and was no doubt influenced by it.[72] In June they took industrial action again, using the machinery of the newly-formed Railway African Staff Association to press for the ending of the colour bar. This was followed in February 1947 by the threat of a general strike, which was averted only by the promise of a further increase in wages.[73] Conflicts emerged, however, between artisans and unskilled workers, with the workers in

---

[68] Blantyre District Annual Report for 1947, MNA NS 3/1/4; *Annual Reports of the Labour Department for 1947 and 1949;* Jack Report, p. 75.

[69] Jack Report, p. 75; Thomas M. Franck, *Race and Nationalism. The Struggle for Power in Rhodesia-Nyasaland* (London, 1960), p. 156.

[70] *Annual Report of the Nyasaland Labour Department,* 1955, p. 18.

[71] *Annual Report of the Labour Department,* 1946, p. 6.

[72] See *Note on the Annual Report of the Labour Department for 1945,* Hailey Papers, Notes on Nyasaland, TNA CO 1018/57.

[73] C.D. James, 'On behalf of the railway African staff' to General Manager, Associated Railways, 5 Feb. 1947, MNA NSB 3/3/6; Annual Report on Blantyre District for 1947, MNA NS 3/1/4.

the lower grades repudiating the leadership of 'so-called representatives' who, they claimed, 'were not empowered to act on behalf of all the African staff'.[74] And these divisions continued after 1950 when the management officially recognised the African Railways Staff Association as the body representing railway workers. Aggrieved at the rising cost of living, workers held a meeting at the Mpingwe compound on February 24 1951 at which they subjected the General Manager to a series of criticisms, called for a doubling of wages across the board as from 1st January and threatened to strike if their requests were not met.[75] However, none of these demands or threats was communicated to management by D.B. Ndovi, the Vice-Chairman and chief negotiator of the Staff Association, who compounded the problem by agreeing to a settlement that provided nothing at all to 30 per cent of the workers – those in the lower grades – and only modest gains to the rest.[76] Ndovi's dismissal by management for what were said to be 'other disciplinary grounds' therefore went largely unremarked by rank-and-file workers who retreated into inaction over the next few years.

Even the foundation in 1954 of the Nyasaland Railway African Workers' Union did not provide them with an effective or representative institution. Two years later, the Protectorate's Labour Officer noted that it was still not properly organised; by 1957 it had attracted only 1,000 paid-up members out of an African staff of over 6,000.[77] In that year its secretary underwent a three-month study course in Japan under the auspices of the Federation of Democratic Youth – the first indication of the internationalisation of trade union activities in Malawi. No organisational benefits appear to have percolated down to the members. Divisions among railwaymen thus continued to persist, although there can be little doubt that a measure of class consciousness emerged among them at this period, explained largely by the organisation of the industry. Some groups of workers were scattered along the line of rail but the great majority was concentrated in the Limbe workshops, a situation facilitating the emergence of a corporate identity. Most lived with their families in the company location at Mpingwe. Many were highly committed to their jobs so that turnover among staff was slow. By the late 1950s some 40 per cent were classified as 'permanent' workers with at least three years' continuous employment in the industry, whereas in the tea industry little more than 25 per cent of the workers were permanent and, in the construction industry, less than ten per cent.[78] To a greater extent than most other wage-earners, therefore, railway employees had an intimate understanding of labour conditions gained over a number of years.

The repeated attempts to develop links of worker solidarity among railwaymen may be compared with the more politically astute yet individualistic action of Blantyre's motor drivers and mechanics under the leadership of Lawrence Makata and Lali Lubani, the most prominent representatives of the new urban culture that emerged in Blantyre-Limbe in the 1940s and 1950s. Born in 1916 into one of the leading Yao families in the Ndirande area, Makata combined membership of the locality's traditional elite with an energy and

---

74 *Annual Report of the Labour Department for 1947.*
75 Nyasaland Political Intelligence Report for Feb. 1951, TNA CO 537/7231.
76 Political Intelligence Report for Mar. 1951, TNA CO 537/7231.
77 *Annual Reports of the Labour Department*, 1956 and 1957.
78 *Annual Report of the Labour Department*, 1957, table E.

shrewdness that was all his own.[79] As a young man, he left school early – turning his back on the conventional path to economic success – and joined Hall's Garage in Blantyre as a driver and mechanic at a time when lorries had only recently supplanted head porterage as the main means of transport in the country.

Makata's subsequent career demonstrates the rich rewards that could be obtained from combining hereditary influence at the village level with a mastery of the skills and opportunities that lorry driving provided. During the Second World War he concentrated on carrying goods for his employer between Blantyre and Salisbury. But in 1947 he responded to the post-war boom in the transport business by joining forces with his fellow Yao lorry driver, the ex-soldier Lali Lubani, to found the Nyasaland African Drivers Association.[80] Some drivers and mechanics were recruited from Conforzi's Tea and Tobacco Company at Cholo where they had recently been involved in a strike over wages. Most, however, worked in Blantyre-Limbe, headquarters of the only bus company in the country as well as of several garages.[81] Dues were set at 5 shillings for entry plus 12 shillings annual fees – a high rate designed to discourage all but skilled workers in the industry.[82] Lubani, the Chairman, affiliated the association to the Nyasaland African Congress and spoke at the fourth annual meeting in September 1947, calling on the Government to arrange a minimum wage for drivers, commensurate with their skills.[83] The next year, the appeal of the association was widened by the replacement in the title of the word 'Drivers' by 'Workers'; a year later, in 1949, it was officially registered as Nyasaland's first trade union.[84] Numbers were kept deliberately small, rising to only 255 by 1957. But their strategic importance was such that employers in the transport business founded a parallel organisation in the same year, 'to enforce the adoption of a uniform scale of wages and of time and overtime in every branch of the business' and to defend 'the interests of its members against combination of workmen'.[85]

Historians have noted the tendency over much of Africa in the post-war period for labour leaders to be ideologically populist and socially ambiguous, supporters of worker solidarity on one hand but with a strong belief in individual advancement on the other.[86] In Blantyre, these tendencies were taken to extremes. For lorry drivers like Makata, Lubani and James Mpunga, a fellow founder of the African Transport Workers Association and also the founder of his own canteen business, combination was a means rather than an end – the end being the furthering of their own economic interests through strategies which involved the mobilisation of networks of dependants. In 1948, while still secre-

[79] Bettison and Apthorpe, 'Authority and residence', pp. 11–12. For further details on Makata see Power, 'African Entrepreneurship', pp. 292–94, 323.
[80] L.L. Lubani for Lawrence Makata (Secretary), Nyasaland African Drivers Association, 5 Aug. 1947, MNA NSB 3/3/6.
[81] Annual Report on the Southern Province for 1947, MNA NS 3/1/12.
[82] Constitution of the Nyasaland African Drivers' Association, 1947, MNA NSB 3/3/6.
[83] Records of the 4th Annual Meeting of the Nyasaland African Congress, 22–26 Sept. 1947, MNA PCC 1/4/1.
[84] *Annual Report of the Labour Department*, 1949.
[85] Provincial Labour Officer to PC, Southern Province, 13 Nov. 1948, MNA NSB 3/3/6.
[86] See Bill Freund, *The African Worker* (Cambridge, 1988), pp. 91–109.

tary of the association, Makata made the transition from wage earner to entrepreneur by purchasing a second-hand lorry from his employer, which he used for
selling firewood in Blantyre. 'He was so successful in this enterprise', according
to his friend and political ally, Orton Chirwa, 'that he soon bought four more
lorries and entered fully into the general transport business.'[87]

> His business then grew by leaps and bounds. He built maize machines, started brick-
> making, timber works and so on. By 1952 his operations extended to such things as bus and
> taxi services between Ndirande and Blantyre. He became well known throughout the
> country as the famous Makata and Sons Ltd. He opened five milling machines, a fabulous
> bar at Lilongwe, a garage; his properties throughout the Southern and Central Provinces
> were worth thousands of pounds. He was the king of all African businessmen.

Yet, like self-made businessmen elsewhere, Makata's success was insecure and
he looked constantly for means to give it firmer foundations. One strategy he
adopted in 1953 was to challenge European and Asian economic dominance by
creating an African Chamber of Commerce, along with a dozen or more other
self-employed businessmen, several of whom had also been involved in the
Motor Drivers' Association only a couple of years earlier.[88] Another was to
develop elaborate ties of patronage with Blantyre's urban poor through the provision of credit on relatively easy terms and through the loan of lorries to mourners
seeking transport to funerals – almost always held in the rural village from which
the deceased had originally come. He also sponsored a primary school in
Ndirande and revived the Ndirande Welfare Club (founded in 1933) as 'a club
run by Africans themselves' and as a focus for political agitation.[89]

One of his key henchmen in all these activities was Lali Lubani, the first
Chairman of the Motor Drivers' Association and, by the early 1950s, a fellow
transporter and store-keeper. Another was Hartwell Solomon, Makata's
successor as Secretary of the Motor Workers' Union, a man who combined a
fine line in Marxist rhetoric with part-ownership of a mobile cinema and a
stake in a furniture factory.[90] Entrepreneurs such as these were representatives
of a new, self-consciously 'modern' type of urban leadership owing little to
mission education. Yet, as Power has noted, they were also acutely aware of
their need to satisfy communal obligations by providing support for their
extended kin. In his role as brickmaker, Makata recruited labourers from the
Lower Shire Valley at wages lower than workers living closer to Blantyre were
willing to accept. Yet he also went out of his way to demonstrate his generosity
through the distribution of favours to those less fortunate than himself.[91] From
this standpoint, Makata's pursuit of the Makata village headship in the mid-
1950s was entirely compatible – because inextricably linked – with his drive to
maximise profits.

[87] Chirwa, obituary of Makata, *Malawi News*, 19 Apr. 1962.
[88] Political Intelligence Report, Nov. 1953, TNA CO 1015/455.
[89] Minutes of a General Meeting of the Ndirande Welfare Club, 15 June 1941; James F. Sangala to DC
Blantyre, 21 June 1947, MNA NSB 3/3/5.
[90] Minutes of a meeting of the Blantyre branch of the Nyasaland African Motor Transport Workers,
25–26 Sept. 1948, MNA NSB 3/3/6; Political Intelligence Report, Oct. 1949, TNA CO 537/4725.
[91] In my analysis here and in the preceding paragraph I am indebted to Power, 'African Entrepreneurship', pp. 334–362.

Urban culture

The last decade of colonial rule was a period of particular importance for Malawi's towns. With the national population now rising at more than three per cent per annum, the influx into all the major towns accelerated although, in Blantyre's case, part of the explanation for the doubling of the population between 1956 and 1966 was the incorporation within its boundaries of peri-urban villages that had previously been excluded from demographic surveys. Even Lilongwe, a sleepy market and administrative centre containing only 400 inhabitants as late as 1936, grew rapidly in the postwar era to reach a population of over 19,000 thirty years later.[92] For urban workers, wages remained 'conspicuously low', as the Colonial Office noted in 1957.[93] However, with food prices in the township market rising only very slightly between 1953 and 1958, the substantial increase in the minimum daily wages in Blantyre, from 10d in 1952, to 1s 4d in 1955 and 2s 6d in 1959, almost certainly involved a real increase in living standards for workers in employment although from a very low base.[94] Job insecurity, however, which had been at a relatively low level in the late 1940s when labour was in short supply, grew very markedly following the downturn in the economy from 1957, the loss of jobs and, for the first time in Malawi's urban history, the growth of substantial unemployment. With the future of the Federation now in doubt, inward investment dried up in 1959 leading to 'a growing volume of unemployment which became so serious about the middle of the year that the Government was asked to accelerate its own programme of public works'.[95]

Urban crime, however, remained at remarkably modest levels by the standards of our time. Although Blantyre rather than Zomba, 'the more respectable and law abiding settlement of Government officials', was the main source of serious crime, according to the Commissioner of Police, figures for murder, manslaughter and housebreaking were distinctly low.[96] Over the whole of Malawi, 85 cases of murder and manslaughter and 2,070 cases of burglary and housebreaking were reported in 1957; by 1960 the figures had risen to only 137 and 3,316 respectively.[97] Occasional professional thieves, like the notorious John Petros Mitende in the 1940s, won legendary status through their exploits in robbing European homes. Theft, however, was normally a low-level activity taking place in peri-urban villages.[98] In 1950, according to the Blantyre police,

---

[92] Cole-King, *Lilongwe*; Half Yearly Intelligence Report ending 31 Dec. 1936 by acting Intelligence Officer, 2 KAR, MNA S2/6ii/27.

[93] J.C. Morgan to Sir Robert Armitage, 12 July 1957, MNA SMP/23050/77 quoted in Iliffe. 'Poor', p. 124.

[94] Figures calculated from *Annual Reports of the Labour Department*, 1952 to 1960. See also David G. Bettison, 'The Poverty Datum Line in Central Africa', *Rhodes-Livingstone Journal*, 27 (1960). This notes that wages in Blantyre were somewhat less than half those in Salisbury in the late 1950s, but that food prices were nearly half as cheap. Overall, however: 'the average wage is in each case well below the cost of goods and services required to keep a family in health and decency.' [pp. 4–5].

[95] *Annual Report on African Affairs*, 1959, PRO CO 624/34. See also *Annual Reports of the Labour Department*, 1958–1961.

[96] W.B. Bithrey, to Chief Sec., 16 May 1939, MNA POL 2/17/3.

[97] *Annual Report of the Nyasaland Police*, 1960.

[98] McCracken, 'Coercion and Control', pp. 134–35.

juvenile delinquents 'prey on bus passengers and market hawkers and indulge in petty pilfering in Indian stores' but their numbers remained very small.[99] Over the whole of the country, about 50 juveniles a year were convicted of theft in the mid 1950s. In 1960, the figure was only 73. In Malawi, as in the rest of Africa, it was no doubt the case that communities were less successful than tradition suggests in caring for the elderly and the infirm.[100] Even in villages where the majority of women had been abandoned by their husbands, however, very few of them allowed their children to run wild. In the late 1890s, so Judge Nunan believed, Ngoni women were being brought by pimps to Blantyre as prostitutes for European men but whether this trade continued in the twentieth century our sources do not tell.[101] By 1953, according to one well informed witness, 'there were innumerable girls [in Blantyre] who earn their living as prostitutes who never come before a court.' Most of these, it has been argued, are likely not to have been professional prostitutes but rather poor women, lacking the support of men, who turned to prostitution as a strategy of survival.[102]

Urban living involved the construction of a variety of new social and ethnic categories. Tribal societies, common in most West and East African towns, were few in number in Blantyre – perhaps because stabilised workers in peri-urban villages were less in need of communal support than were foreign long-term migrants. Such societies as were formed, notably the Alomwe Tribal Representative Association founded by Lewis Bandawe in 1943, were more concerned with pressing a particular case on the government than in providing needy kinsmen with social assistance.[103] Religious affiliation, however, was of importance, particularly in the new government-planned townships at Soche and Kanjedza that lacked the network of traditional authorities that Ndirande possessed. In the late-1950s, so Wishlade has claimed, few African independent churches were active in Blantyre.[104] But the Blantyre Synod of the CCAP and the Roman Catholic Church both played influential social as well as religious roles in disciplining their members and providing them with support. According to figures collected by Bettison, around 36 per cent of Blantyre's African population claimed affiliation to the CCAP in 1957.[105] Although politically radical, the Scottish church was doctrinally conservative, dominated at parish level by cautious and increasingly elderly men. Nevertheless, the Church of Scotland (as it was still described by most of its members) contained within itself a capacity for innovation that was to prove of importance in later years. In 1962, the Rev C. J. Nkunga was appointed as minister to the large new church of St Columba, close to the rapidly expanding settlement at Soche, the bleak new home of many Malawian Christians. Under his influence, contacts were established with the Assemblies of God pentecostal church at Kanjedza, and within a matter of years revival meetings were being held at St Columbia's, to the consternation of other

99 L. Hannon to DC Blantyre, 27 Dec. 1950 quoted in Iliffe, 'Poor', p. 270.
100 The key argument of John Iliffe, *The Poor in the History of Africa* (Cambridge, 1987).
101 McCracken. 'Marginal Men', p. 550.
102 Iliffe, 'Poor', p. 271.
103 Bandawe, *Memoirs*, pp128–29; Vail and White, 'Tribalism', pp. 172–73.
104 R.L. Wishlade, *Sectarianism in Southern Nyasaland* (London, 1965), pp. 31–32.
105 Bettison, 'Demographic Structure of Seventeen Villages', pp. 54–55. Other figures were: Roman Catholics, 26.2%; Seventh Day Adventists, 8.7%; Zambesi Industrial Mission, 4.1%; Watch Tower, 1.5%. In the villages studied only 4.4% of the people questioned declared themselves Muslims.

CCAP leaders, involving people dancing, singing and speaking with tongues. The way was being prepared for the emergence from St Columba's in the early 1970s of a new wave of youthful born-again preachers who would revitalise Blantyre's religious life.[106]

Meanwhile, in the late colonial period, it was through music and politics rather than religion that young people expressed their independence most effectively. *Beni* and *Mganda* were now danced in towns as well as in villages. But they were joined in the 1950s by new musical modes, carried by gramophone, wireless and returned migrant from South Africa – *sinjonjo* (Malawian jive and twist*)*; the 'shocking' *jole* dance (a dance where partners held each other); above all, *kwela*, a passion among adolescents. Born in South Africa in the early 1950s, *kwela* music, played upon metal flutes, popularly known as pennywhistles, swept through Malawi in the 1950s and 1960s only to vanish as rapidly as it had emerged. By the 1970s, its most distinguished performers, Donald and Daniel Kachamba, had to make tours of Europe in order to find an audience. Ex-soldiers like James Kachamba, Donald and Daniel's father, introduced guitar and banjo music to Malawi in the aftermath of the war. It was played to enthusiastic audiences by Soza Molesi and others at popular centres in Chileka and elsewhere.[107]

Football, too, claimed the attention of many young Malawian men. First played in 1880 at the Blantyre Mission, football, so a missionary noted, was taken up by 'natives of all ages and sizes' with a 'zeal which would delight the heart of any disciple of the school of Physical Education'.[108] At Livingstonia, the stern Robert Laws concentrated on drill rather than on games. But at Likoma the Anglican missionaries were enthusiasts for football, convinced that through playing it, students would become imbued with the quintessentially English virtues of self-discipline and fair play. It was they who in 1910 brought out a book of rules, standardising what had previously been a highly informal pastime.[109] In the 1920s other bodies – the police, the prisons, *boma* administrative staff – also took part in football matches. However, it was not until the foundation of the Ndirande Welfare Club in 1933 that the game was organised on a formal basis. Run by a group of mission-educated clerks and businessmen, the club had its own football team and playing field on which it played regular matches against the Jeanes Training College at Domasi and the Nyasaland Railways African Football Team, the first company-sponsored side in Malawi.[110] In Lilongwe, Levi Mumba convened a public meeting in 1937 at which it was agreed 'that immediate steps should be taken to revive the interest of Africans in sport, especially Football, which though it exists in name is not played for lack of ball or ground.'[111] But the key development came with the establishment of the Shire Highlands African League in 1938 and the interest that it aroused among ordinary workers in Blantyre as well as among the educated elite.

[106] Richard A. van Dik, 'Born-again Zealots: The Young Preachers of Malawi. A Report', (unpublished report, 1989), Appendix 2.
[107] Gerhard Kubik, *Malawian Music, A Framework for Analysis* (Blantyre, 1987), pp. 17–31.
[108] Duff Macdonald, *Africana*, Vol. II, p. 224; *Life and Work Blantyre Mission Supplement*, July 1880.
[109] B.W. Randolph, *Arthur Douglas. Missionary of Lake Nyasa* (London, 1912), pp. 85, 137–8, 149, 165, 241; Duff, *Nyasaland under the Foreign Office*, p.81.
[110] *Annual Report on Native Affairs for 1933*, TNA CO 626/12; J.F. Sangala to DC Blantyre, 21 June 1947, MNA NSB 3/3/15.
[111] Notes of a Public Meeting of Africans held at Lilongwe, 26 May 1937, MNA S1/22/38.

In 1939, the Nyasaland Railway Company began to run 'football specials' between Blantyre and Limbe taking fans to some of the matches.[112] By 1946, so it was noted, 'Enthusiasm for sport, that is essentially for football, amongst Africans has grown', leading to the incorporation of teams from Chileka and Lunzu into the Shire Highland League and climaxing in a match played for the Nyasaland Amateur Football Association Cup between the Abraham Team from Blantyre and the Zomba Amateur Athletic Club. In a rare outbreak of multira-cialism, the game was 'played on the grounds of the Blantyre Sports Club' where it 'attracted large crowds and produced some play of high class in its opening stages when the outcome two goals to one goal was decided'.[113] James Frederick Sangala, the founder of the Nyasaland African Congress, was the chief organiser of the League. He was also the manager of the first Malawian team to participate in an international match, the game played in Beira in June 1949 at which a Shire Highlands Select lost to the Beira team, Grupo Desportivo Rebenta Fogo.[114] By this time the Nyasaland African Football Association had been established and under its control football continued to flourish with new teams like the Imperial Tobacco Company taking on existing favourites, Michiru, Abrahams and Ndirande Lions. Educated men continued to dominate the game, at least at a managerial level, although their organisational frailties were demonstrated in the late 1950s when 'inadequate finance, paucity of transport and fatalistic apathy among its organisers' were said to bedevil the game in the Northern Province.[115] Nevertheless, football was now an unequivocally African activity rather than the instrument of cultural imperialism that some early missionaries had tried to forge, with charms being heavily employed in important matches to assist one's own players and to prevent players in the opposing team from scoring. These were of little assistance to the Nyasaland team in October 1962, defeated by 12 goals to 0 by the famous Ghana Black Stars in Nyasaland's first full interna-tional. Nevertheless, this match, followed in June 1964 by a drawn game against Southern Rhodesia in front of 50,000 spectators in the Kamuzu Stadium, was not without significance in the forging of a popular Malawian identity.[116] At a time when regional differences threatened to tear apart the fragile fabric of the new state, the emergence of a generation of 'ninety-minute nationalists', united in their support of Malawi, if only on the pitch, was of no mean value in giving popular meaning to the idea of the nation.

---

[112] Annual Report on the Southern Province for 1939, MNA NS 3/1/8.

[113] *Annual Report on Native Affairs for 1946*, TNA CO 262/24.

[114] D.D. Phiri, *Sangala*, pp. 12–13; Moses T. Dossi, *Football in Malawi: A Way of Life* (Limbe, 1992), pp. 7–8.

[115] *Annual Report on African Affairs*, 1959, TNA CO 626/35.

[116] Dossi, *Football in Malawi*, pp. 9–15.

12
Peasants & Politicians
1943–1953

Introduction

During the 1940s and 1950s, the colonial government of Malawi was faced by mounting opposition larger in scale and more intense in type than anything it had previously experienced. The nature of the opposition varied considerably from place to place. In the Shire Highlands, long-term resentment among tenants over the exaction of *thangata* on European-owned estates deepened from the early 1940s, leading in 1953 to an outbreak of peasant-based violence, the nearest that Central Africa experienced at this period to the Mau Mau revolt in Kenya. Independent peasants in the Central Province were aggrieved by the policies pursued by the Native Tobacco Board. Peasants more widely resented the imposition of *malimidwe*, the new intrusive conservation rules imposed by the Department of Agriculture. Fear of the likely impact of federation added to discontent. This was combined in a number of districts with the appearance of subordinate groups seeking to challenge the system of collaborative alliances with chosen chiefs that had been carefully constructed by the government over the previous half century. Meanwhile, the emergence of a nationalist movement, given organisational form through the creation in 1944 by a group of Blantyre-based intellectuals and businessmen of the Nyasaland African Congress, added an important new centralising element to Malawian politics. Ostentatiously modern in its emphasis on the importance of Western education, Congress in its early years was something of an elitist organisation, with little room for women, the uneducated or the poor. Yet it was also committed to the idea of democracy, at the very least as 'a theory of challenge to the colonial order, a vehicle to contest its hegemony and accelerate its departure'.[1] Nationalists, in consequence, attempted from an early stage – and initially with mixed success – to relate their concerns to the grievances experienced by other Malawians. Ultimately, from the end of the 1950s, nationalism in Malawi would take an exceptionally powerful and popular form. But it is important to recognise that politics were never entirely monolithic: a single movement with a single aim in view. Rather, as in

---

[1]   Crawford Young, 'The African Colonial State and its Political legacy' in Donald Rothchild and Naomi Chazan (eds), *The Precarious Balance: State and Society in Africa* (Boulder, 1988), pp. 25–66.

other countries, Malawi experienced tensions and divisions, regional, ethnic, generational and occupational, both within the dominant party and without.

The crisis of thangata, 1940–1953

By 1945 more than 170,000 Africans were living as tenants on the extensive European-owned estates in the Shire Highlands. A minority of these were descendants of Mang'anja and Yao villagers who had been living in the area prior to the arrival of the Europeans. But many more were descendants of immigrants from the Dedza area ('Ngoni') and in particular from Mozambique ('Anguru' or 'Lomwe') who had been attracted to the estates as labour tenants by the pioneer settlers. Tenants in the mid-1930s had a number of grievances including the refusal of some estate owners to allow the husbands of the daughters of tenants to move onto estate land – a clear breach of matrilocal custom.[2] But they bene-fited during the depression years from the decision of the great majority of owners to abandon direct production of cash crops on all but their tea-growing estates and to rely instead on the crops, mainly tobacco, grown by tenants. In 1939 the scandalous behaviour of the A. L. Bruce estates manager, Captain Kincaid-Smith, in persistently delaying payments to his tenants and factory workers provoked so much bitterness that the Government was forced to inter-vene and arrange for Kincaid-Smith to be despatched by the army to Nairobi.[3] Elsewhere, however, a number of companies, including the British Central African Company, withdrew staff and, for several years, ceased to demand rent on many of their estates. In 1939, for example, no European was resident on the large estates owned by the Blantyre and East Africa Company in the Zomba and Chiradzulu districts. Instead, a single agent living in Zomba made periodic visits, seeking to purchase such tobacco as was grown but otherwise making few demands.[4]

From the early 1940s, however, growing population pressures combined, following the end of the war, with an increase in prices for export crops brought about a change of strategy which fuelled tenant discontent. As he freely acknowl-edged, A. J. Tennett, the owner of the Mangunda Estate in the Cholo district, had gone out of his way in the early 1920s to settle 'Anguru' on his land as labour tenants. By 1936, however, he had become convinced that these people were 'locusts', cutting down his trees for firewood and putting the very fertility of his land at risk.[5] Early in World War II, other settlers joined in the condemnation of 'Anguru'. Renewed attempts were made to ensure that men from Trust Land did not come onto the estates as husbands. Demands were made that rents should be paid in full, even by women abandoned by their husbands who clearly lacked the wherewithal to do so. On the Bruce estates, so often out of line with the rest, the appointment of a new manager, J. Sibbald, led to the virtual aban-donment of *thangata* and a concentration on the production of tenant-grown

[2]   DC Cholo to CS, Zomba 13 June 1936, MNA S1/411ii/33.
[3]   W.S. Phillips to J. M. Ellis, 16 Dec. 1939; Record of discussion at Government House, 23 Dec. 1939, MNA GOB G. 187. A lively discussion of this event is contained in White, *Magomero*, pp.194–98.
[4]   DC Cholo to Chief Secretary, 13 June 1936, ibid.; Annual Report on the Chiradzulu District, 1939, MNA NSD 2/1/4.
[5]   J. Tennett to DC Cholo, 4 Nov. 1936, MNA S1/411ii/33.

tobacco.[6] Elsewhere, however, the war witnessed a marked tightening up of the imposition of *thangata* along with an increase in the number of eviction notices issued against those unable or unwilling to pay. By late 1943, the Southern Province Provincial Commissioner noted, 'there were serious incidents on certain estates in the Blantyre district owing to refusals to leave by several hundreds of natives who had been served with notices to quit in that and the preceding year'; by 1945 the situation had deteriorated further.[7] As successive administrators emphasised, little or no alternative land was now available on the heavily congested Native Trust Land outside the estates. Nevertheless, neither the British Central Africa Company nor Tennett showed any compunction in seeking to eject a total of nearly 700 tenant families in the Cholo District for failing to meet their rent obligations. This was in line with the BCA Company's new policy of bringing more land directly under production and forcing tenants to choose between paying rent in money or labour. Those who chose the latter worked as agricultural labourers for the Company for four months a year at the miserly rate of 8 shillings a month. As many tenants had paid no rent in either money or labour for well over a decade, this belated demand was perceived as 'something of a "ramp"', as H. V. Macdonald, the Cholo DC noted, and one which they had every moral right to reject.[8] P.H. Keppel-Compton, the Provincial Commissioner agreed, in January 1944: 'In my opinion the time is not very far distant when the tenants will refuse to pay rent, or to work in lieu of rent and will in fact act in open defiance of their landlords.'[9] A year later, Macdonald claimed that numbers of people refused to pay rent because they 'do not see what they get out of it. They argue (quite illogically of course) that as Government does not charge rent for Native Trust land why should estate owners do so.' In a prescient note he added:

> Native Trust Land in this district is already heavily crowded and if large numbers of natives on private estates are constantly to be threatened with ejection in this manner, it seems to be certain that it will only be a matter of time before some situation arises which it will be impossible peacefully to control. It is therefore strongly recommended that early consideration be given to amending the law so as to give natives on private estates more security in the tenure of their homes.[10]

It was against this sombre background, in July 1946, that Sir Sidney Abrahams, a former Chief Justice of Tanganyika and a senior member of the Colonial Office staff, arrived in Zomba on a one-man commission of enquiry to discover whether he could succeed, where others had failed, in resolving the question of land.

Few documents in the history of Malawi have generated as much controversy as the Abrahams Report of October 1946. Derided by the settler leader, M. P. Barrow, as 'the most mischievous document that has ever been produced in this country in connexion with one of its most difficult problems',[11] the report, as Dr

6   White, *Magomero*, p. 198.
7   *Report of the Land Commission, 1946* (Zomba, 1946) [hereafter referred as the *Abrahams Report*] p.14.
8   V. McDonald, DC Cholo to PC Southern Province, 27 Aug 1945, MNA 2–8–9F 1476.
9   Quoted in P. H. Keppel-Compton to CS, Zomba, 21 July 1945, MNA 1–8–9F 1476.
10 McDonald to PC Southern Province, 27 Aug 1945, ibid.
11 M.P. Barrow in debate in Legislative Council, Aug 1948, CO 525/207.

Banda was to note in 1962, had the merit that it 'pricked and has pricked ever since the consciousness of the Government of this country in London and Zomba'.[12] Written in October 1946, after a whirlwind tour that took Abrahams to almost every district in the country, the report acknowledged the legitimacy of African grievances that 'Europeans are holding large tracts of undeveloped land while natives are suffering the acute pangs of land hunger.' Abrahams's solution was 'the clear cut one of getting rid of the status of resident native', something which could not be achieved, he acknowledged, 'unless accommodation is found on native trust land for those who wish to live there.'[13] Writing in very broad terms, Abrahams therefore recommended that the Government should seek to acquire from estate-owners all those estates fully occupied by resident tenants as well as large tracts of undeveloped land on estates to which tenants who wished to move could be settled. All Africans remaining on estates would enter into a form of contract with the estate owners by which they would agree to work for a fixed period. Tenant status and thus *thangata* would be effectively abolished. Meanwhile, African access to the newly acquired lands would take place in a controlled and carefully supervised manner. Productive estates, including the visiting tenant estates of the Central Province, would be preserved. Land would be acquired, if at all possible, through negotiation. However, Abrahams did propose that, if landowners refused to negotiate, compulsory purchase should be used as a last resort.[14]

The six years following the publication of the Abrahams Report in February 1947 were marked by a series of concessions, as a result of which radical reform was avoided and the 1953 disturbances became almost inevitable. Abrahams's fundamental aim had been to end *thangata* through the large-scale acquisition of settler estates. Details, however, as to the estates to be purchased or the methods of resettlement used were left to a local Land Planning Committee set up in April 1947 under the chairmanship of the Acting Chief Secretary, Talbot Edwards. Among its members was Abrahams's leading critic, the powerful settler leader, Malcolm Barrow: the next few months were to demonstrate the continuing strength of the settler lobby. Although V. H. McDonald, the Cholo District Commissioner, repeatedly emphasised the urgency of the situation they were facing, the committee as a whole quickly convinced itself of the impracticality of Abraham's proposals. In its report of 1948, the Committee made clear its view that 'no full and clear-cut solution of land problems on the lines suggested was possible.' In areas such as Cholo, where tenants were most numerous, 'practically all estates were already to a great extent developed or earmarked for development' with the result that 'the amount of unoccupied land available for acquisition in these areas was negligible.'[15] Following negotiations with landowners, the Committee recommended that the Government purchase 545,857 acres of freehold land from Europeans, of which 477,454 acres were in the Southern Province. These impressive figures, however, disguised a somewhat less promising reality. Well over half the land recommended for purchase in the Southern

---

12 Speech by Banda introducing the Africans on Private Estates Bill, 31 May 1962, Legislative Council, 76th Session.
13 *Abrahams Report*, p. 17.
14 *Abrahams Report*, pp. 21–23.
15 *Report of the Land Planning Committee, 1948*, MNA LS/GEN/2.

Province was of low fertility and contained few tenants. Several of the estates where congestion and political agitation were greatest (including Tennett's, near Luchenza) were not included as their owners had made clear they would not sell.[16] As a result of Barrow's intervention, a proposal to compulsorily acquire lands belonging to the BCA Company in the southern part of Blantyre district and the northern part of Cholo district was dropped from the published report. Instead, the Committee accepted the extremely dubious assurance of the Company's manager, Kaye Nicol, that in view of the deteriorating political situation he would be prepared to recommend the sale of these estates.[17]

From 1948, concern over the problem of the European estates mounted. Freed from the threat of compulsory purchase, European estate owners took their cue from the British Central Africa Company and reacted with a recklessness that drove Colby to despair. An exceptionally inefficient organisation, notorious in the 1940s for the low quality of its European employees, the British Central Africa Company in 1948 owned 329,353 acres of freehold land of which only 6,340 acres were under the Company's economic crops.[18] Kaye Nicol, nevertheless, was unwilling to give any of this up. Jettisoning his promise to recommend the sale of the BCA's Cholo estates, he provoked a storm of resentment in May 1948 by prohibiting tenants from growing cash crops, as many had done for years. Not until Colby had told him to his face that he would hold him personally responsible for any trouble that resulted, did Nicol reluctantly withdraw the orders.[19]

Further problems arose over the question of land. In 1949 Colby informed Abrahams: 'not only are the large landowners determined to squeeze the last penny out of the Government but they have all tended to reduce the amount of land they are prepared to surrender.'[20] A.L. Bruce led the way. From 1945 onward he had been in negotiations with the Nyasaland Government over the sale of his huge estate with its more than 33,000 tenants. But when new private purchasers, led by Ignaco Conforzi, appeared in 1949 he was quick to grasp the opportunity they provided. In a massive blow to the Government, over 90,000 acres of the Bruce Estates were sold off into private hands, leaving the remaining, least fertile, 72,000 acres to be sold to the Government in 1951.[21] This served as a precedent for the British Central Africa Company. The directors repeatedly refused to sell the well populated Cholo and Blantyre estates but they were glad to be rid of the 130,000 acre Chingale Estate situated in a rain shadow to the west of Zomba Mountain in an area where white farmers had failed in the interwar years. In 1949 they attempted to emulate Bruce in auctioning off the estate to fellow landowners. But when no buyer was forthcoming, they entered into discussions with Colby who was eventually forced to pay a price of 12s 6d an acre for the estate: a good return on what up to then had been an unpromising

16 Minutes of 4th Meeting of Land Planning Committee, 11 Aug 1947, MNA LS GEN/2.
17 Minutes of Meeting of the Land Planning Committee, 10 Oct 1947, MNA LS/GEN 2. For a somewhat different interpretation of the operation of the Land Planning Committee see Colin Baker, *Seeds of Trouble. Government Policy and Land Rights in Nyasaland, 1946–1964* (London, 1993), pp. 47–64.
18 'History of the British Central Africa Company', 1948, TNA CO 525/208/44332.
19 Colby to CO, 3 March 1953, TNA CO 1015.773.
20 Colby to Abrahams, 28 Feb. 1949, TNA CO 525/207/44332.
21 White, *Magomero*, pp. 205–211; confidential appendix to Land Planning Report, 1948, MNA LS/GEN 2.

investment.[22] Other estate owners also opened negotiations, with the result that, by March 1953, the government had purchased a total of 315,598 acres, almost all in the Southern Province.[23] Much of the land so acquired – some three-fifths of what the Land Planning Committee had recommended – was lightly populated, of poor quality and not in the areas of greatest political concern. Nevertheless, it was of value to the government as surplus land on which peasants from more crowded areas could be settled. Between 1951 and 1953, roads, markets and a medical centre were all opened in the Chingale area, bringing in their wake a steady stream of new settlers from elsewhere.[24]

The introduction of higher rents in 1952 brought matters to a head. In 1951, proposals for a new Africans on Estates Ordinance were produced by a committee dominated by the managers of the largest estates, although it contained African representatives. Ostensibly aimed at reducing the number of evictions from estates by abolishing the right of landlords to evict up to ten per cent of their tenants at the end of five yearly periods, the new Ordinance in fact offered less protection than before. Tenants still remained liable to eviction but they could no longer count on the assistance of district officers in helping them find land elsewhere. The male children of tenants were specifically denied the right to remain on the estate after their 18th birthdays. Tenants were restricted even more than previously, both in the land made available to them and in their right to utilise firewood. Above all, a new rents system, tied to the minimum wage, was introduced, resulting in a massive increase from 20 shillings to 52s 6d.[25]

On 11 July the new ordinance was published in a supplement to the Nyasaland Gazette. Early in September A. W. Dixon, Kaye Nicol's replacement as General Manager of the British Central Africa Company, issued his tenants with a notice in Chinyanja setting out the provisions of the ordinance in the starkest terms and demanding payment of rents (before they could be legally enforced, so it later transpired) at the new rate of 52s 6d.[26]

For a brief spell the tenants hesitated. Then the resistance began. Early in December the Cholo District Commissioner received a letter from the leader of the local branch of the independent Church of God, Lumbe, announcing that 'all tenants on BCA land have agreed that it is their intention to refuse to pay the higher rate of rent.'[27] Over twenty village headmen in NA Bvumbwe's sector also announced that they did not intend to pay, and these views were repeated by ordinary villagers who informed the Company's rangers 'that they would neither work nor pay'. When the District Commissioner tried to intervene he was told to his face that 'if the Company sent rent collectors round they would be killed, and that any man who paid would suffer the same fate.'[28] Dixon responded by

[22] 'Land Policy: Purchase of Estates', 1949, TNA CO 525/208 44332/3; Baker, *Seeds of Trouble*, pp. 80–91.
[23] Colby to CO, 3 March 1953, TNA CO 1015/773.
[24] Baker, *Seeds of Trouble*, p. 90.
[25] Colby to CO, 9 May 1951; Report of the Committee appointed to consider the amendment of the Natives on Private Estates Ordinance, 14 April 1951; note by J E Rednall on Colby memo and report, 29 May 1951, TNA CO 525/208/44332.
[26] Colby to CO, 3 March 1953, TNA CO 1015/773.
[27] Quoted in 'Factual Narrative' attached to Colby to CO, 3 March 1953, Ibid.
[28] Ibid.

demanding government support for the eviction of over 3,600 of his tenants. But the Government, now alarmed by 'the prospect of a peasant rising' signalled the need for delay. As the dispute escalated, recalcitrant tenants, some of them active members of the Nyasaland African Congress, announced that 'the day of rents was passed' and that they were not prepared to pay even one shilling. They also claimed that the BCA Company had no legal right to the estates and that the land belonged to the African people.[29]

Meanwhile, the imminent imposition of the Central African Federation crystallised fears of further land alienation by whites and contributed to a surge in support for Congress's non-cooperation campaign. In the early months of 1953 the rent strike spread to other estates, bringing the total number of defaulters involved to between 6,000 and 8,000. Congress agitation increased. Dixon's bravado dissolved. Early in June, at Dixon's insistence, McDonald attempted to serve notices to quit on a group of BCA tenants only to be forced to leave after 'crowds of men arrived from all directions, and whilst making no threatening move made it quite plain that they would not have Europeans in the village in connection with rent or evictions.' McDonald, so Dixon then claimed,

> ...told me that, based on some 23 years of experience as a D.C. or Administrative Officer mostly in the Cholo area, he was certain that if he proceeded with the matter of these evictions there would be what would amount to a pitched battle and that it would spread rapidly through the Southern Province, and that once Europeans were assaulted the situation would assume a very ugly aspect.[30]

Belatedly acknowledging the seriousness of a situation which his own company had done so much to provoke, Dixon therefore changed course and recommended that the BCA Company should waive the right to receive rent from its tenants.[31] Neither the Chairman of the Board nor the Colonial Office was happy with the proposal.[32] But while they delayed, 'the tenants' as Macdonald noted, 'seeing that Government was unwilling to take any action likely to precipitate unnecessary disturbance decided to take the initiative themselves.'[33] Groups of women led the way, 'entering onto undeveloped lands in the possession of estate-owners and cutting trees and making cultivations to demonstrate that these lands belonged to them.' In a general defiance of authority, people also refused to pay taxes, beer fees and other licenses, and boycotted Native Courts.[34] It was against this background that the Cholo disturbances began.

Official accounts of the Cholo disturbances date their origins to 18 August 1953 when rumours spread that the planter, A. J. Tennett and his sons had abducted and then killed two men whom they had discovered stealing oranges.[35]

---

[29] A.C.W. Dixon to Donald Brook, Chairman, BCA Company, 16 Jan. 1953, TNA CO 1015/773.

[30] Dixon to Brook, 14 June 1953 contained in Brook to J.E. Marnham, CO, 19 June 1953, TNA CO 1015/773.

[31] Colby to CO, 13 June 1953, TNA CO 1015/773.

[32] Palmer, 'Workers on Nyasaland Tea Estates', p. 123.

[33] Report by H.V. McDonald on 'Unrest in Estates in the Cholo District', TNA CO 1015/773.

[34] 'Unrest in Estates in Cholo District, ibid.; Political Intelligence Report, July 1953, TNA CO 1015/465.

[35] *Report of the Commission of Inquiry appointed to enquire into disturbances at Magunda Estate, Luchenza on the 18th and 19th August 1953* (Zomba, 1953); Statement by Oliver Lyttelton, Colonial Secretary, in House of Commons, 21 Oct 1953, TNA CO 1015/459.

Unofficially, however, C. W. Footman, the Chief Secretary, believed that the disturbances could be dated to an incident a few days earlier when H. H. Percival, one of the BCA Company's managers, had stripped naked a woman he had come across collecting firewood on his estate.[36] Taken together, the two incidents are indicative of the culture of the plantation economy at that time: highly personal in the face-to-face confrontations involved; imbued with casual violence in the relationship between manager and tenant; and giving rise to the powerful, widely held myth of *chifwamba* – the belief in the white man as cannibal, constantly hungering for African flesh.

On 19 August a large crowd gathered at Tennett's house; the police were called; tear gas was used; a shot was accidentally fired and a man was left dying on the ground. Riots then spread through a substantial part of the Southern Province, presenting a formidable threat not only to the estate economy of the Shire Highlands but to the collaborative mechanisms that upheld it. For several weeks, gangs of armed men in the neighbourhood of Cholo blocked roads with trees and trenches, labourers on tea and tobacco estates refused to work and strikes took place on the railway and at the plywood factory at Luchenza. Telephone wires were cut, European-owned property was damaged, the homes and courts of half a dozen chiefs were destroyed and a handful of tax collectors were beaten.[37] Although violence was focused above all on the estates in the Cholo and Blantyre districts, other areas were not unaffected. Early in September, attacks were made on the group headman's house in the Chingale area by newly established settlers who resented the controls that the Agricultural Department imposed.[38] In Port Herald the headquarters of Chief Mlolo was also attacked by rioters.[39] Colonial control was in danger of collapse.

Prior to 1953, Colby had attempted to improve the efficiency of the Nyasaland police by bringing in a number of battle-hardened European officers from the Palestine Police Force, which had been disbanded in 1948.[40] However, faced by riots on an unprecedented scale, the limitations of the force became glaringly apparent. As early as May, a contingent of constables sent to Ntcheu to arrest Chief Gomani, who had been instructing his people to disregard agricultural rules, proved 'too inexperienced and frightened and were attacked and dispersed by the crowd'.[41] It was only after the arrival of substantial detachments of armed policemen from Northern Rhodesia, Southern Rhodesia and Tanganyika, along with a flight of spotter planes from Salisbury, that colonial authority was reasserted in a hail of rifle fire and tear gas which left 11 Malawians dead and 72 injured. Thereafter, for five weeks, a contingent of the British South Africa police from Southern Rhodesia carried out dawn to dusk patrols in the Cholo, Blantyre, Chiradzulu and Zomba districts, arresting suspected rioters and tax defaulters, searching for weapons and destroying illicit stills.[42]

36 C.W.F. Footman, Chief Sec. to J.E. Marnham, 20 Oct 1953, TNAO 1015/455; Political Intelligence Report, August 1953, TNA CO 1015/465.
37 *Nyasaland Times*, 20 Aug–21 Sept 1953; Westrop, *Green Gold*, pp. 341–53.
38 R. Munro, 'Riots and disturbances – 1953', Chiradzulu District Book, vol. VI, 1953–55.
39 Monthly Intelligence Report, Sept. 1953, TNA CO 1015/465.
40 McCracken, 'Coercion and Control', pp. 138–39.
41 Memoir by Malcolm Llewelyn, RHL Ms. Afr. 1748 (45).
42 Munro, 'Riots and disturbances; Political Intelligence Reports, Sept. and Oct. 1953, TNA CO 1015/465.

It is an important feature of the 1953 disturbances that ethnic and social divisions reinforced grievances over land. The political settlement of the interwar years underlined the distinction made by the British between a 'traditional', officially recognised elite of Yao and Mang'anja chiefs – Yao in the Blantyre, Chiradzulu and Zomba districts, Mang'anja in Cholo and Mlanje – and the majority population of Lomwe commoners, descendants of immigrants from Mozambique. In Cholo, for example, in 1947 four out of the six officially designated chiefs described themselves as Mang'anja at a time when over three quarters of the population, some 79,000 people, were designated as Lomwe and only 23,000 as Mang'anja.[43] Extensive intermarriage meant that ethnic divisions were extremely porous. Yet, when the opportunity arose to use them, it was usually grasped with relish. Questioned by the Land Planning Committee in 1947, the two leading Mang'anja chiefs, Chimaliro and Chimombo, insisted that 'all privately owned land in the Cholo District which was undeveloped' should be handed over to 'the "original" African population of the District.' As for the "newcomers", these could be 'accommodated in compounds on the estates without gardens, or removed from the District to their original homes'.[44]

As the discontent of impoverished tenants intensified, Native Authorities, who were often perceived as little more than the mouthpieces of the government or the estate owners, came under increasing attack. In July 1953, a month before the main disturbances began, a meeting was called in Chiradzulu to arrange the removal of Mpama, one of the senior Yao chiefs in the area. The DC intervened and Mpama's principal opponent and rival, Malika, was arrested by the police.[45] Once rioting began, however, the position of the chiefs deteriorated. In a series of incidents in the Chiradzulu and Zomba districts, angry crowds burnt down the houses and courts of the Yao chiefs, Kadewere, Chitera and Mpama. The same medicine was meted out to Chimombo by a crowd led by the village headman Mberenga[46]. In some cases the dissident leaders were Yao headmen who had lost out in the 1933 settlement. But, in the view of the compiler of the monthly intelligence report, most of those involved were Lomwe. 'That does not mean that members of other tribes are not also active', he wrote, 'but, whereas the mass movement is solidly Alomwe in character, it is only a handful of individuals in each district who come from other tribes.'[47]

In a striking response, harking back to the strategies pursued after the Chilembwe Rising, the colonial authorities went out of their way to enrol Yao ex-soldiers in the para-military Police Mobile Force, formed following the outbreak of disturbances in August.[48] 'These recruits give indication of widespread feeling among the Yaos to give Government every assistance to quell the trouble and restore order', the *Nyasaland Times* commented in an unconvincing attempt to lift flagging settler morale.[49] More relevantly, the Government turned its attention to driving a wedge between the educated leaders of the Nyasaland African Congress and the radicalised peasants on the settler estates. Ralph

[43] Note by H.V. Macdonald, 24 Nov. 1947, Lord Hailey Papers, CO 1018/62.
[44] Minutes of the 4th meeting of the Land Planning Committee, 11 Aug. 1947, MNA LS GEN/2.
[45] Munro, 'Riots and Disturbances'.
[46] *Nyasaland Times*, 3 and 7 Aug., 1953.
[47] Political Intelligence Report, July 1953.
[48] Memoir by Malcolm Llewelyn, RHL.
[49] *Nyasaland Times*, 7 Sept. 1953.

Chinyama, the Congress President, was summoned to an interview with Colby in September after which he publicly repudiated the use of violence and withdrew the civil disobedience campaign. Some minor attacks on property continued in October. Otherwise the Province reverted to an uneasy peace. Tenant agitation in 1953 was not directly caused by Congress. But Congress action did play a part in bringing the agitation to a temporary halt.

The Nyasaland African Congress, 1944–1950

The Nyasaland African Congress, founded in 1944, has been described as a 'logical development' from the Native Associations of the 1920s and 1930s.[50] However, it also contained a number of novel elements that distinguish it from earlier political organisations. First, Congress was an umbrella-type organisation, organised on the lines of the European-controlled Convention of Associations and specifically designed as a vehicle for the expression of African grievances at a territorial rather than a regional or district level. Secondly, Congress evolved as a nationalist movement in the sense that it made use of the doctrine of popular sovereignty in order to justify the right of Malawians to take control of the central instruments of authority in the colonial state. Nationalism was in part an imported doctrine, linked to the quickening pace of political change in West Africa during the war and drawing on ideas obtained from India, South Africa and elsewhere. But it also came to acquire its own characteristics as a result of the impact made by a succession of nationalist leaders.

The foundation of Congress can be credited to James Frederick Sangala, one of the most attractive individuals in the history of Malawian nationalism. A modest, self-effacing figure but a born organiser, Sangala was educated at the Henry Henderson Institute at the Blantyre Mission before following the conventional career path from school teacher to government civil servant. In the late 1930s he helped to organise a variety of civil institutions in Blantyre: the Shire Highland Football League, the Black and White Club (a club aimed at bringing 'educated Africans to mix with Europeans of like mind') and the Parents' and Guardians' Association – an organisation concerned with improving the education of girls. He also played a part in the affairs of the Blantyre Native Association and established a range of informal contacts that were to be useful later in his career.[51] For a brief period in the aftermath of the Bledisloe Commission in 1939, he contemplated the creation of a nation-wide organisation. But, with the coming of war, this was delayed until the victory of the allies against Italy had brought about a more relaxed atmosphere in which political innovations could be tolerated by the colonial authorities.[52] It was thus not until 1 October 1943 and after he had taken soundings from the provincial commissioner, that Sangala signalled his entry into national politics by addressing a circular letter to 'All Africans resident in Nyasaland Protectorate'. In this letter Sangala stated that in

[50] Gray, *Two Nations*, p. 344.
[51] Phiri, *Sangala*, pp. 1–16.
[52] Phiri, Ibid., p. 17; Roger K Tangri, 'The Rise of Nationalism in Colonial Africa: the Case of Colonial Malawi', in B. Pachai, G.W. Smith and R.K. Tangri (eds), *Malawi Past and Present* (Zomba, 1967), p. 112.

previous months 'the community of both Blantyre and Limbe Township met together to discuss the formation of an Association which should be represented by all the Africans resident in Nyasaland':

> The chief object for forming it is because experience has taught us that unity is strength. It is considered that time is ripe now for the Africans in this country to fight for their freedom, progress and development of Nyasaland from one field.[53]

Questioned by colonial officials, alarmed by this language, Sangala responded by pointing to the discrimination to which Africans were still exposed:

> Pass restrictions, particularly those necessary in the Townships, the lack of African representation on Legislative Council and other Official and non-Official bodies, show that the Nyasaland Natives are a subordinate race and they will remain so so long as they do nothing to improve their lot.[54]

Sangala's emphasis on the need for unity and self improvement as a means of overcoming racial discrimination resonated favourably with the growing population of Blantyre-based civil servants and independent businessmen, most of them living in Ndirande. A first taste of the new attitudes was provided in January 1944 when Sangala, his fellow clerk, Charles Matinga and the High School teacher and independent businessman, Sidney Somanje, joined other former members of the Blantyre Native Association in calling for improved education and the direct representation of Africans on the Legislative Council.[55] A week later this message was hammered home at a meeting with Bishop Thorne, the recently appointed representative for African interests on the Council. Matinga bluntly informed Thorne that 'it will be a mistake on our part to leave our interests to be represented by missionaries' before embarking on a lengthy critique of missionary education.'[56] Levi Mumba, the veteran associationist was recruited both to write the constitution and to bring into Congress the important northern dimension which had previously been lacking. And it was Mumba who was elected as President-General at the inaugural meeting held in Blantyre on 21 October 1944. In his presidential address, delivered less than three months before his sudden death in January 1945, Mumba combined a demand for direct representation on the Legislative Council (although not, at this time, for majority rule) with an attack on racial segregation and a call for 'full citizenship and consequent opportunities for all regardless of race, colour or creed'.[57] The Government, as we have seen, turned down the demand for direct representation. It did, however, agree on 20 December 1944 to accord Congress official recognition as 'representing the various African associations in Nyasaland'.[58]

[53] James F. Sangala to 'All Africans Resident in Nyasaland Protectorate', 1 October 1943, MNA NSB 3/3/6.

[54] DC Blantyre to PC Southern Province, 8 October 1943, MNA NSB 3/3/6. See also Gray, *Two Nations*, p. 337.

[55] Rotberg, *Rise of Nationalism*, pp. 189–90.

[56] 'Memorandum prepared by Mr C. J. Matinga and presented to the Bishop of Nyasaland', 28 Jan. 1944, TNA CO 525/199/44379.

[57] Levi Mumba, Presidential Address to Nyasaland African Congress, 21 October 1944, MNA NS 1/3/10.

[58] Quoted in Short, *Banda*, p. 45.

It is a feature of the Nyasaland African Congress in its early years that, for all its weakness as an instrument of national liberation, it remained broadly democratic in intent. Like Thompson Samkange in Southern Rhodesia, about whom Terence Ranger has written, Mumba and Sangala combined a belief in the importance of unity in articulating African interests with an awareness, drawn from their own experiences, of the value of the variety of associations and interests groups representative of civil society. They were 'not in sympathy with a "totalitarian" view of nationalism, in which a single movement would organise and orchestrate the branches of the people's life'.[59] Sangala, for example, combined his role as chief organiser of Congress in the 1940s with active participation in the Parents' and Guardians' Educational Association, and also in the Blantyre African Co-operative Trading Society, a body run by independent African entrepreneurs.[60] Congress, in consequence, developed as an umbrella organisation, initially conceived as the 'mother body...only...concerned with major problems which affect the Protectorate generally' and leaving district associations and societies to continue functioning at the local level.[61] By the time of the inaugural meeting, thirteen district branches had been formed, spreading from Cholo in the south to Karonga in the north. But there were also representatives from four native associations as well as two farmers' groups, the Nyasaland Railways Social and Recreational Association and a branch of Congress established in Johannesburg.[62]

The formation of this branch raised the question of whether it would be better for Malawi migrants in South Africa and Southern Rhodesia to join the ANC and the Southern Rhodesian Bantu Congress or to set up local branches of the Nyasaland African Congress. Sangala initially responded enthusiastically to overtures from Thompson Samkange which aimed to federate the Southern Rhodesian and Nyasaland Congresses. This Pan-Africanist vision was enthusiastically supported by Dr Hastings Banda in London.[63] 'Disunity will only ruin while unity will build us, politically, economically and socially', Banda wrote to Samkange in 1946.[64]

> I quite agree with you that Africans of Nyasaland in Southern Rhodesia should not organise a separate political or industrial body from that organised by their brethren in the Colony. I also agree with you that they should wholeheartedly support the organisation already in existence in Southern Rhodesia.

Banda's plea, however, came at a time when territorial nationalism was beginning to win out over Pan-Africanism at an organisational level. When Charles Matinga, on a visit to Johannesburg in 1946, proposed the creation of a Pan African Congress, Dr Xuma, the President of the African National Congress, was not forthcoming.[65] Matinga therefore changed direction and, in the same

---

[59] Terence Ranger, *Are We Not Men? The Samkange Family & African Politics in Zimbabwe 1920–64* (London, 1995), pp. 120, 159.

[60] For further information on Sangala's involvement in the late 1940s in the Parents and Guardians Educational Association and in the Blantyre African Co-operative Trading Society see MNA NSB 3/3/6.

[61] Rotberg, *Rise of Nationalism*, p. 192.

[62] Minutes of the NAC Committee, 19 Oct. 1944, MNA NS 1/3/10.

[63] Ranger, *Are We Not Men?*, pp. 98–99

[64] Quoted in Ranger, ibid., p. 103.

[65] C.J. Matinga, Presidential Address, Third Annual Conference of NAC, 23 Sept. 1946, MNA PCC/1/4/1.

year, played an active part in founding the first Southern Rhodesian branch of the NAC in Salisbury. Further branches were quickly established in Lusaka and elsewhere, bringing precious funds to Congress's empty coffers. By 1957 over half the total membership of Congress was said to be living in the two Rhodesias and South Africa and the financial support they provided had become essential to Congress's success.[66]

Prior to 1950, Congress's democratic pretensions did not extend to the creation of a popular base. In theory, membership was open from the first to 'all men and women...belonging to the aboriginal races of Africa who are 18 years and over'.[67] In practice, however, only 'educated' men were encouraged to attend meetings along with a tiny handful of women, almost all of whom were the wives of male delegates. At the annual conference in 1946, only two women out of a total of 56 delegates were present, one of them being the wife of the new president, Charles Matinga.[68] Universal suffrage was not a demand; instead, Congress advocated 'the appointment of intelligent progressive Africans in all Government Advisory Committees'.[69] In 1946 the Blantyre branch became actively involved in the claim by local domestic servants for higher wages. But the next year the Governor announced that civil servants should not meddle in labour disputes, and, following this warning, Congress became much more wary in its support for workers' rights.[70] At annual conferences, deliberately held in a different location each year, some issues of widespread popular interest were discussed, among them the pricing policies of the NTB and the alienation of land from Africans. However, attention continued to focus most actively on matters of less immediate concern at village level: the need for improvements in educational standards and in pay and promotion opportunities for school teachers. It was on these issues that Congress achieved its greatest propaganda success of the 1940s: the visit in May 1948 of a two-man NAC delegation to London for a meeting with the Colonial Secretary, Creech Jones.

Congress leaders were thus unashamed modernisers although, as they were soon to realise, Western modernising agendas could at times conflict with African popular opinion. In his long career, Levi Mumba had combined a passionate belief in self-improvement through Christianity and western education with an equally passionate concern for the maintenance of African communal values. His successors, however, were less discriminating. At the annual conference of Congress held in Lilongwe in 1945, the Dutch Reformed Church minister, J. L. Pretorius, launched an attack on the *nyau* societies of the Chewa. Despite the evident sensitivity of the issue, several Congress members came to Pretorius's support and passed a highly controversial motion demanding that *nyau* be 'prohibited' as it hindered the attendance of children at school. Only after George Simeon Mwase had intervened the next day to point out that 'if we stopped this dance we will not unite well our people' was the resolution finally rescinded.[71] Mwase's intervention, however, could not prevent further

---

[66] Intelligence Digest 4. 1957, TNA CO 1015/1748.
[67] 'Nyasaland African Congress: Constitution', 1945, MNA NN 1/4/6.
[68] Record of the Proceedings of the Fourth Conference of the Nyasaland African Congress, September 1947, MNA1/4/1.
[69] Constitution, 1945, MNA NN 1/4/6.
[70] Acting Governor's speech to NAC, 22 Sept. 1947, MNA PCC/1/4/1.
[71] Minutes of the Second Annual Conference of the NAC, 17–18 Oct. 1945, MNA NS 1/3/10.

misjudgements of popular feeling, none greater than the initial response of Congress leaders to the introduction of the Government's bitterly unpopular conservation campaign. As President of Congress, Charles Matinga first invited the director of agriculture, Dick Kettlewell, to expound his ideas at the 1945 meeting, and then added insult to injury by publicly welcoming the new programme in 1946 and by calling on 'all members of the Congress to give our people a hand in trying to preserve the soil'.[72]

Often insensitive to popular feeling, Congress leaders were also lacking in organisational skills. Dr Hastings Banda supplied financial assistance from London, where he had recently established a medical practice, and made repeated suggestions aimed at reorganising the movement on more efficient lines. Matinga, however, was concerned that these reforms might weaken his own position and, in September 1946, persuaded Congress to reject Banda's offer to pay for a full-time secretary-general at a salary of £63 a year.[73] Thereafter, the movement went into decline. Rumours of financial mismanagement spread, fuelled by the failure of the Executive Committee to produce any statements of account between 1944 and 1949.[74] Regional tensions grew stronger, inflamed by Matinga's failure either to visit the two northern provinces or to permit them to establish separate provincial committees.[75] Matters came to a head in 1948, by which time it was said that only the £200 legacy received from a European sympathiser, W. H. Timcke, was keeping the movement afloat.[76] In a peculiarly messy episode, Matinga was removed from office on the double accusation of tribalism and embezzlement: tribalism because he had engineered the replacement on the delegation to London of the northerner, Charles Chinula, by his friend and fellow southerner, Andrew Mponda; embezzlement because he was said to have appropriated £162 from Congress funds.[77] Thereafter, authority in Congress was temporarily shared between the Lilongwe-based provisional President-General, Sam K. Mwase, one of the leading activists in the Achewa Improvement Association, and James Sangala who had quietly re-emerged as chairman of the Blantyre branch. In January 1950, the Blantyre branch, as 'the senior Branch of the Congress', took upon itself the right to act on behalf of the NAC.[78] In August, however, power was transferred to the Central Province. At the annual general meeting held in Mzimba, inaccessible to more than a handful of southerners, Ralph Chinyama, the tall, imposing tobacco farmer, was elected President General. A. J. M. Banda, also from Lilongwe, was elected Secretary-General; they were joined on the nine-man executive committee by three other delegates from Lilongwe, giving that branch a permanent majority. James Sangala, demoted from acting President to Vice President, was one of only two committee members from the south.[79]

---

[72] C.J. Matinga, Presidential Address to NAC, 23 Sept. 1946, MNA PCC/1/4/1.
[73] Minutes of 3rd Annual Meeting of NAC, 23–26 Sept. 1946, MNA PCC/1/4/1. This episode is discussed in some detail in Short, *Banda*, pp. 44–50.
[74] Sec., NAC Blantyre Branch to PC Southern Province, 7 Jan. 1950, MNA PCC/1/4/1.
[75] Minutes of 4th annual meeting of NAC, Zomba, 22–26 Sept. 1947, MNA PCC/1/4/1.
[76] Tangri, 'From the Politics of Union to Mass Nationalism: the Nyasaland African Congress, 1944–59' in Macdonald, *From Nyasaland to Malawi*, pp. 261.
[77] Short, *Banda*, pp. 53–54.
[78] Secretary, NAC Blantyre Branch to PC, Southern Province, 7 Jan. 1950, MNA PCC/1/4/1.
[79] James F. Sangala to Chief Sec., 9 Aug. 1950, MNA PCC/11/4/6.; Phiri, *Sangala*, pp. 34–37.

Thus, at precisely the time that political agitation in the south was beginning to grow, executive power at the centre moved into the hands of a group of prosperous Lilongwe-based tobacco farmers. Congress was developing three distinct, although overlapping centres of influence: Lilongwe-based tobacco farmers, several of whom, like Chinyama, were incomers to the district; the Blantyre branch, radicalised from 1949 by the return to the town of several migrants from the south; finally, Dr Banda – a remote but increasingly influential presence. All of these in turn were affected by the behaviour of discontented peasants in both the south and north of the country, people who still remained independent of Congress but shared a number of its concerns.

Malimidwe & the advent of Federation

From 1950 three separate but increasingly inter-related issues transformed the political temperature in Malawi. Tenant discontent, mounting following the failure of the Government to take decisive action in the wake of the publication of the Abrahams Report, left much of the Shire Highlands in a highly volatile condition. But by now, these grievances were gaining wider ground, fuelled by fears concerning the destructive impact of conservation measures (*malimidwe*) and the impact of Federation. Congress's challenge, which Chinyama ultimately failed to meet, was to harness these various grievances to its political purposes in a way that would allow it to bring concerted pressure on the colonial state.

In Malawi, as in other colonies in East and Southern Africa, the determination to increase agricultural productivity at a time when soil erosion was seen to be accelerating into crisis largely explains the intensification of state intervention in peasant farming following the Second World War. R. W. Kettlewell, one of the most important architects of the new policy of intervention, had been deeply influenced by the alarming account of environmental degradation world-wide contained in Jacks's and White's popular study, *The Rape of the Earth*, published in 1939.[80] On his appointment, in 1943, as Senior Agricultural Officer for the two northern provinces, he therefore took the lead in calling for the implementation of comprehensive land usage legislation.[81] Shortage of staff and money, combined with the reluctance of Ellis, the Provincial Commissioner, to risk provoking the opposition of African cultivators, prevented any major initiatives being taken at the time.[82] But when Kettlewell returned to the attack in the aftermath of the war, his policy was rapidly approved. In a last-ditch stand, the liberal-minded Director of Agriculture, P. B. Garnett, made clear to Kettlewell, 'I was not prepared at this stage to be responsible for, or associated with, the enactment of any mass legislation in respect of soil conservation on Native Trust Land'.[83] But with the arrival of Colby in 1948, the opposition was finally overcome. A firm admirer of Kettlewell's energy and commitment, Colby engineered Garnett's humiliating transfer to the Gambia and Kettlewell's appointment in

---

[80] G.V. Jacks and R.O. Whyte, *The Rape of the Earth: A World Survey of Soil Erosion* (London, 1939). I owe this observation to William Beinart who interviewed Kettlewell in 1982.

[81] Kettlewell to Provincial Commissioner Northern Province, 31 January 1944, MNA NC1/30/1.

[82] Ellis to Kettlewell, 15 June 1944, MNA NC1/30/1.

[83] Garnett to Kettlewell, 16 October 1947, MNA NCL 1/30/1.

6 Malimidwe *in action. Villagers construct contour ridges under the supervision of agricultural instructors, mid-1950s*

his place.[84] A new, comprehensive Natural Resources Ordinance was introduced to replace the comparatively mild ordinance of 1946. Funds were made available on a much larger scale than previously for the enactment of soil conservation measures. The resources of the District Administration were committed to the task of agricultural extension. And, with new staff in place, large-scale schemes were introduced with the double purpose of preserving the fertility of land under threat and of improving the sustainability and productivity of indigenous African farming. The former could be achieved through a territory-wide campaign 'to substitute contour and box ridging for the indigenous system of flat and mound cultivation over as wide an area as possible'.[85] The latter concerned the introduction of a number of land usage schemes, often associated with the movement of peasants from 'congested' to lightly populated land. These typically involved the consolidation of previously scattered gardens, the introduction of crop rotation and the abandonment of intercropping.[86]

In a narrative no less moralistic than those once presented by Scottish missionaries, Kettlewell justified increasingly draconian state intervention on Malthusian grounds by depicting peasant farmers as wreaking terrible havoc on

[84] In fact there was a year's delay, filled by short-term appointments, before Colby succeeded in getting Kettlewell promoted. See Baker, *Development Governor*, pp. 116–18; RHL Mss Afr.S. 1811, R.W. Kettlewell, 'Memories of a Colonial Career' (unpublished typescript).

[85] *Annual Report of the Nyasaland Department of Agriculture for 1944.*

[86] Mandala, *Work and Control*, pp. 202–03.

the environment through their inability to adjust their farming methods to the
rapid growth of population:

> It is a regrettable fact that the radical change in environment which the rapid increase in
> population has brought about has not resulted in the natural evolution of better agricul-
> tural practice to cope with it. The change has been too rapid and the traditional methods
> contain scarcely even the foundation on which improvement might naturally develop.
> There was no consciousness of erosion; crop rotation did not exist since maize with a few
> interplanted legumes provided a fairly adequate diet; livestock were regarded simply as
> wealth; land tenure was on a communal basis; and in the majority of tribes the matrilineal
> system of marriage prevailed.[87]

Matrilocality, ensuring as it did the access of land to women, was seen as a
particularly pernicious obstacle in the Southern and Central Provinces: 'There
is no doubt that this system, by removing the man's personal interest and
responsibility in the land he cultivates, is one of the greatest stumbling blocks to
agricultural progress.'[88] By the 1950s Kettlewell had come to the conclusion that
it was only through a social revolution imposed from above, resulting in the
emergence of 'a class of [male] yeoman farmer with security in the land he farms'
that the problem could be solved. This, he accepted, would have to be combined
with the creation of 'a landless class of workers' and the mass 'emigration by
family units' to Southern Rhodesia, a state of affairs made all the more possible
through the creation of the Central African Federation.[89] The assumption that
there was a link between *malimidwe* and federation, accepted as an article of faith
by many rural Malawians, was thus also shared by the leading conservation tech-
nocrat in the country.

Conservationist strategies were not applied uniformly in Nyasaland, nor did
they have a uniform impact. Ridge terracing was introduced in tobacco growing
areas of the Central Province and in certain hilly parts of the Shire Highlands
from the mid-1930s; although its imposition gave rise to some peasant opposition, ridges did become generally accepted by the late 1940s and cultivation on
mounds was largely abandoned.[90] At the south end of Lake Malawi, however,
and in the Lower Shire Valley the situation was very different. Cultivation here
had traditionally taken place largely on the flat ground, rather than on mounds,
and peasants resented the extra labour involved in constructing ridges, particularly since it did not result in an increase in yields. They also feared that ridges
built in sandy soil would be liable to disintegrate and that they made it easier for
white ants to attack the stems of maize plants.[91] At the south end of the lake,
where Chief Mponda retained the respect of his people, opposition remained
relatively restrained. But in the Port Herald District, where divisions already
existed between the Mang'anja Native Authorities and their largely Sena
subjects, tensions were very much greater. For several years in the early 1940s,
peasants both there and in the Chikwawa district resolutely defied attempts to
make them ridge their land. In this they were, in some instances, backed by chiefs

---

[87] R.W. Kettlewell, *An Outline of Agrarian Problems and Policy in Nyasaland* (Zomba, 1955), p. 2.
[88] Ibid., p. 2.
[89] Ibid., pp. 3, 7.
[90] *Agricultural Department Reports*, 1935–1947; Beinart, 'Soil Erosion', pp. 71–72.
[91] Mandala, *Work and Control*, pp. 226–229; Beinart, 'Agricultural Planning', pp. 106–07; DC Fort Johnston to Deputy PC Blantyre, 23 Feb. 1943, MNA 2–30–8F/3499.

'who absolutely refused to agree to any orders'.[92] In 1948, therefore, the District Commissioner, P. C. Lewis, embarked on a compulsory district-wide drive, assisted by the most 'progressive' chiefs in his area, Mollen Tengani and Liva Mlolo. In the resulting 'war of the ridges' over 2,000 cultivators were arrested and tried in Native Authority Courts, receiving punishments varying from 5 shilling fines to six months in gaol. Many people took refuge in Mozambique. The medium of the Mbona cult joined in the protest, and the story spread that Mbona had withheld rain during the drought of 1949 because of his displeasure that, in his embodiment as a snake, his movements had been restricted by the building of ridges. At the same time, in a significant development, members of the local branch of the Nyasaland African Congress, meeting at Tengani's head-quarters, defied the central leadership by overthrowing the incumbent secretary. They then held several meetings with village headmen at which they 'urged them to exhort their people to show open hostility to the campaign'. Five Congress leaders were subsequently charged with 'attempting to undermine the lawful power and authority of Chief Tengani' but this did not bring resistance in the area to a halt.[93] By the end of 1949, reluctant peasants had ridged well over half the fields in the Port Herald area. No agricultural rules were passed covering the valley floor of the Chikwawa District, much of which remained unridged.[94] Port Herald, too, remained a zone of confrontation. Through the efforts of the DC, Mollen Tengani's chiefship was expanded in the early 1950s. Tengani and Mlolo then embarked on a new campaign in which they demanded strict compli-ance with laws concerning ridging and rigorously punished offenders. Peasants, in their turn, took advantage of the Cholo disturbances in 1953 to launch a large-scale attack on Chief Mlolo's courthouse involving 1,500 people, several of them Congress activists. It was only through the actions of the newly-formed Police Mobile Force, supported by two platoons of the Northern Rhodesian Police, that the rioters could be dispersed.[95]

Elsewhere, resistance to conservation measures was frequently linked to resistance to Federation, as is demonstrated by a women's song sung at Magomero around 1953:

> Federation capitaos
> e – e – e
> Sooner or later you will die
> e – e – e
> Contour ridging capitaos
> e – e – e
> Sooner or later you will die
> e– e – e
> *You will die but you don't know it*[96]

Back in 1945, Congress delegates had expressed their fears about the possible loss of yet more land to an estimated four to five hundred new settlers in Nyasa-

---

[92] Quoted in Beinart, 'Agricultural Planning', pp. 106–07.
[93] Annual Report on the Southern Province for 1948, MNA NS 3/1/13; Lower Shire District Report for 1948, MNA NS 3/1/18; Mandala, pp. 229–31; Schoffeleers, *River of Blood*, pp. 107–08.
[94] Lower River District Report for 1949, MNA NS 3/1/18.
[95] Political Intelligence Report, September 1953, TNA CO 1015/1465; Llewelyn memoirs.
[96] White, *Magomero*, p. 217.

land; with the approach of federation these fears intensified.[97] Ridging campaigns, involving an unprecedented interference by the state in peasant production techniques, were a threat to land security. Even worse were the land resettlement schemes introduced in increasing numbers from the mid-1940s which aimed to dramatically restructure the basis of peasant society. Drawing their inspiration from the Misuku Land Development Scheme in the north, resettlement schemes like those at Livulezi near Ntcheu, at Magomero near Chiradzulu, and at Kakoma in the dry north western part of Chikwawa district were opposed particularly by women who feared that their rights to control over land would be undermined when gardens were consolidated. Such schemes in the Lower Shire Valley had collapsed almost entirely by the mid-1950s, partly because of technical reasons – the poor quality of water produced by bore holes and the absence of fertile soil – but also because of fears of the excessive degree of regimentation involved.[98] Meanwhile, from 1952, the independent church leader, Wilfred Gudu, began to instruct his followers in Cholo to destroy bunds, using the Biblical injunction that 'the waters of the earth shall run free.'[99] The central executive committee of Congress took up the issue, although with some reluctance on the part of the President, Ralph Chinyama, a substantial tobacco farmer, previously the manager of one of Barron's estates, and a leading advocate of 'progressive' farming. Prior to 1952, the Natural Resources Ordinance was not applied to estates with the result that, there, the issues of land and *thangata* remained dominant.[100] Elsewhere, however, the increased emphasis in the years 1950 to 1952 on the large-scale construction of bunds and ridges provoked grievances which flowed into Congress's anti-federation campaign. From 1950 European-supervised teams of African instructors, newly graduated from the Mpemba Agricultural Training Centre, swept across the country marking out contour bunds which peasants were then required to construct. Further teams of rangers, employed by the recently-formed Natural Resources Boards, followed in their wake inspecting the work and hauling off offenders – more than 10,000 a year in the Southern Province alone by 1954 – to Native Authority courts.[101] According to Agricultural Department statistics, an astonishing 15,500 miles of bunds were constructed in 1951 provoking, as the political intelligence report for July noted, 'a growing feeling among Africans of the Southern Province that the Government is interfering too much with their way of life'.[102]

The impact of colonial agricultural policies in the Northern Province was different from that in the south. The absence of *thangata*, of extensive land alienation and of new, large-scale, land settlement schemes meant that an open alliance between politicians and peasants was slower to take shape there than it was in the Lower Shire Valley and the Shire Highlands. Nevertheless, when the

[97] Minutes of 2nd annual executive meeting of NAC, 20 April 1946, MNA NS 1/3/10.
[98] Mandala, *Work and Control*, pp. 218–226; Beinart, 'Agricultural Planning', p. 1124–26.
[99] Robert Boeder, 'Wilfred Good and the "Ana A Mulungu" Church of Southern Malawi', History seminar paper, Chancellor College, 1982.
[100] W. O. Mulwafu, "Soil Erosion and State Intervention into Estate Production in the Shire Highlands Economy of Colonial Malawi, 1891–1964', *JSAS*, 28, 1, 2002, pp. 25–44.
[101] *Agricultural Department Reports*, 1950–52; PC Southern Province to Chief Secretary, 22 Jan. 1959, MNA 15.10.4F 4852.
[102] Political Intelligence Report, July 1951, TNA CO 1015/464.

newly enlarged Agricultural Department moved to prohibit mound cultivation in the north as well as the *visoso* method of growing finger millet, long condemned by missionaries and administrators alike for its destructive effect on indigenous woodlands, peasants, who were acutely aware that no other method of growing millet was nearly as effective, were quick to react. The first concerted steps to introduce the new agricultural rules were taken in 1947, but a year later it was claimed: 'in Ngoni country opposition to contour ridging was general. Rules had been made to prohibit *visoso* and mound cultivation but they had not been properly enforced.'[103] Similar reactions were expressed in the Karonga District where the new DC noted in his diary: 'God how these people loathe the agricultural department.'[104] And a comparable response was recorded in the Chikulamayembe area with the Chief Conservation officer noting: 'Regarding the ridge cropping programme, it is doubtful if this would be maintained without constant supervision by Agricultural Instructors backed by Native Administration Chiefs.'[105]

Not until the end of 1949 were the first gardens in the Mzimba district ridged, a result achieved only through the Herculean efforts of newly appointed rangers who toured the area to check that work on ridging had been carried out and punishing offenders.[106] Some success with this draconian policy was noted in 1950 when, according to the agricultural authorities, 32,000 gardens in the Mzimba district were ridged. But this was only a prelude to the great push of 1951 when 6,400 miles of bunds were said to have been constructed in the Northern Province alone.[107]

As state intervention increased, so the opposition of peasants intensified, although, at this period, in an uncoordinated and largely passive form generally unrelated to Congress activities. At meeting after meeting in the Chinteche District in 1952, the District Commissioner, Griff Jones, faced a barrage of criticism from villagers concerned about the excessive labour involved in digging bunds and by the fear that cassava grown on ridges would rot, as had happened in an earlier experiment in 1942. Concern was also expressed that compulsory bunding was being introduced as a prelude to further European settlement in the district. In addition, 'The Kasitu Valley bunding [in the Mzimba district] is held up as an awful example and they are quite definite that they want none of that nonsense here.'[108]

In the Mzimba district itself, where the attempt to ban *visoso* was construed by women as well as men as being an assault on Ngoni/Tumbuka identity, government measures were even more strongly opposed. 'As a means of testing the reactions of the people to a proposal to prohibit this system and other practices harmful to the soil, *baraza* [public meetings] were held throughout the Mzimba district…at which many thousands of people attended', the Provincial Commissioner noted in 1948. He added:

[103] *Annual Report of the Nyasaland Departments of Agriculture* for 1947 and 1948.
[104] Phillips, *Obscurity to Bright Dawn*, p. 22.
[105] W.J. Badcock, Chief Conservation Officer to Director of Agriculture, 31 December 1946, MNA 1.17.7F/879.
[106] *Annual Report of the Nyasaland Agricultural Department for 1950*, pp. 11–12.
[107] *Report of the Agricultural Department for 1951.*
[108] Griff Jones, 'Ulendo Diary', 1952–53, entry for 14 Jan 1952, RHL Mss Afr. V 123.

The meetings were attended by numbers of women and as it is they who take a large part in food production they were interested parties in the discussion on cultivation methods, and in particular in the 'magadi' system, as this is used largely in growing millet for beer making which is left entirely to the women. It is estimated that 95% of the Angoni resisted the prohibition of 'magadi'.[109]

In 1951, the Northern Provincial Commissioner reported that Native Authority orders imposing conservation measures were 'not being strictly enforced due to the erratic and half-hearted support of most of the Native Authorities concerned'.[110] But when the authorities attempted to make use of government Natural Resources legislation, this proved highly unpopular, as was noted in an intelligence report of July 1951:

> It is reported from the Northern Province that many Africans consider the Natural Resources Board rules a greater danger than Federation because of the cumulative effect on their way of life. It is said that Federation plays on their fears but Natural Resources rules are an ever present source of trouble.[111]

No evidence is currently available to suggest that traditional religious institutions comparable to those operating in the Lower Shire Valley at this period were mobilised against the ridging campaign.[112] But in a suggestive move, young members of the Presbyterian Church (some, like Daniel Mkandawire, also members of Congress) took action in a public protest against bunding held at Livingstonia in August 1953, which resulted in seventeen arrests.[113] With the exception of this and a few other sporadic protests, the north was largely unaffected by the disturbances which convulsed much of the Southern Province in August and September 1953. Nevertheless, at a popular level, grievances were mounting that, from 1956, would be exploited by a new generation of political leaders.

Congress & the anti-Federation campaign

From 1950 the growth of popular discontent brought about significant changes in Congress's character and approach. During the 1940s, leaders of Congress faced by the threat of Federation had turned to the argument that, since Nyasaland was a protectorate, it was the responsibility of the King as 'our Guardian' to protect Nyasas 'from enemies within and enemies without... enemies whose ambitions and aims are to rob us of our land by their cunning and political traps'.[114] By 1951, however, Congress had rejected 'the philosophy that Black men should be ruled by a White aristocracy, however benevolent' and instead was demanding 'our legitimate rights, including the right to self-determination, the right to reach political manhood, the right to govern ourselves'. This involved the

---

[109] *Annual Report on Native Affairs*, 1948, p. 26.
[110] PC Northern Province to Chief Secretary, 13 October 1951, MNA 4.13.8F/3091.
[111] Political Intelligence Report, October 1951, TNA CO 1015/464.
[112] For the impact of the Mbona cult in the Lower Shire valley see Schoffeleers, *River of Blood*, pp. 107–08; Mandala, *Work and Control*, p. 229.
[113] Political Intelligence Report, October 1953, TNA CO 1015/464.
[114] Minutes of the Lusaka Branch of the Nyasaland African Congress, 12 March 1949, MNA NN 1/4/6.

classic request that 'the democratic system of franchise be introduced in the form of adult suffrage'. But it also included the more unusual demand that no chief should be deposed by the Government 'without the consent of the majority of his people in the area'.[115] Popular sovereignty was thus conceived as operating as much at the level of the rural locality as it did at the level of the state. Somewhat belatedly, Ralph Chinyama, the new president-general, took the decision to open up membership of Congress to a wider constituency by reducing the substantial annual fee of 5 shillings to the more realistic sum of 3d. Additional branches were established in the countryside with the result that, by November 1952, Congress was said to have 'representatives in all the main villages, particularly around the Native Authority headquarters'.[116] Paid-up membership rose to about 5,000 in 1953 and the organisation's financial efficiency was improved as a result of Chinyama's insistence that all cash should be held by the central executive except the amount necessary to carry out local branch affairs.[117]

Access to education or involvement in business still remained important criteria for leadership positions, even at a local level. But in an interesting reversal to the position on the Bruce Estates at the time of the Chilembwe Rising, several capitaos on European estates, notably Joseph Phambala, Head Capitao on the Tennett estate and son of the head capitao for the B&EA Company, also became active in Congress. A pioneer member of the NAC, Phambala was president of the Cholo branch from 1952 and later played an important role in linking Blantyre-based Congress leaders with rural tenants.[118] The role of women, which had been envisaged in 1945 as being simply to 'provide suitable shelter and entertainment for members or delegates', was radically revised in 1952, by which time spontaneous demonstrations by women farmers in Cholo, the Lower River and the Mzimba district were beginning to attract attention. In that year, Rose Chibambo, the wife of a Livingstonia-educated civil servant based in Zomba, responded to the growing agitation against Federation taking place in the south by recruiting a number of fellow-wives of civil servants into the newly-established NAC Women's League.[119] This aimed at undermining segregation by organising women to boycott those shops that still insisted on Africans being served through separate windows.[120] Transferred with her husband to Blantyre in 1953, Rose Chibambo continued to play an active political role and was elected treasurer of the local branch of Congress in 1953. There she came into contact not only with James Sangala, the quietly efficient central organiser of the Blantyre branch, but also with a number of more radical and flamboyant figures. They included Hartwell Solomon, who received much of his upbringing in South Africa before returning to Malawi in 1949, and Grant Mkandawire, secretary and then president of the Blantyre branch in the early 1950s. Self-employed

---

[115] Nyasaland African Congress manifesto presented to Colonial Secretary, James Griffiths, 28 August 1951, TNA CO 1015/404.

[116] Political Intelligence Reports for May and November 1952, TNA CO 1015/464.

[117] J.R. Chinyama, memo on 'Raising Money for Congress', 29 Aug 1950, MNA Chinyama Papers Acc. 19.

[118] Political Intelligence Report June 1952, TNA CO 1015/469.

[119] Constitution of the NAC, 1945, MNA NN 1/4/6; 'The Rose Chibambo Story', *Wasi*, 11, 3 (2000), pp. 17–18.

[120] Political Intelligence Report, February 1953, TNA CO 1015/464.

businessmen, and hence free of the restraints imposed on government employees, Solomon and Mkandawire were unabashed populists, influenced at least in the case of Solomon by the language of Marxism acquired in South Africa and not averse to using the rhetoric of violence. By 1952 they had joined forces in seeking to organise a John Chilembwe Memorial day in Blantyre as well as an African Republican League, linking Nyasaland and Northern Rhodesia, and hence striking at the cult of royalty which the British had used to legitimise their rule.[121] Mkandawire had also begun to claim that a response akin to Mau Mau would erupt if Federation were imposed against the wishes of the people.[122]

Mkandawire's rhetoric can be contrasted with the more moderate language employed at this period by Dr Hastings Kamuzu Banda in his attempt to mobilise support against the introduction of Federation. A man of almost precisely the same age and modest height as Sangala, Banda had lived a very different life, taking him from his childhood home in Kasungu to South Africa as a labour migrant and then, thanks to assistance from the African Methodist Episcopal Church, to universities in America in the 1920s and 1930s.[123] In 1938 he had gone to Scotland on what was intended to be the last lap of a protracted education that would allow him to return to Nyasaland as a government or mission doctor. In 1941, however, Banda was rejected for both posts on racist grounds and turned instead to general practice in England, first in working class neighbourhoods in the north, in Liverpool and North Shields and then, from 1945, in the north London suburb of Harlesden.[124] It was in North Shields in 1944 that he met Mrs Merene French, the wife of a wartime major, who was to be his partner, housekeeper and receptionist for the next 13 years.[125] By 1949, in a remarkable demonstration of his ability to transcend the racism of 1940s Britain, Banda had built up a large and flourishing practice in Harlesden and won the trust and respect of his patients, almost all of whom were white. He was a member of the Fabian Colonial Bureau and of the Labour Party for which he had canvassed and voted in the 1945 general election that swept it to power.[126] He was a friend and correspondent of Arthur Creech Jones, the Colonial Secretary, and of several other British politicians including Fenner Brockway, founder of the Movement for Colonial Freedom and Rita Hinden, the formidable secretary of the Colonial Bureau. He had attended the Pan-Africanist Congress in Manchester in 1945 and become both friend and doctor of Kwame Nkrumah whom he treated for pneumonia in 1947, shortly before Nkrumah returned to the Gold Coast.[127]

Banda's consuming concern, however, remained the future of Nyasaland. His involvement in its politics went back to 1938 when the evidence he gave to the

[121] Political Intelligence Reports, July 1952, Feb. 1953, TNA CO 1015/464.
[122] Intelligence Report, Sept. 1952, TNA CO 1015/464.
[123] The best biography remains, Short, *Banda* but see also John Lloyd Lwanda, *Kamuzu Banda of Malawi: A Study in Promise, Power and Legacy* (Kachere, Zomba, 2009).
[124] 'Medical Department, African Personnel – Hastings Banda', TNA CO 7031/19 (1938) 44034/4; Fergus Macpherson, *North of the Zambezi. A Modern Missionary Memoir* (Edinburgh, 1998), pp. 10–11.
[125] Richard Pendlebury, 'The Despot and his Suburban Mistress', *Daily Mail*, 20 Dec. 1997.
[126] Hastings K. Banda to Creech Jones, n.d.[1945], RHL Creech Jones Papers, Mss. Brit. Emp. S 332, Box 7.
[127] Marika Sherwood, *Kwame Nkrumah: the Years Abroad, 1935–1947* (Accra, Ghana, 1966), p. 159.

Bledisloe Commission was highly critical of the proposal to amalgamate Nyasa-land and the Rhodesias. A year later he acted as adviser to the young Chief Mwase, from his own home district, on the chief's visit to London. In 1944 he joined forces with a former Livingstonia missionary, T. Cullen Young, to edit a collection of essays by young Malawians, published in 1946 under the title, *Our African Way of Life*. This contains an introduction in which Banda and Young provide a sympathetic account of the workings of African matrilineal societies that Banda was subsequently to utilise in projecting his personal vision of Malawian society.[128]

With the founding of Congress, in 1944, Banda's involvement in politics increased, only to come to a temporary halt in 1948 at the time of Matinga's fall from grace. However, the emergence, in 1949, of plans for the Federation of Nyasaland with the two Rhodesias brought him back into the fray once more. Convinced, not unreasonably, that this was a scheme designed to maintain white supremacy in Central Africa, Banda wrote a memorandum, published as a pamphlet in 1951, denouncing the proposals and threw himself into the anti-federation campaign. In a slightly surprising passage, drawing a veil over his own personal experiences of discrimination, Banda contrasted the relatively benign behaviour of the British Government towards Africans with the tendency of 'the Government and people of Southern Rhodesia [to] regard the Africans as infe-rior beings, with scarcely any right to a dignified and refined existence'. Feder-ation was simply amalgamation in disguise with the ultimate aim being the creation of a settler-controlled dominion. Only if universal suffrage were granted could Federation be contemplated: 'By universal suffrage we mean adult suffrage. We mean the right of every African man and women, who can read in any language…to register as a voter on the common roll with…other citizens.'[129] In his preface to the pamphlet, written in 1951, Banda consciously distanced himself from the non-confrontational and accomodationist approach he had previously pursued, citing Gandhi and Nehru in India, Sukarno in Indonesia and De Valera in Ireland as examples of politicians branded as 'agitators and extremists' who were now recognised 'as honourable statesmen and respectable leaders of their people'.[130]

Let us be clear about the nature of Banda's involvement in Nyasaland's poli-tics in the early 1950s. By this time, he had succeeded in his long-term aim of acquiring an estate in the Kasungu district managed by the journalist, Elias Mtepuka, but he remained isolated in London. Thus, distanced from the conflicts over soil conservation and even over *thangata*, he had little purchase on the wider peasant struggle.[131] On the issue of Federation, however, Banda's influence was important and it was his strategy of seeking to mobilise a broad coalition of support against Federation in both Britain and Malawi that Congress was to follow for the next three years. One aspect of this campaign, which he was superbly placed to fulfil, was to mobilise his political contacts in the Labour Party, discussing the issue face to face with Creech Jones, following up visits

[128] Cullen Young and Hastings Banda (eds), *Our African Way of Life* (London, 1946).
[129] Banda and Nkumbula, *Federation in Central Africa*. Although Nkumbula's name appears on the pamphlet, it was written by Banda alone.
[130] Banda, Introduction to *Federation*.
[131] A formal application by Banda for land in either the Kasungu or Mzimba district is contained in Hastings K. Banda to E.L. Brown, Chief Sec., 23 Dec. 1949, MNA. See also Short, *Banda*, p.62.

with personal letters and seeking support from the Fabian Bureau and from allies in the Church of Scotland.[132] At the same time, however, he was anxious to persuade Congress leaders to mobilise the support of 'chiefs, councillors, headmen and commoners' in an alliance very much looser than he himself would be prepared to contemplate once he came to power.[133] The issue surfaced over the question of how far it was appropriate to denounce the three Malawian delegates sent by the Protectorate Council to attend the Victoria Falls Conference to discuss Federation in September 1951. Because unity was a fundamental aim of Congress politicians, justifying their claim to speak for the African people of Nyasaland as a whole, the appearance of this small group of chiefs and politicians, publicly flouting Congress's policy of boycotting all discussion of Federation, came as a major blow to the Executive Committee and elicited a fierce response. Such men were 'Quislings', wrote A. J. Banda, the General Secretary of Congress; men who were acting against 'the expressed feelings of the people'.[134] In an ironic touch, it was Banda from his surgery in London who upheld the belief that more could be achieved by courting waverers than by outright condemnation. In a note to Elias Mtepuka, Banda wrote:

> In politics it is often necessary to use tactics and diplomacy... To the authorities we must be as firm as possible and within the law first, but even outside the law when all constitutional and legal means fail to defeat federation. But to our own people, that is those who do not see things the way we see things, we must be very tactful, diplomatic and even lenient to their mistakes and errors which come from their ignorance.[135]

In the next few months, Banda went out of his way to convince Congress leaders of the need to involve chiefs as widely as possible in the anti-federation campaign so that they could speak with a single voice. 'If we do that no British Government, whatever its political colour, will dare to force us into accepting Federation. There is a thing called British public opinion which all Governments really fear.'[136] It was largely through Banda's efforts that a delegation of three chiefs, accompanied by Orton Chirwa and Matthews Phiri, and speaking on behalf of a representative conference of chiefs, visited Britain in February 1953 with the intention 'of representing personally to the Queen the unanimous opposition of their peoples to the proposed Federation.' Sent instead to the new Colonial Secretary, Oliver Lyttelton, the delegation was given a lesson in the limitations of popular opinion. In school-masterly manner, Lyttelton announced that 'he could see nothing new in the memorandum, much of which he regarded as irresponsible.' 'Federation', whatever they thought, 'would be greatly to the advantage of Africans in Nyasaland.' There would be no value in them meeting the Queen.[137] In a separate minute, a senior civil servant at the Colonial Office noted of the widespread opposition: 'I do not think it alters the fundamental factors in the equation: we believe Federation is right; we believe that 90% of the

---

[132] Banda to Creech Jones, 23 June 1951, 27 Oct 1951. RHL Creech Jones Papers, Mss. Br. Emp. 332, Box 7.

[133] Banda, *Federation*, 'Introduction'.

[134] 'The Truth about the African Protectorate Council' by A.J. Mtalika Banda, 9 September 1951, TNA CO 1015/404.

[135] Quoted in Political Intelligence Report, September 1951, TNA CO 1015/464.

[136] Political Intelligence Report, November 1951, TNA CO 1015/464.

[137] Draft note of meeting held at the Colonial Office, 4 Feb. 1953, TNA CO 1015/159.

people affected know little about it, care less, and after some possible initial excitement will scarcely notice that it has happened.'[138]

Dr Banda's miscalculation of the British Government's response can be seen in retrospect as weakening the prospects for democracy in Malawi. As an active supporter of Labour in the landslide election of 1945, at which the Conservative Government was defeated, Banda was one of the very few Malawians in the early 1950s with direct experience of parliamentary democracy in practice.[139] The crushing demonstration provided by the Government in 1953 that this democracy was not for export, and that a policy unambiguously rejected by chiefs and people alike could still be foisted on Nyasaland, came as a blow which temporarily weakened his credibility at home and contributed to a marked harshening of his subsequent political attitudes. One lesson to be learnt was the danger of relying on personal alliances at a time of political change. Had Labour remained in office and had Creech Jones remained Colonial Secretary, there is every likelihood that Banda's strategy would have triumphed and the Federation would not have come into existence. In that sense it was the dismissal of Creech Jones and the loss by Labour of the 1951 election that scuppered Banda's plans. At another level, however, the imposition of Federation was a clear demonstration that Banda had been wrong when he argued in 1949: 'Not only does the Government of the United Kingdom regard the Africans as human beings, but also, it accepts them as British subjects in the full sense of the term.'[140] The harsh truth was that, even in the 1950s, democratic accountability existed in Britain but was absent from her colonies. As this became plain by the early months of 1953, the prospect of a shift in Congress strategy to a campaign of civil disobedience became ever more attractive. 'If federation forced on us, non-violent resistance', the fiery Grant Mkandawire cabled Banda in January. In the same month Ralph Chinyama wrote to the local newspaper repudiating Mkandawire's action.[141]

The events of 1953, culminating in the 'Cholo disturbances' in August and September, brought home at once the autocratic character of the colonial state and the limitations of Congress's leadership. Ralph Chinyama was a highly experienced politician, past secretary of the Central Province Native Association, a former president of the African Farmers' Association and an active member of the executive committee of the Native Tobacco Board. But he was also by temperament and training one of the least appropriate leaders it would be possible to find to head a movement composed of discontented peasants. Not only was he a successful Central Province estate owner with little understanding or sympathy for the plight of tenants in the Shire Highlands, he was also a long-term supporter of conservation measures as a member of the Native Tobacco Board. What is more, for all his imposing appearance, Chinyama at heart was a conciliator, more than slightly in awe of the Governor and reluctant to challenge him to his face. In his personal diary in 1951, he recorded a dream, 'Riding with H.E. on motor bike' (one suspects that Colby was in the driving seat), that provides us with a fleeting glimpse into the psychology of colonial relation-

---

[138] Note by Marnham, 8 Dec. 1952, TNA CO 1015/159.
[139] Banda to Creech Jones, No date [1945], RHL Creech Jones Papers, Mss Brit. Emp. S 332 Box 7.
[140] Banda and Nkumbula, *Federation*.
[141] Short, *Banda*, p.71.

ships.[142] Later, in October 1952, when summoned by Colby to Government House for a lecture on 'the way in which Congress activities had developed in the last two or three years', Chinyama responded meekly, 'thanking His Excellency for his clear exposition, to which he had listened with pleasure' and expressing his regret at 'the incidents which had taken place'.[143]

Chinyama's position, however, was rapidly becoming more difficult. On 5 April 1953, a large crowd, variously estimated at between one and three thousand people, many of them women, flocked into Blantyre market to attend an Emergency Conference of Congress.[144] Chinyama made clear his opposition to the use of unconstitutional methods. But his views were ignored in favour of a resolution that the 'imposition of federation against the expressed opposition of the African people will be met by the strongest non-violent resistance' and that 'a Supreme Council of Action consisting of representative Chiefs, members of the Legislative Council, Congress and people from various organisations be set up immediately, which Council shall consider and direct the resistance movement.'[145] The Conference also resolved that there should be a Protectorate-wide strike by all civil servants and workers on farms, a ban on the payment of taxes, and a boycott of European markets and stores. In a separate section, the Conference came out in support of tenants on estates who 'themselves had decided to refuse any more Thangata either in cash or service', and demanded the abolition of the *thangata* system.[146]

Within a matter of days, a Supreme Council had been formed, chaired by Dr Banda's kinsman, Chief Mwase from Kasungu, and containing a handful of chiefs and a scattering of politicians. Despite his evident misgivings, Chinyama was one of those most prominently involved. He was joined by a group of Blantyre-based leaders, including Lali Lubani, an independent businessman, and trade unionist, Lawrence Mapemba, a fellow union organiser, and the ever-present James Sangala.[147] An early rebuff came towards the end of April when the general strike planned by Lubani and Hartwell Solomon failed to materialise. But in May the campaign achieved a boost through the decision of Chief Philip Gomani from Ntcheu, acting on the advice of his son Willard, to call on his people to disregard agricultural and forestry instructions and to refuse to pay tax.[148] Gomani's action, the support he received from the visionary Anglican clergyman Revd Michael Scott, the botched attempt to arrest them, and Gomani's ultimate banishment to Cholo were all covered in considerable detail by the British press and brought the campaign welcome publicity.[149] More important, over much of the Ntcheu district, peasants responded positively by refusing to dip cattle or to observe agricultural rules.

Elsewhere, the civil disobedience campaign ran into trouble. The attempted

---

[142] J.R.N. Chinyama, diary entry for 1 May 1951, MNA, Chinyama Papers. MNA ACC 19/JRC/3/1.

[143] 'Record of a Meeting held at Government House Zomba, 29 Oct. 1952', Chinyama Papers, MNA ACC 19/JRC/4/1.

[144] A.J.M. Banda to Chief Secretary, 13 April, 1953, TNA CO 1015/464; Phiri, *Sangala*, p. 41–42. This episode is described in some length in Rotberg, *Rise of Nationalism*, p. 250 and Short, *Banda*, pp. 72–73.

[145] Statement by A.J. Mtalika Banda, 6 April 1953, TNA CO 1015/404.

[146] Ibid.

[147] Political Intelligence Report, May 1953, TNA CO 1015/404.

[148] Ibid.

[149] Michael Scott, *African Episode* (London, 1953) and *A Time To Speak* (London, 1958), pp. 282–84.

boycott of the Coronations celebrations for Queen Elizabeth on 2 June were almost completely effective in Blantyre, Cholo and Zomba but worked less well in other smaller towns. Late in May, one Native Authority in the Zomba district, Chief Msamala, followed Gomani in ordering his people to stop paying taxes and to ignore agricultural regulations. But a week later, following a meeting of chiefs in the Zomba/Liwonde area, he withdrew these orders and began to cooperate once more.[150] In all, fifteen chiefs tendered their resignation as Native Authorities but most of these, including Mwase, continued to work with the government, and in only four cases were their resignations formally accepted.[151] Several of the more radical urban-based Congress activists, including the northerners Grant Mkandawire in Blantyre and McKinley Qabaniso Chibambo in Zomba, established a dialogue with disaffected tenants in the countryside but with very mixed results. Chibambo, a senior clerk and the son of one Livingstonia's most respected pastors, was involved in July in an attempt to overthrow Chief Chikowi in the Zomba district which resulted in his arrest and conviction on a charge of sedition. He was then exiled to steamy Port Herald where he remained until 1960.

As violence spread, splits in Congress emerged and the senior leadership took fright. Orton Chirwa, one of the best-educated members of the party, joined Charles Matinga in forming the rival African Progressive Association with an eye on the forthcoming federal elections. Chief Mwase privately informed the Provincial Commissioner that he wished to withdraw his resignation as Native Authority and was prepared to cooperate fully with the Government.[152] Colby sent again for Chinyama, warned him of the 'incalculable damage which you and your associates have done in the previous few months' and threatened him with the fate of his father who had been executed during the Chilembwe Rising.[153] Bowing to this pressure, Chinyama issued a statement early in September 1953 denying 'that directly or indirectly Congress had anything at all to do with the outbreak of demonstrations at Cholo and elsewhere' and criticising the violence that had resulted.[154] A little over a week later, Mwase convened a meeting of chiefs and Congress leaders at Lilongwe at which he appealed to them to call off the non-cooperation campaign. Some last-minute resistance came from chiefs and Congress leaders in the Northern Province, who had only been indirectly involved, but following the intervention of Sangala and of other southern Congressmen the motion was finally passed.[155] On 19 September, Chinyama wrote to all Congress branches announcing that the passive resistance campaign had been withdrawn. He also declared that since Federation was now an accomplished fact, 'Congress will raise no objection for any suitable and properly selected African members to go and represent Africans in the Federal parliament.'[156]

Over the next few weeks, the Supreme Action Council was disbanded. A. J.

[150] Political Intelligence Report, June 1953, TNA CO 1015/404.
[151] Political Intelligence Report, Sept. 1953, TNA CO 1015/405.
[152] Political Intelligence Report, Aug. 1953, TNA CO 1015/465.
[153] C.W. Footman to Chinyama, 10 Sept. 1953, MNA Chinyama Papers, AC 19/JRC/4/1.
[154] Statement by Chinyama contained in A.J.M Banda to P.C. Central Province, 5 Sept. 1953, MNA Chinyama Papers, ACC 19/JRC/4/1.
[155] Political Intelligence Report, Sept. 1953, TNA CO 1015/465.
[156] A.J.M. Banda to all Congress branches, 19 Sept. 1953, MNA Chinyama Papers, Acc 19/JRC/4/1.

M. Banda and then Chinyama resigned. In the Northern Province, and partic-ularly in the Nkhata Bay area, activists continued to hold meetings and speak out against Federation. Elsewhere, however, as Short has noted, 'the mood of the Nyasa people settled into sullen resentment.'[157] At the end of November, there was still 'a good deal of sporadic opposition to the garden preparation and bunding laws' in the Cholo and Chikwawa districts but virtually all Native Authorities, other than Chiefs Mbwana and Mankhambira in the Nkhata Bay district, were said to be cooperating with the Government.[158] In a deeply humil-iating episode, Chief Mwase at a public meeting held at his own court renounced his connections with such unconstitutional bodies as the Supreme Council and declared that in future he would devote his entire energies to the affairs of the Kasungu district alone.[159] Opposition against bunding continued in the Lilongwe district, where Joseph Chateka, a Seventh Day Baptist pastor, led a party of his adherents into the township in October to protest against the convic-tion of one of his members. In Ntcheu, however, such protests were a thing of the past. On 8 October police detachments from Northern Rhodesia, Tanganyika and Nyasaland arrived in the district at the start of a highly coercive campaign aimed at bringing resistance to government rules to an end. Over 1,000 people were fined for their opposition to *malimidwe*. More than 60 Watchtower adher-ents, who ignored the summonses, were rounded up and sent to prison in Zomba instead. Large numbers of tax defaulters were arrested and were not released until they had paid their arrears.[160]

With disillusionment rife, Congress numbers fell from a high point of 5,000 paid-up members early in the year to only a few hundred at the end.[161] The unas-suming James Sangala once more stepped into the breach and took over the Pres-idency of Congress in January 1954, after which he transferred the headquarters back from Lilongwe to Blantyre.[162] Wellington Manoah Chirwa, Chairman of the Students Representative Council at Fort Hare in 1951–52, successfully stood as Congress representative to the federal parliament. Meanwhile, Dr Banda, appalled by what he saw as Chinyama's and Chirwa's betrayal of the nationalist cause, turned his back on Britain and Nyasaland alike. In August he left for the Gold Coast, now moving towards independence under Nkrumah, where he set up his practice in the northern provincial capital of Kumasi. Radicals such as Grant Mikeka Mkandawire and Hartwell Solomon were left equally dismayed. In August they had travelled through the Cholo district with Phambala, head capitao of the Tennett estate, urging the people to continue their struggle; simul-taneously, Chinyama and Mwase in a government-supplied car were calling upon them to stop. The radicals were isolated and embittered, deprived of office in the new central executive and convinced that, through the timidity of Congress's leadership, the opportunity of mounting a radical, peasant-based challenge to the Government had been lost.[163]

The Government, like the nationalists, was deeply affected by the distur-

---

[157] Short, *Banda*, p.74.
[158] Political Intelligence Report, Nov. 1953, TNA CO 1015/455.
[159] Political Intelligence Report, Oct. 1953, TNA CO 1015/465.
[160] Ibid.
[161] 'The Political Situation in Nyasaland at the end of April, 1956', TNA CO 1015/961.
[162] Phiri, *Sangala*, pp. 49–50.
[163] Joey Power, 'Building Relevance: the Blantyre Congress, 1953 to 1956', *JSAS*, 28, 1, 2002, p. 46.

bances. Colby, in striking contrast to Armitage six years later, retained the initiative virtually throughout. Nevertheless, he was acutely aware of the fragility of his position. Onlookers were divided as to whether the situation in the Shire Highlands could best be compared with that of indigo estates in Bihar, of large-scale farms in post-war Italy, or of the White Highlands in Kenya. But they were united in acknowledging that in each and every one of these cases tensions between tenants and landlords had resulted in violence, leading to attempts by peasants to occupy the estates.[164] Fearful of publicity, Colby made up his mind at an early stage that there should be no wide-ranging independent investigation of the causes and character of the riots or of the conduct of the colonial authorities.[165] The insubstantial report that did appear, written by a local commission of inquiry, concentrated entirely on the first three days of the disturbances on Tennett's Magunda Estate, and almost entirely ignored their causes.[166] 'It is clear that the Commission has placed a far narrower interpretation on its terms of reference than the Governor's telegram led us to believe', one disillusioned Colonial Office mandarin noted.[167]

Yet if Colby was anxious to avoid enquiry, he and his advisers were in no doubt that the troubles emerged from 'deeply-rooted grievances' and that these could not be removed by coercive action alone. 'It is not surprising', McDonald had noted, 'that there have sprung from these people some strong supporters of the African Congress, who are now acting as ringleaders. It is erroneous to imagine, however, that merely by impounding these ringleaders the situation would be resolved.'[168] Consequently, Colby developed a two-pronged strategy, aimed at once at strengthening the coercive powers available to the state but also at increasing the pace and extent of land settlement, with the new aim of eventually ending *thangata*.

With the collapse of informal mechanisms of control from the early 1950s, more effective policing was a high priority. One lesson learnt by the British from 1953 was that colonial chiefly authority could no longer be relied on. Another was that African politicians were becoming increasingly adept in reinterpreting the cult of monarchy in a manner that challenged the legitimacy of imperial-directed constitutional change. Whether boycotting the Coronation celebrations or appealing directly to the Queen, Congress leaders were adapting the cult of monarchy to their own political purposes.[169] Consequently, from December 1953, Colby put in train an ambitious programme of police expansion that resulted in the size of the force being trebled in just six years, from a little over 700 policemen to more than 2,500.[170] Priority was given to the Police Mobile Force [PMF], a paramilitary organisation founded at the time of the 1953 troubles and designed 'to provide a striking force for use in disturbed areas'. Led by

---

[164] Lord Hailey, a former provincial governor in India, made the comparison with Bihar. See 'Notes on Nyasaland' [1947], Hailey Papers, TNA CO 1018/62. See also Dixon to Brook, 6 Jan 1953, TNA CO 1017/773.

[165] Colby to Gorell Barnes, 22 Sept.1953, TNA CO 1015/470. See also Palmer, 'Workers', p. 124.

[166] *Report of the Commission of Inquiry appointed to enquire into disturbances at Magunda Estate, Luchenza.*

[167] Note by J.R. Williams, 22 Oct. 1953, TNA CO 1015/470.

[168] Colby to CO, 2 Sept. 1953 enclosing 'Report by...McDonald ...on Unrest on Estates in the Cholo District', TNA CO 1015/470.

[169] McCracken, 'Authority and Legitimacy', p. 174.

[170] *Annual Reports of the Nyasaland Police,* 1958 and 1959.

John Mesurier, a former army officer, the Force consisted in 1954 of fourteen European officers and 200 mainly illiterate recruits with a minimum of five years' military service behind them. Trained mainly in riot control and dressed in distinctive black jerseys, they travelled in blue-painted, purpose-built Bedford trucks to wherever their services were required. In 1954 two platoons of the PMF spent several weeks patrolling extensively in the Nkhotakota district. Later they were used as a blunt weapon in the enforcement of agricultural rules and in the Government's struggle against an increasingly assertive Congress.[171]

Land purchase was the other side of the coin. As Dr Banda was to demonstrate in 1962, the most effective way of ending *thangata* would have been to abolish the obligation on tenants to work for their landlords and to reduce rent to a nominal level: the policy that was recommended by S.R. Simpson, the Lands Adviser to the Colonial Office in May 1954.[172] Colby, however, who was already embroiled in a damaging dispute with the estate owners and their supporters in the Conservative Party in Britain, was not prepared to make any radical change in the relationship between landlords and tenants other than to reduce the level of rent from 52 shillings to 30 shillings Instead, he renewed efforts to force estate owners to transfer to the state undeveloped land or land heavily settled by tenants, using the threat of compulsory purchase if estate owners refused to sell. Oliver Lyttelton, the Colonial Secretary, made a special visit to Nyasaland early in May 1954, nearly brought to an unceremonious end when Lyttelton fell over the banisters at Government House in the middle of the night, hitting the stairs 12 feet below and leaving him covered in bruises.[173] However, he recovered sufficiently to be able to attend a meeting two days later with representatives from the large estates. Dixon led the way in calling on the Government to demonstrate a 'vigorous attitude' in the defence of European-owned land.[174] In reply, however, Lyttelton made it clear to the estate owners that 'compulsory acquisition will not be shirked if they are not prepared to sell voluntarily that part of their land which is irretrievably infested with African tenants or which, though unoccupied, they cannot develop within a reasonable time.'[175] In a public statement, Lyttelton reiterated the long-held belief in official circles in Britain: '…the agricultural development on estates has been the foundation of the economic progress and wealth of the territory and will continue to play an essential part in its economy.' But he also stressed his conviction that 'the Tangata system has outlived its usefulness and should be progressively brought to an end.'[176]

Negotiations were therefore resumed with the BCA Company over the sale of land occupied by tenants in the Cholo District. Once more the Company's chairman, Brook, used every means at his disposal to delay until the highest possible price had been conceded. In June 1955, however, agreement was reached for the purchase from the BCA Company of 48,750 acres of land at the extremely generous price of £1 an acre. Other estate owners, who had held back while the negotiations with the BCA Company were in progress, now came forward, with

---

[171] McCracken, 'Coercion and Control', p. 140.
[172] Baker, *Seeds of Trouble*, pp. 124–27. Baker sides with Colby in taking a highly critical view of this report.
[173] Lyttelton to Prime Minister, Churchill, 4 May 1954, TNA CO 967/276.
[174] Baker, *Seeds of Trouble*, p. 119.
[175] W.L. Gorell Barnes to G.H. Baxter, 14 May 1954, TNA CO 1015/1010.
[176] Ibid. See also Baker, *Seeds of Trouble*, pp. 114–22.

the result that a further 23 estates, over 100,000 acres in extent, were sold to the Government by 1957.[177] From that year forward, CDWF funds from Britain were applied to this purpose but in a remarkable turn of affairs, Colby made use of money from the Native Development and Welfare Fund accumulated through the levy charged on independent peasants. Altogether, in 1955 and 1956 nearly 25,000 tenant families were 'emancipated' (the evocative term originally used in the Abrahams Report). This in turn, however, brought new tensions to the fore as many former tenants were moved off estates that had been retained under European ownership, often to inferior land elsewhere. Land resettlement, rather than being a solution to the problem of rural unrest, simply transferred the problem outwards. Rural grievances were to continue to resonate during the final period of political agitation culminating in the achievement of independence.

[177] Baker, *Seeds of Trouble*, pp. 135–53.

13
The Liberation Struggle 1953–1959

Introduction

The decade ending in 1964 was the most dramatic in the twentieth century history of Malawi. At one level, the key feature was the transformation of Congress from the weak, divided movement of 1953 into the infinitely larger, more united, more powerful Malawi Congress Party that was to dominate Malawian politics in the early 1960s. As modern research has demonstrated, in many parts of Africa the rhetoric of nationalist 'struggle' disguised the reality that political independence was the outcome of a negotiated settlement achieved as much through the input of colonial planners in Europe as it was through the agitation of African nationalists. In Malawi, by contrast, the impact of the nationalist movement brought about a fundamental reassessment of British decolonisation strategies. Widespread popular participation, however, went side by side with a growing intolerance of dissent. Surface unity masked the emergence of increasing ethnic, regional and generational tensions. Alternative models of political mobilisation were marginalised and then eliminated. Independence for Malawi involved not just the formal ending of British rule on 5 July 1964. It also involved the eruption of the cabinet crisis five weeks later and the birth of the Banda dictatorship.

From apathy to agitation, 1953–56

The period from 1953 to 1956 has generally been described as one that marked a low point in the fortunes of the Nyasaland African Congress, although, as Power has demonstrated, disruption at the centre did not mean the ending of all political activity.[1] Sangala did his best to retain contact with the fifteen or so branches still in operation. But his political strategy consisted of little more than issuing occasional statements denouncing federation and calling for self-government. Branches were instructed in the need 'to obey all the laws of the govern-

---

[1]   Power, 'Building Relevance' pp. 45–65.

336

ment and to refrain from doing things which will bring Congress into disrepute or disgrace'.[2] The occasional news-sheet, *Kwacha* (the Dawn), first published in 1952, was expanded into a newspaper in 1955, only to collapse the following year.[3] Manoah Chirwa emerged as the single most influential individual in Congress. But, from mid-1955, much of Chirwa's energy was dissipated in defending himself against a series of challenges from radicals in the party who demanded that he and Kumbikano should resign their seats in the Salisbury parliament as part of the wider rejection of the Federation. Supported by Sangala, Chirwa was able to see off his opponents over more than two years, but only at a cost to Congress. Thwarted in his attempt to force Chirwa's resignation, Masopera Gondwe, one of the most committed of the activists, left Congress in August 1955 to found his own Congress People's Party. Within a matter of months, he had been followed by Kinross Kulujili, Secretary of Congress, and two prominent radicals: Grant Mikeka Mkandawire, President of the Blantyre branch and J. A. Phambala, the Treasurer-General and leading representative of the estate workers.

The decline of Congress did little, however, to dissipate the tensions that had built up during the previous decade. In the Cholo district, for example, the decision of Government in the aftermath of the troubles to impose a reduction on rents, combined with a greater wariness among landlords as to the advisability of collecting rents at all, led to some marginal improvement in the position of tenants. However, the radical new programme of land purchase, started in August 1955 with the acquisition by Colby of nearly 40,000 acres of land in the district, introduced a disturbing new element into relations between tenants and the Government. In the long run, there can be little doubt that this policy, which resulted in the acquisition of at least 170,000 extra acres over what had already been bought by 1953, played a significant part in breaking up the big Shire Highlands estates and bringing *thangata* to an end. By 1958, only 80,000 people (or some 20,400 families) lived on private estates in Nyasaland as compared with over 200,000 people in 1945.[4] Independent Malawi was thus saved from the dangerous obsession with white-owned land that was carried over into independent Zimbabwe.

Resettlement on this scale, however, brought further problems in its wake deriving in part from the insistence of landlords that tenants should be removed from several of the estates they retained. From August 1955, reports were received by Government concerning the discontent expressed by former tenants of the BCA Company in being moved from more to less fertile land without compensation. Special efforts were made to try and ensure that the resettlement programme proceeded smoothly; however, there was a good deal of opposition in the Bvumbe area, the home of Mission Bvumbe, one of Congress's most radical activists. In January 1956, this led to fears of a further outbreak of disturbances.[5] By April, the Government was cautiously claiming that the Cholo resettlement scheme was 'proceeding satisfactorily and without incident, in spite of

[2]   Quoted in Rotberg, p. 268.
[3]   Phiri, *Sangala*, p. pp. 53–54.
[4]   Baker, *Seeds of Trouble*, p. 167–68. According to the *Annual Report on African Affairs for 1957*, only about 15,700 families were left on private estates by 1958.
[5]   Baker, *Seeds of Trouble*, pp. 150–51.

threats of resistance against forcible eviction'.[6] The following year, however, this optimism was countered in a report that noted the extent of resentment that remained. 'The volume of families moving off private estates caused nervousness and unrest among those remaining who had lived on estates, undisturbed, for many years, and also among squatters who had entered illegally in recent years.'[7] At Congress's annual conference in August, a resolution was passed demanding that an investigation should be launched in the Cholo District 'concerning the removal of African villages; these investigations should cover the Southern Province as a whole, since many villages are being removed from place to place.'[8]

In many parts of Malawi, continuing fears over agricultural rules loomed larger than land resettlement policies. Large-scale drives involving the marking out of thousands of miles of bunds reached their peak in 1953, after which they were replaced by more concentrated campaigns aimed at improving conservation standards in particular areas. In 1954, for example, special attention was given to the Tangadzi and Chimombo catchment areas of the Cholo district. Cultivators turned out in their hundreds and the countryside was said to have been transformed.[9] Prosecutions grew for breaches of the Natural Resources legislation, reaching more than 10,000 cases in the Southern Province alone in 1955. Agricultural instructors became increasingly employed as agricultural police with predictably disastrous results. 'We have now finished checking bunds...[and] we have caught many cases', Agricultural Instructor Hoda reported from near Dedza in 1955:

> But what I can also report is that people are not happy with capitaos, they say: We are troubling them, and also they say we are stealing their money... They speak bad words to us, saying we trouble them, and why do we agree with the Azungu [Europeans].'[10]

Opposition in the lakeshore section of the Nkhotakota district was even more fiercely expressed. In 1953, the local Congress leader Dunstan Chijozi had been only partially successful in his efforts to mobilise Chewa peasants against the Nyamwezi/Yao chief, Msusa.[11] However, with the introduction from 1954 of a campaign aimed at forcing peasants to grow their cassava on ridges rather than mounds, opposition intensified, focusing on Msusa as the local representative of the colonial state: 'In the area of Chief Msusa, who remained steadfast in his support of Government, local agitators endeavoured to undermine his authority and also incited a crowd to stage an unruly demonstration.'[12] A contingent of the Police Mobile Force was sent to restore order but was unable bring about any fundamental change. Local people continued to argue that cassava would rot if it were grown on ridges. They combined this complaint with the charge, strongly made by the Achewa Improvement Society, that Msusa should be replaced by a

---

6   'The Political Situation in Nyasaland at the end of April 1956', TNA CO 1015/961.
7   Annual Report on the Progress of Land Acquisition and Resettlement in the Southern Province of Nyasaland, 1957–58, TNA CO 1015/1337.
8   Resolutions of the 13th Annual Conference of the Nyasaland African Congress, 3–5 August 1957, TNA CO 1015/1748.
9   *Agricultural Department Report for 1954*, p. 17.
10 Report by Agricultural Instructor Hoda, 20 Jan. 1955, MNA 15/1/4F 7325.
11 Political Intelligence Report, Oct. 1953, TNA CO 1015/465.
12 *Annual Report on Native Administration for 1954.*

Chewa chief. In 1956, conditions on the lake shore 'continued to be very unsettled' and it was claimed that

> opposition to the ridging of cassava gardens remains as firm as ever and the latest reports indicate that local Headmen, backed by the local people, are unchanged in their determination to refuse to comply with Government's orders if they are required to cultivate their crops in ridged gardens in the future.[13]

Even the decision taken by the government, on a territory-wide level in 1956, to relax the policy of compulsion and concentrate on punishing flagrant offenders, had little effect in reducing tension in the area. Villagers continued to refuse to ridge their cassava gardens and the local branch of Congress made this issue a focal point of its campaign. In June of that year, the intelligence digest noted: 'Political activity in the Kota Kota district... where opposition to the ridging of cassava gardens on sloping ground has always been a main feature of Congress propaganda, has been stimulated by the holding of ten public meetings of Congress, one of which was attended by over four hundred people.' In speech after speech, Andrew Sonjo, Secretary of the local branch, 'deplored the manner in which Europeans were taking land away from the Africans and criticised Federation and the Natural Resources Board Rules.'[14]

Similar reactions could be found in other parts of the country. In the Northern Province by 1955 a clear majority of Native Authorities were giving support, direct or tacit, to the protestors, with the result that the authority of the state found itself increasingly challenged. In the Misuku hills, hundreds of cultivators went unpunished when they flouted bunding rules; elsewhere Natural Resources legislation was routinely ignored.[15] Near the mission station at Ekwendeni, for example, L. N. Gondwe was leader of a soil conservation team charged with marking bunds that local villagers were then required to build. Gondwe's report to his supervisor captures the strained atmosphere in which he worked:

> No garden owner assisted in the work of cutting pegs ...each one entirely refused, so the team had to provide pegs and marked all the gardens, no work has been done from that time. Only few people have made traces. Often and often we are visiting this village but we cannot find people at the village or in their gardens; they always desert when they have seen or heard us coming...The village has given us troubles for a very long time, since 1950 they have been accused for many times and fined many times in Mtwalo's court but no change.[16]

The agricultural supervisor complained at the low level of fines that Mtwalo's court imposed (five to ten shillings for an offence against bunding regulations; fifteen to twenty shillings for those found guilty of cultivating *visoso* gardens). But with his authority hanging in the balance, there was no question of the chief imposing more.[17]

---

13 *Annual Report on Native Administration for 1956*; 'The Political Situation at the End of April, 1956', TNA CO 1015/961.
14 Intelligence Digest, June 1957, TNA CO 1015/1748.
15 Waterfield, 'Nyasaland Disturbances N.W. Karonga', 6 May 1959, RHL Devlin Commission Papers, Box 8.
16 L.N. Gondwe to Agricultural Supervisor, Zombwe, no date [1955], MNA 9.4.11F/16100.
17 Agricultural Supervisor, Zombwe to Agricultural Officer, Mzuzu, 29 October 1956, MNA 9.4.11F/16100.

Rural discontent was combined with the articulation in Blantyre of a number of urban-based grievances. Racial discrimination, as represented by the continued existence of a pass system in the township, had been identified by Sangala in 1943 as one of the central factors behind the creation of the Nyasaland African Congress. In subsequent years, members of the Malawian urban elite, supported from 1949 by the Provincial Commissioner, made repeated efforts to have the curfew lifted or else extended to cover people of all races. Time and again the Blantyre and Limbe town councils turned down these requests, giving way reluctantly only in March 1954 on the advice of the Nyasaland police.[18] The ending of one grievance, however, was accompanied by the extension of another. As Power has demonstrated, many Africans were bitterly opposed to the plan, unveiled in 1951, to restructure Blantyre into commercial and industrial zones as well as into high, medium and low density residential areas. In Chichiri in particular, Congress politicians such as Mikeka Mkandawire and Hartwell Solomon constructed buildings without planning permission, only to have them demolished by the Government. Squatting flourished from 1953 resulting in further conflicts with the authorities and the growing belief that land was being alienated to serve the purposes of the Federation.[19] At the same time, in a process indicative of the fluidity of class relationships in Blantyre, independent businessmen, politicians and labour leaders joined together in a number of overlapping alliances. In November 1953, Lawrence Makata and Lali Lubani were instrumental in forming an African Chamber of Commerce along with other businessmen in politics such as Mikeka Mkandawire and James Mpunga.[20] They were also active in providing a house for Chief Gomani when he was exiled from Ntcheu, and transport for fellow-Congressmen during the 1953 disturbances. In the mid-1950s, Lali Lubani and Hartwell Solomon both continued to play active administrative roles in the African Motor Transport Workers' Union despite their transition several years earlier from employee to employer. In 1953 several strikes took place in Blantyre-Limbe involving workers in the construction industry, in a tobacco grading company and in the ITC factory at Limbe.[21] In the following year, 1954, the Nyasaland Railways African Workers Union was officially registered. Paid up trade unionists remained few in number – not more than 1,500 in 1957.[22] Nevertheless, the number of strikes and industrial disputes continued to grow from 11 in 1954 to 14 in 1956, including three in the building industry. In that year, Wellington Manoah Chirwa was reported as 'having recently been interested in the Nyasaland African Railway Workers Union'. But the Special Branch noted that 'until the Unions develop and gain the support of the majority of the workers, it is unlikely that Congress will attempt to achieve its aims through this medium.'[23]

[18] Blantyre Town Council minutes, 15 Aug. 1949; 15 Jan. 1952; 26 Jan. 1953; 12 Oct. 1953; 8 March 1954; MNA BL 2/1/1/14 and 2/1/1/15.
[19] Power, 'Building Relevance'.
[20] Political Intelligence Report, Nov. 1953, TNA CO 1015/455.
[21] Mapopa Chipeta, 'Labour in colonial Malawi: the growth and development of the Malawian wage labour force during the colonial period, 1890–1964', Ph.D. dissertation, University of Dalhousie, 1986, p. 388.
[22] *Annual Reports of the Labour Department for 1957 and 1958.*
[23] Political Intelligence Report for April 1956, TNA CO 1015/961; *Annual Report of the Labour Department for 1956.*

The new politics, 1955–1958

From 1955 two developments took place that were to transform the character of politics in Malawi. Modest constitutional changes at the territorial level provided the incentive for radical nationalist politicians to seek to enter the Legislative Council. At the same time, a new generation of politicians emerged – almost all of them deeply influenced by ideas and experiences gained outside Malawi – who were to construct a powerful and increasingly popular political movement out of the disparate grievances already in existence.

Rather surprisingly, it was the Nyasaland Government rather than the Colonial Office which set in motion the discussions leading to constitutional change. Colby reacted to the introduction of the Federation by recommending, in November 1953, that Africans should be given parity with non-African unofficials in the Nyasaland Legislative Council.[24] Lyttelton and his advisers turned down this proposal, which came 'as rather a shock' to the Colonial Office, on the grounds that Huggins would be likely to oppose such a radical measure.[25] Colby, however, continued to press for limited reform, in part because he was anxious to reduce the political influence of European settlers. Federal inaction prevented any decisions being taken during Lyttelton's visit to Nyasaland in May 1954. But a year later, Colby was summoned to meet the new Colonial Secretary, Lennox-Boyd, in London where a decision was finally taken. On Colby's recommendation, no provision was made for the appointment of an African to the Executive Council as had recently happened in Uganda.[26] However, the number of Africans on the Legislative Council was increased from three to five (as compared with six European unofficials). Most important of all, it was agreed that the African members would be elected by the 120 or so chiefs and others who were members of the three African Provincial Councils rather than being selected by the Governor from a panel of names submitted to him by the councils as had happened in the past.[27] Neither parity nor anything approaching democratic participation was thus involved in this new system. But it did mean that, whereas previously African membership of the Council was automatically confined to moderates such as Alexander Muwamba, who were content to work within a colonially dominant system, now there was the possibility of the election of radicals who would challenge the state outright.

The sweeping victory achieved by Congress candidates in the elections of March 1956 marked a significant shift in the nature of Malawian politics. The three former African members of the Legislative Council were swept away, receiving only six of the 119 votes cast in the three provinces. By contrast, two new young radical politicians were easily elected. Kanyama Chiume, aged 27, born in Usisya in the Nkhata Bay district but educated entirely in Tanganyika and Uganda, received 16 out of a possible 22 votes in the Northern Province. Henry Masauko Chipembere, aged 26, a Fort Hare graduate and former admin-

---

[24] Colby to Gorell Barnes, 4 Nov. 1953, TNA CO 1015/549.
[25] Gorell Barnes to Colby, 27 Nov. 1953; TNA CO minute 19 Nov 1953, CO 1015/549.
[26] Colby to Gorell Barnes, 19 Jan. 1955, TNA CO 1015/1011.
[27] Williams to Footman, 4 May 1955, TNA CO 1015/1011.

istrative officer, received 21 out of 48 votes in the Southern Province.[28] Little real change took place in the Central Province where the comparative weakness of Congress was demonstrated by the fact that one of its candidates, Richard Katengeza, was defeated and that the second, Ralph Chinyama, epitomised the old style of Congress politician. Overall, however, the elections showed that by 1956 a large majority of the Chiefs on the Councils had become broadly supportive of Congress aims and were prepared to embrace a new, more confrontational agenda. A lengthy report produced by the Special Branch concluded:

> In fact, there is no doubt that support for Congress aims is not confined to an extremist minority but that many ordinary, as well as educated Africans, share the political aspirations of Congress, particularly in those areas where grievances, e.g. in respect of land resettlement, agricultural rules and the like, have been or may be exploited by Congress.'[29]

Within a matter of months, Chipembere and Chiume had grasped the initiative in the Legislative Council to a remarkable extent. The culture of deference that had previously reigned was decisively abandoned. Instead, these two led their colleagues in a sharp-witted assault on colonial policies and the iniquities of Federation that turned the official *Hansard* into a best-selling broadsheet. James Sangala ('an able man... hampered by the lack of a good education', so Chiume was later to write[30]) resigned as Congress's president to be replaced in January 1957 by the younger, although as it turned out, less incorruptible T. D. T. Banda (no relation to Dr H. Banda). Chipembere initiated a renewed campaign against the continued presence in the Federal Parliament of his former mentor and fellow-student at Fort Hare, Manoah Chirwa. This eventually resulted, in August 1957, in the expulsion of Chirwa and Kumbikano from Congress. Fresh funds flowed into the coffers of the central executive committee in consequence of the support provided by Congress branches in Southern Rhodesia.[31] Finally, Chiume, a restless, energetic and brilliantly effective propagandist, spearheaded a recruiting drive which raised Congress's paid-up membership from around 1,000 in April 1956 to 13,000 in October 1957.[32]

Blantyre, Limbe and Zomba remained important centres of Congress activity. However, in striking contrast to the early 1950s, much of the movement's new growth took place in the Northern Province which had been left largely untouched by the 1953 disturbances. Chiume took the lead in 1955 by revitalising the Usisya branch of the NAC prior to embarking on the campaign aimed both at building up support for coffee growing in the Nkhata Bay area and in creating a personal political platform.[33] Dunduzu Chisiza joined the action from January 1957, following his expulsion from Southern Rhodesia, setting up branches of Congress at Karonga, Kaporo, Florence Bay and Livingstonia.[34] He was later joined by Flax Katoba Musopole, recently returned from South

---

[28] Extract from *East Africa and Rhodesia*, 22 March 1956; extract from Political Intelligence Report, March 1956, TNA CO 1015/1011.
[29] 'Political Situation in Nyasaland at the end of April 1956', TNA CO 1015/961.
[30] Chiume, *Kwacha*, p.66.
[31] Political Intelligence Reports, March, May 1957, TNA CO 1015/1748.
[32] Political Intelligence Reports, Oct., Nov. 1957, TNA CO 1015/1748.
[33] Chisiza, *Kwacha*, pp. 66–67.
[34] Nyasaland Intelligence Reports for January and February 1957, TNA CO 1015/1748.

Africa, who founded a branch of Congress in the Misuku hills of the Karonga district following a visit there by Kanyama Chiume.[35]

As the campaign spread, assisted by the recruitment of networks of women traders in the Rumpi district, so the number of branches in the Northern Province increased: from 13 in April 1957 to 21 six months later, and to 34 in May 1958 out of a total of 46 branches in the whole country.[36]. Through the efforts of Chipembere and of Gilbert Kumtumanji, a former KAR medical orderly expelled from Salisbury to Blantyre in 1957, membership of Congress among civil servants and villagers expanded in the Southern Province but only to a limited extent. Cholo remained a major centre of activism but, as late as March 1958, Chipembere had failed in his efforts to revive the Fort Johnston branch.[37] In the Nkhotakota district the local branch of Congress remained active in its opposition to agricultural rules. Elsewhere in the Central Province, the high prices now being paid for tobacco and groundnuts meant that discontent over the activities of the marketing board temporarily slackened, leaving peasant involvement in politics limited. It was not until November 1957 when the independent businessman, Richard Chidzanja, took over the presidency of the Lilongwe branch, that a new more dynamic element was added to local organisation.

Meanwhile, in the Northern Province, the Karonga district and particularly the Misuku hills emerged as the foremost arena of confrontation. As we have seen, this district was the locus for the Misuku Land Usage Scheme, one of the earliest and ostensibly one of the most successful of Nyasaland's land usage schemes but one which, in 1948, was still provoking considerable opposition. With the return to his homeland of Flax Katoba Musopole in 1955, this opposition was given a central direction. A largely neglected figure in Malawi historiography by contrast with his colleagues Chiume and Dunduzu Chisiza, Musopole appears to have spent some time at Livingstonia before migrating to South Africa in the late 1940s. During the heady days of the Defiance Campaign he attended lectures at the University of Cape Town and almost certainly became linked to the South African Communist Party.[38] It is likely that the Party sponsored his award of a scholarship in 1957 (denied to him by the colonial authorities) at the Moscow State University.[39] The new, confrontational style that Musopole brought to politics was demonstrated shortly after his return home in an article he wrote for the left-wing South African periodical, *New Age*, entitled 'Nyasas Preparing for Strikes and Boycotts' and calling for the creation of a 'mass and militant organisation.' Musopole was ideally positioned to act in the Karonga district of the 1950s: he was dealing with a resentful Sukwa peasantry, a weak police force numbering only a dozen constables and an ineffectual administration. T. D. T. Banda, as late as February 1958, refused to commit the central executive committee of Congress to supporting the local Nkhotakota branch in its campaign against Natural Resources rules.[40] By contrast, Musopole, a radical

---

[35] K.J. Waterfield, 'Nyasaland Disturbances N.W. Karonga', 6 May 1959, RHL, Devlin Commission Papers, Box 8.
[36] Intelligence Report for May 1958, TNA CO 1015/1749.
[37] Nyasaland Police Digest, March 1958, TNA CO 1015/1749.
[38] *Proceedings of the Malawi Parliament, 3rd Meeting, 1st session, 27–30 Oct 1964*, p. 180.
[39] Intelligence Report for August 1957, TNA CO 1015/1748.
[40] Intelligence Report, Feb. 1958, TNA CO 1015/1749.

Marxist, had no hesitation in using grievances over conservation as a means of building a peasant base. Coming from one of the leading coffee-growing families in the district, he was well placed to utilise the Misuku Coffee Producers' Co-operative Society, founded in 1950, as a base for his operations.[41] By 1956 he had begun to organise opposition to coffee rules. The next year he carried this further, holding frequent branch meetings of the Nyasaland African Congress throughout the Karonga district and calling on the people to boycott dipping tanks and to flout agricultural rules.[42] By August 1958, membership of Congress in the Karonga district had risen from fewer than 200 a few months earlier to 2,200. In a studied rejection of government policy, bush fires were lit all over the Misuku hills, so that when Dr Banda visited the area in September, only two months after his much heralded return to Nyasaland, the Misuku was literally 'ringed with fire'.[43] 'At the same time, palm trees were cut without permit and widespread *visoso* cultivation was practised in the Karonga hill area.'[44]

The gathering storm

The decision to invite Banda to take over the leadership of Congress was a pivotal event in the modern history of Malawi. Given the progress that had been made since 1955, it is perhaps surprising that Chipembere and his colleagues felt the need to look elsewhere. On the one hand they had little faith in the ability of T.D.T. Banda as more than a stopgap leader, yet on the other believed themselves to be too young to take over the leadership outright. Dr Banda's venerable age (he was approaching sixty), his reputation as an intellectual and perhaps also his lack of first-hand familiarity with Malawi were all attractive credentials for ambitious young politicians anxious to retain the option of rising to the top. There is more than a touch of naivety in Chipembere's assertion in a letter to Banda dated 14 May 1957: 'It will be the greatest shock of my life if I learn later you (or anyone else) have any feeling that I might be doing all this in order to prepare a place for myself.'[45]

Chipembere made clear that much time would have to be spent in building up Banda's reputation: 'there is on the whole not widespread knowledge of what you are or what you can be for us.' Nevertheless, he was convinced that, faced by the perils of Federation, 'every true Nyasa should desperately look round for a kind of saviour...and my feeling is that you can at least be of great help in this connection, if you can't actually liberate the country.'[46] Banda should not be alarmed if he was heralded as the political messiah. Publicity of this sort 'would

---

[41] *Annual Report on Native Affairs for 1950*, p. 45; Mulwafu, 'The development of the coffee industry'; Waterfield, 'Nyasaland Disturbances N.W. Karonga' RHL Devlin Commission Papers, Box 8.

[42] Nyasaland Intelligence Report for quarter ending 31 March 1958, TNA CO 1015/1749.

[43] Waterfield, 'Nyasaland Disturbances N.W. Karonga'; C. Haskard, Provincial Commissioner's 'Report on the Disturbances in the Northern Province of Nyasaland, February/April 1959 and the events leading up to them'. Banda frequently claimed that he had 'set the whole of Nyasaland on fire' but this is usually read metaphorically.

[44] Haskard, Provincial Commissioner's Report, February/April 1959.

[45] Chipembere to Banda, 14 May 1957, RHL Devlin Commission Papers, Box 12.

[46] Chipembere to Banda, 14 May 1957, Ibid.

cause great excitement and should precipitate almost a revolution in political thought'.[47]

At first the suggestion was for Dr Banda to be involved in 'national leadership' in an unspecified role. But this proposal was briskly rejected by Banda who insisted that he would return only if guaranteed the presidency of Congress. In March 1958, T. D. T. Banda, now mired in accusations concerning the misappropriation of funds, was suspended from office; this cleared the way for Dr Banda's arrival at Chileka airport on 6 July. Greeted by a crowd of three thousand with an enthusiasm which spoke volumes for the energy and skill with which Chiume and the other young militants had promoted his public image, he moved decisively to concentrate power in his own hands. In the months leading up to his departure from London, Banda, according to a friend, had often been 'deeply distressed and had little faith in himself as a leader... He has never sought this responsibility and it is a terrible burden to him.'[48] Fired by the adulation of the crowds, however, he demonstrated a new-found confidence as well as a capacity for popular oratory that surprised even himself.[49] Formally elected President-General at the annual general meeting of Congress held at Nkhata Bay from 1–5 August, he stamped his authority on the movement through his insistence that the constitution be amended to permit him to appoint all office-holders and to suspend or expel any member. A few days later he announced the composition of the central body. Young militants filled the most influential positions: Chipembere as Treasurer-General; Chiume as Publicity Secretary; and the impressively hard-working Dunduzu Chisiza as Secretary-General. In a shrewd move, Banda also found places for Blantyre's leading bosses, Lawrence Makata and Lali Lubani, businessmen with access to funds and transport and with links to the urban poor. Rose Chibambo was called upon to revive under Banda's control the Women's League which she had founded on her own initiative in 1952. The youth organisation, 'the Kwaca Boys', created by T. D. T. Banda in 1957, was transformed into the Congress Youth League. For the first time, a public address system was employed, manned by the motor mechanic, Thomas Karua.[50]

The nine months between Banda's arrival at Chileka and the declaration of a state of emergency in March 1959 witnessed an acceleration in the pace of political agitation, leading to the virtual collapse of colonial authority in substantial parts of the territory. In many countries in Africa by the late 1950s a politician like Banda, pro-Western, anti-Communist, and leading a broadly based popular movement, would have been regarded by the authorities as the ideal interlocutor to whom power could safely be transferred over an appropriate period of time. In Nyasaland, however, Banda's implacable opposition to what he repeatedly described as 'this stupid Federation' turned him from a potential ally of Britain into one of her most troublesome foes. Back in April 1957, Banda's worst fears had been aroused by the announcement that a conference was to be convened in 1960 to consider the constitutional future of the Federation and its possible move to dominion status. In response, T. D. T. Banda had led a delegation to Govern-

[47] *Devlin Report*, p. 13.
[48] Lorna Micklem to Devlin Commission, 19 June 1949, RHL Devlin Commission Papers Box 17.
[49] *Devlin Report*, p. 27.
[50] Intelligence Reports for August and September 1958, TNA CO 1015/1749.

ment House to demand an African majority, elected by universal suffrage, in the territorial Legislative Council, only to be met by evasion and delay. The new governor, Sir Robert Armitage, who had taken over from Colby in April 1956, quickly became convinced, as he explained to Gorrell Barnes at the Colonial Office, 'that the only form of constitution which could be regarded as permanent and towards which we should plan must be full and responsible self-government within the framework of the Federation, i.e., a form of regional autonomy'. But he also believed 'that an advance to that particular stage is out of the question for the present. It would mean an African majority in the Legislative Council and in the Executive Council and I could not advise you that this is yet desirable.'[51]

The consequence was that Banda's repeated demands for self-government within the Commonwealth and secession from the Federation were studiously ignored. Armitage's draft proposal for constitutional advance (produced in October 1958 after interminable meetings with every strand of political opinion in the country) was a weak document which envisaged keeping an official majority on the Legislative Council – something which Colby had been prepared to abandon in 1953 – while increasing the number of elected Africans on it from five out of eleven elected members to seven out of fourteen; this was far short of what Banda or any other nationalist leader could have accepted. By December, Armitage had progressed to the view that

> a statement, agreed by H.M.G., Welensky and this Government, should be made to the effect that the future of Nyasaland lies in achieving regional autonomy within the Federation and that, in the circumstances of Nyasaland, an African controlled government will eventuate and be welcomed.[52]

This proposal, however, was bitterly attacked by Benson, the Governor of Northern Rhodesia, on the grounds that it would be used by politicians there to push for an African majority; subsequently Lennox-Boyd made clear that he had no intention of pursuing the matter further.[53]

It was against this background of constitutional inaction that the new wave of political campaigning took shape. A later myth, sedulously promoted by Banda himself, was that he was single-handedly responsible for extracting Nyasaland from the Federation – a claim that falls away when one considers the rising tide of political activity from 1953 onwards. Nevertheless, it cannot be denied that Banda, in Armitage's words, 'brought to Congress the drive and co-ordinated direction which they [sic] had formerly lacked'.[54] To some observers, the new leader, clothed in his three-piece suit, wearing a black homburg hat, delivering his speeches in English and refusing to eat *nsima,* was an unconvincing nationalist, 'to all intents and purposes a white man'.[55] As Chilembwe and John Gray Kufa had demonstrated before him, however, to wear European clothing could be a mark of African pride rather than of cultural inferiority. Banda's clothes, totally unlike the baggy shorts and stockings favoured by colonial officials,

[51] Armitage to Gorell Barnes, 8 Oct 1958, TNA CO 1015/1605.
[52] Armitage to Colonial Secretary, 6 Dec 1958, TNA CO 1015/1605.
[53] Benson to Colonial Secretary, 8 Dec 1958, TNA CO 1015/1605.
[54] Armitage to Lennox-Boyd, 9 Jan 1959, enclosing paper entitled 'The African National Congress Problem in Nyasaland', TNA CO 1015/1749.
[55] Chiume, *Kwacha,* pp. 90–91.

conveyed metropolitan elegance rather than colonial imitation.

Here was a leader, experienced in the white man's world, who with every word and gesture implicitly challenged the myth of colonial superiority. By August he had abandoned the conciliatory tone he had adopted in his early speeches in favour of the more strident style that became his hallmark in subsequent years. Travelling through the Central and Northern Provinces, he attracted attentive crowds, two to three thousand strong, who responded enthusiastically to his anti-Federation message. The basic theme, repeated time and again, was the need for African self-government. But it was a strength of Congress under Banda that this message was combined with a sensitivity to local issues that the central executive of Congress had previously lacked. From the beginning of August, when the annual general conference passed a resolution that 'the Agricultural Rules should only be enforced in areas where their implementation did not interfere with the successful growing of crops', Banda pursued a strategy in which he declared his support for soil conservation in principle while condemning the manner in which it was applied.[56] Congress militants in the Chingale area declared that, with the coming of self-government, agricultural rules would be abolished. Following Banda's visit to the Fort Johnston district on 14 September, the same message spread there, leading to widespread disregard of the rules, threats to agricultural staff and the dispatch to the district in October of two platoons of the Police Mobile Force.[57]

By this time, challenges to colonial authority were coming from an increasingly wide variety of sources: civil servants at Mzuzu, secondary school students at Blantyre, former labour tenants at Cholo, imprisoned in the 1953 disturbances. Livingstonia, in the far north, was not immune from the infection. In a remarkable little episode, striking in its demonstration of the extent to which colonial rituals of loyalty had been undermined, Girl Guides wearing Congress badges greeted the Governor General of the Federation with shouts of 'Kwacha' and 'Get Out' to the evident pleasure of the Principal, Fergus Macpherson, a long-term friend of Banda.[58]

Constitutional negotiations continued. On 24 October Banda had an inconclusive meeting with the Secretary for African Affairs, John Ingham, followed on 30 October by 'a very cordial' discussion with Armitage at which he indicated to the Governor that he was prepared to make some concessions in the demand for universal suffrage.[59] In the absence of new Government initiatives, however, tensions began to build. On several occasions, starting with the so-called 'Clocktower Incident' at Blantyre on 26 October, crowds of young men came out on the streets of Blantyre and Zomba, 'shouting political slogans and abusing Europeans and Asians', sometimes stoning cars and in general demonstrating the resentment of a poor and marginalised group, some of whom had been recently made unemployed following a downturn in the Federal economy.[60]

[56] Intelligence Report for August 1958, TNA CO 1015/1749.
[57] Intelligence Reports for August and October 1958; extract from *Gwelo Times*, 31 Oct 1958, TNA CO 1015/1749.
[58] Intelligence Report for August 1958, TNA CO 1015/1749.
[59] *Devlin Report*, pp. 28–30.
[60] Intelligence Report, October 1958, TNA CO 1015/1749; P.F. Wilson, 'Events leading up to the declaration of a State of Emergency in Nyasaland on March 3 1959', RHL, Devlin Commission Papers, Box 9.

By the end of the year, they were joined by increasing numbers of women activists in Mzimba, Zomba and elsewhere who spoke at political meetings and participated in public demonstrations. Across the country, teachers, churchmen and others associated with the Livingstonia and Blantyre synods of the Church of Central Africa Presbyterian identified themselves closely with the nationalist cause, although less support was forthcoming from active members of the Roman Catholic, Anglican and Dutch Reformed Churches, all of whose leaders attempted to distance themselves from politics. From April 1958 onwards, hardly a single month went by when the intelligence reports produced by the Nyasaland police did not comment on 'the irresponsible attitude' of the CCAP towards Federation and on its readiness to support 'political programmes in the name of religion'. Malawian and Scottish churchmen alike were accused of giving 'encouragement to Africans to oppose Federation by unconstitutional means'; Livingstonia's schools were said to be 'positive breeding grounds for Congress leaders of the future'.[61] Partly in consequence of this, peasant involvement remained at its greatest in the Northern Province: the site of 48 out of a total of 63 branches of Congress in existence in October 1958.[62] Elsewhere, popular rural support continued to be patchy: strong in the Cholo, Lower Shire and Nkhotakota districts where ethnic divisions interacted with economic grievances; weaker in other parts of the country. Chiefs in the north were now virtually unanimous in backing the Congress line. In the south and centre, however, significant divisions still existed with some chiefs aligning themselves to Congress and others to the colonial state.

By January 1959 the battle-lines had been drawn. In a lengthy memorandum written on the 2nd of the month, J. C. Morgan set out the Colonial Office position.[63] The power and influence of Banda, his associates and the Nyasaland African Congress generally was steadily growing, he noted, making it likely 'that unless some counter-action is taken Banda and his associates will in the near future enter on a course of deliberately fomented strikes, boycotts, general civil disobedience and so on' which would almost inevitably result in 'outbreaks of violence.' Faced with this situation, the Government had to determine whether it intended to keep Nyasaland in the Federation or not.

> If HMG is prepared either now or in the context of 1960 to permit Nyasaland to secede from the Federation and become an African state with self-government (even if that self-government is to be achieved in some stages) then the attitude towards Banda is immediately altered and he becomes a 'respectable' and 'normal' African leader, with whom we should lose no time in doing business and coming to terms.

If, however, the Government was determined to keep Nyasaland in the Federation, opposition to this policy became illegitimate and seditious and Banda would have to go. Almost no constitutional reforms could be proposed that had

---

[61] Intelligence Reports for April and May 1958, TNA CO 1015/1749.

[62] Intelligence Report for October 1958, TNA, CO 1015/1749. The precise number of Congress branches fluctuated considerably. According to a paper entitled 'The African National Congress Problem in Nyasaland' [PRO CO 1015/1749], 42 out of 83 Congress branches were located in the Northern Province on 30 November 1958.

[63] J.C. Morgan, draft memo on 'Nyasaland: problem at the end of 1958', 2 Jan 1959, TNA CO 1015/1606.

any hope of success without 'the early liquidation of Dr. Banda and the Congress'. Morgan had expressed his own personal conviction in a visit he had made to Nyasaland in November. Banda was 'a nasty little man', he told officials, adding, not entirely seriously, that they ought to find someone to get rid of him: 'Shall we not get a friend to do it?'[64]

Morgan's rhetoric was more than matched by that of the Congress leaders. Early in December, while attending the All African People's Conference in Accra, Banda took the decision, fully supported by Chipembere and Dunduzu Chisiza, to mount a non-violent resistance campaign of a type very likely to escalate into open confrontation.[65] Over the subsequent weeks, relations between Congress and the European community continued to decline, reaching a low point on 20 January when the arrest in Zomba of 40 women waiting to greet Banda was followed by an attack on the police station of a crowd some 500 strong. Four days later, Congress held an emergency conference in Blantyre attended by about 150 delegates. Much of the discussion in the opening session focused on the tactics to be followed should Banda be arrested; and the decision was taken to call out civil servants, railway and road transport workers in a general strike and to seek support from the trade unions. With that in mind, the delegates agreed to try to oust Weston Chisiza from his post as General Secretary of the Nyasaland Trade Union Congress, founded in 1956, on the grounds that he was insufficiently radical.[66]

The next day, in the absence of Banda, the delegates met in secret session on scrubland near Limbe under the chairmanship of the businessman, Lawrence Makata. No completely authoritative account of the meeting has been produced. But it is generally accepted that the delegates agreed to draw up a 'black-list' of African 'stooges and quislings', headed by Manoah Chirwa, who had fallen foul of Congress, and to approve a policy of sabotage and civil disobedience. As Chipembere noted, '…for the first time, Congress adopted "action" as the official policy – and "action" in the real sense of action.'[67] Approval was given 'to a policy of sabotage – cutting of telephone wires, blocking of roads, destruction of bridges and the like – and of defiance, such as holding meetings without asking permission.'[68] In addition, it was agreed to resist with violence any attempts to enforce agricultural laws and to arrest individuals who broke them. 'End European Agriculture. Hit or tie Kapitaos. Forestry Kapitaos are not wanted', a delegate subsequently noted.[69] There was much talk of violence against Europeans, but little in the way of detailed planning. Action to be taken following the arrest of Banda was to include 'To hit Europeans or cut throat' according to the delegate previously quoted. But he also noted in a more conciliatory tone: 'If a person is arrested because of Congress the case must be taken to senior Europeans.'[70]

[64] Baker, *Sir Robert Armitage*, p. 219.
[65] Short, *Banda*, p. 103.
[66] Special Branch memo on 'The Emergency Conference of the Nyasaland African Congress held at Blantyre on 24/25 January 1959', 13 Feb 1959, RHL Devlin Commission Papers, Box 6.
[67] H.B. Chipembere to M.W.K. Chiume, 2 Feb 1959 in *Devlin Report* p. 144.
[68] *Devlin Report*, pp. 50–51.
[69] 'Translation of Chinyanja notes relating to meeting of 25 January, 1959' reproduced in *Devlin Report*, p. 146.
[70] Ibid.

The nature of the 'bush meeting', as it subsequently became known, and in particular, the question of whether Congress leaders plotted to kill large numbers of Asians and Europeans is a highly contentious issue. As no undercover policemen had been able to infiltrate the meeting, Philip Finney, the recently appointed Head of the Special Branch, ex-Indian policeman and ex-Guinness salesman, was forced to base his report on evidence obtained from informers, only one of whom had been present in the bush. Completed on 13 February, and supplemented by a further paper sent to the Governor five days later, Finney's report is a dramatic document that accused the Congress leadership of planning nothing less than a pogrom. On Banda's arrest, Chipembere, Chisiza, Chiume and Rose Chibambo would take over the leadership and notify branches of 'R-Day', the day on which violence would begin. According to the Commissioner of Police, Mullin, this would involve 'the mass murder throughout the Protectorate of all foreigners, by which is meant all Europeans and Asians, men, women and children, to take place in the event of Dr Banda being killed, arrested or abducted'. Mullin added: 'I am satisfied that this information is correct and must be accepted seriously.'[71]

Much of the literature concerning Malawian nationalism has tended, with good reason, to downgrade the significance of the 'the murder plot'. But in one respect at least its importance should not be underestimated. As the Devlin Report was later to demonstrate, there are strong grounds for believing that the violent rhetoric that was undoubtedly a feature of Congress at this period was not matched by a determination to kill the Governor and his council in order to bring colonialism to an end. 'That would have been tantamount to declaring war on the United Kingdom', Dunduzu Chisiza later noted. 'We were not equipped to fight with the Nyasaland Government let alone the United Kingdom Government. You cannot kill a representative of the Queen and expect the people of the United Kingdom to take the whole thing lying down.'[72] Nationalist behaviour – whether it involved men throwing stones at cars in Blantyre or women making 'grossly insulting gestures' at European club members at Mzuzu – can be construed as part of a wide-ranging project aimed at destroying the cultural basis of European dominance. But, even at the height of the disturbances, no attempt to assassinate Europeans was ever made, even on occasions when it would have been easy for a Congress crowd to do so.[73] Whether, as some police officers believed, the murder plot was a fabrication by Nyasaland intelligence officers anxious to force the Government into taking decisive action to put down the disorders, is an intriguing question to which no final answer can be given.[74] What one can say is that Armitage and his colleagues do not appear to have allowed their belief in the plot to significantly influence their actions. On the Governor's instructions, the Chief Secretary continued negotiations with Banda on 20 February. Later, a report on the security position in the Karonga district argued, with considerable accuracy, that the local Congress leaders 'will continue to hold

---

[71] Mullin to Footman, 18 Jan 1959 with Finney to Mullin attached, RHL Devlin Commission Papers, Box 9.

[72] D.K. Chisiza interviewed by Devlin Commission, 18 May 1959, RHL Devlin Commission Papers, Box 12.

[73] *Devlin Report*, pp. 84–86.

[74] See Colin Baker, *State of Emergency: Crisis in Central Africa, Nyasaland 1959–1960* (London, 1997) pp. 177–78.

meetings and to advocate all forms of illegal action including riots and damage to property but stopping short of incitement to murder.'[75]

Congress restraint in the face of Europeans, however, was combined with a growing intolerance of African dissent which discussions at the emergency meeting did much to dramatise. Back in 1951, Dr Banda had advocated the use of leniency and diplomacy in dealing with fellow nationalists at odds with Congress strategies but, by late 1958, he had abandoned this view. On his visit to Salisbury in December of that year, he went out of his way to denounce 'moderates' and 'Capricorns' such as his former ally, the veteran politician Thompson Samkange, with a vehemence that astounded other politicians in Zimbabwe.[76] Chipembere and Chiume were no more restrained either in their criticisms of colonial rule or in their denunciation of backsliding colleagues, notably 'the rotten' Manoah Chirwa, but also Charles Matinga, T. D. T. Banda and others – condemned not just as political opponents but as traitors to the nationalist cause. The Devlin Report was later to argue that 'intimidation was practised mostly at lower levels' and not by Banda and the Congress leadership.[77] But while this may have been true in the sense that actual physical assaults, threats to kill and the burning of houses were undertaken by members of Congress rather than by leaders, it was the latter who provided the justification for such actions. By February 1959, teachers and clergymen, such as Stephen Kauta Msiska, the Moderator of the Livingstonia Synod, who remained neutral on political issues, were being subjected to a campaign of abuse; politicians who came out in opposition to Congress fared even worse. Manoah Chirwa was repeatedly warned that he would be killed; Charles Matinga's house in Ndirande was attacked and its windows broken.[78] At numerous Congress branches, chairmen compiled 'black lists' of 'stooges' which were sent to Headquarters in Blantyre.[79]

For the Nyasaland Government, the growing belligerence of Congress signalled the emergence of a crisis of authority deeper and more widespread than any it had hitherto faced. Back in 1953, the troubles had been confined largely to a limited area in the Southern Province and the Congress leadership had been quickly cowed into submission. Now, however, Banda and his colleagues were resolute in refusing to condemn violence and all three provinces found themselves affected by the disturbances. Trouble, arising from a series of meetings called without official permission, began on 8 February in the Karonga district where the police were at their weakest and where Congress, under the leadership of Musopole, was particularly strong. Within a matter of days it had spread through much of the Central and Southern Provinces with a variety of separate incidents involving clashes between rioters and the police being reported from Visanza, Dowa, Nkhotakota, Blantyre and elsewhere. As the level of violence increased, the Northern District once more became the main scene of action: Karonga was taken over by a crowd some 600 strong on 19 February; the Fort

[75] *Devlin Report*, pp. 86–87.
[76] Ranger, *Are We Not Men?* p. 170.
[77] *Devlin Report*, p. 20.
[78] Jackson, *Send Us Friends*, pp. 79–81; Fergus Macpherson to Dr Banda, 20 Feb 1959, EUL, Helen Taylor Papers; G.R.H. Gribble, Analysis of Covert Intelligence made available to the Governor of Nyasaland during the period Jan/Feb, 1959, 14 July 1959 TNA CO 1015/1546.
[79] *Devlin Report*, p. 54.

Hill airfield was occupied on the following day. According to a security appreci-ation, all Congress branches in the district 'were engaged in activities to arouse people to illegal disturbances':

> The degree of support is 100% in the Misuku area and widespread in all other areas ...The standard of Congress leadership is comparatively very high and the organisation of women and children is growing rapidly. The power of the Chiefs is insufficient to over-come Congress leadership.[80]

In the remote Misuku Hills, hostile gangs forced the agricultural officer and a family of Pentecostal missionaries to flee. Elsewhere in the country, five Congress members were killed in separate clashes between the demonstrators and the military. 'Negotiations won't do ... we mean to create disturbances from Port Herald to Karonga even if it means every person dies', Yatuta Chisiza flam-boyantly announced.[81]

Nearly three and a half years earlier, Armitage had been replaced as Governor of Cyprus because of his failure to control the political crisis there, and he was determined not to fail again. Writing on 20 January, the day of his last meeting with Banda and five days before the Congress meeting in the bush, he ranged over various options available to him for crushing Congress and bringing its leaders' influence to an end. Congress could be declared an unlawful society and its leaders restricted to an inaccessible area. This would be difficult to accom-plish in a country as small as Nyasaland. Banda could be charged and imprisoned (but where was the evidence to bring about a successful conviction?). Best of all, he and his fellow Congress leaders could be deported to another country, ideally Southern Rhodesia, until such time as an alternative, more compliant leader-ship had emerged.[82] This would involve the declaration of a state of emergency. By the end of the month, the Chief Secretary was hard at work preparing the necessary documents and arranging with the Federal Government for the 'hard core' of Congress leaders to be detained in Gwelo and Khami prisons.[83] Mean-while, secret plans were drawn up to construct a Nyasaland-based detention camp at Kanjedza, the site of an artisan training centre five miles from Blan-tyre.

With the growth in violence, the issue of security became increasingly pressing. Under the Federal constitution, law and order (and hence the police) remained a territorial responsibility – much to the annoyance of Welensky who openly pressed for it to be taken over by the Federal Government. But defence (and hence the army) was an exclusively Federal subject. Since 1953, the Nyasaland Government had made strenuous efforts to strengthen internal security: it built up the Police Mobile Force to nine platoons, reformed and enlarged the Special Branch and increased the total number of policemen to 130 European officers and 2,200 African constables, this last a rise of over 300 per cent in just six years.[84] Nevertheless, the police force, as Mullin stressed

---

[80] Appreciation of the Situation as at 0900 hour, Monday 25 February 1959 by the Provincial Opera-tions Committee, Mzuzu, RHL, Devlin Commission Papers, Box 8.
[81] Quoted in *Devlin Report*, p. 71.
[82] Armitage to Gorell Barnes, 20 Jan 1959, TNA CO 1015/1519.
[83] Baker, *Armitage*, p. 218.
[84] McCracken, 'Authority and Legitimacy', pp. 175–76.

on 18 February, remained 'numerically very weak' and subject to disturbing political influences. Certain of the younger men in the force were known to be in sympathy with the aims of Congress; 'in a crisis there might be a reluctance to fire.'[85]

Mullin's recommendation was that a battalion of British troops be flown out from the United Kingdom. But this was something that Welensky, neither then nor later, was prepared to countenance. As he was to inform Lord Home, who offered him a battalion stationed in Kenya along with helicopters and light aircraft from Cyprus: 'I see no reason whatsoever to consider that British troops will be needed here ... I would consider that the Federal Government had failed in its responsibilities if the situation deteriorated so far as to require outside help.'[86] Instead, so Benson believed, Welensky was anxious to provide his own reinforcements as the first step in achieving Federal 'control over Police and internal security' in Nyasaland.[87] Armitage, initially, was reluctant to accept this assistance but on 20 February he changed his mind and requested reinforcements. The next day the first battalion of the King's African Rifles was dispatched to Nyasaland from Lusaka and detachments of the white settler Royal Rhodesian Regiment were airlifted from Salisbury to Blantyre. A week later they were reinforced by platoons from the Tanganyika and Northern Rhodesian police forces. By the beginning of March, well over 2,500 additional troops had been ferried to the Protectorate, nearly five times as many as were normally stationed in the territory. On 2 March, according to Orton Chirwa, 'The whole country is at present a battlefield in that you meet a soldier at every corner in Blantyre and Limbe. ... This action by the government has killed dead whatever little sympathy there may have been for the Federation on the part of Africans.'[88] On the same day, Armitage signed the documents to bring the state of emergency into force. From just after midnight, the Nyasaland African Congress, the Youth League and the Women's League were proscribed as unlawful organisations: persons continuing as members of Congress would be liable to seven years in gaol.

Early next morning, on 3 March, Operation Sunrise was launched. Within 24 hours 149 nationalists had been arrested, with many of the 'hard-line' being flown to Bulawayo for despatch to Khami Prison where they were immediately subjected to rigorous interrogation. Banda, Chipembere and D. K. Chisiza, whom Armitage regarded as the main organisers, were sent separately to Gwelo Prison. Meanwhile, in an emergency debate in the House of Commons, Lennox-Boyd justified the Governor's actions on the grounds that 'plans had been made by Congress to carry out widespread violence and murder of Europeans, Asians and moderate Africans; that, in fact, a massacre was being planned.'[89]

[85] Commissioner of Police to Chief Secretary, 18 Feb 1959, RHL Devlin Commission Papers, Box 9.
[86] Personal message from Lord Home to Sir Roy Welensky, 1 March 1958; Welensky to Home, n.d. [March 1959], ZNA F 236 CX 27/3/1.
[87] Benson to Gorrell Barnes, 2 March 1959, TNA CO 1015/2056.
[88] Orton Chirwa to Margaret Gardner, 2 March 1959, quoted in Baker, *State of Emergency*, p. 37.
[89] Speech by Lennox-Boyd in the House of Commons, 3 March 1959, TNA CO 1015/1515.

State of emergency

Historians are united in regarding the state of emergency as a decisive turning point in the post-war history of Central Africa but they divide sharply on the question of the effectiveness of British colonial policy in this episode. One view, expressed with spirit by Colin Baker, asserts that despite the variety of obstacles placed in their way, the much maligned colonial authorities followed a rational, far-seeing policy that was ultimately successful in resolving the crisis.[90] Another, taken by John Darwin, argues rather more plausibly, that the Nyasaland emergency was the supreme example in the era of decolonisation of colonial – and imperial – failure.[91] Where they agree is in emphasising the transformation in colonial policy that the state of emergency engendered.

> Before the emergency the British government was adamant that the Federation was a permanent institution; after the emergency they recognised that its survival was in the gravest doubt and then decided to abandon it. ... Before the emergency independence for Nyasaland appeared to be at least a decade, and probably longer away; after the emergency it was clear that it would follow in a matter of a very few years. Before the emergency Banda was generally seen by the governments concerned as representing relatively few, ambitious, self-seeking political activists ... after the emergency he was clearly recognised as the undisputed leader of a committed mass movement involving almost the whole of the African population of Nyasaland.[92]

The unravelling of Armitage's new interventionist policy began on the day on which it was revealed. A short time earlier, the Southern Rhodesian government had encountered little or no resistance when it declared its own state of emergency and arrested 400 members of the Southern Rhodesian African National Congress. In Malawi, however, the smooth progress made by Operation Sunrise in the early hours of 3 March in peacefully detaining leading members of Congress came to a rapid halt at Nkhata Bay. There, after a protracted stand-off, white territorial troops of the Royal Rhodesian Regiment opened fire on an unarmed crowd, killing at least twenty and wounding twenty-nine.[93] To John Brock, the local District Commissioner, this was a 'betrayal of all that we had been working for'. He felt 'utter dejection that my career had come to this'.[94] Over the next few days Africans were killed by the security forces in five separate incidents covering all three provinces and bringing the total number of deaths to over 50. There were numerous disturbances in which crowds were dispersed with tear gas and with baton charges and many examples of strikes by estate workers and civil servants. On 3 March, protesters brought Blantyre to a virtual halt by going on strike, building roadblocks and stoning or

---

[90] Baker, *State of Emergency*, pp. 203–48.
[91] John Darwin, 'The Central African Emergency, 1959', *Journal of Imperial and Commonwealth History*, 21, 3 (1993).
[92] Baker, *State of Emergency*, p.vii.
[93] The total number of protestors at Nkhata Bay who were killed or who subsequently died of their wounds is now calculated at 28. My thanks to Professor Wiseman Chirwa for supplying me with this revised figure.
[94] Brock, interviewed on 'End of Empire' series, Granada Television, repeat, 1 March 1987.

7 Stop and search operation in the Mulanje area, carried out by territorial soldiers from the Royal Rhodesian Regiment, March 1959

burning cars.[95] But there, as in other parts of the Southern Province, this resist-ance proved to be relatively short-lived. On 5 March the Railway Workers Union quietly instructed its members to return.[96] A day later, the Governor noted that the atmosphere in Blantyre was still 'rather tense and unsettled' but that 'labour in urban areas [is] now reported normal and clerical and other staff have returned to work.'[97]

Elsewhere, however, and particularly in the Northern Province, resistance was more tenacious. With the security forces 'thin on the ground', Flax Katoba Musopole was able to evade arrest. And with his freedom secured, he travelled widely through the Karonga District, appearing 'one day at Ngerenge, another at Misuku, another at Balambaya', leaving behind him a trail of torched build-ings and sabotaged bridges. By 23 March, 26 bridges in the north had been damaged, ten completely destroyed and 79 houses burnt to the ground.[98] As the Devlin Report noted, for at least a week in March 'large areas of the Northern Province have passed out of government control and in many places gangs under

95 Operations Control Diary, 3 Mar 1959, RHL Devlin Commission papers, Box 9.
96 Ibid., 5 Mar 1959.
97 Governor, Zomba to Federal Prime Minister, Salisbury, 6 Mar. 1959, ZNA F 236 CX 27/3/1.
98 Federal Intelligence and Security Bureau, report on sabotage in Nyasaland, 8 July 195, ZNA F 236/CX27/3/3 9.

Congress leadership were behaving as they liked.'[99] In an act of ritual cleansing, all traces of the Misuku Land Usage Scheme were removed with the burning by Musopole and his followers of the European supervisor's house and the houses of all six of his African staff.[100] Not even the dispatch of military reinforcements to the north in April brought Musopole's activities to an end. Aided by the active support of what Armitage, described as a 'generally very truculent' population, he successfully avoided capture during 'Operation Crewcut' by taking refuge in the remote Misuku hills or in neighbouring Tanganyika.[101] Even after his arrest in August 1959, sporadic disturbances in the Karonga and Rumphi districts continued. As late as November, two Congress gangs still operated in the area, committing various acts of arson.[102]

Continued resistance brought in its wake colonial retribution and the hardening of political attitudes. As military and police reinforcements grew – to a maximum of about 4,500 men – Armitage launched a 'campaign of harassment' designed to rebuild colonial prestige and 'eradicate Congress leadership and doctrines.'[103] Frequent patrols – searching houses, seizing documents and making arrests – were sent throughout the countryside. Although the intention, ostensibly, was that they 'should give an impression of firm friendliness', the reverse was often true. The Devlin Commission subsequently rejected allegations of rape and torture made against soldiers operating in the Misuku hills.[104] But the burning of houses did frequently take place along with the imposition on villages of collective fines. By the end of April the military had extracted the remarkable sum of over £30,000 from bitterly hostile villagers.[105] There was a good deal of aggressive and bullying behaviour involved in the searching of villages; cattle, bicycles and other property were stolen by soldiers; people were often beaten with rifle butts or fists. 'To stamp out Congress' became the central aim of the Nyasaland Operations Committee, with the major drawback, as the Committee admitted in mid-April, that 'sympathy and support for Congress aims are still widespread and deep-rooted and often reinforced by bitterness and resentment.'[106] This attitude was most marked, the Committee noted, 'in the Northern Province, the Chewa areas of the Central Province and throughout the Southern Province except for the areas of certain loyal chiefs in Blantyre, Zomba and Port Herald'. Support for Congress was also strong among civil servants in Blantyre and Zomba. 'In detention camps the attitude of detainees is said to be unrepentant.'[107] By this time, some 1,300 people had been detained without trial and over 2,000 had been gaoled for political offences.[108]

[99] *Devlin Report*, p. 125.
[100] Waterfield, 'Nyasaland Disturbances NW Karonga', 6 May 1958, RHL, Devlin Commissions Papers, Box 8.
[101] Armitage to Colonial Secretary, 30 March 1959 TNA CO 1015/1494; Nyasaland Operations Committee, Operations Instructions No. 3/59, 13 April 1959, CO 1015/1517; MILLIA Salisbury to War Office, 21 April 1959.
[102] Short, *Banda*, p. 117; Intelligence Report for November 1959, TNA CO 1015/1518.
[103] Baker, *State of Emergency*, p. 63; Nyasaland Operations Committee, Instructions No. 2/1959, 7 March 1959TNA O 1015/1494.
[104] For these allegations see H.M. Taylor, 'Security Forces in Karonga Hills', no date [1959], EUL Helen Taylor Papers.
[105] *Devlin Report*, p. 139.
[106] Nyasaland Operations Committee, Instructions No. 3/59, 13 April 1959, TNA CO 1015/1495.
[107] Ibid.

For the Government, failure in the Malawian countryside was compounded by political embarrassment at home. For all the fissures that existed within colonial society, missionaries and government as far back as the 1920s had tended to come together in a tacit alliance when fundamental questions concerning the colonial system were raised. On the question of Federation, however, most Scottish missionaries and most of their Malawian colleagues and parishioners moved steadily from cautious criticism in 1953 to full-scale opposition in 1958, placing them alongside Congress and in opposition to government.[109] The Blantyre synod of the CCAP called publicly for the dissolution of the Federation in 1958; Dr Banda, a personal friend of Fergus Macpherson, the Principal at Livingstonia, was invited to speak in its churches.[110]

The significance of this rupture became increasingly clear in the wake of the declaration of the state of emergency. Armitage's strategy was heavily dependent on his ability to discredit Congress by painting Banda and his colleagues not as legitimate politicians but rather as men of violence embroiled in a murder plot. It was this theory that Lennox-Boyd had seized on in justifying the arrests to parliament. The emergence, therefore, of an alternative voice, well informed, making use of first-hand evidence and able to mobilise national opinion in Scotland, came as a peculiarly painful blow to the authorities both in Nyasaland and Britain. Eyewitness accounts by missionaries complaining of the brutality of the police were printed in British newspapers and made use of by opposition spokesmen.[111] Allegations of a 'murder plot' were dismissed as 'a fabrication by paid informers'.[112] In a particularly dramatic episode, members of the Church of Scotland General Assembly responded to an appeal from the former moderator, George Macleod, by calling in overwhelming numbers for a 'daring and creative transfer of power' to the African people of Nyasaland and the immediate release of the detainees.[113] Labour politicians added their voice to the debate. In London, former patients of Banda presented a petition to the Colonial Office demanding the release of their 'beloved doctor'.[114]

Faced by questions in the House of Commons and extensive comment in the British press, the Government had little room for manoeuvre. Some form of official enquiry into the disturbances would be necessary – and not of the unobtrusive local type that Colby had convened in 1953. On 6 April 1959 the composition of the four-man Devlin Commission was announced. All were fully paid-up members of the British ruling class: a former colonial governor, an Oxford college head, a Scottish lord provost and a high court judge – the chairman Sir Patrick Devlin, one of the most brilliant lawyers of his day. Lord Perth, the

[108] According to Armitage, the total figures for the whole of the emergency were 1,339 persons detained and 2,160 convicted of political offences. Armitage to Macleod, 6 June 1960, ZNA F236 CX27/2.
[109] See John McCracken, 'Church and State in Malawi: the Role of the Scottish Presbyterian Missions, 1875–1965' in H. G. Hansen and M. Twaddle (eds), *Christian Missionaries and the State in the Third World* (James Currey, Oxford, 2002), pp.182–89.
[110] 'Statement of the Synod of Blantyre of the CCAP concerning the present state of unrest in Nyasaland' March 1958 printed in *First Report of the General Assembly's Committee anent Central Africa* (Edinburgh, 1959).
[111] Letter by Albert McAdam in *Manchester Guardian*, 4 March 1959.
[112] Tom Colvin, 'Notes on the Present Position in Nyasaland and Causes of Disturbances', n.d., EUL Kenneth Mackenzie Papers.
[113] *The Scotsman*, 26 May 1959.
[114] Short, *Banda*, 119 footnote.

junior minister in the Colonial Office, had known Devlin all his life and assured Lennox-Boyd that 'we could not have anybody more sensible.'[115]

Any implication that Devlin could be relied on to deal gently with the colonial administration was quickly shown to be untrue. Demonstrating from the start a determination to remain socially aloof from Government House, Devlin and his colleagues went about their business with an earnestness that shocked colonial officials to the core. By late May they had become seriously concerned that the Commission might not vindicate government action in all respects. If this were to be the case, Major Nicholson, the choleric Provincial Commissioner for Southern Province, declared: 'the Kwaca cock would crow like mad' and the consequences would be devastating. Even if the report was entirely favourable to Government, 'it is unlikely that its findings will to any great extent stifle African nationalism, curb local African aspirations or demands, or muzzle or discredit the Nyasaland African Congress, the Church of Scotland Mission or the left wing lunatic fringe.' If, on the other hand, the Commission castigated Government and exonerated Congress, Nicholson, in jingoist vein, could only 'hope that Sir Roy Welensky will throw a Monkey Bay Tea Party.'[116]

Ian Nance, the Provincial Commissioner for the Central Province, was more restrained but equally downbeat in his views. If the inquiry condemned Congress's plan for violence but absolved Dr Banda of responsibility for it, Banda, he believed, would have to be released and offered a ministerial portfolio and a seat on the Legislative and Executive Councils. Even if Banda was not absolved but the Government was criticised for the use of unnecessary force, there was certain to be a resurgence of Congress activity. Whatever the outcome, 'Government will have to govern by force, or the threat of force, for so long as Federation in its present form persists. There can be no hope of government by consent until such time as Nyasaland is withdrawn from the Federation.' In an ominous aside, Nance suggested that this could not be delayed indefinitely: '...attention must be paid to the fact that the ordinary members of the security forces – Police and Military – cannot be expected to continue to work loyally and effectively for more than a limited period to implement a political policy with which most of them do not agree.'[117]

It is an indication of the stunning impact of the Devlin Report, handed in draft form to Lennox-Boyd on 13 July 1959, that its conclusions were more critical than anything that the provincial commissioners had feared. The Commission was careful to clear Armitage of two accusations that had been laid against him: that he had declared the emergency at the request of Welensky and that he was not justified in doing so in the circumstances. But it also reached three conclusions that undermined the Government's case. First, there was no murder plot or plan, although there had been talk of beating and killing Europeans. Second, Congress under Banda was a genuinely popular movement, feeding on the widespread dislike of Federation. Third, during the security operations the police and military had employed illegal and excessive force. During frantic discussions with ministers and officials, anxious to limit the damage before publication, Devlin agreed to excise the summary and some of the more striking

---

[115] Lennox Boyd to Armitage, 27 March 1959, TNA CO 1015/1533.
[116] P.F. Nicholson to Commissioner of Police, 9 June 1959, TNA CO 1015/1544.
[117] I.T. Nance to Commissioner of Police, 26 May 1949, TNA CO 1015/1544.

passages from the report.[118] But, because he was never asked, he did not remove the single most controversial sentence, conveniently placed on the very first page:

> Nyasaland is – no doubt only temporarily – a police state, where it is not safe for anyone to express approval of the policies of the Congress party, to which before 3rd March, 1959 the vast majority of politically-minded Africans belonged.[119]

It was to banner headlines – '"Police State" Charge' and 'No Murder Plot in Nyasaland' – that the British public awoke on 24 July.[120]

There are good grounds for arguing that the Devlin Report was the final nail in the coffin of Nyasaland's continued involvement in the Federation. But, at the time, this was the view of neither the British nor the Nyasaland Government. In a damage limitation exercise that extended from Zomba to the Cabinet Office in Whitehall, a high-level working party including several cabinet ministers set to work drafting a despatch that was to appear under Armitage's name, refuting the findings of the commission. Lennox-Boyd, already under pressure over the Hola detention camp atrocity in Kenya where eleven Mau Mau detainees had been beaten to death, offered to resign only to be persuaded to stay by the Prime Minister, Harold Macmillan, after the issue had been discussed in cabinet.[121] Rebellious Conservative backbenchers were brought into line with the result that when the issue was debated in parliament, a government motion rejecting the Report was passed with a comfortable majority.[122] Macmillan belatedly confided to his diary that Devlin had been a disastrous choice. 'I have since discovered that he is (a) *Irish* – no doubt with that fenian (sic) blood which makes Irishmen anti-government on principle, (b) a *lapsed* Roman Catholic. His brother is a Jesuit priest.' Devlin's motive in criticising government policy, Macmillan alleged, was resentment at 'my not having made him Lord Chief Justice'.[123] William Kirkman, *The Times* Africa correspondent, took a more accurate view. The Cabinet decision to reject the Commission's findings was 'by any standards a depressing example of the triumph of expediency over principle'.[124] The Conservative Government had bought time which allowed it to come unscathed through the October 1959 General Election. But, in so doing, it had delayed confronting the question of Nyasaland's future. Not until after Macmillan's appointment, that month, of a new colonial secretary, Iain Macleod, was the issue to be squarely addressed.

Back in Zomba, Armitage and his colleagues attempted to make the best of what, for them, was a very bad job. Internal security remained the highest priority because, although an uneasy calm had now fallen over most of the terri-

---

[118] Details of the incisions are provided in CO to Sir E. Baring for Governor Nyasaland, 17 July 1959, TNA CO 1015/1545. There is a copy of the draft report in Rhodes House Library. For further details see Richard Lamb, *The Macmillan Years 1957–1963* (London, 1995) pp. 235–36.

[119] *Devlin Report*, p. 1; Devlin to Perth, 21 Sep 1959, TNA CO 1015/1547.

[120] *The Scotsman*, 24 July 1959, *Manchester Guardian*, 24 July 1959.

[121] Eleven Mau Mau detainees at Hola camp were beaten to death by warders in March 1959 following their refusal of a work order. The incident caused a political furore in Britain which had implications for the treatment of detainees in Nyasaland.

[122] For detailed accounts of this episode from different perspectives see Baker, *State of Emergency* and Lamb, *Macmillan Years* pp. 235–42.

[123] Alistair Horne, *Macmillan 1957–1986* (London, 1989), p. 181.

[124] Quoted in Lamb, *Macmillan Years*, p. 237.

tory, the risk of renewed disturbances was believed to be high. In a measure that demonstrates how serious the British authorities were in their effort to retain the initiative during the latter years of decolonisation, a massive programme of police expansion was approved, involving both the recruitment of another 1,100 policemen, 100 of them European, and also the expenditure of £1,500,000 on the construction of new stations and quarters. A new pay scale was introduced, backdated to 1 January, resulting in increases in pay of between 7 and 18 per cent. Thirty seven officers were seconded to Nyasaland from Britain; 700 more Africans were recruited to the force. By 1960, expenditure on the police was double its 1957 figure; there were almost as many European police officers (215) as there had been Europeans in total number (238) employed in all branches of the government in 1938.[125]

Nyasaland, other than in the special circumstances of the emergency, had not been a 'police state' prior to 1959. It was now in danger of becoming one, as the treatment of detainees, in particular, demonstrated. Numbering in total 1,339 people – almost of them men but also including Rose Chibambo, Vera Chirwa, Gertrude Rubadiri and several other women – the detainees provided Armitage with a conspicuous demonstration of intransigent nationalism and hence of the limits of his interventionist policy. One possible solution, recommended to him by John Pinney, an officer from Kenya seconded to Nyasaland in 1959, was to make use of the methods employed against Mau Mau detainees in forcing the prisoners to carry out compulsory work as a means of breaking their spirit and conditioning them for rehabilitation. With the example of Hola fresh in their minds, officials from the Colonial Office acted quickly to ban this practice.[126] Nevertheless, although conditions in Gwelo were good and in Khami tolerable after the early days of violent interrogation, those in the Kanjedza camp near Blantyre were decidedly harsh. Detainees were often beaten and stripped naked before being forced to exercise with their hands on their heads and without coats, underwear and shoes even in the coldest weather.[127] It is an irony that in the Banda era, from 1964, former inmates were to use the benchmark of their Kanjedza experience in imposing even worse conditions on a new generation of detainees.

On the central issue, the resolution of the political crisis, Armitage had little to offer other than the conviction that no solution was possible that did not involve the elimination of Banda and the Nyasaland African Congress. 'Until we can show that Banda and company will not be seen for many years, we shall not get neutral and uncommitted people to come and take their places as moderate leaders of the public.'[128] From March onwards he repeatedly requested the Colonial Office to sanction the introduction of new legislation that would allow him to exclude Banda from Nyasaland when he was eventually released from detention or else to detain him indefinitely after the emergency had ended.

[125] *Annual Reports of the Nyasaland Police*, 1959 and 1960. See also McCracken, 'Coercion and Control', p. 141.
[126] Armitage to Morgan, 18 April 1959 CO 1015/1839; Baker, *State of Emergency*, p.141–43.
[127] Dingle Foot to Armitage, 19 May 1959, CO 1015/1518; *Dissent*, 4 June 1959; Edward Mwasi, 'Reminiscences of My Detention', *Society of Malawi Journal*, 59, 2, 2006. For a full discussion see John McCracken, 'In the Shadow of Mau Mau: Detainees and Detention Camps during Nyasaland's State of Emergency', *JSAS*, 37, 3, 1911, pp. 535–50.
[128] Armitage to Lennox-Boyd, 18 March 1959, TNA CO 1015/1517.

But the Government, fearful of public opinion at home, refused to accede to these demands.[129]

By October 1959, the obstacles confronting Armitage seemed, even to him, to be almost insuperable. Not only had popular opposition to Federation hardened as a consequence of the introduction of the state of emergency, but so too had support and veneration for Dr Banda, outside Nyasaland as well as in. 'In the United Kingdom and in the United States, as well as elsewhere, he has links which will keep him in the public eye, wherever he may be, and enlist support for his political aims, whatever they are.' Banda, in Armitage's opinion, was 'extremely emotional, especially if criticised', possessed 'no administrative ability' and could not be relied on 'as a person with whom Her Majesty's Government could ever treat with any confidence that he would keep his side of the bargain'.[130] Nevertheless, the hard fact was that 'the influence of the Congress is so great and the messiah-like concept of its leader, Dr Banda, still so alive that the great majority of Africans, particularly would-be politicians, continuously see the shadow of Dr Banda over their shoulder' and were reluctant to put forward any views which did not conform with his.

Back in April, Armitage had attempted to begin the process of filling the political vacuum by having private talks with Manoah Chirwa and T. D. T. Banda, now linked in an unlikely (and largely Tonga-based) alliance as joint leaders of the Congress Liberation Party, but by October he had dismissed them as a credible alternative, since they were unable to attract the support of more than 500 people.[131] Charles Matinga's Progressive Party was even less influential. But 'one redeeming feature' remained – although Armitage admitted 'It is but a straw in the wind.'

> There are signs of change of heart in the case of some Africans who appear to be prepared to follow political parties with aims very different from those of the parties they have left, and to cooperate with Europeans and Asians. ... If this catches on and…the United Federal Party can…get a really strong following, then the bogey of fear and intimidation may be laid and it will be possible to look forward to the resumption of normal political life.

Lord Perth's comment on this bizarre suggestion (the UFP was almost universally hated in Nyasaland) puts a fitting gloss on Armitage's views: 'Read with interest and depression! The idea of the UFP being the leading party is very hard to believe.'[132]

In the recesses of Armitage's mind, however, racial paranoia was fast taking over from rational dialogue. Only a few years before, Armitage had served alongside Nkrumah as a minister in the Gold Coast's first elected government. But this experience had done nothing to diminish the contempt for African political aspirations that he now displayed. 'I believe that the evil, all perverting and inescapable horrors of intimidation as practised in Africa…cannot be really appreciated by those who do not know the African mind in an African environment', he wrote in a savage aside. 'Of course, once an African state gets inde-

---

[129] Armitage to Lennox-Boyd, 28 April 1959, TNA CO 1015/1839; brief for the visit of Governors of Northern Rhodesia and Nyasaland to Colonial Office, Nov 1959, CO 1015/1518.
[130] Armitage to Lennox-Boyd, 6 Oct 1959, TNA CO 1015/1839.
[131] Armitage to Gorrell Barnes, 13 April 1959, TNA CO 1015/1607.
[132] Note by Lord Perth, 13 Oct 1959, TNA CO 1015/1839.

pendence it is fully justified as being part of "the African way of life".'[133] In the Colonial Office, Gorell Barnes dryly minuted:

> I need only say here that I think it is as yet too early to assess whether any move *vis-à-vis* Dr Banda is desirable and would add that the conduct of the negotiation which would be necessary is not the sort of business for which Sir Robert Armitage's qualities obviously fit him.'[134]

Less than a week later, Iain Macleod became Colonial Secretary.

British ministers do not, by and large, play an important part in the 20th century history of Malawi but Iain Macleod is the exception. A highly ambitious politician, perhaps the most distinguished of the younger generation of Conservatives who transformed their party in the 1950s, Macleod had not visited a single British colony at the time of his appointment and had no expertise whatever in this area.[135] Yet by the time of his departure from the Colonial Office in October 1961 he had carried through a transformation in British decolonising strategies not just in Central Africa but in East Africa too. It was Harold Macmillan, at least partly in response to the passionate debate over the Devlin Report, who set in motion a reassessment of British colonial policy but it was the sharp-witted Macleod, ruthless, pragmatic but also clear-sighted in his ultimate objectives, who forced through the policy to fruition – at times against ferocious opposition. Many of the details of the fierce and protracted debate in which he became involved with Armitage, Macmillan, Welensky and Lord Home[136] over the timing and circumstances of the release of Dr Banda and the other detainees can safely be consigned to the chroniclers of British decolonisation. But the basic outline of the story needs to be told. Its central paradox was that the two main protagonists played precisely the reverse roles that might have been expected, given the nature of their posts. The Colonial Secretary, a career politician, was under pressure from the settler-supporting right wing of his party not to make substantial concessions to African nationalists. Yet it was Macleod who took the lead in pressing for the early release of Banda, even although it was clear that this would have profound and dangerous consequences for Britain's relations with Northern and in particular Southern Rhodesia – consequences with which he and his colleagues would ultimately have to cope. Conversely, the Governor of Nyasaland, an appointed bureaucrat, was principally responsible for the well-being of the Protectorate and was largely immune from settler pressures. Yet it was Armitage who stood out against negotiations with Banda and his colleagues, despite the indications that only through a rapprochement with the nationalists could some kind of normality be achieved.

For Macleod, the key issue that confronted him on entering the Colonial Office was whether any political solution in Nyasaland remained viable that did not involve Banda and, by extension, Nyasaland's exit from the Federation. As he quickly came to recognise, there was no mileage in Armitage's suggestion

[133] Armitage to Lennox-Boyd, 6 Oct 1959, TNA CO 1015/1839.
[134] Note by Gorell Barnes, 12 Oct 1949, TNA CO 1015/1839.
[135] For an excellent discussion see Robert Shepherd, *Iain Macleod: A Biography* (London, 1994).
[136] As Secretary of State for Commonwealth Relations, Home had primary responsibility for dealing with the Federation and Southern Rhodesia. He was subsequently Foreign Secretary (1960–63) and, as Sir Alec Douglas Home, Prime Minister (1963–64).

concerning the United Federal Party, but Orton Chirwa, the leader of the recently formed Malawi Congress Party, appeared to offer a more promising alternative. Was there not a chance that the 'civilised and charming' Chirwa, a Lincoln's Inn barrister with a wide range of European friends, might provide the flexibility that had previously been lacking?[137] On 11 November, Chirwa flew to London where he was immediately subjected to a charm offensive at the Colonial Office involving three separate meetings with Macleod, one with his deputy, Lord Perth, and another with Lord Monckton, the newly appointed chairman of the commission to consider the Federation's future. Chirwa's resolute refusal to offer even the hint of a compromise confirmed Macleod in his judgement that the key to Nyasaland 'lay in the person of Banda'.[138] According to Chirwa, 'he [Banda] was in fact the only person on the African side who was in a strong enough personal position to make compromises with us and in these circumstances his release from detention offered the only hope we could have of fruitful negotiation.'[139]

On 2 December 1959, the day after his last meeting with Chirwa, Macleod met the Livingstonia missionary, Fergus Macpherson, and informed him of his conviction that while it would be beneficial on economic grounds to maintain some form of federation, 'if it will not work, it will have to go, as we cannot rule by bayonets.'[140] Little more than a fortnight later, he flew to Dar es Salaam where he and Armitage had the first of several increasingly frosty discussions. First, Macleod insisted, against Armitage's protests, that the release of the 470 people still held in detention must be speeded up – although it was accepted that a hard-core of perhaps 49 'extremists' would remain. Second, he announced his intention of releasing Banda soon, as a prelude to opening constitutional discussions with him.[141]

From our vantage point, it is not always easy to see why the debate over the timing of Banda's release (as opposed to the debate over whether he should be released at all) took such a heated and contentious form. But in many respects the two issues overlapped. Macleod's central aim, once he had taken the decision to release Banda, was to press ahead as rapidly as possible in the belief that getting him quickly involved in constitutional discussions would reduce the risk of further disturbances breaking out. It would also make it more likely that some partial compromise could be reached concerning Nyasaland's continued associ-ation with the Federation. In the final analysis, however, Macleod felt that a smooth transfer of power in Nyasaland – especially if it excluded the 'extremists', Chipembere, Chiume and the Chisiza brothers – was of even greater importance than the maintenance of the Federation itself. For rather different reasons, Welensky, Armitage and Home were all deeply opposed to this line of action: Welensky and Home because they believed the release of Banda would have disastrous consequences for the Federation at a time when its constitutional future was still unresolved; Armitage because he remained deeply suspicious of

[137] H. Rolfe Gardner to Lord Perth, 23 Feb 1959, TNA CO 1015/1606; file on Orton Chirwa's visit to London, CO 1015/2119.
[138] Shepherd, *Iain Macleod*, p.188.
[139] Monson to Armitage, 3 Dec 1959, TNA CO 1015/2119.
[140] F. Macpherson, note on his meeting with Iain Macleod, 2 Dec 1959, EUL Helen Taylor Papers.
[141] Note by Secretary of State on Nyasaland Emergency, 24 Dec 1959 with covering memo to the Cabinet, 24 Dec 1959, CO 1015/1518; Baker, *Armitage*, pp. 240–42.

Banda and was convinced that his release would trigger major disturbances.

Macleod's announcement, telegraphed to Armitage on 4 January 1960, that the cabinet had approved the release of Banda from 1 February thus came as a considerable shock to the governor who replied by demanding that, if Banda were to be released, he should be sent in exile to Britain.[142] On 25 January, when Macmillan arrived in Zomba on the fifth leg of his six-nation African tour, the matter remained unresolved. In an acrimonious discussion lasting many hours, Armitage accused the Prime Minister of being prepared to risk lives in the colonies for the sake of votes in Britain, a charge that Macmillan regarded, not surprisingly, as 'most offensive'.[143] Under pressure from Welensky and even more from Home, Macleod agreed to delay the release, first to a date in February, then to 1 April. But he remained insistent that no conditions would be attached and that Banda would be brought from Gwelo straight to Zomba. On reflection, he and Macmillan decided not to dismiss Armitage, who remained resistant almost to the end. Rather, Macleod took the decision to accelerate the appointment of Glyn Jones, Commissioner for Native Development in Northern Rhodesia, as the new Chief Secretary and, a year later, as Armitage's successor.

Banda's release, under conditions of strict secrecy, on 1 April marked a victory for Macleod who was waiting in Zomba to meet him. In the preceding weeks, the Colonial Secretary had put his career on the line by rejecting the advice given by Armitage and others that, with Banda free, Malawians would indulge in 'large and disorderly illegal public meetings' leading to 'serious riots' and the likely loss of life.[144] In the event, on this, as on other matters Armitage proved mistaken. Since the previous September, the Malawi Congress Party under Orton Chirwa's leadership had taken off as a genuinely popular movement. But there had never been any real doubt in the minds of its members that Banda would return sooner rather than later to lead the country to independence. In that sense, ordinary Malawians were better prophets than many politicians and officials. Banda himself, moreover, shared the popular view. In his last major discussion with a colonial official prior to his release, he told Glyn Jones:

> His present incarceration was a necessary stage in his progress towards leadership of his people in a free Nyasaland. His imprisonment was part of an inevitable series of vicissitudes such as other historical figures like Gandhi, de Valera, Nehru, Nkrumah and others had suffered. … For these reasons he was philosophical about his detention – he knew he would come out and lead Nyasaland to self-government or die in gaol, in which case others would succeed him and attain his ambition.[145]

The result was that that the release took place without incident and in a mood of jubilation. 'Congratulations Macleod! Good wishes Armitage!' the *Malawi News* proclaimed.[146] Banda went out of his way to call on people to be peaceful

---

[142] Macleod to Armitage, 4 Jan 1960, CO 1015/2233.

[143] Baker, *State of Emergency*, p. 196.

[144] 'Note of appreciation of possible turn of events if Dr Banda is released to Nyasaland in near future', Jan 1960, TNA CO 1015/2439. According to Macleod, it had been Sir Malcolm Barrow's view that '10,000 Africans would be killed in the riots that would follow Banda's release.' Shepherd, *Iain Macleod*, p. 201.

[145] 'Report on discussions between Dr Banda and the Chief Secretary' in Glyn Jones to Monson, 16 March 1960, TNA CO 1015/2458.

[146] *Malawi News*, 2 April 1960.

and to leave the fighting to him.[147] 'So all our precautions were not needed and the warnings of immediate disaster that have poured on us for months past unjustified', Macleod commented, with well-earned relish to his rival, Alec Home.[148] On 5 April, Orton Chirwa handed over the presidency of the MCP to Banda and reverted to the position of executive committee member along with Rose Chibambo, Lawrence Makata, and Lali Lubani. They were joined a month later by Kanyama Chiume, who had been out of the country when the emergency was declared and had spent much of the intervening period in London agitating on Congress's behalf. Notably absent were the 'extremists,' Chipembere and the Chisiza brothers, who had been kept in detention along with 17 other 'hard-liners' at Armitage's wishes and with the approval of Macleod.

Banda, in consequence, was the dominant MCP figure at the constitutional conference convened by Macleod at Lancaster House in London on 25 July. Home, as usual, urged caution from the sidelines. 'I think a programme of advance culminating in independence for Nyasaland and Northern Rhodesia by 1970 would be accepted as reasonable and swallowed, although with great difficulty, by Southern Rhodesia', he wrote to Macmillan in June. 'Anything shorter would, I fear, surely provide a campaign for the extremists on either side and give no chance of stability.'[149]

Macleod, however, had every intention of moving faster. In the course of an exceptionally delicate set of negotiations involving representatives from the MCP, UFP, Congress Liberation Party, chiefs and others, he persuaded the delegates to agree unanimously to a new transitional constitution. For the first and last time, Banda made significant concessions by agreeing not to push his initial claims for universal suffrage and for an assured African majority in the Executive and Legislative Councils. What he did obtain, however, would transform the nature of politics in Malawi. For the first time, Africans would be directly elected to the Legislative Council through an immensely complicated dual-roll system enfranchising about 100,000 voters; this would almost certainly provide an African majority. The Governor plus five officials would retain a slim majority on the Executive Council. But there would also be five unofficials drawn from elected members of the Legislative Council; this would make possible the introduction of some kind of ministerial system.[150] Macmillan, somewhat duplicitously, tried to persuade Welensky that white rule remained intact. Banda, more accurately, presented the new constitution as the key to self-government and to eventual independence.

---

[147] Intelligence Report, 6 April 1960, TNA CO 1015/2444.
[148] Macleod to Home and Perth, 4 April 1959, TNA CO 1015/2438.
[149] Quoted in Lamb, *Macmillan Years*, p. 252.
[150] For details see Short, *Banda*, pp. 133–38; Baker, *Armitage*, pp. 275–79.

14
The Making of Malawi
1959–1963

The Malawi Congress Party, 1959–1961

The reconstitution of the Nyasaland African Congress from September 1959 as the Malawi Congress Party (MCP) marked the beginnings of a significant shift in the character of Malawian politics. Often regarded as the NAC by another name, the MCP quickly emerged as one of the most popular, dynamic and successful nationalist parties in Africa, infinitely larger than its predecessor, much more consciously 'traditionalist' in style, distinctly more illiberal in its attitudes and drawing support from regions into which Congress had barely penetrated. It was also important that while the Nyasaland African Congress was, above all, an anti-colonial protest movement seeking national liberation, which individuals joined often at considerable personal risk, the MCP, following Dr Banda's release from gaol in April 1960, was conceived increasingly as a government in waiting, with considerable powers of patronage from which people disassociated themselves only at their peril.

An element of controversy surrounded the launch of the MCP. Orton Chirwa, its urbane founder, had played an active part the affairs of Congress in the early 1950s when he was financed for a time by a grant from Dr Banda in London. But his involvement in 1953 in the short-lived African Progressive Association had left him distrusted by nationalists, some of whom alleged that the colonial government had arranged his early release from Khami prison in August in the hope that he would guide nationalist sentiment into new and more moderate channels. Kanyama Chiume, then in exile in London, initially warned his supporters in the Northern Province against involving themselves with the party; and although in December 1959 he and Chirwa published a joint statement calling on Malawians to support the MCP, the damage had already been done.[1] In both the Southern and Central Provinces, people flocked to join the party but, in the north, branches were concentrated in a limited number of places such as the CCAP stations at Loudon and Mzuzu, leaving other areas unrepresented. By December 1959, only three northern branches had been opened as

---

[1]   Intelligence Reports for December 1959 and January 1960, TNA CO 1015/2444. See also Chiume, *Kwacha*, pp. 128–32.

compared with 31 in the south and eighteen in the centre. The next month, Karonga-born Patrick [later Pemba] Ndove, the dynamic young National Organising Secretary, led a recruiting drive in the north, which raised the number of card-carrying members there to around 7,000 scattered in twelve branches. However, by this date, there were already 20,000 members in 28 branches in the Central Province and 40,000 in 37 branches in the south.[2] New areas of MCP strength were being created, particularly in the Lilongwe and Fort Manning districts, the Chewa heartland of Malawi. By the same token, the north was losing its ground as an area of exceptional popular strength.

The regional shift in support of the MCP was accompanied by the establishment of formal links between the party and the trade union movement. As Armitage noted, one of the weaknesses of the NAC in the early months of 1959 was 'the complete lack of cohesion between the Trade Union movement and Congress', and hence the failure of attempts to organise workers in a general strike.[3] Trade Unions, in consequence, remained unbanned during the emergency at a time when Congress, the Youth League and the Women's League were all proscribed. Aleke Banda, the newly-appointed secretary-general of the MCP, was determined to rectify this problem. The son of Nyasa parents, born in Northern Rhodesia and educated in Bulawayo, Aleke Banda was aged only nineteen when his schoolboy political activism resulted in his legally dubious deportation to Nyasaland. Nevertheless, he already possessed elements of the administrative competence that was to be a constant feature of his political career. Initially based in the office of Nyasaland Trades Union Congress, he produced a cyclostyled paper for workers, *Ntendere pa Nchito*, which was widened in scope in December and given a new title, the *Malawi News*. In January, the TUC affiliated itself to the MCP. In the same month, John Ngwire and C.C.M. Msisya of the TUC joined forces with Orton Chirwa in a delegation to meet the British prime minister, Harold Macmillan.[4] In later months the evident reluctance of some trade unionists to subordinate themselves to the party led to growing friction, culminating in a public attack on the trade union leadership launched by Aleke Banda in the *Malawi News* in May.[5] Nevertheless, there can be little doubt that in its early weeks the organisational muscle provided by the trade unions was vital to the MCP's success.

The expansion of the MCP from twelve branches in October 1959 to 112 in February 1960 and a remarkable 1,842 in October 1961 made it one of the fastest growing political parties in East and Central Africa. However, figures for total membership must be treated with caution. In the view of the Special Branch, which had no reason to inflate numbers, the paid-up membership climbed from 8,100 at the end of October, reaching 67,000 in February 1960 – figures that strikingly demonstrate popular support for national liberation. They rose again following Banda's release and the build up to the August 1961 elections, to a figure in excess of 100,000 in September 1961 (the Special Branch evaluation) or 600,000 according to the MCP.[6]

---

[2]   Intelligence Reports for January and February, 1960, TNA CO 1015/2444.
[3]   Armitage to Colonial Secretary, 6 October 1959, TNA CO 1015/1755.
[4]   Intelligence Report for January 1960, TNA CO 1015/2444.
[5]   *Malawi News* 7 May 1960.
[6]   Political Intelligence Report for February 1960, TNA CO 1015/2444; Special Branch report on The Malawi Congress Party, fourth edition, 14 October 1961, CO 1015/2445. The MCP claimed 300,000 members in April 1960 (*Malawi News* 9 April 1960) and 600,000 in October 1961.

8 Dunduzu Chisiza, Masauko Chipembere, Qabaniso Chibambo and Yatuta Chisiza at Nkhotakota in their prison graduate gowns, following their release from Kanjedza, 27 September 1960

Little attempt was made by the Blantyre-based leadership in the first four months to exercise control over district branches, which therefore grew in a 'loose and uncoordinated manner'.[7] But in January 1960 Pemba Ndove, recently returned from study in Britain, was appointed as National Organising Secretary and quickly imposed his authority on the internal organisation. By the time that he was ousted from office by Dr Banda in April, on the charge that he had acted independently of Chirwa and the central executive, Ndove had created a network of 18 district organising secretaries, all of them directly responsible to him. 'Dr Kamuzu Banda is taking over a colossal organisation, well disciplined and determined', Orton Chirwa announced during the official handover on 5 April. In addition to a large paid-up membership, the party could boast 'a landrover [sic], an electric duplicator, a large staff and a bank balance of over £2,000'.[8]

[7] Intelligence Report for December 1959, TNA CO 1015/2233.
[8] *Malawi News*, 5, 9 April 1960.

The removal of the officials appointed by Ndove was only the first step in a process aimed at refocusing power on the leader. Aleke Banda and, following his release from detention, Dunduzu Chisiza, took over the day-to-day running of the party. New full-time organising secretaries were appointed, paid by the party and directly responsible to the president.[9] Provincial executive committees were brought into existence under loyalist party bosses: M. Q. Chibambo in the Northern Province, Richard Chidzanja in the centre, and G. W. Kumtumanji in the south. Party members who had previously paid only the two shilling entrance fee to join the MCP were instructed of the need to pay an additional annual subscription fee, also of two shillings.[10] 'Kamuzu' badges (cardboard badges containing a photograph of the leader) costing two shillings and sixpence were introduced in October 1960 and quickly became near obligatory adornments. Malawians in South Africa and Southern Rhodesia continued to provide support but, whereas in the 1950s their financial assistance had been vital, by 1961 the sums contributed by the South African branch to the election fund (£1,000) were little more than that produced by an average district such as Dowa.[11]

The increased funds went on a rash of new offices, on salaried staff and on a fleet of cars – vital for the effective organisation of an election campaign. By the time of the elections in August 1961, the single Land Rover owned by the party sixteen months earlier had been replaced by 22 vehicles, ten of these Land Rovers paid for by Kwame Nkrumah and the government of Ghana.[12]

Of even greater importance for the future was Dr Banda's decision to set up an independent printing and publishing company to produce the *Malawi News* and other promotional literature.[13] Aleke Banda leased a warehouse in Limbe in which he installed a second-hand printing machine, purchased in Salisbury by Peter Mackay, a European sympathiser who for several months had been producing a lively pro-nationalist journal, *Tsopano*. A team of talented young journalists was recruited, among them the school-leaver Thandika Mkandawire (many years later to become Director of the United Nations Research Institute for Social Development).[14] Additional members of staff were appointed to the printing, advertising and administrative departments. In February 1961 the first issue of the new style *Malawi News* was published, edited by Aleke Banda and proudly proclaiming on its masthead that it was 'The only newspaper in East, Central and Southern Africa owned, printed and published by Africans themselves at a press that is owned and managed by Africans themselves.'[15] Those words concealed the fact that while the Malawi Congress Party has spent some £4,000 of subscribers' money in setting up the press, its legal owner was Malawi Press Ltd, a private company floated in January 1961 with Aleke and Kamuzu Banda, its two shareholders, each holding a nominal £1 share. What this meant in practice was that Dr Banda had gained possession of an economic instrument

9 *Malawi News*, 14 July 1960.
10 *Malawi News*, 4 September 1960.
11 *Malawi News*, 29 October 1960; Special Branch appreciation, 'The Malawi Congress Party Fourth edition', 14 October 1961, TNA CO 1015/2445.
12 Ibid.
13 The account that follows is drawn largely from Peter Mackay, *We Have Tomorrow: Stirrings in Africa, 1959–1967* (Norwich, 2008) pp. 109–12, 128–9, 139–44.
14 According to Mackay, it was Mkandawire who coined the praise-name *Ngwazi* for Dr Banda.
15 *Malawi News*, February 1961.

that he would subsequently employ with considerable skill in building up his power base. Thus, the distinction between what was his and what was the party's had been fundamentally breached. Kanyama Chiume, now installed as Publicity Secretary, made the same point in the new nationalist song that became an MCP anthem: *Zonse zimeni za Kamuzu Banda* (Everything belongs to Kamuzu Banda). What was nationalist hyperbole in the early 1960s became disconcertingly close to the truth during the next two decades.

For sympathetic observers of the MCP at this time, the clear evidence of widespread village-level support, with the active involvement of peasants as well as teachers and of young as well as old, made it a movement of exceptional attraction. Writing of his visit to Malawi in June 1960, the anonymous editor of the radical broadsheet, *Dissent* (in fact the historian, Terence Ranger) emphasised 'the solidity and solidarity of Malawi support' which he compared a little wistfully with his experience of nationalist divisions in Southern Rhodesia.

Yet as Ranger noted, if his first impression had been of 'the strength and popularity of Malawi', his second impression was of 'Malawi's problems' – problems that arose 'from the very fact that Malawi is a national movement, containing within itself so many elements which under other circumstances would be competitive or hostile':

> How is it going to be possible to reconcile the interests and influence of the village headman and the "emergent" Malawi branch officers?. ... And then what of the Youth League, as they march down the hillside twenty minutes or so after the meeting has begun, with drums and chants and peculiar home-made Party uniforms of their own?

What in particular of the 'respected elder … beaten up as a "stooge"' or of the 'able and patriotic headmaster persecuted with libel, threat and open disobedience by his own pupils'?[16]

Ranger's emphasis on the significance of generational conflict is an important insight which historians of Malawi have been unwise to ignore. All over Africa, nationalism was above all a young people's movement and this was particularly true in Malawi, a country steeped in patriarchal values. Here, a commitment to national liberation could also serve as a bid by the young to stake out ground for themselves in the unending struggle against the elders. Protests and demonstrations in schools were a regular feature of political activity from the late 1950s. According to one source, at least fifty per cent of the crowds flocking to hear Banda in Blantyre after his release were under 20; not more than ten per cent were over the age of 40.[17]

The League of Malawi Youth, formed on the initiative of Pemba Ndove at a meeting held at Limbe on 24 December 1959, acted as a focus for youthful discontent. In its initial form, the Youth League was an urban-based movement, attracting some 400 members by February 1960 and drawing disproportionably for its leaders on the children of Blantyre's entrepreneurial elite. Constance Makata, the first vice-chairman, was the daughter of the wealthy businessman Laurence Makata, who was then incarcerated in Khami gaol. Even at this stage, however, the Government regarded the Youth League as 'as clear potential

---

[16] 'Return to Malawi', *Dissent*, 9 June 1960, pp. 1–5.
[17] Intelligence Report and Appreciation, 6 April 1960, TNA CO 1015/2444.

danger', responsible for the disturbances that erupted close to Ryall's Hotel, during the visit of the British prime minister Harold Macmillan on 25 January.[18] John Chikwakwa, the chairman of the League and an employee of the Electricity Supply Commission, was believed to have ignored Orton Chirwa's call for calm in seeking to provoke the police.[19]

With the reorganisation of the Youth League in April, the movement spread into the countryside, taking on a less elitist, more vigorous and more socially radical character. Dr Banda attempted to assert his control by appointing a new chairman, C. D. Chidongo, a stalwart of the banned NAC Youth League, who had recently been released from Gwelo. It was under Chidongo's leadership that the League's membership grew to around 40,000 in September 1961, divided into 551 branches spread throughout the country. Loosely organised into units of the 'Malawi Police', they acted as stewards at public meetings, checked the credentials of delegates, and provided guards of honour for Banda, dressed in para-military uniforms consisting of white drill bush shirts, black trousers and black berets. Chidongo's attempt in January 1961 to gain greater autonomy for the Youth League by granting it control of its own funds was decisively rejected at an emergency meeting held on 21–22 January 1961 where the League's subordination to the MCP at all levels was re-emphasised.[20] Nevertheless, there were many occasions on which militant Youth Leaguers took the initiative in confrontations with the police or in assaults on political opponents. These included the destruction, early in December 1960, of the house of Chester Katsonga, the leader of the Christian Liberation Party, for which John Chikwakwa and four other leading members of the League were charged.[21] Then, as later, Banda proved highly adept in publicly distancing himself from acts of violence of which he may well have privately approved. Nevertheless, considerable strains existed in his relationship with MYP leaders at this time resulting in his decision, taken in 1961, to establish a more compliant, better disciplined youth movement. It was not until after the suspension of John Chikwawa in early 1964 following on the creation of the Young Pioneers, closely modelled on the Young Pioneers of Ghana, in 1963, that his control of the youth movement became fully established.[22]

Women were also attracted to the MCP, although there were restrictions on their full participation. Back in the 1950s, women farmers had frequently been in the forefront of popular protests against *thangata* and *malimidwe* but, with the exception of Rose Chibambo, they played a lesser role in the affairs of the NAC. Time and again in the early months of 1959, women took part in demonstrations, sometimes pushing themselves to the front in the belief that the police would use less violence on them than on men. However, male nationalist leaders

[18] Armitage to Colonial Secretary, 1 February 1960, TNA CO 1015/2444.
[19] Special Branch report on the League of Malawi Youth, 29 January 1960, TNA CO 1015/2444.
[20] Special Branch evaluation, 'The League of Malawi Youth.' Third Edition, 31 October 1961, TNA CO 1015/2445.
[21] Special Branch, 'The Malawi Congress Party.' Fourth Edition, 14 October 1961, TNA CO 1015/2445.
[22] Nyasaland Intelligence Committee, 'The Extent of Opposition to and Criticism of Dr Banda & the Malawi Congress Party at 5th January 1962', TNA CO 1015/2445; Aleke Banda, 'The History of the Youth Movement' in *Youth in Malawi. Security and Progress with Malawi Young Pioneers* (Department of Information, Blantyre, 1965); Intelligence Report, March 1964, TNA DO 183/137.

tended to respond with exaggerated displays of chauvinist chivalry, thus drama-tising the differences between the sexes. When 50 women were arrested in Zomba in January 1959, Chipembere's response was to call on men to come to their aid in words that emphasised male responsibility for protection: 'We the men of Nyasaland should never sleep or be happy until these women are released. If we are men and not women we must see that the women are released now, this very instant.' [23] Less than a dozen women out of a total of more than 1,300 people were detained during the emergency including Rose Chibambo, who was removed to Zomba gaol with her six-day-old child; Vera Chirwa, the wife of the MCP president; and Gertrude Rubadiri, one of the very first Malawian women to attend Fort Hare.[24]

In the absence of Rose Chibambo, who was restricted to the Mzimba district following her release, it was Vera Chirwa who took the lead in founding the League of Malawi Women. Eleven branches were quickly formed, all but one in the Southern Province and in July 1960 a National Dress was introduced, the prede-cessor to the distinctive *chirundu* that members of the Women's League would wear following independence.[25] On Banda's insistence, Rose Chibambo returned in October 1960 as Chairman of the League and as a member of the MCP's National Executive. But virtually no other women obtained administrative respon-sibility alongside men. Only one woman out of 118 members was elected to MCP district councils in July 1960.[26] No women, not even Rose Chibambo, were among the twenty MCP candidates chosen by Banda for the Legislative Council elec-tions in 1961. Banda went out of his way to argue during the Lancaster House discussions that some women should have the vote – notably literate women who had obtained the age of 'responsible motherhood' (later defined as those who had been married for ten years or more).[27] But his depiction of Malawi women as his *mbumba* did little to enhance their decision-making role. Rose Chibambo, even at this time, had no doubt that members of the Women's League should play a full part in the political process. In practise, however, in the run up to the election their main task appears to have been 'to turn out as a body to greet Dr Banda at his public appearances' and to sing and dance in Banda's honour.[28]

The emphasis on dancing as a means of popular mobilisation was a funda-mental feature of the MCP, dramatising its character as a movement set on cultural as well as political liberation and hence distinguishing it from the Nyasa-land African Congress. On his first visit to Lilongwe in July 1958 Dr Banda had been welcomed by a public performance of *Gule Wamkulu*, the Great Dance of the secret *Nyau* society, but in general the young leaders of the NAC were at best ambivalent about the value of indigenous culture and made little effort to incorporate it within the movement.[29] Following his release from gaol in April 1960, however, Banda went out of his way to encourage the use of dancing as a means of obtaining popular support – and with dramatically successful results.

23 Transcript of speech by H.B.M., Chipembere, 21 January 1959, RHP, Devlin Papers, Box 5.
24 'The Rose Chibambo Story', *Wasi*, 11, 3, 2000, pp. 17–21; Rotberg (ed.), *Hero of the Nation*, p. 147.
25 *Malawi News*, 23 April, 14 July 1960.
26 *Malawi News*, 14 July 1960.
27 *Malawi News*, 20 August 1960, 21 January 1961.
28 Lucy Mair, *The Nyasaland Elections of 1961* (London, 1962), p. 33.
29 *Proceedings of the Nyasaland Legislative Assembly, 9–16 June, 1963*; speeches by Richard Chidzanja and Banda; Forster, 'Culture, Nationalism and the Invention of Tradition', pp. 488–89.

Wherever he travelled on his triumphal tour of the Northern and Central Provinces in June 1960, people gathered in their thousands to dance *nyau*, *malipenga*, *chioda* and *visikese* in a striking assertion of African values.[30] Later, the First Annual Delegates' Conference of the MCP, held at Nkhotakota in October 1960, was transformed into a celebration of Malawian culture, with dancers outnumbering delegates by nearly five to one.[31] To the bemusement of Special Branch observers, Banda's main speech at the conference was devoted, not to a statement of policy, but rather to a prolonged criticism of European missionaries for condemning African dances.

Banda's emphasis on popular cultural nationalism was symbolised for him, although not for all leaders, by the change from 'Nyasaland' to 'Malawi' in the title of the party. The term 'Nyasaland African Congress' had emphasised a particular brand of nationalism, derived from the shared experience of Africans living in an artificially-created colonial state, many of whom had also shared the experience of labour migrancy. The label 'Nyasa' was one widely used from the 1920s on the Copperbelt and in Southern African mines; by the 1950s it had come to provide the basis for a form of national identity defined in territorial terms. For Banda, by contrast, 'Malawi' assumed the existence of a 'Malawi people' sharing a common culture and heritage. His interest in the history of the Malawi or Maravi people appears to have first developed in Chicago in the early 1930s where he collaborated with an American scholar on a grammar of 'Chichewa' (a term he preferred to the more commonly used 'Chinyanja'). It was further strengthened in the mid-1940s when he was persuaded to join the Scottish missionary/antiquarian Cullen Young in editing a collection of essays, *Our African Way of Life*. Their joint preface contained the first modern reference to the *aMaravi*, the correct shared name, the two authors claimed, for a variety of peoples, all speaking a common basic language, who had expanded out of a single Chewa homeland.

Banda's subsequent use of 'Malawi', first in the name of the company he launched unsuccessfully in 1951, the Malawi Trading and Transport Company, and second in the title of the MCP, was no doubt in part a tactical measure, designed like Kwame Nkrumah's employment of 'Ghana' as the new name for the Gold Coast, as a means of dramatising his rejection of colonialism. But there can be no doubt that, during his long years in exile, Banda, as he explained to Glyn Jones while still imprisoned in Gwelo Gaol, had become convinced of the existence of a '"Malawi Nation" … homogenous and divided by tribal differences to a much smaller extent than the people of Northern Rhodesia'. At different times he was to give different accounts of which peoples were incorporated in that nation. His early insistence in 1946 that *aMaravi* ought to be the shared name for all 'so-called Nyanja-speaking peoples' spreading from Nyasaland into Northern Rhodesia and Mozambique was replaced by 1960 by the more ambitious claim that out of the Malawi kingdom 'broke Achewa, Anyanja, Ayao, Angoni, Alomwe, Tumbuka, Henga, Tonga and so forth' – all the peoples of Nyasaland as well as many elsewhere.[32] What was consistent, however, was his

---

[30] For a vivid account of the tour see the report by Aleke Banda in *Malawi News*, 14 June 1960.
[31] Report by Nyasaland Police on 'MCP First Annual Delegates' Conference', 7 Oct 1960, TNA CO 1015/2445.
[32] Speech by Dr Banda while opening Soche Hill Teachers Training College. *Malawi News*, 8 March 1963.

repeated assertion that superficial differences among Malawi's people masked a fundamental cultural unity, owing nothing to colonial boundaries, which found its modern expression in the MCP. During the time that Orton Chirwa was leader, nationalist speakers regularly distinguished between 'Malawi', the party, and 'Nyasaland', the country. But from the time of his release Banda popularised a new rhetoric, quickly imitated by others, in which 'Malawi' was used with deliberate ambiguity as the term embracing both the party and the territory.[33] Moreover, there is evidence to suggest that many Malawians, particularly those from the centre and south of the country who could identify with the cultural symbols that Banda employed – his self-identification as the matrilineal 'uncle' of his people, 'Nkhoswe Number One' – responded with enthusiasm to the new approach. Equally, in the Northern Province, there were those such as the veteran Congress leader, Charles Chinula, who were left bemused by the new cultural rhetoric, puzzled by what 'Malawi' might mean and unable to empathise with the symbolism now being employed.[34]

There is no simple explanation for the growing absolutism and intolerance demonstrated from April 1960 by the MCP. Fear of disunity – fear too of Machiavellian colonial rulers intent on dividing and ruling – were certainly factors. And so too was the renewed concern to build up Banda's public image as the unchallenged leader – concern given added urgency following the release of Chipembere and the remaining detainees in September 1960 on the eve of the Nkhotakota conference. Three days after their release, Banda was proclaimed as Life President of the Party. Of particular note is the fact that the younger politicians in general, for all their idealism and generosity, were no less illiberal than Banda in their political attitudes. Henry Masauko Chipembere is a particularly interesting example. Regarded in colonial circles as 'rabidly racist' and 'mentally most unstable', Chipembere was in fact a thoughtful, sensitive individual, whose well-earned reputation for violent rhetoric was at odds with his 'natural external politeness or shyness'.[35] On issues of parliamentary democracy, however, his views were predominantly negative. 'Let us not listen to those who talk of party-politics', he wrote in 1957, in a passage that at least contemplated the possibility of change:

> This is not the stage for party-politics for us. Party-politics are a dangerous thing during pre-liberation views. They are the ideal thing when you have achieved independence, or are near the achievement of independence. But now we are in the stage of struggle and what we need in this stage is one solid powerful mass movement embracing all people and enjoying the active support of our Chiefs.[36]

By 1960, however, Chipembere's political vision had hardened. Writing in the *Malawi News*, he denounced the multi-party system as 'a system of Government with a built-in subversive mechanism' and rejoiced that 'In Africa, fortunately this political ailment seems likely to be avoided.'

[33] See *Malawi News* 21 May, 4 June and 29 October, 1960.
[34] Author's interview with Revd Charles Chinula, 25 July 1964.
[35] Quoted in Colin Baker, *Revolt of the Ministers: the Malawi Cabinet Crisis, 1964–1965* (I.B. Tauris, London, 2001), p. 10; leaflet entitled *Mr Masauko Chipembere* (Malawi Press Limited, Limbe, n.d., c. 1961).
[36] Henry B. Chipembere, 'A Letter to the African People of the Southern Province of the Nyasaland Protectorate', May 1957, TNA CO 1015/1748.

The new independent African states have all shown themselves to be keen to inherit only the good fruits of Western thinking and to reject all its destructive myths and political superstitions. They are developing what Britons deride as "monolithic" States. This is nothing to worry about. Africa must evolve systems that suit her people's attitudes and temperament.

He concluded by noting that, even in Europe, parliamentary democracy was not the only system employed. 'Half the population of Europe lives under one type of authoritarian state or another, and they are none the worse for it.'[37]

Chipembere's comments were occasioned by the founding of the Christian Democratic Party, launched on 17 October 1960 by Chester Katsonga, owner of a famous *chibuku* bar at Blantyre market and one of the city's leading entrepreneurs.[38] An ill-conceived venture, aimed specifically at Nyasaland's large Catholic population, the CDC received support from Archbishop Theunissen of Blantyre in the vain hope that it would act as a Catholic counterweight to the Presbyterian-dominated MCP. At that level, Theunissen was seeking – against the wishes of his fellow Catholic bishops – to introduce into Nyasaland the tradition of religious-based political parties that existed in his homeland, Holland.[39] Yet if the MCP leadership had good reason to react strongly against what it perceived as a cynical example of divide and rule, perpetrated by a religious leader who, for all the genuine concern he had shown on social and educational matters, had previously been notably indifferent on the issue of political advancement, it was less than justified in the intensity of its response. Even before the founding of the CDP, interest groups sympathetic to but independent of the MCP had become targets of criticism. 'All churches are ONE AND THE SAME whatever their names', Aleke Banda asserted in the *Malawi News* in April 1960 in a generalised assault on mission-based churches, including the CCAP. 'When we get our own government such things will have to be put to a stop or else Africans will start their own National Church. Education will, of course, be "nationalised" so that no propaganda for imperialism can be continued in schools.' [40]

The formation of an opposition party dedicated, according to its manifesto, to 'safeguarding the Christian faith' and 'protecting the country from the threat of despotism' resulted in an even fiercer response.[41] In a wide-ranging denunciation of 'Vatican Imperialism', which took up a complete issue of *Malawi News*, Aleke Banda revealed his immaturity – he was still only 21 – in arguing that the creation of the CDP formed a link in the attempt of the Catholic Church to achieve world domination.[42] Chiume and Chipembere kept up the pressure in a series of fiery speeches, culminating in Chipembere's call at a public meeting held at Ndirande on 4 December for 'real bloodshed, real killing of our enemies.'[43] This in turn was followed by the burning of Katsonga's house and

---

[37]   H.B.M. Chipembere, 'Something about Opposition Parties', *Malawi News*, 26 November 1960, TNA CO 1015/2445. Matthew Schoffeleers is mistaken in ascribing this quotation to Aleke Banda in his book, *In Search of Truth and Justice* (Blantyre, 1999), p. 22.

[38]   For Katsonga see Lamani Kamdidi, 'Reminiscences', *SOMJ*, 50, 1 (1997).

[39]   The key study of the CDP is Schoffeleers, *In Search of Truth and Justice*, pp. 17–60.

[40]   *Malawi News* 23 April 1960. See also Albert de Jong, *Mission and Politics in Eastern Africa* (Limuru, Kenya, 2000), pp. 247–307.

[41]   Schoffeleers, *In Search of Truth and Justice*, p. 17.

[42]   *Malawi News*, 22 October 1960.

[43]   Special Branch, 'The Malawi Congress Party', 14 October 1961, TNA CO 1015/2445.

subsequently by a number of violent assaults made by Youth League vigilantes on members both of the CDP and of T.D.T. Banda's rival Congress Liberation Party.[44] Dr Banda, who had no desire to force a confrontation with the Vatican, attempted to close the breach with the church authorities in a hastily convened meeting with the liberal-minded Bishop Fady of Lilongwe. But it was not until after he had called for 'peace and calm at all costs' at an MCP conference held in Blantyre late in January 1961 that the disturbances were brought to an end.[45] A short time later, and with the tacit approval of Banda, Chipembere was convicted of sedition on account of his speeches and sentenced to three years' imprisonment. Just as he had in July 1960, at the time of the Lancaster House negotiations, so in 1961 Banda entered the election campaign with his main internal rival safely incarcerated in a colonial gaol.

The new Governor

The final stages in the transition from colonial rule to independence were domi- nated by two men: Dr Banda and Armitage's successor as Governor, Sir Glyn Jones. A taciturn figure, Jones had been plucked from what had been a respectable but humdrum career in the district and provincial administration of Northern Rhodesia to take on 'the most difficult job in the colonial empire' (as it was described to him by Macleod). He was in many respects the archetypical colonial administrator, keen on games, an enthusiastic fisherman and shot, and a prodigious walker through the African countryside he loved. But, unlike many of his profession, he appears to have entirely lacked prejudice against national- ists and over the years formed firm personal links not only with Banda but also with some of the Colonial Office's 'hard core of extremists', notably Dunduzu and Yatuta Chisiza.[46]

Jones's appointment early in 1960 as Chief Secretary and, unofficially, as Governor in waiting, marked the first stage in an extensive shake up of Nyasa- land's senior administration – an event given added urgency by Macmillan's dismay, expressed following his ill-fated visit to the country in January, at the entrenched attitudes taken by Armitage and his advisers. 'If you would prefer to find a new Governor you could count on my full support', he told Macleod: 'in other words I think the course you recommend is right, but I doubt very much whether you have got in Nyasaland the men to carry it through.'[47]

Jones's arrival brought a breath of fresh air to proceedings. Appointed with the fisherman's brief of 'keeping Banda in play', he travelled to Gwelo in March 1960 for a meeting with the Doctor that left both men positively disposed towards each other. Jones, according to Banda, was 'thoughtful and considerate'. Banda, so Jones reported, was 'intelligent and shrewd when his mind was not confused by emotional fervour.'[48] Back in Nyasaland, following Banda's release, he renewed the relationship in a series of sometimes heated discussions at which

[44] Ibid.; Schoffeleers, *In Search of Truth and Justice*, pp. 55–7.
[45] Short, *Banda*, pp. 141–2.
[46] For an account of Jones' career prior to his appointment to Nyasaland see Colin Baker, *Sir Glyn Jones. A Proconsul in Africa* (London, 2000). I have also made use of my interview with Jones, Goudhurst, 21–22 August 1982.
[47] Macmillan to Macleod, 29 January 1960 quoted in Shepherd, *Iain Macleod*, p. 193.

Banda attempted to build on the gains achieved at Lancaster House, while Jones, on Macleod's instructions, tried to persuade him of the benefits to be obtained from maintaining some form of federal connection. A central issue concerned the fate of the last dozen detainees. Banda pressed for their release, conscious of the anomaly of their continued detention while he was free. But Macleod was initially reluctant to respond, having convinced himself that while Banda was a moderate favouring a non-violent approach to constitutional change, Chipembere and the Chisiza brothers were 'extremists' committed to a campaign of violent confrontation. There was little recognition that Banda's 'moderation' masked an implacable ruthlessness in obtaining his objectives or that Chipembere's shrill rhetoric was at odds with his thoughtful, even gentle personality. As Acting Governor in the absence of Armitage, Jones shared with Macleod his concern that 'Chipembere was a violent young man whose behaviour in detention showed that he was resolved to be as bitter and difficult at he could be.'[49] But he also felt the force of Banda's skilfully presented argument that unless the men were released he would lose control of his followers. Macleod agreed, on condition that Banda give an undertaking to cooperate with the Government and prevent any further disorders. This was accepted, and on 27 September Jones ordered the lifting of all restriction orders and the release of the remaining detainees. They were freed just in time to be paraded by Banda at the opening session of the MCP convention at Nkhotakota.

The release of the detainees was only one among a number of developments transforming the position of the MCP. Almost all settlers and many administrators continued to regard Banda and the party with loathing and contempt. But Jones had no doubt of the extent of the latter's support and the need to respond positively to it. A symbolic action – aimed particularly at challenging the ingrained racism of many Europeans – was his decision to resign as patron of the Zomba Gymkhana Club until it dropped its opposition to African membership. Of greater practical importance was his insistence that government officers seek to actively cooperate with the party rather than treating it uniformly as the enemy. In a carefully worded directive, provincial and district commissioners were informed that 'an increasing measure of circumspection must be exercised by... government servants, not to take courses of action which will precipitate political strife and prevent peaceful progress towards the end of responsible government.' Unqualified support should no longer be given to chiefs. Minor breaches of the law by nationalists could safely be disregarded. 'No Government should instruct its agents not to enforce the law, but...a discretion exists and political judgment must be exercised in furtherance of those political solutions on which the ultimate peace of the country must depend.'[50] In the months following Armitage's return in November, this message was interpreted conservatively so as to allow the prosecution not only of Chipembere but also of several local MCP leaders: at one point, Armitage even considered prosecuting Banda

---

[48] Banda to Jones, 16 March 1960 quoted in Short, *Glyn Jones*, p. 67; Jones, 'Report on Discussions between Dr. Banda and the Chief Secretary' enclosed in Jones to Monson, 16 March 1960, TNA CO 1015/2438.

[49] Note on meeting between the Chief Secretary and Dr Banda, 20 June 1960, Jones Papers, quoted in Baker, *Glyn Jones*, p. 69.

[50] Chief Secretary to Provincial Commissioners, 22 September 1960, quoted in Baker, *Sir Glyn Jones*, pp. 85–6.

– an action that would have put further negotiations at risk.[51] But when Jones took over as Governor in April 1961, the guidelines were relaxed once more, with predictable results. On the one hand, relations between MCP leaders and senior officials tended to improve, particularly if the officials were newcomers to Nyasaland: men appointed after the state of emergency had been lifted. On the other, assaults on opponents of the MCP could take place virtually unhindered by the state.

The 1961 elections

The elections of August 1961 marked the high point of democracy in colonial Malawi. For the first and last time prior to 1994, a significant number of ordinary people had the opportunity to vote for the party of their choice. Serious restrictions on full democratic accountability existed including, most obviously, the nature of the franchise, which limited the vote to little more than 110,000 people, of whom only 10,000 were women. Some cases of intimidation occurred in the run-up to the election. Nevertheless, there can be no doubt that the MCP, in its crushing victory, truly represented the voice of the people.

The electoral system, agreed at Lancaster House and refined by a constitutional working party whose recommendations were accepted by Macleod in December 1960, was a transitional arrangement, falling far short of Banda's demand for 'one man, one vote', yet considerably in advance of anything that had existed previously. Twenty-eight seats in the Legislative Council would be open for election, eight on the higher roll and 20 on the lower roll. The higher roll, although technically colour-blind, was aimed overwhelmingly at members of the small European and Asian communities. The much larger lower roll was open predominantly to Africans. On average, the electorate for each lower roll seat was nearly ten times higher than for each higher roll seat.

The nature of the franchise strongly favoured people with education, money or status. On the lower roll over 10,000 chiefs, headmen and councillors were enfranchised as a consequence of their position. Others were required to be literate in one of a number of languages, to have a minimum income, or to possess a certain amount of property. In a deliberate attempt to keep out youthful militants, literate tax payers were made eligible but only those who had paid tax continuously for up to ten years, a qualification that in practice raised the age level for most voters from 21 to 28. A contentious issue was the position of women. Dr Banda pressed for their enfranchisement only to meet considerable opposition, some of it from within his own party. The agreed compromise gave literate women the vote – but only if they had been married for up to ten years. In all, 10,185 women voters were registered. Of the 107,000 voters registered on the lower roll in a four week period of intense activity, all but 600 were African. On the higher roll, 2,895 voters out of a total of 4,401 (66%) were Europeans; 1,035 were Asians.[52]

The electoral campaign was the only one in the history of Malawi prior to 1994 in which more than one party was even marginally involved. MCP strength was overwhelmingly demonstrated in the remarkable number of branches it now

[51] Baker, *Armitage*, pp. 300–301.
[52] Lucy Mair, *The Nyasaland Elections of 1961* (Athlone Press, London, 1962), pp. 10–26.

possessed, approaching 1,800; in its phalanx of enthusiastic organisers, skilfully marshalled by the hard-working Dunduzu Chisiza; in its improving financial state; and in its access to a fleet of vehicles, some of them donated by Nkrumah, others by Julius Nyerere. A conspicuous feature was the extent to which Banda came to personify the party during the campaign. Acclaimed Life President, in contradiction to the original constitution of the MCP which stated that elections for the president would be held every three years, he strengthened his personal power by personally nominating all MCP candidates, in some cases in the face of opposition from within constituency branches.[53] In the campaign itself individual candidates were reduced to the position of 'representatives of Kamuzu'; party songs, on instructions from headquarters issued following Chipembere's imprisonment, praised only Banda and no other leader. At frequent meetings, Banda hammered home the central choice facing Malawians: 'SLAVERY WITHIN FEDERATION OR FREEDOM AND INDEPENDENCE OUTSIDE THE FEDERATION.'[54] But he also gave space to other issues: to the ending of *malimidwe* and to his personal campaign for women's rights.

The MCP's opponents in the election, the United Federal Party and the newly formed Christian Liberation Party, formed two minority strands in Malawian politics, neither of which should be entirely ignored. The Nyasaland branch of the UFP, now under the leadership of the Blantyre-based lawyer, Michael Blackwood, suffered from its reputation as a rump of the Rhodesian-based party, established with the aim 'to protect and further the interests of Europeans in Nyasaland'.[55] However, in the aftermath of the state of emergency it picked up several conspicuous African members, among them Matthews Phiri and Ralph Chinyama, both former NAC presidents; also Harry Jonga, a Blantyre trader who became party organiser for the Southern Province in February 1961.[56] Its electoral ambitions were concentrated largely on carrying all the higher roll seats and winning one or two on the lower roll. However, its non-racial pretensions were weakened both by its failure to nominate a single African, not even the party vice-president, Matthews Phiri, to an upper roll seat and by its frequently expressed opposition to any attempt to widen the franchise. Much of its activities in the run-up to the elections were devoted to complaining of MCP intimidation. This was a valid concern up to January 1961 but less so in the later stages of the campaign when, in the words of a report by the Special Branch, the Party's 'instructions to avoid provocative action which might lead to incidents were, generally, implicitly obeyed'.[57] Blackwood, supported by the UFP President, Welensky, attempted unsuccessfully to have the elections postponed following an incident late in July when nine houses, four of them owned by UFP members, were destroyed by fire. Later, the UFP candidate for the area and six other UFP supporters were convicted of having carried out the acts of arson themselves.[58]

[53] Ibid., pp. 45–6, 84.
[54] *Malawi News*, 1 May 1961 quoted in Short, *Banda*, p. 150–51.
[55] This was one of the aims included in the programme drawn up for the party in 1956. See Mair, *Nyasaland Elections*, p. 43.
[56] Ibid., p. 44.
[57] Special Branch, 'The Malawi Congress Party. Fourth Edition', 14 October 1961, TNA CO 1015/2445.
[58] Short, *Banda*, p. 152; Jones to Macleod, 4 October 1961, TNA CO 1015/2491.

Although it was electorally negligible, the Christian Liberation Party was in some senses a more significant organisation. Its origins lay in two separate parties: T. D. T. Banda's Congress Liberation Party and the Christian Democratic Party headed by Chester Katsonga. Both men fell into the category of disappointed NAC politician, Banda because he had been removed from the presidency of the NAC prior to Dr Banda's appointment; Katsonga because the financial sacrifices he had made in chairing the reception committee to greet Banda on his return to Nyasaland in 1958 had not been rewarded with promotion to senior office. Nevertheless, it would be wrong to dismiss their efforts too quickly. For a time, T. D. T. Banda did possess a degree of popular support, not only in his own district, Nkhata Bay, but also in Cholo and Mulanje where he was admired for his work among labour tenants. As for the CDP, Katsonga's frailties as a politician must be placed against the steadfast commitment to democracy demonstrated by some fellow-members of the party. Gilbert Pondeponde, co-founder and secretary of the CDP, is a particularly striking example.[59] A book-keeper employed by Lever Brothers, Pondeponde resigned from the MCP in protest against Dr Banda's appointment as president for life and later published a courageous article justifying the founding of the CDP on the grounds that 'One party is not enough for the political discussion in a country' and that 'This party wants everybody to be free to speak his mind without being intimidated.'[60] When in April 1961 the CDP amalgamated with the CLP under the new name of the Christian Liberation Party, Pondeponde became its secretary. Later still, after the electoral obliteration of the party in August he stuck to his principles, joining a further small opposition party, *Mbadwa*, in 1963. His murder at the hands of an MCP militant on Christmas Eve 1963 silenced a remarkably tenacious and independent-minded individual.[61]

The elections took place on 15 August. Although the final weeks of the campaign were largely free of blatant acts of political violence, the social pressure on members of minority parties was undoubtedly intense. Nevertheless, the commitment of ordinary people in expressing their views was not in doubt. By 6.30 am, when the polling stations opened, most voters had already gathered in silent queues. At one Central Province station, hundreds of voters assembled the night before.[62] In all lower roll constituencies, the turn-out was well over 90 per cent, an exceptionally high figure, while on the higher roll, an average of 85 per cent of those registered voted, ranging from 75 per cent in the Northern Province to 91 per cent in Limbe. In five lower roll constituencies, the MCP candidates were unopposed. Leaving them aside, 76,353 people went to the poll out of a total of 80,108 who had the opportunity to vote, a remarkable figure of 95.1 per cent.[63]

The results were a triumph for the MCP. In figures reminiscent of those obtained in the Soviet bloc, the Party took all 20 lower roll seats with an average of 99 per cent of the poll. Only in Lilongwe, where Chinyama was still remembered with affection, did an opposition candidate achieve more than 100 votes.

[59] For more on Pondeponde see Schoffeleers, *In Search of Truth*, pp. 86–90.
[60] Ibid., pp. 86–8.
[61] Ibid., pp. 88–90; de Jong, *Mission and Politics*, pp. 302–3.
[62] Mair, *Nyasaland Elections*, p. 79.
[63] Mair, p. 80; Governor's Address, *Second Meeting of the Seventy-sixth Session of the Legislative Council*, 28 November 1961.

On the higher roll the MCP also made significant inroads despite the deep hatred with which it was still regarded by many Europeans. Both of its two candidates were successful: Mikeka Mkandawire in the Northern Province and I. K. Surtees in the Central Province. Both, it was calculated, must have obtained a limited number of European votes. In addition, Colin Cameron, an MCP-supporting independent, won Soche, defeating an Asian UFP candidate through the support he obtained from MCP-voting Asians. All the other five higher roll seats went to the UFP but on lower majorities than it expected. No less than 43 per cent of higher roll votes went to candidates opposed to the UFP.[64]

The MCP's massive victory transformed the political climate. Up to then the Colonial Office had expected that the new Government as represented in the Executive Council would consist of five colonial officials, two UFP ministers and three from the MCP. On most crucial issues the UFP ministers could be counted on to vote with the officials thus leaving control in colonial hands. The MCP's success in taking seats on the upper roll drastically changed the equation. Blackwood initially argued that the UFP was still entitled to two ministers. But Jones rejected this request, and Blackwood, for his part, rejected Jones's compromise offer of one. The UFP, therefore, went into opposition leaving all five seats in MCP hands. In theory, Jones still had power to determine who should be ministers and for what portfolios. In practice, he largely deferred to Banda on this issue as he did on an increasing number of concerns. The fisherman 'playing' Banda was now himself being played. Despite Jones's reservations as to the wisdom of taking on two portfolios, Banda assigned to himself the important ministries of Natural Resources and Local Government. Kamwana Chiume was appointed Minister of Education; Augustine Bwanausi, a Makerere graduate in whose Blantyre house Chipembere and Chiume had planned their rise to power in 1955, became Minister of Labour.[65] Under the Lancaster House agreement, two ministries had to go to politicians elected on the higher roll. Cameron, a young Scottish lawyer closely associated with his fellow Scots in the CCAP, became Minister of Works. Mikeka Mkandawire, the one-time radical firebrand, was appointed Minister without Portfolio – a consolation prize for having reluctantly agreed to Banda's decision to nominate Chiume for Mkandawire's constituency, Rumphi. Two parliamentary secretaries were also appointed: Orton Chirwa for Justice and Dunduzu Chisiza for Finance. Both could complain that they had not been made ministers, but it was Banda's intention that they should shadow their expatriate ministers and take over from them when the time was ripe. Nevertheless, Dunduzu Chisiza in particular had grounds for regarding himself as ill-treated. A man of exceptional talents, who had 'greatly impressed' Jones on their first meeting, Chisiza had participated in discussions in Gwelo with Banda and Chipembere on the makeup of a Malawi government, never once believing that he would not be centrally involved.[66] It was the first sign that relations between him and Banda were becoming strained.

The composition of the newly elected legislative council provides a useful demonstration of the character of the Malawi Congress Party's political elite at this time and over the next two parliaments leading up to independence and

[64] Mair, pp. 80–81.
[65] Chiume, *Kwacha*, p. 65.
[66] Baker, *Glyn Jones*, p. 66; Baker, *Revolt of the Ministers*, p.38.

beyond. In making his nominations, Dr Banda had been constrained by a number of factors, including the requirement that candidates be proficient in English (a regulation that disqualified Lawrence Makata, the influential Blantyre businessman) and that they be at least 25 years of age (thus ensuring that Aleke Banda could not stand). More troublesome for him was the need he felt to dampen potential ethnic and regional divisions by ensuring that, as far as possible, candidates stood for their own home districts. This rule was breached in the case of Kanyama Chiume who was nominated, in the face of considerable local opposition, for the Rumphi seat to allow his fellow-Tonga, Orton Chirwa, to stand for the Nkhata Bay constituency. But it was enforced in the case of Yatuta Chisiza who had to cede the Karonga seat to his younger brother, Dunduzu, while witnessing nonentities of the correct ethnic background being nominated to Cholo and Lilongwe North. Overall, however, the composition of the council accurately reflected the nature of the MCP's leadership. Dr Banda, now aged 63, with his numerous degrees and his lengthy experience in professional employment in Britain, stood separate from the rest, who were broadly divided into two overlapping categories: students turned politicians and party bosses.[67]

The largest group, eight in all if Chipembere is included instead of his father, who took his place as representative for Fort Johnston during the former's time in gaol, was composed of students turned politicians – men drawn from the tiny group who had completed secondary education and, in the case of all save Dunduzu Chisiza, had gone on to university. Aged only 32 on average (Orton Chirwa was the oldest at 42, John Tembo the youngest at 29), these men had all spent several formative years outside Nyasaland and, in several cases, had participated together in the Nyasaland Students' Association prior to their active involvement in the NAC.[68] From 1956, initially under the leadership of Chipembere and Chiume, they had spearheaded political advances in Nyasaland. Now, as members of the Legislative Council, they had every expectation that their superior academic qualifications would lead them almost automatically into ministerial office. All but one of the first group of ministerial appointments (the exception was Mikeka Mkandawire) fit into this category as do two additional appointments, John Msonthi and Willie Chokani, made in March 1962.

The second group, 'party bosses', formed an alternative and, in the long run, more successful source of power: men who owed their position primarily to their skill in maintaining and expanding the party machine at local and regional level. They were generally somewhat older than their rivals, with an average age of 38 in 1961. They were also much less well qualified academically (only the youngest in the group, the 26–year-old Gwanda Chakuamba, had been to secondary school). Nevertheless, the varied experiences and strong sense of survival that characterised these men made them formidable opponents. Richard Chidzanja, the MCP regional chairman for the Central Province, personified these trends. A Chewa militant, born near Nathenje in the heart of the Central Province tobacco industry, Chidzanja left school after standard three and spent several years working in South African hotels. He then returned to Nyasaland and, like

---

[67] The details that follow are drawn largely from a series of brief biographies of MCP lower roll candidates, *Malawi News*, 20 July 1960. See also *Malawi News*, 19 October 1962 and 15 March 1963.

[68] Chiume, *Kwacha*, p. 51; Rotberg (ed.), *Hero of Nation*, 143.

several other leading politician-businessmen, used his savings to start his own business as a road haulier. Frustrated by the near-monopoly established by European and Indian transporters over the movement of crops purchased by the Agricultural Produce and Marketing Board, he became an active member of the African Road Transporters' Association as well as district, later regional chairman of the NAC. Initially suspicious of Kamuzu Banda as one of the *machona* who had lost touch with their homeland, Chidzanja developed a fierce loyalty towards him, as did other party bosses, once it became clear that Banda's Western tastes were combined with a passionate belief in the importance of traditional Chewa/Malawian values. Others who fit within this category include the two other regional chairmen, Qabaniso Chibambo, exiled to Port Herald for eight years by the British, and Gomile Kumtumanji, a one-time medical assistant who had been deported back to Blantyre from Southern Rhodesia on account of his political activities. Gwanda Chakuamba, although the youngest of the group, had already spent eight years of his life immersed in the politics of the Lower River where he was MCP district chairman. And he in turn was joined by several journeymen organisers, including Hexter Massa, born near Dowa and for several years treasurer of the important NAC Northern Rhodesian branch.

Groups that that were barely or not at all represented are also worthy of attention. No women candidates were chosen in 1961, no trade unionists, and only one Catholic, the schoolteacher, John Msonthi, although by this period Catholics were the most numerous group of Christians in Nyasaland. By contrast, at least 13 members had been brought up in the CCAP (four in the DRC section, nine in the Livingstonia and Blantyre spheres). Only one Muslim, Kumtumanji, the powerful Southern Province Regional Chairman, and one 'Coloured', Ismail Kassam Surtees, the leader of the Coloured Association, were nominated by Banda. The son of a prominent Indian trader with a string of stores in the Central Province, Surtees was elected on the higher roll.[69] His presence alongside that of Colin Cameron demonstrated the non-racist pretensions of the party. Regional representation strictly followed the provincial allocation of lower roll seats. However, four out of the six Africans nominated by Banda for government office came from the north: a matter of some subsequent grievance to southerners but recognised at the time as a pragmatic decision based on the abilities of the men concerned.

The road to secession

Two main issues confronted the new Government between 1961 and 1963: constitutional change and the nature of the new Malawi. On a number of levels, these demonstrate Banda at his best: shrewd, determined, skilful in his alternative deployment of charm and threat in negotiations with the British; utterly focused on his long-term objectives. Even after independence, it was only occasionally that a Malawian government acted as effectively as it did at this time. Yet, as Matthew Schoffeleers has noted, this period was also 'decisive as regards the founding of the MCP's police state'.[70] Moreover, this was the time in which divisions among MCP

---

[69] *Malawi News*, October 19 1962.
[70] Schoffeleers, *Truth and Justice*, p. 15.

politicians and within Malawian society began to be clearly articulated.

There was never any doubt that Banda – and Banda alone – would conduct negotiations with the British. 'Banda has on several occasions emphasised both to me and to Foster [the new Chief Secretary] that he is himself solely responsible for M.C.P. policy and the policy to be adopted by the elected members of Executive Council', Jones told Macleod only a few weeks after the elections. 'He has told me that he lays down the policy without consulting them. "If they do not like this they can lump it or sack me, but I have made quite plain from the start that I impose my own policy on the party."' [71]

The central issue, returned to time and again in meetings not only with the Governor but with a succession of high-ranking British ministers, was that of Nyasaland's secession from the Federation. Following his visit to Nyasaland in January 1960, Macmillan had reached the conclusion, already accepted by Macleod, that 'the cause of Federation was almost desperate because of the strength of African opinion against it.'[72] Further ammunition was supplied in the report of the Monckton Commission, published in October 1960. Set up to review the federal constitution in the face of considerable nationalist suspicion, the Commission recommended the need for widespread changes in the structure of the Federation and, crucially, advised the British Government to permit territories to secede in certain defined circumstances.

Nevertheless, the MCP's overwhelming victory left a number of questions to be resolved. In a striking reverse of Armitage's position, Glyn Jones now operated as a staunch ally of Banda, noting in a meeting with Colonial Office officials on 30 October, that 'Dr Banda won the recent election on a clear "secession" platform and it was certain that this policy had almost universal support.'[73] Time and again in subsequent meetings and despatches, he returned to the theme, emphasising that 'Banda has over 90 per cent support in Nyasaland for his secession policy' and warning of the disturbances that would result if his concerns were not fully met.[74]

For ministers in London, however, tacit acceptance that Nyasaland would eventually become independent was accompanied by recognition of the virtues of delay. The central problem, as in the late 1950s, was the likely consequences of Nyasaland's secession on developments in Northern and Southern Rhodesia where the existence of substantial European minorities raised the possibility of an attempted white-backed *coup d'état* to throw off British rule. Reginald Maudling, who replaced Macleod as Colonial Secretary in October 1961, shared his predecessor's belief in the need for continued constitutional change but he was also keenly aware of the antagonisms that Macleod had aroused within powerful sections of the Conservative Party in Britain where support for Roy Welensky remained strong. His main concern, therefore, on a short visit he made to Nyasaland in November, was to respond sympathetically to the proposal that Banda should be given the title of 'Chief Minister' as the other ministers had suggested, but not to commit himself officially on the issue of secession.[75]

[71] Jones to Macleod, 4 October 1961, TNA DO 158/25.
[72] Macmillan, *Pointing the Way*, pp. 148–49.
[73] Note of a meeting held at Church House on 30 October 1961, TNA DO 158/25.
[74] Jones to Maudling, 20 February 1962, TNA CO 1015/2255.
[75] Baker, *Glyn Jones*, pp.105–07.

More substantial proposals, when they emerged, came from an unexpected source. Duncan Sandys, the son-in-law of Sir Winston Churchill, was an energetic hard-line right-winger appointed by Macmillan in July 1960 as Commonwealth Secretary in succession to Lord Home. In February 1962 he met Banda in Zomba and was left in no doubt concerning his views. 'He will not negotiate with anybody about anything until Nyasaland is out of the Federation', Sandys reported. 'He said that if Welensky wished to keep Nyasaland in the Federation, he would have to send in his army.' Sandys's response was influenced by the proposal, currently being floated by the Southern Rhodesian Prime Minister, Edgar Whitehead, for the creation of a Bantustan-type arrangement in which Nyasaland would be allowed to secede along with the poorest parts of Northern Rhodesia, leaving Southern Rhodesia to join with the Copperbelt and the Central district of Northern Rhodesia in a slimmed-down, white-dominated Central African state.[76] With this in mind, Sandys, according to Jones, 'promised that the British Government would let Banda know one way or the other within a month, whether it would allow him to secede from the Federation'. Jones further commented: 'Mr Sandys repeatedly said that he could not commit the British Government one way or the other but the discussion was such that I am pretty certain that Banda has been left with the impression that the answer will be favourable to him.' [77] In a separate note, Sandys suggested: 'The best and most dignified procedure would be for Welensky to take the initiative himself by declaring that he has no wish to retain an unwilling partner in the Federation and that he is therefore asking the British Government to make arrangements for the secession of Nyasaland, in accordance with the wishes expressed by its people.'[78]

Sandys' ill-timed promise (made in a territory over which he had no responsibility and without the agreement of the British cabinet) marked the beginning of a period of intense diplomatic activity. On 13 February, Duncan Watson, a senior official in the Colonial Office, drafted an initial response. Gone were the obfuscations of earlier reports. His first sentence read: 'It is now apparent that the present Federation creates an unreal and unworkable political situation, which will explode violently very soon if it is not otherwise resolved.' All attempts to reconcile Africans with the Federation had failed. 'It is now abundantly clear that Nyasaland cannot be held within the present Federation.' Yet it was a fallacy to believe that the two Rhodesias could be held together once Nyasaland had gone. His conclusion was that 'the situation…should be faced immediately and the demise of the present Federation accepted, as the starting point for an energetic attempt to create a form of association on a realistic basis.'[79] Sir Edgar Hone, the Governor of Northern Rhodesia, added to this analysis although from a different direction. Sandys's proposals for the division of Northern Rhodesia he regarded as totally unacceptable: 'I pointed out the very considerable and in my view fundamental objections to any proposal for

[76] 'Review of Recent Discussions with Political Leaders in the Federation on the Future of the Federation', Central African Office, May 1962. TNA DO 183/142; Sir Edward Hone to Maudling, 17 February 1962, TNA CO 1915/2255. See also Wood, *Welensky Papers*, pp. 1000–004, 1028–033.

[77] Jones to W.B.L Monson, Colonial Office, 17 February 1962, TNA DO 158/25.

[78] Sandys to the Cabinet, 12 February 1962, TNA DO 158/25.

[79] N.D. Watson, 'The Elements of the Federal Problem in Central Africa, 13 February 1962, TNA CO 1015/2255.

carving up Northern Rhodesia in this manner.' Popular consent could not be obtained. The interests and feelings of the people would be flouted.[80]

In London, however, powerful factions still favoured caution. Sir Leslie Monson, Head of the Africa Desk at the Colonial Office, shared Watson's view that the Federation had failed but urged delay in going public on the issue. As he shrewdly noted, 'I imagine that in terms of the political situation in this country Ministers would prefer not to have to take the initiative in making a statement unless there was no other way of resolving the dilemma available to them.'[81] Sure enough, Macmillan, faced by an irate Welensky who made a sudden visit to Britain early in March, moved with conspicuous lack of haste. Whitehead's partition proposal, now supported by Welensky, was discussed at several high level meetings but without any decision being taken. Welensky was questioned on how to respond to Banda but refused to give a positive reply.[82] By the time that Macmillan, on 16 March, had taken the overdue step of creating a single ministry to deal with Central African Affairs under the immensely experienced R. A. Butler, no further progress had been made.

The effective dialogue established between Butler and Banda was a significant feature in Nyasaland's smooth transition to full self-government and then to independence. In many respects, it was Banda who made the concessions. Butler came to his new post already convinced that the Federation had no future but anxious to seek 'a composite solution' to its problems rather than making a unilateral decision on Nyasaland alone.[83] He was therefore prepared to renege on the undertaking given to Banda by Sandys that the British Government would give him an immediate answer on the question of Nyasaland's secession. 'The Conservative party were not prepared for an announcement on secession and there would be inevitable criticism that it was too soon', he told a specially convened meeting of Governors. 'He had not yet had time to consult the Cabinet or his supporters, and this proposal would come as a shock.'[84] Instead, he proposed the appointment of a commission of advisers under the chairmanship of Sir Roger Stevens of the Foreign Office to examine 'before any final conclusion is reached, the economic and financial consequences for Nyasaland of withdrawal from the Federation.'[85] The fact that Duncan Watson, the author of the anti-Federation report quoted above, was one of its members provided an indication of what its findings were likely to be.

At an earlier stage, Banda might well have reacted angrily, cutting off negotiations in response to what he could legitimately argue was a breach of trust. But now, as the leader of a governing party actively involved in putting through a radical reform programme, his inclination was to compromise. On 9 April he discussed the proposals with Jones and received from the Governor his personal assurance that they were made in good faith and not as a delaying tactic.[86] He therefore agreed to a delay until 8 May, when Butler announced in the House of Commons the appointment of advisers and, in somewhat Delphic tones,

80 Hone to Maudling, 17 February 1962, CO 1015/2255.
81 Note by W.B.L. Monson, 14 February 1962, CO 1015/2255.
82 Wood, *Welensky Papers*, pp. 1011–19.
83 Lamb, *Macmillan Years*, pp. 272–73; Baker, *Glyn Jones*, p. 126.
84 Quoted in Baker, *Glyn Jones*, p. 127.
85 Quoted in W.P. Kirkman, *Unscrambling an Empire* (London, 1966), p. 124.
86 Baker, *Glyn Jones*.

acknowledged the right of Nyasaland to secede. A week later, on 15 May, Butler flew to Zomba. Over the next four days he held a series of meetings with Banda during which the two men developed a real measure of mutual respect. Butler from the first allowed it to be understood that the appointment of advisers was a necessary step on the inevitable path to Nyasaland's secession. Banda, for his part, made clear that whatever the advisers recommended, he and his people were determined to secede.[87] The central discussions, therefore, focused not on the political outcome, about which both men were in broad agreement, but rather on the procedure and timing, over which several heated arguments ensued. Banda initially pressed for full self government in July 1962 and independence in April 1963; Butler replied that this programme was much too fast. Butler demanded that a further conference should be held before Nyasaland's constitution was changed; Banda was initially opposed but finally agreed. Butler pressed for the continuation of some kind of association with the Rhodesias after independence, Banda made clear that any association would be token at the best.[88]

Several historians have utilised the self-congratulatory accounts of British ministers and officials to emphasise the skill with which Butler 'handled' Banda during the negotiations. Butler is presented as an Olympian figure, 'standing firm' when Banda became 'very heated'; 'calling his bluff' when Banda resorted to threats; acting tactfully when Banda was 'petulant' and behaving reasonably when Banda was in an 'excitable mood'.[89] But if the end result was 'a remarkably successful piece of negotiation' for Britain (the words of a colonial official), it was also in a very real sense a triumph for Malawi.[90] For all his occasional and often deliberately staged volcanic rages, Banda was a realist when it came to the transfer of authority, perfectly prepared to compromise on the precise date of independence as long as there was no dispute concerning the reality of power. What Butler gained was a few more months in the interminable debate with Welensky and the right wing of the Conservative party before the fate of the Federation was finally settled. What Banda obtained was much more important: Britain's tacit acceptance, reinforced in October by the report of Butler's advisers, that Nyasaland would secede and the promise of constitutional changes that would bring about the transfer of power.

The mechanisms for change were hammered out at the Marlborough House Conference convened in London on 12 November 1962. Banda in his opening speech expressed his basic aims:

> When I came here in 1960 I said I came in a spirit of give and take. This time I have come in a spirit of take – to take what is mine by conquest at the ballot box and by successful and creditable performance in office.[91]

The agreement, announced at the end of the conference on 23 November, shifted power irretrievably into Malawian hands. Constitutional change would

---

[87] Lamb, *Macmillan Years*, pp. 272–25.
[88] For details of the discussions see Lamb, ibid.; Baker, *Glyn Jones*, pp. 133–33.
[89] See Baker, *Glyn Jones*, pp. 131–35; Lamb, *Macmillan Years*, pp. 273–75; Lord Butler, *The Art of the Possible* (London, 1971) pp. 210–22.
[90] Quoted in Baker, *Glyn Jones*, p. 135.
[91] Quoted in Short, *Banda*, p. 159.

take place in two steps, the first to be completed by February 1963. Banda would become Prime Minister (he had rejected the earlier proposal that he be called Chief Minister because the change in name did not involve a substantial increase in powers). There would be a cabinet of ten selected by the Prime Minister and including for an interim period Henry Phillips, the Financial Secretary, who would become Minister of Finance. As a second step, there would be a new constitution, an increased number of members and the widening of the franchise (in effect, the introduction of universal suffrage). One man one vote would become a reality – the irony was that in practice no voting would take place in parliamentary elections for the next 40 years.[92]

Issues of contention were discussed not in open sessions but in private meetings between Banda and Butler. Even before the conference began, Butler told Banda in confidence that he was now committed to announce in Parliament in the week beginning 17 December that Nyasaland could withdraw from the Federation.[93] No agreement was reached on the precise date of independence but Butler conceded that it would not be far off Banda's proposed target of April 1964. A potentially contentious issue was the respective powers of the Governor and Prime Minister, although such was Banda's faith in Jones that he was prepared to make concessions in this area, knowing that Jones was likely to delegate authority to him. Responsibility for the civil service for a limited period, therefore, remained in the Governor's hands; Jones promised to consult Banda on appointments and promotions. By the same token, the Governor retained responsibility for public order and public safety, including the operations of the police, but with the important provision that he could delegate this authority to the Prime Minister as, in practice, he was to do.[94] At Banda's insistence, it was agreed that Peter Youens, the deputy chief secretary and his long term acquaintance, would become secretary to the Prime Minister and the cabinet.[95] Even at this stage, it is clear that Banda was anxious to surround himself with expatriates he could trust.

The official announcement made by Butler in the House of Commons on 19 December, that Nyasaland would secede from the Federation, brought to an end one of the most tortuous episodes in the history of British decolonisation. Exactly when secession became inevitable is by no means easy to determine, but three aspects of the process are worthy of note. First, it is clear that the events of 1959 – the extent and severity of violent opposition on the ground in Nyasaland, the continuing evidence of popular opposition even after the arrest of the NAC leaders, and the publication of the Devlin Report – combined to bring about a political crisis that could be resolved only by actions that would put the future of the Federation at risk. Once Banda was accepted as a legitimate politician to be negotiated with rather than kept in continued imprisonment, the likelihood was always that sooner or later British politicians would agree to make concessions to him. His release and the Lancaster House agreement were not intended to bring Federation to an end but it is difficult to see how they could have had any other outcome.

[92] Short, *Banda*, p. 160.
[93] Baker, *Glyn Jones*, p. 151.
[94] Ibid., pp. 154–56.
[95] Ibid., p. 155. Youens was the colonial officer deputed to accompany Banda on his release from Gwelo prison on 1 April 1960.

The second point leads directly from the first. Banda's key card from April 1960, regularly produced in negotiations but never played, was the threat, couched in a variety of ways that if he did not obtain his objectives through negotiation then large-scale disturbances would result. As he told Sandys in February 1962, 'If the British Government wished to maintain the Federation as constituted at present it would have to send an army to Nyasaland to deal with the revolt that would ensue.'[96] The crucial issue was how policy makers responded to the warning, and here it is important to recognise that politicians in Britain by the early 1960s, with the example of France's long struggle in Algeria before them, were becoming increasingly anxious not to be drawn into unwinnable colonial wars. This was a matter on which Macleod and Macmillan reached full agreement when they met to discuss the future of the Federation in November 1960. 'The Prime Minister and the Colonial Secretary...said that they did not want an Algeria. That was the crux of the matter.'[97] Lessons from outside Central Africa, moreover, were compounded by the particular problems of colonial defence within. As Prime Minister of the Federation with responsibility for defence, Welensky made every effort to exclude British troops from the area. But by the same token, in the aftermath of the state of emergency, Armitage and later Jones repeatedly vetoed the employment of white Federal reservists whose presence in Nyasaland would have been regarded as dangerously provocative.[98] With Macmillan's agreement, the strength of the police force was nearly doubled between early 1959 and June 1961 at a cost to Britain of £1,523,000 – an indication that Britain was determined to avoid a repeat of the disastrous disintegration of authority experienced in the Congo at the time of the Belgian withdrawal. Nevertheless, in the final analysis, successive ministers were always readier to make concessions to Banda and the MCP than they were to risk a violent confrontation that they were ill equipped to pursue.[99]

The final point concerns the trajectory of colonial policy. Reading the diaries and reports of the stream of important visitors who made their way to Zomba in the aftermath of the publication of the Devlin Report, it is clear that hardly one – not Burke Trend of the Cabinet Office in October 1959, not Macmillan nor David Hunt, his assistant from the Commonwealth Relations Office in February 1960 and not Macleod in April 1960 – had any doubt that Nyasaland, to quote Trend, 'must become a black state in the not too distant future' and that Federation was almost certainly doomed.[100] Translating inner conviction into public policy, however, was a very different matter. Not only did policy makers continue to emphasise the economic advantages of Federation and the irrationality demonstrated by nationalists in opposing it, they also increasingly backed away from any clear public statement, fearful of the political damage that would result. On any rational grounds, the MCP's crushing victory in the elections of August 1961 made secession certain as long as Banda continued to press for it. But it was

---

[96] Quoted in Baker, *Glyn Jones*, p. 118.
[97] Note by Wyndham on discussions between Macmillan and Macleod, 13 November 1960 quoted in Shepherd, *Iain Macleod*, p. 212.
[98] McCracken, 'Authority and Legitimacy', pp. 176–78.
[99] Ibid., p. 178; McCracken, 'Coercion and Control', pp. 140–41.
[100] Quoted in Lamb, *Macmillan Years*, p. 243. For Hunt's account see Hunt to Clutterbuck, 2 February 1960, TNA CO 1015/2255; Sir David Hunt, *On the Spot. An Ambassador Remembers* (London, 1975), p. 108.

not until February 1962 and Duncan Watson's paper, that senior officials in the Colonial Office were prepared to state in writing what Jones had been telling them for months. Even then, it was not until 3 November that Butler officially informed Welensky that he had taken the decision to let Nyasaland go.[101]

The MCP in Government, 1961–63

It is difficult to appreciate the sense of sheer excitement felt by MCP ministers in the aftermath of the 1961 elections. With one exception, that of Chiume, no one – not even Banda – had experience of sitting in a Legislative Council, far less of holding a ministry. Now as they moved into their new offices, staffed even down to the secretaries, largely by Europeans, there was a sense of cultural as well as political revolution in the air. On the European side, particularly among junior staff, there was plenty of apprehension, fear that a way of life was ending, concern about pensions, and disdain for 'Malawi spivs ... Africans with shiny briefcases ... talking in loud, convoluted English', who now frequented the corridors of the Secretariat.[102] According to one keen observer of fashion, European staff took to shorts and open-necked shirts at precisely the time that the first African ministers arrived, dressed like Banda in smart dark suits.[103] Similar suspicions were not unknown among the ministers. Allocated one of the first African secretaries, a beautiful young woman aged about 21 (or so he tells us), Kanyama Chiume became obsessed with the notion that she was a Federal spy, sending papers from his office to Welensky's agents in Salisbury.[104]

Yet if mutual suspicions abounded, this was a period when a number of significant government initiatives were taken. Banda led the way as Minister of Natural Resources by introducing three key measures of profound importance for Malawi's peasantry at that time and for many years to come. Despite his genuinely impressive grasp of European and world history, Banda's insights into development were confined to a limited number of propositions including considerable scepticism concerning the relevance of fashionable Marxist approaches and a belief in the importance of stimulating agricultural growth in a predominantly agricultural country. On certain specific issues, however, his mind was clear. First, *malimidwe*, the notorious agricultural regulations must go, to be replaced by a gentler conservation regime in which persuasion replaced compulsion as the guiding principle. Second, *thangata* must be finally ended, some 15 years after Abrahams had first recommended that it be abolished. Third, the whole system of marketing peasants' crops must be reformed, although Banda was initially unclear as to what would take its place. Altogether, these reforms involved an immensely popular response to genuinely widely-held peasant grievances. But they also provided Banda with the opportunity to introduce economic structures that that he would use to his own advantage after independence.

There is good reason for arguing that by 1959, *malimidwe* was to all intents

[101] Alport to Butler, 3 December 1962, TNA DO 183/232.
[102] Davidson, *The Real Paradise*, pp. 452–3.
[103] Ibid., p. 454.
[104] Chiume, *Kwacha*, p. 145.

and purposes dead. Even before the emergency there had been a marked decline in convictions for agricultural offences in Native Courts – from a figure of about 8,100 in 1956 down to 1,800 in 1959.[105] All over Malawi, land reorganisation schemes were abandoned under the pressure of popular opinion. Bunds were frequently broken without any punitive action being taken in return.[106] By May 1960, so Kettlewell explained to Banda in one of their very few meetings, agricultural staff had largely abandoned coercive actions. 'It was… now their sole aim and wish to see Government's policy of helping the more progressive farmers made effective.'[107] In an isolated incident in 1960, the District Commissioner at Port Herald sent a contingent of the Police Mobile Force into Mollen Tengani's area in an attempt to enforce *malimidwe* and bolster the chief's flagging fortunes. So strong, however, was the response of Banda and the MCP to this that the action was not repeated. Enraged by reports that villagers, including women, had been beaten and ill-treated, Banda went in person to Port Herald where he publicly rebuked both the chief and the district officer.[108] In a follow up move, he published a notice in the *Malawi News*, calling on chiefs and district commissioner to abide by Kettlewell's assurance 'that no persons will be prosecuted any more for failure to observe the agricultural rules'.[109]

With Banda's appointment as Minister of Natural Resources in September 1961 colonial soil conservation policy was finally put to rest. Shunning the advice of Kettlewell, who was now moved to the Department of Lands, Surveys and Geology prior to his departure from Nyasaland, Banda immediately informed agricultural staff that from now on the agricultural rules should be applied by persuasion only.[110] Ten months later, in May 1962, he introduced the Land Use and Protection Bill to replace the now discredited Natural Resources Ordinance of 1952 – a measure, so Banda noted, that had 'regimented' the African farmers of Nyasaland 'almost as rigidly as farmers behind the iron curtain or the bamboo curtain.'[111] In his speech, as in all his interventions on the subject, Banda went out of his way to support the principle of 'scientific' farming designed to conserve natural resources while totally rejecting the methods that had been used. In his view, 'you cannot coerce people into good farmers. You only embitter them … Farmers the world over are conservative by nature and very independent. They do not like being treated like children by anyone.' His methods instead were 'those of persuasion and not coercion.' A Land Use and Protectionary Advisory Council would be established linked in turn to a number of area committees. In theory at least peasants would be intimately involved in the working of the committees. Serious offences, such as the diversion of water channels could still be punished by imprisonment and fines of up to £50. Otherwise, all punishments would be abolished.[112]

[105] *Agricultural Reports for 1956, 1958 and 1959;* Kettlewell to Acting Director, Agriculture, 14 May 1960, CO 1015/2349.
[106] *Annual Report on African Affairs,* 1959, CO 626/36.
[107] Kettlewell to Acting Director of Agriculture, 14 May 1960, reporting on his meeting with Banda, CO 1015/2349.
[108] *Malawi News,* 17 September 1960. See also Mandala, *Work and Control,* pp. 236–37.
[109] *Malawi News,* 17 September 1960.
[110] Speeches by Banda, *Proceedings of the Legislative Council, 28 November 1961; 30 May 1962;* Kettlewell, 'Memories of a Colonial Career'.
[111] Speech by Banda, *Proceedings of the Legislative Council, 30 May 1962.*
[112] Speech by Banda, ibid., 32 May 1962.

In a separate initiative, the Master Farmers' Scheme, aimed at encouraging the emergence of a group of 'progressive' farmers, was brought to an end and most of the surviving land reorganisation schemes were halted. Banda, unlike several of his ministers, continued to insist on the importance of maintaining contour ridges (*misere*), now widely adopted in Nyasaland and perhaps the most important positive legacy of the colonial government's soil conservation programme.[113] Other colonial initiatives, however, suffered a more uncertain fate. Colonial advice on early planting continued to be followed, but over much of the country, bunds appear to have been abandoned. Of greater concern, encroachment on forests accelerated despite Banda's call for continued preservation.[114] Land improvement schemes suffered particularly badly. Out of 30 in existence in 1959 covering a total area of some 200,000 acres all that remained in 1963 were a few stray ends of fencing around land given over to grazing and the odd barely discernable hummock where bunds and ridges had once been.[115]

In later years Dr Banda repeatedly boasted of two central achievements: that he had broken the 'stupid Federation' and that he had brought *thangata* to an end. Both claims are exaggerated but just as there is a kernel of truth in the first assertion so there is in the second. By 1958, well over 400,000 acres of European-owned land had been purchased by the Government, bringing the number of tenants living on private estates in the Shire Highlands down to less than 80,000 from over 170,000 in 1945. This, however, had been done through financial inducements rather than by legislative action, with the result that many undeveloped estates still survived into the early 1960s, situated alongside areas of highly congested Trust Land. For over three years, no further estates were given up and tension once more grew, fuelled by the restrictive 1952 Ordinance which denied rights of residency to the children and dependents of tenants and banned them from cutting building materials or firewood.[116] The continuation of *thangata*, Armitage noted in December 1960, was one of the greatest threats the government faced. 'I am deeply concerned about the potential danger to our security situation created by the progressive worsening of this festering sore in one of the most sensitive parts of the Protectorate and the one contributing most to the economy.'[117]

It was against this background that Banda, in one of his most impressive parliamentary performances, introduced the Africans on Private Estates bill in May 1962. Abandoning the gradualist approach that had dominated previously, he made clear his conviction that 'the process of acquiring land by the Government from the estate owners is far too slow... As a solution to the problem of *thangata* it cannot be entirely relied upon to achieve the result which the seriousness and urgency of the situation demands.'[118] His solution was not to attack the property rights of estate owners directly but rather to put pressure on them either to sell the land to the government or to farm it through the employment

[113] *Malawi News*, 2 November 1961.

[114] *Malawi News*, 15 February 1962.

[115] Peter F.M. McLoughlin, 'Land Reorganization in Malawi, 1950–60: its pertinence to current development' in Sayre P. Schatz (ed.), *South of Sahara: Development in African Economics* (Philadelphia, 1972), pp. 130–32.

[116] Central African Department, 'Land and the Thangata System', brief for the Secretary of State's visit to Central Africa, February 1960, TNA CO 1015/2161. See also Baker, *Seeds of Trouble*, pp. 167–68.

[117] Armitage to W.L. Gorrell-Jones, 1 December 1960, TNA CO 1015/2161.

[118] Opening speech by Banda, *Proceedings of the Legislative Council*, 31 May 1962.

of wage labourers. Tenant rights were vastly increased over those introduced in 1952 through the provision that children and dependents would be counted as residents. Restrictions on the collection of firewood or the cultivation of food crops were abandoned. Rents were reduced to a nominal £1 a year and many people were exempted entirely, including unmarried women and the wives of resident men. No tenant would be required to work for an estate owner. Equally, he or she could offer to work outside the rainy season and the estate owner could not refuse. Overshadowing everything was Banda's clear warning to estate owners: 'My intention is to abolish *thangata* altogether but I have drafted this Bill to give them a chance … to sell their land, wherever there are Africans, to the Government so that the Government can use that land the way it wants to use.'[119]

In retrospect, Banda's campaign against *thangata* is as important for what it did not contain as for what it did. Presented as a radical measure, the bill made no provision for compulsory purchase and indeed, in its general approach, went little further than the recommendations made in 1954 by the Land Adviser to the Colonial Office, S. R. Simpson, for the abolition of labour requirements and the reduction of rent to a nominal sum.[120] However, while Simpson's proposals had provoked a successful counter-attack from settlers and the Nyasaland government, Banda's, in 1962, were received with a surprising measure of acceptance. Michael Blackwood, the settler leader, went out of his way 'to urge all estate owners to co-operate to the full with the Government in solving this problem and solving it quickly'[121] and the Colonial Office, alarmed by evidence that squatters were beginning to move onto estates, also gave Banda's measure its support. Following extensive negotiations throughout 1961, colonial officials had persuaded an initially reluctant Treasury to free over £400,000 from CDW funds to allow the last group of Shire Highland estate owners to be bought out on favourable terms, with the surplus being used to resettle families on the land.[122] With generous compensation now available, most estate owners had little hesitation in complying. In 1962, they sold 133,000 acres to the Government; in 1963, they sold another 102,272 acres.[123] Even the British Central Africa Company, for long the most reluctant to relinquish land, accepted the new approach. Shortly before the Company was bought out by Lonrho – the first of the aggressive new concerns that were to dominate post-colonial enterprise in Malawi – the chairman signalled the change of policy:

> In my view it would be entirely unrealistic today to envisage that the Company can retain large tracts of land which are surplus to its requirements … there is an ever growing hunger for land … and in these circumstances we may expect to be approached by Government with a view to the acquisition of all land at present owned by the Company and not required for its tea and sisal operations. The extension of Government areas may be expected to help in the very pressing problem of encroachment on the Company's existing plantations.[124]

[119] Concluding speech by Banda, *Proceedings of the Legislative Council*, 31 May 1962.
[120] Baker, *Seeds of Trouble*, pp. 124–26.
[121] Speech by Blackwood, *Proceedings of the Legislative Council*, 31 May 1962.
[122] Armitage to Colonial Secretary, 10 April 1961; K. J. Neale, Colonial Office, to E.G. Burnett, Commonwealth Relations Office, 7 September 1961; R.L. Baxter to E.G. Burrett, Treasury, 21 June 1961, CO 1015/2161.
[123] Baker, *Seeds of Trouble*, p. 170.
[124] Quoted in ibid., p. 166.

What, in fact, was envisaged was a tacit agreement where underutilised land or land heavily occupied by tenants was given up and land used in tea planting or in other intensive estate operations remained in private hands. At the same time, estate owners now turned to the new Government for support in blunting the threat of landless squatters who had begun to move in increasing numbers and with growing confidence onto the remaining Mulanje and Cholo estates.

The challenge from landless squatters was overshadowed for estate owners in the Central Province by the threat that Banda's proposals appeared to pose to the visiting tenant system. Prior to 1962, settlers in the area had believed that the MCP would concentrate the full weight of its reforming energies on the Shire Highlands, leaving the north relatively unscathed. In the debate on the Africans on Private Estates Ordinance, however, such hopes were rudely shattered. In introducing the bill, Dr Banda confined his comments to the Shire Highlands but when John Msonthi, the member for Dedza, called for its measures to be extended to his area, Banda responded positively:

> Whether you call it *thangata* in the Southern Province or visiting tenants in the Central Province, it is the same thing and I was not going to be deceived and confine this Bill to the Southern Province. I mean to extend it to Lilongwe, Fort Manning, Kasungu, Dowa, Kota Kota, right up to Karonga.[125]

Banda once more emphasised that he had no objection to private landlords employing direct labour but tenant schemes would not be allowed, 'and if that means I am driving anyone away from this country, then I say he can pack up and go.' All tenants under the new Bill would automatically become permanent residents, thus destroying the right to evict tenants that landlords had previously enjoyed. Control over the production of commercial crops on estates would pass into the hands of the Minister, who would normally not permit tenant-tobacco to be grown.[126]

The complex process by which the visiting tenant system was first saved and then greatly extended under Banda's own personal control is worth studying for the light it throws on decision-making in the transition period leading up to and just after independence.[127] Initially, white farmers followed traditional tactics: direct appeals made both to the British Government in the person of the new Minister for Central African Affairs, Butler, and to the Governor, Glyn Jones, who met a delegation of Central Province farmers in July 1962.[128] But with the growing recognition that these approaches were no longer effective, a different strategy was devised. Late in July Bruce Barron, son of the founder of the Central Province tobacco industry, enlisted the support of Michael Blackwood, now recognised by Banda as the legitimate representative of the European community. Here was a man whose basic instincts were much closer to Banda's own than were those of the more radical Europeans who had identified themselves with the nationalist cause. Blackwood spent several days negotiating with officials in the Ministry of Natural Resources with the result that when the

---

[125] Speeches by Msonthi and Banda, *Proceedings of the Legislative* Council, 31 May 1962.
[126] See Central Province Association, 'Memorandum on the Visiting Tenant System', July 1962, MNA Central Province Association Papers.
[127] For an extended discussion see McCracken, 'Share Cropping', pp. 52–59.
[128] John Foot to Richard Warren, 23 July 1962, MNA, CPA Papers.

Africans on Private Estates Ordinance was promulgated on 10 August, it was not applied to the Central Province. Instead, estate owners were obliged to accept a new tenancy agreement giving tenants greater rights and the Ministry more influence in their respective dealings with landlords. Estates were given permission to grow burley tobacco for a further year. However, it was made clear 'that the Minister's avowed intention' was still 'to ultimately end the visiting tenant system.'[129]

With a stay of execution won, Banda's conversion became the central objective. After several postponements, Barron and Wallace, the leading spokesmen for the Central Province Association, obtained an audience with him in November 1963. They were met by a series of objections. Drawing on his American experience, Banda complained: 'That the present system appeared to be the same as the Share Cropper system practised in the Southern States of America, where the tenant is very seldom out of debt to the landlord.' Furthermore, the burden of risk was unequally divided, with the landlord making all the profit in a good year and the tenant suffering all the losses in a bad.[130] Barron responded by suggesting that no debts incurred in one season should be carried over to another and that tenants should be assured a minimum sum for the tobacco they grew. But these recommendations were decisively rejected.[131] Instead, Banda responded by appointing T. V. Watson, a former Director of Agriculture in Uganda, to carry out an investigation into the visiting tenant system and the production of burley tobacco. Should it continue to be produced only on estates as had been the practice since 1952 or was there a case for permitting smallholders to grow burley too? Above all, how economically effective was the visiting tenant system?

There can be no definitive answer as to why Banda backtracked on his original decision and decided to seek expert expatriate advice on the future of tenant production. Perhaps this was a case similar to others described by his European admirers, where Banda's private pragmatism overruled his public rhetoric.[132] Scientific evidence, rather than emotion, would determine the final decision. An alternative suggestion is that the economic interests of Banda and his fellow African estate owners were now entering into the equation. During the debate over *thangata*, John Msonthi, with the impetuosity of youth, had called out: 'Doom to Settlers'.[133] But while 'settler' could be convincingly defined as European or at least as non-African, 'estate owner' was an economic term, synonymous with European over most of the colonial period but not by the mid-1960s. Banda himself, with his farm at Kasungu, another near Mzuzu, and several more coming into existence was rapidly turning himself into the largest landlord in Malawi. He was also being joined by other members of the Malawi political elite for whom estate owning was to become a source both of status and of wealth. Earlier African rural entrepreneurs, whether men like Ralph Chinyama or the much derided Master Farmers, had been exponents of 'straddling', in the sense that they often combined wage employment with a direct commitment to the

---

[129] Blackwood to Central Province Association, 11 August 1962, MNA CPA Papers.
[130] Report by R.P. Warren on a meeting with the Prime Minister, 10 November 1963, MNA CPA Papers.
[131] Report by the special sub-committee on proposals for a profit sharing scheme and other alterations to the visiting cultivator system, December 1963, MNA CPA Papers.
[132] See Phillips, *Obscurity to Bright Dawn*, p. 145.
[133] Intervention by Msonthi in speech by Banda, *Proceedings of the Legislative Council*, 31 May 1962.

land. The new generation of estate owners, however, had neither the time nor the inclination to farm directly and thus found the employment of tenants, who would do the work for them in exchange for a share of the proceeds of the crop, an immensely attractive alternative.

Watson's report, produced shortly after independence in October 1964, thus provided welcome backing not only to European landlords in the Central Province but also, although less directly, to all those Malawians who fancied themselves as estate owners. Watson acknowledged that some estate owners were prone to pass on risks to tenants but denied that this was an integral feature of the system. Instead, he emphasised its positive features: the rapid increase in the amount of burley grown since 1953; the substantial amount of credit made available to the 5,200 tenants working on Central Province estates (at least £71,000 in 1964) and the effective technical advice and instruction provided. These permitted tenants to achieve yields that were more than twice as good as those obtained by Trust Land producers and to earn considerably more money for their crops. In the three seasons up to 1964, tenants' annual income averaged £32 per head, almost double that received by Trust Land growers. His conclusion was, 'that the tenant or visiting cultivator system is potentially not only a progressive system of farming but also one which is very suitable for local conditions. It is clear that under efficient and enlightened management it has already proved itself to be agronomically sound and profitable to both tenants and estate owners alike.'[134]

In striking contrast, Watson's recommendation as to who should be allowed to grow burley was markedly less favourable to the estate owners. Noting that 'there is now an increasing desire on the part of the Trust Land growers to be allowed to grow Burley', he reviewed the possible objections before coming to a compromise solution. Some independent peasants, he recommended, should be permitted to grow burley but only those living in specific areas where adequate supervision could be provided. Otherwise, there was a danger that too much low quality leaf would be grown, resulting in a collapse of the market.[135] There was no case, however, for maintaining the existing monopoly.

On many issues Banda displayed a vigorous scepticism concerning the validity of expatriate advice; his reaction to Watson's report was no exception. In February 1965 he approved a three-year extension to the period during which tenant production of burley would be allowed, thus demonstrating his qualified support for the system. However, he also decided not to involve Trust Land growers in the production of the crop, thus rejecting one of Watson's key recommendations.[136] European estate owners had been given a new lease of life although considerable uncertainty existed as to how many would be able to survive alongside the new generation of Malawians who were now beginning to acquire estates, some by obtaining leases on customary land, others through the transfer of land from absentee Europeans. Not until the period 1969–1971 was the situation to be finally resolved by the forced buy-out of the greater part of European-owned land in the Central Province and its redistribution to Malawian

[134] *Report of the Burley Tobacco Industry Commission*, 1964, p.11, CPA Papers.
[135] *Report of the Burley Tobacco Industry Commission*, pp. 18–19.
[136] Minutes of meeting of the Central Province Association, 1 March 1965; Warren to Dewar, Permanent Secretary Ministry of Natural Resources, 10 October 1966, MNA CPA Papers.

farmers. Virtually all European lease-holders who remained resident in Malawi were allowed to retain possession of at least one estate but there were few whose landholdings were not drastically reduced. Ignaco Conforzi was forced to give up all of the 35,000 acres he leased in the Central Province but retained his extensive Shire Highlands tea estate. Barron lost nine estates but kept three, including Mbabzi, the pioneer, which remained a model of successful tenant production. Warren survived with only one.[137] Some land was taken over by smallholders on settlement schemes but even more by Malawian estate owners. A new chapter in the history of tenant farming had begun, dominated in the 1970s by the remarkable expansion of tobacco estates, many of them owned, either directly or through Press Holdings, by Banda and by his close associates.[138]

Banda's attempt to reform the agricultural sector did not end with the abolition of *malimidwe* and the transformation of *thangata*. Ever since the early 1930s, the marketing and production of peasant grown cash crops had been dominated by parastatal organisations – first the Native Tobacco Board and from 1956, the giant Agricultural Production and Marketing Board. By 1961 some of the more questionable features of this organisation had already been addressed. Africans were represented on the Board, as they had been since 1946. The number of markets had grown, although the Northern Province in particular was still starved of trading opportunities. From 1958, under the instructions of Armitage, an attempt had been made to bring the price paid to Trust Land growers into line with world market prices.[139] Nevertheless, as Banda noted when bringing forward the Nyasaland Farmers Marketing Ordinance, 'the Board was not loved by the African… People demanded the abolition of the Board. And after the Election the clamour for abolition of the Board or opening trading in tobacco, groundnuts and cotton to free competition became vociferous and acrid.'[140] The relations between growers and supervisors had collapsed. Staff morale was at an all time low.[141]

Faced by a breakdown in communications, Banda contemplated abolishing the Board and opening up trading to free competition but quickly put the thought behind him. 'We are not living in the days of Adam Smith but of John Maynard Keynes', he was later to note. 'We are not living in the days of *laissez faire* economic policy; we are living in the days of regulation, control and even guidance.'[142] His actions were thus largely cosmetic. In an attempt to restore confidence, he changed the name to the Farmers' Marketing Board and severed links with the Agricultural Department.[143] The number of African members on the Board was increased from three to 11, three parliamentarians and eight elected by provincial committees of farmers.[144] Greater Africanisation, however,

---

[137] McCracken, 'Share-Cropping', pp. 58–9; Wilshaw, *Century of Growth*, p. 109.
[138] Jonathan Kydd, 'Development Policies and Economic Change' in Centre of African Studies, *Malawi*, pp. 320–21.
[139] *Report of the Working Party on Cotton and Tobacco Bonuses* (Zomba, 1958), MNA 3–15–R/9725/34049; McCracken, 'Share-Cropping in Malawi'.
[140] Speech by Banda, *Proceedings of the Nyasaland Legislative Council,* 7 March 1962.
[141] Thandika Mkandawire, 'Marketing Board must be in Hands of Able People', *Malawi News*, 25 January 1962.
[142] Speech by Banda, *Proceedings of the Legislative Council*, Dec. 1963.
[143] In 1971 the name was changed again to the Agricultural Development Marketing Corporation (ADMARC).
[144] *Malawi News*, 2 November 1961.

was not synonymous with the democratisation of the Board in the sense that its affairs were placed in the hands of African farmers. Banda claimed and was given unprecedented powers to appoint or dismiss any employee he wished.[145] All 11 members proudly wore their Kamuzu lapel badges at the first meeting they attended as a signal of where their primary loyalty lay.[146] The control previously exercised by European agricultural officials was decisively broken. However, the opportunity for independent-minded members to ask hard questions, as Chinyama had done in the early 1950s, virtually disappeared as well.

There can be no doubt that in the initial stages of African majority rule, Dr Banda's priority was to develop peasant agriculture. To the Board's credit, renewed energy was put into expanding market facilities and encouraging increased production. As Kydd has noted, 'almost all of the Ministry of Agriculture's local resources were allocated to smallholder projects.'[147] In the first development plan, prepared by Dunduzu Chisiza in 1962, the focus was almost entirely on achieving peasant growth.

At the same time, pricing policies were followed that had interests other than those of the growers in mind. The decision to maintain a 'stabilisation' fund was a particular case in point. Like Colby before him, Banda was anxious to maintain a wide gap between world market prices and those paid to the growers so that surplus funds could be accumulated for investment. As Parliamentary Secretary for Finance, struggling with the costs of development, Dunduzu Chisiza welcomed this approach. The Board, he argued, 'cannot perform only the function of stabilizing prices; it must also help the government in siphoning off money from the growers for further development.' This, he noted, would be facilitated by a provision in the bill that allowed the Board to invest or lend the money it accumulated – perhaps to the Ministry of Finance if it found itself in difficulties.[148] In a curious reversal of roles, the only support for the growers came from the opposition benches. Chisiza's remarks 'about siphoning off the money from the growers for development projects' were 'surprising', Blackwood commented. 'I always understood that this was one of the things that growers objected to, and that they always required the right price for their crops and not some hidden tax put on them by Government.'[149] In practice, prices paid by the Farmers Marketing Board in the 1960s do not appear out of line with what had been paid before.[150] However, the mechanism was in place whereby, under the auspices of the FMB's successor, the Agricultural Development Marketing Corporation (ADMARC), massive surpluses were generated from the artificially low prices paid to peasants.[151]

If growers failed to benefit as much as might have been expected from Banda's reforms, independent businessmen did much better. Prior to 1961, African lorry owners had resented the near monopoly held by Europeans over the transport

---

[145] Speech by Banda on Farmers Marketing (Amendment) Bill, *Proceedings of the Legislative Council,* 13 July 1962.

[146] *Malawi News,* 1 March 1962.

[147] Kydd, 'Malawi in the 1970s. Development Policies and Economic Change', p. 319.

[148] Speech by Chisiza, *Proceedings of the Legislative Council,* 7 March 1962.

[149] Speech by Blackwood, ibid.

[150] See *Compendium of Agricultural Statistics, 1977* (Zomba, 1977), tables 18 and 19, pp. 46–7.

[151] J. Kydd and R. E. Christiansen, 'Structural Change in Malawi since Independence: consequences of a development strategy based on large scale agriculture', *World Development,* 10, 5, pp. 355–375.

of crops handled by the Board; now they were in a position to act. Richard Chidzanja, himself a leading lorry owner who had suffered financially during the emergency, led the attack in the first session of the post-election Legislative Council and was joined by several fellow businessmen.[152] In response, Banda appointed Chidzanja to the Board and announced, 'I am allowing those African businessmen and traders who own lorries and trucks to share in the business of the Board by acting as transporters and carriers of tobacco, groundnuts and cotton.'[153] New licenses were quickly issued with the result that, by May 1962, virtually all tobacco sold through the Board in the Southern Province as well as 50 per cent sold in the Northern Division (the Central and Northern Provinces combined) was transported in African-owned lorries.[154] For some politicians at least, nationalism was also good business. Obtaining political power had become the key to economic success.

Initiatives in education

The determination to restructure the agricultural sector went side by side with an attempt to expand secondary and higher education as a means of Africanising the civil service and ancillary professions at a time when the country was approaching independence. The magnitude of the exercise must have impressed even the resolutely upbeat Kanyama Chiume, the new minister, as he perused the findings of the Phillips Commission, laid on his desk late in 1961.[155]

Written in somewhat Olympian style by a Scottish professor, the report laid bare 'the low standard of education at all levels' that still existed in Nyasaland, 90 years after the establishment of colonial rule and despite the threefold increase in the funds set aside for education between 1954/55 and 1960/61.[156] Wastage, particularly in unassisted primary schools, was colossal; the standard of teaching, with very few exceptions, was poor; results were disappointing. Places in secondary schools were available for only 13 per cent of standard six primary school leavers; a mere trickle of leavers from secondary schools was going into higher education. In 1961, only two pupils from Nyasaland's schools passed the necessary exams to qualify for entry to university.[157] Others figures, not contained in the report, were equally depressing. In settler-dominated Southern Rhodesia, 6,675 African students were enrolled in 34 secondary schools, several of much higher standard than any that Nyasaland possessed. Nyasaland, by contrast, had just 1,505 pupils in 17 schools, only five of which taught the full secondary syllabus.[158] It was a far cry from the days when Livingstonia and Blantyre had made Nyasaland the leading centre of education in central Africa.

Not even Chiume's best friends would deny that he had an exceptionally

---

[152] Speeches by Chidzanja, Nyasulu and Katengeza, *Proceedings of the Legislative Council*, 28 November 1961.
[153] Speech by Banda, 7 March 1962, *Proceedings of the Legislative Council*, 7 March 1962.
[154] *Malawi News*, 10 May 1962.
[155] *Report of the Committee of Inquiry into African Education* [the Phillips Report]. (Zomba, 1962).
[156] Ibid., pp. 12, 20.
[157] Ibid., p. 13.
[158] *Legislative Council Proceedings*, 29 November 1961, p. 137.

abrasive personality.[159] But he was also a man of remarkable energy and imagination, well equipped to revitalise what had become a demoralised and apathetic department.[160] Travelling across the country, visiting schools, interviewing teachers and reading files, he came to three conclusions that were to shape educational policy in the years up to independence and beyond. First, he accepted Phillips's recommendation that priority must be given to the expansion of secondary education, although with the important qualification that while Phillips had envisaged a relatively slow growth in secondary enrolment from 1,500 in 1960 to around 4,080 in 1967, he was determined to achieve a much faster increase – up to between 5,000 and 6,000 young people in secondary education by the end of 1963. Philips's ambitions had been restricted to converting the 12 junior secondaries, teaching up to Form II, into full secondary schools. Chiume, however, took the imaginative if dangerous decision to reduce expenditure on primary schools, cut down the number of boarding schools and use the surplus created to build new day secondary schools in almost every district of the country. Severely limited in the money he could spend, he devised a system, similar to self-help schemes in other African countries, by which the government provided £18,000 for each new secondary school to construct some buildings on condition that the newly democratised local education authorities came up with an additional sum to complete the buildings. By July 1963 six new schools were in the process of construction; a year later, nine further were built.[161] In a remarkable, completely unacknowledged development, first-year primary enrolments, already in decline as a percentage of the school age population, fell severely after 1962, thus pioneering a trend that was to continue into the 1970s.[162] However, secondary school recruitment increased much faster than had previously been planned.

Chiume's second conclusion was to reject the voices of caution in his department by seeking a rapid expansion in access to higher education. Decisions on the nature, timing and siting of a university were reserved exclusively to Banda, who had decided to create a University of Malawi at Khondowe in honour of Robert Laws as part of the Gwelo Plan he had developed while in detention. Up to 1963, the only tangible advance that had been made was the establishment of a small committee of expatriate experts to consider the feasibility of the project. Chiume's initiative thus had to take a different form. Under his direction, negotiations were conducted with the American government, now committed under President Kennedy to providing significant financial aid to Africa, leading to the construction of the polytechnic at Blantyre in 1963. Chiume was also responsible for the short-lived junior college, established at Livingstonia as a nucleus for the university. But his more significant initiative was to develop a scheme for sending students abroad on undergraduate courses, some to Makerere and to its fellow colleges at Dar es Salaam and Nairobi in the newly created University of East

[159] See Chipembere, *Hero of the Nation*, p. 229–30.
[160] For positive evaluations of Chiume by expatriate colleagues who worked with him see Phillips, *Obscurity to Bright Dawn*, pp. 144–45; Mullins, *Retreat*, p. 83.
[161] Chiume, *Kwacha*, pp. 146–47; speeches by Phillips and Chiume, *Legislative Council Proceedings*, 12 July 1963.
[162] Williams, *Malawi*, pp. 159, 287. According to Williams, the proportion of school-age children attending primary school decreased by 30 per cent in the decade up to 1970 at a time when access to education was improving almost everywhere else in Africa.

Africa; others to Britain, the United States and beyond.[163] Passports to opportunity for the fortunate, these grants and scholarships quickly became objects of grievance for others who resented the policy of allocating them to those students with the best qualifications –often from the north – rather than spreading them more widely across the country. By the beginning of 1963, Chiume had become the target for a widespread whispering campaign which accused him of favouring his fellow-Northerners at the expense of students from the Southern and Central Provinces.[164]

Chiume's final conclusion was the most controversial of the three. Backed by Banda, he took the view that the missionary hold over education – already much eroded – must be ended and that control should be firmly vested in the hands of the state. The bill he introduced in March 1962 was a wide ranging measure, broadly acceptable to the Protestant churches but initially greeted with considerable suspicion by Roman Catholic leaders, several of whom remained shaken by their bruising encounter with the MCP only five months earlier. However, in negotiations with the Church's Secretary General for Education, the liberal-minded Father van der Asdonk, Chiume was able to quieten fears and reach an acceptable compromise.[165] Chiume insisted that he supported the teaching of religion in schools and was not opposed to missionary involvement. However, he and Banda also made clear that unsubsidised schools would have to come to an end and that in future all schools would be organised through a network of elected educational committees controlled from the top by the minister.[166] Deprived of control over textbooks and syllabi, most Montfortians concluded that their work would have to change. 'The traditional missionary methods and unquestioned docility have had their day. We are being increasingly forced back into the sacristy.'[167]

In some respects, the construction of secondary schools was of less importance than the quality of the teachers who filled them. Chiume, a keen proponent of Africanisation, went out of his way to appoint Malawian headmasters to the new schools he was building.[168] But he was painfully aware that for several years to come there would be no possibility of more than a handful of qualified teachers emerging from the Soche Hill Teacher Training College, which opened its doors in 1963. The answer, in Malawi as in many other countries in Africa, lay in the recruitment of young American members of the Peace Corps, established on the instructions of President Kennedy in 1962. The first twenty Peace Corps volunteers arrived in Nyasaland in 1963 and were joined by a larger contingent a year later. By the time of their expulsion in 1969, as many as 179 Peace Corps teachers were employed: on one calculation, over half of the total teaching strength of Malawi's secondary schools.[169]

---

[163] Chiume, *Kwacha*, p. 149; speech by Chisiza, *Legislative Council Proceedings*, 11 July 1962.
[164] *Malawi News*, 22 February 1963.
[165] de Jong, *Mission and Politics*, pp. 250, 310–11.
[166] Speeches by Chiume and Banda, *Proceedings of the Legislative Council*, 6 March 1962.
[167] Quoted in de Jong, *Mission and Politics*, p. 312.
[168] Chiume, *Kwacha*, p. 146;
[169] Carolyn McMaster, *Malawi. Foreign Policy and Development* (London, 1974), p. 67; Bruce T. Williams, *Bambo Jordan. An Anthropological Narrative* (Prospect Heights, Ill.,1994), p. 125. Three years earlier, in 1966, there were 136 Peace Corps teachers in Malawi secondary schools, 35 British VSO graduates and 14 French teachers. See *Annual Report of Ministry of Education for 1966*.

No study has been made of the involvement of the Peace Corps in Malawi but there can be little doubt of its importance, certainly to the volunteers and probably to their students as well.[170] Over the previous decade, Malawian students had been exposed to a wide variety of British teachers: some dedicated enthusiasts, hard-working and encouraging, like Florence Walker, the inspirational headmistress at Malosa, but virtually all socially distant from their African colleagues and pupils.[171] The arrival of the young Peace Corps volunteers, brimming with idealism and enthusiasm, contemptuous of colonial divisions, thirsting for new experiences and intrigued by Malawian bars, brought a refreshing new note to the history of colonial, and soon, of postcolonial encounters. Dr Banda was right to be concerned that their sloppy clothes, flowing locks, dissident music and relaxed teaching styles could encourage the emergence of an element of personal protest among Malawi youth – one that in practice was largely restricted to the sporadic employment of an American accent and an enthusiasm for American music. Nevertheless, there can be little doubt that when Banda finally expelled the Peace Corps, his decision was welcomed by many rural elders who saw in the volunteers a threat to their hegemonic control.[172]

[170] The most perceptive and thoughtful account by a former Peace Corps volunteer is Williams, *Bambo Jordan*, pp. 7–144. Paul Theroux, the best-selling author, has also written extensively about his experiences in both fictional and factual form. See, for example, Paul Theroux, *Sunrise with Seamonsters* (London, 1986), pp. 63–75, and *My Secret History* (London.1996), pp. 191–274.

[171] Rotberg (ed.), *Hero of the Nation*, pp. 85–86.

[172] McMaster, *Malawi. Foreign Policy and Development*, p. 67.

15

Prelude to Independence
Unity & Diversity

Internal divisions

At the Marlborough House conference in November 1962, Dr Banda looked back with justifiable pride on his party's 'successful and creditable performance in office'.[1] A range of important legislative measures had been introduced; Chiume, Chisiza and particularly Banda himself had delivered a number of eloquent and forceful speeches in the Legislative Council; all the ministers had demonstrated a capacity to master their portfolios that the experienced Henry Phillips found very impressive.[2] Banda could legitimately deride the many critics who had forecast administrative and financial disaster. Yet, these early sessions of the Legislative Council had also brought into focus tensions that were to erupt into open division less than two years later.

A key issue concerned the conduct of proceedings. In the early meetings, backbenchers and ministers alike raised questions and brought up sensitive issues with a frankness that would later be regarded as unthinkable. Dunduzu Chisiza led the way in calling for Chipembere's release from prison and in advocating the abandonment of English as the sole language to be used in parliament.[3] Other members followed his example by raising questions on such sensitive issues as the differential treatment of black and white civil servants in the allocation of houses and provincial variations in the allocation of bursaries.[4]

Within a matter of months, however, this display of very limited independence had been largely abandoned. In the first session, Banda made clear, in comments greeted with laughter and applause, that, 'Under our custom... I here am the father of all my boys behind me. ...when I leave the house I go home, I talk to them like children and they shut up.'[5] He alone was responsible for making policy, he insisted; even Kanyama Chiume, a brilliant debater and a much more experienced parliamentarian than himself, was pronounced to be

[1] Short, *Banda*, p. 159.
[2] Phillips, *From Obscurity to Bright Dawn*, pp. 144–46.
[3] Speeches by Chisiza, *Legislative Council Proceedings*, 28 Nov. 1961, 29 May 1962.
[4] Questions by Chibambo and Katengeza, *Legislative Council Proceedings*, 28 Nov. 1961.
[5] Speech by Banda, *Legislative Council Proceedings*, 29 Nov. 1961, p. 101.

merely a child in his eyes. Chiume was 'the Honourable Minister of Education to the rest of you', he announced, 'but to me he is just my boy, Kanyama.'[6] By late 1962, the questioning of ministers by Malawian backbenchers had virtually ceased; Banda had taken to intervening in speeches by his ministers to correct their pronunciation and to curtail debates to ensure that measures were quickly passed.[7] With the exception of the generally muted comments of opposition members, debates in the Council were degenerating into praise sessions in which Banda's talents were extravagantly extolled.

In a parallel initiative, in July 1962 Banda set up a sub-committee of the MCP Central Executive under Orton Chirwa to advise on ways in which party discipline could be strengthened. The report, adopted in February 1963, only days after Banda had been sworn in as Prime Minister, marked a further extension of his authority as Life President of the Party. Any member, from the most junior up to his senior colleagues, could be 'dealt with in such a manner as the President in his absolute discretion may think fit' if he suspected them of disloyalty or rumour-mongering. A list of epithets, including Saviour and Messiah, was set aside for his exclusive use. No statement on any aspect of policy could be made by a minister unless it had received Banda's approval. The message to his fellow leaders was clear: in Malawi, the Party was now supreme; as Supreme Leader of the Party, Banda ruled unchallenged over all.[8]

Banda's success in extending his overbearing style of leadership to the legislative council came at a time when factionalism was increasing both within the leadership and without. The MCP's victory in the August elections changed the nature of politics by shifting the focus away from the achievement of independence to the sensitive issue of the allocation of resources. One consequence, at a rank and file level, was that growing personal rivalries took an increasingly regional and/or ethnic dimension. The construction of regional identities is often perceived as a relatively straightforward process, resulting from a combination of colonial administrative policy (the division of Nyasaland into Northern, Central and Southern Provinces) and linguistic policy (the decision of Livingstonia to employ Tumbuka in virtually all schools in the north at a time when Chinyanja was being spoken elsewhere in the Protectorate).[9] In reality, however, the process was a complex one, involving most pertinently the differential impact of mission education in northern and central Malawi, and resulting in the emergence of identities that were far more fluid and tentative than is often imagined.[10] For most Malawians, tribal, racial and indeed national identities remained quite as important as regional identities, into the 1950s and beyond. Nevertheless, increasing competition for jobs, first in the wider southern African labour market and later in Nyasaland itself, threw into profile genuine differences between the educational skills possessed by the Tumbuka, Tonga and Ngoni job-seekers from Livingstonia's sphere of influence and those of the Chewa migrants from the Central Province, much of whose education had been obtained in low-grade unassisted schools.

6 Ibid., p. 144.
7 Intervention by Banda in speech by Msonthi, *Legislative Council Proceedings*, 16 July 1962, p. 484.
8 Short, *Banda*, pp. 169–70, quoting the *Malawi Party Constitution*.
9 The classic analysis can be found in Vail and White, 'Tribalism'.
10 McCracken, 'Ambiguities of Nationalism', pp. 68–70.

Subsequent efforts made by frustrated Chewa migrants and intellectuals to redress the balance in favour of their own ethnic group played an increasingly important role in internal Malawian politics. Launched in 1946, with the founding in Johannesburg of the Achewa Improvement Society, the campaign moved into a new gear two years later when the Association's founder, D. S. Kamangeni, visited Chief Mwase and became involved in an attempt by him and the politician Sam K. Mwase to persuade Dr Banda to provide bursaries for the training of deserving Chewa students.[11] This was followed in 1952 by the establishment in Zomba of the Achewa Welfare Association, dedicated 'to trying to discover the causes of the backwardness of the Achewa people and how to get rid of such causes'.[12] Banda's brand of cultural nationalism, focusing on a particularly Chewa version of Malawian identity, breathed new life into the campaign, although up to the mid-1960s, there is little evidence to suggest that he took a blatantly pro-Chewa or anti-northern attitude to politics. Just as in the late 1940s he had provided financial support to Malawian students from a variety of ethnic backgrounds, so now the appointments he made betrayed no signs of regional bias. Indeed, one of the criticisms most regularly voiced in the early 1960s concerned the high concentration of northerners employed in senior positions in the party and the government. This in turn reflected suspicions over the allocation of resources. Even before the 1961 elections, the Special Branch reported 'some jealousy of the prominent part played by "North-erners"' among party activists from other provinces;[13] following the swearing-in of the ministers, criticism increased. By October 1961, the three Blantyre-based businessmen, Laurence Makata, Lali Lubani and Sydney Somanje, were said to have founded a southern-based bloc in the MCP Executive opposed to that formed by the Chisiza brothers and bitterly hostile to Chiume on account of his 'arrogance and the apparent favouritism shown by him in his capacity as Minister of Education, towards the Northern Province'. This, in the view of the author of a Special Branch report, 'is not tribalism in the popular idea of the word or of the Kenyan pattern, rather it is Provincialism'. Banda, he believed, was 'in something of a dilemma over the clash between the Northern and Southern groups within the MCP Executive, particularly as the Northern Province group are clearly more able and efficient than their counterparts'.[14] More accurately, Banda at this stage was content to play off his lieutenants against each other, to assert his authority more effectively.

By February 1963, regional cleavages within the MCP had begun to take a more public and popular form. With grants and studentships for a variety of higher education courses suddenly becoming available, it was natural that party activists should be divided as to whether they should go to those with the very best qualifications – often from the north – or should be spread more widely across the country. When Kanyama Chiume once more came under attack for his alleged tendency to favour fellow-northerners, Banda responded directly in a

11 Charles Matinga, President's Address, 3rd Annual Conference of the Nyasaland African Congress, 23 September 1946; Woods, 'Chief Mwase and the Kasungu Chewa'.
12 J.W. Kadzamira to D.C. Zomba, 21 May 1951, MNA NS 1/3/1 quoted in Wood, ibid.
13 Special Branch, 'The Malawi Congress Party', 4th edition, 14 October 1961, TNA CO 1015/2445.
14 Nyasaland Intelligence Committee, 'The Extent of Opposition and Criticism of Dr Banda and the Malawi Congress Party as at 5th January 1962', TNA CO 1015/2445.

highly ambiguous speech made to the Malawi Disciplinary Conference. Politicians, he noted, were arguing 'to the effect that the people from the North are dominating the people in the Central and Southern Provinces'.[15]

> They are saying that all the important jobs in the Party, in the Government and in all other walks of life in this country are held by people from the Northern Province. Not only that, they are also saying that most of the Scholarships are awarded to the students from the Northern Province; most of the places in our Secondary Schools throughout the country are given to the children from the Northern Province.

Banda's answer to the charge was that this was not so: 'it is the ability and suitability of the individual that always decides who is to hold which and what job.' But many of his listeners remained unconvinced and were to bring up the allegations again during the emergency debate following the resignation of the ministers in September 1964.

Banda's ability to situate himself above the competition for resources was also apparent in his relations with other ministers. In theory, it might be imagined that his highly confrontational leadership style and aloof, patronising manner would have provoked an early clash with his lieutenants, few of whom had ever been invited to share a meal with him or even to enter his home. 'If they do not like this they can lump it or sack me', he informed the Governor, 'but I have made it quite plain from the start that I impose my own policy on the party.'[16] Sacking Banda, however, was the very last thing that ministers wanted in the run-up to independence. In later years, Kanyama Chiume was to express his contempt for Banda but at this time he had nothing but praise. Writing to him from New Delhi in January 1962, he emphasised the importance of 'solidarity and unity' and added: 'We in Nyasaland must count ourselves as being extremely lucky that God gave us your leadership... "To serve Kamuzu to death" must be the motto of every sane nationalist in this country.'[17]

Even Dunduzu Chisiza was anxious to avoid confrontation. 'Without Dr Banda's leadership this country would go to the dogs', he informed Glyn Jones, at a moment when he was contemplating resigning from his post. 'It is no exaggeration to say that Doctor Banda is the most important asset of this country.'[18]

With a direct challenge to Banda off limits, the ministers turned on each other. Kanyama Chiume was the principal source of dissension. A politician of exceptional talents, Chiume was also a dedicated schemer, almost continuously at odds with Orton Chirwa, his old opponent, and increasingly distrusted by other ministers who resented the personal influence over Banda he appeared to exert by the early months of 1962.[19] As in governments across the world, the dispute centred on issues of ministerial responsibility. Chiume was dissatisfied with the assistance provided by Cameron, the Minister of Works, for his school buildings programme; other ministers were resentful of Chiume's criticism (the more hurtful because it was at least partly true) that he alone had succeeded in

---

[15] *Malawi News*, 22 February 1963.
[16] Jones to Macleod, 4 October 1961, TNA DO 158/25.
[17] Chiume to Banda, New Delhi, 17 January 1962, TNA DO 158/25. For his private opinion see Chiume, *Kwacha*, pp. 90–91, 153–54.
[18] Chisiza to Jones, 4 August 1962, quoted in Baker, *Revolt*, p. 53.
[19] Monthly intelligence report, May 1962, TNA DO 183/136.

wresting control of his ministry from the permanent officials. Matters came to a head on the last day of July and the beginning of August in a flurry of accusations and counter-accusations made at meetings first with Banda and then with Jones at which Dunduzu Chisiza attacked Chiume for 'indulging in activities which make the work and life of his elected colleagues… impossible.'[20] Disappointed by Banda's failure to respond, he, Cameron and Mkandawire then proffered their resignations to the Governor. It was only after a further meeting with Jones, who had previously discussed the matter with Banda that they agreed to continue to serve.[21] Less than a month later, on 3 September, Chisiza died when his car plunged off the Blantyre road a few miles south of Zomba.

Dunduzu Chisiza & the democratic alternative

Nearly 50 years after Dunduzu Chisiza's death, many people in Malawi continued to believe that, far from dying in a car accident, he had been murdered on Banda's instructions.[22] The matter has been investigated in some detail by Joey Power who demonstrates beyond reasonable doubt that the death was almost certainly accidental.[23] Whatever his other crimes, Dr Banda was not involved in high-level political assassinations in the early 1960s. The widespread contemporary rumours of misdoing, however, do point to an important conclusion. Even at this time, two years before independence, many ordinary people far from the inner circles of power had begun to question whether the top leadership of the MCP was as united as official propaganda proclaimed. Many had come to believe, however incoherently, that a fundamental rupture had emerged with Chisiza on the one side and Banda on the other.

Although he lacked the popular charisma of Chipembere or Chiume, Dunduzu Chisiza is perhaps the most significant of the younger generation of Malawian politicians in being the only intellectual rival of Dr Banda and the one MCP activist to provide a coherent democratic alternative to his views. Born at Florence Bay in the Karonga District, he was educated at Livingstonia up to standard six and then attended the Aggrey Memorial College near Kampala, Uganda, where he involved himself, along with Kanyama Chiume in the activities of the Makerere branch of the Nyasaland Students' Association.[24] Unlike Chiume and several of his contemporaries, he did not go on to university, instead working as an interpreter for American members of the Baha'i faith in Rwanda and Burundi before taking up employment in 1955 with the Indian High

---

20 Chisiza to Jones, 4 August 1962, Jones Papers quoted in Baker, *Revolt*, p. 53.
21 Jones to Central African Office, 7 August 1962, DO 183/168. This episode is discussed in detail in Baker, *Revolts*, pp. 50–54.
22 Joey Power, 'Remembering Du: an episode in the Development of Malawian Political Culture', *African Affairs*, 97, 388 (1998), pp. 386–96. See also Power, *Political Culture and Nationalism*, pp. 156–76, which concentrates particularly on the power of rumour.
23 Power, ibid., pp. 383–86. This conclusion is confirmed by the Special Branch, Monthly Intelligence Report, September 1962. TNA DO 183/136. There is a sad irony in the fact that 'car accident' is often used as a euphemism for murder in a country with one of the world's highest rates of genuine car accidents per vehicle. In the few months prior to Chisiza's death, he had been involved in one serious road accident, Chiume had been involved in two, and Lawrence Makata had been killed in another.
24 For a useful biographical introduction see D.D. Phiri, *Malawians to Remember. Dunduzu K. Chisiza* (Longman, Blantyre, 1974). See also Power, 'Remembering Du', pp. 373–83.

Commission in Salisbury, Southern Rhodesia. There he played a leading part in the founding of the radical City Youth League prior to his deportation back to Nyasaland in August 1956.[25] Later, in 1957, he was admitted to study economics in England at Fircroft College, Birmingham, only to withdraw in less than a year after Banda invited him back as Secretary General of Congress.

Writing to Banda in 1957, Chipembere described Chisiza as 'a self-made intellectual of no university attainments but one who surprises us all with his mental powers'. [26] A voracious reader, lacking any systematic ideology, he was particularly receptive to new ideas. As a convert to the Bahai faith, he was a convinced believer in religious toleration. But he was also a passionate cultural nationalist with a consuming interest in the struggle of the Malawian people against colonialism, the subject of a book that he once planned to write.[27] Chisiza's internment in Gwelo gaol extended his intellectual horizons. Instructed by Banda to 'master Economics', he read up to 70 books on the subject and started a regular correspondence with the fiercely anti-communist Walter Rostow, Professor of Economics at the Massachusetts Institute of Technology.[28] Rostow sent him draft chapters of the book on which he was then working, *The Stages of Economic Growth*, an ambitious attempt to provide a non-Marxist model of economic development in the context of democratic capitalism.[29] It was in part through his contacts with Rostow, now appointed to Washington as one of President Kennedy's key advisers, that Chisiza obtained the funds that allowed him to mount the ambitious Nyasaland Economic Symposium in July 1962.

Chisiza's importance in the shaping of Malawian nationalism can be seen both at an intellectual level and at the level of everyday politics. As Parliamentary Secretary to the Minister of Finance, his major responsibility was to prepare a three-year development plan which he presented to the Legislative Council in a notably articulate and well organised speech in July 1962. Dr Banda's Gwelo Plan, developed while in he was in prison, focused on three narrow but eminently achievable objectives on which Banda stamped his personal authority: the founding of a university at Livingstonia, the building of a lakeside road from Fort Johnston to Karonga and the creation of a new capital: the site still unnamed, although it was always intended to be Lilongwe. Banda thus gave notice of a feature of his strategic vision that was to become more prominent in later years: his tendency to take personal ownership of certain identifiable projects for which he could assume direct credit (the Kamuzu Academy was to become the best known) leaving other, more intractable concerns (the educational system as a whole) in the hands of ministers and officials.

Chisiza's task, although at one level little more than the creation of a shopping list of projects that could be passed round among prospective donors, was an altogether more ambitious exercise. Following virtually all development plan-

---

[25] For an admiring account of Chisiza's role in Southern Rhodesian politics see Nathan Shamuyarira, *Crisis in Rhodesia* (London, 1965), pp. 26–28.

[26] *Report of the Nyasaland Commission of Inquiry*, p. 14.

[27] See the account by George Shepperson, with whom Chisiza corresponded between 1956 and 1960, in Macdonald, *From Nyasaland to Malawi*, Introduction.

[28] Speech by Banda, *Proceedings of the Legislative Council*, 16 October 1962; Mackay, *We Have Tomorrow* pp. 46–48; George Shepperson, 'Africans Studied in Prison', *The Scotsman*, 17 November 1960.

[29] Shepperson, Ibid.; Godfrey Hodgson, obituary of Walt Rostow, *The Guardian*, 17 February 2003.

ners and politicians of the period, he started with the contentious assumption that colonialism *per se* was a major obstacle to growth whose removal would automatically stimulate development. 'The Plan before the Council', he announced in July 1962, 'is designed to take up the anchor which has held Nyasaland in stagnation.'[30] With the anchor raised, it would be time for the implementation of Rostow's strategy for economic modernisation from the top through intervention by a powerful and dynamic state. This, he explained to officials in Washington in October 1961, would involve a three-pronged approach concentrating 'first upon better land use, secondly upon the creation of the infrastructure for a modern industrial state: roads, harbours, railways etc; thirdly upon a determined and vigorous programme to train up Nyasalanders to run their own country.'[31] One distinctive feature was his belief that, 'Only when we have a clear understanding of the qualities of our people ... are we likely to tap their dynamism for the reconstruction of the nation.'[32] He therefore rejected calls for individual land tenure to be introduced, arguing instead that 'it will be possible to foster increased cash crops under the traditional system of land tenure.'[33] Questioned on the discrepancy between his vision and Banda's more limited objectives, he replied that 'these were essential too, as a monument to future generations of the faith and courage of their forefathers.'[34] Banda would build monuments to the past; Chisiza, so he optimistically hoped, would plan the transformation of the economy for the future.

In Gwelo, while Banda worked on his still unpublished autobiography, Chisiza contemplated the challenges facing post-colonial Africa. His analysis, articulated both in his pamphlet, *Africa – What Lies Ahead*, published in India early in 1961, and in the paper he wrote for the Economic Symposium in July 1962, contains three main elements intimately linking his economic strategy to his wider political vision.[3] These were: a generalised account of the communal character of African culture; an emphasis on the importance of the role of the state in economic modernisation; and a hard-headed discussion of the difficulties facing African rulers in reconciling the demands of the state with the variegated interests of the people. As an unabashed convert to modernisation theory, Chisiza was convinced of the need for 'strong man government', which he defined, quoting an American professor, 'as a dictatorship which the citizens choose to put up with'.[36] But his concern with state-led economic growth was qualified by his liberal beliefs in a modern state in which 'respect for the dignity of the human individual and the sanctity of his personality shall be recognised' and in which 'basic human rights shall be guaranteed'.[37]

Chisiza's attempt to reconcile these two contradictory concerns is a central

[30] Speech by Chisiza, *Legislative Council Proceedings* 11 July 1962.
[31] Account of Chisiza's discussion in the State Department, J.D. Hennings, British Embassy, Washington to K.J. Neale, 26 October 1961, TNA DO 158/25.
[32] Speech by Chisiza, *Legislative Council Proceedings*, 11 July 1962.
[33] Interview with Chisiza, *Scotsman*, 20 Oct. 1961.
[34] Account of Chisiza's discussion, Hennings to Neale, 26 October 1961, PRO DO 158/25.
[35] D.K. Chisiza, *Africa – What Lies Ahead* (New Delhi, 1961); 'The Temper, Aspirations and Problems of Contemporary Africa' in E.F. Jackson (ed.), *Economic Development in Africa* (Oxford, 1965), pp. 1–18. This was summarised under the title, 'The Outlook for Contemporary Africa' in *The Journal of Modern African Studies*, 1, 1 (1963).
[36] Chisiza, 'Temper, Aspirations and Problems', p. 8.
[37] Ibid., p. 3.

feature of his writings. It pervades his discussion of the relationship between governments and opposition parties, between the state and trade unions, between central governments and chiefs and, above all, between the leader and his lieutenants. (Chisiza is also concerned about the relationship between the leader and the masses but in a distinctly less urgent manner.) In all of these cases, Chisiza's own preference is for a political approach which accepts the need for a strong central government while recognising the legitimacy of sectional interests. Thus, opposition parties should continue to function but ideally as co-opted members of 'national governments – the type of all-party government that Britain had during the world war'. The trade union movement should be free from political control while accepting its 'voluntary subordination' to the nationalist movement. Chiefly authority should be protected but the central government must take over some of the functions previously performed by traditional rulers. 'A distinction must be very clearly drawn between enemies of the state and enemies of ones party', with the former being 'dealt with in accordance with the law of the land' and the latter protected from victimisation.[38]

Chisiza saw dictatorship as one of the most pressing dangers to be faced, not least because of the difficulty in drawing 'the line between a strong man and a dictator'. The following passage, taken from his address to the Economic Symposium, can be read as a commentary on the experiences of men like Chipembere, Chiume and himself, who built up Banda as a leader only to discover, too late, that he had established an authority beyond their control:

> If a nationalist movement is to achieve the goal of independence, it is vitally important that one of the leaders should be elevated well above the others; that his former equals should look upon themselves as his juniors; and that they should accept his decision as final; and that they should pledge loyalty to his leadership. But once independence has been achieved, the problem of reconciling submissiveness to the top leader and individual initiative on the part of second-level leaders arises. To a man who has been surrounded by submissive associates for a long time, the exercise of initiative by his associates is easily misconstrued as a sign of rivalry and disloyalty.[39]

In his pamphlet, *Africa – What Lies Ahead*, Chisiza approached the argument from a different direction, bluntly underlining the limitations of politicians:

> The real problem is posed by those leaders who will lapse into dictatorial tendencies either because their countrymen trust them too much or too little. When too much trust is reposed in a leader (sometimes) the thing goes to his head and makes him believe that he is infallible. Such a man is not likely to brook criticism or to welcome alternative suggestions. It is his idea or nothing. On the other hand, when a brilliant, self-assured, well-meaning leader is begrudged trust or is dealing with a dense populace, he too will tend to force his measures through in a dictatorial manner believing that the masses will appreciate what he is doing later.

What such leaders required, he suggested, was 'a dose of humility'.

> They need to remind themselves that getting to the top of the political tree does not necessarily mean that they are more intelligent than other people. Indeed politics, the world

---

[38] Chisiza, *Africa*, p. 11.
[39] Chisiza, 'Temper, Aspirations and Problems', p. 8.

over, has the uncanny knack of attracting the most mediocre of brains… In framing policies and designing measures, therefore, leaders must rely [more] on public opinion and the
opinions of colleagues than on their imagined superior intellects. The task of leadership
involves following as well as leading.[40]

Chisiza's language is refreshingly different in tone from the stifling political
rhetoric of the Banda years. But it would be wrong to push the contrast too far.
An advocate of the interventionist state, Chisiza, like Banda, was an unabashed
believer in strong government. Like Banda, he was in favour of politicians
entering actively into business.[41] Like Banda (and Colby too) he did not doubt
that if investment capital was to be obtained internally, it would have to come
from squeezing the peasants. His statement that the Farmers Marketing Board
should 'help the Government in siphoning off money from the growers for
further development' was a logical outcome of their shared beliefs.[42] On social
issues, he proved no more enlightened. Banda advocated giving votes to women
but only because of his profoundly paternalist belief that they would return the
favour by accepting him as their male protector (*Nkhoswe* Number One). Chisiza
by contrast, had little to say on women's political rights but much on the need
for them to obtain the domestic and social skills required by their male partners.

> Modern African young men want their wives (a) to know how to prepare traditional as well
> as western dishes; (b) to know how to rear children in the modern way; (c) to share in their
> social interests such as dancing etc.; (d) to maintain a modern home which they can be
> proud of; (e) to be able to entertain guests both the African and western way depending
> upon the type of guests; (f) to know enough English to be able to read useful manuals and
> to converse in English when necessary; (g) to master the art of washing and ironing clothes,
> and (h) to know how to dress like film stars without playing the part.[43]

If Rose Chibambo had opinions on this passage they have not been recorded.
Yet if some of Chisiza's views mirrored the conventional attitudes of the time,
others went well beyond them. In one incautious passage he came close to
implying that the essence of democracy was popular acceptance of a dictator.
But, in practice, it is clear that he rejected such an absolutist posture and instead
reverted to a position closer to that of James Sangala in the late 1940s in its recognition of the virtues of diversity. It was a far cry from Dr Banda's definition,
made to the annual convention of the MCP in 1965 but to all intents and
purposes in place by 1963: 'A Government chosen by the people themselves –
whether it is a dictatorship or not, as long as it is the people who choose the
dictator, it is not a dictatorship. That's all. That is what democracy is.'[44]
Historians are divided on the extent to which Chisiza mounted a political as
opposed to an intellectual challenge to Banda.[45] His interventions in the Legislative Council – calling for Chipembere's release, advocating the use of local

---

[40]   Chisiza, *Africa*, pp. 16–16. There is a misprint in the final sentence which I have corrected here.
[41]   Chisiza, 'Temper, Aspiration and Problems', p.8.
[42]   *Proceedings of the 3rd Meeting of the 76th Session of the Legislative Council*, 6–7 March 1962, p. 159.
[43]   Chisiza, *Africa*, p. 22.
[44]   Quoted in Short, *Banda*, p. 260.
[45]   For alternative views see Andrew Ross, 'Some Reflections on the Malawi "Cabinet Crisis" 1964–65',
       Religion in Malawi, 7 (1992), pp. 7–8 and Baker, *Revolt*, pp. 48–62. Power, 'Remembering Du', pp.
       378–83 provides an admirably balanced analysis.

languages in parliament and setting out the case for a genuinely non-aligned stance in foreign affairs – were all examples of his independence of mind but in no case added up to a systematic campaign for changes in policy.[46] A more striking intervention was his involvement in 1962 in discussions with Kaunda, Nyerere and his brother Yatuta Chisiza (at that time not even a member of parliament) on the sensitive issue of Malawi's federation with Tanzania and Zambia.[47] However, the fact that Banda did not immediately dismiss Dunduzu for interference in a matter over which he had no ministerial responsibility suggests that these talks were little more than casual conversations. Back in 1960 Banda and Nyerere enthusiastically supported the idea of union between their two states as the prelude to the creation of a wider Eastern African federation but by 1962 both had abandoned any serious interest in the project, at least until after Malawi's independence had been won.[48]

Banda, however, may well have become concerned at the extent of the international attention given to Chisiza at the time of the star-studded economic conference he convened in Blantyre in July 1962.[49] And he was certainly aware that it was Chisiza who took the lead in criticising Chiume (ironically, for intervening in other ministers' affairs) only a few days later. On his side, Chisiza's reservations concerning Banda's style of leadership deepened at this time, although it is again ironic that the event that precipitated his offer to resign was not some dictatorial action but rather the failure of Banda to get rid of Chiume. His declaration to Jones – 'Without Dr Banda's leadership this country would go to the dogs' – is a significant demonstration that as late as August 1962, Chisiza remained convinced of the pivotal importance of Banda in the making of Malawi.[50] But by this time, he had also made abundantly clear through the freshness of his approach and the liveliness of his arguments that it would not be possible to constrain him for long in the political system that Banda was creating. In that sense, villagers and party activists alike were right in seeing his death as a significant event – one that fatally weakened the case for a democratic society.

The labour movement

Chisiza's efforts to construct a zone of intellectual independence free from Banda's all-embracing control has its parallel in the sudden eruption of a radicalised labour movement in the early 1960s. For several historians of Malawi, the increased activity displayed by trade unionists and workers was simply a by-product of the expansion of mass nationalism at this period.[51] However, while the

[46] Speeches by Chisiza, *Legislative Council Proceedings*, 28 November 1961, 29 May, 16 July 1962.
[47] Andrew Ross, 'Some Reflections'.
[48] Short, *Banda*, pp. 176–7, 183–4.
[49] Among those who presented papers were Nicolas Kaldor, advisor to Harold Wilson and one of the most influential left-wing developmental economists of the 1960s, and Peter Bauer, subsequently advisor to Margaret Thatcher and a leading opponent of state regulation.
[50] Chisiza to Jones, 4 August 1962, quoted in Baker, *Revolt*, p. 53.
[51] Mtafu Manda, *The State and the Labour Movement in Malawi* (Glasgow, 2000), pp. 22–30; Tony Woods, '"Bread with Freedom and Peace": rail workers in Malawi 1954–1975', *JAS*, 18 (1992) pp. 727–38; Lewis Dzimbiri, 'Industrial Relations, the State and Strike Activity in Malawi' (Ph.D. dissertation, University of Keele, 2002), pp. 101–07.

great majority of workers were nationalists, many of the actions they took between 1960 and 1962 were only indirectly influenced by the MCP. Furthermore, a significant number of workers in this period avoided not only the embrace of the dominant party but of also that of trade union officials. Their story testifies to the fact that for a limited period of time, some workers were able to achieve a significant improvement in conditions through their own independent action.

No one factor can explain the rapid expansion of worker militancy in Malawi in 1960. Economic circumstances no doubt had their part to play. Some improvement in basic living standards probably took place in the Blantyre-Limbe area from the early 1950s but wages remained remarkably low by contrast with the other Central African territories: slightly less than half those in Salisbury, according to one contemporary study.[52] In 1960, the statutory minimum wage in Blantyre was only three shillings a day; in 1957, in Dar es Salaam, probably the poorest city in British East Africa, it was approximately 3s. 4d..[53]

To endemic poverty (often a cause of inertia rather than of radicalism) should be added the increased resources made available to Malawian trade unions by international bodies as well as the new mood of confidence that the success of nationalism engendered. From 1959, the American-based International Confederation of Free Trade Unions (ICFTU) began to channel financial support to selected union leaders as well as funding attendance at overseas courses.[54] Also important was the determination of government following Dr Banda's release to avoid unnecessary confrontations with workers. It is a striking feature of labour disputes in 1960 that whereas, previously, state power all over Central Africa was frequently used to crush opposition from workers and bring strikes to an end, now government intervened repeatedly to negotiate compromise settlements between employees and employers.

Whatever the causes, the overall result was a rapid upturn in labour activity at a number of levels. Trade union membership increased from the low figure of 1,300 in 1957 to 3,400 in 1958, 7,000 in 1960 and approximately 13,000 in 1962 (out of some 130,000 workers in the industries represented), before falling rapidly in the 18 months leading to independence to about 5,520 in 1967.[55] All the major unions expanded: the Railway Workers Union from 2,100 members in 1958 to 4,000 in 1963 (more than 80 per cent of the work force); others by equally significant amounts. The African Motor Transport Workers Union, which changed its name to the Transport and Allied Workers Union in 1959, increased its membership from 660 in that year to over 4,000 in 1960. New, independent-minded union leaders also emerged, several of them influenced by Marxist ideas of class struggle. The most important were C. C. M. Msisya and Susgo Msiska, Chairman and General Secretary of the Transport and Allied Workers Union, and Chakufwa Chihana (in the 1990s founder of the opposition party AFORD) who became Acting General Secretary of the General and

[52] David G. Bettison, 'The poverty datum line in central Africa', *Rhodes-Livingstone Journal*, XXVII (1960).
[53] *Annual Report of the Labour Department for 1960*. The figure for Dar es Salaam is taken from an unpublished manuscript by Andrew Burton.
[54] Stevens to Short, 27 August 1959, MRA; *Malawi News*, 4 June 1969.
[55] Figures drawn from *Annual Labour Reports, 1957* and *1960*; Monthly Intelligence Report for February 1963, TNA DO 183/136.

Commercial Workers Union in 1960 at the youthful age of 21.[56]

Trade union expansion was combined with a significant increase in strike activity. Strikes in Malawi were relatively few in number between 1947 and 1953, the year of the Southern Province disturbances, when they rose suddenly to 15 with about 3,300 workers involved. This number was not exceeded over the next six years, including 1959, when only nine strikes took place. In 1960, however, there was a sudden surge in labour activity resulting in 77 strikes (by far the largest number recorded prior to 1992) involving an estimated 23,000 workers. Some stoppages were relatively minor; others, however, were much larger. In January, following a lengthy dispute, the road haulage industry was convulsed by a strike involving 610 workers. Later in the year, 5,100 workers on the extensive tea estates owned by Conforzi Ltd went on strike, to be followed a few weeks later by 4,000 railwaymen employed by Nyasaland Railways.[57] The dispute in the motor industry was quickly settled in favour of the workers; those on the tea estates and the railways were much more protracted affairs, placing great strains on worker solidarity and lasting for 15 and 51 days respectively. In the first two of these strikes, the influence of a new strand of radical unionism, as represented by the Transport and Allied Workers Union came to the fore. Other stoppages, however, most notably the railway workers' strike, were examples of popular workers' movements, controlled by rank-and-file employees and owing little or nothing to official trade unions or even, directly, to the intervention of the MCP. Indeed, in the years leading up to independence, the Party increasingly operated more as an opponent of the labour movement than as a supporter.

Table 15.1
Strike Activity in Malawi 1947–63[58]

Year	No of Strikes	No of Workers	Year	No of Strikes	No of Workers
1948	4	470	1956	14	NA
1949	7	724	1957	13	NA
1950	3	681	1958	15	1,283
1951	3	388	1959	9	NA
1952	6	889	1960	77	23,929
1953	15	3,286	1961	25	7,182
1954	11	797	1962	24	3,421
1955	9	Na	1963	20	7,315

The years between 1960 and 1963 mark a particularly intense phase in the history of MCP-union relations. In the initial period, up to June 1960, Aleke Banda worked to bring the unions affiliated to the Nyasaland Trade Union Congress into the anti-colonial struggle. Some support was forthcoming from C. C. M. Msisya of the Transport and General Workers Union who declared that the 'Trade Union movement ... [is] indissolubly linked up with the struggle

---

[56] For Chihana see *Malawi News*, 29 June 1961.
[57] *Annual Report of the Labour Department for 1960.*
[58] Adapted from Dzimbiri, 'Industrial Relations', p. 102, with additional material from annual Labour Reports.

for the political freedom … of our continent.'[59] But Weston Chisiza, the General Secretary of the NTUC, was not prepared to subordinate his organisation to another's will, particularly as he was now in receipt of considerable funds from the ICFTU and from the Trades Union Congress of Britain.[60] Relations between the MCP and the NTUC therefore deteriorated, culminating in a series of public attacks launched in May and June 1960 by Aleke Banda on the leadership of the trade union movement. In his judgement, only the Transport and Allied Workers Union was 'trying, in spite of its financial and other difficulties, to do some honest, militant and real trade unionism'.[61] This no doubt played a part in the founding by C. C. M. Msisya in October 1960 of the breakaway National Council of Labour, and in the removal of Chisiza from office in an internal coup mounted in spring 1961.

Changes in trade union leadership, however, did nothing to halt the growing tendency for workers to pursue their own agendas without reference to the MCP. There can be little doubt that the stoppages of early 1960 demonstrated a significant degree of interaction between nationalists and workers. In January, MCP activists warmly supported the campaign mounted by the Transport and Allied Workers Union to force the Nyasaland Transport Company to give it union recognition. By early November, however, when the large-scale railway workers' strike broke out, the situation had changed. Confidence among railwaymen is likely to have been boosted as a result of the spectacular advances made by the party in the previous months. But the dispute that erupted at the beginning of the month focused exclusively on an economic issue – the disappointingly low increases contained in the new wage scales introduced in October.[62]

The most conspicuous feature of the strike that followed was the extent to which ordinary workers took control of their own affairs with little or no support either from the African Railway Workers' Union or from the MCP.[63] Railway workers were unique in Malawi in being able to draw on a sense of solidarity rooted in their shared experience of living together in the large company compound at Limbe and of working in the industry for several years. By the late 1950s some 40 per cent were classified as 'permanent' workers with at least three years' continuous employment in the industry; in the tea industry, by contrast, little more than 25 per cent of the workers were permanent and in the construction industry less than ten per cent.[64] Common understanding of labour conditions, however, was combined with a growing exasperation with the leaders of the union, perceived by many rank-and-file workers as being too closely identified with the small minority of elite employees – drivers, foremen, firemen and senior clerks – paid several times more than the average unskilled worker. The result was that, by a deliberate decision of the workers, officials of the African Railway Workers' Union were excluded from negotiations during the disciplined, two-weeks-long strike involving over 4,000 men that closed down Nyasaland's rail-

[59] *Malawi News*, 22 October 1960.
[60] H.W. Stevens to R.A. Short, 27 August 1959, MRA; *Malawi News*, 4 June 1960.
[61] *Malawi News*, 4 June 1960.
[62] 'Memorandum on the Nyasaland Railway Strike handed to Lord Rupert Nevill by Lord Perth', 25 November 1960, Malawi Railway Archives [MRA].
[63] For a full discussion of this strike see John McCracken, 'Labour in Nyasaland: an assessment of the 1960 Railway Workers' Strike', *JSAS*, 14, 2 (1988), pp. 279–90.
[64] *Annual Report of the Labour Department for 1957*, Table E.

ways in November. Instead, the strikers resorted to what Iliffe has described as an 'anonymous, ostensibly leaderless type' of action in which they systematically refused to send representatives to negotiate with the company on the grounds that in the past 'anybody who has stood up to Management ... was believed to have been either dismissed or promoted or transferred to some unpleasant spot where he could be no trouble' – a charge accepted by the Acting Manager as being broadly correct.[65] Not until the management had backed down by agreeing to the appointment of a tribunal of inquiry did the strikers come together in a mass meeting as members of the union. And when they did, they dismissed the whole committee of the Nyasaland African Railway Workers' Union and elected a new committee drawn from the leaders of the strike.[66] The tribunal's awards, made public a few days later, vindicated the use of these tactics. In a rare victory for workers in Malawi, wages of unskilled labourers were increased by 25 per cent and those of junior clerical staff and artisans by between 15 and 20 per cent.

Equally detached was the leadership of the Malawi Congress party, now preoccupied in the run-up to the 1961 elections with maintaining industrial harmony. Government officials perhaps over-simplified the situation by arguing of the strike that 'there was no evidence whatever of instigation by any political party'.[67] But although a handful of Malawi Youth Leaguers were active, so the General Manager claimed, in preventing people returning to work, leaders of the party kept their distance.[68] Masauko Chipembere and Dunduzu Chisiza refused to intervene when approached by strikers anxious to break the deadlock. And although Orton Chirwa offered his assistance, it was with the aim of bringing the strike to an end.[69] By mid-November, MCP leaders were being openly described as 'Capricorns' by disillusioned railwaymen, who preferred to discuss matters with the one external 'agitator' of substance to contact them, C. C. M. Msisya, the ambitious chairman of the newly formed National Council of Labour.[70]

The year 1960 marked at once the high point of the labour movement and the beginning of its rapid decline. With the MCP moving from a position of limited and largely rhetorical support for worker interests to one which gave priority to the control of wages, labour leaders were confronted with a difficult choice. One response, followed by Stewart Nkholokosa, a former guard who became Secretary General of the African Railway Workers' Union in the aftermath of the 1960 strike, was to seek an accommodation with the Congress Party. An astute campaigner, Nkholokosa in March 1962 mobilised support from fellow-southerners to oust the northerner, Kelvin Nyirenda, from his post of General Secretary of the Nyasaland Trade Union Congress. Thereafter, he resisted a series of challenges to his position by giving his unswerving support to party policies, even when, as with the Trade Union (Amendment) Ordinance of 1963, they involved an assault on the independence of the trade union movement.

[65] Iliffe, 'Wage labour and urbanisation', pp. 286–87; B.M. Strouts to E.A. Short, 20 November 1960, MRA.
[66] Strouts to Short, 23 November 1960, MRA.
[67] Memo handed to Nevill by Perth, 25 November 1960, MRA.
[68] Strouts to Short, 18–20 November 1960, MRA.
[69] Woods, 'Rail Workers', pp. 731–32.
[70] Woods, 'Rail Workers', pp. 731–32; McCracken, 'Labour in Nyasaland', p. 283. Among politically active Central Africans in the 1960s, the term 'Capricorn' was synonymous with 'stooge' or 'sellout'.

Suzgo Msiska and Chakufwa Chihana took the alternative approach. General Secretaries respectively of the Transport and Allied Workers Union and of the Commercial and General Workers Union, both men committed themselves to a radical position involving the defence of workers' rights even when this conflicted with the wishes of the party. Conflict came as early as September 1961, within weeks of the MCP's success in the August elections, when Msiska called more than 800 workers in the motor transport business out on strike in a demand for higher wages. On 14 September, the *Malawi News* condemned the strike, which collapsed within a few days once the workers became aware that they lacked political support.[71] Msiska led his supporters in a demonstration to the head office of the MCP only to have his complaints firmly rejected. In June 1962, he and Chihana became the first individuals to be suspended from membership of the MCP, an action that was eventually to bring their labour careers in Malawi to a close.[72] In a statement of official policy, the *Malawi News* trumpeted: 'In this country the Trade Union movement should be part of the mass movement and in all its activities it must conform with the policies and programmes of Ngwazi Dr Kamuzu Banda who, alone, knows best what is good for this country.'[73]

With considerable courage, the labour leaders brushed off a diatribe launched against them by Banda in August and rallied support from their members to prevent them being expelled from office.[74] Government disapproval mounted, however, from February 1963 when they came out in public opposition to the Trade Union (Amendment) Ordinance, a measure introduced by Chokani that gave the Government control over the external affiliations of trade unions as well as the power to bar any person from becoming an officer; this time they had no defence.[75] Deserted by a substantial portion of the membership of the Transport & Allied Workers Union, Msiska resigned as Secretary-General in May and a year later left Blantyre for Moscow.[76] Chafukwa Chihana remained in office up to the end of January 1964 when he too resigned, to the disappointment of most members of his union who were said to have regretted 'the loss of an individual who, they consider, had worked so hard on their behalf'.[77] Meanwhile, confidence in the remaining leaders of the trade union movement slumped, 'since it is believed by the rank and file that they dare do nothing in opposition to the Government's employment and wages policy'.[78] Many were subsequently absorbed into the civil service or else into the party bureaucracy. As Woods has demonstrated, railwaymen at the Limbe yards continued to demonstrate their discontent through a variety of overt and covert means.[79] But when in 1963 the multinational company, Lonrho, the new owners of Nyasaland Railways, made 1,600 employees redundant the process was completed almost without inci-

[71] *Malawi News*, 14, 21 September 1961.
[72] *Malawi News*, 29 June 1962; Monthly Intelligence Report, June 1962, TNA DO 183/136.
[73] *Malawi News* 29 June 1962.
[74] Monthly Intelligence Report, August 1962, TNA DO 183/136; *Malawi News*, 17 August 1962.
[75] Speeches by Chokani and Blackwood, *Proceedings of the Legislative Council*, 5 March 1963; Monthly Intelligence Reports, February, March, April 1963, TNA DO 183/136.
[76] *Malawi News*, 17 May 1963; Monthly Intelligence Reports, May 1963, TNA DO 183/136 and May 1964, DO 183/137.
[77] Monthly Intelligence Report, February 1964, TNA DO 183/137.
[78] Monthly Intelligence Reports, August, 1963, TNA DO 183/136.
[79] Woods, 'Rail Workers', pp. 737–78.

dent.[80] Several, small-scale, unofficial strikes took place on expatriate-owned tea estates. However, with the trade union movement now firmly subordinated to the party, the room for independent labour action was limited. Not until 1992, after the Banda regime had begun to collapse would an effective workers' movement re-emerge.[81]

Coercion, control & the MCP

It is a tragic feature of the absolutist mass party that the demands it makes frequently press most hard on the most harmless members of society. Those, like Aleke Banda, who argued for a Christianity with genuine Malawian roots had no need to look further in the early 1960s than to the Jehovah's Witnesses with their origins in Eliot Kamwana's Watchtower movement from 1909 and to the Providence Industrial Mission (PIM) founded by John Chilembwe in 1900. But while Chilembwe and Kamwana were now lauded by the MCP as 'our national heroes and martyrs', their successors were fatally impeded by their religious conviction that they should not register for elections or purchase Party cards.[82]

In the aftermath of the 1961 elections, this detachment was regarded by MCP vigilantes as tantamount to treason. The first wave of attacks on Jehovah's Witnesses by militant members of the Malawi Youth League took place between March and June 1962 but came to a halt when Dr Banda expressed his disapproval.[83] However, the start of the pre-independence election campaign late in 1963 was marked by a further wave of political violence actively encouraged by several MCP leaders (including Gwanda Chakuamba and Aleke Banda, so the Special Branch reports alleged).[84] Virtually no incidents were reported from the Northern Province. But in other parts of the country attacks on members of religious sects totalled over 600 reported cases (434 involving Jehovah's Witnesses) in January 1964 at the height of the registration period, and to more than 1,200 in the following month. In the majority of instances the damage was confined to the burning of houses and crops and the beating up of men and women, but at least eight Witnesses and a member of the PIM were killed. In one incident in the Dedza district, Youth League vigilantes attacked a PIM church during a service, killing one member of the congregation and beating several others severely. In two separate cases on the Lilongwe Plain, a total of five Witnesses were murdered by youths dressed as *Nyau* dancers – an indication of the fact that even before independence the secret village-based *Nyau* society was

---

[80]   Monthly Intelligence Report, July 1963, TNA DO 183/136. Lonrho's short-lived involvement in Nyasaland (Malawi) Railways (from 1962 to 1966) is described in S. Cronje, M. Ling and G. Cronje, *Lonrho: portrait of a multinational* (London, 1976), pp. 26–28.

[81]   According to the figures collected by Dzimbiri, 'Industrial Relations and Strike Activity', the number of strikes in Malawi fell from 77 in 1960 to 20 in 1963. In the 13 years from 1966 to 1978 there was an average of 12 strikes a year, most of them very small and short-lived. In the next 13 years, up to 1991 only 26 strikes were recorded, an average of two a year. But with the beginning of the breakdown of the Banda regime, the number soared to 88 strikes in 1992 and 66 in 1993.

[82]   The quotation is contained in Dunduzu Chisiza to George Shepperson, 28 October 1956, Shepperson Papers, EUL.

[83]   Monthly intelligence reports for March, April and August 1962, TNA DO 183/136.

[84]   Intelligence reports for January and February 1964, TNA DO 183/137.

being utilised by elements within the MCP as an instrument of rural oppression.[85] Not until the belated intervention of Dr Banda on 23 February did the number of violent incidents fall, helped no doubt by the reluctant decision of the PIM leader, Dr Malekebu, in January, to abandon his earlier policy and instruct his members to register.[86] As late as May, however, cases of assault continued to be reported.

The campaign launched against Jehovah's Witnesses is best understood in the light of changing political circumstances in the 18 months leading up to independence. Back in March 1962, Dunduzu Chisiza had warned that the very success of the MCP in persuading the British Government of the need for independence would create a political vacuum that would be hard to fill:

> Disengagement from political action really means that the thousands of people who are engaged in the political struggle with us will suddenly find themselves without useful tasks to perform. It will, in a way be a sort of anticlimax for them – an anticlimax which, if mishandled, might easily deteriorate into disillusionment.[87]

By the end of that year, villagers in the Mulanje and Cholo districts, calling themselves the Land Freedom Army, had begun to encroach on tea estates to the embarrassment of the MCP leadership. Within a matter of months, their discontent had been mirrored by that of smallholders in the Lilongwe and Dowa districts, disappointed at the low prices being paid in FMC markets for their tobacco and maize, despite Banda's well-publicised reforms. At six markets dissatisfied tobacco growers staged one-day boycotts. At Lombadzi they abused the local MLC, Massa, and stoned his car.[88] Tobacco production fell. Across the country, the first serious economic depression since the Second World War was making its presence felt.[89]

In later years, Banda's favourite tactic in responding to the emergence of village-level unrest was to refocus resentment on a popular scapegoat and it seems likely that he did the same at this time. Jehovah's Witnesses were generally law-abiding and industrious but their very success in achieving prosperity without sharing the proceeds with members of the wider community often made them deeply disliked. Many villagers, therefore, thoroughly approved of the MYP campaign of harassment.[90] The election campaign, of which it was a part, appears to have been equally popular. As Banda noted in December 1963, he was under no obligation to call an election before independence (the assembly elected in 1961 did not need to be dissolved until 1966). However, by agreeing to an election he could mobilise popular support and isolate the small group of political opponents that remained, headed by Pemba Ndove and largely organ-

---

[85] Intelligence reports for December 1963 and for January and February 1964, TNA DO 183/136, DO 183/137. These reports were made available to Dr Banda but not to other ministers.
[86] Intelligence reports for January, March 1964, TNA DO 183/137.
[87] Chisiza quoted in monthly intelligence report, March 1963, TNA DO 183/136.
[88] Monthly intelligence reports, October, December 1962, June 1963, TNA DO 183/136; *Malawi News*, 22 November 1962.
[89] Williams, *Malawi*, pp. 210–12.
[90] For a discussion of the response of ordinary Christians to the persecution of Jehovah's Witnesses from 1963 to 1975 see Klaus Fiedler, 'Power at the Receiving End: the Jehovah's Witnesses' Experience in One-Party Malawi' in Kenneth R. Ross [ed.], *God People and Power in Malawi* (Kachere Monograph, Blantyre, Malawi, 1996).

ised in the coalition party, Mbadwa. In what was to become standard form, Banda denounced these men by name before declaring: 'I want them to come forward now and put up candidates and see what is going to happen to them.'[91]

If there were any doubts as to their fate, it was soon to be dispelled. Within days of Banda's statement, attacks on Mbadwa members began, culminating in the killing of Gilbert Pondeponde on Christmas Eve. By early January virtually every opposition leader had fled the country and it had become clear that all MCP candidates would be returned unopposed and hence that no formal elections would be held.[92] Nevertheless, the MCP organised a huge registration campaign that combined genuine popular enthusiasm with frequent cases of assault. At Magomero and in other parts of the country, Youth Leaguers drove away people who did not have MCP cards; independent trade unionists were subjected to vitriolic abuse. In an important development, senior British officials placed themselves tacitly on the new Government's side. Following discussions with Banda, Foster, the Chief Secretary, ordered the interception of postal communications with ten named critics of the Prime Minister, among them Chihana and Souzgo Msiska, and eight organisations including all opposition parties and the two most independent trade unions.[93] State and Party were coming together in a formidable alliance.

Foster's action is evidence of the decisive shift of power within Malawi that took place around the time of Banda's swearing in as Prime Minister on 1 February 1963. Ever since the 1961 elections, Jones had trod a cautious path in seeking to maintain the basic structures of law and order while accommodating himself to the dominant nationalist party. From February 1963, however, his attempts became increasingly cosmetic. In theory, British policy-makers still clung to the aim, enunciated by Creech Jones in 1948, of encouraging the emergence of independent liberal democratic states with viable economies. In practice, however, just as the policy of no independence without economic viability had now been abandoned, so too had the Government's short-lived concern for democratic rights. Butler, as he explained to the cabinet in 1962, was convinced that it was 'imperative to retain Dr Banda's co-operation' if stability was to be maintained, and Jones adopted a similar non-confrontational approach.[94] In private letters, he frequently urged Orton Chirwa, the newly-appointed Minister of Justice and Attorney-General, to assists the Director of Public Prosecutions in bringing charges against MCP officials believed to be guilty of assault.[95] But when his requests were rejected, he had nothing further to offer. Late in June 1963 a relatively minor incident – an assault on two European teenagers by 'Malawi Police' escorting Banda – provoked widespread hostile comment in the Rhodesian and overseas press as well as an ill-judged telegram sent to Butler by a group of disaffected civil servants protesting at the breakdown of law and

---

[91] Speech by Banda in *Proceedings of the Legislative Assembly*, 12 December 1963.
[92] Monthly intelligence report for December 1963, TNA DO 183/135; Schoffeleers, *In Search of Truth and Justice*, pp. 89–90.
[93] K.H. Towsey to J.M. Greenfield, Federal Minister of Law and Home Affairs, 28 April 1963, ZNA F 236/CX/27.2
[94] Butler to Cabinet, 1 May 1962 quoted in H.A. Badenoch, 'Banda and the British: Anglo-Malawian Relations in the 1960s', Undergraduate thesis, University of Cambridge, 2002. I am indebted to Mr Badenoch for giving me a copy of his excellent thesis.
[95] Baker, *Sir Glyn Jones*, pp. 191–95.

9 Dr Banda, after being sworn in as Prime Minister, Zomba 1963
(Photograph reproduced by kind permission of Peter Mackay)

10 Waiting for Kamuzu to return from a foreign visit: Chileka Airport, 1963

order.[96] Butler, however, although expressing his concern to Jones at the 'profoundly unfavourable image to Nyasaland' that such incidents demonstrated, was more interested in facilitating the smooth transition to independence. He therefore rejected the request by the Chief Justice, Unsworth, for a commission of enquiry into the way justice was being administered under the new Government.[97] Instead, in September, Butler invited Banda to London, where they reached agreement that the date of independence should be 6 July 1964.

Decisions taken in the last months leading up to independence are important for the light they shed on the nature of the Banda regime and on its relationship with Britain. The starting point was the dissolution of the Federation at the end of 1963. On Banda's insistence, from 1961 links had been severed with many institutions associated with the Federation, including the University College of Rhodesia and Nyasaland, the one university operating in Central Africa at that time. Under Banda's express instructions, Federal financial support of some £3m for the ambitious Nkulu Falls hydro-electric scheme on the Shire River had been rejected. Nevertheless, the imminent ending of Federation resulted in a further unravelling of ties. In a complex operation, which left Malawi dangerously short of doctors and nurses, responsibility for health was transferred back from the Federation to Nyasaland.[98] Plans for a Malawi currency were introduced along with a Reserve Bank of Malawi to replace the Federal Reserve Bank; Air Malawi came into existence, initially under the auspices of the Central African Airways.[99] Careful consideration was given to the fate of 1 and 2 KAR, the two battalions from Nyasaland that had previously come under the control of Central Africa Command. Given the need for strict economy, Banda agreed that one battalion, 2 KAR, should pass into the army of Zambia at the time of independence, thus cutting the potential military strength available to him by half. But he also insisted that that the pay and conditions in the new Malawi Rifles (formerly 1 KAR) should be reviewed and that after independence, he alone would have responsibility for the army.[100] There would be no place in Malawi for army mutinies such as those that took place in Kenya, Tanzania and Uganda in January 1964. On a more pragmatic note, Banda signed a trade agreement with Winston Field, the new Prime Minister of Southern Rhodesia, and sanctioned the continuing of labour recruitment to Southern Rhodesia, where some 200,000 Malawians now worked. Ending the Federation would not alter Malawi's economic relations with the south.

Pragmatic considerations were also apparent in Banda's relations with the British. During earlier discussions Banda had been quick to dismiss concerns expressed by British ministers over the financial consequences for Nyasaland of its withdrawal from the Federation. But as independence approached the two

---

[96] The matter is discussed at some length and from a strongly anti-MCP perspective in Baker, *Sir Glyn Jones*, pp. 170–74 and less critically in Phillips, *Obscurity to Bright Dawn*, p. 167, 172–4.

[97] Baker, *Sir Glyn Jones*, pp. 176–81.

[98] Baker, 'Government Medical Service', pp. 306–07. In May 1964 only 12 out of 25 Medical Officer posts were filled, there was no Psychiatrist, only one Surgeon and no Senior Medical Superintendent. Only three out of 13 District Hospitals possessed doctors. *Annual Report of the Nyasaland/Malawi Ministry of Health for 1964*.

[99] Phillips, *Obscurity to Bright Dawn*, pp. 191–92.

[100] Lovering, 'Authority and Identity', pp. 42–3; Baker, *Revolt of the Ministers*, p. 74.

sides moved closer together. Reassured by the optimistic forecasts of Sir Roger Stevens and the Oxford economist, Arthur Hazlewood that an independent Malawi could become financially self-sufficient within a decade, Butler agreed to provide British grants in aid to cover the shortfall in Malawi's recurrent expenditure.[101] At the same time, Banda promised to make substantial economies before independence. Between 1962 and 1964 Britain provided development aid from the CDC of some £5 million, including a loan of £1.85 million to help finance the Nkulu Falls project.[102] With the end of the Federation, Britain intervened further, providing budgetary aid in 1964 of £4.25 million, no less than 31.4 per cent of the Malawi Government's recurrent expenditure. In that year, according to Morton, 'British aid accounted for over 98 per cent of Malawi's gross aid receipts and financed nearly half of total government expenditure.'[103] Whereas for much of the colonial period, Britain had starved Nyasaland of financial support, now and for nearly a decade, Malawi was to become one of the largest single recipients of British aid in terms both of receipts per head and its share of the total sum.[104]

Meanwhile, Banda kept his side of the bargain. Earlier, countries moving to independence, like Kwame Nkrumah's Ghana, had been able to utilise the rise in cash crop prices to dramatically increase expenditure on social services. But in Malawi, the situation was reversed. Pressed by Jones, Banda in 1963 persuaded Chiume, the Minister of Education, to make major cuts in expenditure on primary education before embarking on a further round of savings.[105] Under the scrutiny of Henry Phillips, who Banda kept on as Minister of Finance up to independence, the cost of all former Federal services, including health, was reduced by 15 per cent, and there were also cuts in the budget of the Ministry of Works and Administration.[106] Particularly contentious was the report made by T. M. Skinner on local civil service salaries and conditions of service. Released early in 1964 and approved by Banda and the Cabinet, it recommended that civil servants should pay rent for government housing as well as contributing 7.5 per cent of their salary in pension contributions.[107] Its implementation shortly before independence provoked 'a considerable amount of grumbling among civil servants' who were threatened by a real fall in their standard of living. Some of the most aggrieved in Zomba and Blantyre proposed to submit a memorandum to the prime minister deploring the contents of the report and requesting that it be amended.[108]

What were the objectives of the British Government in providing aid to Malawi on such a large and hitherto unprecedented scale?[109] A simple answer, utilising a Marxist neo-colonial model, would be that aid was intended as an instrument to protect British (or Western) investments in the country. But this

---

[101] Phillips, *Obscurity to Bright Dawn*, pp. 157–58.
[102] McMaster, *Malawi Foreign Policy*, p. 44.
[103] Kathryn Morton, *Aid and Dependence* (London, 1975), pp 62, 83.
[104] Ibid., p. 57. British budgetary aid was not phased out until 1972. Between October 1964–1968 Britain provided £32 million in aid to Malawi (Badenoch, p. 37).
[105] Baker, *Sir Glyn Jones*, pp. 163–64.
[106] Phillips, *Obscurity to Bright Dawn*, p. 177.
[107] Ibid., pp. 192–93.
[108] Intelligence Report for May 1964, TNA DO 183/137.
[109] For useful discussions see Morton, *Aid*, pp.57–6 and Badenoch, pp. 33–41.

is almost certainly untrue. With no exploitable minerals and only a small expatriate agriculture sector centred on the tea industry, Malawi did not register strongly in the spectrum of Britain's economic interests. On one estimate, only 3.8 per cent of British exports to the Third World went to Malawi in 1965; only 0.8 per cent of British assets in developing countries were invested in the territory.[110]

More convincing is the argument that Malawi's survival as an economically viable and politically stable state was of crucial importance for the success of Britain's new decolonisation policy in Central Africa. Once the decision had been taken to allow the three territories in the Federation to go their separate ways, it was essential that Malawi, economically the most fragile, should be seen to succeed. At all events, it was important to avoid the precedent of the Congo, where the rapid Belgian withdrawal in 1959 had been followed by economic and political collapse. Butler acknowledged in 1962 that, 'The economic and financial consequences of secession for Nyasaland are serious, and a claim upon HMG for substantially increased assistance over the next few years at least is to be expected.' He concluded, however, that if this assistance was provided, 'There is ... at least a prospect of launching Nyasaland into independence on a reasonably stable basis and of negotiating a "tapered off" financial settlement which in the circumstances is the best solution we can hope for.'[111] Some Conservatives in Britain, he later claimed, 'would have preferred that Nyasaland should be left to "stew in its own juice"' but this was not an option he could contemplate.[112]

The question of the nature of Malawi's relationship with Britain at this period also requires exploration. Did Banda's acceptance of large-scale British aid transform him into a 'puppet of neo-colonialism' or a 'tool of imperialism', as Chiume later suggested?[113] Or did he remain an autonomous agent, largely free from British control, as Badenoch has argued?[114] Although Badenoch's analysis is mainly focused on the decade following the cabinet crisis of 1964, it holds equally good for the months leading up to independence. Banda's strength as a potential ally of the British was that, once the issue of the Federation was out of the way, his views on several key issues were similar to their own. At a time when Cold War rivalries were at their most intense, Banda was unusual among politicians in Africa in stating that 'so far as we are concerned in Central Africa, there is no attraction to communism at all.'[115] In theory, he proclaimed his belief in 'discretional alignment', thus not committing Malawi in advance to any political grouping from the East or the West. In practice, however, as he demonstrated in a talk given in 1964 to the Zomba Debating Society, his reading of European history had led him to the then unfashionable conclusion that Communism was the product of the particular circumstances of Russia's past – in particular the continuation of feudalism there long after it had died out in the West – and had little relevance to Africa.[116] Stalin was as much an empire-builder as Peter the

[110] Morton, *Aid*, p. 59.
[111] Butler to Alport, Jones and Hone, 25 October 1962 quoted in Baker, *Sir Glyn Jones*, p. 149.
[112] Baker, *Sir Glyn Jones*, p. 164.
[113] Chiume, *Kwacha*, pp. 230–31.
[114] Badenoch, pp. 51–74.
[115] Quoted in Short, *Banda*, p.173.
[116] Address given by Banda to the Zomba Debating Society, April 1964 reprinted in the *Nation* (Malawi), 23 December 1997.

Great or Tsar Nicholas. The threat posed to Malawi by 'communist imperialism' was real.

Banda's ideas concerning economic development, therefore, coincided largely with the British position, although he did not shrink from taking an independent line when he believed it necessary to do so. In a meeting with Butler in 1963, he rejected out of hand Kettlewell's recommendation (made on his retirement from Nyasaland) that responsibility for Trust Land should be vested in an independent Land Board rather than in government ministers. And he was equally robust in refusing to recognise the existing system of land titles or to guarantee outright that he would never confiscate any settler-owned land.[117] However, as he made clear in introducing the Malawi Development Corporation Bill, he was opposed to large-scale nationalisation and in favour of the MDC working in partnership with private capital.[118] And he was also not averse to accepting the stringent budgetary demands that Butler asked for – in part because he himself believed in restraining expenditure on social services. Even before Skinner reported, Banda committed himself to looking for cuts in civil servants' allowances.[11] At the same time, he rejected requests for increased social support for workers on the grounds that, as most Malawian workers had access to land, they should be capable of looking after themselves.[120]

Banda's relationship with Lonrho, the one major new company to invest in Malawi, is particularly interesting for the insights it provides into the distinctive character of the emerging post-independence regime. In 1961 the London and Rhodesia Mining Company (as it was originally known) was one of several companies speculating in land and mining in Southern Rhodesia with very indifferent results. In that year, however, Lonrho fell into the hands of R. W. ('Tiny') Rowland, an unscrupulous, charismatic entrepreneur, who quickly transformed its fortunes by investing in Africa at a time when many more cautious businessmen were distancing themselves from the continent.[121]

Rowland's involvement in Malawi pioneered the approach he was to follow in other African countries in later years. Early in 1962 he attracted Banda's attention by purchasing a controlling interest in Nyasaland Railways from the federal government. They met for the first time in March, and quickly developed a mutually beneficial alliance that was to survive for over 30 years.[122] In 1963, Lonrho embarked on a buying spree in Nyasaland, purchasing the leading motor distributor, Halls Motors, as well as the British Central Africa Company, one of the original 'big three' in the Shire Highlands. It also announced its intention of developing a huge, 14,000 acre sugar plantation and refinery in the Lower Shire Valley (Sucoma), a striking demonstration of the confidence invested by Rowland in the new state of Malawi in the period leading up to its existence.[123]

---

[117] R.W. Kettlewell, 'Land Policy in Future Stages of Constitutional Development' with note by N.W. Watson, 5 April 1962, TNA DO 183/110; Note of a Meeting held on 24 September 1963 between Butler, Jones and Banda, DO 183/104.
[118] Speech by Banda, *Proceedings of the Legislative Assembly*, 7–10 Jan. 1964, pp. 1180–81.
[119] Speech by Banda, *Proceedings of the Legislative Assembly*, 15 July 1963.
[120] Speech by Banda, *Proceedings of the Legislative Assembly*, 25 Feb. 1964.
[121] Tom Bower, *Tiny Rowland. A Rebel Tycoon* (London 1993), pp. 50–71; Cronje, Ling and Cronje, *Lonrho*.
[122] Bower, pp. 72–4, 602.
[123] Ibid., pp. 63, 75–76.

Banda's response, as he indicated at a party he gave for the company in November 1963, was positive: 'I have told these people they are welcome. … Once I was sure Lonrho didn't want to turn the country into a sugar republic or a banana republic, like they have in South America and those places, then I welcomed them.'[124] What he did not say publicly was that from this time on, Lonrho benefited in Malawi from being granted a highly privileged position in which it paid virtually no taxes and enjoyed a near monopoly over the production of certain commodities. Nor did he note that from 1963 Lonhro began to pay secret donations as a form of political investment both to Banda personally and to the MCP.[125] Favours were not dispensed to Malawian politicians alone. Following his retirement in 1966, Peter Youens, Banda's closest expatriate adviser and Secretary to the Prime Minister and Cabinet, was appointed as one of Lonrho's directors.[126] By the early 1970s, the company controlled 22 subsidiaries in Malawi including the textile manufacturers, David Whitehead, and a highly profitable brewery that had gained the franchise to produce *chibuku*, African beer. Only Banda's own company, Press Holdings, had a larger stake in the country. Together they demonstrated the striking institutional overlap that now existed between political and economic power.

Regime change in Malawi involved continuity as well as transformation. Despite concern in Whitehall at 'Governors soldiering on after independence', Glyn Jones was approved as Malawi's first Governor General in January 1964.[127] 'It would be something of a miracle if anyone else was found who could establish the same relations with Dr Banda or exercise the same quiet influence', an official in the Colonial Office minuted.[128] There would be important places in the new regime for Youens as Secretary to the Prime Minister and Head of the Civil Service, for Bryan Roberts as Solicitor-General, for Peter Long as Commissioner of Police and for Douglas Lomax, who had served in the Nyasaland police since 1950, as Head of the Special Branch. Lieutenant Colonel Paul Lewis, Officer Commanding Nyasaland, was appointed Commander of the Malawi Army.[129] Many expatriate officers resigned before independence but, with Banda's approval, nearly half stayed on, some for up to eight or ten years.[130]

Changes in the composition of parliament, the cabinet and the party had the effect of consolidating Banda in power. As in 1961, he personally selected all 50 of the MCP candidates elected unopposed in April, including Katoba Musopole, the militant leader of the violent anti-colonial resistance movement in the Karonga district, who had been released from prison to a hero's welcome in March 1962.[131] Also elected was Rose Chibambo, the first woman to sit in parliament, who had been chosen by Banda in the face of considerable male opposition to fill a vacancy in August 1963. A few weeks later, Banda appointed her as Parliamentary Secretary to the Ministry of Natural Resources, a post she

[124] Quoted in McMaster, *Malawi-Foreign Policy*, p. 46.
[125] Bower, pp. 107, 366–67.
[126] Ibid., p. 105. On his retirement from Lonrho in 1994, Youens received a pay-off of £300,000. See obituary of Sir Peter Youens in the *Daily Telegraph*, 25 May 2000.
[127] J. L. Chadwick to Garner, 14 November 1963, TNA DO 183/444.
[128] Note by S P Whitley, 8 November 1963, TNA DO 183/444.
[129] Lovering, 'Authority and Identity', p. 157.
[130] Mullins, *Retreat from Africa*, p. 94.
[131] McCracken, 'Ambiguities of Nationalism', p. 85.

continued to hold in the independence government.

Further changes took place in the cabinet. Chipembere, who had entered the cabinet in February 1963 following his released from Zomba gaol, became Minister of Education; Chiume, deprived of his Education portfolio, combined the offices of Minister of External Affairs and Minister of Information; Yatuta Chisiza entered the cabinet as Minister of Home Affairs; John Tembo, the youngest member, became Minster of Finance. In a move that demonstrated the growing influence of Tiny Rowland on Banda, Colin Cameron, who had attempted to rein back the privileges vested in Lonhro as managing agent for Nyasaland Railways, was switched to the Ministry of Works, with John Msonthi taking the former's position.[132] Chipembere had been re-instated as Treasurer-General of the MCP on his emergence from prison but, requested by Banda to make frequent overseas visits, he had little time to carry out duties in this area. Instead, control of the Party moved into the hands of a group of Banda loyalists: the three regional chairmen, dominated by Richard Chidzanja for the Central Province; Aleke Banda, the Doctor's bright young acolyte, reinstated as Secretary-General following Dunduzu's death; finally Albert Muwalo, a tough functionary, appointed by Banda as Administrative Secretary in April 1964.[133]

Banda's intervention in reorganising the Malawi Youth constituted the final change. In March 1964 Jomo Chikwakwa, the hot-headed but independent-minded leader of the Youth League, was suspended from the MCP.[134] Seven months earlier, on 10 March 1963, Banda opened the first training course of the Young Pioneers in an attempt to create a smaller, better disciplined, more subservient organisation in the model of the Young Pioneers of Kwame Nkrumah's Ghana, drawn predominantly from unemployed and uneducated youth.[135] Initially, it was organised by a committee chaired by Chiume under the auspices of the Ministry of Education. But in November 1963, Banda transferred control to the Office of the Prime Minister and appointed Aleke Banda as National Chairman. When the Malawi Youth now acted they would do so in obedience to Dr Banda's direct command.[136]

All over Africa in the decade starting with Ghana's independence in 1957 colonial dependencies were transformed into independent nations but the routes they took varied dramatically from one country to another. In much of West and Equatorial Africa, decolonisation was a process controlled and mediated by the departing powers. In Algeria, by contrast, independence was the result of a brutal and lengthy war that became unbearably costly to France. Malawi's independence was achieved following neither of these models. Despite the loss of life experienced by activists both in 1953 and 1959, violence was not a key feature of Malawi's nationalist struggle but neither was the path to independence determined by strategies initiated in Britain. Instead, and to an extent that many Malawians today do not fully recognise, nationalists and the threat that they could muster played a key role in forcing British politicians to abandon their

[132] Phillips, *Obscurity to Bright Dawn*, p. 193–95.
[133] Ross, 'Reflections on the Malawi Cabinet Crisis'.
[134] Monthly intelligence report for March 1964, TNA DO 183/136.
[135] Intelligence reports for November 1962 and September 1963, TNA DO 183/136; Aleke Banda, 'The History of the Youth Movement' in *Youth in Malawi. Security and Progress with Malawi's Young Pioneers* (Department of Information, Blantyre, 1965).
[136] Banda, 'History of the Youth Movement'.

preferred strategies of disengagement. In what is a remarkable paradox, this led to a situation where, for Malawi to survive as a viable state, large scale British investments (financial and human) were required. This paradox is matched by another, demonstrating the improbable alliances established by the nationalists in opposing the colonial regime. During the independence celebrations from 4 to 7 July 1964, the new national anthem, a somewhat lugubrious piece, strongly influenced by Presbyterian hymns, was frequently played. But on the steps of Mua mission, perhaps at other churches in the Central Region too, *Nyau* dancers triumphantly performed.[137] Nationalism in Malawi was a genuinely popular movement, drawing support from conservative members of society as well as from the new elites. Only with the eruption of the cabinet crisis shortly after independence would the full implications of this fact emerge.

---

[137] Phillips, *Obscurity to Bright Dawn*, p. 204; Linden, *Catholics,* p. 131.

16
Revolt & Realignment
1964–1966

The cabinet crisis

According to older narratives, the lowering of the Union Jack at Rangeley (later Kamuzu) Stadium at midnight on 5 July 1964 marked a watershed, the moment when Malawi became free. Modern historians, more sceptical about what precisely independence entailed, might point to alternative events as marking the key transition: the two-day emergency debate in Parliament on 8–9 September, when Banda won a vote of confidence over his younger cabinet colleagues; Chipembere's failed coup d'état in February 1965, the point at which it became clear that Banda's regime would not be overthrown by force; perhaps even the economic crisis of the late 1970s and early 80s, which brought a lengthy period of economic growth, dating from the 1940s, to an unceremonious halt. Nevertheless, the formal ending of colonial rule was not simply a matter of ceremony. For the great majority of those packed into the stadium, even more for those who attended the many hundreds of village celebrations held a week later, independence meant the culmination of a struggle for liberation, although what that liberation might involve remained to be seen.[1] In his last speech in parliament before independence, Yatuta Chisiza, perhaps the bravest and most generous of all the ministers, put into words what many felt by quoting the poet Langston Hughes: 'We have tomorrow/Bright before us/Like a flame.'[2] Yet only three years later, Chisiza was to meet his death while leading a tiny group of guerrillas dedicated to overthrowing Banda by force.

This chapter seeks to explore the events surrounding what has been labelled both 'the cabinet crisis' and 'the revolt of the ministers': the attempt made by a group of senior politicians to challenge Banda only seven weeks after the independence celebrations and Banda's successful response.[3] There is nothing unusual about political upheavals in newly-independent African countries. In

---

[1]   Or so it seemed to the author who attended both the national celebrations in the Kamuzu Stadium and also a village ceremony in the Mulanje District a week later.
[2]   Speech by Chisiza, *Proceedings of the National Assembly*, 29 May 1964, p. 117.
[3]   The most detailed and accurate account of these events is contained in Baker, *Revolt of the Ministers*. However, there is still much of value in Short, *Banda*, pp. 197–230.

Malawi, however, the crisis had a particular resonance. Not only was Malawi's leadership nearly decimated, a whole generation of able young men and women was forced into exile, some of them for nearly 30 years. Families were permanently split; many hundreds of nationalists were herded into detention camps and treated with terrible brutality. Hopes for a democratic transition were dashed; at the same time, hitherto unexplored fissures within Malawi's society opened up, demonstrating to some commentators the existence of ideological, generational and regional divisions of a depth much greater than had previously been imagined. The purist might argue that an account of Malawi under colonial rule should end with the formal transfer of political authority. But just as the transfer of power to Banda and the MCP got under way not in July 1964 but rather in 1961, following the first elections, so British officials played a key role in the politics of Malawi at least up to 1966. Indeed, there are grounds for arguing that these years, straddling independence, form a single period; that it is not until the challenge from the ministers had been removed that a distinctive new phase in Malawi's history began – the era of the Banda dictatorship.

For many observers, the independence celebrations in July 1964 were a remarkable demonstration of Malawian unity. Yet even at this time, some outsiders detected signs of tension. Lord Alport, the former British High Commissioner in Salisbury, had a lengthy talk with Banda that evening, 'and noted the increasing degree to which he was holding himself apart from the other members of the Malawi Hierarchy'.[4] Peter Moxon, an ex-army major, married to a Malawian and an enthusiastic supporter of the nationalists provided an irreverent analysis of why this was so. Ministers, he claimed were not only resentful of the large number of portfolios Banda had kept to himself, they also deplored his failure to consult them on a range of issues including the identity of candidates nominated to the independence parliament. Yatuta Chisiza was irked by Banda's insistence that he should give up drink and reduce his social contacts with Europeans; more significantly, other nationalists had begun to find Banda's repetitive speeches 'faintly ridiculous'; several had taken to mimicking them in private.[5]

Events in the next few weeks brought tensions to a head. On 8 July, Banda left Malawi to attend meetings in London and Cairo. Shortly after his departure, Youens announced that Msonthi had been dropped from the cabinet; a routine measure explained by Banda's puritanical insistence on sobriety among his ministers, but one nevertheless that seriously alarmed his colleagues.[6] Banda's speech, made at Chileka airport on his return on 26 July, further increased their fears. At the OAU conference in Cairo, Banda had fallen out with Chiume following his delivery of a controversial speech emphasising that Malawi's geographical position would not allow him to sever all ties with the white-dominated countries of the south. Still angry when he arrived home, he deliberately reached over the heads of the assembled ministers to seek the support of the Party rank-and-file:

[4]   Lord Alport, *Sudden Assignment* (London, 1965).
[5]   Unpublished paper by Peter Moxon, York University Conference.
[6]   Paper by Moxon; Baker, *Revolt*, pp. 91, 95.

You the common people are the real Malawi Congress Party. Watch everybody! Even Ministers – and I tell you when they are present right here. Watch them, everybody! If they do what you do not think is good for the Malawi Congress Party, whether they are Ministers or not, come and tell me. It is your job to see that nothing injures or destroys the Party.[7]

Banda's speech had the effect of at least temporarily uniting the ministers. Previously, they had been divided into factions but now they came together in a single group which even Chiume was invited to join. Their unity was tested at the cabinet meeting held on 29 July at which Banda brought forward proposals for the reintroduction of detention without trial in the absence of a state of emergency. None of the ministers, the Head of the Special Branch believed, was in favour of the measure, 'some of them fearing no doubt that it might be used against themselves'. Only Colin Cameron, however, took the extreme step of resigning on the grounds that 'Banda was introducing the things which he, Cameron, had been highly critical of in the British Administration, and…he was not prepared to be associated with it.'[8]

With Cameron gone, the ministers made a further effort to defend their position. Up to now, none of them, not even Chipembere, had been prepared to criticise Banda to his face. However, at a meeting on 10 August, from which Chiume was absent, they plucked up sufficient courage to complain of the 'slighting references' to them that Banda had made in his speeches and to question whether it was wise for him to keep so many government responsibilities to himself.[9] Banda's muted response only increased their confidence. By this time, news of the strains within cabinet had begun to spread to senior diplomats and civil servants, leading Jones to fear that 'at some stage Dr Banda will declare an emergency, lock up all his Ministers and replace them with stooges.'[10] In the event, it was the ministers who took the initiative. On 19 August Chipembere departed for an educational conference in Canada. Despite his absence, his fellow-ministers felt the time was ripe to force a confrontation with Banda either to persuade him to change his ways or else to get him to resign. The chosen venue was the cabinet meeting on 26 August. Chiume, Chisiza and Chirwa, supported at times by Tembo, launched into a litany of grievances. These ranged from the lack of respect shown to them by senior European civil servants and Banda's failure to Africanise to 'his policies towards Portugal and Southern Rhodesia which made Malawi contemptible in other African eyes.'[11] According to the British High Commissioner, 'As they warmed to the task they lost their timidity and addressed the Prime Minister critically and almost threateningly.'[12] Tembo complained that 'Africans in the civil service had suffered as a result of the Skinner recommendation'; others argued against signing a new labour agreement with WNLA.[13] Banda, although outwardly calm and restrained, was inwardly appalled by the verbal assault to which he was subjected.

---

[7] Quoted in Short, *Banda*, p. 203.
[8] D. L. Cole, British High Commissioner, to K. J. Neale, 12 August 1964, TNA DO 183/168.
[9] Baker, *Revolt*, p. 103.
[10] Cole to Sir Arthur Snelling, 20 August 1964, TNA DO 183/168.
[11] Cole to Sandys, 14 October 1964, TNA DO 183/457.
[12] Ibid.
[13] Baker, *Revolt*, pp. 109–117.

They all attacked me. ... I was shocked...because there was the Prime Minister isolated, deserted by every one of his Ministers. No one tried to support me. Not one of them tried to defend me.[14]

In an ambiguously stated response, Banda announced: 'If my present policies are disapproved by you I should go now', only for the ministers to reply that this was not what they wanted. The next day, after a further meeting, the ministers agreed that Banda should discuss the matter with the Governor General. When he did, Jones recommended that he should stay. In an attempt to heal the split, Jones also suggested that Banda should give up two of the six ministries he held and seek to consult ministers more on policy decisions.[15]

It is not easy to determine whether Banda ever had any serious intention to resign. Some observers believed that he was at least temporarily demoralised by the ministers' united attack; others, including Peter Youens, that he was simply playing for time. At all events, from this point his attitude hardened and the rift widened. On 27 August, Chiume convened a meeting of a group of ministers, not including Tembo, at the Kuchawe Inn on Zomba plateau. There they drew up the Kuchawe Manifesto, a list of 'matters on which ministers want immediate action taken'.[16] The tone it struck was infinitely more aggressive than anything previously produced. Banda was informed in peremptory terms that 'Government must not be or appear to be the personal property of an individual. ... Favouritism and nepotism, intended or apparent, e.g. the Tembo family is favoured, must stop for the good of the country... Equally, people like Aleke Banda must not be treated ... as the favoured pets of the Prime Minister.' The decision to move the capital to Lilongwe must be reversed. So must the decision (taken directly by Banda) to introduce a charge of three pence a day in government hospitals. Cuts in the salaries and conditions of service of African civil servants must be abandoned; the Civil Service itself must be immediately Africanised. Secret diplomacy of the type Banda had previously indulged in must be abandoned; true cabinet government must be introduced, with the ministers being given real power.[17]

There can be no doubt that had Banda made major concessions to this remarkable document he would have surrendered the reality if not the appearance of power. Instead, he responded by giving ministers the impression that he was prepared to compromise while, in fact, setting out to defeat them. His initial task was to mobilise support. In quick succession, starting on 27 August, he reappointed Msonthi as a minister, thus reducing his isolation in the cabinet, and met Muwalo and Aleke Banda, the two key Party administrators, who informed him that news of the dispute was now current in Blantyre. Bolstered by the arrival of anonymous letters, accusing the ministers of plotting against him, he held further meetings with a number of loyalists including Chidzanja and Kumtumanji, his ministers for Southern and Central Region and Alex Nyasulu, the Speaker of the Parliament; all of them assured him that he continued to enjoy the support of the MCP. Encouraged by this, he rejected any

[14] Speech by Banda, *Proceedings of Parliament,* 8 September 1964.
[15] Baker, *Revolt,* p. 117, 121–23.
[16] Ibid. p. 128.
[17] Ibid. pp. 129–32.

hint of compromise with the ministers when they met on 2 September, and instead appealed over their heads to members of parliament. At a hastily convened informal meeting held on 7 September, Nyasulu, the Speaker, informed them that a vote of confidence in the Prime Minister would be proposed next day. At almost the same time, Banda dismissed three of the ministers, Chirwa, Chiume and Bwanausi, as well as Rose Chibambo, Parliamentary Secretary for natural resources, who was accused of organising women's groups against him. Yatuta Chisiza decisively resigned, followed by Chokani and, with less conviction, by Msonthi. A few hours later, however, Msonthi withdrew his resignation having talked over the issue with John Tembo, who had swung back in support of Banda following the criticisms he made in the meeting on 26 August.

The parliamentary debate on 8–9 September was an intensely dramatic event yet there is good reason to believe that any question concerning its outcome had already been decided at the informal meeting of parliamentarians on the previous day. The former ministers, still lacking the involvement of Chipembere, who was now making his way back by plane from Canada, had failed to devise a coherent strategy aimed at overthrowing Banda and, in consequence, were driven onto the defensive. None of them appears to have made a concerted effort to win over their fellow-parliamentarians in advance, with the result that not one rallied to their cause at the meeting on the 7th.[18] Nevertheless, when parliament met next day to discuss a motion of confidence in the prime minister and his policies the atmosphere was electric. Civil servants, many from the adjacent Government Press, cheered the ex-ministers as they arrived and frequently intervened during the debate itself, particularly on the first day when loudspeakers broadcast the proceedings to the assembled crowd. Banda opened the debate in a powerful and controlled speech that received an ovation from his backbenchers. Starting with a rhetorical flourish, he bemoaned the collapse of the four cornerstones, unity, loyalty, discipline and obedience, before describing the various meetings he had held with the ministers and the complaints they had presented to him. He made no bones of the fact that 'I run this State as if it were my own property.' But he claimed that this was done to prevent his colleagues making 'their Ministries a source of fabulous wealth by bribery and corruption'. The ministers, he suggested, were involved in a conspiracy against him, fuelled not simply by ambition and avarice but also by the sinister machinations of Communist China orchestrated by its ambassador in Dar es Salaam. He concluded by asserting that, had they believed they could get away with it, they would have murdered him in cold blood.[19]

Banda's speech set the tone for the ensuing debate. With the exception of Kanyama Chiume, who spelt out his criticisms of Banda's policies in some detail, the ministers restricted their remarks to reiterating their loyalty to the Prime Minister and asserting that it was their duty to bring to his attention the views of the people. This, however, did not protect them from being denounced as 'power-hungry maniacs', 'traitors' and 'conspirators'.[20] Rose Chibambo, the one

---

[18] The one partial exception was Rose Chibambo who raised with the Speaker the question why the Prime Minister was not in attendance.

[19] Speech by Banda, *Proceedings of Parliament*, 8 Sep.1964, pp. 10–19.

[20] Speech by Chakuamba, 8 September 1964, p. 38.

woman in the House, came in for particularly virulent abuse. Denounced by Banda as a dangerous schemer who had encouraged women in the north to protest against the introduction of hospital fees of 3d a day ('tickies'), Chibambo was subjected to a torrent of interjections whenever she attempted to speak, demonstrating the strength of anti-female prejudice among male Malawian politicians.

The arrival of Chipembere brought proceedings in parliament to a climax. During the last stage of his journey home on 8 September, he was joined in Dar es Salaam by Qabaniso Chibambo, who begged him to make one final attempt to achieve reconciliation between Banda and the ministers. Following his return to Zomba, Chipembere therefore approached the Governor General in the hope that he could persuade Banda to postpone the debate so that he could meet the ministers in the morning. Banda's rejection of this proposal dashed any hope of reconciliation. At 9.20 on Wednesday 9 June Chipembere formally resigned as minister before driving to parliament where he joined his ex-colleagues on the back benches to cheers from the visitors' gallery. Ten minutes later, Banda entered the house in a rage, threw his fly whisk down, and – according to the official record of proceedings – demanded to know who was organising the people demonstrating outside. He then shouted that the debate would continue without break for lunch or tea until a decision had been reached.[21]

Read today, many of Chipembere's speeches come over as populist diatribes, superficially eloquent but lacking in substance. But this cannot be said of his last and greatest parliamentary performance. As D. L. Cole, the British High Commissioner noted in his penetrating discussion of the crisis, most speeches delivered by Banda's supporters in the debate 'were adulatory, frequently threatening and sometimes incomprehensible'.[22] Chipembere, by contrast, spoke in a tone of dignified regret that was all the more impressive because of its evident restraint.

> It gives me a really heavy heart that Malawi, which was so proud of its unity, so famous for its stability, that Malawi, which people were regarding as a paragon of political organization and discipline and understanding, has now broken down. Broken down to the extent of the members of the one party, the mighty Malawi Congress Party, attacking one another in public here, in the presence of *atsamunda,* or our former enemies, calling one another traitors. Wherever Welensky is today, he must be rejoicing. He must be celebrating. There must be a cocktail party somewhere in Salisbury as a result of what is taking place here. We are in utter disgrace.[23]

Taking each minister in turn, but concentrating particularly on Yatuta Chisiza, he sought to demonstrate the absurdity of describing them as traitors. 'If there is a name…that risked his life, it was Yatu. And for his performance, his loyalty, his energy, his obedience to the Ngwazi, let the Ngwazi's own praises in recent months speak for themselves.' He personally had resigned because he believed that the problem should have been solved through open discussion at

---

[21] The official transcript reads: '*The Prime Minister*: Organizing those people, chaos! Civil Servants, ridiculous. Until a decision is reached. I mean until a decision is reached, Mr Speaker'. *Proceedings of Parliament*, 9 September 1964, p. 49. According to Peter Moxon, 'There in front of the entire house… the P.M. leaped to his feet, hurled his fly whisk down on the cushions, and rais[ing] his arms above his head he started to scream.'

[22] Cole to Secretary of State for Commonwealth Relations, 14 October 1964, TNA DO 183/457.

[23] Speech by Chipembere, *Proceedings of Parliament*, 9 September 1964, p. 89.

a meeting of the Malawi Congress Party rather than through dismissals. This, as the Prime Minister had frequently advised, was the appropriate action for a minister to take. He also expressed his general support for the various points the ministers had raised, starting with their emphasis on the need for collective responsibility: 'both in our custom and modern custom, it is necessary that we must consult when we do things.' He ended by promising to serve Banda loyally 'in any capacity.... I am perfectly convinced that one of these days the Prime Minister will evolve a solution to this problem and that once more we shall be calling one another brothers and not attacking each other as monsters.'[24]

By the time he came to wind up the debate, Banda knew that his motion would receive unanimous approval and he was prepared to be magnanimous: 'This is not a Cabinet crisis at all.... This is a family affair, in which no outsider must try to meddle.' If any outsider attempted to 'make political capital out of this', he warned, 'these very same men [the six ministers] will be the very first ones to be on that man's neck.'[25] Public magnanimity, however, could not conceal the deep divisions that had been exposed during the debate. Not only had many speakers expressed their intolerance of any disagreement, however small, with Banda, they had also demonstrated the dislike felt for the small coterie of graduates by less well educated, often older men who believed they had been shouldered aside in the race for the spoils of office. 'If you will be deserted by these graduates', one speaker told Banda, 'then we the uneducated will follow you until death.' Educated people were power hungry; by contrast: 'It is uneducated savages in the villages who followed you first, Ngwazi. Those are the people who are following you.'[26]

Resentment over educational privilege reflected the growth of regional and ethnic rivalries. The ministers' accusation that Banda had practised nepotism and favouritism led several speakers from the Central and Southern Regions to point to the accumulation of posts in the hands of northerners. Three of the dissident ministers came from the North; about 300 northerners were being educated on scholarships overseas.[27] None of the resigning ministers drew attention to regional differences in their speeches. But two of Banda's closest allies from the Central Province took a very different stance. Provoked by hostile comments from the packed crowd of civil servants – many of them from the north – F. R. J. Bundaunda, the member for Kasungu North, accused an unnamed northern politician of claiming that he was 'not prepared to be ruled by the primitive people of the South and Central Regions'. He then launched into an attack on Chiume whom he accused of 'favouritism in employing and granting scholarships in which one Region is favoured'.[28] Richard Chidzanja, the newly-appointed Minister for the Central Region, expressed a similar, deeply felt view. A self-made businessman who had left school early, Chidzanja echoed the concerns of the organisers of the Achewa Improvement Society back in the 1940s, in a speech shot through with resentment at the way in which he and his fellow Chewa had been treated by better-educated northern politicians:

[24] Speech by Chipembere, ibid., pp. 98–99.
[25] Speech by Banda, ibid., p. 141.
[26] Speech by E. Z. K. Banda, ibid., p. 63.
[27] Ibid., p. 62.
[28] Speech by F. R. J. Bundaunda, 8 Sep. 1964.

Who practises tribalism? Not me. I believe in unity, but somebody mustn't despise me because I am Nchewa; there I am bitter, Mr Speaker *(Applause)*. It is true that Achewa people were regarded as inferior people for years – it is hard to believe that someone can find someone like Chidzanja – when they come from other areas they think they are going to find stupid Achewas. That is why they follow us, when I tell them no, no that is finished. Now we are equal. They don't mind to despise us, that is when I am bitter, and then they know what I always talk but I've never been a tribalist, a provincialist or regionalist, all my friends are not from my region.[29]

In a message of support, directed to Dr Banda, he added: 'All of these things, known as Zinyao, of course, in Central Region are in full swing behind me. *(Applause)* ... They will never run away from you. Nothing, no threats by anybody, will move them away from you; they are with you.' It was a clear state-ment that members of *nyau* societies, who had been engaged since January 1964 in attacks on Jehovah's Witnesses on the Lilongwe Plain, would now be employed to intimidate the Prime Minister's opponents within the MCP.

Studies of the cabinet crisis have tended to focus on the role of the ex-minis-ters. Yet, it is arguable that the conduct of politicians who remained loyal to Banda is equally worthy of attention. In particular, it is worth exploring the behaviour of Katoba Musopole, at one level the quintessential northern politi-cian, one of Malawi's most authentic freedom fighters, yet also the man whose intervention in parliament in March 1966 can be seen as leading to the enshrine-ment of Chichewa as Malawi's single national language and hence, in some views, to the marginalisation of northern culture

There is no simple explanation for Musopole's transition from Marxist freedom-fighter to MCP loyalist. Following his arrest in Tanganyika in August 1959 he spent two and a half years in Zomba gaol and was released to public acclaim on 22 March 1962.[30] He then returned to a hero's welcome in the hill areas of the Karonga district, from where he began a correspondence with his fellow left-winger, Attati Mpakati, at that time a student in Leningrad.[31] Given his unashamedly Marxist views at this time it is unlikely that the more conser-vative-minded Dr Banda regarded him with other than suspicion. Nevertheless, Banda, who may have been aware of the rumours that Musopole was planning to join forces with Pemba Ndove in the short-lived Nyasaland African National Union, took steps to incorporate him within the MCP by selecting him as candi-date and thus member for the Karonga Hills constituency in the parliamentary elections of April 1964.[32] Chipembere, who had spent some time with Muso-pole in Zomba gaol, welcomed him at the first meeting in May as 'the General from Fort Hill', a man 'of modern and left-wing notions'. Musopole, on his own account, did nothing to dispel this impression. In a rousing maiden speech he attacked the British flag as 'a symbol of imperialism, imperialism which has for ages stood for oppression, exploitation, slavery, misery and all sorts of evil.'[33]

29 Speech by Chidzanja, 9 Sep 1964.
30 Monthly Intelligence Report for March 1962 TNA 183/136; *Malawi News*, 29 March 1962.
31 Monthly Intelligence Report, August 1963, TNA DO 183/136. Mpakati later emerged as the leader of the exiled Socialist League of Malawi (LESOMA). He was murdered in Harare in 1983.
32 For the background of this party see TNA CO 1015.2445, 'The Extent of Opposition to & Criticism of Dr Banda'.
33 *Proceedings of First Session of the National Assembly*, 26–29 May 1964, speeches by Chipembere and Musopole.

There can be little doubt that for Musopole, as for many Malawians, the emergency debate of September 1964 involved an acutely agonising choice, not made easier by the fact that the dissident ministers failed to coordinate their strategy with potential sympathisers. Since every member was called upon to speak, silence was not an option. The Member of Parliament for Karonga South, Akogo Kanyanya, spoke out in support of the ministers in a short but effective contribution.[34] Musopole, by contrast, while acknowledging that several of the ministers were his friends as well as his colleagues, found himself unable to go this far. In a halting speech, marked 'inaudible' in several places in the parliamentary record, he pledged his loyalty to Banda and repeated the slogan, "The Doctor knows best." At one point he started to diverge from official policy by claiming in relation to Communist China, 'if I am not mistaken, we are going to remain neutral.' But his central, still slightly ambiguous argument was: 'Leave everything to Ngwazi Kamuzu, he knows best, but some of us they think we know better, we can do best, we can do better than Kamuzu – we are becoming new trouble makers.'[35]

Kanyama Chiume, Musopole's comrade in arms in 1957, continued to believe that although 'Mr Musopole … had supported Banda in parliament … deep in his heart he was not with the regime'.[36] But, Musopole himself, whatever his private reservations, took an increasingly loyalist position in public. Promoted to Parliamentary Secretary in the Ministry of Community and Social Development, he led the way during a further debate in October in denouncing Chiume as 'Lucifer' and in reaffirming his support for Banda. The terms he used suggest that he remained sensitive to criticisms of his new-found, unquestioning loyalty:

> Some people say: "Oh we praise today, Kamuzu knows best", just because we want to gain favour, or because we want that we should be good boys, but that we are just "Yes men", "Yes, Sir, yes, Sir". It is not that… When we know that Kamuzu knows best, we know what we are talking about.[37]

Other politicians found their loyalties equally divided. In pledging their support for Banda, Qabaniso Chibambo distanced himself from his sister-in-law, Rose, just as J.L. Pangani, the MP for Mulanje South, distanced himself from his brother-in-law, Bwanausi. Their personal dilemmas were to be replicated across Malawi in the next few weeks for scores of individuals confronted by a desperately hard decision of which the outcome was to affect their lives, in many cases permanently. Some, like the senior civil servant, Gomo Michongwe, and the newly-appointed ambassador to the United Nations, the poet and novelist David Rubadiri, were to end in exile. Others, following the example of Msonthi and Chibambo, were to throw in their lot with Banda and become prominent members of the new regime.

In the days following the emergency debate, the conflict spread into the streets and villages, taking an altogether more popular and more violent form. On the evening of the 9th, the ex-ministers met briefly and agreed to take their

[34] *Proceedings of Malawi Parliament, Second Meeting, First Session*, 8–9 May 1964, speech by Kanyanya.
[35] Ibid., speech by Musopole.
[36] Chiume, *Kwacha* p. 223.
[37] *Proceedings of Parliament, Third Meeting, First Session*, 27–30 Oct, 1964, speech by Musopole.

message to the constituencies with the intention of mobilising popular support.[38] Warned that there might be an attempt on his life, Chiume left Zomba secretly at night and drove to Nkhata Bay where he met up with Chisiza and Chirwa. Together they held meetings all over the north – in Mzuzu, Rumphi, Karonga, Chirumba and Chitimba – where they received the support of the M.P. for Karonga, Kanyanya, before separating to visit their respective constituencies. Despite Chibambo's attempts to prevent people attending, Chiume held a large meeting at Livingstonia, the site of the junior college.[39] In the south, Chipembere addressed a meeting at Fort Johnston where he attacked the slow pace of Africanisation and, according to one account, claimed that 'The present Malawi Government is worse than Welensky's Federal Government.'[40] Other ex-ministers, lacking Chipembere's popular support, took a more circumspect approach. Chokani, joined later by Bwanausi and Chisiza on his return from the north, held several meetings with the Governor General at which the question of their return to the Cabinet was discussed. Banda, despite denouncing his former colleagues at a public rally as 'hyenas conspiring against him in the night', left open the possibility that at least those who had resigned might be admitted back. But as the days went by, 'attitudes hardened and speeches became more and more vitriolic.'[41] Having dismissed the ministers from the MCP executive, Banda on 15 September suspended them from the party and banned members from attending their meetings. Chipembere responded on 19 September by holding a 'cocktail party' in Blantyre at which he criticised Banda's policies; Banda replied next day by denouncing the ministers for their 'criminal irresponsibility' at a rally attended by about 5,000 people at Ngabu in the Lower Shire Valley.[42]

Less than a week later, violent rhetoric descended into physical violence in the first of a series of clashes that pitted Banda's Malawi Youth against civil servants and Chipembere's supporters. According to Banda, the violence was initiated on Friday 25 September by a group of Chipembere loyalists who attacked Kumtumanji and the veteran businessman, Lali Lubani, at a meeting at Mponda's village near Fort Johnston from which Kumtumanji escaped only by firing his gun.[43] The next day Banda gave orders that all public meetings and processions in the Southern Province should be banned; he then departed for Lilongwe on the first stage of what was intended to be a triumphal tour of the Central and Northern regions. Meanwhile, 200 Youth Leaguers were brought by lorry into Limbe where they became involved in a fight that left more than 20 people injured. On Sunday 26th, the violence escalated still further. Despite his meeting being banned, Chipembere addressed 300 supporters in the Blantyre suburb of Soche. There they were attacked by Youth Leaguers armed with clubs and iron bars but fought back, driving off their opponents. That evening, Youth Leaguers set up a road block at Ntondwe on the Zomba-Blantyre road where they stopped all vehicles and burned two, including one owned by Orton Chirwa who escaped only by running into the bush.

[38] Chiume, *Kwacha*, p. 216.
[39] Ibid., pp. 216–19.
[40] Short, *Banda*, p. 216.
[41] Cole to S. of S. for Commonwealth Relations, 14 October 1964, TNA DO 183/457.
[42] Baker, *Revolt*, p. 178.
[43] Speech by Banda, *Proceedings of Parliament*, 29 October 1964, p. 251.

In the following week, Zomba became the centre of confrontation. The clashes began on Monday 28 September when Youth Leaguers and Pioneers, bussed into town the night before, attempted to eject traders from Zomba market and to intimidate civil servants on their way to work. The civil servants reacted by arming themselves with sticks, setting fire to the Congress Party headquarters and burning down the store owned by the local MCP Chairman. During a series of scuffles, Muwalo, recently appointed as a minister, was attacked, as was Chakuamba, who was dragged from under a bed in the hospital where he had taken refuge and severely beaten. A further clash took place the following day in which one person was killed.

By Wednesday, pro-Chipembere supporters, some from outside Zomba, had taken over the town. According to Cole, who witnessed the events at first hand,

> …by that morning the general intimidation was such that the entire African community refrained from going to work, they all wore white bands on their wrist to indicate that they were not Youth Leaguers, and they all carried clubs and cudgels. All shops were closed and eventually Government departments also closed down. Large crowds gathered in the market area, with the supposed purpose of defending Zomba against an attack by Dr Banda's followers from the nearby villages.[44]

Not a single Malawian minister remained in the capital; instead it was left to Youens to address the crowd assembled in the market. Not until the next day was peace restored when police and soldiers moved into the residential area where they were welcomed by civil servants as their protectors against further attacks from the Malawi Youth.

In October the shape and nature of the conflict became clear. An early casualty was the ministers' fragile unity. Chokani and Bwanausi had demonstrated considerable solidarity by refusing to contemplate a return to government without their colleagues. But following Banda's rejection of negotiations, they had nothing further to offer. At the end of September, they left for Northern Rhodesia where they were to attempt to carve out new careers as schoolteachers.[45] Chiume and Chisiza, the two most powerful northern politicians, were equally unsuccessful. An effective popular speaker and organiser, Chiume suffered from a reputation for scheming and unreliability and hence failed to mobilise large-scale support. By 1 October he had become cut off in the north, fearing to return south through Kasungu because of the threat posed by the Young Pioneers, and isolated from his fellow ministers. Faced first at Karonga and later at Fort Hall [Chitipa] by angry crowds seeking to attack his car, he made his way over the border to Tanzania with the help of a friendly police officer.[46] There he met up with Yatuta Chisiza who had crossed the border on the same day, having told the officer that he intended to return to 'remedy the ills of this country … sooner rather than later.'[47]

With their colleagues departed, Chirwa and Chipembere reacted in different ways. An instinctive moderate, Orton Chirwa set about achieving a rapproche-

[44] Cole to Secretary of State for Commonwealth Affairs, 14 October 1964 TNA DO 183/457.
[45] Bwanausi was killed in a car crash in 1968 but Chokani was one of those who returned to Malawi in 1994.
[46] Chiume, *Kwacha*, pp. 20–224.
[47] Quoted in Baker, *Revolt*, p. 198.

ment with Banda – although the fact that it was he who had handed the abusive Kuchawe Manifesto to the Prime Minister ensured that this would always be an uphill task. In an act of calculated cruelty, Banda invited him to his house on the pretext of discussing Chirwa's appointment as a judge before setting his bodyguards on him and having him beaten up. Chirwa then left for Tanzania around 22 October, having hidden on a boat departing from Fort Johnston.[48] Chipembere, by contrast, avoided all direct personal contact, either with Banda or with Jones, and concentrated on building up his personal support. Banda attempted to reduce his movements by signing an order on 30 September restricting him to a four-mile radius of his home at Malindi. But this was only partly successful; Chipembere organised a contingent of some 1,000 supporters to protect the approaches to his house and received visits from sympathisers arriving by lorry from Blantyre, Zomba, Chiradzulu and elsewhere. Tension mounted with the murder in Zomba on 23 October of the Tonga sub-chief, Timbiri (a death initially blamed on Orton Chirwa). It rose again over the next two days when, at an emergency conference of the MCP, Banda issued a warning that the ex-ministers were plotting to overthrow him by force. 'I'll face Kanyama Chiume with his foreign allies', Banda informed the party. 'We must be ready for anything. Every man and women will have to be taught to use a gun – even a machine-gun.'[49] Aware that parliament was about to meet to approve Banda's proposal for the reintroduction of detention without trial, Chipembere decided to pre-empt the inevitable by going into hiding. The news was announced by Banda in parliament on 28 October. 'Henry Chipembere has run away from Malindi. He has run away; he is missing. I have ordered full search for him and I want him brought here, alive if possible, but if not alive then any other way.'[50] A new stage in the struggle had been reached.

The Chipembere rising

For many observers in the days following the emergency debate it seemed likely that, if armed resistance to Banda should break out, it would do so in the Northern Region. Not only had Banda's new-style cultural nationalism, predicated on the superiority of Chewa institutions, exacerbated regional divisions, so too had the increasingly open criticisms made of 'arrogant' northerners by politicians from elsewhere, culminating in Chidzanja's speech in parliament on 9 September. Many, although not all of the civil servants disillusioned by economic cutbacks and the slow pace of Africanisation, came from the north. So too did four of the seven leading dissident politicians. What is more, it was in the Northern Region and particularly in the Karonga district that armed opposition to colonialism had operated most effectively in 1959, and most of the leaders of that resistance still remained active in politics.

Yet if the north was to be the scene of widespread disaffection in the aftermath of the crisis, it was in the southern districts of Zomba, Kasupe and, particularly,

---

[48] Baker, *Revolt*, pp.190–98. Such was Chirwa's persistence, that having narrowly escaped being assaulted at Banda's house at an abortive meeting on 19 October he went back again on the 20th.

[49] Short, *Banda*, pp. 224–25.

[50] Speech by Banda, *Proceedings of Parliament*, 28 October 1964, p. 164.

around the south-east arm of Lake Malawi that the most dramatic confrontations took place. Although this can be explained in part, in the case of Zomba, by the existence there of substantial numbers of the ex-ministers' most obvious allies – civil servants and young educated nationalists – it is not true of the other districts, notably Fort Johnston, which was one of the most educationally undeveloped in the country. There one must look both to the appeal of Chipembere as the most prominent local politician but also to the complex interrelationship of economic interests and ethnicity in what, for much of the colonial period, had been a highly marginalised area.

A photograph of Chipembere survives, taken in January 1965 when he was hiding in the mountains east of Malindi, less than a month before he attempted to overthrow Banda's regime by force. It shows a dumpy, somewhat overweight man, wearing a long raincoat almost down to his feet and carrying a black umbrella. Che Guevara – then about to embark on his final, ill-fated Bolivian campaign – he was not. Yet if the diabetic Chipembere, like his hero John Chilembwe, lacked military skills, he shared with the latter the ability to reach out beyond his natural constituency to convert others to his cause. Of Nyanja stock (both his parents were born in Mozambique[51]) and brought up in a strictly Anglican family, he was an unlikely role model for disaffected Muslim Yao headmen and villagers who were doubly marginalised in the newly independent state by their lack of access either to the jobs that come with education or to major cash crop opportunities. However, as the dominant local political leader, he combined a reputation for 'extremism' attractive to the young with respect for his role as an influential political fixer, energetic in his support of local interests. In this respect it seems more than likely that Chipembere's experience as a fish trader (an occupation he combined with politics from 1956) was of value in allowing him to establish links with fellow traders and fishermen who rallied to his support in 1964.[52] He was thus able to build up a network of supporters and sympathisers consisting of fellow politicians, civil servants and youthful activists, and also of some Yao chiefs and headmen in the Fort Johnston and Zomba areas, among them Jalasi, Mwambo and Kumtumanji (a cousin of the minister). The two fellow members of parliament from the area, George Ndomondo and Thengo Maloya, also threw in their lot with him as did most of the members of the Fort Johnston and Kasupe district councils. As late as the end of October 1964, supporters loyal to Chipembere blockaded the road at Kasupe and Liwonde with the intention of forcing delegates from the MCP conference to remove their Kamuzu badges.[53] When Youth Leaguers visited Fort Johnston in November, Chipembere loyalists forced them to retreat.

With Chipembere in hiding, rumour and reality became increasingly intertwined. A central theme was that the ex-ministers were using witchcraft in order to achieve their ends. Chipembere, it was claimed, had been sleeping on a grave in order to obtain greater power. Orton Chirwa had consulted a *singanga* at Mulanje and promised him £500 for finding *mankhwala* [medicine] and £1,200 if this *mankhwala* succeeded in bringing about Banda's death.[54] Further

---

[51] Henry Chipembere, *My Malawi Ancestors* (privately published pamphlet, August 1969).
[52] Wiseman C. Chirwa, 'Fishing Rights, Ecology and Conservation along Southern Lake Malawi, 1920–1964' *African Affairs*, 95, 380 (1996), p. 374.
[53] Speeches by Musopole and Muwalo, *Proceedings of Parliament*, 28 October, 1964, pp. 181, 187.
[54] Speeches by Banda and Muwalo, *Proceedings of Parliament*, 28 October 1964, pp. 164, 189.

rumours focused on the likelihood of invasion across the Songwe River from Tanzania, organised by Chiume and Yatuta Chisiza with the assistance of an Eastern European power. For four days people in the Central Region searched Dzalanyama forest near Budu for the remains of six Youth Leaguers, said to have been machine-gunned by guerrillas. There were rumours that Banda was about to flee and that Chipembere would take his place; that Banda's fly whisk (a potent source of strength) had disappeared and that a photograph of Chipembere had mysteriously appeared in his pocket; that he had dismissed his African bodyguards and replaced then with mercenaries hired from Europe. It was also claimed that an illicit collection of arms and ammunition had been discovered near the northern border. This, in fact, was true, although the arms were destined not for the ex-ministers but for Frelimo, the Mozambican liberation movement, which had carried out its first raid against the Portuguese in September 1964. Chipembere was confidently rumoured to be in Tanzania: perhaps in Dar es Salaam with the other ministers; perhaps with the father of Oscar Kambona, Chipembere's childhood friend.[55] It was not until the rising began that officials learned for certain that, far from retreating into Tanzania, Chipembere had spent the previous 14 weeks in a secret training camp named 'Zambia' in the forest north of Malindi. It was from there that he emerged on the night of 12 February with a contingent some 200 strong, set on overthrowing the Banda regime.

It is difficult not to see in Chipembere's abortive insurrection the same combination of courage, idealism, brutality and incompetence that had characterised the Chilembwe Rising almost exactly 50 years earlier. On his own account, Chipembere's original intention in going into hiding was to organise a campaign of civil disobedience. But faced by the government's restriction and, from January, the detention of many of his sympathisers, he changed his mind and determined to strike at the centre.[56] His precise plan remains shrouded in mystery but it certainly involved a first stage in which his tiny army would move by night from Malindi to Zomba – a distance of 100 miles – crossing two ferries and gathering transport and arms as they went. What he expected to happen at Zomba, not only the capital but also the headquarters of the Malawi Rifles, is by no means clear. Possibly he thought that elements in the army and the police would come to his support and turn against their expatriate commanders as had happened just over a year previously during the army mutinies in Kenya and Tanzania.[57] Sympathisers in government offices and Radio Malawi would also come to his aid and, with power transferred in the capital, the rest of the country would fall in line.[58] John Okello, he may have reflected, had been successful in seizing power in Zanzibar in January 1964 with fewer supporters

---

[55] Oscar Kambona's career has certain parallels with that of Chipembere. Of Malawian stock, he rose to be Secretary-General of TANU and Minister of Education in Tanzania before falling out with Nyerere in 1967 and going into exile.

[56] Baker, *Revolt*, p. 208.

[57] There is some evidence that Chipembere had received assurances of support from sympathetic policemen or soldiers prior to the revolt. See A. Ross, 'A Return to Malawi,' *Edinburgh University History Graduates Association Newsletter*, 30, October 1998, pp. 12–20. The evidence is reviewed by Baker, *Revolt*, pp. 219–221.

[58] For a somewhat garbled account of rumours current in Zomba see Bill Jackson, *Send Us Friends*, p. 285.

and on the basis of an even more improbable scheme.[59]

In the event, Chipembere's rebellion was doomed almost from the start. Although rumours of a possible insurrection had circled in Zomba from January, the precise timing came as a complete surprise and Chipembere and his men were able to cross the ferry to Fort Johnston unmolested, having already acquired a lorry, a Land Rover and rifles at St Michael's College, Malindi. No resistance to them was offered by the police or the expatriate district officer at Fort Johnston. They were therefore free to occupy the police station, release the prisoners from the gaol, seize guns and ammunition from the armoury, acquire further vehicles and cut the telephone wires. They also killed the wife and child of an unpopular Malawian Special Branch Officer, Inspector Changwa, and burnt down five houses, including the court-house in the neighbouring village of Chief Mponda, one of the few Yao chiefs to have thrown in his lot with Banda. They then drove by lorry towards Liwonde, confidently assumed to be a Chipembere stronghold where, as a result of a spectacular failure of planning, they found the ferry moored on the Zomba side of the river. With no prospect of getting to Zomba before the alarm had been raised, they retreated to Fort Johnston, now pursued by contingents of the Malawi Rifles, whose commander had been alerted to their attack around 3 a.m., some six hours after it had begun. In the pursuit, one of the lorries was destroyed and several of the rebels were captured or killed. The army then pushed on to 'Zambia' camp where soldiers discovered a suitcase belonging to Chipembere in which, in a staggering breach of security, he had left a batch of documents listing the names of 300 of his followers. During the next week, more than 50 individuals named on this list were captured by the security forces in a series of stop and search raids.[60]

With Chipembere's forces scattered, the process of reasserting state power began. Back in October 1964, the army and police had functioned almost as neutral umpires in the frequent clashes between Youth Leaguers and civil servants but as the threat of insurrection grew, any sense of neutrality was abandoned. Instead, the police reluctantly came to accept the Young Pioneers as semi-autonomous allies authorised to set up roadblocks, search suspects and make their own arrests. Banda fiercely rejected criticism made in the overseas press of their bullying behaviour. Rather, in April, he introduced a measure making them an integral part of the security services.[61] Later in the year, in an amending act, the police were expressly forbidden from arresting any Young Pioneer without his commander's agreement – a measure that to all intents placed them above the law.

In an exhibition of remarkable courage, villagers at the south east end of the Lake resisted all attempts by the security services to obtain information leading to the capture of Chipembere. But efforts by a small band of his supporters led by the ex-soldier, Medson Silombela, to take the fight to the government were unsuccessful. Late in February, attacks on the police station at Ntaja and on

---

[59] For Okello see Michael F. Lofchie, *Zanzibar: Background to Revolution* (Oxford, 1965), pp. 274–77; John Okello, *Revolution in Zanzibar* (Nairobi, 1967).

[60] A detailed contemporary account of the rising and its aftermath can be found in a speech by Banda, *Proceedings of Parliament,* 6 April 1965, pp. 504–13. Further additional information is provided by Baker, *Revolt,* pp. 208–18.

[61] Speech by Banda, *Proceedings of Parliament,* 12 April 1965, pp. 610–14.

Chief Chikowi near Zomba were both repulsed. In the far north of the country, raids launched from Tanzania in March by fighters loyal to Chisiza proved equally abortive. Two fighters were hacked to death by Young Pioneers near Chitipa after the chairman of the local MCP branch had been killed, leaving the rest of the band to retreat across the border in disarray.

The end of the rising was signalled by Chipembere's flight. Despite the government offer of a reward of £1,000 for anyone providing information leading to his arrest, Chipembere was able to move virtually unhindered from house to house and village to village throughout the Fort Johnston district in the two months following his raid, leaving large detachments of soldiers and Young Pioneers scrambling in his wake. However, ill with diabetes and increasingly isolated, he contemplated ending the conflict. In a lengthy letter written to Jones about 7 March he offered to end the fighting if the prime minister agreed to declare an amnesty. If this were done, Chipembere would be happy to go into exile or else live in isolation on Likoma Island. If Banda refused, he would continue the war using guerrilla tactics.

> I have read enough about hit and run methods to know that a guerrilla war is not easy to crush. Fifty armed men operating in three or four forests can do a lot of havoc before they are crushed and I'm a man who can raise thousands of men for this purpose in six districts of the Southern Region.[62]

A key difference between Banda and the dissident ministers is that while he, after an initial wobble, set himself implacably to retain his grip on power, they treated the crisis almost as they might have treated an episode in the nationalist struggle, in which an initial rebuff could be easily turned, perhaps with the cooperation of their opponents, into a striking victory. For Chipembere (even more, for Chirwa) a rapprochement with Banda was always on the cards. For Banda, by contrast, no outcome would be tolerable that did not leave his opponents humiliated and utterly crushed. Indeed, at the very time that Chipembere was writing his letter, Banda was planning to make the death sentence mandatory for anyone convicted of treason.

Banda's response was thus to reject any contact with Chipembere and to order an intensification of the army campaign. Through much of March and April, army units loosely supported by Young Pioneers swept to and fro across the area east of Fort Johnston, systematically burning houses, looting property and beating recalcitrant villagers with a vigour that more than equalled the worst excesses of the emergency of 1959. Chipembere still retained his freedom, protected by villagers who, at immense personal risk, hid and fed him and provided advance warning on the movement of troops. But with over 400 of his followers now captured, any hope of success had gone. At the beginning of April he contacted the US ambassador to ask for assistance in gaining admission to an American university. Banda, when consulted, made clear that he would not prevent Chipembere leaving Malawi as long as he agreed not to plot against him in America. Lomax, the British Head of the Special Branch, was brought in to mastermind the operation in which the Scottish missionary, Andrew Ross, was involved as a trusted link between Chipembere and the Americans. On 26 April,

[62] Chipembere to Jones, 7 March 1965 quoted in Baker, *Revolt*, p. 225.

after much clandestine planning, a Special Branch Officer met Chipembere at a designated spot some three miles from Fort Johnston and escorted him to Zomba airport, from where he flew to Salisbury and then to London and New York. Not until 21 May, however, did Banda publicly announce that Chipembere was now in America.[63]

In later correspondence, Chipembere claimed that he had been given assurances that his followers would be amnestied following his departure from Malawi. In the event, pressure on Banda's remaining opponents increased. Many of them were detained in the notorious Dzeleka camp near Dowa, opened on Banda's instructions in 1965.[64] Run by Youth Leaguers under the direction of four officers personally chosen by Chidzanja, Dzeleka quickly won a fearsome reputation for the systematic brutality to which its inmates were exposed. 'There were authentic stories of beatings, under-feeding, over-exercising, flooding of rooms, prisoners forced to eat human excreta, etc.,' the British High Commissioner reported at the end of March.[65] In the Fort Johnston area, whole villages were deliberately destroyed by the security forces in retaliation for raids by rebels. There, as in other parts of the country, individuals were denounced on the basis of anonymous accusations, sometimes brought through a desire to settle old scores. Medson Silombela continued to carry out occasional hit and run raids but in November he was finally captured. Convicted of murder, he was hanged in front of a crowd of about 400 people in Zomba prison after Banda had turned down a plea for clemency made by his friend of former years, Nkrumah. A public or, in this case, semi-public execution was necessary, Banda argued, because Chipembere 'had, through his agents managed to propagate the idea that he and his army commanders had medicine that made them invisible.' The execution would demonstrate 'that Chipembere and his henchmen are not superhuman beings.'[66]

The final flicker of resistance came in 1967. The bearded Yatuta Chisiza, former police officer and one-time personal bodyguard for Banda, was, of all the dissident ministers, the one best qualified to mount a guerrilla campaign. Following the failure of his raids in the north, he spent some time training in China and then returned to Tanzania to plan a last excursion, this time into the Mwanza district, where he lacked personal support but could benefit from an element of surprise. In mid-September he and his 16 companions made their way from their camp near Lusaka in Zambia into Mozambique. They crossed the border into Malawi on 30 September and were spotted by a police patrol three days later. Over the next few days, detachments from the Malawi Rifles captured nine members of the small band of insurgents. On 11 October, they caught up with Chisiza, who was killed after a fierce battle lasting over two hours.[67] In the aftermath, Banda insisted that Chisiza's mutilated body should be displayed in public and that no one, not even his mother, would be allowed to publicly mourn his death.[68]

---

[63] Short, *Banda*, p. 230.
[64] Speech by Banda, *Proceedings of Parliament*, 25 January 1965, p.459.
[65] Cole to Commonwealth Relations Office, 23 March 1965, York Conference Papers.
[66] T. K. Owusi, Ghana High Commissioner in Malawi to African Affairs Secretariat, Accra, 19 January 1966, Banda-Nkrumah Correspondence, York Conference Papers.
[67] The most detailed account of Chisiza's venture, based on evidence from the five survivors is contained in Peter Mackay, *We Have Tomorrow*, pp. 327–55. See also Baker, *Revolt*, pp. 279–82; *Annual Report of the Malawi Police Force*, 1967, p. 4.
[68] Malawi *Freedom News*, 1 (1967), York Conference Papers.

Cabinet crisis: interpretations

Analyses of the cabinet crisis have tended to divide around two clusters of questions: the first focusing on relations between Banda and his ministers; the second on the social forces brought into play and the wider significance of the revolt. On the first issue there is broad consensus that the seeds of the crisis lay in differences in personality and approach that can be traced back to Banda's return to Malawi in 1958, but there is less certainty as to when the breakdown became inevitable. Colin Baker, following his colonial source, has suggested that as early as the evening of Banda's return, Chipembere and associates agreed to support Banda as leader only so long as he accepted their views.[69] But Chipembere specifically rejects this allegation in his autobiography, written in America in the 1970s, and instead presents a surprisingly respectful account of Banda, emphasising his personal resolution as well as his effectiveness as a speaker.[70] By the early 1960s, ministerial irritation with the prime minister had become more apparent, although even Dunduzu Chisiza, for all his thoughtful comments on the dangers of dictatorship, was not prepared to challenge him outright. Hence, it was not until after independence that the ministers mounted a reasonably coherent challenge to Banda's authority, and even then they do not appear to have agreed on what were their ultimate objectives and how best to mobilise support. Banda subsequently alleged that Chiume and Chipembere had been scheming against him for up to two years prior to September 1964 but in fact, what most distinguished their challenge was its impromptu, uncoordinated nature.

Banda, by contrast, had been meticulously careful in his planning. In the six years since he returned to Malawi he had not only gained a formidable reputation as a powerful leader, he had also constructed a system of personal authority that made him well nigh impossible to dislodge. Not only did he have the support of the European-officered security forces, substantially enlarged since 1960 as a result of the substantial sum of extra money, £1,523,000 in all, invested in the police by the British government, he could also rely on the Young Pioneers, specially chosen members of the Malawi Youth who came under his direct command.[71] Furthermore, through the assistance of loyalists like Richard Chidzanja and Albert Muwalo, he controlled the central organs of the MCP, although at district level in both the Northern and Southern Regions his authority was less secure. By 1965 the system of personal patronage that Banda was to employ with great effect in the 1970s was still only in the process of coming into being. But in the Central Region particularly, and in parts of the Southern Region too, he had developed contacts with chiefs, headmen and religious authorities that would stand him in good stead. The increasing involvement of members of the *Nyau* cult in operations against supporters of the ministers was an indication that Banda's neo-traditional brand of Malawi nation-

[69] Baker, *Revolt*, pp. 3, 303–305.
[70] Chipembere, *Hero of the Nation*, p. 307, 341–42; Chipembere, 'Malawi in Crisis: 1964', *UFAHMU*. 1, 2 (1970), p. 81.
[71] McCracken, 'Authority and Legitimacy', pp. 178, 181.

alism resonated effectively at village level in many of the Chewa-speaking parts of the country. Finally, Banda benefited from the rewards he could provide to members of parliament, every single one of whom had been nominated by him. Rose Chibambo, for years a special favourite of Banda's, was thrown out of the party and forced into exile when she attempted to articulate the complaints of women against the imposition of hospital charges.[72] Katoba Musopole, by contrast, received a ministerial salary and house after he had distanced himself from his former colleagues. It would not be surprising if he and Qabaniso Chibambo, a fellow former northern radical, who had suffered a lengthy period of imprisonment and restriction under the British, came to believe that continued loyalty to Banda was the key to ensuring that their sacrifices would not go unrewarded.

Historians are divided in their interpretations of the nature of the conflict. In a pioneering analysis, Andrew Ross, one-time Presbyterian Chaplain at Kanjedza and a friend of several of the ministers, puts forward the argument that Banda's success lay in his ability to mobilise conservative and 'traditionalist' elements in Malawi against the modern and progressive forces represented by the ministers. Nationalism in its initial form was a liberating movement, created by young educated, Christian men and appealing to labour migrants and to graduates from Presbyterian mission schools, many of whom happened to be Tumbuka-speakers from the north or else Mang'anja or Yao from the south. Banda, by contrast, in a successful attempt to create a personal power base, turned 'not to a tribe, but to the whole class of people left aside by the rise of the new men' – people who were uneducated, often non-Christian, and enmeshed in traditional society. Many of these 'backward' people were also Chewa but it was principally because of their feelings of inferiority that they responded to Banda rather than because he was a Chewa too. Banda's support increasingly came from traditionalist sectors of society – chiefs, headmen, witch-finders and the anti-Christian *Nyau* cult, as well as from an older generation of politicians who had been shouldered aside by the younger, better educated men. Those attached to him came predominantly from the most backward districts in the country – not just the Central Region but also the Chikwawa and Port Herald districts where mission schools were relatively few. 'The apparent tribalist revival in Malawi, on closer examination, seems to be a counter-revolution.'[73]

Ross's path-breaking analysis, based on his own experience as a minister at Balaka, is still important for what it has to say about the interrelationship between ethnic and class divisions during the crisis. However, its central argument on the clash between the forces of modernity and of tradition is difficult to sustain.[74] Although most of Banda's leading supporters were less well educated than their opponents, they were no less modern in their experiences

---

[72] Rose Chibambo and her husband moved first to Lusaka, where she worked as a shop assistant, before being forced to flee to Tanzania after she had received several death threats. See speech by E. Z. K. Banda, *Proceedings of Parliament,* 18 January 1966, p. 369.

[73] Andrew Ross, 'White Africa's Black Ally', *New Left Review,* 45, (September/October 1967), pp. 85–95.

[74] For a general discussion of the impossibility of disengaging modernity from tradition in Africa see Jean and John Comaroff, 'Introduction' in Jean Comaroff and John Comaroff (eds), *Modernity and Its Malcontents. Ritual and Power in Postcolonial Africa* (London, 1993).

and attitudes. Richard Chidzanja, for example, although he had left school early, stood in a line of Malawian nationalist entrepreneurs, including Lewis Makata and Lali Lubani, who were at the cutting edge of the capitalist economy. Nor was it only the educated and progressive elements who supported the ministers or only the uneducated and traditional who supported Banda. At a very broad level, divisions between northern supporters and Chewa opponents of the ministers mirror the distinction; a high proportion of the best educated Malawians of the independence generation ended in exile. However, few Muslim, Yao-speaking villagers in the Kasupe and Fort Johnston district had access to education. Yet it was from these districts that Chipembere drew his most loyal support.[75] Furthermore, the contrast Ross draws between the rationality of the ministers' approach and the tradition-bound attitudes of Banda and his supporters should not be carried too far. Banda undoubtedly benefited from his readiness to embrace *Nyau* and from his ability, using Chidzanja and others as intermediaries, to enlist many of its members in his support. By 1965, teams of *Nyau* dancers from Dedza and Lilongwe were being bussed down to the Ntcheu district in defiance of the Chief Gomani, an Ngoni and a Christian, who had previously opposed their activities.[76] However, although the ex-ministers were slower than Banda to associate themselves with traditional culture, it would be wrong to assume that they failed to do so entirely. During the course of his revolt, Chipembere was widely believed to be making use of 'witchcraft' (a generic term applied to the acquisition of magical powers) in order to make himself invisible. Whether he or Orton Chirwa actually consulted *singanga* in an attempt to achieve their purposes is largely irrelevant. What is more important is that many people – supporters and opponents alike – believed that they had.

What part did ethnic divisions play in the cabinet split? Vail and White have persuasively argued that the MCP, up to 1964, was a coalition of predominantly economic interests articulated in regional and ethnic terms but that it was following the collapse of the coalition that these tensions were brought most fully into the open.[77] Chiume, Chisiza and Chipembere, the latter with the greatest success, all drew their main support from their own home areas; and so did Banda, who, in the aftermath of the revolt, found his most reliable allies among his own Chewa people. In a breakdown of 54 named supporters of the ex-ministers who participated in military training in Tanzania in 1965, 46 came from the Northern Region, 12 from the south and none at all from the centre.[78] All 12 of the Members of Parliament expelled from the MCP at this time came from the north or south. A similar picture emerges from Banda's efforts to strengthen his control over the institutions of local government, by ridding them of elements sympathetic to the ministers. Under the direction of the Home Affairs minister, Richard Chidzanja, three out of five District Councils in the north were dissolved (Karonga, Nkhata Bay and Rumphi) as were four out of ten in the

---

[75] A point made vigorously in parliament where it was claimed; 'in Kasupe and Fort Johnston most of the people there are illiterate.... Therefore it is possible for a person like Henry [Chipembere] and his fellow Maloya...to dictate these people.' See speech by Chipungu, *Proceedings of Parliament*, 28 October 1964, p.241.

[76] Ross, 'White Africa's Black Ally', p. 90.

[77] Vail and White, 'Tribalism', p. 179.

[78] Calculated from figures given in speech by Banda, *Proceedings of Parliament*, 9 November 1965, pp. 271–73.

Southern Region but none at all in the Centre.[79] Meanwhile, contingents of Young Pioneers from the Central Region were sent to the north to protect the newly-appointed parliamentarians selected by Banda to replace the MPs who had been expelled.[80] A parallel development took place in the police, although more gradually and over a longer period of time. Faced by the need to strengthen security, Banda responded by seeking recruits from those sections of the population, notably his own Chewa people, in whom he felt he could rely most confidently. Between 1960 and 1970 the percentage of Chewa policemen in the force rose from 12.6 to 20.5; the percentage of Yao policemen fell from 14 to just over 10.[81] The recruitment of Lomwe policemen took a similar form. Heavily recruited into the Police Mobile Force by the colonial authorities in the 1950s, Lomwe recruits remained much in demand under Banda as a counterweight to Chipembere's Yao supporters. Throughout the 1960s, they continued to represent around 20 per cent of all policemen in the service.[82]

It is important to emphasise that Dr Banda's concern with mobilising Chewa support was always part of a larger project. By the time he arrived at Blantyre in 1958, Banda had already developed a strong sense of cultural nationalism based on two interconnecting beliefs: support for African culture as expressed in traditional dances, ceremonies and secret societies; and pride in his identity as a Chewa, in his view, the tribe most closely associated with the ancient Maravi Empire. His particular brand of Malawian nationalism therefore involved a strong assertion of the country's indigenous values in the face of the cultural imperialism propagated by generations of missionaries as well as an insistence on the special authenticity of Chewa culture and, in particular, of the Chewa language. As early as 1963, he had made clear his desire to have a single national language: 'not Chi-mission … or Chi-planter' (the then standard version of Chinyanja promoted in the famous Scott-Hetherwick dictionary dating from 1892 and revised by Hetherwick in 1929), but rather 'a real Chichewa as spoken not in Blantyre and Zomba but Lilongwe, and even in Lilongwe not as spoken in Lilongwe town but as it is spoken in the villages'.[83]

Yet if Banda tended to perceive Chewa and Malawi culture as being virtually synonymous, there is little evidence to suggest that he went out of his way prior to the Cabinet Crisis to favour his Chewa supporters. Indeed, many of the symptoms of ethnic unrest demonstrated in the period 1960 to 1964 took the form of grumbling by politicians from the Southern and Central provinces against the over-representation of Northerners as ministers in his early cabinets and against the disproportionate number of Northerners awarded scholarships abroad. Certainly Banda frequently insisted that 'I am a Chewa' before going on to denounce signs of tribalism in others. But this was part of a formula, expressed most clearly in his draft autobiography, written in Gwelo, in which he stated 'I

---

[79] McMaster, *Malawi*, p. 65 suggests that six of the District Councils in the Southern Province were dissolved but I have only seen evidence for four (Kasupe, Fort Johnston, Chiradzulu and Chikwawa). Ross, followed by Vail and White and others confuse the dissolution of these councils with changes in the membership of MCP district committees.

[80] Speeches by W. G. M. Mkandawire and N. Mwambunga, *Proceedings of Parliament*, 9 November 1965, pp. 264–65.

[81] McCracken, 'Coercion and Control', p. 144.

[82] *Annual Reports of the Nyasaland Police*, 1960, 1967, 1970.

[83] Speech by Banda, *Proceedings of the Legislative Assembly*, 15 July 1963, p. 844.

value my being a Chewa only so far as my being a Chewa enhances my being a Nyasa.'[84] Up to 1964, as Chipembere conceded, 'as far as the party generally was concerned, he [Banda] did admirable work in maintaining unity and authorized stern action against any evidence of nascent factionalism.'[85] Although he played off members of the cabinet against each other in this period, the key divisions were personal rather than ethnic. Indeed, even after the revolt of the ministers had begun, Banda was careful to seek support not just from fellow Chewa politicians like Chidzanja but from others, including Aleke Banda, Kumtumanji, Chakuamba and Qabaniso Chibambo, drawn from both the north and south of the country. Just as in the 1940s he had provided financial assistance to both Chewa and non-Chewa students, so in the 1960s he was sufficiently astute to ensure that his political base was not confined to the Central Region alone. By the same token, while he now went out of his way to encourage the Mang'anja people of the south to regard themselves as Chewa, he also focused his traditionalist appeal more widely – on chiefs and headmen from across the country.[86] As Forster has noted, Banda's vision of African values was strongly influenced by the Tumbuka concept of the 'good village,…where the headman and all the elders are respected by all: and where they too have regard for all, even the children'.[87] Young Pioneers, he argued, could learn from the discipline imposed on pre-colonial Chewa youth sitting in the *bwalo*. But they could also learn from the example of good citizenship provided by Mbelwa's Ngoni or by Chaka's Zulu.[88]

How far did the Cabinet Crisis reflect fundamental divisions as to the nature of Malawi's political culture? In his valedictory speech in parliament, Chipembere placed emphasis on the importance of consultation before decisions were made. But this hardly makes him a 'staunch and committed democrat', as Rotberg has suggested.[89] Indeed, in his public denunciations of multipartyism and in his criticisms of the rule of law (made in August 1963 after the battle for independence had already been won) Chipembere expressed opinions that were virtually identical to Banda's.[90] The views of the other ministers, now that Dunduzu Chisiza's voice had been silenced, also suggest that many of their differences with Banda were more matters of style and personality than they were of basic principle. It is doubtful if any of them disagreed with Kanyama Chiume when he looked forward on the eve of independence 'to the day when this country will be so organised that there will be no opposition at all and all of us will be sitting like in a real *mphara*' [traditional meeting place]. However, few would have gone as far as Chiume in arguing that God's expulsion of Satan from Heaven 'is an indication that there is absolutely nothing wrong in dictatorship, and, therefore, if we, through the Malawi Congress Party, established a dictatorship here, we can only be described as the loyal servants of God.'[91]

[84] Speech by Banda, *Proceedings of Parliament*, 10 November 1965.
[85] Chipembere, 'Malawi in Crisis', p. 83.
[86] Foster, 'Culture, Nationalism', pp. 493–94.
[87] Ibid., p. 493.
[88] Banda, *Address to the Young Pioneers at Kanjedza*, 7 October 1966, Ministry of Information.
[89] R. I. Rotberg, 'Introduction', in Rotberg (ed), *Hero of the Nation*, p. 15.
[90] Speeches by Chipembere, *Proceedings of the Legislative Assembly*, 10 July 1963, pp. 745–49; 14 August 1963, pp. 961–63.
[91] Speech by Chiume, *Proceedings of the National Assembly*, 26–29 May, pp. 124–25.

Nevertheless, Guy Mhone is entirely justified in arguing that by the time of independence the MCP was already exhibiting 'incipient tendencies toward hero-worship, centralized authoritarianism, exclusiveness and a low toleration for criticism or internal opposition', although he might have added that, in some respects, it continued to function as a genuinely liberating force.[92] David Cole, the British High Commissioner, perceived 'a certain nobility in the claim of the ex-Ministers that all they have been trying to do is to make the voice of the people heard in the counsels of the Cabinet'.[93] But while it is undoubtedly the case that, with their fall, hopes for a democratic transition receded, this does not mean that prior to the crisis they demonstrated any great readiness to tolerate minority views. Chipembere's explanation of why the ministers did not resign *en masse* over Banda's plan to reintroduce preventative detention is relevant in this context. According to Chipembere, Banda's initial intention, which the ministers appear to have approved, was to use the bill to imprison nationalist politicians like Manoah Chirwa and Matthews Phiri who had fallen out with the MCP. 'Those among them who were chiefs had been deposed, but it had been difficult to punish those who were businessmen, farmers etc.' This, he claims, was such a popular issue that the ministers were not prepared to oppose it in public whatever dangers it presented to them personally.[94] Writing in exile in 1966, Chipembere expressed certain reservations concerning the one-party state, of which, as he admitted, he had once been 'an enthusiastic advocate'.[95] But how far these views would have influenced his behaviour had he been successful in seizing power two years earlier it is impossible to tell. All that one can say is that, with the departure of the ministers, any possible counterweight to Banda had been eliminated. Within Malawi for the next 30 years, the contribution made by these politicians to the anti-colonial struggle was systematically ignored. Instead, a new version of history was inculcated – one that grossly exaggerated Banda's role while minimizing the activities of anyone else.[96]

There is a central paradox concerning the role of the British in Malawi during and after the crisis. To the alarm of their expatriate subordinates, Glyn Jones and the other senior colonial administrators went a long way towards ceding authority to Banda and his fellow ministers in the eighteen months leading up to independence when Britain still officially continued to rule. But in the two years that followed, prior to the establishment of a Republic, they played an important, some would say a decisive part in sustaining Banda in power. Their activities at this period are of significance in understanding the role of the imperial power and its agents once colonial rule had formally ended.

For the British Government, the Cabinet Crisis was an unwelcome and embarrassing development. David Cole, the newly-appointed High Commissioner, was personally sympathetic to the ministers, whom he believed to be 'men of courage, ability and consequence'. But he had no doubt as to where British

---

[92] Guy Mhone, 'The Political Economy of Malawi: an Overview', in Mhone (ed.), *Malawi at the Crossroads* (Harare, 1992), p. 4.
[93] Cole to Secretary of State for Commonwealth Relations, 27 October 1964, TNA DO 183/457.
[94] Chipembere, 'Malawi in Crisis', p. 92.
[95] H.B.M. Chipembere, 'Dr Banda's opposition in exile', *Manchester Guardian*, 7 July 1966.
[96] Owen J.M. Kalinga, 'The Production of History in Malawi in the 1960s: the Legacy of Sir Harry Johnston, the Influence of the Society of Malawi and the role of Dr Kamuzu Banda and his Malawi Congress Party', *African Affairs*, 97, 1988, pp. 540–41.

interests lay. 'A compromise, involving the retention by Dr Banda of most of his powers and policies but some outward signs of respect to his Ministers would have been the ideal outcome', he wrote.[97] But with that option gone, support for Banda was the only realistic alternative. 'The whole concept of independence for Malawi was framed around Dr Banda.' He alone could provide the 'strong and paternalistic Government' which Malawi desperately needed. 'Most of Dr Banda's external policies are, in the circumstances of Malawi, sensible and realistic. Many of them are helpful to the West.' By contrast, if Chipembere and Chiume obtained power, they 'would probably, willy nilly, take Malawi very quickly down hill and perhaps into the arms of Peking.'[98] Ministers and officials in the Commonwealth Relations Office concurred with this conclusion. In a draft note the new Secretary of State, Arthur Bottomley wrote: 'It is agreed that … in current circumstances the only prospect of stable government in Malawi and the continuance of a regime calculated to serve British interests and policies in Central Africa rests with Dr Banda.'[99] Britain refused Banda's requests for military reinforcements to suppress the Chipembere insurrection.[100] However, under the Labour Prime Minister Harold Wilson, financial aid continued to flow despite the reservations expressed by Cole concerning Banda's increasingly dictatorial methods.

For Jones and the British officers who continued working in Malawi the situation was particularly fraught. As Governor General, Jones was placed in a delicate constitutional position where, as representative of the Queen but no longer of the British state, he could advise but not act without the authorisation of the Malawi Government. As he demonstrated in his frequent meetings with Banda and with individual ex-ministers, Jones's constant aim was to bring about a reconciliation between Banda and at least some of his former colleagues. But this ambition was secondary to his overriding conviction that his duty lay in sustaining Banda in office. Whether his advice had any influence on the outcome of the crisis is problematic. But at least it was the case that, for several months, Jones acted as a privileged intermediary between almost all the warring parties; Chiume alone refused to become involved.

In his analysis of the crisis, Chipembere emphasised the role played by British civil servants and security officers both in turning Banda against the ministers and in using their control over the security services to defeat them. On the first point, he was almost certainly mistaken in believing that intelligence officers had deliberately submitted misleading reports to Banda in a successful attempt to sow the seeds of suspicion in his mind. But on the second, it appears more than likely that officials did resent the open attacks made upon them by Chipembere and Chiume and hence were ready to believe that they 'were potentially, if not actually, communist sympathizers and would lead the country into the communist camp'.[101] The consequence was that, when the revolt erupted, Youens, Roberts and the heads of the security services committed themselves to the government side with a zeal that did not stem from their undoubted profes-

[97] Cole to Commonwealth Relations Office, 14 October 1964, TNA DO183/457.
[98] Cole to Bottomley, 27 October, 1964, TNA DO 183/457.
[99] Draft from Bottomley to Cole, no date [November 1964], TNA DO 183/457.
[100] Badenoch, 'Banda and the British', p. 28.
[101] Chipembere, 'Malawi in Crisis', pp. 80–95.

sionalism alone. For a brief period, late in September 1964 when Banda was absent in the Central Region, not a single loyalist government minister remained in Zomba and effective control passed into expatriate hands.[102] Banda made effective use of Youth Leaguers and Young Pioneers in the assault on Chipembere's supporters. But it was only through the active cooperation of the European-led police and army that they were able to achieve success. In one of the more bizarre episodes in a bitterly contested struggle, British Special Branch officers organised almost every detail of Chipembere's flight, including the humiliating requirement that he should coat his face with black dye, acquired from the Zomba Dramatic Society, in order to prevent recognition on the plane.[103] Thereafter, senior expatriate officials retreated to a less exposed position although one in which they continued to play an important part in the maintenance of Banda's regime. Bryan Roberts, Attorney-General and, from 1965, Permanent Secretary to the Office of the President and Head of the Civil Service, had a particularly pivotal role. Diplomats in the British High Commission had no doubt of his importance as the President's right-hand man but they increasingly perceived him as an instrument at Banda's disposal rather than as a source of independent advice. In 1967, the acting High Commissioner was 'horrified by what he describes as the complacency and servility of the senior expatriate officials who lend an aura of respectability and "Britishness"' to the regime.[104] Roberts, it was said, was 'afraid to proffer advice'.[105]

The consolidation of the Banda regime

On 5 July 1966, a day before Malawi became a Republic, Sir Glyn Jones flew out from Chileka airport, following the enactment of one of the many elaborate ceremonies that marked the arrival and departure of senior dignitaries. The British connection was by no means over. British officers continued to head several of the key administrative departments as well as the army and police force. A Scottish academic, Ian Michael, had taken up office as first Vice-Chancellor of the University of Malawi. Fifty-six per cent of the posts in the civil service were still held by European expatriates.[106] As Banda announced with typically robust candour to the MCP annual convention: 'if Britain stopped to help us with our Recurrent Budget and our Development Budget tomorrow, we could not stand and function a single day as a State.'[107]

Yet if the British presence still continued to be felt, it now operated in an arena where Banda's dominance was greater than ever before and colonial influence had substantially diminished. The consolidation of Banda's personal authority that took place from the low point of September 1964 to his unopposed election in July 1966 as the executive president of the newly constituted

---

[102] Cole to Secretary of State for Commonwealth Relations, 14 October 1964, TNA DO 183/457.

[103] Baker, *Revolt*, pp. 237–42.

[104] Cole to Monson, 29, May 1967, TNA FCO 31/102 quoted in Badenoch, 'Banda and the British', pp. 88–89.

[105] Scott to Monson, 23 June 1967, PRO FCO 31/102 quoted in Badenoch, ibid., p. 89.

[106] Speech by Banda at the opening of the MCP convention, 12 October 1966, Malawi Information Department, Blantyre.

[107] Ibid.

one-party state was the result of a number of factors among which the continued support of the expatriate-led police force and army was only one. Despite suggestions to the contrary, there is little reason to believe that the MCP effectively collapsed in the aftermath of the crisis but it is certainly the case that over the next two years extensive changes were made in the leadership at both local and central level resulting in the creation of a party machine whose central rationale was loyalty to the president.[108] Some individuals appointed to parliament following the resignation of the ministers proved grossly inadequate: Nelson Mwambungu, Yatuta Chisiza's successor as MP for Karonga North, was convicted of raping a 17-year old schoolgirl in December 1966 only months after he had demanded that political opponents be subjected to public executions at which they would first be tortured and then slowly hung to death.[109] Others, however, headed by Aleke Banda and John Tembo brought administrative competence to their posts. In a deliberate effort to prevent any regional or district party leader becoming too powerful, Banda forbade MCP district chairmen from giving orders to members of the Youth League and the Women's League, both of which came directly under him.[110]

At the same time, the Young Pioneers, the elite formation within the Youth League, was considerably expanded both as an instrument of control and as a means of training young people in agricultural techniques. The number of training camps increased from 9 in 1965 to 16 in 1968. Only 1,153 young men and 73 young women were in these camps in 1965 but they were supplemented by some 40,000 acting Young Pioneers spread throughout the country. Over the next year they were active in carrying out security searches, targeting suspected dissidents and in checking people at markets or on buses for paid-up party membership cards.[111] In 1967, following a resolution passed at Banda's behest at the Malawi Congress Party Convention in Mzuzu, they launched a ferocious onslaught on Jehovah's Witnesses (targeted once more for their failure to buy party cards) which involved the destruction of crops, burning of houses, physical torture of both men and women and general beating, sometimes resulting in deaths.[112]

Banda's employment of the Young Pioneers as an irregular coercive force was combined with an attempt to reinforce his popular base through a number of different methods. Despite his reputation for rigidity in policy matters, Banda was a natural populist, ready to make limited concessions to public opinion on matters that did not conflict directly with his central aims. Back in September 1964 he had tacitly dropped the 'ticky' charge at government hospitals when the full extent of opposition became clear. Later, in 1965, he set out to remove the most contentious elements in the Skinner Report as a means of reaching a partial

---

[108] See Vail and White, 'Of Chameleons and Clowns. The Case of Jack Mapanje', in Vail and White, *Power and the Praise Poem* (London, James Currey, 1991), p. 289.

[109] *Malawi News*, 20 January 1967; Speech by Mwambunga, *Proceedings of Parliament*, 10 November 1965, pp. 252–53.

[110] Closing address by Banda at Political Education Conference, Soche Hill College, 18 April 1966, issued by Department of Information.

[111] Aleke Banda, 'The History of the Youth Movement' in *Youth in Malawi. Security and Progress with Malawi's Young Pioneers* (Department of Information, 1965); A.W. Wood, 'Training Malawi's Youth: the work of the Malawi Young Pioneers', *Community Development Journal*, 5,3 1970, pp. 130–38; Short, *Banda*, p. 257; Williams, *Malawi*, pp. 247–49.

[112] Klaus Fiedler, 'Power at the Receiving End', pp.154–6.

rapprochement with the civil servants.[113] In June the provision that civil servants should contribute to a Pension Fund was rescinded. The next year, the money they had paid in contributions was returned and all public servants, including teachers, policemen and soldiers were rewarded with a generous pay rise of 6 per cent.[114]

Equally important was Banda's new strategy of actively soliciting the support of chiefs, in part at least as a means of reducing reliance on the educated elite. Back in the period of self government from 1961, the powers of Native Authorities and District Commissioners had been considerably restricted as a result of wide-ranging changes in the nature of local government. New Local Courts had been established, manned by magistrates trained at the Mpemba Institute of Public Administration, to take the place of Native Courts, previously chaired by Native Authorities.[115] District councils had been democratised through the introduction of a universal adult franchise and the ending of the right of all chiefs to sit as *ex officio* members.[116] Following the cabinet crisis, however, aspects of this policy were reversed. Banda went out of his way to insist that chiefs should be formally recognised in the new republican constitution and that their role should be accepted as complementary rather than subordinate to that of party leaders. They would 'look after ... those aspects of life where custom and traditional laws still function', leaving the rest to the Party and the Government.[117] What this would mean in practice was not easy to determine. Central control over local government was in fact strengthened in 1966 by the decision to abandon elections for district councils and move instead to a system of patronage in which Banda or his nominees took over responsibility for making appointments. By the same token, Banda embarked on a policy of selecting and de-selecting chiefs according to his own interpretation of Malawian history. Chiefs, it was clear, were now to be recognised as authentic exponents of Malawian culture rather than as colonial stooges, yet they were expected to operate within the constraining context of the Banda autocracy. It would not be long before Banda, in a further reversal of policy, turned Local Courts into 'Traditional Courts', dispensing justice according to 'custom' and utilising the services of selected traditional leaders alongside Mpemba-trained magistrates.[118]

It is hardly surprising that the two major historic themes of land and identity featured large in the months leading up the establishment of the Republic. Land had been a central issue ever since Harry Johnston had approved large-scale acquisitions by white settlers in the early 1890s and although by 1964 the assault on *thangata* had done much to ease the problem, a number of unresolved issues remained. One of these, unique to the Mulanje and Cholo districts, was the continuing presence of land hunger in an area still dominated by large-scale, expatriate-owned tea estates. Encroachment by landless peasants on to these estates began on a significant scale in 1962 but expanded in 1964 following independence when some 5,500 acres were settled, mostly on unused forest that had

[113] Speech by Banda, *Proceedings of Parliament,* 13 April 1965.

[114] Opening Speech by Banda to Malawi Party Convention, 12 October 1966.

[115] Speech by Orton Chirwa, *Proceedings of the Legislative Council,* 19 May 1962, pp. 192–96.

[116] Speech by Banda, *Proceedings of Legislative Council,* 27 September 1961, pp. 39–41.

[117] Speech by Banda, *Proceedings of Parliament,* 13 July 1965, pp. 198–99; *Opening speech by Banda to Malawi Party Convention, 12 October 1966.* (Ministry of Information, Blantyre, 1966).

[118] *Speech by Banda to Parliament,* 28 July 1970 (Ministry of Information, Blantyre, 1970).

not been cleared for tea planting.[119] As an official in the British High Commission noted, the take-over was 'highly organised':

> Areas for encroachment are clearly allocated and a concerted movement on the land by as many as a 100 at a time takes place. Often women with hoes are the shock troops, and they are prepared to use, and have used, violence on estate workers, bulldozer drivers etc. The land occupied is in many instances in the very heart of an estate almost surrounded by developed tea. In one estate in Cholo the organisers set up an 'office' with a properly stencilled signboard saying in Chinyanja "Office of Hunger. Hunger in Malawi"; from this office the intruders were directed on to a particular piece of land.[120]

Rows of banana plants were planted to mark the new boundaries. Whole villages were constructed on the newly occupied land.

There is good reason to believe that had the ex-ministers sought to champion the squatters they would have been able to widen their popular base. But with their appeal focused on salaried employees, the opportunity was not taken up. Instead, the organisers of the encroachment campaign were predominantly local MCP officials and activists, including the MP for Mulanje West, J.W. Chikwita, who continued to support Banda on issues of wider policy. Many of the assaults on estate workers, *capitaos* and clerks that took place in the latter months of 1964 were presented as attacks on Chipembere's supporters although, in the view of one knowledgeable outsider, they involved the paying off of old scores by marginalised peasants, envious of those of their neighbours who had obtained salaried employment on European estates.[121]

As for Banda, the squatters' actions came as a potentially embarrassing challenge to his authority requiring a carefully modulated response. As he frequently boasted, Banda was the self-proclaimed destroyer of *thangata*, but this did not mean that he approved of peasants acting on their own initiative. Instead, he followed a deliberately low key policy of turning a blind eye to what he must have recognised were highly popular encroachments while at the same time doing nothing to give them official support.[122] The crunch came in April 1965 when, with the challenge of the ministers rebuffed, Banda felt free to stamp his authority on proceedings. The Malawi Land Bill he introduced that month was, as he noted, 'very, very controversial'[123] both in the sense that it provided the government with immense powers over the ownership of land and also in that it signalled the government's determination to protect landowners from the depredations of the landless:

> If anyone trespass on anyone's land, whether the individual got the land under Certificate of Claim or by buying it from someone else or by lease from the Government, that is an offence. If he encroaches on it, that is an offence. If he occupies it without right, that is an offence.[124]

[119] Report by John Nicholas in Cole to Watson, 3 December 1964, TNA DO 183/110.
[120] Ibid.
[121] Ibid.
[122] 'Visit of the Prime Minister of Malawi. Brief No.1 General Political Situation', December 1964, TNA DO 183/110. According to this brief, 'Dr. Banda himself has not been very helpful [in opposing encroachments on tea estates] probably because he fears that serious intervention could damage his popularity in the area.'
[123] Closing speech by Banda on Malawi Land Bill, *Proceedings of Parliament*, 12 April 1965, p. 660.

From then on, patrols by the police mobile force into the tea-growing areas increased as a means of bringing encroachment under control, although this remained a sporadic and low-key operation in which the eviction of squatters was frequently followed by further cases of encroachment.[125] European estate-owners continued to face the threat of compulsory purchase, notably in 1970 when a new programme of forced buy-outs resulted in the distribution of thousands of acres into Malawian hands. However, this action predominantly benefited the new class of estate-owners, many of them members of the political elite, and offered comparatively little to the landless and the poor.[126]

By 1966 the issue of Malawian identity was in the process of being redefined. The central question was, who was a Malawian citizen? Banda's answer, as provided in the Malawi Citizenship Bill of 1966, was very different from the compromise constitution which he had reluctantly accepted in 1964. During the run-up to independence, British ministers had been anxious to prevent sections of the population becoming stateless with the result that Malawi citizenship had been broadly defined to include everyone born in Malawi irrespective of racial origin as well as all those who had resided in the country for seven years or more. Banda, by contrast, took a position adopted very widely in Africa at this time, in arguing that only Africans or people born of an African mother could be Malawian citizens as of right. Europeans and Asians might apply for citizenship but this would be granted only as a favour if the government so decided.[127] Some Asians could claim residence in the country going back two generations or more but this did not entitle them to citizenship rights.

The citizenship of Africans was equally contentious. In common with the overwhelming majority of leaders in Africa, Banda by the 1960s had abandoned his earlier vision of shared black African citizenship across the continent. But he still retained his belief in a Malawi nation defined as much in cultural as in territorial terms; in consequence he went out of his way to offer citizenship rights to Africans living on the Mozambique side of the border with relatives in Malawi as well as to Africans who had lived in Malawi for any length of time who had been born in Mozambique.[128] The one reservation – once more, common across Africa – was that citizenship was a matter of family rather than of individual identity; that an individual without a demonstrable ancestry could not be regarded as an authentic Malawian citizen. Banda, who had come under just such an accusation from Kanyama Chiume, ridiculed Chipembere in similar terms.[129] What was at issue was not just that Chipembere's parents and grand-

---

[124] Opening speech by Banda on Malawi Land Bill, *Proceedings of Parliament*, 12 April 1965, pp 653–58. See also Williams, *Malawi*, pp. 242–43.

[125] *Annual Report of the Malawi Police Force for 1976*, p. 5; Simon Thomas, 'Economic Developments in Malawi since Independence', *J SAS*, 2, 1 (1975), p. 43; Speeches by E.C. Peterkins, *Proceedings of Parliament*, 7 July 1965; 17 January 1966.

[126] Thomas, 'Economic Developments in Malawi since Independence', *JSAS*, 2, 1 (1975), pp. 39–41; Williams *Malawi*, pp. 244–46.

[127] Speeches by Banda, *Proceedings of Parliament*, 29 October 1964, pp.221–26; 18 May 1966, pp. 581–84.

[128] Speech by Banda, *Proceedings of Parliament*, 18 May 1966, p. 583.

[129] Allegations that Banda came from Ghana or America and not from Malawi date back to the late 1950s and continued to be made up to and after his death. See Chiume, *Kwacha*, p. 89; Harri Englund, 'Between God and Kamuzu: the transition to multiparty politics in central Malawi' in R. Werbner and T. Ranger (eds), *Postcolonial Identities in Africa* (London, 1996), pp. 107–31.

parents had not been born in what became Malawi, it was rather that, according to Banda, no one could say where his family came from or what was their village or district. The underlying accusation is that Chipembere was the descendant of freed slaves, lacking kin and hence ineligible for citizenship status.[130] So seriously did Chipembere take the matter that he responded with a pamphlet setting out his ancestry, aimed at his fellow-Malawians in exile.[131]

Defining Malawian citizenship involved a consideration of national identity. Critics of Banda have argued that he pursued a brazenly tribalist agenda in the aftermath of the cabinet crisis but this is to ignore the extent to which his policies at the time contained a hard pragmatic edge. Economic concessions were made to civil servants; there was no systematic assault on educated Northerners (that was to come later in the 1970s); some were retained as members of the political elite. ADMARC's purchasing policy provided even prices to peasants across the country with the consequence that Central Province peasants close to the market subsidised those in more outlying areas. What is clear, however, is that there was a further shift in the concept of the nation involving not simply the change from 'Nyasaland' to 'Malawi' but an additional refinement in what 'Malawi' meant. A diversity of ethnicities was not only tolerated but celebrated, as in the great dancing festivals that became a routine part of Banda's public appearances. But with the marginalisation of minority languages and the replacement of the name 'Chinyanja' by 'Chichewa', Chewa culture and language was placed at the heart of the nation state.

Change & continuity

The establishment of the Republic of Malawi under Dr Banda marked the opening of a new chapter in the country's history and the removal of the last traces of formal British authority. Yet, in a number of respects, influences dating from the colonial era continued to shape the character of the post-colonial state. Parliamentary democracy, symbolised by the new parliament building opened in Zomba shortly before independence, was paraded by the imperial power as being of particular significance. However, under British rule the democratic tradition had been conspicuous only by its absence; faced in the early 1960s by the growing authoritarianism of the MCP, the colonial authorities had tacitly abandoned their short-lived concern for democratic rights. It was not until nearly three decades later that Malawians, through their own efforts, succeeded in establishing functioning, if fragile institutions of democracy. Much more important in the 1960s were the instruments of control utilised by the colonial government: the newly-expanded police force, the army, now back out of Federal hands, and the Special Branch with its network of informers. Added to these was the tradition of press censorship, dating from the aftermath of the Chilembwe Rising and soon to be taken to new levels with the foundation of the Malawi Board of Censorship. At the administrative level, the prefectural system, involving the employment of district officers, most of them now trained locally at the Institute

---

[130] *Address by Banda to Mass Rally at Malindi, Fort Johnston*, 30 April 1967 (Ministry of Information, Blantyre, 1967).
[131] Chipembere, *My Malawian Ancestors*.

of Public Administration at Mpemba, remained unchanged, as did the failure of the central government to introduce viable, elected local councils with real authority. Official chiefs survived in diminished form in the era of the one-party state but subsequently regained influence when respect for politicians and parties declined.[132]

At an economic level, one important element was the continuation into the late 1970s of the cash-crop boom that began in the late 1940s, faltered during the period of political transition and then took off at greater speed from the late 1960s, although without improving the lot of the majority of Malawian cultivators. This was marked both by the key role that continued to be held by government-controlled marketing boards (now unified in the giant ADMARC) in the sale and supervision of peasant-produced crops and also by the continued importance of 'visiting tenants' in the production of those crops. In an unexpected turn, independence was followed by a major expansion of the estate sector, now largely in African hands.[133] Labour migration expanded rapidly up to 1974 when the Malawi Government banned recruiting for South African mines following the deaths of 74 Malawian migrant workers in a plane crash. Although recruiting was resumed in 1977, numbers fell sharply: from over 123,000 in 1973 to an average of around 17,000 in the decade after 1978.[134]

Almost as important as the survival of colonial economic structures was the pervasive influence of Christian missions, the earliest of all European actors on the Malawian stage and the ones that remained there long after colonial officials had departed. Scholars are divided as to whether missions in Malawi should be labelled as agents of imperialism, a view most enthusiastically espoused today in departments of religious and cultural studies, or seen, as is argued in this book, as imperfect transmitters of 'a religion to which Africans turned to suit their own purposes: spiritual, economic and political'.[135] Whichever side one takes, however, there can be no dispute that their legacy extended widely: from the introduction of football to the spread of the English language and from a distinctively sober style of dressing to the creation of organised groups of Christian women. For a brief spell in the run-up to independence it seemed possible that, as mission-controlled schools and hospitals contracted with the emergence of the new government, the influence of churches would decline. In subsequent years, however, it became rapidly apparent that Christian churches, now largely Africanised, were of greater importance than ever, not least because of their role in providing Christians with precious spaces separate from, but not necessarily antagonistic to, the new regime.

The final influence to be considered is the deepest and most long-lasting of all. Rural communities entered independence facing the same fundamental challenges they had encountered throughout the colonial period: the need to eke out

[132] Oyvind Eggen, 'Chiefs and Everyday Governance: Parallel State Organisations in Malawi', *JSAS*, 37, 2, 2011, pp. 313–331.

[133] Kydd and Christiansen, 'Structural Changes in Malawi since Independence', pp. 355–375; J. Kydd, 'Malawi's Economy and Economic Policy in the 1970s', pp.293–380.

[134] J. Kydd and R. Christiansen, 'The Return of Malawian Labour from South Africa and Zimbabwe', *Journal of Modern African Studies*, 21, 2, 1983, pp. 311–26; Chirwa, 'Rural Labour Migrancy and Fishing', pp. 472–74.

[135] McCracken, *Politics and Christianity*, 3rd edition, 2009, p. 17 quoting Norman Etherington, 'Recent Trends in the Historiography of Christianity in Southern Africa', *JSAS*, 22, 2, 1996, pp. 209–10.

a living and feed themselves in an often harsh and uncertain environment where seasonal hunger was for many households a regular and predictable event.[136] They were confronted by population growth exceeding three per cent per annum by 1966 with consequent increased shortages of fertile land, soil erosion and deforestation. Yet, as in previous generations, rural Malawians responded with skill, invention and resilience in squeezing surpluses out of the land. Much of the last third of this book is devoted to the activities of national and local politicians. Yet it is not, I hope, too romantic to suggest that the true heroes of colonial Malawi were those villagers in the countryside, men and women, who maintained the viability of rural communities in the face of the myriad threats to which they were exposed.

[136] See Mandala, *The End of Chidyerano*.

Bibliography

ARCHIVAL SOURCES

Malawi National Archives, Zomba (MNA)

The records contained in these archives constitute the main source for this book. They can be divided as follows:

1. Secretariat and departmental records, including annual provincial and district reports, mainly but not exclusively covering the period from 1919 (the date of a fire in the archives) up to the early 1950s when detailed cataloguing ends. Of particular importance are those holdings that throw light on the aims, attitudes and behaviour of individual Malawians. They include the evidence given to the Commissions of Inquiry into the Nyasaland Rising of 1915, North Nyasa Lands, 1929, the Tobacco Industry, 1938 and the Fishing Industry, 1956.
2. District books, periodically updated by district officers.
3. Annual reports of the departments of Agriculture, Education, Labour, Medicine, Native Affairs, Native Administration, Police, Public Works etc.
4. Private holdings donated to the archives
   Edward Alston diary, 1894–96
   Wordsworth Poole Papers, 1895–96
   J.R.N. Chinyama Papers
   Central Province Association Papers
   Livingstonia Mission papers
   Church of Scotland papers (including Dr Hetherwick's correspondence)
   Blantyre Town Council Minutes
   Limbe Town Council Minutes

Malawi Railway Archives (MRA)

I have used files on staff recruitment from the 1920s, on labour relations and on the 1960 strike, c1959–1969.

National Archives, Kew (TNA)

The following series of files have been consulted:

FO 2 and FO 84, correspondence relating to Malawi region up to 1905
CO 525, correspondence between the Nyasaland Government and the Colonial Office, 1907 to 1951; CO 1015; CO 952, 1950–1962. These files not only contain correspondence between the Colonial Office and the Nyasaland Government, they also include monthly intelligence reports produced for the Nyasaland Government, copies of opposition newspapers and a significant amount of material relating operations during the Nyasaland State of Emergency
CO 626: printed annual Nyasaland departmental reports

CO 1018. Working papers of Lord Hailey preparing the Nyasaland section of his *Native Administration in the British African Territories*

DO 158. Files generated by the Commonwealth Relations Office, Central Africa concerning Nyasaland, 1959–62

DO 183. Records of the Central Africa Office, 1962–64, including information on the Cabinet Crisis

Rhodes House Library, Oxford (RHL)

The Devlin Commission Papers deposited by Lord Devlin are an important source for the events surrounding the 1959 State of Emergency. In addition I have used the following personal collections obtained through the Oxford Colonial Records Project: the Colby Papers; the Hoole Papers; R. W. Kettlewell, 'Memories of a colonial career'; Griff Jones, 'Ulendo Diary', 1953–53; Mss Afr. S. Papers relating to Nyasaland'. I have also consulted the Creech Jones Papers as they relate to Dr Banda

Edinburgh University Library (EUL)

The diaries of Frederick Morrison, 1882–1887, provide vivid insights into life on Malawi's trading frontier in the 1880s. I have also used the papers of Kenneth Mackenzie, Helen Taylor and Professor George Shepperson, all of which provide information on post-1945 Malawian politics

National Library of Scotland (NLS)

Foreign Mission Records of the Church of Scotland: Letter-book of the Secretary, John T. Maclagan

Diary of Rev. Duff Macdonald, 1879–80

Letter-book of the Secretary of the Livingstonia Committee, 1901–34

Letters from Livingstonia missionaries to secretaries, Livingstonia committee, 1874–1924

Letters from officials and missionaries to Dr Laws, 1875–1900

Cape Maclear Journal, 1875–1880; Bandawe-Kanangina Journals, 1887–79; Bandawe Journal, 1881–87

Foreign and Commonwealth Library

Record of evidence heard by the Rhodesia-Nyasaland Royal Commission [the Bledisloe Commission], 1938

Record of evidence heard by the Hilton Young Commission, 1929

Imperial War Museum

War diary of Major-General Sir Edward Northey

Zimbabwe National Archives, Harare

I have consulted three series of files: the H.H. Johnston papers; files on the Watchtower Movement, 1920s; correspondence concerning the 1959 State of Emergency in the Federal Archives.

Fort Hare University Library, Alice

Student Records

York University Conference Papers, 1992

Photocopied papers relating to the Cabinet Crisis, 1964–66

Newspapers

Aurora
British Central Africa Gazette
Central African Planter
Central African Times (later *Nyasaland Times*)
Church of Scotland Home and Foreign Missionary Record
Free Church of Scotland Monthly Record
Life and Work in British Central Africa (subsequently *Life and Work in Nyasaland*)
Malawi News
Dissent

Official Publications

Abrahams, J.C., *Report on Nyasaland Natives in the Union of South Africa and in Southern Rhodesia* (Zomba, 1937)

Bell, Sir Robert, *Report of the Commission Appointed to Enquire into the Financial Position and Further Development of Nyasaland* (London, 1938)

Burden, G.N., *Report on Nyasaland Native Labour in Southern Rhodesia* (Zomba, 1938)

Burden, G.N., *Report on Nyasaland Natives in the Union of South Africa* (Zomba, 1940)

Census of the Nyasaland Protectorate, 1911, 1921, 1931

Correspondence relating to the Recruitment of Labour in the British Central Africa Protectorate for Employment in the Transvaal, 1903, Cmd. 1531

Correspondence relating to the Recruitment of Labour in the Nyasaland Protectorate for the Transvaal and Southern Rhodesian Mines, 1908, Cmd. 3993

Correspondence respecting Operations against Slave Traders in British Central Africa, 1896, Cmd. 7925

Kettlewell, R.W., *An Outline of Agrarian Problems and Policy in Nyasaland* (Zomba, 1955)

Malawi Population Census, (Zomba 1966)

Mitchell, B.L. and B. Steele, B., *A Report on the distribution of Tsetse Flies in Nyasaland and Some Recommendations for Control* (Zomba, 1956)

Nyasaland Protectorate Report, 1907–08, Cmd. 3729; *1908–09*, Cmd. 4448; *1909–10*, Cmd. 4964; *1910–11*, Cmd. 5467; *1911–12*, Cmd. 6007; *1912–13*, Cmd. 7050; *1913–14*, Cmd. 8822; *1914–15*, Cmd. 6172

Papers relative to the suppression of Slave-Raiding in Nyasaland, 1892, Cmd. 6899

Papers relative to the suppression of Slave-Raiding in British Central Africa, 1893–1894, Cmd. 7031

Pearson, E.O. and Mitchell, *B.L., Report on the Status and Control of Insect Pests of Cotton in the Lower River Districts of Nyasaland* (Zomba, 1945)

Proceedings of the Nyasaland Legislative Assembly, 1958–64

Proceedings of the Malawi Parliament, 1964–66

Report by Commissioner Johnston of the First Three Years' Administration of the Eastern Portion of British Central Africa, 1894, Cmd. 7504.

Report by Commissioner… Johnston… on the Trade and General Conditions of the British Central Africa Protectorate, 1895–96, Cmd. 8254

Report by Consul Sharpe on the Trade and General Condition of the British Central Africa Protectorate, 1896–97, Cmd. 8438

Report on the Trade and General Conditions of the British Central Africa Protectorate, 1902–03, Cmd. 1772; *1903–04*, Cmd. 2242; *1904–05*, Cmd. 2684; *1906–07*, Cmd. 3729

Report of the Commission appointed … to inquire into various matters and questions concerned with the Native Rising within the Nyasaland Protectorate (Zomba, 1916).

Report of a Commission to enquire into and report upon certain matters connected with the occu-

pation of land in the Nyasaland Protectorate (Zomba, 1920) [the Jackson Report]
Report on an Economic Survey of Nyasaland, 1958–59 (Salisbury, 1959)
Report of the Committee appointed to enquire into Emigrant Labour, 1935 (Zomba, 1936)
Report of the Committee of Inquiry into African Education (Zomba, 1962) [the Phillips Report]
Report of the Land Commission (Zomba, 1946) [the Abrahams Report]
Report of the Commission of Inquiry appointed to enquire into disturbances at Magunda estate, Luchenza on the 18th and 19th August 1953 (Zomba, 1953)
Report of the Nyasaland Commission of Inquiry, Cmd. 814 (London, 1959) [the Devlin Report]
Smith, Eric, *Report on the Direct Taxation of Natives in the Nyasaland Protectorate* (Zomba, 1937)
Speeches by Dr Banda, 1966–1970 (Ministry of Information, Blantyre)

Selected Secondary Sources

Abdallah, Y.B., *The Yaos*, Zomba, 1919
Alpers. Edward A., *Ivory and Slaves in East Central Africa*, London, 1975
Alpers, E.A., 'Trade, State and Society among the Yao in the Nineteenth Century' *Journal of African History*, 10, 3, 1969
Alpers, E.A., 'Towards a History of the Expansion of Islam in East Africa: the Matrilineal Peoples of the Southern Interior', in T.O. Ranger and I. Kimambo (eds), *The Historical Study of African Religion*, London, 1972
Agnew, Swanzie, 'Environment and history: the Malawian setting', in B. Pachai (ed.), *The Early History of Malawi*, London, 1972
Badenoch, H.A., 'Banda and the British: Anglo-Malawian Relations in the 1960s', Undergraduate thesis, University of Cambridge, 2002
Baker, Colin, *Seeds of Trouble. Government Policy and Land Rights in Nyasaland, 1946–1964*, London, 1993
Baker, Colin, *Development Governor: A Biography of Sir Geoffrey Colby*, London, 1994
Baker, Colin, *State of Emergency: Crisis in Central Africa, Nyasaland 1959–1960*, London, 1997
Baker, Colin, *Retreat from Empire: Sir Robert Armitage in Africa and Cyprus*, London, 1998
Baker, Colin, *Sir Glyn Jones. A Proconsul in Africa*, London, 2000
Baker, Colin, *Revolt of the Ministers: the Malawi Cabinet Crisis, 1964–1965*, London, 2001
Bandawe, L.M., *Memoirs of a Malawian*, Blantyre, Malawi, 1971
Barnekov, T. K., 'An Inquiry into the Development of Native Administration in Nyasaland, 1888–1937', MA Syracuse University, 1967
Beinart, William, 'Agricultural Planning and the Late Colonial Technical Imagination: the Lower Shire Valley in Malawi, 1940–1960' in Centre of African Studies, *Malawi: An Alternative Pattern of Development,* Edinburgh, 1984
Bettison, D.G., 'The demographic structure of seventeen villages, Blantyre-Limbe, Nyasaland', *Rhodes-Livingstone Communications*, XI, Lusaka, 1958
Bettison, D.G. and Apthorpe, R.J., 'Authority and Residence in a Peri-Urban Social Structure – Ndirande, Nyasaland', *Nyasaland Journal*, 14, 1, 1961
Birch de Aguiler, Laurel, *Inscribing the Mask: Interpretations of Nyau Masks and Ritual Performance among the Chewa of Central Malawi*, Fribourg, Switzerland, 1996
Boeder, Robert, *Alfred Sharpe of Nyasaland*, Blantyre, 1981
Blood, A.G., *The History of the Universities' Mission to Central Africa 1907–1932*, London, 1957
Bone, David, 'Islam in Malawi', *Journal of Religion in Africa*, 13, 2 1982
Bone, David (ed.), *Malawi's Muslims: Historical Perspectives*, Blantyre, 2000
Bower, Tom, *Tiny Rowland: A Rebel Tycoon*, London, 1993
Buchanan, John, *The Shire Highlands*, Edinburgh, 1885
Centre of African Studies, *Malawi: An Alternative Pattern of Development*, Edinburgh, 1984
Chanock, Martin, 'Ambiguities in the Malawi Political Tradition', *African Affairs*, 74, 296, 1975
Chanock, Martin, 'The New Men Revisited' in Roderick J. Macdonald, *From Nyasaland to Malawi*, Nairobi, 1975

Chanock, Martin, *Law, Custom and Social Order: the Colonial Experience in Malawi and Zambia*, Cambridge, 1985

Chipembere, H.M., 'Malawi in Crisis: 1964', *UFAHMU*, 1, 2, 1970

Chipembere, H.M., *Hero of the Nation. Chipembere of Malawi: An Autobiography*, edited and introduced by Robert I. Rotberg, Kachere, Blantyre, 2001

Chipeta, Mapopa, 'Labour in a Colonial Context. The growth and development of the Malawian Wage Labour Force during the colonial period', PhD dissertation, Dalhousie University, Halifax, Nova Scotia, 1986

Chirwa, Wiseman C., '"Theba is Power": Rural Labour, Migrancy and Fishing in Malawi, 1890s – 1985', PhD dissertation, Queen's University, Kingston, Ontario, 1992

Chirwa, Wiseman C., 'Fishing Rights, Ecology and Conservation along Southern Lake Malawi, 1920–1964', *African Affairs*, 95, 380, 1996

Chisiza, D.K., *Africa – What Lies Ahead*, New Delhi. 1961

Chisiza, 'The Temper, Aspirations and Problems of Contemporary Africa' in Jackson, E.F. (ed.), *Economic Development in Africa*, Oxford, 1965

Chiume, M.W.K., *Kwacha. An Autobiography*, Nairobi, 1975

Cole-King, P.A., *Lilongwe. A Historical Study*, Zomba, 1971

Coleman, G., 'The African Population of Malawi: An Analysis of the Censuses between 1901 and 1966', *Society of Malawi Journal*, 27, 1, 1974

Coleman, G., 'International Labour Migration from Malawi, 1875–1966', *Malawi Journal of Social Science*, 2, 1973

Coleman, G., 'Regional and District Origins of Migrant Labour from Malawi to 1966', *Malawi Journal of Social Science*, 6, 1970

Cronje, S., Ling, M. and Cronje, M., *Lonrho: Portrait of a Multinational*, London, 1976

Darwin, John, 'The Central African Emergency, 1959', *Journal of Imperial and Commonwealth History*, 21, 3, 1993

Davidson, Ann M., *The Real Paradise: Memories of Africa 1950–1963*, Edinburgh, 1993

Davies, W. Twiston, *Fifty Years of Progress. An Account of the African Organisation of the Imperial Tobacco Company 1907–1957*, Bristol, n.d.

Dawe, J.E., 'A History of Cotton-Growing in East Central Africa: British Demand, Africa Supply', PhD dissertation, University of Edinburgh, 1993

Deane, *Colonial Social Accounting*, Cambridge, 1953

De Jong, A.H. *Mission and Politics in Eastern Africa: Dutch Missionaries and African Nationalism in Kenya, Tanzania and Malawi, 1945–1965*, Nairobi, 1900

Dixie, F., 'The Distribution of Population in Nyasaland, *Geographical Review*, 18, 1928

Donaldson, John, 'The African Lakes Corporation – an analysis of its role in the economy of East Central Africa', BA dissertation, University of Stirling, 1995

Dossi, Moses T., *Football in Malawi: A Way of Life*, Limbe, 1992.

Dotson, Floyd and Dotson, Lillian O., *The Indian Minority of Zambia, Rhodesia and Malawi*, New Haven CT 1968.

Dzimbiri, Lewis, 'Industrial Relations, the State and Strike Activity in Malawi', PhD dissertation, University of Keele, 2002

Elton, J.F., *The Lakes and Mountains of Eastern and Central Africa*, London, 1879

Faulkner, Henry, *Elephant Haunts*, London, 1868

Fiedler, Klaus, 'Power at the Receiving End: the Jehovah's Witnesses' Experience in One Party Malawi' in Kenneth R. Ross (ed.), *God, People and Power in Malawi*, Blantyre, 1966

Fields, Karen E., *Revival and Rebellion in Colonial Central Africa*, Princeton NJ, 1985

Foskett, R. (ed.), *The Zambesi Journal and Letters of Dr John Kirk*, Edinburgh, 1965

Forster, P. G., 'Culture, Nationalism and the Invention of Tradition in Malawi', *Journal of Modern African Studies*, 32, 3, 1994

Fraser, Agnes R., *Donald Fraser*, London, 1934

Fraser, Donald, *Livingstonia*, Edinburgh, 1915

Gamitto, A.C.P., *King Kazembe and the Maravе, Cheva, Bisa, Bemba, Lunda, and Other Peoples of Southern Africa* (translated by Ian Cunnison), Lisbon, 1960

Gelfand, Michael, *Lakeside Pioneers*, Blackwell, Oxford, 1964

Good Jr., Charles M., *The Steamer Parish*, Chicago, 2004

Gray, Richard, *The Two Nations*, London, 1960

Groves, Zoe R., 'Malawians in Colonial Salisbury: a social history of migration in Central Africa', PhD, University of Keele, 2011
Hailey, Lord, *An African Survey*, London, 1938
Hailey, Lord, *Native Administration in the British African Territories, Part II*, London, 1950
Hanna, A.J., *The Beginnings of Nyasaland and Northern Rhodesia*, Oxford, 1956
Handbook of Nyasaland, Zomba, 1908 [1st edition]
Hazlewood, A. and Henderson, P.D., *Nyasaland: The Economics of Federation*. Oxford, 1960
Hazlewood, A., *African Integration and Disintegration*, London, 1967
Hastings, Adrian, *The Church in Africa, 1450–1950*. Oxford, 1994
Helly, Dorothy O., *Livingstone's Legacy: Horace Waller and Victorian Mythmaking*, Athens, OH, 1987
Hetherwick, A., *The Romance of Blantyre,* Dunfermline, n.d.
Hokkanen, Markku, *Medicine and Scottish Missionaries in the Northern Malawi Region, 1875–1930*, Lampeter, 2007
Hodges, G.W.T., 'African Manpower Statistics for the British Forces in East Africa, 1914–1918', *Journal of African History*, 19, 1, 1978
Holmberg, Ake, *African Tribes and European Agencies*, Goteborg, 1966
Hynd, 'Law, Violence and Penal Reform: State Responses to Crime and Disorder in Colonial Malawi, c. 1900–1959, *Journal of Southern African Studies*, 37, 3, 2011
Iliffe, John, *A Modern History of Tanganyika,* Cambridge, 1979
Iliffe, John, *Africans: the History of a Continent*, Cambridge, 1995
Iliffe, John, 'The Poor in the Modern History of Malawi' in Centre of African Studies, *Malawi: An Alternative Pattern of Development*, Edinburgh, 1984
Irvine, A.G., *The Balance of Payments of Rhodesia and Nyasaland 1945–1954*, London, 1959
Jack, J.W., *Daybreak in Livingstonia*, Edinburgh, 1901
Jackson, Bill, *Send Us Friends* (privately printed, n.d.)
Jeal, Tim, *Livingstone*, London, 1973
Johnson, W.P., *Nyasa, The Great Water*, Oxford, 1922
Johnston, H.H., *British Central Africa*, London, 1898
Jones, T.J., *Education in East Africa*, London, 1925
Kachapila, Hendrina, '"Remarkable Adaptability": Gender, Identity and Social Change among the Chewa of Central Malawi, 1870–1945', PhD dissertation, Dalhousie University, 2001
Kadalie, Clements, *My Life and the ICU: the Autobiography of a Black Trade Unionist in South Africa*, London, 1970
Kalinga, Owen, *A History of the Ngonde Kingdom of Malawi*, Berlin, 1985
Kalinga, Owen, 'The British and the Kyungus: A Study of the Changing Status of the Ngonde Rulers during the period 1891–1933', *African Studies*, 38, 2, 1979
Kalinga, Owen, 'The 1959 Nyasaland State of Emergency in the Old Karonga District', *Journal of Southern African Studies*, 36, 4, 2010
Kettlewell, R.J., 'Agricultural Change in Nyasaland: 1945–1960', *Food Research Institute Studies*, 5, 1965
King, M. and King, E., *The Story of Medicine and Disease in Malawi*, Blantyre, 1992
Kjekshus, Helge, *Ecology Control and Economic Development in East African History*, London, 1977
Kopytoff, Igor and Miers, Suzanne, *Slavery in Africa*, Madison, Wisconsin, 1977
Krishnamurthy, B.S., 'Economic Policy: land and labour in Nyasaland, 1890–1914' in B. Pachai, *The Early History of Malawi*, London, 1972
Kuczynski, B.R., *Demographic Survey of the British Empire*, Vol. II, London, 1949
Kuik, Gerhard, *Malawian Music: A Framework for Analysis*, Blantyre, 1987
Kydd, J. and Christiansen, R., 'Structural Changes in Malawi since Independence: Consequences of a Development Strategy based on Large-Scale Agriculture', *World Development*, 10, 5, 1982
Kydd, 'An Account of Malawi's Economy and Economic Policy in the 1970s' in Centre of African Studies, *Malawi: An Alternative Pattern of Development*, Edinburgh, 1984
Lamba, I.C., 'The History of Post-War Western Education in Colonial Malawi, 1945–61: A

Study of the Formulation and Application of Policy', PhD dissertation, University of Edinburgh

Lamb, Richard, *The Macmillan Years 1957–1963*, London, 1995

Langworthy, H.W., 'Swahili Influence on the area between Lake Malawi and the Luangwa River', *African Historical Studies*, 4, 3, 1971

Langworthy, H.W., *"Africa for the Africans": the Life of Joseph Booth*, Kachere, Blantyre, 1996

Laws, Robert, *Women's Work at Livingstonia*, Paisley, 1886

Linden, Ian, *Catholics, Peasants and Chewa Resistance in Nyasaland 1889–1939*, London, 1974

Linden, I., 'Chewa Initiation Rites and *Nyau* Societies' in T.O. Ranger and J. Weller (eds), *Themes in the Christian History of Central Africa*, London, 1975

Linden, I. and Linden, J., 'John Chilembwe and the New Jerusalem', *Journal of African History*, 12, 4, 1971

Livingstone, David and Charles, *Narrative of an Expedition to the Zambesi and its Tributaries*, London, 1865

Livingstone, W.P., *Laws of Livingstonia*, London, 1921

Lovejoy, P., *Transformations in Slavery*, Cambridge, 1983

Lovering, Timothy, 'Authority and Identity: Malawian Soldiers in Britain's Colonial Army, 1991–1964', PhD dissertation, University of Stirling, 2002

Lucas, C.P., *The Empire at War*, London, 1921

Lwanda, J. L., *Kamuzu Banda of Malawi: A Study in Promise, Power and Legacy*, Zomba, 2009

McCracken, John, *Politics and Christianity in Malawi*, Cambridge, 1977

McCracken, John, 'Experts and Expertise in Malawi', *African Affairs*, 81, 322, 1982

McCracken, John, 'Planters, Peasants and the Colonial State: the Impact of the Native Tobacco Board in the Central Province of Malawi', *Journal of Southern African Studies*, 9, 2, 1983

McCracken, John, 'Sharecropping in Malawi: the Visiting Tenant System in the Central Province, c. 1920–1968' in Centre of African Studies, *Malawi: an Alternative Pattern of Development*, Edinburgh, 1984

McCracken, John, 'Coercion and Control in Nyasaland: Aspects of the History of a Colonial Police Force', *Journal of African History*, 27, 1, 1986

McCracken, John, 'Fishing and the Colonial Economy: the Case of Malawi', *Journal of African History*, 28, 3, 1987

McCracken, John, 'Labour in Nyasaland: an Assessment of the 1960 Railway Workers' Strike', *Journal of Southern African Studies*, 14, 2, 1988

McCracken, John, '"Marginal Men": the Colonial Experience in Malawi', *Journal of Southern African Studies*, 15, 4, 1989

McCracken, John, 'Colonialism, Capitalism and Ecological Crisis in Malawi: a Reassessment' in Anderson, D. and Grove, R. (eds), *Conservation in Africa: People, Policies and Practice*, Cambridge, 1987

McCracken, John, 'Economics and Ethnicity: the Italian Community in Malawi', *Journal of African History*, 32, 2, 1991

McCracken, John, 'Authority and Legitimacy in Malawi: Policing and Politics in a Colonial State' in D. Anderson and D. Killingray (eds), *Policing and Decolonisation*, Manchester, 1992

McCracken, John, 'Blantyre Transformed: Class, Conflict and Nationalism in Colonial Malawi', *Journal of African History*, 39, 2, 1998

McCracken, John, 'Church and State in Malawi: the Role of the Scottish Presbyterian Missions 1875–1965' in H.G. Hansen. and M. Twaddle (eds), *Christian Missionaries and the State in the Third World*, Oxford, 2002

McCracken, John, 'Conservation and resistance in Colonial Malawi: the "Dead North" Revisited' in William Beinart and JoAnn McGregor (eds), *Social History and African Environments*, Oxford, 2003.

McCracken, John, 'Imagining the Nyika Plateau: Laurens van der Post, the Phoka and the making of a National Park', *Journal of Southern African Studies*, 32, 4, 2006

McCracken, John, 'Mungo Murray Chisuse and the early History of Photography in Malawi', *Society of Malawi Journal*, 61, 2, 2008

McCracken, John, 'In the Shadow of Mau Mau: Detainees and Detention Camps during Nyasaland's State of Emergency', *Journal of Southern African Studies*, 37, 3, 2011

Macdonald, Duff, *Africana or the Heart of Heathen Africa*, 2 vols, London, 1882, reprinted 1969.

Macdonald, R. J., 'A History of African Education in Nyasaland, 1875–1945', PhD dissertation, University of Edinburgh, 1969

Macdonald, Roderick J. (ed.), *From Nyasaland to Malawi: Studies in Colonial History*, Nairobi, 1975

Mackay, Peter, *We Have Tomorrow: Stirrings in Africa, 1959–1967*, Norwich, 2008

McMaster, Carolyn, *Malawi Foreign Policy and Development*, London, 1974

Macmillan, H.W., 'The Origins and Development of the African Lakes Company, 1878–1908', PhD dissertation, University of Edinburgh, 1970

Macmillan, H.W., 'The African Lakes Company and the Makololo, 1878–84' in R.J. Macdonald (ed.), *From Nyasaland to Malawi*, Nairobi, 1975

Macmillan, H.W., 'Notes on the Origins of the Arab War' in B. Pachai (ed.), *The Early History of Malawi*, London, 1972

Mair, Lucy, *The Nyasaland Elections of 1961*, London, 1962

Mamdani, Mahmood, *Citizen and Subject: Contemporary Africa and the Legacy of Late Colonialism*, London, 1996

Mandala, Elias C., 'The Kololo Interlude in Southern Malawi, 1861–95', MA dissertation, University of Malawi, 1977

Mandala, Elias C., 'Capitalism, ecology and society: the lower Tchiri (Shire) Valley of Malawi, 1860–1969', Ph.D. dissertation, University of Minnesota, 1983

Mandala, Elias C., *Work and Control in a Peasant Economy*, Madison, WI, 1990

Mandala, Elias C., *The End of Chidyerao: a History of Food and Everyday Life in Malawi, 1860–2004*, Portsmouth NH, 2005.

Mandala, Elias C., 'Feeding and Fleecing the Native: How the Nyasaland Transport System distorted a new Food Market, 1890s-1920s', *Journal of Southern African Studies*, 32, 3, 2006.

Maugham, R.C. F., *Africa as I Have Known It*, London, 1929

Mfuni, J.H.C., 'Labour Migration from Northern Mzimba', History seminar paper, Chancellor College, University of Malawi, 1981/82

Morris, Brian, *The Power of Animals: An Ethnography*, Oxford, 1998

Morton, Geoffrey J., *Just the Job: some experiences of a colonial policeman*, London, 1957

Morton, Kathryn, *Aid and Dependence*, London, 1975

Moyse-Bartlett, H., *The King's African Rifles*, Aldershot, 1956

Mullins, Patrick, *Retreat from Africa*, Edinburgh, 1992

Mulwafu, Wapulumuka O., *Conservation Song: A History of Peasant-State Relations and the Environment in Malawi, 1860–2000*, Cambridge, 2011

Murphy, Philip (ed.), *British Documents on the End of Empire: Central Africa*, London, 2005

Murray, S.S., *A Handbook of Nyasaland*, Zomba, 1922 [2nd edition]

Murray. S.S., *A Handbook of Nyasaland*, Zomba, 1932 [3rd edition]

Mwase, G.S., *Strike a Blow and Die*, Cambridge, MA, 1967

Myambo, Simon S., 'The Shire Highlands Plantations: A Socio-economic History of the Plantation System of Production in Malawi, 1891–1938', MA dissertation, University of Malawi, 1973

Newitt, Malyn D.D., *Portuguese Settlement on the Zambesi*, London, 1973

Newitt, Malyn D.D., *A History of Mozambique*, London, 1995

Norman, L.S., *Nyasaland Without Prejudice*, London, 1934

Oliver, Roland, *Sir Harry Johnston and the Scramble for Africa*, London, 1959

Pachai, Bridglal (ed.), *The Early History of Malawi*, London, 1972

Pachai, Bridglal, *Malawi: the History of a Nation*, London, 1973

Pachai, Bridglal (ed.), *Livingstone: Man of Africa Memorial Essays 1873–1973*, London, 1973

Pachai, Bridglal, *Land and Politics in Malawi, 1875–1975*, Kingston Ontario, 1978

Page, Melvin E., *The Chiwaya War. Malawians and the First World War*, Boulder, CO, 2000.

Page, Melvin E., 'Malawians in the Great War and After, 1914–1925', PhD dissertation, Michigan State University, 1977

Page, Melvin E., 'The War of *Thangata*: Nyasaland and the East African Campaign, 1914–1919', *Journal of African History*, 19, 1, 1978

Palmer, Robin, 'Johnston and Jameson: a comparative study in the imposition of colonial rule' in B. Pachai (ed.), *Early History of Malawi*

Palmer, Robin and Parsons, Neil (eds) *The Roots of Rural Poverty in Central and Southern Africa*, London, 1977

Palmer, Robin, 'White Farmers in Malawi: before and after the Depression', *African Affairs*, 84, 334, 1985

Palmer, Robin, 'The Nyasaland Tea Industry in the Era of International Tea Restrictions, 1933–1950', *Journal of African History*, 26, 2–3, 1985

Palmer, Robin, 'Working Conditions and Worker responses on Nyasaland Tea Estates, 1930–1953', *Journal of African History*, 27, 1, 1986

Phillips, Henry, *From Obscurity to Bright Dawn*. London, 1998

Phiri, D.D., *Malawians to Remember: James Frederick Sangala*, Lilongwe, 1974

Phiri, D.D., *Malawians to Remember: Dunduzu K. Chisiza*, Blantyre, 1974

Phiri, D.D., *Malawians to Remember: Charles Chidongo Chinula*, Blantyre, 1975

Phiri, D.D., *Let Us Die for Africa*, Blantyre, 1999

Phiri, Isabel A., *Women, Presbyterianism and Patriarchy: Religious Experience of Chewa Women in Central Malawi*, Limbe, 1997

Phiri, Kings M., 'Chewa History in Central Malawi and the Use of Oral Tradition', PhD dissertation, Wisconsin University, 1975.

Phiri, Kings M., 'Pre-Colonial Economic Change in Central Malawi: the Development and Expansion of Trade Systems 1750–1875', *Malawi Journal of Social Science*, 5, 1976.

Phiri, Kings M., 'Northern Zambezia from 1500 to 1800', *Society of Malawi Journal*, 32, 1, 1979

Phiri, Kings M., 'Some Changes in the Matrilineal Family System among the Chewa of Malawi since the Nineteenth Century', *Journal of African History*, 24, 1983

Phiri, Kings M., 'Production and exchange in Pre-Colonial Malawi' in Centre of African Studies, *Malawi: An Alternative Pattern of Development*, Edinburgh, 1984

Pike, J.G. and Rimmington, G.T., *Malawi: a Geographical Study*, London, 1965

Power, Joey, 'Individual enterprise and enterprising individuals: African entrepreneurship in Blantyre and Limbe, 1907–1953', PhD dissertation, Dalhousie University, 1991

Power, Joey, 'Race, Ethnicity and Anglo-Indian Trade Rivalry in Colonial Malawi, 1910–1945', *International Journal of African Historical Studies*, 26, 3 1993

Power, Joey, 'Remembering Du: an episode in the development of Malawian political culture', *African Affairs*, 97, 388, 1998

Power, Joey, 'Building Relevance: the Blantyre Congress 1953 to 1956', *Journal of Southern African Studies*, 28, 1, 2002

Power, Joey, *Political Culture and Nationalism in Malawi: Building Kwacha*, Rochester NY, 2010

Ranger, T.O. and Kimambo, I. (eds), *The Historical Study of African Religion*, London, 1972.

Ranger, T.O., 'Mcape and the Study of Witchcraft Eradication', unpublished paper, Conference on the History of Central African Religious Systems, Lusaka, 1972.

Ranger, T.O. and Weller, J. (eds)., *Themes in the Christian History of Central Africa*, London, 1975

Ranger, T.O., *Dance and Society in Eastern Africa 1890–1970*, London, 1975

Ransford, Oliver, *Livingstone's Lake*, London, 1966

Read, Margaret, *The Ngoni of Nyasaland*, London, 1956

Read, Margaret, 'Migrant Labour in Africa and its Effects on Tribal Life', *International Labour Review*, XLV, 6, 1942

Retief, M.W., *William Murray of Nyasaland*, Lovedale, 1958

Ross, Andrew C., *Blantyre Mission and the Making of Modern Malawi*, Zomba, 1996

Ross, Andrew C., 'Some Reflections on the Malawi Cabinet Crisis, 1964–65', *Religion in Malawi*, 7, 1992

Ross, Andrew C., 'White Africa's Black Ally', *New Left Review*, 45, 1967

Ross, Kenneth R. (ed.), *Christianity in Malawi. A Source Book*, Zomba, 1996

Rotberg, R.I., *The Rise of Nationalism in Central Africa*, London, 1966

Rotberg, R.I., 'Psychological Stress and the Question of Identity: Chilembwe's Revolt Reconsidered' in R.I. Rotberg and A. Mazrui, (eds), *Protest and Power in Black Africa*, Oxford & New York, 1970

Rowley, R.H., *The Story of the Universities Mission to Central Africa*, London, 1866

Rennick, Agnes, 'Church and Medicine: the Role of Medical Missionaries in Malawi 1875–1914', PhD dissertation, University of Stirling, 2003

Shepherd, Robert, *Ian Macleod: A Biography*, London, 1994

Schoffeleers, J.M., 'Livingstone and the Mang'anja Chiefs' in B. Pachai, *Livingstone: Man of Africa*, Longman, London, 1973

Schoffeleers, J.M., 'The Interaction of the M'Bona Cult and Christianity, 1859–1963', in T.O. Ranger and J. Weller (eds), *Themes in the Christian History of Central Africa*, London, 1975

Schoffeleers, J.M., and Linden, I., 'The Resistance of the Nyau Societies to the Roman Catholic Missions in Colonial Malawi' in T.O, Ranger and I. Kimambo (eds), *The Historical Study of African Religion*, London, 1972

Schoffeleers, J.M. and Roscoe, A.A., *Land of Fire: Oral Literature from Malawi*, Lilongwe, 1985

Schoffeleers, J.M., *Guardians of the Land*, Gwelo, 1979

Schoffeleers, J.M., *River of Blood: The Genesis of a Marty Cult in Southern Malawi, c. A.D. 1600*, Madison1992

Schoffeleers, J.M., *Pentecostalism and Neo-Traditionalism*, Amsterdam, 1985

Schoffeleers, J.M., *In Search of Truth and Justice*, Blantyre, 1999

Shepherd, R.H.W., *A South African Medical Pioneer: the Life of Neil Macvicar*, Lovedale, 1952

Shepperson, George and Price, Thomas, *Independent African*, Edinburgh, 1958

Shepperson, George, 'External Factors in the Development of African Nationalism with particular reference to British Central Africa', *Phylon*, 22, 3, 1961

Shepperson, George, 'The Jumbe of Kota Kota and some aspects of the history of Islam in British Central Africa' in I.M. Lewis, *Islam in Tropical Africa*, London, 1966

Short, Philip, *Banda*, London, 1974

Sim, A.F., *The Life and Letters of Arthur Fraser Sim*, London, 1896

Soko, B.J., 'An Introduction to the *Vimbuza* Phenomenon', *Religion in Malawi*, 1, 1, 1987

Soko, B.J., 'The *Vimbuza* Possession Cult: the Onset of the Disease', *Religion in Malawi*, 2, 1, 1988

Soko, B.J. and Kubik, G., *Nchimi Chikanga: the Battle against Witchcraft in Malawi*, Kachere, Zomba, 2008

Stokes, E. and Brown, R., *The Zambesian Past*, Manchester, 1966

Stokes, E., 'Malawi Political Systems and the Introduction of Colonial Rule, 1891–1896' in E. Stokes and R. Brown (eds), *The Zambesian Past*, Manchester, 1966

Stuart, R.G., 'Christianity and the Chewa: the Anglican Case 1885–1950', PhD dissertation, University of London, 1974

Tangri, Roger, 'From the Politics of Union to mass nationalism: the Nyasaland African Congress, 1944–59' in R.J. Macdonald (ed.), *From Nyasaland to Malawi*

Terry, P.T., 'African Agriculture in Nyasaland', *Nyasaland Journal*, 14, 2, 1961

Thompson, T.J., *Christianity in Northern Malawi*, Leiden, 1995

Thompson, T.J., *Touching the Heart: Xhosa Missionaries to Malawi, 1876–1888*, Pretoria, 2000

Thompson, T.J, 'The Origins, Migration and Settlement of the Northern Ngoni', *Society of Malawi Journal*, 34, 1 1982

Vail, H.L., 'Suggestions towards a reinterpreted Tumbuka history' in B. Pachai (ed.), *Early History of Malawi*

Vail, H.L., 'The Making of an Imperial Slum: Nyasaland and its Railways, 1895–1935', *Journal of African History*, 16, 1, 1975

Vail, H.L., 'Railway Development and Colonial Underdevelopment: the Nyasaland Case' in Robin Palmer and Neil Parsons (eds) *The Roots of Rural Poverty in Central and Southern Africa*, London, 1977

Vail, H.L., 'The Making of the "Dead North": A Study of Ngoni Rule in Northern Malawi, c. 1855–1907' in J.B. Peires (ed.), *Before and After Shaka: papers in Nguni History*, Grahamstown, 1981

Vail, H.L., 'The State and the Creation of Colonial Malawi's Agricultural Economy' in Robert

I. Rotberg (ed.), *Imperialism, Colonialism and Hunger: East and Central Africa*, Lexington, 1983

Vail, H.L., 'The Political Economy of East-Central Africa' in David Birmingham and Phyllis Martin (eds), *History of Central Africa*, Vol. Two, London, 1983

Vail, Leroy and White, Landeg, *Capitalism and Colonialism in Mozambique*, London, 1980

Vail, Leroy and White, Landeg, 'Tribalism in the Political History of Malawi' in Leroy Vail (ed.), *The Creation of Tribalism in Southern Africa*, London, 1989

Vail, Leroy (ed.), *The Creation of Tribalism in Southern Africa*, London, 1989.

Vail, H.L. and White, L, *Power and the Praise Poem: Southern African Voices in History*, London, 1991

Van der Post, Laurens, *Venture to the Interior*, London, 1952.

Van Onselen, Charles, *Chibaro. African Mine Labour in Southern Rhodesia, 1900–1933*, London, 1976

Van Velsen, Jaap, 'Labour Migration as a Positive Factor in the Continuity of Tonga Tribal Society' in Southall, I. (ed.), London, 1961

Vaughan, Megan, 'Social and Economic Change in Southern Malawi: A Study of Rural Communities in the Shire Highlands and Upper Shire Valley from the Mid-Nineteenth Century to 1915', PhD dissertation, University of London, 1981

Vaughan, Megan, 'Food Production and Family Labour in Southern Malawi: the Shire Highlands and Upper Shire Valley in the Early Colonial Period', *Journal of African History*, 23, 3, 1982

Vaughan, Megan, *The Story of an African Famine*, Cambridge, 1987

Vaughan, Megan, *Curing Their Ills: Colonial Power and African Illness*, Cambridge, 1991

Waller, Horace (ed.), *The Last Journals of David Livingstone*, London, 1974.

Wallis, J.P.R. (ed.), *The Zambesi Journal of James Stewart, 1861–1863*, London, 1952.

Webster, J.B., 'Drought, Migration and Chronology in the Lake Malawi Littoral', *Transafrican Journal of History*, 9, 1 and 2, 1980

Webster, J.B., 'From Yao Hill to Mount Mulanje', History Seminar Paper, University of Malawi, 1977

Weller, John C., *The Priest from the Lakeside*, Blantyre, 1971

Werner, Alice, *The Natives of British Central Africa*, London, 1906

Westrup, Arthur, *Green Gold*, Bulawayo, n.d.

White, Landeg, *Magomero*, Cambridge, 1987

White, Landeg, '"Tribes" and the Aftermath of the Chilembwe Rising', *African Affairs*, 83, 333, 1984

Williams, Dora, *What We Do in Nyasaland*, Westminster, 1911

Williams, T. D., *Malawi: the Politics of Despair*, London, 1978

Wilshaw, Colin, *A Century of Gold: Malawi's Tobacco Industry, 1893–1993*, Blantyre, 1994

Wilson, Godfrey, *The Constitution of the Ngonde*, Rhodes-Livingstone Papers No. 3

Wright, F.C., *African Consumers in Nyasaland and Tanganyika*, London, 1955

Wright, M. and Lary, P, 'Swahili Settlements in Northern Zambia and Malawi', *African Historical Studies*, 4, 3, 1971

Wright, M., *Strategies of Slaves and Women*, London, 1993

Wood, J.R.T., *The Welensky Papers. A History of the Federation of Rhodesia and Nyasaland*, Durban, 1983

Woods, Tony, 'Chief Mwase and the Kasungu Chewa: Ethnicity, Nationalism and Political Rhetoric in Colonial Malawi', History seminar paper, Chancellor College, University of Malawi, n.d.

Woods, Tony, '"Bread with Freedom and Peace": Rail Workers in Malawi, 1954–1975', *Journal of Southern African Studies*, 18, 4, 1992

Young, E.D., *The Search for Livingstone*, London, 1868

Index

Abrahams, J.C., 224
Abrahams, Sir Sidney, 306-08
Abrahams Report, 306-07, 318, 335, 390
Achewa Improvement Society, 233, 283, 317, 338, 405, 435
Achewa Welfare Association, 405
Adams, Osman, 177, 286
African Chamber of Commerce, 299, 340
African Farmers' Association, 251, 329
African Industrial Society, 133
African Lakes Company (ALC), origins 48–54, 57, 60, 62, 70, 77, 79 83–4, 88; during 1915 Rising, 127, 136, 140–41; transport and trade between wars, 158, 178, 180, 195, 228; and Mandala 284, 286
African Motor Transport Workers' Union, 340
African National Church, 212
African Presbyterian Church, 213
African Progressive Association, 331, 366
Agricultural Produce and Marketing Board, 243, 247
African Road Transporters' Association, 383
African soldiers, 61, 64–6, 71, 94, 103, 137; First World War 147–51, 155; Second World War, 214, 238–40; ex-soldiers, 302, 312; post-war politics, 353, 356, 439, 442–4, 455, *see* also *askaris*
Alpers, Edward, 101
Alport, Lord, 430
Alston, Lieutenant Edward, 64
Amanda, Sam, 156
Amery, Leo, 221
Anti-witchcraft movements, 122, 126, 210–11, 214
Arabs, 22, 26, 53
Arabs, 'north-end', 58, 62–4, 68
Armitage, Sir Robert, 242, 249, 274, 333, 346–7, 350, 352–4, 356–65, 367, 376–7, 384, 389, 392, 397
Asians, in colonial economy 163, 174, 219, 262; political involvement, 270–4, 279, 347, 350, 353, 361, 378, 381; in towns, 279, 282, 286, 288, 291–2, 296, 299;

citizenship, 457, *see also* Indians
askaris, 66, 70–1, 79, 80, 94, 129, 137, 141, 145, First World War 148–51, 153, 155, 157; Second World War 239–40, *see also* African soldiers

Baker, Colin, 242, 354, 446
Banda, A.J.M., 317, 328, 331–2
Banda, Aleke, 367, 369, 375, 382, 414, 418, 427, 432, 454
Banda, Dr Hastings Kamuzu, early life 153, 182, 325; in Britain, 228, 262, 268, 276, 315, 317–18, 326–29, 332; as NAC leader 344–51; during State of Emergency, 353–4, 357–8, 360–64; as leader of MCP, 365–6, 368–74, 376–82, 383–89; as Minister of Natural Resources, 252–3, 307, 390–99; on education, 400–02; leadership style, 403-07; relations with Dunduzu Chisiza, 407-09, 411–12; with trade unions, 417; assault on opponents, 418–20; relations with Britain, 422–26; cabinet crisis, 427, 429–39; suppresses risings, 440–45; explanations for his success, 446–53; construction of personal regime, 453–58
Banda, John Afwenge, 104
Banda, T.D.T., 342–3, 345, 351, 361, 376, 380
Bandawe, 46–7, 79, 83, 103–05, 118, 185, 211
Bandawe, Lewis, 233–4, 301
Bandawe, Sergeant, 60–1, 63
Barron, A.F., 164–6, 170–71, 179, 190, 205, 252
Barron, Bruce, 394–5, 397
Barron, Marjorie, 252
Barros Gomes, 53
Barrow, Malcolm, 167, 272–3, 279, 306–8, 364
Baptist Industrial Mission, 107, 115
beer, pre-colonial 7, 12, 23, 25, 33, 36–7; attempts to control production of, 226, 290–91, 310, 324; and Lonhro, 326
beeswax, 88, 93

472